MONEY AND BANKING

MONEY
AND
BANKING
Theory, Policy, and Institutions

HELEN B. O'BANNON
Carnegie-Mellon University

DAVID E. BOND
Public Service of Canada

RONALD A. SHEARER
University of British Columbia

HARPER & ROW, PUBLISHERS
New York, Evanston, San Francisco, London

Sponsoring Editor: John Greenman
Project Editor: Elizabeth Dilernia
Designer: T. R. Funderburk
Production Supervisor: Will C. Jomarrón

Portions of this book have previously appeared in *The Economics of the Canadian Financial System: Theory, Policy, and Institutions* by David E. Bond and Ronald A. Shearer, published by Prentice-Hall of Canada, Ltd. © 1972 by Prentice-Hall of Canada, Ltd., Scarborough, Ontario.

Money and Banking: Theory, Policy, and Institutions

Library of Congress Cataloging in Publication Data

O'Bannon, Helen B   Date–
    Money and banking
    Earlier ed. by D. E. Bond and R. A. Shearer published in 1972 under title: The economics of the Canadian financial system.
    Includes index.
    1. Financial institutions. 2. Money. 3. Banks and banking. I. Bond, David E., joint author.
II. Shearer, Ronald Alexander, 1932–   joint author.
III. Bond, David E. The Economics of the Canadian financial system. IV. Title.
HG173.O17 1975   332   74-9212
ISBN 0-06-044877-6

To

CAROLYN SHAW BELL
Professor of Economics, Wellesley College
teacher, critic, and friend
whose scholarship and continuing concern for her students
encourage them to persist

and

JOSEPH A. CRUMB
Professor Emeritus, The University of British Columbia
teacher, critic, and friend
whose passionate interest in monetary economics
attracted many students to the field

and

ROBERT E. HUKE
Professor of Geography, Dartmouth College
teacher, scholar, and friend
whose inspired teaching and thirst for knowledge
are an example to all

and

ELIZABETH, RENATE, AND GEORGE

with love

CONTENTS

PREFACE

This book is intended as a textbook for undergraduate courses in money and banking. The level of the analysis presumes a standard course in the principles of economics.

Over the years, a rather standard format has developed for textbooks in money and banking. With some exceptions, most of the widely used books are variations on a basic theme. The structure and content of this book reflect our dissatisfaction with the standard model. We are critical of the model in general and have consciously departed from it in several important respects.

First, we take the view that we must be concerned with microecenomics as well as macroeconomics. Indeed, to the limited extent that is is possible, the macroeconomic analysis should build on microeconomic foundations. The standard textbook does have a microeconomic section, but we believe that the relevant microeconomics is more than just a description of banking institutions and their operations.

Institutions must be described, and we have devoted considerable space to that task, but we do so on the presumption that the proper scope of the discussion is the whole financial system, including both the banks and non-bank financial intermediaries of all types, and the money and capital markets in both their domestic and their international dimensicns. At the same time, we have attempted to avoid presenting a mail-order catalogue of financial institutions. It is important that the institutions be viewed as an integrated system that performs certain basic economic functions (in the spirit of Gurley and Shaw). To this end, their operations must be interpreted in terms of a systematic body of economic theory. We have attempted to do so, using as our foundation an elementary and slightly modified version of what has come to be called portfolio balance theory.

We also take the view that the purpose of economic analysis is the exposition of public policy and policy alternatives. Therefore we have devoted considerable space to the discussion of the development of public policy with respect to the structure of the financial system in the United States, and to the discussion of some of the major issues that have been troubling economists concerned with microeconomic policy in this area.

Our second major departure from the standard model is in our treatment of historical topics. The typical textbook has major sections on the history of money and of banking institutions, and perhaps an extended discussion of the history of monetary theory. Although we recognize the value of a historical perspective on theory and institutions, these are specialized topics with an already abundant and readily accessible literature. In this book, we could only add another superficial survey. While there are many historical references scattered throughout the text, we have confined our historical chapters to an analysis of the evolution of the structure of the financial industry and the development of government policy toward the financial structure. Given the orientation of our microeconomic analysis, these are important topics and, unlike other historical topics, are less adequately developed in the literature that is readily available to undergraduate students.

Our third major point of departure from the standard textbook is in the treatment of international finance. In the standard textbook, international finance is discussed separately in a section at the end of the book, almost as an afterthought. It is our impression that many instructors never get to this section, or, if they do, they deal with it very superficially. We take the position that the discussion of international finance can no longer be omitted from courses in money and banking nor relegated to the back of the book alone. We feel that the discussion of international finance must be *fully integrated* with the discussion of monetary theory and monetary policy. There is no longer any excuse for leaving the student with a model of monetary policy appropriate only for a closed economy.

While our discussion of the macroeconomic aspects of international finance does come toward the end of the book, we have developed the analysis as an extension of the models of monetary policy examined in previous chapters. We have tried to adapt the familiar *IS-LM* model to demonstrate the balance-of-payments constraint on monetary policy in a regime of fixed exchange rates, and to explore the implications of a regime of flexible exchange rates. We have also investigated such topics as speculation in foreign exchange markets and the international liquidity problem from the perspective of their implications for monetary policy.

Finally, as a fourth major departure, we take the view that wherever possible the conclusions of economic theory must be considered relative to the findings of empirical research. It is difficult and frustrating to attempt to interpret for undergraduate students the often conflicting findings of empirical researchers (the subtleties of methodological controversies defy explanation). But wherever it seemed relevant, we have attempted to do this. We refer frequently to the results of empirical research, and the second to last chapter is entirely devoted to a survey of research on the effectiveness of monetary policy.

We acknowledge the particularly useful observations of Carol Clark, Basil Moore, Philip Neher, Douglas Purvis, John Chant, Tom Maxwell, A. A. Shapiro, and John Borcich. We also appreciate the assistance of Helen Terry and Liane Norman. We owe a special debt of gratitude to all who have typed the various versions of the manuscript, particularly Marilyn Russell, who coped with illegible insertions and difficult copy.

H. B. O.
D. E. B.
R. A. S.

MONEY AND BANKING

1

THE FUNCTIONS OF THE FINANCIAL SYSTEM

To the average citizen, finances, financial activities, and the financial system have an aura of mystery. Successful practitioners of the financial arts are widely held in awe—although it is also fair to say that many people regard these financial experts with somewhat the same skepticism as they do astrologers and fortunetellers. On the one hand, reports of fortunes created overnight, almost magically, stir the imaginations and gambling instincts of many. Likewise, reports of bankruptcies under mysterious circumstances and losses of life savings by "innocent" investors stir rumors, allegations, and public outcries for investigations of fraud and deceptive financial "manipulations." Some of these investigations, in fact, reveal practices that are either illegal or ethically suspect. Partly as a result, the financial industry is surrounded by more government rules and regulations than perhaps any other industry, and new laws are being added to the books almost every year. On the other hand, public forums on the somber issues of government economic policy are seldom considered complete unless they include the considered advice of bankers or investment analysts. Yet back room discussions of the economic problems of our time commonly center on the theme of the conspiracy of the bankers, domestic or international.

1

THE FINANCIAL INDUSTRY

Myths about finance are embedded in our culture. An anthropologist or sociologist could undoubtedly write a fascinating analysis of the social functions performed by invocations of the financial spirits. To an economist, however, the financial system is but another industry in the economy. True, it is a particularly important industry that frequently has a far-reaching impact on society and the economy, but stripped of its occult trappings, it is, like any industry, a group of firms that combine factors of production (land, labor, and capital) under the general direction of a management team and produce a product or cluster of products for sale in financial markets. These markets have varying degrees of competition and are regulated by the forces of supply and demand within a general context set by government laws and regulations. It is not quite the same thing as the widget industry, but the general principles applied to the analysis of the widget industry in introductory principles-of-economics courses can also be applied to the financial industry.

THE OUTPUT OF THE FINANCIAL INDUSTRY

The product of the financial industry is not tangible, as are automobiles, food, or clothing. Rather, it is an intangible service such as those produced in the barbering or laundry industry. Indeed, it is incorrect to refer to *the* product of the industry. We are not talking about a single service but a collection of services. It is true that some financial firms specialize in the provision of a single service (or a cluster of very closely related services), but many, including some of the very largest, are complex multiproduct firms. The industry as a whole, including specialized and diversified firms, produces a wide range of services, but all of these services are related directly or indirectly to assets and liabilities, that is, *claims* on people, corporations, institutions, and governments. These are the forms in which people accumulate much of their wealth.

It is not important that we have a complete catalog of the services offered by the industry, but it is useful to identify the most important ones. Basic to almost all the activities of financial firms is the systematic collection and interpretation of information on almost all aspects of economic activity. Some of this information is passed on to clients in the form of professional advice on investments and other personal economic problems. On the basis of such information certain financial firms will also undertake to manage the economic affairs of clients (or their estates) on a *trusteeship* basis. Comprehensive, detailed, and accurate information is an essential input into almost all the activities of a financial firm, including what we call brokerage and financial intermediation. Many financial firms serve as *brokers* in the sense that they bring borrowers and lenders together, thus arranging a transaction (for a fee) without being a party to the transaction themselves.

Perhaps more familiar are the activities of financial firms as *financial intermediaries*. In this capacity they act simultaneously as borrowers and lenders. Like a broker, a financial intermediary brings borrowers and lenders together, but unlike a broker it is a party to the transaction. The financial intermediary actually borrows from one group in society (who are often happy to trust the financial intermediary, whereas they would not trust those to whom the intermediary lends) and lends to another, thus putting itself at risk should some of the loans be defaulted. The activities of a financial firm as an intermediary are sometimes confused in the popular mind with another service: the provision of safekeeping for valuable property. Thus, depositors in a bank frequently fail to recognize that they are creditors of the bank: They have in fact lent the bank money. Safekeeping is provided by the safe-deposit box department of the bank, not through the teller windows. Furthermore, safekeeping is a minor service to customers, incidental to the main business at hand. Finally, we must note that the financial system provides facilities for the transfer of purchasing power from individual to individual or from firm to firm, both within the country and internationally. It thus arranges the financial side of almost all exchanges consummated in markets in the economy, and in the process it provides a detailed set of records of transactions, both for the use of the individuals concerned and, in different forms, for government agencies and the public at large. The financial system is a primary source of statistics used in analyzing national and international economic activity.

VALUE ADDED IN THE FINANCIAL INDUSTRY

So much for the nature of the products of the financial industry. How important is this industry relative to the total economy?

The accepted measure of the aggregate output of the economy is the gross national product. Correspondingly, the appropriate measure of the output of any single industry is "value added" in that industry. Value added is defined as the difference between the market value of the product produced and sold by the industry and the cost of all materials purchased from other industries (e.g., raw materials, component parts, fuel, advertising services, etc.). It is thus equal to the payments for the services of all factors of production directly employed in that industry (rents, wages, interest) plus any residual profit earned by the owners of the firms. In other words, it is the value of "income originating" in the industry. Since such a calculation avoids the error of double counting—of counting as output in one industry what is in fact the output of another industry, as when you simply add up the value of sales by industry—value added is the best measure of the relative contribution of any industry to aggregate national output.

In attempting to measure value added in the financial industry, certain complications arise that are discussed in books on national income accounting. The problem arises in the treatment of interest. In accounting for value

3

added in a normal industry, interest received is deducted from the income of the firms on the ground that this does not represent payment for services of capital employed in production in that industry. If this procedure is carried out for financial intermediaries, the value added by the industry is almost invariably negative. According to national income accountants this answer is "unacceptable," so they resort to imputations; that is, they assign an arbitrary value to the services provided by the financial intermediaries to their customers. The resulting estimates are severely criticized by some economists and must be regarded as approximations. Further complications arise in attempting to use the published estimates, since value added by the financial industry is not shown separately but is included in the category "finance, insurance, and real estate." In recent years this category has accounted for slightly more than 10 percent of gross national product. The financial industry proper (excluding real estate but including insurance) has probably accounted for 3 percent of gross national product.

Put differently, the financial industry directly accounts for perhaps one-thirtieth of the gross output of goods and services produced in this nation. This clearly establishes it as a major industry. But can we take this as sufficient indication of the importance of the financial industry?

ECONOMIC FUNCTIONS OF THE FINANCIAL SYSTEM

The economic significance of the financial system and its operations cannot be assessed in the same way as that of the widget industry. It is not simply a matter of adding up value added and expressing that as a portion of national output. If the widget industry were removed from the economy, perhaps by an act of Congress, repercussions might be felt in many segments of the economy. Suppliers of materials would find that part of their market had disappeared, and hence they would have to adjust the scale of their production. Employees in the widget industry, and probably in supplying industries, would have to seek new employment. Purchasers of widgets would have to make do with substitutes, and if the widget were an essential input into some other industry perhaps that industry would be faced with impossible difficulties. Depending on the size of the industry and the nature of its relations with other industries, the repercussions could be felt over a wide circle of economic activity. In some cases the adjustments could be painful and protracted. However, given time, the economy would adjust. Without the widget industry economic activity would be different, but it would carry on.

If the financial industry were removed in the same way, we could not be so optimistic about the outcome. Unlike the widget industry, the financial industry provides services that are essential to every industry in the economy. In this sense, financial activities are complementary to all other economic activities. While the financial industry may not be unique in this respect, it nonetheless means that the importance of the industry transcends that indicated by the relative size of value added in the industry. It performs certain essential functions for the economy, including maintenance of the payments system, collection and allocation of the savings of society, and creation of a variety of stores of wealth to suit the preferences of individual savers.

THE PAYMENTS SYSTEM

The payments system is the set of institutional arrangements through which purchasing power is transferred from one participant in an exchange to another, that is, from the buyer to the seller.

Why do we consider this to be an essential economic function? Ever since the discipline of economics was established as a systematic analysis of economic activity, economists have been asserting that specialization in productive activities is a necessary (but not sufficient) condition for the achievement of a high general standard of living. Without an elaborate division of labor into specialized tasks, the application of modern technology would be inconceivable. But the counterpart of specialization is exchange. The man who specializes in the activity of dog catching must somehow obtain the variety of goods and services that he and his family wish to consume. He must exchange his services for the products of other specialized producers. Efficient exchange also implies an intermediary that we call money. Money, in a sense, is generalized purchasing power: something that all of the participants in the economy are willing to accept in payment for goods and services, not because they want to consume it but because they know that they can exchange it with some other person, now or later, for the things they desire. The use of money in the exchange process is quite apart from any utility that the monetary medium itself might yield as a commodity. Indeed, it is not necessary that the monetary medium be something that is desired as a commodity: It can be marks on the books of a banker as well as some tangible object such as pieces of gold or paper. We will return to the concept and properties of money later in the book. Suffice it to note at this point that any number of things have been used as money under varying circumstances. But whatever the instrument, and whatever the concrete historical circumstances of its evolution as the monetary medium, confidence that others would accept it in the normal course of business has always been a necessary condition for anything to serve as money.

It is difficult, but not impossible, to conceive of an exchange economy without money. All exchange would have to involve direct bartering of goods for goods. But barter can be an efficient method of exchange only when there occurs a *double coincidence of wants*, that is, when each party to the exchange has precisely what the other party desires, at the time required, and in quantities appropriate to the exchange. In a large, complex society this implies a remarkable coincidence of events in time and space. Under other circumstances, that is, under normal circumstances, barter must involve a series of indirect exchanges. Each individual must take payment in kind, consume what he wishes, and store or perhaps transport the excess until the time and place are right for him to exchange it for the items he requires. Clearly, such a system would be highly wasteful of time and resources.

What we have referred to as the payments system is simply a set of institutional arrangements for the transfer of money from person to person, frequently among people who are widely separated geographically, often in different countries using different moneys. Our interest in the payments system is that of an economist and not that of a financial expert, an accountant, or a geographer. We are not concerned with the techniques of effecting payments or with techniques of recording payments, or even with what the patterns of payments tell us about the geographical patterns of production and trade. Granted that a payments system is essential to an exchange economy, what further questions might an economist ask about it?

The answer is twofold: he must be concerned with the efficiency of the payments mechanism and with its neutrality with respect to the essential economic decisions of society.

As we have described it, effecting payments is essentially a mechanical activity, one increasingly performed by electronic equipment. Still, it is not a costless activity: It absorbs scarce resources (labor and capital) that have alternative uses. The less labor and capital absorbed in effecting a given value of payments, the greater the efficiency of the payments system, the greater the supply of these scarce resources available for other productive employments, and hence the greater the potential output of the economy. This, then, must be a primary interest of economists in the payments mechanism.

Although efficiency is a primary interest of the economist, it must be only part of his concern with the payments mechanism. The economic system is, at root, a social mechanism for making certain decisions: for effecting social choices relating to what is to be produced, how and where it is to be produced, and to whom it is to be distributed. As a mechanical counterpart of the exchange process, the payments system is involved in this decision making. But apart from the fact that the participants in the process must bear the cost of effecting transactions emanating from their decisions, the payments system itself should be essentially neutral as among possible outcomes. The operations of the payments mechanism should not discriminate among transactors or among types of transactions except on the basis of different marginal costs of effecting transactions. Given the pervasive involvement of the payments mechanism in the exchange processes of the economy, the economist must ask if this neutrality is in fact achieved.

THE ACCUMULATION AND ALLOCATION OF SAVINGS

In principles-of-economics courses it is demonstrated that an exchange economy can be characterized as two reciprocal flows: a flow of real goods and services and a reverse flow of payments. The real flows are our ultimate concern. These are what determine our standard of economic well-being. However, the financial flows are not irrelevant, for they elicit and guide the real flows.

Thus, consumer expenditures (or expectations of such expenditures) elicit production of appropriate items. Likewise, income payments from business firms elicit flows of productive services. On the real side of this scheme, households appear as consuming units with distinct preferences and as providers of productive services with distinct characteristics. Business firms appear as producing units motivated by profits and as units that absorb productive services to produce the goods and services demanded by households (and by other firms and government agencies). The government has an ambiguous role. In some respects it is a unit for collective consumption; in other respects it is a producer of goods and services; in still other respects it is a vehicle for the establishment and administration of public policies. Like other producing units, it participates in the circular flow as an absorber of productive services. Unlike the consumer and business units, it does not normally respond to market indicators in its decisions on what to produce.

In real terms each of these groups of units has distinct functions and characteristics. However, they are all alike in that they are all *spending units;* all receive funds from various sources and spend funds for the purchase of goods and services. Each spending unit has sources of revenue: primarily the sale of productive services in the case of households, the sale of products in the case of business firms, and tax collections in the case of governments. In a general way, the expenditure of any spending unit is linked to its revenue. However, revenues do not have to control expenditures on goods and services during any period of time. A spending unit's revenues may well exceed its expenditures on goods and services, and in this sense it may have a *surplus* budget. On the other hand, its expenditures on goods and services may exceed its revenues, and for that period it may have a *deficit* budget.

These financial surpluses and deficits have their counterparts in real terms. A financial surplus implies that during that period the spending unit has chosen not to acquire all of the goods and services that its revenues would permit. A financial deficit implies that during that period the spending unit has been able to acquire more goods and services than its revenues would permit. Taking the two together, there is a transfer of command over resources from the surplus spending units to the deficit spending units. The transfer is arranged through the financial system. This, then, is the second major function of the financial system: It collects the surpluses of the surplus spending units and makes them available to the deficit spending units.

Stated this way, it sounds like a mechanical process similar in effect to the payments mechanism. But there is much more involved than the mechanical acts of collection and transfer. The financial surpluses (and their real equivalents) are, after all, scarce resources capable of many alternative uses. It is necessary to adjust the total available supply and the total demand (by adjusting either the demand or the supply or both), and to allocate the actual supply forthcoming among all of the competing demands. That is, the financial system must act like a market—a market in which prices are formed and adjusted to variations in supply and demand so as to clear the market. This is far from the mechanical type of process described in the discussion of the payments system.

The prices that are formed in financial markets are interest rates. While they perform the same general role, they have significance somewhat different from that of other prices in the economy. Interest rates indicate the market rate of exchange between dollars for present use and dollars for use at some time in the future. In this sense they reflect the opportunity cost of funds devoted to current consumption by households, and thus they should affect household decisions regarding the division of income between consumption and saving. Likewise, they represent the opportunity cost to corporations of funds devoted to particular capital projects. They provide a standard against which the probable profitability of any project can be assessed to determine whether the project should be undertaken. Thus, even if the agency of the financial system is not directly involved, the information provided by the financial system should be highly relevant to a broad range of economic decisions, that is, those relating to the balancing of future gains and present costs.

Throughout this discussion (with one exception) we have studiously avoided the terms *saving* and *investment* in describing this function of the financial system. As a result, in place of the straightforward statement that the financial system transfers command over resources from savers to investors, we have had to use the cumbersome phrase "from surplus spending units to deficit spending units." While it sounds pedantic, we have chosen this expression quite deliberately and with another purpose in mind. Saving and investment are technical terms in economic analysis with important and widely recognized meanings. They are not necessarily the same as the financial surpluses and financial deficits to which we refer. Investment implies expenditures to acquire physical capital goods, to expand the productive capacity of the firm and hence of the economy. But a spending unit may be in deficit for reasons unrelated to capital formation. A household, for example, may require funds simply to support a level of consumption in excess of its current income. Likewise, a spending unit may save and yet not have a financial surplus in the sense in which that term is used here. This would be true, for example, of a firm that finances its capital formation (investment) out of its undistributed profits (savings).

It is true, however, that the bulk of the transfers to which we are referring are related to the process of capital formation. They involve the collection of the financial counterpart of the saving of the society and its allocation to competing demands for capital formation. The efficiency of the financial system in collecting and transfering funds will affect the cost and hence the level of capital formation. This means that the operations of the financial system are vital to the pace and structure of the growth of the

8

economy. However, we must not forget that some of the transfers are to households to acquire consumer goods and services and to governments for assorted purposes, including collective consumption.

What are the questions that an economist would ask about the functioning of the financial system as an allocative mechanism? The answer is quite simple: He would be concerned with its effectiveness in directing funds to uses with the highest social value at the margin and doing so at least cost, and with the mechanism's flexibility in adapting to changing patterns of demand and supply. Inevitably, as in any market, the quest for such information leads the economist to an analysis of competitive conditions in financial markets.

FINANCIAL INTERMEDIATION

Assets, liabilities, and *wealth* are central concepts in our analysis of the financial system. These are familiar concepts to accountants; indeed, they are the stuff of which accounts are made. The terms refer to market values (even though the market value is frequently estimated rather than determined by actual transactions) measured in terms of the unit of value, or unit of account, the dollar. Thus, one's assets are the things of value owned. Assets derive their value either from the fact that they are capable of yielding income in the future (as a factory might yield income to its owners) or from the fact that they have qualities that are prized by others, who are therefore willing to pay to obtain them (as a work of art might be prized and hence valuable). One's liabilities are the value of his obligations, what he owes. Wealth is simply the difference between the value of assets and that of liabilities.

An individual, a family, or a nation becomes wealthy through the process of accumulating assets in excess of liabilities. This is normally done through the acts of saving and investing. If we leave aside the possibility of accumulating claims on residents of other countries, a nation can accumulate wealth in basically two forms: physical capital goods and the intangible skills, knowledge, organizational patterns, and work habits of its population (what is sometimes called human capital). These are the assets that are capable of producing output and hence income to the inhabitants of the nation in the future. However, through the financial system any individual in the nation has a much wider range of choices open to him as to the forms in which he can accumulate wealth. He is not restricted to the accumulation of physical and human capital. He can hold financial instruments or securities that represent claims on other individuals or organizations. Hence, he can participate, directly or indirectly, in the income stream generated by the human and physical capital held by others. This indirect participation is made possible through the financial system.

You may well ask, How significant is this fact? Is not our ultimate concern real income and wealth? Is it not true that, for society as a whole, income and wealth can only be produced by the underlying physical and human

9

assets to which we referred earlier? Indeed, if we set out to measure the wealth of society, all of the complex layers of financial claims would cancel themselves out, leaving only the underlying human and physical capital assets. This follows because every claim that appears as one person's assets is simultaneously someone else's liability. When you measure the wealth of the two combined, the asset of one (positive wealth?) cancels out the liability of the other (negative wealth?). Thus, if Jones owns a $1 million claim on Smith and Smith owns a factory worth $2 million, the wealth of the two combined is $2 million, not $3 million; that is, it is the value of the underlying capital asset. If we say Jones' wealth is $1 million, then Smith's is only $1 million: the value of his asset less the value of Jones' claim. We can push it a step further by noting that if Smith and Jones could exchange promissory notes (promises to pay), each would acquire an asset, his claim on the other, and each would acquire a liability, the other's claim on him. In the extreme, they could create a truly staggering total of paper assets for each of them. Note, however, that in spite of all this financial activity no real wealth would be created. Can we not conclude, therefore, that as economists interested in the real income and wealth of society we can well afford to ignore the complex of claims and counterclaims generated through the financial system? Do they appear as a veil, obscuring the real processes of saving and investing that create the real wealth of society but having no vital significance of their own? Perhaps we would do better to allocate our scarce analytical resources to the study of the real processes themselves.

Reverting to the Jones-Smith example, everyone would presumably agree that it is possible that without Jones' indirect participation Smith might not have had the resources to build the factory. In this sense the creation of financial claims may have some significance. But this is just another aspect of the process we have already discussed. The financial system serves as a vehicle for collecting the surpluses of surplus spending units and transfering them to deficit spending units. The surplus unit (Jones) is given a financial instrument as evidence of its continuing command over the scarce resources of the economy. This is nothing new. This transaction simply amounts to Jones and Smith pooling their resources to achieve an objective that, at that point in time, neither could achieve alone. It perhaps illustrates the point that financial instruments are *divisible* in a fashion in which real capital assets may not be, but that is about all.

The fact of divisibility is important, however. At a maximum it permits the pooling of the small financial surpluses of many isolated individuals to finance a venture of considerable magnitude. Thus, divisibility is important for the efficient collection and use of the savings of society, especially where these savings occur in small, isolated quantities.

Beyond this, divisibility also permits a *diversification* of asset holdings that would not otherwise be possible. Let us refer to any individual's collection of assets as his *portfolio*. We have said nothing about the form of Jones' claim on Smith. Perhaps it takes the form of a claim to half of the profits earned by the factory. In agreeing to share in Smith's venture in this way, Jones must recognize that the returns from the factory are conjectural. If they occur at all, they will occur in the future. The magnitude of the possible profits cannot be known now with any degree of certainty. Market conditions could emerge in which heavy losses are sustained by the venture. On the other hand, the returns could be much in excess of any expectations that the two men might have at the outset. There is some element of *risk* involved; returns may be large or small, and in the extreme the asset could become worthless. By holding only this asset in his portfolio, Jones bears the full burden of this risk. If the factory fails, his wealth is correspondingly reduced (of course, if the factory should prosper beyond all expectations, his wealth would increase correspondingly).

However, Jones does not have to commit all his resources to Smith's venture. Even if he splits his resources between two ventures that are in some sense equally risky, the total risk on his portfolio would be reduced, at least if the success of one of the ventures is not in some fashion related to the success of the other (i.e., if the risks are independent of each other). This follows because it is less likely that two independent ventures will fail at the same time than that either of them will fail individually. The risk on his portfolio could be reduced even further by spreading the funds over a variety of ventures, each with risks independent of each other. The financial system makes such diversification feasible for even relatively small portfolios.

But the financial system goes even further than that. It creates financial instruments that have properties completely unlike those of physical or human assets. It creates a variety of assets that are virtually—indeed, in the extreme, completely—free of the risks inevitably attached to the real capital assets on which the value of the financial instruments ultimately rest.

As a step in that direction, we might again consider the claim Jones has upon Smith, and particularly the form of that claim. So far, we have implicitly assumed that it took the form of a claim to a share of the potentially variable earnings of the venture. That is, we assumed that it was a *variable income security*. This is not the only form possible. The agreement between Smith and Jones might call for a specified dollar payment to Jones periodically (and perhaps a final payment on a certain date, after which the claim would no longer exist). Then the claim would take the form of a *fixed income security*. In the case of the variable income security, Jones bore part of the risk of fluctuation in the venture's earnings. In the case of a fixed income security, Smith bears all of this risk. Jones is entitled to a certain fixed payment, whether the earnings of the venture are large or small. Of course, there is a still larger risk that Jones cannot escape in this way. There is the risk that the venture will fail completely, that is, the risk that Smith will be unable to meet his commitment. This risk can only be hedged against by diversification. The certainty of payment on a fixed income security is only certainty in the small, that is, in the absence of major catastrophes to the venture.

The financial system facilitates diversification in another way. Not only does it permit the division of real assets and income streams into smaller parcels, it also provides markets in which the financial instruments can be traded among individuals. Securities vary in *marketability* as the characteristics of the underlying concerns are or are not known to a wide circle of potential investors. However, through efficient, organized markets, billions of dollars worth of transactions in all types of securities occur every day in the United States.

Our man Jones has wealth of $1 million at his disposal. He can obtain a considerable range of diversification among his assets and yet have a significant sum invested in each venture. This is not true of the typical individual, who may have only a few thousand dollars at his disposal (over and above his own earning power, which is normally his major asset). However, what is possible for an individual through diversification of his portfolio is also possible for specialized financial institutions. We call such institutions *financial intermediaries*, and the function they perform in the economy we call *financial intermediation*. These institutions hold a diversified portfolio of claims, each of which may have a substantial degree of risk, and issue their own liabilities, which are largely (but not necessarily completely) devoid of such risk. Standing as an intermediary between the ultimate lender and the ultimate user of the funds, they absorb risk and thus completely alter the range of investment opportunities open to individuals, particularly the small investor. Financial intermediaries provide financial instruments that incorporate the advantages of portfolio diversification by being claims on diversified portfolios.

Indeed, through the vehicle of the financial intermediary, the financial system carries the process a step farther. The system provides a variety of financial instruments—each of which is a claim on a diversified portfolio of claims—with widely varying characteristics designed to appeal to the specific preferences of very differently situated asset holders. We will have occasion to examine some of these later on, but one type of instrument requires special mention at this point. Financial intermediaries create assets that have the property of *liquidity*, or convertibility into a fixed amount of money on demand. Indeed, what we widely use as money, the demand deposit or checking account, is precisely such a financial instrument. Many economists argue that this provision of liquidity is the most significant aspect of financial intermediation. While holding essentially illiquid assets themselves, intermediaries are able to create liquid assets to be held by the ultimate savers in the economy.

What, then, is the significance of the fact that the financial system creates a wide variety of financial instruments and markets on which they can be traded efficiently? What is the economic importance of financial intermediation? Have we answered our earlier objection that all this financial activity is so much window dressing, a curtain obscuring our view of the true processes of saving and investing in the economy? What is the economist's interest in it all?

Underlying our analysis is the assumption that individuals have preferences as to the form in which they accumulate their assets. By creating a diverse range of assets, the financial system permits more complete satisfaction of these preferences and in this sense permits an increase in economic welfare. This includes making available relatively risk-free and highly liquid assets as well as assets in which the degree of risk is accentuated and that therefore are calculated to appeal to people with gambling instincts.

Beyond this are the implications for public policy designed to influence the level of income, employment, and prices in the economy. If individuals have preferences among assets, they presumably alter their portfolio choices as the characteristics of assets change, and particularly as the relative yield on assets change. Thus, a decline in the yield on a particular asset may induce many individuals to select something else. On the one hand, a general decline in the rates of return on financial assets may well induce the selection of nonfinancial (real) assets in their place. On the other hand, the decline in rates may encourage some to borrow so as to acquire a real asset. Such *substitution effects* can have important implications for the level of economic activity.

We have discovered over time that the government, primarily through the agency of the central bank, is able to alter the supply of certain types of financial instruments, particularly money and claims on the central government. This affects the rate of return on these assets and hence produces substitution effects of the type just noted. The end product should be change in the demand for real capital assets and hence an effect on aggregate demand, the level of income employment, and prices in the economy. This suggests the possibility of a monetary policy, by which we mean a policy designed to use these financial linkages for constructive social purposes, particularly the stabilization of the economy. Proper policy proposals, then, are a matter of major interest to the economist. How can such a policy be effected? What rules ought to guide it? How powerful will its effects be? How successful have we been in using this tool? These matters, of profound significance to every citizen, are the subject matter of the second half of this book.

THE SOCIAL INTEREST IN THE FINANCIAL SYSTEM: OUR APPROACH TO THE ANALYSIS

After this rather academic discussion of the functions of the financial system, it may be well to extract the essence of what we have said about the social interest in the financial system. Why should students of economics be concerned with money, banking, and finance?

Our first proposition is that the payments mechanism is part of the financial system, and its efficiency affects the overall efficiency of the economy. Secondly, the financial system is a vehicle by which a scarce resource, savings, is allocated among competing alternative uses. The use of the flow of savings affects both the rate of growth of the economy and the structure of economic activity. It is a matter of basic importance. Thirdly, the financial system is the repository of the claims to wealth of most families in this country, who have selected financial assets partly because of their belief that these assets are safe. It is important that this not be an illusion, for the consequences of financial collapse are grave. Finally, we have suggested that the interrelationships within the financial system give rise to the possibility of monetary policy designed to influence the level of income and employment in the economy. This alone should be sufficient to create an interest in the economics of money and finance.

SUMMARY

The financial industry as a whole produces a range of services, all of which are related directly or indirectly to assets and liabilities, that is, financial claims on people, institutions, corporations, and governments.

The financial industry provides services that are essential to the functioning of every industry and sector of the economy. It maintains the payments system, the collection and allocation of the savings of society, and the creation of various instruments in which society can hold its wealth.

The financial industry maintains the institutional arrangements that enable money to be transfered from person to person. As economists we are concerned with the efficiency of this mechanism and its neutrality with respect to society's essential economic decisions. The financial system also provides for the transfer of financial surpluses of the surplus spending units to the deficit spending units. The bulk of these transfers are related to the process of capital formation. However, a portion of the transfers are to households and governments.

The allocation of surpluses to deficit spending units occurs in financial markets at prices, called interest rates, that are determined by the supply of and demand for those surpluses. Financial intermediaries provide a wide choice of financial instruments by becoming participants in the process of bringing surplus and deficit units together. A financial intermediary actually borrows from one group giving a claim on itself and lends to another group accepting its claim. This range of financial instruments created by intermediaries has the advantage of portfolio diversification and divisibility, reducing the risk to the holder and giving his portfolio increased liquidity.

MONEY AND THE PAYMENTS SYSTEM

Money is a commonplace phenomenon. It is involved in all of our personal economic activities and is so much a part of our everyday life that we tend to take it for granted. Occasionally, perhaps following a casual visit to a numismatic shop or a discussion with a coin-collecting friend, we may be amused by the diversity of things that have been used as money in different times and places. Or we may struggle with strange coins and unfamiliar denominations in another country and wonder at how such different "moneys" can coexist in the world. But seldom do we stop and carefully consider how the "money system" works. Why can I obtain what I want at a store by handing over pieces of paper? Why will only certain pieces of paper do? How can I be sure that if I write and mail a check to pay a bill in a distant city (or perhaps another country) my creditor will in fact be paid? And if he is paid, what are the mechanics of the transfer? If we pause to consider, these and many similar questions may occur to us.

THE MONEY SUPPLY

MONEY DEFINED

What is money? A suitable definition might be: *anything that is normally accepted when a transfer of purchasing power takes place.*

15

Long philosophical treatises have been written about the essence of "moneyness," attempting to explain why money is money—why certain objects are "normally accepted when a transfer of purchasing power takes place." Our definition, however, is pragmatic, not probing the essence of moneyness but rather acknowledging as money anything that is in fact used as a customary and normal medium of exchange.

The words *customary* and *normal* are important. Our definition rules out things that may emerge on an occasional ad hoc basis as an intermediary in isolated and irregular exchange but at the same time admits the possibility of a wide variety of objects performing this function in different times and places: cigarettes in prisoner-of-war camps; cowrie shells in the primitive native trading economies of the precolonial Pacific Islands and the coasts of Africa; tobacco or warehouse receipts for tobacco in the colony of Virginia; playing cards in New France; gold and silver in the form of bullion, dust, or coins; and paper promissory notes of governments throughout the world.

What money is, then, is a matter of customary practice. The nature of the money supply in any particular area will evolve over time as customary practices adapt to changing circumstances. A list of items to be considered money at one point in time may be inappropriate at another. Moreover, at any given point in time such a list may seem somewhat arbitrary. Whether a particular item qualifies as money or not involves a matter of judgment: Is it a "normal and customary medium of exchange"?

COMMODITY VS. FIAT MONEYS

The story of the evolution of money in different historical, geographical, and cultural contexts is fascinating. Many people have sought general principles underlying this evolution, and it may be that such principles do exist. However, it is not part of our purpose to attempt to identify them, such a quest being more suited to the sociologist or anthropologist than the economist. As one scholar has noted, "Money does not exist in a vacuum. It is not a mere lifeless object, but a social institution."[1] However, we must take some interest in the form of the basic monetary medium because it affects the possibility for deliberate manipulation of the money supply as an aspect of government economic policy. The significant fact from this point of view is that while the process has been neither steady, one-directional, nor complete, the development of modern monetary systems has involved the displacement of *commodity moneys* by intangible claims or *fiat moneys*.

In early history the object used as money tended to be one with intrinsic value as a commodity (as well as certain other desirable properties) or to be representative of such a commodity and freely convertible into it on demand. This commodity is normally referred to as the *standard money*. The most widely recognized monetary commodities are, of course, gold, and to a lesser extent silver, and as a result the historical literature on monetary systems abounds with references to types of gold standards, silver standards, and bimetallic standards (with both metals as standard moneys). Indeed, in spite of the passing of a formal gold standard, many people still regard gold as money *par excellence*.[2]

One effect of having a commodity base for the money supply was to place the size of the money supply largely (but seldom completely) beyond the control of the government. It was strongly influenced by forces governing the availability of the standard commodity. Thus, with a gold standard, the money supply would be affected by forces affecting the output of newly mined gold (including erratic discoveries of new rich deposits), the flow of gold in international trade, and the absorption of gold by industry for non-monetary purposes.

In modern times this link to a commodity has largely been broken. The coins issued by a modern state tend to be simply tokens, the value of the metal they contain being far less than the value of the coin as a coin. Similarly, the notes that are issued as currency are generally not convertible on demand into any standard commodity (except in the sense that any holder of money can presumably purchase whatever commodities he prefers in the open market). Modern currencies are fiat moneys. They are issued by governments, are not representative of any commodity, and are not redeemable in terms of such a commodity. By government fiat or decree, they are *legal tender*. That is, creditors are legally obligated to accept such currencies in settlement of debts. Since there is no legal link to a commodity, modern monetary systems are generally referred to as inconvertible paper standards. The possibilities for deliberate manipulation of the money supply—for good or evil—should be apparent.

There is another aspect of an inconvertible paper standard that should also be of interest to a student of economics. When the money supply is based on a commodity such as gold, an expansion of the money supply can be accomplished only by employing scarce productive resources to produce more of the commodity (or by attracting more of the commodity from alternative possible uses). A substantial economic cost is involved, equal, at the margin, to the value of the money created. With inconvertible paper money, the creation of more money is virtually (but not completely) costless. It does not absorb anywhere near the same value of scarce productive resources. As a result, by economizing on the scarce resources of the world while performing exactly the same economic function, inconvertible paper money permits the attainment of a (slightly) higher overall standard of living.

In fact, in any modern economy both token coins and fiat paper currencies constitute but a fraction of the money supply and account for an even smaller fraction of the total value of payments in the economy. By far the most important medium of exchange is the bank deposit, which is convertible into currency on demand and is transferable among individuals by check. By our definition these deposits are money, although they are not legal tender. They are "normally accepted when a transfer of purchasing

17

power takes place." Yet they are completely intangible. They are claims on a private institution, a bank, taking the form simply of entries in a ledger book. Such money is commonly referred to as *bank money* or *credit money* or, since it is based on trust in the soundness of the institution, fiduciary money.

THE AMERICAN MONEY SUPPLY

Armed with our pragmatic definition of money, what would we have to count if we set out to measure the money supply of the United States? The most obvious items on which we would all immediately agree are the coins and notes used for hand-to-hand circulation. While the term *currency* is frequently used only with reference to paper notes, we can properly use it to refer to both coins and notes.

Coins. Coins are manufactured and issued by the Bureau of the Mint, a branch of the Department of the Treasury. These coins are intended to be tokens. That is, the face value of each coin is intended to be substantially greater than the market value of the metal contained in the coin. Since the coins are in effect sold to the public at their face value, the manufacture and issuance of coins is normally a profitable business. The difference between the face value of the coins and the value of the coins as metal is known as *seignorage*, and, after allowing for the other expenses related to the operation of the mint, it provides a source of revenue for the government. In fiscal 1972, for example, the Bureau of the Mint reported seignorage of $580.6 million.

Although coins are intended to be tokens, they do contain metal that has market value as a commodity. Since that market value can change under the combined pressures of supply and demand for alternative uses, it can happen that the value of the metal as a commodity comes to exceed the face value of the coin. This happened most recently during the 1960s. The price of silver in the open market rose sharply during this period. Silver was being mined only on a limited basis, and worldwide demand for silver in industrial uses increased rapidly. Speculators began to withhold many silver coins from circulation as the commodity value of the silver in the coins exceeded its value as coin. Although illegal, it was profitable for speculators to melt the coins for their silver content. The Treasury recognized that there was a coin shortage but failed to recognize the reasons behind it. It attributed the shortage, even in the face of stepped-up production of silver coins, to numismatists rather than to speculators. Finally in 1965, with congressional approval, the mint began production of its sandwich coins, a copper and nickel alloy on a copper core that satisfied the constraints of the mint's machinery as well as the vending-machine industry's requirements for coins of a certain density and electrical conductivity. At the same time that the new coins were put into circulation, the silver coins were quietly withdrawn from circulation by Federal Reserve banks. Collectors and speculators also continued to accumulate and stockpile these coins.

On May 31, 1972, the Treasury reported that there was $7 billion in coin outstanding, excluding coin held by the Federal Reserve banks and the Treasury itself. This figure is termed coin in circulation. However, it should be obvious from the preceding discussion that not all of this coin is actually available as a medium of exchange. Some coins have greater value to the collector than their value in use would command. Data are not released on the actual amount of predominantly silver coin still in circulation.

Paper Currency. The issuance of paper money today is also a monopoly of the federal government through its agent, the Federal Reserve System. *Federal Reserve notes* are the only form of paper money being issued today to add to the paper component of currency. Federal Reserve notes are liabilities of the Federal Reserve System and direct obligations of the U.S. government. The Federal Reserve must deposit an equivalent amount of eligible securities of U.S. government debt obligations with its Federal Reserve agent before the Reserve banks receive the paper currency. The Federal Reserve banks then fill requests from commercial banks as the public demands more currency at certain periods throughout the year.

It is only recently that the Treasury has ceased supplying any net additions to the stock of paper money. Before the silver crisis of the 1960s mentioned earlier, the Treasury had issued silver certificates in $1, $5, and $10 denominations in exchange for silver dollars or bullion. It became increasingly apparent that it was no longer appropriate to redeem silver certificates with silver dollars or bullion whose free-market value was greater than the paper certificate. The Federal Reserve was issuing notes in $5 and $10 denominations, and in 1963 it began to issue its own $1 Federal Reserve note. Simultaneously, the Treasury stopped issuing silver certificates.

On June 30, 1968, the Treasury officially ceased commodity redemption of these certificates. It is withdrawing them from circulation as they appear at Federal Reserve banks. At the end of May 1971, there were $218 million silver certificates still outstanding, although undoubtedly many of these are now in private collections.

The Treasury still maintains a fixed amount of *United States notes* outstanding ($322.5 million). Known also as greenbacks or legal tender notes, they were first issued in 1862 as part of Civil War financing. They were unredeemable in any commodity form at that time, but in 1900 Congress finally approved a separate gold redemption fund. This still exists, and the Treasury continues to replace worn-out notes as they appear at Federal Reserve banks.

The issuance of notes for circulation was not always a government monopoly. We see in collections or, at times, even in circulation remnants of other paper currency issues. Before August 1935, privately owned, federally chartered national banks could issue their own bank notes. These had to be backed by specific U.S. bonds. These notes circulated as currency and were specifically guaranteed by the Treasury so as to promote their acceptability.

Since they were also backed by federal bonds, they were indirectly Treasury obligations. In 1935 the Treasury undertook to pay off the bonds that had backed many of these notes with profits from the revaluation of the gold stock that had occurred in 1934. Legislation for issuance of new national bank notes expired, and national bank notes remaining in circulation became part of the Treasury's currency. As they appear at Federal Reserve banks, they are retired. In 1935, $650 million worth were reported to be in circulation (13 percent of the currency at that time). By the end of May 1971, the Treasury reported that there were still $20 million in national bank notes "in circulation." The term *in circulation* refers to currency not in Federal Reserve banks or the Treasury's holdings. Not all of this currency serves as a medium of exchange; rather, some small fraction has been lost or withdrawn for its greater value to collectors than as a medium of exchange.

In the United States both coin and paper currency must be accepted at face value in payment of all debts, whether public or private. Our currency is thus legal tender. All paper currency printed since 1963 bears the words "This note is legal tender for all debts, public and private." Prior to that time paper notes also included a meaningless phrase "and is redeemable in lawful money at the United States Treasury or at any Federal Reserve Bank."

Declaring its currency legal tender is one device a government may use to promote general acceptability and use of its currency. Another method is to guarantee that the paper currency could be redeemed in a commodity. Until 1934 paper currency could be redeemed for the commodity that backed it—gold. Until 1968 silver certificates could be redeemed for silver bullion. Today our paper currency is no longer redeemable in commodity, yet it continues to be accepted and used by the public. Another device used by governments to limit the production of paper currency is to back it with a commodity like gold. In this way, it is believed, the government is constrained from "turning on the printing presses." Since 1968 our currency has not been backed by a metallic commodity but only by an equivalent amount of eligible securities.

Paper currency is a form of government debt, but it is non-interest-bearing debt that need never be retired. Since the face value of Federal Reserve notes exceeds the value of the paper as a commodity, the government also earns seignorage on its issue. While it is difficult to determine the value of this seignorage, it cost the Federal Reserve System only $31 million in 1972 for about 2.7 billion pieces of paper money. This is a significantly small price to pay to maintain and add to a paper component of the total money supply of more than $50 billion.

Bank Money. As in other modern economies, the bulk of the money supply in the United States is bank money, the deposit liabilities of private, commercial banks. Just as paper currency is in effect government debt, so bank money is private debt. Bank depositors have made a loan to the bank. They are creditors, the bank's debtors. What happens in the payments process, therefore, is a transfer of ownership of the debts of banks.

There are many types of deposits issued by commercial banks and by other financial institutions called near banks. Not all of them qualify as money by our definition. That is, not all deposits are designed to be used as a medium of exchange, and hence not all deposits are customarily used as such. The essential technical requirement for a deposit to be money in the narrow sense in which we have defined it is that ownership of the deposit can be readily transfered from individual to individual, that is, that it be *checkable*.

A *check* is a written order from a depositor instructing his banker to pay a specific sum to a third party whenever the third party presents the order for payment. It is the instrument through which the transfer of purchasing power is effected. Only commercial banks issue deposits that are checkable. Therefore, by our narrow definition of money, we should include only coin, paper currency, and demand deposits in the money supply.

Commercial banks issue other deposits, which, although not transferable by check, can be easily converted into a checkable account. If our concern is with the impact of the money supply on the behavior of firms and households, we would want to think twice about excluding such deposits. If they can be so readily transformed into "money," should not the holder of such an account behave as though he had money in his hands?

We have defined the money supply narrowly to include coin, paper currency, and demand deposits. We also take note of deposits that can easily be converted into a medium of exchange. Since the concept of *near money* plays a prominent role in our analysis in later chapters, when we will define it more precisely, we include a brief introduction here.

Commercial banks issue three categories of time (in contrast to demand) deposits. In one category are deposits in amounts of $100,000 or more that are accepted for a period of at least 30 days in exchange for a *certificate of deposit*. The bank usually issues these certificates in a specific amount for a fixed period that may range from 1 to 12 months. The certificate is issued with a fixed rate of interest that is payable to the holder at maturity. Negotiable certificates of deposit have become an important money market instrument as well as an important method by which commercial banks can attract large amounts of funds for relatively short periods. The holder of a certificate of deposit can convert the certificate into payments money prior to maturity only by selling it in the open market, that is, drawing payments money from some other party. The issuing bank is under no obligation to redeem the certificate until it matures. These deposits are not considered a part of the narrowly defined payments money supply but are a near money and should be considered a significant component of a more broadly defined money supply that would include other near moneys.

Perhaps the nearest of the near moneys, however, are other time deposit accounts of commercial banks. One type of open time deposit is the *passbook savings account*. Passbook savings accounts may be held only by individuals and nonprofit institutions. They are evidenced by the passbook and, although not checkable, can be transfered into a form that is a medium of exchange merely by presenting the passbook. In general, commercial banks try to discourage frequent turnover of these accounts and have the legal right to require notice prior to withdrawal. In fact, banks rarely exercise this right.

Commercial depositors can also obtain interest on funds, if they are willing to lend them to commercial banks for a minimum of thirty days. These accounts are called *open-account time deposits*. The holder of this type of deposit may add to it at any time and may leave funds with the bank beyond the minimum period with interest continuing to accumulate. Banks again have the legal right to notice of intention to withdraw funds, but they typically waive this right or reduce the time of notice. The difference between open-account time deposits and savings accounts is that the former often require that the depositor keep a larger minimum balance. Moreover, depending on the length of time they are left on deposit, open account funds may earn higher rates of interest than passbook savings.

What we have been considering, however, is the money supply. None of these types of time deposits is a part of the narrowly defined money supply that can be used directly in its present form as a medium of exchange, but the size of these deposits influences the money supply because these deposits may be quickly and easily converted to a form of payments money as we have already defined it.

In referring to these deposits we have used the expression *near money*. We might well ask if it is necessary for the time deposits to be with a bank for them to be considered near money. The answer is unequivocally no. There are a large number of institutions that accept deposits on essentially the same terms as savings deposits with commercial banks. These institutions are frequently referred to as near banks and consist of mutual savings banks, savings and loan associations, and credit unions. We will examine their activities in greater detail in later chapters. What is relevant at the moment is that they hold deposits that are very close substitutes for savings deposits with commercial banks, which, as we have seen, are close substitutes for demand deposits and currency.

In Table 2.1 we set out the items most actively used as a medium of exchange: coins; currency in circulation outside the vaults of commercial banks, Federal Reserve banks, and the Treasury; and adjusted demand deposits. The latter figure excludes the deposits of banks with other banks (interbank deposits) and the deposits maintained at commercial banks by the federal government. The total of these components we call the money

Table 2.1. The U.S. Money Supply, August 31, 1973
(Not Seasonally Adjusted) (Billions of Dollars)

Payments Money	
Currency (coin and paper notes in circulation outside banks)	$ 60.0
Demand Deposits (excluding interbank and federal government deposits)	200.8
Total	$260.8
Near-Money Deposits	
Time Deposits at Commercial Banks (excluding negotiable certificates of deposits in denominations of $100,000 or more)	$286.3
Certificates of Deposit (negotiable in denominations of $100,000 or more)	68.4
Savings and Loan Association Deposits	220.8
Mutual Savings Bank Deposits	95.4
Credit Union Savings[a]	21.7
Total	$692.6
Total Money Supply and Near Money	$953.4

Source: Federal Reserve *Bulletin*, October 1973, pp. A16, A38; [a]National Credit Union Administrator, *Annual Report* (Washington, D.C., 1972), p. 4.

supply. This conforms to one of the definitions of the money supply (M_1) on which the Federal Reserve System regularly publishes data.[3] We also include in Table 2.1 the near-money deposits of commercial banks and near banks for comparison and reference.

Composition of the Money Supply. There are, then, several items that can be used as money. What determines the composition of the money supply? Is the composition constant over time?

In considering these questions, the important principle to keep in mind is that while the various types of money in use in the United States are not officially convertible into any commodity like gold or silver, they are freely convertible into each other. Thus, the holder of a demand deposit in a bank can at any time (at least while a bank or grocery store is open) convert his deposit into currency. Likewise, a holder of Federal Reserve notes can readily convert them into coins or into a demand deposit or into a personal savings deposit at any of the banks or near banks that hold such deposits. This means that the *composition* of the money supply depends simply on the relative demands of the public for each type of money. (We italicize the word *composition* because this is not true of the *size* of the total money supply.)

Why might the public have different demands for each type of money? A major explanation (apart from habit) must be that each type of money is efficient for different purposes.[4]

As is evident from Table 2.1, deposits, transferable by check, constitute the largest part of the money supply: about 75 percent by the narrow definition. This refers to the stock of money held at any point in time. What is not shown in the table is the fact that the actual transfer of such deposits accounts for an even larger portion of the total value of payments. Some authorities estimate that between 85 percent and 90 percent of the value of transactions is effected by check.

The users of money clearly find demand deposit money the most convenient form for most purposes. As an asset, bank money is safer than currency. It can be withdrawn only by the owner of the deposit, whereas currency can be lost through theft, fire, natural disaster, and so on. So there is much less risk of loss as long as the bank itself is sound. Additional safety is provided by the Federal Deposit Insurance Corporation, which insures individual deposits up to a maximum of $20,000. Ninety-eight percent of commercial banks are covered by this insurance.

The check is a convenient and (at least for large transactions) relatively cheap method of making payment. It can be drawn for exactly the correct sum and can be readily transported over long distances through the mail at very low cost. The shipment of currency, by contrast, can be expensive and in addition involves risk of loss. There are alternative transfer arrangements with currency, such as postal money orders or telegraphic transfers, but again these are relatively expensive compared to checks. It is also worth noting that checks leave a very convenient record for the firm or individual using them.

Bank money, then, is relatively convenient for most commercial purposes, but there is always some demand for currency from individuals who do not trust or do not understand banks. There is probably some demand from individuals who find the fact that checks leave a record of transactions to be a disadvantage, for example, people trying to avoid income taxes or engaged in illegal transactions. Moreover, given the normal practice of many banks, which charge a flat amount per check (regardless of the magnitude of the check), checks can become costly for small transactions. (In several major metropolitan areas free checking is offered by the major commercial banks.) In addition, a bank customer drawing a check for cash at his bank increasingly has to go through the inconvenient and time-consuming routine of identifying himself at his own bank and indeed even proving that he has an account with that bank. Such inconvenience deters and embarrasses many depositors, but commercial banks may have begun to improve this aspect of their service by introducing automated tellers that will cash small amounts. Active use of coin and paper currency is closely related to the retail trade, particularly "small ticket" retail sales and vending-machine use.

Research shows a relatively strong downward long-run trend in the ratio of currency to the total money supply, at least until 1930. There were major increases in the ratio in the depression of the 1930s (when there was a widespread loss of confidence in the banking system as a result of a wave of bank failures) and during World War II (perhaps because of increased foreign hoardings of U.S. dollars, and increased use of currency for illegal transactions and tax evasion). Thus, although the long-run trend seemed to reemerge after World War II, by the late 1960s the ratio of currency to money was much higher than in the prewar period (the 1920s, for example).

Within each year (and each month, and each week), there are also striking patterns in the use of currency relative to deposits, following mainly the retail trade (and, for shorter periods, payroll arrangements). Thus, the ratio of currency to money systematically rises to a peak in December, with the burst of retail activity related to the Christmas season, and has several minor peaks during the year, also related to retail activity.

THE PAYMENTS SYSTEM

Payment by currency is a straightforward affair, about which little more need be said. However, as we have already pointed out, currency is a relatively inconvenient medium of exchange and, except for small, local transactions, accounts for a rather small share of the total value of transactions. The arrangements for transfering purchasing power by check are necessarily more complicated, although the principles involved are in fact very simple.

Payment by Check. To illustrate the principle underlying payment by check, we can trace what happens when you have purchased some major item, received the bill, and written a check in payment. The check, you will recall, is nothing other than a written order to your banker to pay the appropriate amount to the merchant. When the merchant receives the check and deposits it in his bank, the bank must collect and return the check to the bank on which it was drawn. That bank, in turn, debits your account and returns it to you as evidence that payment has been made.

If both you and the merchant have accounts in the same branch of the same bank, that branch's bookkeeping department makes the appropriate entries on its books. The merchant's account is credited and your account is debited. Purchasing power is transfered with a few strokes of the bookkeeper's pen (or, more likely, a few punches on a bookkeeping machine).

If you have accounts with different branches of the same bank, the check is sent to the central bookkeeping department to be credited to and debited against the individual accounts. If the check is drawn on one local bank and deposited in another, then it is sent to the clearinghouse division of the merchant's bank to be sent to the local clearinghouse.

The Clearinghouse. A clearinghouse is an association of local banks whose primary function is to aid in the exchange of local checks with a minimum movement of funds. Each local bank sorts all clearinghouse checks by drawee bank and computes the sum owed to it by that bank. At an appointed time each day, each bank sends a delivery clerk and a settling clerk to the clearinghouse. Each other bank has a list of items owed to it by the other banks. The items are netted out and, depending on the agreement of the local association, settlement may be made through the district Federal Reserve bank, through the drawing of checks in favor of the creditor bank by the debtor banks, or through the debiting and crediting of the banks' own accounts with the clearinghouse. When the exchange is over, the clerks return to their own banks with checks and other items that must then be debited from the appropriate depositors' accounts.

The principle of local clearinghouses is common to all banking systems. However, the arrangements for the clearing and collection of out-of-town checks differ from one country to another.

In the United States there are some 14,000 different banks. Many of these have extensive branch organizations in limited areas, but branching across state boundaries is not permitted. Although the term is not fully accurate (since there are many branch banking firms), the U.S. banking system is generally referred to as a *unit banking system*. Perhaps the term *fragmented* would be more descriptive.

Another feature of our banking system is that not all banks are required to maintain deposits with the central bank, that is, the Federal Reserve System. The term *system* is quite appropriate. The central bank is in fact a network of 12 regional Federal Reserve banks coordinated by the Board of Governors of the Federal Reserve System in Washington, D.C. The fact that not all commercial banks belong to the Federal Reserve System is a product of the dual character of arrangements for chartering banks. Both the federal and state governments can issue bank charters. National banks are required to be members of the Federal Reserve System and to hold deposits with the regional Federal Reserve bank. State banks, if they meet certain minimum requirements, are permitted to join the System but are not required to do so.

Let us return to your check written to the merchant. If the check is deposited in another bank outside the clearinghouse area, the check can be collected and returned to the drawer's bank in one of two ways.

The Central Bank as a Check Collection Agency. The Federal Reserve System is actively involved in the collection of out-of-town checks. Each Federal Reserve bank will accept checks from member banks (and under some circumstances from nonmember banks also), which it will then forward to the appropriate cities for collection. The Reserve bank, meanwhile, credits the reserve account of the merchant's bank with the full amount of the check and debits the reserve account of your (the drawer's) bank, and sends it back to your bank for debit from your demand deposit account.

If your bank is in another Federal Reserve district, the check will first be sent by the merchant's bank to its Federal Reserve bank. That bank will credit the merchant's bank's reserve account with full payment, but only after a stipulated period not exceeding two days. The check is sent on immediately, however, to the Reserve bank of your district, where that bank debits your bank's reserve account and sends it on to your bank for collection from your deposit account.

In this case, differences in balances between the Federal Reserve district banks can occur. These differences are settled through another clearinghouse arrangement—this one is for the 12 Federal Reserve banks only. At the Interdistrict Settlement Fund, each of the 12 Reserve banks maintains deposits of gold certificates that are moved among the 12 banks as changes in balances dictate.

Gold certificates are assets of the Federal Reserve. They are claims against the nation's gold stock, which the Treasury owns. When the Treasury buys gold, it normally creates and issues to the Federal Reserve an equal value of gold certificates. When it sells gold, it usually retires an equivalent amount of gold certificates. Thus, changes in the monetary gold stock affects the assets and liabilities of the Federal Reserve.

The Correspondent Banking System. Although the Federal Reserve's check collection service is free, most out-of-town checks are not collected through the agency of the Federal Reserve System. Indeed, a recent study revealed that while the larger banks (i.e., those with deposits of $100 million or more) collected between 55 percent and 60 percent of the value of their out-of-town checks in this way, the smaller banks (e.g., those with deposits of $10 million or less) used the facilities of the Federal Reserve System to collect less than 10 percent of the value of their out-of-town checks. The rest of the out-of-town checks were collected through an alternate system, a network of correspondent banks. Thus, as the study concluded, "the Federal Reserve System only supplements—it did not supplant—the correspondent banking system."[5]

Correspondent banking relations involve banks maintaining deposits with each other and performing certain services for each other. Generally speaking, smaller banks in outlying areas maintain deposits with correspondent banks in larger cities in the region, which in turn hold deposits with correspondent banks in still larger cities. However, the structure of the system is not a simple pyramid. Many banks, particularly the larger banks in larger cities, both hold deposits for other banks and maintain deposits with these same correspondents. Moreover, the larger banks will have correspondent relations with many banks, including many foreign banks. Thus, according to the study cited earlier, the large city banks (deposits of $100 million or more) on the average are correspondents for over 240 banks and hold correspondent balances with over 30 banks. One large New York City bank is reported to hold correspondent balances for over 4000 banks.

City correspondent banks provide a variety of services for their country correspondents. This includes participation in loans too large for the small bank to handle, advice on investments, assistance in trading in government securities, and sometimes assistance in the recruitment and training of personnel. But the main service, and the only one of interest to us, is the clearing and collection of out-of-town checks. Correspondent banks act as agents for other banks in the collection of checks. Thus, instead of using the facilities of the Federal Reserve System, a bank receiving a check drawn on an out-of-town bank has the option of sending it to a correspondent bank in that city for collection and having the proceeds deposited in its account with that correspondent. Similarly, a bank having to make payment in another city can do so by drawing drafts on its correspondent balances.

Two clearing systems coexist in the United States partly because many banks do not belong to the Federal Reserve System. But even member banks make heavy use of the correspondent system. Because of the increased deposits that it provides to them, many city banks have found it profitable to compete actively for correspondent business. The result of their competition is fast, efficient service in collecting checks (plus all of the other services that go along with correspondent relations), which many banks find preferable in some respect to the service provided by the central bank. In general, clearing checks through correspondents does not require the same degree of sorting that the Federal Reserve does. Nor do they adhere to as strict a deadline as the Federal Reserve. Further, a correspondent will credit the bank's deposit immediately, regardless of how long it estimates it will take for the check to actually clear and for it to receive the funds. This feature is particularly important to banks in periods of tight money and is in sharp contrast to the Federal Reserve System's crediting schedule. A final point is that correspondents do not insist on par clearing.

Par Clearing. The involvement of the Federal Reserve System in the check collection process has had another important effect on the payment system. The Federal Reserve System has insisted on what is called *par clearing.*

Since its beginning in 1913, the Federal Reserve System has attempted to eliminate exchange charges on checks and hence to impose the principle of par clearing. It has done this in two ways. Initially it made par clearing compulsory for member banks. When this did not achieve the desired results (because many banks chose not to join the system), it gave nonmember banks access to its check clearing and collection service on the condition that they accept the par clearing principle.

The Federal Reserve's efforts have been largely successful. It had been common practice for most banks to pay less than the stated amount for checks presented by mail. If a check for $100 was presented, the drawer's account was debited by the full amount; but the bank sent back $99.90 to the bank that had presented the check for payment. In order to encourage the use of checks and the acceptance of checks by merchants, the Federal Reserve refused to accept nonpar checks for collection. Only about 3 percent of all banks in the United States are still nonpar banks. They tend to be small country banks concentrated in the rural areas of the Southeast and Midwest.

The Federal Reserve has pursued the principle of par clearance because it was interested in an efficient, low-cost check payments system. Nonpar clearing led to circuitous routings of checks to avoid exchange charges, with consequent delays in payment. Equally important, the exchange charges had discriminatory effects. Not all bank depositors were treated alike, and the differences were not necessarily related to costs of handling. Banks were accused of exploiting whatever monopolistic power they had, making the levying of exchange charges a profitable activity. (It is still true that a nonpar bank is typically the only bank in any given town.) The principle of requiring the recipient rather than the remitter to pay the cost of a payment can also be questioned. Perhaps the appropriate place to levy charges is on the deposit, with the charges related to the activity of the account.

Service Charges. The process of clearing and collecting checks, however, is far from costless. Banks do incur expense in the handling of their demand deposit accounts. Indeed, the costs associated with the servicing of checking accounts are among the major costs incurred by banks. It has been estimated that between 40 percent and 50 percent of all bank employees are assigned to the check-processing function. On an average business day millions of checks will be written; and while the volume of activity depends on the size and location of the banking office, major banks will handle many thousands of checks drawn on out-of-town banks. In fiscal year 1970, the Federal Reserve handled nearly 8 billion checks with an aggregate value of over $3.5 trillion.

The costs in question arise in connection with the handling of all the documents and bookkeeping entries involved in transfering funds by check. This has provided fertile ground for automation; and while there are large numbers of items, the costs involved depend more directly on the number of checks handled than on the total value of payments transfered. Thus, it should cost no more to handle a check for $1 million than it does to handle a check for $1.00 (provided that it is cleared through the same channels).

It can be argued that a charge for this service is both fair and economically efficient. It would be economically efficient on the ground that those who use scarce resources of the economy ought to pay a price equal to the value of those resources in their alternative uses; that is, they ought to pay a price equal to the marginal cost of the service.

Banks attempt to recover the costs of handling these payments in two ways. First, they do not pay interest on demand deposits. Thus, in effect the depositor makes an interest-free loan to the bank, forgoing interest income for the privilege of writing checks. The bank can use the money to make loans or purchase securities and then use the interest income to help cover the costs of providing checking facilities.

Another method used by banks is to assess a *service charge*. This charge is related to the activity of the account, the number of checks written, the number of deposits made, the size of the minimum balance maintained on the deposit (which affects the interest income the bank can earn on the funds deposited), and other peripheral conditions. This charge bears more heavily on checks drawn for small sums of money than on those drawn for large sums. This is one factor making the check a relatively more efficient instru- ment for large payments than for small ones.

In some areas free checking is normal. In using this device, the bank relies solely on the interest income to defray the costs of servicing checking accounts. Further, it is a device that is used to attract new customers or first-time checking account holders. The extra inflow of funds enables the bank to expand its loan and investment activity. Banks resort to free checking when there is vigorous competition and during periods of tight money conditions.

FOREIGN PAYMENTS

So far we have examined how transfers of purchasing power are made possible within the confines of a nation. But what about payments to or from places outside the nation's boundaries? Such payments introduce two com- plications: The U.S. bank may not have branches in the relevant foreign center (although U.S. banks do have agencies in many important financial centers), and the payment involves another currency besides the dollar.

Assume you live in Minneapolis and that a bill you owe in Toronto, Canada, is payable in Canadian dollars. The bill could just as well be made payable in London, Cairo, Tokyo, or Moscow. You could go to your local bank and buy Canadian dollars in exchange for your dollars. The Canadian currency could then be mailed to Toronto, completing the transfer. This method involves the same risk of theft or loss as mailing currency domesti- cally and would be suitable for small transactions only. More safely, you could purchase a bank draft payable in Canadian dollars and send it to Toronto. This draft is, in effect, a check written by the U.S. bank on an account it holds in a Canadian correspondent bank. The recipient of the check in Toronto deposits or cashes the draft, and it is then put through the clearing system just as if it were any other check written on a Canadian bank. The U.S. bank has reduced its holdings of Canadian dollars (i.e., its deposits with its Canadian correspondent) and increased its holdings of U.S. currency if you paid cash, or reduced its deposit liabilities by an equivalent amount if you wrote a check. For providing this service the bank charges a fee for the draft and for exchanging U.S. dollars for Canadian dollars.

A second question then arises: How does the American bank obtain Canadian dollar deposits to sell to its customers? There are two possibilities. First, corresponding to the payments by Americans to foreigners are reverse payments by foreigners to Americans. To the extent that the American recipients of these payments are customers of your bank, it has a flow of Canadian dollars out of which it can meet its customers' demands. However, with so many banks and so many different currencies that customers might want, the bank must have an alternative source. Thus, if the demands for Canadian dollars exceed the funds that the bank has available, it can enter the foreign exchange market, centered primarily in New York City, and purchase the required Canadian funds from other banks that have a surplus. This market is an essential part of the international payments process. We will examine it in more detail in a later chapter.

In summary, the crucial institutions involved in international payments are an international network of correspondent banks and foreign exchange markets in which foreign moneys can be bought and sold just as if they were commodities like wheat or rice.

ECONOMIC ISSUES IN THE OPERATIONS OF THE PAYMENTS SYSTEM

So much for a description of the institutions of the payments system. What are the economic issues posed by the operations of this system in the United States? As noted in Chapter 1, the relevant questions are twofold: Is the system efficient, and is it neutral? In raising the question of efficiency we mean to ask: Does the existing system accomplish its task with the minimum amount of resources required? Would some alternative system accomplish the task with fewer resources? The question of neutrality, on the other hand, is concerned with whether the existing payments arrangements induce people to discriminate in favor of one method of payment rather than another, with some consequences for the allocation of resources in the economy. The evidence on which to base our answers is at best only circumstantial. Indeed, a search for quantitative answers to these questions is a virtually untouched field for economic research.

EFFICIENCY OF THE PAYMENTS SYSTEM

The Supply of Currency. Discussions of the efficiency of the payments system inevitably focus on arrangements for payment by check. We should not forget, however, that provision of the currency supply also absorbs real resources and hence involves costs that should be minimized in the interest of efficiency. There are two types of costs involved: the costs of operating the institutions that produce and distribute currency, and the value of the resources embodied in the currency media. In 1972 the production and shipment of Federal Reserve notes cost $31 million and accounted for approximately 8 percent of the total operating costs of the Federal Reserve. (This does not include costs incurred by commercial banks in handling currency.) This might be a low estimate, then, of the cost of maintaining and providing for one year's increase in the supply of paper money (some 2.7 billion new pieces). Furthermore, the operation of the mint cost an additional $70 million. This can be taken as an estimate of the cost of maintaining and providing for one year's increase in the stock of coins. The annual operating cost of this side of the payment system, then, is significant but nonetheless

31

small. It accounts for substantially less than 0.001 percent of the gross national product; and even if there were evidence of substantial inefficiencies (which there is not), the total savings in the aggregate would be very small indeed (i.e., a fraction of a small fraction).

Such calculations ignore the value of metal embodied in the outstanding stock of coinage by including only the value of metal embodied in the annual increase in the coinage. As noted earlier, the United States does not have a commodity currency. The largest part of the currency supply consists of paper notes and hence probably embodies the least amount of scarce productive resources possible, given the necessity of some type of tangible currency. The balance of the currency supply consists of coins, which embody a relatively larger value of scarce resources per dollar of money in circulation. The changeover to cuproclad—copper and nickel—coinage has resulted in substantial economies in this portion of the payments system. However, the changeover had complications. One of the major uses of coins is in vending machines, which must have a device to select good coins from slugs. The existing coin selectors had to be adjusted to work with the new coinage. The vending-machine industry was therefore faced with a major problem and a considerable investment in adapting to the new coinage. As a result of economies in the public sector, some additional one-time costs were incurred in the private sector.

Payment by Check. We have already referred to the substantial and rising costs involved in processing checks through the banking system. Check processing is basically a series of mechanical activities involving several different sortings of items and recording of amounts. Not surprisingly, this has proved to be fertile ground for the application of automated techniques. Thus, for example, the coding of relevant information on the face of each check in magnetic ink has permitted the processing of checks through high-speed sorting equipment connected to electronic computers. The cost reductions from this technological advance apparently have been dramatic.

It is frequently suggested that the check is outmoded as a method of payment. The volume of paper work and sequence of mechanical handlings of the payment order can be significantly reduced, critics argue, by adopting alternative, allegedly cost-saving, payments arrangements.

The Federal Reserve has already begun to urge wire transfers of large sums of money rather than transfer by check. In 1972 the Federal Reserve handled over 9 million such transfers, for a value of over $17 trillion. Nonetheless, as mentioned earlier, it is the number of pieces of paper that must be reduced or contained if the system is not to drown in its own paper.

Computer Technology and the Checkless Society. A proposal of revolutionary consequences involves extension of the application of computer technology and the credit card to the payments process. This combination may augur the end to checks as a means of transfering demand deposit liabilities. In one version it is suggested that a modern form of the telephone connected to the computer, coupled with a plastic identification card, could be used to effect payments. For example, if you made a purchase you would present your card to the merchant. The merchant, using a computer terminal linked to the banking system's central computer, would feed the appropriate information. Immediate credit would be given to the merchant's account, immediate debit made from your account. The transfer of purchasing power would be accomplished in a few seconds. Installment credit could be arranged with a few additional instructions to deduct periodic payments from your account and credit them to the merchant's account. The computer would record the transaction and continually update both the merchant's and your balances.

One can envision businesses having terminals that direct the bank to transfer funds to a creditor. The banking system's computer could be tied to the Federal Reserve banks as well. Interdistrict clearing between regions could be accomplished immediately without the prescribed wait that results in "float."

Clearly the system possesses many technical and legal problems, including that of security. In the absence of a written document, the bank (or depositor) runs severe risks of the sort that are familiar to all users of credit cards, particularly as a result of loss or theft of the identification card. In addition, with a fragmented banking system it would be a mammoth job to tie all banks into a centralized clearing and payments system. The problem of providing merchants with terminals is being solved by new telephone technology. Without question this is a system of the future, not the present. Yet test areas where merchants can check to see if your account has sufficient funds, the encouragement by the Federal Reserve of wire transfers, and rapid technological advances are bringing the checkless society out of the domain of science fiction.

NEUTRALITY OF THE PAYMENTS SYSTEM

The neutrality of the payments system seems to center on the elimination of nonpar clearance. This is a relatively minor problem. The existence of a few nonpar banks causes some concern, since it affects the neutrality of the payments system, but only in a minor way.

Encouragement of more rapid clearing of checks, as mentioned above in discussing the efficiency of the payments system, carries over to the question of neutrality. In recent years there has been increased demand for immediate transfer of payments funds so that purchasing power is transfered instantaneously. We see this in the growth of the "federal funds" market, the increase in wire transfers of money, the inclination of commercial banks to clear checks through the less stringent system of correspondent banking relationships, and the movement toward computer application to the payments system. Time has become increasingly expensive, and this fact has altered some of the traditional methods of payment.

MONEY AND THE FLOW OF PAYMENTS

In our later analysis the concept of the demand for money will play a central role. Monetary policy—one of the central concerns of this book—involves manipulation of the supply of money.

What is the nature of the demand for money? What factors govern the quantity of money demanded at any point in time? We are not yet ready to examine these questions in any detail. However, our discussion of money as a medium of payment does suggest one factor of consequence. Surely, if money is a medium of payment, then the quantity of money demanded must be related in some way to the value of payments to be made. This is correct, but the exact nature of the relationship is neither simple nor obvious.

The complication that arises in specifying the relationship between the value of transactions and the demand for money is that these are variables in different dimensions. The value of payments is a flow variable. It is something that occurs over a period of time: a day, a week, a month, or a year. By contrast, money is a *stock variable*. It is something that can be measured at a point in time: at a particular minute on a particular day. Thus, we cannot talk about the stock of money in the year 1974 in the same sense as we talk about the gross national expenditure in 1974. The stock of money must be measured at some particular point in time, such as the end of the business day, June 12, 1974. For purposes of analysis, of course, we might want to measure the average stock of money in existence during the year 1974. In principle, we should be measuring the average stock in existence at each successive instant during that year. In fact, we would probably only measure the stock once a week or once a month and average these observations to obtain the annual average.

It is true that the flow of payments involves money. Payments are effected by money changing hands. However, over any given period—such as a year—the same piece of money can change hands many times. Thus, the total flow of payments during the year can be many times the average stock of money in existence during the year. If money changes hands rapidly —if it has a high *turnover rate* or *velocity of circulation*—a very small average stock of money can support a very large flow of payments. If velocity is high, each piece of money is held for a short time between payments. A small stock of money is required to support a given flow of payments. If velocity is low, each piece of money is held for a long time between payments. A larger stock of money is required to support a given flow of payments. Clearly we cannot derive the demand for money from knowledge of the flow of payments without knowing something about the determinants of the velocity of circulation. That is a very complex topic, which we are not yet ready to explore.

An analogy is sometimes helpful in thinking about these concepts. Such an analogy might be a fountain that continuously recirculates the same water supply by means of a mechanical pump. We might insert a meter into the pipe of the fountain and measure the total flow of water past that point in an hour. That would be analogous to the flow of payments in the economy at any given point in time. The total flow of water past our meter is effected by the continuous recirculation of the same water supply, and the magnitude of that flow depends directly on the speed at which we run the pump, that is, the velocity or rate of turnover of the water supply. We cannot say how much water we require in the reservoir for any given flow of water per hour unless we know how fast the pump runs.

SUMMARY

Money is anything that is normally accepted when a transfer of purchasing power takes place. Our money supply consists of coins, paper currency, and bank money. Not all bank money, that is, deposits held by commercial banks, can qualify as money. To be readily transfered, only bank deposits that are checkable are included in a narrow payments definition of the money supply.

In addition to demand deposits of commercial banks, which clearly satisfy our definition of money, commercial banks also issue interest-bearing deposits that can often be quite readily converted into some form of direct-payments money, currency or checkable deposits. Often economists are concerned with the impact of changes in the money supply on the economic behavior of firms and households. A broader definition of the money supply, which would include commercial bank near moneys as well as interest-bearing deposits at near banks, is more useful in interpreting changing economic conditions.

The transfer of purchasing power when accomplished by coin or paper currency is direct and simple; when accomplished by check it is more complicated. Payment by check frequently involves complex bookkeeping and clearing arrangements when payments are made across geographic areas because of the existence in the United States of a large number of independent banks, many of which choose to clear checks through a private and informal system of correspondent bank relationships rather than through the facilities of the central bank.

When payment is to be made across international boundaries, the mechanism relies on two different sets of institutions and an additional market mechanism for converting one currency into another.

The cost of maintaining the money supply is one indication of its efficiency and drain on scarce resources. The cost of supplying coin and paper currency is quite small. However, there are substantial costs involved in collecting and clearing an increasing volume of checks. Application of computer technology to this area has undoubtedly speeded the transfer of payments as well as held down rising costs. Today experiments are being conducted in various parts of the country to see if electronic transfer of demand deposit liabilities would be applicable to the banking system at large and to determine if it would be more efficient than current methods.

NOTES

1. P. Einzig, *Primitive Money* (London: Eyre & Spottiswoode, 1948), p. 25.

2. Why has gold been so widely selected as the commodity to be used as money? While there are clearly many cultural factors to be taken into account, early monetary economists argued that gold was technically superior to most commodities for this purpose. Since it is also limited in supply, it has "intrinsic" value; that is, it would have value as a commodity even if it were not used as money. The supply is physically limited, apart from occasional major gold discoveries; and it tends to maintain its value over time. It has a relatively high value in relation to its weight and in this case is relatively portable. It is virtually indestructible. It is homogeneous and readily divisible. Finally, it is quite easily recognizable. A classic exposition of the "technical" requirements for a monetary commodity is provided by W. S. Jevons, *Money and the Mechanism of Exchange* (New York: Appleton, 1902), pp. 29–39. How does paper money compare with gold in terms of these technical desiderata? (Remember that while paper money is far from "indestructible," a worn-out note is easily and relatively cheaply replaced.)

3. For example, see Federal Reserve *Bulletin*, November 1971, pp. 880–893.

4. It is interesting to note that no new large-denomination bills have been printed since the late 1940s. On May 31, 1971, only $462 million, or less than 1 percent of the paper currency in circulation, was in bills of denominations of $500 or larger.

5. U.S. Congress, House Committee on Banking and Currency, *A Report on the Correspondent Banking System*, 88th Cong., 2d sess. 1964.

FINANCIAL INSTRUMENTS
AND FINANCIAL MARKETS

In our economy the collection of financial surpluses and their allocation among alternate uses is primarily a market process. Individuals exchange their savings for financial instruments, claims on borrowers that entitle lenders to (certain or uncertain) returns in the future. The interaction of supply (from borrowers) and demand (on the part of lenders) in the market for financial instruments determines their market prices and in the process regulates the size, composition, and direction of financial flows in the economy. In this chapter we will discuss the characteristics of the most important types of financial instruments and some of the basic institutions of financial markets. In subsequent chapters we will develop a theoretical analysis of how these markets work.

THE CHARACTERISTICS OF FINANCIAL INSTRUMENTS

DEFINITION

A financial instrument originates in an act of borrowing and lending—a transfer of purchasing power from a surplus spending unit to a deficit spending unit. It is what the borrower gives to the lender as evidence of the debt. In a more general way, we can define a financial instrument as a claim

37

to a future stream of payments. It is a contract between a creditor (who will receive the payments) and a debtor (who will make the payments), one that in general can be bought and sold in the market at a market-established price. Thus, the initial creditor need not remain a creditor. He can sell the claim to someone else. A major part of our problem is to explain the price at which such transactions will occur.

Our definition of a financial instrument is perfectly general. Individual instruments will differ in a number of ways. First, we have not specified the number of payments to be received. It can range between a single payment and an infinite number of payments. Second, we have not specified the timing of the payments, only that they be made in the future or at some unspecified time in the future. Third, we have not specified the magnitude of the payments. They may be large or small, of equal or different size; indeed, they may vary in size from time to time. Finally, we have not specified that the payments will necessarily be made. A financial instrument is a claim to such payments: That claim may in fact be honored in whole, in part, or not at all. At the moment we cannot know what will happen, since the claim is for future payments.

BONDS AS FINANCIAL INSTRUMENTS

The most common of all financial instruments is what we shall call a *bond*. It has the amount of each payment and the number of payments (the length of the payments stream) specified in the contract. It is a *fixed income security*.

We are using the term *bond* in a very broad, generic sense to refer to all fixed income securities, regardless of the term to maturity, the number and type of payments, or the various provisions for the security of the bondholder (which will be set in a deed of trust accompanying the bond). In fact there are many types of bonds, and, without attempting to provide a complete catalog, it may be useful to note the characteristics of some of the major varieties.

Term to Maturity. A major consideration in classifying bonds is the term to maturity, that is, the time that must elapse before the final payment is due. At one extreme is a peculiar class of bonds issued by some governments, variously called *consols* or *perpetuities*. The contract calls for annual payments to the owner in perpetuity. By contrast, most bonds have a definite term to maturity. Those with a maturity date of 10 years or over are normally classed as *long-term* bonds, those with maturities in the range 3 to 10 years might be called *intermediate-term* bonds, and those with a maturity of less than 3 years, *short-term* bonds. The shortest-term bonds are those payable on demand, that is, at any time specified by the holder.

Why is this classification by maturity important for our analysis? One of the characteristics of financial instruments that will assume importance in our analysis is the relative stability of market price in the face of changing interest rates. In general, stability of market price depends on the term to maturity. Bonds with a short term to maturity tend to have a more stable price than those with a long term to maturity. This is a result of some importance, which we will establish in Chapter 5.

Security of the Bondholder. Another major consideration in classifying bonds is the provision for the security of the bondholder. Some bonds are secured by a formal pledge of certain physical assets of the debtor. These are *mortgage* bonds, and in modified form are well known in real estate transactions. By contrast, some bonds are simply a charge against the general assets and earning power of the debtor and are not secured by a pledge of any specific assets. These bonds are commonly called *debentures*, although if they are for a very short term they are more likely to be referred to as *promissory notes*, or *notes* for short. Some bonds also have a provision for a sinking fund and hence are called *sinking fund* bonds. This form of bond requires that the debtor set aside a certain sum of money each year (frequently through the purchase of part of the outstanding issue of bonds) to provide for eventual retirement of the issue. This is supposed to provide additional security to the bondholder. Municipal governments generally issue *serial* bonds instead of sinking fund bonds to achieve the same purpose. A serial bond is in fact a package of bonds, each with a different maturity such that a portion of the total issue comes due for retirement each year during the term of the issue.

This brief survey hardly does justice to the variety of possible types of provisions for the security of bondholders and hence to the possible types of bonds. However, they are only relevant in the present context because they have some bearing on the risk attached to the bond, and that is a factor of some interest for our analysis.

Credit Risk. Our definition of a bond stresses that it is a claim to a series of payments of fixed magnitude to be made in the future. However, the future can never be known in advance. There will always be some uncertainty about whether the payments will ever be made. Circumstances may change so that even the most carefully formulated plans and expectations do not materialize; the debtor may be unwilling or unable to meet his obligation. In some cases this may only create costs of collection that cannot be fully recovered. In other cases it may involve partial or total default on the obligation, with partial or complete loss to the creditor. In this event the provisions for the security of the bondholder referred to in the previous section may take on more than academic significance.

We refer to the risk that the contractual payments may not be forthcoming as planned as the *credit risk*. In a sense it is a one-sided risk. The actual payments may be less than those called for in the contract, but they will never be more.

For reasons that we will explore more fully in Chapter 5, credit risk enters into the determination of the market price of bonds. In brief, other things being equal, investors will normally prefer less risky securities to riskier ones. As a result, if the promised stream of payments is the same for two securities, investors will offer a higher price for the less risky one. But if risk is to enter into the investment decision, investors must be able to assess differences in credit risk. This calls for specialized skills in financial analysis. As a result, an industry has developed as an adjunct of financial markets that provides information and professional advice to investors.

Nature of the Payments Stream. Another characteristic with respect to which bonds may differ is the nature of the stream of payments involved. In general, a bond will call for equal semiannual payments (the interest or coupon payments) and a larger lump-sum payment on the maturity date (variously called the *face* value, the *par* value, or the *redemption* value of the bond). Bonds are normally issued in denominations of $1000 (although there are many exceptions to this). That is to say, the redemption value is $1000. This should not be confused with the market price of the bond. A bond that has a redemption value of $1000 may trade in the market at a price either greater or less than $1000. If its price is less than its face value, the bond is said to be trading at a *discount*; and if its price is greater than its par value, the bond is said to be trading at a *premium*. Bonds, even at their initial offering, frequently sell at a discount or a premium. That is, the original issuer of a bond with a face value of $1000 does not necessarily receive $1000.

The annual interest payments (normally two coupons) can be expressed as a percent of the par value of the bond. Thus, a $1000 bond, bearing semi-annual coupons for $25 each, would normally be referred to as a 5 percent bond. That is, the annual interest payment of $50 is 5 percent of the face value of the bond. This is termed the *coupon rate* and is merely a nominal rate of interest. Just as the market price of the bond may depart significantly from its par value, so the true rate of interest (what we shall call the *yield*) may depart significantly from this coupon rate. Indeed, as just noted, at the time the bond is first issued, the issuer may receive less than the face value of the bond (he may sell it at a discount). As a result, he in fact pays a higher rate of interest on the money he has actually obtained than that indicated by the coupon rate. The only significance of the coupon rate is to fix the size of the semiannual coupon payments.

Not all bonds will be in this coupon form, however. A particularly important variant is what we shall call a *bill*. This is a security calling for a single payment on a fixed date in the future. There are no periodic interest payments, only the final payment for the redemption value of the bill. Such bonds normally have a very short term. Perhaps the most important are the Treasury bills issued by the federal government maturing in less than one year. They play an important part in the financial system, and we will have occasion to refer to them frequently.

Negotiability. One characteristic that many, but not all, financial instruments possess is negotiability. This is a legal quality that has evolved through time as a result of asset holders' need to purchase assets with clear title. Without negotiability, when title to property is transferred the new owner normally cannot obtain a better title than that possessed by the original holder. Therefore, if the seller had obtained the property improperly, the buyer would be assuming the risk that the true owner could reclaim the property. In the transfer of real assets, there may be time to search the title; with financial instruments, time may mean money lost. Therefore, while nonnegotiable instruments may be sold or assigned, a negotiable credit instrument provides the holder or assignee with an unconditional promise or order to pay. The security can then be bought and sold freely without doubts about the title. If legal specifications are met, a credit instrument becomes negotiable, facilitating the transfer of these instruments from person to person and thus enhancing their marketability.

Marketability. Another salient characteristic that may or may not be possessed by bonds and other financial instruments is marketability. This refers to the ability of the holder to sell the security to someone else on short notice at a reasonably predictable price. Some instruments are not marketable because they are not transferable. That is, the sale of the security to a third party is prohibited. For example, U.S. savings bonds contain the condition: "This bond is not assignable nor transferable." Other instruments are not marketable simply by virtue of the fact that an active market does not exist.

Such a statement must seem puzzling to a student of economics. A market exists whenever transactions occur. Thus, the very fact that the present purchaser of the security has purchased it must indicate that a market exists. Moreover, it is in general possible to find a buyer for most securities at some price.

In this connection it is useful to make a distinction between the primary and secondary markets for securities. By the *primary market* we mean transactions involving the issuance of new securities. By the *secondary market* we mean transactions in outstanding securities. Thus, the supply of securities in the primary market comes from individuals, firms, and government agencies raising money for diverse purposes. The supply of securities in the secondary market comes from asset holders selling securities out of their portfolios.

While every credit transaction can thus be construed as a transaction in the primary market, the range of securities continually traded in significant volume in the secondary market is relatively limited. These tend to be securities of well-known creditors whose credit worthiness can be relatively easily assessed and of which a relatively large volume is outstanding. Only these securities can be said to be highly marketable. True, most other transferable securities can be sold at some price, but perhaps only after considerable searching for a buyer, some delay, perhaps substantial cost, and possibly only then at a low price. The secondary market for such instruments is irregular and unorganized.

A marketable security is a security for which there is a developed secondary market in which there is a relatively large volume of continual trading of the security.

41

COMMON STOCK AS A FINANCIAL INSTRUMENT

While the type of financial instrument that will occupy most of our attention in this book is the bond, there are other financial instruments in which the amount of each payment is not specified in the contract between creditor and debtor. The prototype of such securities is the common stock of corporations. Whereas a bond entitles its owner to a series of fixed payments, a share of common stock entitles its owner to a *pro rata* share of such dividends as may be declared from time to time by the directors of the corporation. Dividends are normally thought of as a share of profits, although they are not rigidly tied to profits. The directors of a corporation might decide to retain some or all of the profits to finance the growth of the corporation, and on occasion they may decide to pay dividends even though the corporation is not making profits or perhaps is suffering losses. However, in general dividend payments will tend to reflect the profits of the corporation.

Also unlike most bonds, common stock does not have a definite maturity date. There is no fixed lump-sum redemption value, although the stockholders do own residual rights to the assets of the corporation (i.e., after all other claims are allowed for).

The important point for our analysis is that just as the profits of a corporation may vary from time to time, so the dividend payments to the stockholder may vary over a wide range. Accordingly, we refer to such a financial instrument as a *variable income security*.

Stockholders as Creditors. Since our definition of financial instruments involves the concepts of debtor and creditor, it may seem that we are stretching a point to include common stock. The owners of the common stock of a corporation are in law the owners of the corporation, not its creditors. Moreover, since they have a claim to a *pro rata* share of the profits (or better, the declared dividends) of the corporation, their "instrument" has many of the characteristics of titles to physical capital rather than what we might normally think of as a financial instrument.

These points are valid and important. However, we should distinguish between the corporation and its stockholders or owners; and it is convenient to treat the stockholders simply as creditors of the corporation with a particular type of claim on that corporation, a variable income claim. We should remember that the corporation is in itself a "legal person" with certain rights and obligations. The stockholders are not responsible for the actions and debts of the corporation, except to the extent that they may lose their investments in the corporation should it be unable to meet its obligations. Indeed, it is this fact of the "limited liability" of the stockholders—the fact of their separateness from the obligations of the corporation—that makes the corporation such an effective form of business organization for ventures involving risk.

As a subsidiary point, it might be noted that while all stockholders have the right to vote at stockholders' meetings (which generally must be held at least once a year), in a typical corporation most do not participate actively in the management of that corporation. They treat their stock as an investment in someone else's venture, and they hold it in anticipation of an appreciation in market price and a series of dividend payments whose magnitude is beyond their direct control. Even if a stockholder is in the management of the corporation, we should nonetheless regard his stock simply as a claim on a separate entity, the corporation. It is true that the fact of his ability to influence or control corporation policy may add an important dimension, a valuable characteristic to that particular financial instrument; nonetheless, it is a financial instrument that provides a claim to a (probably variable) future stream of payments.

Other Variable Income Instruments. The common stock is the best-known type of variable income security. However, there are several other types of instruments that have variable payments streams. Basically they combine some of the features of common stock with some of the features of bonds. There are many subtle variations on the central principles; we can only mention some of the main types.

Perhaps the best known of such instruments is *preferred stock*. Unlike a bond, preferred stock does not have a fixed maturity, although it may be redeemable in the sense that the corporation has the option of retiring it on specified terms. The owner of preferred stock has a prior claim to dividends, up to a specified maximum rate, before any dividends can be paid on common stock. Moreover, some preferred stocks are *participating*. That is, they have the prior claim to dividends, but once dividends are paid on common stock at a certain specified rate, the owners of the preferred stock share in any additional dividends declared. Thus, the specified rate is in fact a minimum rate, not a maximum.

There are also two classes of bonds that have variable payments streams, *income* bonds and *participating* bonds. These are bonds in the sense that they have a fixed redemption date and a fixed redemption value. However, in each case the annual interest payment is contingent on the earnings of the corporation, with participating bonds having the additional feature of a guaranteed minimum annual payment.

The endless varieties of financial instruments, with subtle differences in their characteristics, are evidence of the ingenuity of the participants in the financial system in designing instruments to suit the specific preferences of both debtors and creditors (including taking advantage of many complex provisions of the tax laws).

MONEY AS A FINANCIAL INSTRUMENT

In the previous chapter we offered as a general definition of money "anything that is normally accepted when a transfer of purchasing power takes place." Our concern was with the payments system, and our interest in money was as a medium of exchange. However, the very fact that money will normally be accepted in exchange for goods and services means that it is an asset. It is something that can be held as a store of wealth. Today money is simply one type of financial instrument that has the peculiar property of being acceptable at face value in exchange for goods, services, and other financial instruments.

To some students this may seem a paradox. Financial instruments are claims for future payment. Future payments will be made in money. How, then, can money be both the means of payment and a claim for payment? Are we simply talking in riddles?

Perhaps no problem arises in connection with bank money. Checkable bank deposits can be regarded as claims for payment in legal tender money— claims that may be effected at the option of the depositor in whole or in part at any time in the future. We can take this as a limiting case in our definition of a financial instrument. It can be a claim for a single payment (the shortest possible stream of payments) payable on demand of the creditor (the shortest possible term to maturity).

This still leaves the problem of legal tender money, however. As we noted in the previous chapter, legal tender in the United States means all coin issued by the Treasury and notes issued by the Federal Reserve for use as currency. They have formal status as liabilities of the Treasury and the Federal Reserve System, respectively. In what sense can we say that legal tender money is a claim for payment?

Unit of Account. In order to answer this question we require another concept, that of the *unit of account*. This is the abstract unit by which we measure, record, and compare market values, the unit in which we keep our personal and business accounts. In the United States the unit of account is the dollar (which is subdivided into 100 cents).

It is sometimes said that one of the functions of money is to serve as a unit of account. However, such a statement confuses two concepts. *Money* is an object, a financial instrument or (in some times and places) a commodity. It is something that changes hands in the process of exchange. The unit of account is an arbitrary unit in which we measure market value, including the value of money. It should be thought of in the same vein as one thinks of the ounce as an arbitrary unit in which we measure weight and the degree as the arbitrary unit in which we measure temperature. It is true that money is normally issued in denominations corresponding to the unit of account. That is not necessary, however. For example, in England values are frequently measured in guineas, a unit of account for which there is no monetary counterpart.

Money as a Generalized Fixed Price Claim. In what sense, then, is money (particularly legal tender money) a claim for future payment? We should not regard it as a claim against any specific debtor (even though the government issues it). Rather, it is a claim for payment in that it is universally acceptable in exchange for goods, services, or financial instruments of a given value, with the value measured in terms of the unit of account. A $10 Federal Reserve note can always be exchanged for goods, services, or financial instruments whose market value equals $10. The Federal Reserve note—legal tender money—is a general claim against society that can be effected at any time at the option of the holder.

Fixed Price vs. Fixed Purchasing Power. It is important to remember that to say that the price of money is fixed in terms of the unit of account is not to say that the purchasing power of money is always constant. A given quantity of money may not always command a fixed quantity of goods and services, only a fixed market value of goods and services. The prices of goods and services measured in terms of the unit of account may rise over time, and money, which always commands a fixed value of goods and services, will buy a smaller quantity of those goods and services. The purchasing power of money will have fallen. This process is called inflation, and one of the major tasks of monetary theory is to explain its causes, consequences, and cures.

Summary: The Concept of Liquidity. In summary, we can say that money is a peculiar type of financial instrument. Regardless of the form in which it appears, money should be regarded as a claim against society as a whole rather than against any single debtor. It is a financial instrument whose price, measured in terms of the unit of account, is fixed. This is a vital property not possessed by most other financial instruments (or commodities).

The holder of shares of corporate stock or of government bonds faces the risk that their market values will fall. By contrast, the holder of money faces no such risk.

We call this property of money *liquidity*. It is possessed by other assets in varying degrees. That is, their market prices, measured in terms of the unit of account, are more or less stable. Money, since its price is fixed, is the most liquid of financial instruments.

THE INSTITUTIONS OF FINANCIAL MARKETS

To an economist the concept of a market does not necessarily imply a fixed location or any particular set of institutional arrangements or pattern of organization of exchange. A market exists whenever buyers and sellers agree to exchange, regardless of whether they are located in the same physical place and regardless of how their mutual interests are brought together. The tangible evidence of a market is not a structure of buildings or a particular set of institutional arrangements; it is simply a series of exchanges. In this sense, then, an economist would consider the financial market to be conterminous with the entire financial system. The financial system is basically a set of markets for particular types of financial instruments.

However, when we use the term *financial market* we have a narrower concept in mind. We can divide all financial transactions into two types, loan transactions and investment transactions. In the former category we place all transactions involving face-to-face negotiations between borrowers and lenders. The promissory notes involved are not normally designed to be resold, and hence they tend to remain lodged in the lender's portfolio (although this is not necessary, of course). In the second category we place all transactions in "public issues," financial instruments designed to be sold on an impersonal basis to any and all buyers. Inevitably, the distinction between the two categories is fuzzy at the margin. It is not clear whether certain transactions (e.g., negotiated private placements of long-term marketable bonds with a single institutional lender) should be considered loan or investment transactions. There is, however, a difference of substance. When we speak of financial markets in the narrow sense, we refer to the second type of transaction—impersonal transactions in marketable financial instruments.

For most purposes of economic analysis, complete details on the institutional arrangements of markets are not necessary. Indeed, such details frequently get in the way of clear analysis. The institutions tend to adapt themselves to the particular market situation; and although they may have some impact on the efficiency and neutrality of the exchange process, they are seldom crucial to the outcome. This is equally true of the financial system. While it is important to know that certain types of markets exist and to understand the institutions of those markets in broad outline, it is seldom important that all of the details of those arrangements be understood. All that is required here is a brief overview of the major institutions involved in exchanging financial instruments.

BROKERS, DEALERS, AND UNDERWRITERS

The central institutions of financial markets are a group of business firms called investment houses. They function as intermediaries in the marketing process, as brokers, as dealers, or as underwriters.

A *broker* is a pure intermediary in market transactions. He is not a party to any transaction himself. Rather, he acts as an agent for his clients, be they buyers or sellers. He uses his information on the market—the basic ingredient in his activities—and his contacts to bring buyers and sellers together at mutually acceptable prices and provides the technical facilities necessary for the execution of the transactions. For his services the broker charges his client a fee or *commission* that is normally related to the value of the transaction.

A *dealer* is also an intermediary in the exchange process. However, in contrast to the broker, the dealer actually becomes a party to market transactions. In the jargon of the trade, he "makes markets." He holds an inventory of securities, buys in the market to add to that inventory, and sells out of his inventory to other buyers, perhaps at a different time or place. He hopes to make a profit on a spread between buying and selling prices.

While techniques of underwriting vary depending on the circumstances, an underwriter is basically a dealer who handles new issues of securities. He buys them and then sells them into the market, hoping to make a profit on the spread between the selling and the buying price. Again, information and market contacts are the essential ingredients in the underwriter's activities.

Earlier in this chapter we distinguished between primary and secondary markets for securities. We can identify underwriting with the primary market and the main operations of brokers and dealers with secondary markets. This is in part an oversimplification, because not all new issues of securities go through a formal process of underwriting. One vitally important group of bonds, those issued by the Treasury, are sold in the first instance through sealed bids to a large group of buyers and distributors, including commercial banks, mutual savings banks, savings and loan associations, corporations, life insurance companies, and government bond dealers. Similarly, a significant portion of corporate and municipal bonds are "direct placements" with large institutional lenders. The issuers negotiate directly with the lenders, generally with the assistance and advice of an investment house but without benefit of an underwriting arrangement. This is an extension of the brokerage function to the new-issue market.

The identification of underwriters with primary markets and of brokers and dealers with secondary markets is also an oversimplification, because it is difficult to separate the three activities. Investment houses, with some exceptions, do not narrowly specialize in one or the other line of activity.

PATTERNS OF ORGANIZATION IN FINANCIAL MARKETS

In the United States the securities industry is a regulated one. The Securities and Exchange Commission (SEC) acts to assure the investing public that there will be adequate publicity and disclosure of pertinent information when new securities are publicly offered for sale. The Commission also enforces laws designed to protect the investing public from illegal acts by dealers, brokers, and specialists. Through the National Association of Securities Dealers, the Commission registers firms in the industry. In 1973, there were over 5000 firms in the securities industry operating in the United States. Despite this large number, all aspects of the industry are dominated by a few very large firms, several of which operate through nationwide branch offices. (See Chapter 13.) Nonetheless, taking the industry as a whole, we are talking about a comparatively large number of firms that trade among themselves (wholesale transactions) and with the general public (retail transactions). How are their activities organized so as to produce an effective national market in securities?

Over-the-Counter Markets vs. Organized Exchanges. Perhaps the best-known—and certainly the most spectacular—institutional arrangement for buying and selling securities is the organized stock exchange. The stock exchange provides the physical facilities for transactions to occur in a manner resembling an auction. In the United States there are twelve registered exchanges. Two others are extremely limited and exempt from direct SEC regulation. The two major national exchanges—the New York Stock Exchange and the American Stock Exchange—account for more than 85 percent of the value of stock traded on all exchanges.

A stock exchange is an association of members, and membership in the exchange may be limited. The New York Stock Exchange, for example, has only 1366 memberships. These are owned by individuals or firms, who then may act as commission brokers, buying and selling for the investment house they represent, or may be floor traders, buying and selling for their own account, or specialists, who "make the market" in a few securities.

Only a limited number of corporations meet the listing requirements of the various exchanges. The New York Exchange lists about 1700 different corporations. Only these companies' stock may be traded through the New York Stock Exchange facilities. Although some trading in bonds also takes place on the organized exchanges, the volume is small compared to the total volume of bonds traded each year.

Another network for trading the enormous volume of stocks and bonds not listed on organized exchanges has been developed. The participants—brokers, dealers, and specialists—in this over-the-counter market are linked by electronic communications equipment. They can quickly bring together offers to buy and sell new securities, existing unlisted shares, and most of the corporate, municipal, and federal bonds that are traded each year. The result is an efficient, well-organized market. Prices in over-the-counter trading are usually determined by negotiation rather than auction. The market is dominated by dealers, who acquire and sell from inventories of securities in which they are interested, and brokers representing a range of potential buyers and sellers. A computer network of quotations called NASDQ provides instant information on bid and ask prices for a large number of more actively traded over-the-counter securities. Since the inception of NASDQ the volume of shares traded through over-the-counter markets has increased dramatically.

A National and an International Market. The investment houses, many of them with nationwide networks of branch offices, linked together through the stock markets and the over-the-counter markets in stocks and bonds, provide the institutional arrangements for a truly nationwide market in all types of securities. Changes in demand or supply in any section of the country will be felt almost immediately in all of the others.

In part, this transmission of market changes will result from formal arbitrage operations. *Arbitrage* involves the simultaneous purchase and sale in separate markets of any commodity to take advantage of a price differential. In stocks, for example, if a particular stock listed on both the New York Stock Exchange and the Midwest Exchange should fall in price on the Midwest Exchange, an alert investment house (probably with seats on both exchanges) could buy shares in Chicago and sell them in New York virtually simultaneously, making a profit in the transaction. The increased quantity demanded in the Midwest and the increased quantity offered in New York would tend to eliminate the price differential between the two markets.

Arbitrage of this sort appears to account for a small but significant portion of the activity in the organized stock exchanges. However, equally important in transmitting the changes in supply or demand among market areas are the activities of brokers and dealers in the over-the-counter market. In virtually constant communication with each other, traders at the leading investment houses seek out the best prices for their customers who wish to buy or sell, and are constantly alert for profitable buying and selling opportunities for the firm's own portfolio. The result is a fluid and continuous coast-to-coast market.

The market connections established through the network of investment houses and formal stock exchanges are not confined to the boundaries of the nation. There are equally important international connections as well. Some Canadian stocks are traded on stock exchanges in the United States, and United States stock in Canada. Leading investment houses have branch offices in several other countries. Security dealers and brokers are in virtually continuous telephone and telegraphic contact with their counterparts in leading financial centers abroad. These connections permit international arbitrage in both American and foreign securities and facilitate American transactions in foreign securities and foreign transactions in American securities. The institutions of the financial market are international as well as national in scope, and as a result, market transactions flow easily across the country and across national borders. This, as will become evident, is important for U.S. monetary policy.

THE SECONDARY BOND MARKET

As we will discover in a later section of this book, a major portion of the day-to-day operations of the Federal Reserve, including the implementation of monetary policy, involves purchases and sales of bonds in the open market. These are operations in the secondary bond market, and the nature and scope of that market can affect the magnitude, timing, and nature of the operations that the central bank can effectively carry out. Hence, since it has particular significance for our later analysis, before we leave our brief description of financial markets we should examine the dimensions of the secondary bond market.

No statistics on the secondary bond market are collected and published as a matter of course. Bond houses act as dealers buying and holding inventories in the hope that these securities can be sold at a significant price spread to bring a profit. There are no regulations as to how much of a spread is in good taste. These local houses perform the function of making local securities more marketable and enable investors to purchase both municipal and corporate bonds with the knowledge that a secondary market for these securities exists. Bond houses report their approximate inventory of bonds available for sale each day. However, they vigorously guard specific details, since the market is extremely competitive. What information is available is an approximation of inventories. Industry publications report that on the average between $600 million and $1 billion in municipal securities is available for sale each day.

By comparison, trading in U.S. government securities is more carefully documented. This market is maintained by a group of about 20 bank and nonbank dealers. The average daily transactions for the month of August 1973 was $3.4 billion, of which 70 percent was in short-term government securities maturing within one year. Inventories held by government securities dealers fluctuated widely. Government bond dealers held $4.7 billion on a daily average in January 1973 and only $1.8 billion on a daily average in August 1973. Still, their inventories are significantly larger than reported inventories of municipal securities. In a recent report for the House Banking and Currency Committee, a government agency estimated the 20 bond dealers' total transactions for 1970 at $738 billion.

The market in short-term U.S. government securities is part of what is known as the money market, an open market in short-term securities of selected "blue chip" borrowers. The money market has taken on an institutional identity of its own and has developed a peculiar significance within the financial system.

THE MONEY MARKET

The money market is an active open market in selected short-term financial instruments.

Treasury Bills. These debt instruments of the federal government are the major element in the money market. Each week the Treasury issues about $3 billion in bills to mature in 91 days and in 182 days. At regular intervals it also issues about $1.8 billion of 52-week bills. Then, throughout the year, the Treasury issues tax anticipation bills, which have no set length of maturity. Rather, these issues generally mature a few days after corporate tax payments are due to the Treasury, and the Treasury accepts them at par on the tax due date in payment for federal tax liabilities, or it redeems them in full at the maturity date.

Treasury bills have no coupon rate. The yield on such securities to the investor and the interest cost to the government is determined by purchasing them at less than their par or redemption value. At the initial offering the Treasury sets the bottom price it will accept, effectively putting a ceiling on yields for that issue. Sealed bids are proffered at the weekly auction.

A primary function of the money market is to permit financial and

50

nonfinancial institutions to make adjustments in their holdings of liquid assets. Treasury bills, because of the quantity outstanding, frequent maturity, and high quality, dominate transactions in the money markets. They can be readily bought and sold after the initial Treasury offering.

The Federal Reserve relies heavily on government bond dealers and the smooth functioning of the money markets to implement monetary policy. Through its open-market operations the Federal Reserve implements prevailing monetary policy directives deemed in line with current monetary and economic conditions. By buying or selling government securities the Federal Reserve can also effect a policy change, alter the maturity of its large portfolio of government securities, or seek to maintain the present degree of availability of bank reserves in the system.

Some sales and purchases of government securities by the Federal Reserve are done outright; that is, the Federal Reserve bank receives funds or securities "to keep." Other transactions, made at the initiation of the Reserve bank, are under agreements to sell and then buy the securities back within a specific period, or to buy securities now from those nonbank dealers and resell them at a later date. These transactions are called *repurchase agreements*. In each case the time involved is short, usually not more than fifteen days. In the latter case the Federal Reserve bank agrees to a spread in price so that it will receive a yield, but that yield is typically less than the going market rate of interest on similar short-term funds. Through this device the Federal Reserve can extend low-cost credit to nonbank dealers and aid the entire money market. In the agreements to sell and buy back, the Federal Reserve again agrees to buy back at a price that will yield the dealers a bit more than they would expect to receive in the market.

Through repurchase agreements, then, the dealers obtain low-cost financing and are able to tailor the repurchase dates to their specific liquidity needs.

Day-to-Day Loans. Loans extended by banks to bond dealers are *call loans*. Call loans have no specific maturity and are extended with securities as collateral.

Before 1946, loans of this type were made impersonally to brokers and dealers through the New York Stock Exchange's money desk. Banks would readily call these loans for payment to adjust their liquidity and reserve positions. If many banks were in a tightening reserve position and the general condition necessitated calling such loans, brokers and security dealers would have to sell securities to cover the call. This generalized selling would, in turn, depress the market price of securities and compound a decline in these prices and a decline in the market value of the collateral backing the loans. It would become more difficult to repay the loan, and more pressure would be exerted by banks for repayment.

Since 1946, brokers and dealers have obtained loans directly from their own banks on a personal basis. Banks may call these loans but as a rule do

51

not. Only loans to government securities dealers are called by banks on a regular basis as a normal method of adjusting reserve positions. Recently, bank loans to dealers averaged about $1.2 billion per day.

Commercial Paper. *Commercial paper* is a term that is often applied to a variety of short-term instruments such as acceptances, finance paper, and repurchase agreements. Here we use the term more narrowly. Commercial paper is an unsecured promissory note maturing in less than 270 days. Its growth in the 1960s was attributed to the rapid increase in the demand for funds from several sectors of the economy accompanied by a general tightening of available credit from traditional sources.

Commercial paper is issued by three different types of borrowers. The first and largest issuer is the group of finance companies. Their paper has traditionally been their major source of funds and is highly rated in the money market. Much of it is placed directly by such companies as Commercial Credit, General Motors Acceptance Corporation, Sears Roebuck Acceptance Corporation, and Household Finance Corporation.

A second, smaller amount of paper is issued through dealers and smaller brokerage houses by corporations that use commercial paper less frequently or have smaller amounts outstanding than the finance companies. It is this group of issuers that grew so rapidly during the 1960s. Many companies sought short-term funds from commercial banks during that period. Banks were under increasing pressure from tightening monetary conditions and had to turn away many requests for funds. The corporations looked to other sources and found the commercial paper dealers eager. Within the decade of the 1960s the number of issuers doubled to 650 corporations.

A third group that turned to the commercial paper market were one-bank holding companies. One-bank holding companies also became popular in the 1960s. The bank itself generally forms a new parent holding company that controls only that bank. The parent company, however, is quite free to engage in other corporate businesses without the restraint of state or federal banking regulations. When interest rates rose in 1969, one-bank holding companies found that by issuing commercial paper in their own name they could deposit the proceeds of the issue with their bank and provide it with an injection of new moneys that, in turn, could form the basis for additional loan commitments. Bank-related commercial paper grew from $1.2 billion outstanding in June 1969 to $7.8 billion outstanding 13 months later. In September 1970 the Federal Reserve imposed reserve requirements on funds acquired through one-bank holding company commercial paper, eliminating much of the advantage of these funds to commercial banks. By August 1973 only $1.4 billion was outstanding. Part of this decline was a result of easier credit conditions and a general decline in short-term interest rates that enabled banks to attract moneys through more traditional means.

During the summer of 1970, however, the entire commercial paper market experienced an abrupt shock. When the Penn Central Corporation

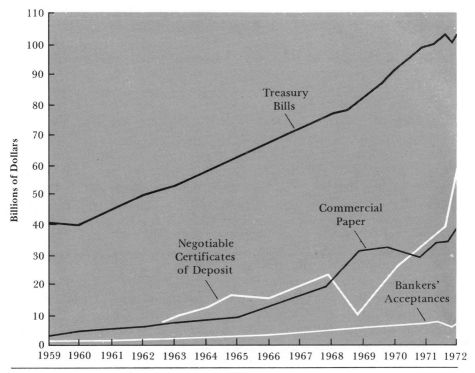

Figure 3.1 **Growth of Money Market Instruments, 1959–1972**
SOURCE: Federal Reserve *Bulletin*, various issues.

filed for bankruptcy at the end of June 1970, it had $85 million in commercial paper liabilities outstanding that it would not be able to pay off. Previous buyers of commercial paper turned fickle and looked for more secure situations for their investable funds. Corporations that had borrowed funds through the commercial paper market had to seek new sources of short-term funds. The Federal Reserve quickly moved to ease credit conditions by removing the ceiling on the interest rates banks could pay on time deposits (Regulation Q). It moved in its open-market operations and at the discount window to supply adequate bank reserves so as to avoid a liquidity crisis and the collapse of the financial markets.

Figure 3.1 illustrates the change that has occurred in the commercial paper market, but unlike government securities, the secondary market is nearly nonexistent. When commercial paper is issued to be placed directly, it is tailored to the asset holder's needs in terms of amounts and maturities. When sold to a dealer for resale, the asset holder or potential buyer realizes that he will not be able to sell that paper but must hold it until maturity.

Commercial paper has its advantages to the issuer. It is sold at a discount rather than with a coupon rate of return. The issuer then has full use of the funds without the bothersome compensating balance requirements of banks. Often the effective rate of borrowing is lower than the prime rate of major banks.

Bankers' Acceptances. Another short-term source of funds for the business sector is the bankers' acceptance. This financial instrument is a draft drawn by an individual or firm on its bank, ordering the bank to pay a specific sum to a third party at a specific future date. Usually these are drawn for a 30- to 180-day period. If the bank accepts the draft, the bank is then essentially guaranteeing that the drawer will pay his debt at maturity and is, in fact, substituting its credit rating for the drawer's.

The advantage to the drawer is that he has obtained time before funds are due and may also receive the goods he is trying to acquire. The lender of the funds, in this case the third party who is willing to take payment in the future (not the bank), receives the draft knowing that he can hold it to maturity and be guaranteed of payment or can readily sell it in an active secondary market. This secondary market is made by approximately six dealers who also deal in other money market instruments.

The bank in this case is the intermediary. In accepting a draft it loses no funds immediately but does acquire a contingent liability. Most of the banks that accept such drafts are centered in New York City and San Francisco. They are well known, and their acceptance of the drafts make these bankers' acceptances one of the prime quality money market instruments. This quality is attested to by the fact that the Federal Reserve System will take bankers' acceptances as collateral from borrowing member banks.

Acceptances, like Treasury bills and commercial paper, carry no coupon rate but rather are sold at a discount to determine their effective yield. The volume of acceptances outstanding grew rapidly in the 1960s. (See Figure 3.1.) At the close of 1959, $1.2 billion was outstanding; by August 1973, $7.7 billion was outstanding, of which more than 65 percent was based on financing imports and exports.

Acceptances are held and traded in the secondary market by corporations, financial institutions, commercial banks, foreign banks and businesses, and the Federal Reserve System.

Certificates of Deposit. So far we have mentioned the money market instruments issued by the federal government sector and the business sector. Now we turn to the commercial banking sector. (Commercial paper is issued by one-bank holding corporations, not by the banks themselves.) In an effort to acquire new sources of funds, commercial banks have turned to issuing large-denomination *negotiable certificates of deposit* (CDs). These certificates are issued in specific denominations, usually for $100,000 or more, for a specific period by about 3000 banks. They bear a coupon rate that is paid to the bearer at maturity. First issued in negotiable form in 1961, they attracted some $2 billion in funds that year. Undoubtedly some of the banks saw their liabilities being rearranged as buyers of CDs moved funds from demand deposits or time deposits with that bank into the higher-yielding CDs. But they also attracted new funds that corporations had been investing in the money market directly. Negotiable certificates of deposit continued to grow in the 1960s until the end of 1968, when the amount outstanding was $24 billion.

Certificates of deposit, however, are unique as a money market instrument in that the maximum coupon rate is controlled by the Federal Reserve System under Regulation Q. The effect of this ceiling was to encourage CD holders to find more attractive short-term securities (i.e., commercial paper) during 1969, when free-market interest rates hit historic highs. Unable to compete with these market-determined rates, banks experienced a rapid decline in the quantity of certificates demanded. Certificates of deposit declined by $12.5 billion, to $11.5 billion, or about half of their previous holdings. As economic conditions changed again, asset holders turned away from commercial paper and Treasury bills and back to certificates of deposit. As of September 30, 1973, some $69 billion was outstanding in negotiable certificates of deposit of $100,000 or more.

There is an active secondary market for the certificates that are issued by the largest and best-known banks. Holders of these certificates of deposit find them marketable and easily disposed of prior to maturity. The important characteristic of this instrument is that it is negotiable. This doesn't insure its marketability, however.

Federal Funds. The trading in federal funds began 50 years ago. In 1921, New York City banks discovered that at any one time some of the banks would have excess required reserves on deposit with the Federal Reserve Bank of New York, while others were short of reserves and were having to borrow directly from the Reserve bank at the discount rate—a fixed rate of interest that may be quite different from a rate that would reflect the supply of excess reserves and the demand for those reserves. The banks found that they could make money themselves or pay less by working through a private federal funds market.

Federal funds or, more precisely, legal reserve balances of member banks on deposit with the Federal Reserve banks are an extremely desirable means of payment. If payment is in federal funds, the amount is transfered from the reserve account of one bank to the reserve account of the other bank the same day, almost instantaneously. Contrast this with payment by check. The check may be written and delivered today to the drawee, who then deposits it in his bank. The earliest the reserve accounts of the two banks are altered is the following day. These payments are often called clearinghouse funds. Can one day be so significant? This is one of the tenets of cash management—that time costs money. If a bank with excess reserves of $3 million can loan them for one day at an annual rate of 5 percent, it would receive $400 in addition to its $3 million the following day.

The market for federal funds is made primarily by commercial banks. The center of the market is New York City, with New York banks generally borrowing funds. Funds are supplied by other commercial banks, usually smaller banks outside New York and Chicago, that typically keep more excess reserves as a cushion in their own portfolio policy. Government security dealers use payment in federal funds as a way of having funds transfered immediately. Corporations may demand federal funds in payment for securities they have sold.

The growth of the federal funds market has been dramatic. In the early 1960s daily average volume of federal funds purchases and sales combined was about $2 billion. In the early 1970s it had reached $13–$18 billion per day. More banks are learning about this market for investing their idle reserves. In the Fourth Federal Reserve District (Cleveland) alone, the number of banks in the federal funds market grew from 10 in 1948 to 330 in 1969. Not all of these banks are regular traders; in fact few are, but trading is now on a wider geographic base and among a much larger number of banks.

A continuous market for federal funds is facilitated by one large brokerage firm, a few large money market banks that act in part as dealers accumulating funds and also in part as brokers, and the network of correspondent bank relationships through which information about potential lenders and borrowers of funds is transmitted.

The existence of the federal funds market has enabled credit conditions to be diffused about the country more easily. In addition to altering holdings of Treasury bills, buying and selling federal funds has become the major method by which commercial banks adjust their liquidity positions on a day-to-day basis.

THE ROLE OF THE MONEY MARKET IN THE FINANCIAL SYSTEM

The basic function of all financial markets is to mobilize the financial surpluses of the nation and to allocate these among competing deficit spending units. The money market, however, has another important role to play in the financial system. It provides a place where spending units and financial intermediaries can adjust their holdings of liquid assets and where the central bank can adjust the liquidity position of the entire economy. The vital quality of the money market is its breadth, activity, and stability, which can absorb substantial short-term shocks without excessive gyrations in market prices. Thus, corporations, banks, or other financial intermediaries with temporarily surplus cash can put it to work at a competitive rate of interest in the money market and be reasonably secure in the knowledge that the funds can be recalled on very short notice if needed. Likewise, corporations, banks, or other financial intermediaries that are short of cash can obtain it on short notice and for short periods of time, if that is desirable, by borrowing in the money market or selling in the market any money market instruments they may have been holding.

The money market thus makes it possible for all types of firms and financial intermediaries to manage their financial affairs more efficiently and particularly to economize on their holdings of money. It also provides a convenient point for the central bank to intrude into the operations of the financial system. The central bank can sell Treasury bills and other short-term government securities in the money market in order to absorb what it might consider excess cash in the financial system. Likewise, it can purchase such money market instruments in exchange for cash if it feels that there is not sufficient cash in the system. We will have many occasions as we progress through this book to refer to the money market and its importance for financial intermediaries and the operation of monetary policy.

SUMMARY

A financial instrument originates in the act of borrowing and lending. It is a written contract between a creditor and a debtor. It is a claim to a future stream of payments. Many, but not all, types of financial instruments can be bought and sold in financial markets at a market-established price. If a financial instrument is negotiable, it is more easily transfered from owner to owner. Some financial instruments are difficult to sell; that is, they are not readily marketable. A marketable security is one for which there is a developed secondary market having a relatively large volume of continual trading in that security.

The most common financial instrument is a debt obligation or bond. It is a claim to a specified number of payments in fixed amounts. Because it is a claim to future payments, there is always some uncertainty about whether the payments will actually be made as specified. This is termed *credit risk.*

There are other financial instruments in which neither the amount of each payment nor the number of payments is specified. Common stock is a convenient example of such a variable income security.

Money, too, may be considered a financial instrument. It is the one financial instrument whose price is fixed. It is therefore the most liquid financial security.

Financial markets enable the financial surpluses of the nation to be channeled and allocated among competing deficit spending units. Our concern is with financial markets for impersonal securities or investments rather than with the markets for direct loans. Financial intermediaries such as investment houses and, more specifically, brokers and dealers make the markets in various types of impersonal securities. Perhaps the best-known institution for selling financial instruments is the organized stock exchange, particularly the New York Stock Exchange. Common stock is also traded through other registered exchanges and in over-the-counter markets. Secondary markets in corporate and municipal bonds are made most often by dealers on an informal basis rather than through the facilities of an organized exchange.

The term *money market* is applied to a number of markets for short-term financial debt instruments. The money market is of particular interest because it provides a place where spending units and financial intermediaries adjust their liquidity positions and the central bank can operate to adjust the liquidity position of the entire economy.

NOTE

1. Until early in 1970 Treasury bills could be bought in multiples of $1,000. As interest rates rose in late 1969 and 1970, small investors withdrew savings from financial intermediaries and invested directly in money market instruments—primarily Treasury bills. The savings and loan associations and commercial banks pressured the Treasury to raise the minimum purchase of bills to stop the outflow of funds. In addition, the Treasury found issuing so many more small-denomination certificates at high rates of interest costly. In 1970, with these two points in mind, the Treasury raised the minimum purchase of Treasury bills to $10,000. Treasury notes may still be purchased in $1,000 multiples.

ELEMENTARY THEORY
OF FINANCIAL MARKETS

Part 1: The Demand
for Wealth

In Chapter 3 we described the major instruments exchanged in financial markets and discussed the more important institutions of these markets in the United States. It is now time to turn to the more difficult task of exploring the process by which prices are formed in such markets. That is the purpose of this and the following two chapters.

When asked, "What determines prices in a financial market?" the average economics student will instinctively respond, "supply and demand." This is true in a general sense, since all prices are determined by supply and demand, but unless we can put some content into these concepts, such an answer will not take us very far toward understanding the behavior of financial markets.

THE DEMAND FOR FINANCIAL INSTRUMENTS

THE BASIC DECISIONS

The demand side of the market for financial instruments includes at various times virtually every spending unit in the economy—households, financial intermediaries, business firms, nonprofit institutions, and government agencies. Any spending unit with a need or desire to accumulate wealth will probably enter this market from time to time.

The role of financial intermediaries in financial markets raises special issues that are best considered separately. We will discuss them in Chapter 8. At the outset we also prefer to leave aside discussion of the demands of business firms, nonprofit institutions, and government agencies. With a few exceptions, particularly relating to the demand for money, they are peripheral to the main demand forces in financial markets. Thus, in this and the next chapter we will be focusing attention almost exclusively on household demands for financial instruments.

We will cast our analysis in terms of two basic decisions that every household must make: (1) a decision on the size of total wealth holdings, and (2) a decision on the composition of wealth holdings. Wealth is the central concept in the analysis. Indeed, we will argue that financial instruments take on significance to households simply as forms in which wealth may be accumulated.

The first decision is the subject of this chapter, the second decision that of the next chapter.

WEALTH AND SAVING

If wealth is to be the central concept in the analysis of demands for financial assets, then the first task must be to define the concept of wealth and to explore the process by which wealth is accumulated. Our objective is the development of a theory of wealth accumulation.

THE CONCEPT OF WEALTH

As a start, we might define the household's wealth as *the value of the household's net equity in the things the household owns.* Although complex, this definition is designed to emphasize three essential elements. First, the concept of wealth relates to things that have value in the economic sense (i.e., market value). Second, it implies ownership—the right of the household to exclude others from the enjoyment of these valuable things. Finally, the definition recognizes that the household may formally "own" valuable things of greater aggregate value than the total wealth of the household. The difference is the aggregate value of the debts or obligations of the household. Thus, to cite the most familiar example, a family may "own" its house and at the same time have an outstanding debt or mortgage against it equal to a substantial portion of the market value of the house. The contribution of the house to the family's wealth is the difference between the value of the house and the value of the mortgage—the family's *equity* in the house.

THE ACCOUNTING FRAMEWORK

Three basic accounting relationships provide a simple framework for our analysis of the demand for wealth. Each of these can be expressed in the

60

form of an equation that is an *identity*. The two sides of the equation are equal by definition. One can take the left-hand side of each equation as a formal definition of the variable on the right-hand side. Unlike equations that embody *functional relationships*, identities do not tell us anything substantive about the demand for wealth. They do not purport to describe the behavior of participants in the financial system. Rather, they specify constraints on behavior. They tell us that certain combinations of events or activities are logically impossible. For example, the first identity tells us that it is impossible for a household's assets to increase while both its liabilities and its net worth are falling.

The Balance Sheet Identity. *Assets* are values that the household owns. *Liabilities* are the values that it owes. The difference between assets and liabilities is the equity in the value of things owned—the household's net worth or *wealth*. This fundamental relationship can be expressed in the balance sheet identity:

$$\text{Assets} - \text{Liabilities} = \text{Wealth} \tag{4.1}$$

Wealth need not always be positive. The assets of the household could exceed or fall short of liabilities, and accordingly wealth could be positive or negative. If wealth is positive we can refer to the household as a *net creditor*, and if it is negative we can refer to it as a *net debtor*.[1]

The Saving Identity. The second basic identity is a definition of net saving. For every household, and indeed for the nation as a whole, it is true by definition that:

$$\text{Income} - \text{Consumption} = \text{Saving} \tag{4.2}$$

This identity is simply a statement of the fact that consumption and savings are alternative uses of the same scarce resources, the household's (or the nation's) income. In order to save, the household must choose to forgo current consumption, and in this very basic sense current consumption forgone is the cost of saving. The decisions on consumption and saving are two sides of the same coin. If you explain one, you explain the other.

There is nothing in the saving identity that says saving must be positive. Saving can be negative as long as current consumption exceeds current income (negative saving is sometimes called dissaving). Thus, saving is an economic variable that must be assigned an algebraic sign as well as a magnitude.

The Accumulation Identity. Assets, liabilities, and wealth are *stock variables*. They are values measured at a point in time. Income, consumption, and saving are *flow variables*. They are values measured over a period of time. The third identity—the accumulation identity—establishes a logical link between the stocks and the flows. It simply states that during any given period of time:[2]

$$\text{Saving} = \Delta \text{ Wealth} \tag{4.3}$$

where Δ wealth means the net change in wealth.

The logic of this equation should be self-evident. If it is not, consider briefly what is involved in the act of saving. If the saving of a given household is positive during a particular month, the household receives more income than it spends on consumption during that month. What can the household do with the balance of its income? There are three possibilities. It might use this portion to acquire real or financial assets. This is a nonconsumption use of the household's income, which results in an increase in its net asset holdings and hence in its wealth. As an alternative, the household might use this portion of its income to pay off debts. Again, this is a nonconsumption use of its income, which, by reducing liabilities, increases the household's wealth. If it neither purchases assets nor pays off liabilities, then the household must simply accumulate money in the amount of the excess of its income over its consumption. But money is also an asset. Its accumulation implies an equal increase in the household's wealth. Positive saving implies a corresponding increase in wealth.

The same points can be made regarding negative saving. If consumption is to exceed income, the household must somehow finance its deficit budget. It must either borrow, and thereby increase its liabilities and hence reduce its wealth, or draw down its assets, whether money or other assets, with the same effect on its wealth. Negative saving implies a corresponding reduction in wealth.

THE ECONOMIC THEORY OF THE SAVING DECISION

On any particular date, which we can choose arbitrarily as the starting point for our analysis, each household in the population will have a measurable stock of wealth (positive or negative) and will expect a certain flow of income during the following time period—say, one year. The household may plan to increase, decrease, or make no change in its wealth holdings over that year. For our analysis this is the fundamental decision to be made by each household—a decision about the size of its wealth holdings.

Equation 4.3 tells us that saving is the method by which any household adjusts the size of its wealth. This suggests that we should call this fundamental decision the *saving decision*. (It is important to remember that saving may be either positive or negative; wealth may be increased or decreased).

SPECIFIC MOTIVES FOR SAVING

If we asked people why they save part of their income we would probably be given a great variety of specific motives. It is quite likely that we would discover many instances in which saving was alleged to be quite fortuitous—an unplanned, inadvertent, and perhaps random event. Aside from such short-term aberrations, however, we would probably discover that most households had in mind a fairly deliberate plan for saving. In some cases it might involve a general income objective, such as the provision of a pension during years of retirement from active participation in the labor force or otherwise to increase the household's income in later years. In other instances we might be told about some specific target the household has in mind, such as the purchase of a new house, a new automobile, or some other major durable good, or even an intangible item such as a prolonged vacation, perhaps involving a trip to "the old country," or a university education or an inheritance for the household's children. In other instances we might discover that saving was simply an attempt to provide for general or specific contingencies that might occur in the future. Thus, a household might buy life or disability insurance on the main income earner, or it might build up a bank account "against a rainy day" or to take advantage of unexpected future opportunities.

The variety of possible motives for saving is virtually endless, and no single theory can encompass all of them in detail. The problem is to distill from the complexities of reality a few generalizations that capture the essence of the behavior of saving. In recent years this has been the subject of much theoretical and empirical research. Without attempting a detailed review of the resulting literature, it is pertinent to note some of the highlights.

INCOME AND THE SAVING DECISION

The Keynesian Hypothesis. The theory of saving developed in most principles-of-economics textbooks is that embodied in the Keynesian consumption function. Its originator, J. M. Keynes, asserted that "the amount of aggregate consumption mainly depends on the amount of aggregate income," and this relationship exists because there is a

> fundamental psychological law, upon which we are entitled to depend with great confidence, both a *priori* from our knowledge of human nature and from the detailed facts of experience . . . that men are disposed, as a rule and on the average, to increase their consumption as their income increases, but not by as much as the increase in their income.[3]

As Equation 4.2 demonstrates, consumption and saving are complements. They are alternative possible uses of income, and if you explain one you necessarily explain the other. Thus, Keynes' consumption function can be readily translated into a saving function that says "the amount of aggregate saving mainly depends on the amount of aggregate income," and "men are disposed, as a rule and on the average, to increase their saving as their income increases, but not by as much as the increase in their income." In most elementary economic theory it is assumed that the relationship between aggregate income and saving can be described by a straight line, such as that depicted in Figure 4.1. At low levels of income saving

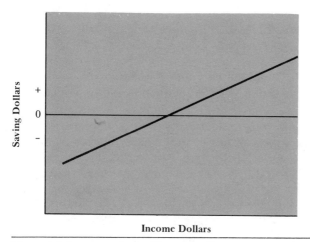

Figure 4.1 Aggregate Saving Function: Keynesian Hypothesis

is negative. At higher levels of income it is positive and is an increasing function of income. The portion of income saved (the average propensity to consume) thus depends on the level of income, but the increase in saving is always a constant proportion (the marginal propensity to consume) of any increase in income.

This assumed relationship between income and saving seems plausible enough. Since the accumulation of wealth is but one among the many competing demands on the limited income of each household, it would be surprising if the level of saving in the household were not affected by the household's income. Households with relatively high incomes are able to buy more of everything, including wealth, than households with relatively small incomes. Moreover, at a low level of income present consumption needs are likely in general to seem relatively more urgent than future requirements. We would therefore expect low-income households to save a smaller portion of their income than high-income families.

As it has been used in economic theory, the Keynesian hypothesis is primarily a relationship between *aggregate* income and *aggregate* saving. It is clear, however, from his "fundamental psychological law" that Keynes thought of his relationship applying at the *microeconomic* level as well— as explaining differences in individual households' saving habits. The validity of the hypothesis has been tested at both levels in a large number of studies. The aggregative studies have examined the relationship between income and saving for the nation as a whole over varying periods extending well over half a century in length. The microeconomic studies, by contrast, examine the saving behavior of a cross-section of households during a given period, normally one year.

At first glance, both the micro and macro studies appear to confirm the Keynesian hypothesis, at least in a general way. While the relationship may not be strictly linear, there is a clear, unmistakable positive relationship between saving and income, both in the aggregate and on the average for a cross-section of the population. The latter is illustrated in Table 4.1. However, in spite of this evidence many economists have lingering doubts about the adequacy of the hypothesis.

These doubts are based in part on theoretical reasoning involving the relationship between saving and wealth accumulation that we have already established. A low-income household that is dissaving must be simultaneously reducing its wealth by either disposing of assets or increasing liabilities. The assumption that saving depends solely on income (if it is to conform to the facts of Table 4.1) implies a further assumption that households with chronically low incomes have unlimited means to finance consumption in excess of income. They must have unlimited assets that can be sold, or they must be able to increase their debts without limit. In general, this assumption is implausible.

Households with incomes above the zero saving level must be accumulating wealth. This includes the bulk of the households in the population. The hypothesis that saving depends only on the level of income implies the further hypothesis that households whose income remains continuously in this range have insatiable demand for wealth. While it does not do as much violence to our preconceptions about the world as does the first assumption (unlimited credit or assets for sale), this is also implausible. Households presumably demand wealth for any of the variety of purposes we have noted earlier. None of these suggests an insatiable demand for wealth at moderate to high income levels regardless of all other considerations.

Empirical research appears to confirm these theoretical doubts. A careful sifting of the evidence shows that the Keynesian hypothesis does not adequately explain all of the significant variations in saving behavior among households or all of the significant fluctuations in national saving behavior. The Keynesian hypothesis appears to identify one important consideration in household saving, but as a total theory of saving it is at best only a first approximation.

The Permanent Income Hypothesis. One of the interesting regularities discovered in cross-sectional studies is that the saving behavior of households that have recently experienced a significant change in income is different from that of households that have the same present income level but have not experienced a change in income. Households that have experienced a decline in income tend to save less than comparable households with a steady income, and households that have experienced a rise in income tend to save more than comparable households with a stable income. One possible explanation for this phenomenon is to be found in the so-called permanent income hypothesis.

According to this hypothesis, a household's consumption does not depend directly on its current income. Rather, if we ignore a random or

Table 4.1. Income and Saving by Income Class, 1963

Disposable Income

	Under $1,000	$1,000– 1,999	$2,000– 2,999	$3,000– 3,999	$4,000– 4,999	$5,000– 5,999	$6,000– 7,499	$7,500– 9,999	$10,000– 14,999	$15,000 and Over	All Classes
Average Disposable Income	$ 367	$1,482	$2,521	$3,489	$4,483	$5,506	$6,742	$8,663	$11,887	$23,780	$5,832
Saving[a]	−479	−328	+353	+526	+866	+862	+931	+1,491	+2,944	+5,094	+971
Saving as a Percentage of Income	−130.5	−22.1	14.0	15.1	19.3	15.7	13.8	17.2	24.8	21.4	16.6

[a]Saving includes the purchase of automobiles, which is often treated as a consumption expenditure, and includes saving in the form of retirement contributions.

SOURCE: Board of Governors of the Federal Reserve System, Survey of Changes in Family Finances (Washington, D.C., November 1968), p. 9.

"transitory" component in consumption expenditures, it depends on the household's "permanent income." The concept of permanent income is somewhat complex, and a formal definition is beyond our present exposition. However, we can roughly interpret it as the level of income the household has come to expect as its normal income. The actual income may fall short of or exceed permanent income as a result of random "transitory" factors.

Illness or unexpected unemployment might reduce income below permanent income. Similarly, an unexpected gift or a sudden rise in the market price of a product produced and sold by members of the household would raise current income above permanent income. Thus, both income and consumption have a permanent component (planned or expected) and a transitory component (a product of unexpected chance variations).

The permanent income hypothesis is normally presented as a theory explaining the behavior of consumption expenditures. However, Equation 4.2 permits us to reinterpret it as a theory of the behavior of saving. According to this hypothesis, both income and saving have permanent and transitory components. Permanent (or planned) saving depends directly on permanent income, but actual saving may fluctuate about permanent saving as a result of chance factors. In most formal presentations of the permanent income hypothesis it is assumed that permanent saving is a constant portion of permanent income—that the permanent marginal propensity to save is a constant.[4] The relationship observed in Table 4.1 is explained in terms of the transitory components of income and saving.

The permanent income hypothesis, if correct, provides a fundamentally different interpretation of the relationship between income and saving than does the Keynesian hypothesis. Moreover, the difference is a matter of considerable consequence for economic policy, as we will see in later sections of the book. Tests of the hypothesis have thus had a relatively high priority in empirical economics in recent years. Unfortunately, none of the variables involved—permanent income, permanent consumption, or permanent saving (or, for that matter, the corresponding transitory components)—can be observed directly. They are theoretical constructs. As a result, all of the tests have had to be indirect. Perhaps for this reason we must regard the formal statistical tests as inconclusive. Much of the evidence is favorable to the hypothesis, but the evidence is far from decisive.

The Life Cycle Hypothesis. In the simple form in which we have presented it, the permanent income hypothesis does not provide us with many insights into the saving decision. It only tells us that in part the saving decision is deliberate and in part it is a product of chance variations in income. It does not tell us what considerations govern the level of planned saving. (By definition, we cannot have a theory to explain the "random" component.) This is not a fault of the theory, but of our exposition, since we have not explored the theoretical foundations of the hypothesis.

The theory of household behavior underlying the permanent income hypothesis is in all essentials the same as that underlying another contemporary theory of saving behavior, the so-called *life cycle hypothesis*, which starts with the familiar assumptions that households seek to maximize utility and that they derive utility only from the consumption of goods and services (and perhaps from leaving bequests to the next generation). However, households have a normal life span well beyond one year. Hence, the household will presumably seek to maximize the utility it derives from consumption over its entire life span. This calls for a lifetime plan for consumption expenditures in the light of expected lifetime income.

A basic fact of life that the household must recognize is that the most desirable lifetime pattern of consumption will probably not conform exactly to the lifetime pattern of income the household expects to receive. A typical life cycle is illustrated in Figure 4.2. In early years, as the household is formed, acquires the necessary durable goods, and raises and educates children, it is quite probable that income will not exceed planned consumption by a substantial margin, and in many cases it may fall substantially short of planned consumption.[5] In the middle years of the life span, by contrast, planned consumption will normally fall substantially short of earned income as the children grow up and leave home. In later years, income from employment will probably drop substantially, particularly following retirement. Planned consumption will then greatly exceed income from employment.

Under these circumstances, the maximization of utility from consumption requires a redistribution of purchasing power between years of "surplus" income and years of "deficient" income. In addition, the household may wish to accumulate a reserve for contingencies, such as illness or unemployment, that might have a short-term impact on either income or consumption expenditures. The method of achieving both of these objectives is through saving. In years of surplus income the household can accumulate wealth (positive saving); in years of deficient income it can reduce its wealth, either through a reduction in asset holdings or through an increase in liabilities (negative saving).

Some aspects of the life cycle in income and wealth for American households are illustrated in Figure 4.3.

EXPECTED YIELD AND THE SAVING DECISION

The central variable in the Keynesian, permanent income, and life cycle hypothesis is income. While the relationship between income and saving will depend in part on transitory factors and in part on the household's stage in the life cycle, it is conceded in general that the higher the level of income, the higher will be the level of saving. There is also a

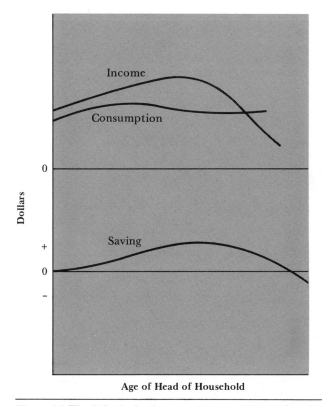

Figure 4.2 **The Life Cycle: Income, Consumption, and Saving**

second variable affecting the saving decision that has received much attention in the literature; this is the *expected yield on assets.*

Expected yield is the interest rate implicit in the relationship between the stream of future payments and the market price of the asset that provides those payments. A more precise formulation of the concept is developed in the appendix to Chapter 5. However, in a very crude sense it is the ratio of the expected future payments to the current cost of the asset.

That expected yield should be a primary determinant of the demand for wealth should not be surprising. As we have already noted, the accumulation of wealth implies the sacrifice of current consumption in order to accumulate the means for larger future consumption. Depending on preferences between future and present consumption, saving—and hence the net demand for wealth—should be more or less sensitive to changes in the yield on assets.

While saving should be sensitive to yields on assets, the direction of the effect is not always clear. From one perspective, the effect of higher

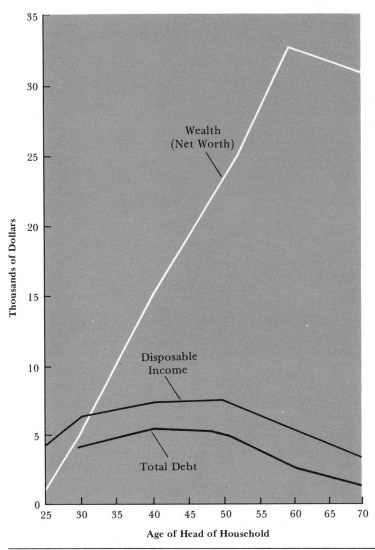

Figure 4.3 **The Life Cycle: Income, Debts, and Wealth, 1963**
SOURCE: Total debt: Dorothy Projector and Gertrude Wise, *Survey of Financial Characteristics of Consumers* (Washington, D.C.: Board of Governors of the Federal Reserve System, 1966), p. 130; wealth and income: Board of Governors of the Federal Reserve System, *Survey of Changes in Family Finances* (Washington, D.C., 1968), pp. 52, 214.

yields is to provide a larger stream of future benefits from any given present sacrifice (e.g., a larger pension or a larger estate for one's heirs). Since larger benefits are to be preferred to smaller, higher yields should stimulate saving. From a different perspective, however, the higher the yield, the smaller the current sacrifice necessary to achieve any given future objective (e.g., a new house or a round-the-world tour). A higher yield could conceivably reduce the incentive to save on the part of "target savers."

There is also another aspect to any increase in expected yields on assets. Higher yields also imply higher costs of borrowing funds (an interest cost to the borrower is an expected yield to the lender). The higher cost of credit should deter households from borrowing and hence increase their saving for precautionary purposes.

In summary, higher expected yields mean more favorable "terms of trade" between future and present. This should induce saving and hence increase the demand for additions to wealth. However, households with fixed targets for wealth accumulation can now achieve those targets with less saving.

SOCIOECONOMIC FACTORS IN THE SAVING DECISION

Current income, permanent income, stage in the life cycle, and expected yield are all "objective" factors affecting the saving decision. They are factors in the outside world to which the household reacts. We should not ignore the "subjective" or personal elements in the decision. The tastes or preferences of households as between future and present consumption and with respect to the provision of an estate for future generations may differ markedly. In technical terms, they may have very different "time preferences." Some differences in time preference may be related to other social or economic characteristics. Thus, survey researchers have discovered many interesting differences in saving behavior between urban and rural families, homeowners and tenants, and people with different occupations, levels of education, or racial backgrounds.

SUMMARY

The theory of demand developed in elementary economic theory has its foundations in the concept of utility. People demand goods and services because consumption of these goods and services yields utility directly to the consumer. In general, however, financial instruments are not in this category. They do not yield utility directly in the same sense that the consumption of a cup of coffee or a candy bar yields utility. The demand for financial instruments is a demand for something to be held—an asset—not a demand for something to be consumed. If households seek to maximize the utility derived from the use of their limited incomes, why should they allocate part of their limited incomes to the accumulation of financial instruments that do not yield utility? Is their behavior inconsistent with the general assumption of utility maximization? Are asset-accumulating households acting irrationally?

In general, the answer to this last question is no. It may be quite rational for a household that is seeking to maximize utility to devote part of its limited income to the accumulation of financial instruments, even though these instruments are not objects of consumption and hence do not yield utility directly in the same sense as do consumer goods. The rational head of the household must take a lifetime perspective on utility maximization. He must plan his household's expenditures with an eye to the future as well as the present. It may seem rational to him to deliberately reduce the consumption of the household below its potential levels in the present in order to permit higher levels of consumption in the future. Such a redistribution of income and consumption from the present to the future requires an accumulation of wealth, and one of the basic forms in which wealth may be accumulated is in the form of financial instruments. The demand for financial instruments is rooted in the desire to accumulate wealth, and the desire to accumulate wealth, in turn, is based on the desire to redistribute income and consumption over time.

NOTES

1. This accounting definition of wealth is deceptively simple. We are in fact glossing over many of the complexities in the measurement of wealth, particularly in the measurement of the value of assets. In particular, we have ignored intangible assets, such as the earning power of the members of the household—what some economists call human wealth. The measurement of the value of human assets is complicated by the fact that markets for such assets do not exist and as a result it is impossible to quote market values. Markets exist for the services of human beings, of course, but since the abolition of slavery there are no markets in which the asset that yields the services can be traded. This does not mean that the measurement of the value of the human asset is impossible. In the appendix to the next chapter we develop the concept of present value. Measuring the value of a human resource—like measuring the value of any resource—is a problem in the calculation of present value.

If the value of human assets is included in the household's balance sheet, it is less likely that wealth could ever be negative.

2. The validity of this identity depends on the appropriate definitions of income and consumption in Equation 4.2 and hence on the definition of saving. The problems arise because of three elements in the household's financial accounts: gifts, taxes, and changes in the market values of assets (capital gains or losses). We must make adjustments for each of these items. Capital gains and losses and gifts received must be counted as income (capital losses reduce income, of course). Gifts made by the household might be considered as a consumption use of income, but it is probably better to group gifts with taxes paid as a deduction from income to obtain the household's disposable income.

3. J. M. Keynes, *The General Theory of Employment, Interest and Money* (New York: Harcourt Brace Jovanovich, 1936), p. 96.

4. This is not a fully accurate statement of the position of the permanent income theorists. They argue that the ratio of permanent consumption to permanent income is independent of the level of permanent income. It does depend on a variety of other factors, however, including the level of interest rates and the household's "tastes and preferences for consumption versus additions to wealth." In the latter category, such objective factors as the size and age composition of the family and the variability of the household's income are suggested as important considerations. However, with all of these factors given, the ratio of permanent saving to permanent income will be the same at

all levels of permanent income. Cf. M. Friedman, *A Theory of the Consumption Function* (Princeton, N.J.: Princeton University Press, 1957), p. 26.

5. It should be noted that the statistical relationship between age and savings depends on the definition of saving. This is particularly true in the early stages of the life cycle, when the household is typically making heavy expenditures on durable consumer goods, including the purchase of a house. If all consumer durables are considered assets and hence included in the measurement of net worth, then only the "consumption" (i.e., depreciation) of these assets will be included in consumption expenditures. Saving is less likely to be negative under these circumstances than if these goods are not included in the measurement of net worth. Most statistical studies omit most of these consumer durables, largely because of the lack of reliable data. In Figure 4.2 saving excludes automobile purchases and contributions to retirement plans. In Figure 4.3 assets include equity in home, business, and automobile, as well as the value of financial assets. It excludes equity in retirement plans because of the unreliability of the estimates.

ELEMENTARY THEORY OF FINANCIAL MARKETS

Part 2: The Portfolio Balance Decision

The demand for wealth—the saving decision—is fundamental to household demands for financial assets. However, it is simply a decision about the size of total asset holdings; it must be accompanied by a decision about the composition of the collection of assets to be held.

It is convenient to term this collection of assets an *asset portfolio—portfolio* for short. In selecting his portfolio the asset holder must be concerned with the balance between real assets and financial assets, and, of primary concern to us at the moment, within the category of financial assets he must be concerned with the balance between the different types of financial instruments discussed in Chapter 3. He must make choices among the great variety of financial instruments available in the market. The portfolio balance decision thus translates a general demand for assets into specific demands for specific assets.

For the sake of convenience we shall focus on choices among financial assets only. As we will see eventually, the same principles apply to the choice between real and financial assets.

In the first section of Chapter 3 we outlined the diversity of financial instruments in use today. This survey, although far from exhaustive, provided too great a range of characteristics to be manipulated in a general theoretical analysis. For this we need a small set of concepts that capture the essential characteristics of the diverse financial instruments. While we will have occasion to discuss a few others, three concepts are basic: expected yield, credit risk, and liquidity.[1]

EXPECTED YIELD AND THE CHOICE
AMONG FINANCIAL INSTRUMENTS

The central theoretical issue in any discussion of the portfolio balance decision is why any one financial instrument should be chosen over any other as the form in which the household accumulates wealth. One important factor in this choice should be quite obvious. Other things being equal, a rational asset holder will always prefer an asset with a high expected yield to one with a low expected yield.

THE CONCEPT OF EXPECTED YIELD
AND ITS RELATIONSHIP TO MARKET PRICE

We have already encountered the concept of expected yield in our discussion of the saving decision. You will remember that it is the interest rate implicit in the relationship between the market price of the financial instrument and the expected stream of future payments associated with that instrument. We noted that the effect of expected yield on the total demand for wealth was ambiguous. A higher yield might lead to greater or less saving. However, no such ambiguity exists in the effect of expected yield on the demand for particular assets. Since all assets are substitutes for each other as forms in which wealth may be accumulated, the demand for any particular instrument, other things being equal, will be greater the higher the expected yield.

Here we have emphasized a positive relationship between demand for an instrument and its yield, rather than the negative relationship between demand and price that is usually stressed. The fact is that for any financial instrument, market price and expected yield are inversely related. With the stream of future payments fixed by contract, the yield on a bond can rise only if the market price of the bond falls. This is implicit in the definition of expected yield.

An example may clarify these relationships. In 1959 the Treasury issued a series of 21-year bonds to mature in February 1980. The coupon rate was fixed at 4 percent, such that the total annual interest payments on a $1000 (par value) bond is $40. These securities trade freely at prices determined in the market. In 1965 the bond traded at a market price of approximately $940. At this price the yield was about 4.5 percent per annum. Subsequently bond prices fell again. By 1966 the price of a "4s 1980" was about $870, returning a yield to the investor of 5.2 percent. Note that as the price of the bond fell, the yield rose. By 1970 the price fell more, to $710, indicating a yield of 8.1 percent. Conversely, a year later the same bond was selling at $860 to yield 6 percent.

It follows, then, that the statement that the demand for a financial instrument is directly related to its expected yield is the same as the statement that the demand for the instrument is inversely related to its market price.

The whole subject of market prices and yields on assets is so important, not only for our analysis but also in any decisions relating to fixed assets, that we have taken pains to develop and explore the concepts more carefully and systematically in the appendix to this chapter.

RISK AND THE CHOICE AMONG FINANCIAL INSTRUMENTS

If expected yield were the only consideration in portfolio choices, then the rational asset holder, faced with the alternatives of one security yielding 5 percent and one yielding 10 percent, would always choose the latter. In the market, attempts of individuals to sell the 5 percent securities to purchase the 10 percent securities should drive the price of the former down (and the yield up) and the price of the latter up (and the yield down). The end result should be a rough equalization of yields on the two securities. In fact we observe in the market that the yields on different securities differ markedly and consistently. Why is this? The answer is that there are other factors that affect choices among assets, including credit risk, liquidity, the possibility of capital gains or capital losses, the risk of inflation, and differential taxation. We shall examine each of these factors in turn.

The first factor we want to consider is the possibility of the actual yield on the security being considerably different from the expected yield. We call this possibility credit risk. We shall see that credit risks associated with different securities differ markedly and that differences in yield in the market place are in part a reflection of these differences in credit risk.

THE CONCEPT OF CREDIT RISK

A financial instrument is a claim to a stream of future payments. Since those payments are to occur in the future, there will always be some uncertainty about whether the payments will in fact be made and, particularly in the case of variable income securities, about the size of such payments. Correspondingly, there must be some uncertainty about the actual yield on any given financial instrument, since this yield depends on the size of the payments actually made in the future. It is because of this uncertainty that credit risk exists.

We can formalize the concept of credit risk by assuming that for any given financial instrument there is a range of possible yields at the present market price. If large future payments are made, the yield will be high; if small future payments are made, the yield will be low. Indeed, if the future

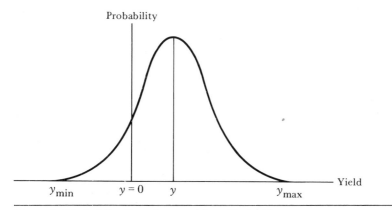

Figure 5.1 **Probability Distribution of Possible Yields**

payments are very small or, in the extreme, nonexistent, the yield will be negative. It must be stressed that we refer to the actual yield on the investment—what actually materializes.

The individual contemplating the purchase of this security cannot know what the outcome will be. However, if he is to make a rational decision he must somehow assess the likelihood of alternative possible outcomes and select the outcome that seems most likely. It is this value to which we refer when we use the expression *expected yield*. Note that the expected yield is not the only outcome regarded as possible, nor is it necessarily the outcome that will materialize.

For the purpose of theoretical discussion we can formalize these elements of the portfolio selection process by assuming that the asset holder has in mind a subjective probability distribution of possible yields on the asset, such as that drawn in Figure 5.1.

The area under the bell-shaped curve is equal to 1, indicating that in the judgment of the asset holder (but not necessarily in fact) one of the possible alternative yields listed along the base of the curve must occur. That is, he feels that there is a probability of 1 (perfect certainty) that the actual yield will be among those listed on the base. The probability that any particular one of these yields will materialize is significantly less than 1. The yield ($\bar{y}$) that he feels has the greatest probability of occurrence —the most likely outcome—is under the highest point of the probability distribution. In his judgment every other possible outcome has a probability of occurrence.

What we mean by credit risk is the dispersion of possible yields around the expected yield. Consider Figure 5.2, which shows two probability distributions of the type plotted in Figure 5.1. Each of these distributions represents the asset holder's subjective judgments about the possible yields on two different securities. Each security has the same expected yield. However, they differ

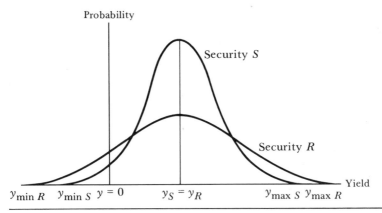

Figure 5.2 **Two Probability Distributions: Same Expected Yield, Different Risks**

markedly in the associated degree of credit risk. In the case of security S (for "safe"), the alternative possible yields are clustered closely about the expected yield. In the case of security R (for "risky"), the alternative possible yields are more dispersed. The asset holder has less confidence that the actual yield will be the expected yield in the latter case. He subjectively assigns probability to the expected outcome and is willing to admit the possibility of a wider range of alternative outcomes.

Standard Deviation as a Measure of Risk. It is convenient for theoretical analysis to have a simple measure of risk in this probability sense. A number of possible measures are available. Perhaps the simplest measure would be the range of possible outcomes, that is, the difference between the highest (y_{max}) and the lowest (y_{min}) yields the asset holder would admit as possible outcomes. Formally, the range is

$$\text{Range} = y_{max} - y_{min}$$

As a measure of risk, the range is seriously defective because it takes into account only one of the two dimensions of risk. While it allows for the fact that the outcome may be different from the expected yield, it ignores the possibility that the asset holder implicitly assigns different probabilities to the alternative possible outcomes. Two securities might have the same range of possible yields, and yet one might appear less risky than the other because the asset holder assigns a lower probability to the extreme values and hence has greater confidence in the accuracy of his estimate of the expected yield. This possibility is sketched in Figure 5.3.

What we need as a measure of risk, then, is a number that takes account of both dimensions, that is, of the range of possible outcomes and of the probability of each outcome. This measure is provided by a statistic called the *standard deviation*, commonly represented by the Greek letter sigma (σ), a complicated measure both in its computation and in its meaning. For now, all we need know is that it is a measure of the dispersion of the probability

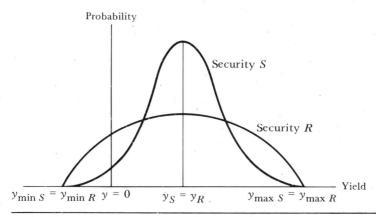

Figure 5.3 **Two Probability Distributions: Same Range, Different Risks**

distribution about the expected yield. The more dispersed the distribution (i.e., the larger the standard deviation), the greater the probability that the actual yield will be different from the expected yield and hence the greater the credit risk associated with that security.

CREDIT RISK AND THE CHOICE AMONG FINANCIAL INSTRUMENTS

We are now in a position to provide a major element in our formal theoretical answer to the question of why yields on two different securities of the same general term to maturity can be continuously and consistently different in the marketplace. While there are some factors on the supply side to be considered, the major consideration on the demand side is asset holders' reactions to credit risk.

Suppose an asset holder were faced with the two securities represented by the probability distributions in Figure 5.2. Both securities have the same expected yield ($\bar{y}_S = \bar{y}_R$). However the distributions of possible alternative yields about the expected yield are notably different. Would the asset holder nevertheless be indifferent as to which security he took into his portfolio?

The answer is, surely not. He cannot ignore the fact that security R is riskier. While the expected yields are the same on the securities, he is less confident that this yield will materialize in the case of Security R than in the case of Security S. Is this not a factor that he should take into account in choosing between the two assets? That is, should he not react to the credit risk on each of the two securities quite independently of the yield on each?

In deciding how he should react, we must remember that the risk we are talking about has two sides. On the one hand, in the asset holder's judgment, there is a much greater probability that the yield on Security R

79

will be less than the expected yield than is true in the case of the yield on Security S. On the other hand, there is also a greater probability that the yield on Security R will exceed the expected yield than is true in the case of the yield on Security S. If the asset holder chooses the "safe" security he is also giving up the greater "risk" of a higher return. Which will he choose?

Risk Aversion. In general, it is assumed that most asset holders are risk avoiders; that is, faced with the alternatives illustrated in Figure 5.2, the typical asset holder will always choose the less risky asset (S). A risk avoider places a higher subjective value (or utility) on the avoidance of extremely small yields (including negative yields) than he does on the possibility of unusually large gains. A risk avoider would demand a larger expected yield on the riskier security before he would choose it over a less risky security.

Not everyone is a risk avoider. Some asset holders, although they appear to be in the minority, are better described as risk seekers, in the sense that they value the chance of larger returns more than the risk of smaller returns. Such individuals, faced with securities R and S under the circumstances of Figure 5.2, would choose security R.

SUMMARY: RISK AND EXPECTED YIELD IN THE CHOICE AMONG FINANCIAL INSTRUMENTS

Perhaps it would be helpful to summarize the argument to this point. We started with the general proposition that expected yield is the primary determinant of the demand for financial assets. However, we noted that since a financial instrument is a claim to payments to be made in the future, and since the future is unknown, the asset holder cannot be perfectly certain about the yield on financial assets. He must form an opinion about the range of possible outcomes and, in a general way, the likelihood of the alternative possibilities. In other words, he must form an opinion about the degree of risk attached to each security. For theoretical analysis we formalized this judgment into probability distributions of alternative yields on securities, with credit risk represented by the standard deviation of the distribution. The demand for any financial asset, then, depends not only on the expected yield but also on the degree of credit risk. All financial instruments are substitutes for each other as forms in which wealth may be accumulated. However, securities with different degrees of credit risk attached are not perfect substitutes. The greater the difference in credit risk, the more imperfect the substitute relationship.

We assume that most asset holders are risk avoiders, that is, other things being equal, they prefer a less risky security. If a risk avoider is to purchase a riskier security, he will require a higher expected yield than that obtained on a less risky security. If most asset holders are of this frame of mind, the structure of yields in financial markets will reflect it. In general, yields on riskier securities will be higher than yields on less risky securities—and this is what we observe, as noted above. Credit risk is a major factor affecting relative yields on financial instruments.

THE DETERMINATION OF CREDIT RISK

Our exposition of the concept of credit risk and its role in the demand for financial assets has been abstract and theoretical. While such formal constructs are indispensable for theoretical analysis, we cannot realistically assume that each individual asset holder constructs a probability distribution of possible yields for each asset that he might consider taking into his portfolio and calculates both the expected yield and the standard deviation. And yet each rational asset holder must form some impression not only of the expected yield but also of the degree of credit risk.

In truth, little is known about how this is done. Sometimes people rely on hunches or moon phases or "inside information" or just some feeling about each asset. For concerned wealth owners, however, there are a group of professional investment counselors whose advice is frequently sought and presumably used. These counselors employ any of a variety of techniques of security analysis and frequently provide ratings of securities.

Past performance generally weighs heavily in such analysis, although the past is frequently a very poor guide to future prospects and history must be tempered with a careful assessment of the implications of current and pending developments. In the market, particularly the market for bonds, certain more or less standard rules of thumb have emerged, and these are reflected in relatively standard differentials between yields on bonds of different types of borrowers.

In Figure 5.4 we have plotted the average yields on long-term bonds of several classes of borrowers over a number of years. Note that the chart must be looked at from at least two different points of view. For our analysis let us examine the yields for long-term Treasury bonds, corporate Aaa, and corporate Baa bonds first. Among these three, the yields on U.S. Treasury bonds are lower than those on the other two classes of borrowers. They are widely regarded as riskless bonds. Yields on bonds of the other classifications of corporate borrowers range upward by risk. Of course, within each category there will be a wider range of yields, even among borrowers with similar credit ratings.

Let us now examine briefly the bottom three curves. Here we see that state government bonds on the average had lower yields than municipal bonds rated Aaa. Moreover, municipals and state bonds both had lower yields than the long-term U.S. Treasury bonds. Does this mean that municipal and state governments are more credit worthy than the federal government? No, the primary differential is one of tax treatment. Interest on both state and municipal bonds is exempt from taxation by the federal government and frequently is not taxed by the issuing area. While the federal government bonds are riskless, interest received is subject to federal income taxa-

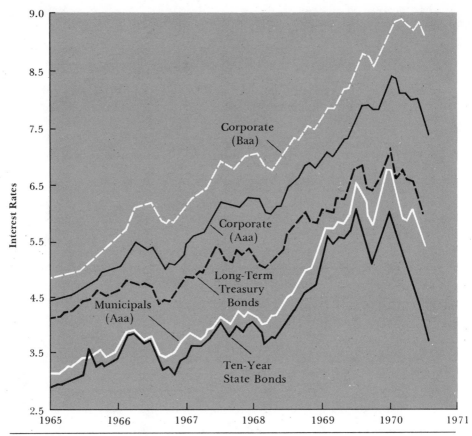

Figure 5.4 **Comparison of Yields on Different Long-Term Bonds, 1965–1970**
SOURCE: Moody's Investors Service, *Moody's Municipal and Government Manual,
1971* (New York, 1971), pp. a16–a22; Moody's Investors Service, *Moody's Industrial
Manual, 1971* (New York, 1971), pp. a18–a19.

tion. Here we see that state bonds compare in tax status with municipal
bonds but usually come with slightly lower yields. This differential reflects
the view that the larger authority has the greater taxing authority and hence
an enhanced ability to repay its indebtedness. The differential between these
bonds and the Treasury bonds is a reflection of risk plus tax status.

LIQUIDITY AND THE CHOICE AMONG FINANCIAL INSTRUMENTS

Our analysis of credit risk has taken us a long way in explaining how
there can be different expected yields on different instruments in the market
at the same time. However, differences in credit risk cannot fully explain
the differences in yields that can be observed. There are other factors that

must be taken into account, one of which is the *relative liquidity* of different instruments.

THE YIELD CURVE FOR GOVERNMENT BONDS

As evidence for the proposition that credit risk alone is not sufficient to explain observable and persistent differences in expected yields on financial instruments we need only consider yields on different financial instruments issued by the same debtor and for which credit risk is not a significant consideration. The one debtor that meets this requirement is the U.S. government. Bonds issued by the U.S. government can be regarded as riskless securities in that there is almost no chance that the contractual payments will not be made. Not only are the bonds backed by the general taxing powers of the federal government, but also the contract calls for payment in legal tender and the federal government has the ultimate power to manufacture legal tender. If all else fails, the government can "print" the money to meet its legal obligations. Thus, if credit risk were the only consideration, yields on all federal government bonds should be approximately the same.

This is seldom the case. A fairly typical situation is depicted in Figure 5.5. On this chart we have plotted the yields on almost all U.S. government

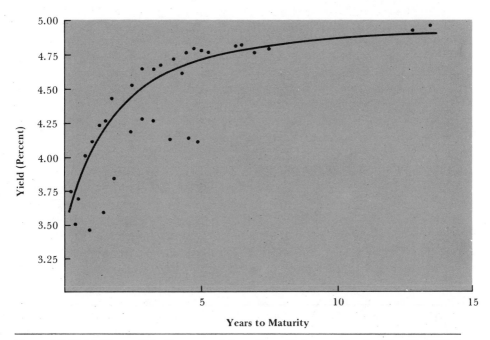

Figure 5.5 **Yield Curve: U.S. Government Securities—Notes and Bonds, May 25, 1967**
SOURCE: Adapted from *The New York Times*, May 26, 1967. © 1967 by The New York Times Company. Reprinted by permission.

bonds outstanding on May 25, 1967, with the bonds arranged in ascending order of term to maturity. The yields plotted on this chart were calculated on the basis of prices quoted in the market on that day and on the assumption that the promised future payments (interest and redemption value) would in fact be made. A line—commonly called a *yield* curve—has been drawn indicating the general relationship between yield and term to maturity on that date. Not all yields lie exactly on the yield curve, but the curve is broadly representative.

The striking thing about this yield curve is that yields on very short-term bonds are as much as 30 percent lower than yields on bonds maturing in five years. The curve initially rises very sharply to the right and then tapers off and is relatively flat for all bonds maturing after four years.

One common theory offered to explain the fact that yields on short-term bonds are typically lower than yields on long-term bonds is that asset holders demand a premium for tying up their money for a longer period. While it is probably true that a premium yield would be demanded if the asset holder actually had his funds tied up, that is, if he could not get his money out until the bond matured, this argument neglects an essential feature of these bonds: They are marketable. A secondary market exists so that the holder of these bonds can sell them at the established market price at any time he chooses. With this option his money is not "tied up." What, then, is the explanation for this rather typical shape to the yield curve?

The Demand for Liquidity and the Yield Curve. One hypothesis, broadly consistent with the facts, that has been advanced to explain this typical shape of the yield curve is that asset holders are willing to pay a premium for liquidity. In Chapter 3 we defined a liquid asset as one whose market price is relatively stable. Thus, money, a financial instrument whose market price is fixed in terms of the unit of account, is the most liquid of assets.

On the basis of this hypothesis, substantiated by Figure 5.5, we may assume that the short-term government securities have the greater degree of liquidity and that asset holders are willing to sacrifice yield to obtain this greater degree of liquidity. As liquid assets, the market prices of short-term government bonds must be relatively stable, although not necessarily fixed. If they are considered more liquid than long-term government bonds, their market price must be more stable than long-term government bond prices.

The Determinants of Liquidity. Three general factors tend to produce variations in the market price of financial instruments: the size of the expected future payments, the risk associated with those payments, and the expected yield on alternative assets. A change in any one can be expected to produce a change in market price.

Clearly, a variable income security could not be a liquid asset. If the size of future payments is subject to change, then the market price of the instrument can be expected to change also, and perhaps over a very wide range. Thus, common stock in corporations cannot qualify as a liquid asset.

Similarly, a fixed income security, such as a corporate bond, subject to substantial credit risk cannot be a liquid asset. If there is substantial risk of default on the promised payments, substantial price changes cannot be ruled out. While they are more liquid than explicitly variable income securities, such bonds could still not be considered highly liquid.

These two points help us narrow the range of instruments that can be considered liquid. To be highly liquid, a financial instrument must be a low-risk claim to fixed future payments. A third factor that might produce fluctuations in the market price of even riskless claims to fixed future payments is a change in the general level of yields on financial instruments, or, in other words, in the general level of interest rates. *The assertion that short-term government bonds (riskless, fixed income securities) are among the most liquid of assets is an assertion that their prices are not significantly affected as their yields rise or fall in sympathy with the general level of interest rates.* This is a property of short-term bonds not possessed by long-term bonds.

Price Stability and Term to Maturity. We leave the basic mathematical exposition of the relationship between yield and maturity and market price to the appendix to this chapter but for clarification include a simple example here. Last year we bought two government bonds, both with coupon rates of 5 percent at par $1000. This year the general level or structure of interest rates has risen, and the market rate of interest on similar credit riskless securities is 6 percent. If we were to sell our bonds today, we would receive less than $1000. However, the two bonds we own have different maturities; one matures in 1 year, the other in 20 years. If we sold the bond maturing next year, we could probably obtain at least $980 for it. The new owner would receive the $50 in interest plus $1000 in 1 year when the bond matured, for a capital gain of $20. (This is about a 2 percent return from capital gains on a $980 investment and more than 5 percent for the year in interest payments of $50 on an investment of $980.)

If we sold the bond with 20 years to maturity at the new level of interest rates, we could not expect to receive more than $880. Here the interest payments figure more heavily in the calculation of market price, since the expectation of gain at maturity is far in the future.

As the holder of both bonds, we know that the market price of the short-term security will fluctuate over a narrower range than that of the long-term security. If we wished to sell either security before maturity, the risk of loss from changing interest rates would be less on the short-term security; hence, we might be willing to pay a premium for the liquidity of this instrument.

We have plotted the actual yields and market prices for two Treasury bonds during the period 1966–1970. Figure 5.6(A) shows a security that matured on August 15, 1972. At the beginning of the period it had $6\frac{1}{2}$ years until maturity. By the end of the period it was nearly a short-term instru-

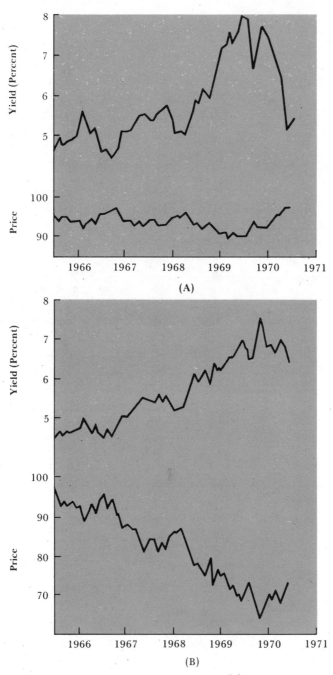

(A)

(B)

ment. By contrast, the bond in Figure 5.6(B) was a long-term security throughout the period. Maturing in August 1992 and callable in 1987, it had a term to maturity of almost 20 years at the end of the period.

To illustrate this point, refer again to Figures 5.6(A) and 5.6(B). Assume that the holder of the long-term bond purchased it at the end of March 1967 for a market price of $941. If held to maturity, the bond would have yielded him 4.6 percent per year. However, suppose the pressure of unanticipated expenditures forced him to sell it in March 1968. He in fact held the bond for 1 year, received $42.50 in interest, and then sold it for $822, or $119 less than he paid for it. Instead of the expected yield of 4.6 percent per year, his annual yield was negative, —8 percent.

On the contrary, if he had bought the short-term bond in March 1967 he would have paid $970 and expected a yield of 4.4 percent per year. Again he had to sell it a year later, and he received only $932. But he also received interest payments of $40 and came out even, losing nothing and making nothing.

Conversely, buying the short-term bond at the end of 1969 and selling it a year later would bring a gain of $75 for each $1000 bond sold, or a return of 8.4 percent in capital gains alone. The longer-term bond, bought and sold during the same period (1969–1970), would bring a gain of $70 but a return of 11 percent in capital gains on a $640 investment.

In this sense, then, the demand for liquid assets is a reaction to a type of risk, that of having to make unexpected future payments. If we may be allowed a play on words, the demand for liquid assets exists because as time passes every asset holder must expect to have unexpected expenditures. As we will see, this is of vital concern to certain types of financial institutions, such as banks.

The contrast between the behavior of yields and prices on the two bonds is striking. First, the yield on the short-term bond actually moved over a much wider range than did the yield on the long-term bond. However, the market price of the short-term bond showed much greater stability, varying over a range of $900–$970, than did the price of the long-term bond, which varied from $960 to $660.

Since we have defined liquidity in terms of stability of market price, it is clear that we must consider the short-term bond of Figure 5.6(A) a much more liquid security than the long-term bond of Figure 5.6(B). Why

Figure 5.6 (A) **Prices and Yields on a Short-Term 4 Percent U.S. Government Bond Maturing August 15, 1972**

Figure 5.6 (B) **Prices and Yields on a Long-Term 4.25 Percent U.S. Government Bond Maturing August 15, 1992 (Callable in 1987)**

SOURCE: Adapted from *The New York Times*, various issues. © 1966, 1967, 1968, 1969, 1970 by The New York Times Company. Reprinted by permission.

should this be a significant consideration in the minds of asset holders? In particular, why should the typical asset holder be willing to pay a premium price (that is, accept a lower yield) for the stability of the market price of the short-term bond?

THE DEMAND FOR LIQUIDITY

The particular motives of individual asset holders will vary, of course, depending on individual situations. However, two major types of demand for liquid assets can be identified, one related to specific expenditure plans in the near future and the other related to uncertainty.

Specific Expenditure Plans. Part of the demand for liquidity is to create a bridge between the receipt of income and planned expenditures in the near future. An individual householder might have a checking account with a commercial bank into which he deposits his monthly paycheck in anticipation of paying assorted bills during the forthcoming month. Similarly, corporations will accumulate liquid assets of various types in anticipation of future payrolls and other current expenditures.

The significant thing about this type of demand for liquid assets is that it represents a matching of assets and liabilities in terms of period to maturity. It follows that an asset holder who has only very definite long-term liabilities may well have little demand for liquid assets. Indeed, he might prefer long-term, relatively illiquid assets to short-term, relatively liquid assets.

Uncertainty. The second major element in the general demand for liquid assets rests in our assumption that most asset holders are risk avoiders and in the fact that the future is replete with uncertainty. An asset holder cannot always anticipate when he will sell his assets. As time passes he may encounter unexpected expenses, calls for payment of debts, interruptions to his employment and income, perhaps unusual opportunities to purchase major real or financial assets, or simply a change in his desires to purchase goods and services now as opposed to the future. Each of these contingencies involves unanticipated payments, calling for a sale of assets. If forced to sell when asset prices are low, he will incur substantial losses. However, if he holds short-term liquid assets he can make the unanticipated payments without incurring these losses.

The Demand for Money and Other Liquid Assets. In the last section of Chapter 2 we raised the question of what determines the quantity of money demanded at any point in time. The answer we gave was that since money is essentially a medium of exchange the quantity of money demanded will depend in some way on the value of payments to be made. As we shall see in Chapter 18, the relationship between the flow of transactions and the demand for money is not that simple; nonetheless, in a monetary economy the workings of the exchange mechanism will create a *transactions demand for money.*

We have shown, however, that while money is the most liquid of assets, it is not the only highly liquid asset. There are other financial instruments that can be held as close (if imperfect) substitutes for money. Short-term federal government bonds and Treasury bills are in this category. Savings bonds issued by the federal government that are not marketable or negotiable are liquid. While they are nominally long-term bonds, the government has agreed to repurchase them at a fixed price at any time the holder requests. In effect they are demand notes and highly liquid. In our survey of the money market we also noted the existence of many private short-term issues. From the point of view of banks, federal funds and call loans to government securities dealers are highly liquid assets. Similarly, certificates of deposit, bankers' acceptances, and commercial paper can be considered highly liquid to the asset holders. It should also be noted that a line of credit with a bank under which a corporation is entitled to loans up to a certain nego-tiated maximum over a given period is also a liquid asset of considerable importance. As we discuss the various types of financial intermediaries in subsequent chapters, we will discover that they also issue highly liquid finan-cial instruments that can be held as substitutes for money. Indeed, we have already referred to such financial instruments as near moneys.

In satisfying their demands for liquidity, then, asset holders can choose from a wide range of instruments, including money. The choice actually made should depend, among other things, on relative yields on the various liquid assets. Thus, the demand for money as an asset should be sensitive to interest rates on other short-term financial instruments. The higher the level of short-term interest rates, the smaller the quantity of money demanded as an asset.

SPECULATION AND THE CHOICE
AMONG FINANCIAL INSTRUMENTS

We now have three characteristics of financial instruments that enter into the demand for those instruments: expected yield, credit risk, and liquidity. In general, we have concluded that, other things being equal, asset holders desire to avoid risk and prefer liquidity. As a result, expected yields on risky assets should normally be higher than expected yields on riskless assets, and expected yields on liquid assets should be lower than expected yields on illiquid assets.

A careful examination of Figures 5.6(A) and 5.6(B) should raise at least two sets of significant questions in your mind.

First, we have asserted that most asset holders are willing to sacrifice yield for liquidity, a set of preferences that implies that short-term bond yields should be lower than long-term bond yields. However, it is evident that the yield on the short-term bond in Figure 5.6(A) was actually higher than the yield on the long-term bond on at least three occasions, that is, in the late summer and fall of 1966, from mid-1967 to mid-1968, and from

March 1969 to September 1970. Is this simply a peculiar aberration of the two bonds in question? Or is it a common phenomenon in financial markets? If it is common, how can we reconcile it with our earlier assertions about the general superiority of liquid financial instruments?

Second, in discussing the implications of changes in the market price of long-term bonds we laid great stress on the risk this implied for the asset holder. However, as we have seen, it also creates opportunities. A sharp operator in the market could anticipate movements of bond prices and profit · by purchasing when bond prices are low and selling when they are high. The capital gain he would make is in addition to the interest payments he would receive during the period he held the bond. By switching his funds in and out of long-term bonds at the appropriate times, he could avoid incurring capital losses during periods of declining market prices and rising interest rates.

The issues raised by these two sets of questions are interrelated. Let us briefly consider the empirical question first: Are long-term bond yields always higher than short-term bond yields?

OTHER YIELD CURVES

The answer is no. As evidence we have plotted yield curves for three other dates. In Figure 5.7(A) we have replotted the yield curve for May 25, 1967, shown in Figure 5.5. This curve is often referred to as "normal" in that under normal conditions we would expect short-term rates to be lower than long-term rates. In the lower section we have plotted the yields of government bonds on July 30, 1969. This yield curve is the inverse of the "normal" curve, showing a consistent downward slope. Yield curves of this shape occur in periods of relatively high interest rates.

In Figure 5.7(B) we have plotted yields on government bonds for August 25, 1966 in the upper section and for August 30, 1971 in the lower section. Both of these yield curves show a pronounced hump. The very short-term yields are low, but in the upper section the yields on bonds maturing in two to three years are higher than on the long-term bonds. In the lower section the hump is in the bonds with five to seven years to maturity.

The shape of the yield curve thus changes from time to time. Indeed, there is a fairly regular cyclical pattern to these changes. When the general level of interest rates is relatively low, the yield curve tends to have the shape of that in the upper section of Figure 5.7(A). As interest rates rise, short-term rates tend to rise more rapidly than long-term rates. From Figure 5.6(A) we saw that short-term yields move over a wider range than long-term yields. As a result, the yield curve becomes flatter. In periods of relatively high interest rates, the yield curve may become "humped," as in Figure 5.7(B) or, at the extreme, downward sloping throughout, as in Figure 5.7(A).

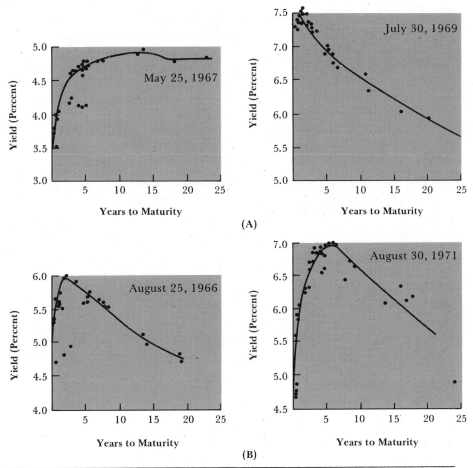

Figure 5.7 (A) Two Yield Curves: U.S. Government Securities
Figure 5.7 (B) Two "Humped" Yield Curves: U.S. Government Securities
SOURCE: Adapted from *The New York Times*, (A) May 26, 1967, and July 31, 1969; (B) August 26, 1966, and August 31, 1971. © 1966, 1967, 1969, 1971 by The New York Times Company. Reprinted by permission.

SPECULATION IN OTHER FINANCIAL MARKETS

Our discussion of speculation as a factor in the choice among financial assets has focused on the government bond market. This is far too narrow a perspective. Speculative transactions are not confined to portfolio adjustments between long-term and short-term government bonds in anticipation of changes in the general level of interest rates. Clearly, whatever forces affect the market for government bonds must also affect the market for private bonds. This is evident from Figure 5.4. In the market for corporate stock, speculation as we have defined it (i.e., purchases in anticipation of short-term capital gains, or sales to avoid short-term capital losses) takes on a different character and assumes much greater importance. In contrast to speculation on relatively regular and somewhat constrained movements in the general level of bond yields, speculation in the stock market involves anticipations of possibly spectacular changes in corporate fortunes. There are almost no limits to the possible changes in the market value of a share of stock, at least in the upward direction.

Speculation in Stock Markets. You will remember from our discussion in Chapter 3 that a share of common stock is a claim to a *pro rata* share of the profits of the corporation (or at least to the portion of the profits paid out as dividends). Just as the profits of the corporation can vary over a wide range, with abrupt changes in both magnitude and direction, so too can the market price of a share of stock of the corporation experience very sharp and very large changes. This is clearly fertile ground for the speculator acting on hunch, rumor, or inside information.

These speculative activities are seen in their most dramatic form in the market for shares of stock in small companies engaged in exploration and development of oil and mining properties. The discovery of a rich body of ore or of a potential oil well will mean large long-run profit prospects for the company and hence a rise in the market value of its outstanding shares of stock. The mere hint of such a discovery will attract speculative buying, which will send the share prices shooting upward. A demonstration that the hints are false will "prick the bubble," producing an equally precipitous decline.

INFLATION AND THE EXPECTED YIELD ON FINANCIAL INSTRUMENTS

Inflation is a rise in the general level of prices of consumable goods and services, where prices are measured in terms of the unit of account. Since the price of money is fixed in terms of the unit of account, inflation can also be defined as a *decline in the purchasing power of money*. A unit of money will buy a smaller quantity of goods and services. Indeed, inflation involves a decline in the real value of anything whose nominal value (in terms of the unit of account) is fixed.

SPECULATIVE DEMANDS FOR BONDS

We cannot develop a complete analysis of changes in the shape of the yield curve until we have considered the supply side of financial markets. However, a major part of the explanation for these gyrations rests in what we might call the speculative demand for financial assets.

Speculation and the Shape of the Yield Curve. Speculators can be expected to shift between long-term bonds and either short-term bonds or money in anticipation of changes in the market prices of long-term bonds.

They seek to capture anticipated capital gains by purchasing long-term bonds (and selling short-term bonds, including money) when they expect interest rates to fall (and hence long-term bond prices to rise significantly). Similarly, they seek to avoid anticipated capital losses by selling long-term bonds (and purchasing short-term bonds) when they expect interest rates to rise (and hence long-term bond prices to fall).

Clearly, such activities will create pressures in financial markets tending to produce the characteristic changes in the shape of the yield curve. Thus, when interest rates are low and expected to rise, speculators will tend to sell long-term bonds and purchase short-term bonds or hold money. Their activities should therefore tend to further depress long-term bond prices and raise short-term bond prices, or, what is the same thing, raise long-term bond yields relative to short-term bond yields. The activities of the speculator, therefore, will tend to accentuate the "normal" slope of the yield curve under these circumstances.

By contrast, when interest rates are high and are expected to fall, speculators will tend to purchase long-term bonds and sell short-term bonds or reduce their holdings of money (or perhaps borrow on short-term notes). Their activities in the market therefore should tend to support the price of long-term bonds and depress the price of short-term bonds, or, what is the same thing, raise short-term bond yields relative to long-term bond yields. Depending on the intensity of the speculative pressures, this could produce the characteristic flattening of the yield curve or the occasional reversing of the slope.

Successful speculators must be well informed or lucky. They must also be prepared to take risks. Moreover, it should be noted that speculation tends to add supply and demand pressures in the market that push prices in the direction the speculators anticipated. Thus, speculation tends to eliminate the basis for speculation and hence accelerate the transition to the new level and structure of interest rates. Therefore, the successful speculator must act early—he must outguess the market and respond quickly to signs of change.

Expected Yield for Short Holding Periods. Thus, a reasonably complete analysis of financial markets must take speculation into account. It should be apparent, however, that to do so it is not necessary to make a major departure from our analysis. What is involved is simply an application of the concept of expected yield. When we first developed this concept we assumed that the security would be held to maturity. We defined expected yield as the interest rate implicit in the relationship between the present market price of the security and all expected future payments to the holder of that security. In the interest of precision, perhaps we should call that concept *expected yield to maturity*. The present discussion of speculative capital gains and losses involves explicit recognition of the fact that the expected yield for shorter "holding periods" may be quite different. Thus, an asset holder seeking to maximize the return on his portfolio of assets may find it appropriate not to hold all assets until maturity. Periodic rearrangements of the balance of assets in his portfolio—involving active trading in anticipation of changes in market prices (it does little good to act after the fact)—may be highly profitable.

INFLATION AND THE "REAL" YIELD ON BONDS

It should be evident from this statement that money is not the only financial instrument whose real value is affected by inflation. While there are few other financial instruments whose market prices are fixed, it must be remembered that bonds are claims to future payments that are fixed in terms of the unit of account. In a period of inflation the real value of these payments will steadily decline. Thus, the bondholder suffers continual erosion of his wealth.

Recognition of the possibility of inflation does not necessarily call for a radical revision of our analytical framework. It is significant because it is presumably the real rate of return on assets that is of concern to asset holders in both their saving decisions and their portfolio balance decisions. But this means that the expected rate of inflation must be allowed for in calculating the expected yields on financial assets and, by implication, that alternative possible rates of inflation must enter into the evaluation of the risks involved in holding bonds or money. What we have done, then, in introducing the possibility of inflation is to add another set of general considerations that must enter into the rational asset holder's calculations of expected yields and risks. Thus, to take a simple example, if an asset holder expects inflation at an annual rate of 1 percent per annum, then he must regard a bond with a nominal yield of 5 percent as having an expected real yield of 4 percent per annum. If he also considers, say, a 10 percent rate of inflation as a possibility, then he must allow for this in evaluating the risks involved in holding bonds or money. Indeed, given the possibility of inflation, even government bonds and money cease to be riskless assets. In making their portfolios, asset holders should be responsive to both the expected rate of inflation and the risk of inflation.

INFLATION AND THE "REAL" YIELD ON CORPORATE STOCK

Corporate stock differs in one vital respect from bonds, and this is significant in assessing the impact of inflation. Common stock is not a claim to a stream of fixed future payments but rather to a share of profits that can be expected to rise in sympathy with any general rise in the price level. That is not to say that profits are tied directly to the price level. Many diverse factors affect profits for individual firms and in the aggregate. As a result, the profits of any individual company can move quite independently of the price level, depending on circumstances peculiar to that company and its industry, and profit levels in all or most industries can show wide short-term variation that has little or no apparent connection with movements in the general price level. These are all risks that the stockholder assumes. Nonetheless, the important point is that as the general price level is rising, the prices of things that business firms sell are rising as well as the prices of things that they buy. For a broad cross-section of firms (in the long run), this should mean that their profits have a built-in mechanism for adjustment to changes in the price level.

There are many qualifications to this conclusion, and many interesting and unsettled empirical questions can be raised about the relationship between prices, costs, and profits. However, the important point for our analysis is that, unlike the bondholder who has a claim on fixed payments of declining real value, the stockholder has a claim on a variable payment, the real value of which is not necessarily eroded (and indeed may be enhanced) through inflation.

The Redistributive Effects of Inflation: Adjustment of Prices and Yields. Does this analysis mean that the bondholder invariably loses real wealth through inflation while the stockholder invariably gains? In order to answer this question, let us briefly consider the adjustments that might occur in the face of a newly expected inflation.

Given the preexisting market prices of stocks and bonds, the initial effect of a new but widely held belief in the likelihood of inflation should be an attempt of holders of bonds (whose expected real yield is now lower in proportion to the expected annual rate of inflation) and money (whose expected real yield is now negative in proportion to the expected annual rate of inflation) to attempt to shift from these assets to common stocks. This shift in demand patterns should produce downward pressure on the price of bonds and upward pressure on the price of stocks. The existing holders of bonds will suffer capital losses, and the existing holders of common stock will experience capital gains. Thus, because the expected rate of inflation had not entered into the previous valuation of these securities, that expectation will now produce a redistribution of wealth from bondholders to stockholders.

It should be noted, however, that the expectation of inflation, by lowering bond prices, will simultaneously increase bond yields. Therefore, someone who purchases a bond at its new market price will not necessarily lose as a result of inflation. The higher yield implied by the lower market price will tend to compensate him for the continual erosion of purchasing power as a result of inflation. Indeed, if inflation actually proceeded at the expected rate, and if expected yield were the only factor affecting demands for assets (i.e., ignoring credit risk and liquidity), the yield on the bond might adjust upward so as to fully compensate the holder for the rate of inflation. Thus, if the preexisting equilibrium yield on bonds was 5 percent per annum, the expectation of inflation at an annual rate of 1 percent per annum might result in a decline in bond prices until the new nominal yield was 6 percent per annum. This would just compensate for the expected (and actual) 1 percent rate of inflation and would reestablish the preexisting real yield on bonds of 5 percent per annum. In this sense the purchaser of bonds at the market price will not suffer from inflation. (By the same token, the holder of bonds cannot improve his situation by selling those bonds in the market— he has already incurred his capital loss, and now the bonds he is holding are as good an investment as ever at their new, lower market price.)

This analysis of the impact of inflation on financial markets is far too simplistic to be useful beyond our very limited purposes. It implicitly assumes that the returns to the holder of common stock are adjusted upward in proportion to the expected rate of inflation so that the inflation establishes the preexisting real rate of return. It is far from obvious that this exact readjustment will occur. Moreover, the analysis ignores the fact that risk is also a factor in portfolio selection. Inflation, like other factors affecting the yield on securities, is a factor that cannot be foreseen with certainty. Thus, the risk of inflation may well affect choices between money, bonds, and stock. In particular, an increase in the risk of inflation, quite independently of an increase in the expected rate of inflation, should reduce demands for bonds and money and increase demands for common stocks. This should have repercussions on the market prices of these instruments in addition to any effects produced by a change in the expected rate of inflation.

CONCLUSION: INFLATION AND THE CHOICE AMONG FINANCIAL INSTRUMENTS

Inflation reduces the real value of fixed payments. It thus reduces the real value of money and bonds. The expectation of inflation therefore should induce a shift in demand from money and bonds to common stocks, producing a decline in the price of bonds and an increase in the price of stock (the price of money is fixed).

Thus, inflation that has not been accurately anticipated will involve a redistribution of wealth among money holders, bondholders, and stockholders. As a result, the possibility of inflation is a risk that must be taken into account in portfolio choices. Both the expected rate of inflation and the risk of inflation should affect the demands for financial instruments.

TAXATION AND THE EXPECTED YIELD ON FINANCIAL INSTRUMENTS

There is one other important factor affecting the choice among financial instruments that requires comment. That is the effect of a taxation system that involves differential tax rates on income obtained in different forms. Some of the differential effects of the tax system, such as the depletion allowances for mining and petroleum firms, affect the relative earning capacity of firms in different industries. They also affect the choice among financial instruments indirectly by affecting the relative profit rates in different industries and hence the expected yields on their securities (particularly their common stocks). Other provisions of the tax system have a direct impact on the choice among financial instruments.

For example, the reduced rate of taxation of capital gains makes a dollar of income in the form of capital gains worth substantially more to an asset holder than a dollar of income in the form of interest and dividend payments. Securities offering capital gains become that much more attractive. Of course, speculation on capital gains carries with it the risk of capital loss. However, many studies have shown that the possibility of capital gains is a primary consideration in portfolio choices, particularly those of wealthy individuals. For people with high incomes the marginal income tax rate is significantly higher, making capital gains income that much more attractive since it is taxed at a maximum rate of 25 percent on the first $50,000 of long-term capital gains.

Another aspect of the effect of the tax laws on portfolio choices is the exemption from all federal income taxes of interest income paid on municipal securities. *Municipal* is a generic term referring to bonds issued by state and local governments. The degree to which tax-free interest benefits individual asset holders depends on their own marginal income tax bracket. The higher the marginal tax bracket, the greater the advantage to the asset holder of municipal securities. Attempts to purchase tax-free interest bonds should drive the prices of these securities higher than the prices on securities of similar maturity, liquidity, and credit risk whose interest is taxable. We saw in Figure 5.4 that the yields on local and state government bonds were lower than on issues of the federal government. This differential reflects in part the premium that asset holders are willing to pay to obtain tax-exempt interest income.

As in the case of anticipated inflation, the attempts of asset holders to adjust their portfolios to take advantage of differential tax rates should have the effect of adjusting the relative prices of securities to compensate for the tax differential. Thus, attempts to purchase securities that seem to promise capital gains or tax-exempt interest income should tend to drive up the price of these securities and depress the prices of securities with more heavily taxed interest or dividend income. This adjustment in prices could eventually eliminate any incentive for further adjustments in portfolios.

SELECTION OF A PORTFOLIO

This chapter has introduced a large number of concepts. The problem now is to draw them together to see what they tell us about the nature of demands for financial instruments.

THE CONCEPT OF A PORTFOLIO

A basic concept, introduced early in the analysis, is that of a portfolio of assets. An asset holder's portfolio is simply the collection of assets that he chooses to hold.

We have already drawn certain strong conclusions about normal (i.e., risk-averse) asset holder's preferences. We cast our analysis in terms of such abstract concepts as expected yield, credit risk, and liquidity, which we considered attributes of individual financial instruments. To complete our analysis we must consider the problem of choice among assets in the context of the selection of a complete portfolio. To that end, we must develop concepts of expected yield, risk, and liquidity as attributes of portfolios.

THE EXPECTED YIELD OF A PORTFOLIO

Since he is only one among a great many participants in the market, each asset holder must take the expected yields on individual financial instruments as given. He cannot control them. He can only choose to hold or not hold the instrument. However, within limits set by the expected yields on instruments available in the market, each asset holder can control the expected yield on his portfolio through careful selection of the instruments to be included in the portfolio.

Expected Yield on a Portfolio. The expected yield on a portfolio is simply the weighted average of the expected yields on the individual assets included in the portfolio—with the expected yield of each asset weighted by the portion of the portfolio represented by that instrument.[2] Any asset holder can increase the expected yield on his portfolio by increasing the portion of his portfolio invested in relatively high-yielding assets, and he can reduce the yield on his portfolio by increasing the portion invested in relatively low-yielding assets.

Yield Preference. We have assumed that each asset holder has a strong preference for yield. The reason for this lies in our discussion of the saving decision (Chapter 4). Each household is presumably striving to maximize utility from its lifetime consumption potential. To accumulate wealth for the support of future consumption it must forgo current consumption. The higher the expected yield on a portfolio, the greater the future consumption that any given current wealth accumulation can be expected to support, that is, the greater the lifetime consumption, and hence total utility, available to the household. A utility-maximizing household must therefore be attracted by higher yields. It must have a preference for yield. Faced with a choice between two financial instruments, other things being equal, it would choose the one with the highest yield.

What Does the Asset Holder Maximize? But what is the import of the "other things being equal" assumption? What other things? Can we not assume that each asset holder simply maximizes expected yield without any qualifications?

We know that the answer to this last question is no. If expected yield were the only consideration in the portfolio balance decision, asset holders would always choose instruments with high yields over those with low yields. Faced with assets with different expected yields, each asset holder would include only one asset in his portfolio—the one that appeared to promise the highest expected yield. It does not take a sophisticated statistical survey to show that few asset holders have portfolios consisting of only one asset.

There is another interesting implication of asset holders maximizing expected yield. If all asset holders had roughly the same expectations with respect to each asset, equilibrium in the market would require identical expected yields on all assets. As asset holders attempt to purchase instruments promising high expected yields, they create excess demand in the market, which tends to drive up the price of those instruments. At the same time, they will be selling instruments that promise low expected yields, tending to drive down the price of those instruments. Remember, the market price and the expected yield on any instrument vary inversely. When the price of high-yielding instruments increases, the yield correspondingly drops, and vice versa for low-yielding instruments. The end result should be a rough equalization of expected yields on all securities. At that time, if yield were the only consideration asset holders would be indifferent between financial instruments. The instruments would be perfect substitutes for each other as forms in which wealth can be accumulated.

In general, we cannot observe either an equalization of expected yields or single-asset portfolios. Asset holders must react to other attributes of financial instruments besides expected yield. One of these attributes is credit risk. The asset holder must be concerned not only with the expected yield on his portfolio but also with the risk on his portfolio.

RISK

We developed the concept of credit risk as an attribute of individual financial instruments. Like expected yield, the riskiness of an instrument is something over which an asset holder has no control. However, within limits, he can control the degree of risk on his portfolio through careful selection of the assets to be included in it. What is the relationship between the degree of credit risk on individual assets and the degree of risk on the portfolio?

The Riskiness of a Portfolio. By the risk on a portfolio we mean the standard deviation of the expected yield on the portfolio. The concept is parallel to that developed for the credit risk on individual assets, and indeed the risk on the portfolio depends on the risk on the individual assets included in that portfolio. However, unlike the relationship between the expected yields on the portfolio and the assets that comprise it, in all but the simplest case the risk on a portfolio is not a simple weighted average of the risks on the individual assets. The relationship is much more complex. Nonetheless, we can assume that in most cases an asset holder will increase the riskiness of his portfolio if he increases the proportion of relatively risky securities contained in that portfolio.[3]

99

INTERDEPENDENCE OF RISK AND EXPECTED YIELD

An asset holder can vary the degree of risk and the expected yield through a careful selection of the assets to be included in his portfolio. However, he cannot choose the degree of risk and the expected yield independently of each other. Since risk and expected yield are both attributes of individual financial instruments, when the asset holder selects a particular group of assets to be included in his portfolio he not only obtains the expected yield provided by that combination of assets but simultaneously obtains the degree of risk provided by those assets. To obtain a different degree of risk on his portfolio he must select a different combination of assets, and that means he will obtain a different expected yield on his portfolio.

In general, higher degrees of risk are associated with higher expected yields. Thus, to obtain a higher expected yield on his portfolio the asset holder must include a higher portion of relatively risky assets, and that generally means a higher degree of risk in the portfolio as well.

Risk Aversion. We have assumed that asset holders in general are risk avoiders. Risk is something they prefer to avoid, and they have to be bribed to take on higher degrees of risk through the expectation of a higher yield. In general, a risk avoider will not select the portfolio of assets with the highest expected yield. That would provide too high a degree of risk. Similarly, in general a risk avoider will not select the portfolio with the lowest degree of risk. That would provide too low an expected yield. Because there is a subjective trade-off between risk and expected yield in his system of preferences, he will normally select a portfolio consisting of more than one asset, and one that is somewhere between the two extremes of maximizing expected yield and minimizing risk.

The Equilibrium Portfolio: Risk and Expected Yield. We have demonstrated the nature of the choice between risk and yield in a particularly simple case in Figure 5.8.

For the purposes of this diagram we have assumed that there are only two assets. One, a government bond, is regarded as perfectly safe (zero credit risk). The other, a corporate bond, has a higher yield, but it also has a relatively high degree of credit risk. If these are the only instruments available, what combination of the two will the asset holder choose?

In this figure, the expected yield on the portfolio (y_p) is measured along the vertical axis. It is the weighted average of the expected yields on the safe (y_s) and the risky (y_r) securities, with the weights being the proportions (a_s, a_r) in which the two assets are included in the portfolio. That is,

$$a_s + a_r = 1 \tag{5.1}$$

and

$$y_p = a_s y_s + a_r y_r \tag{5.2}$$

100

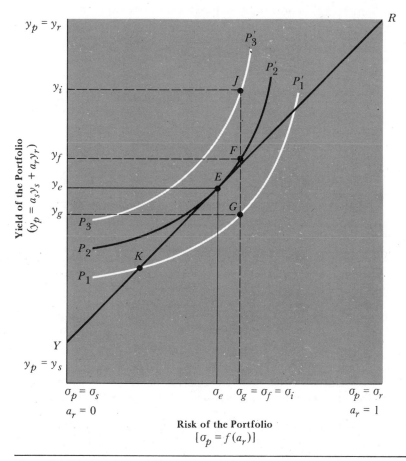

Figure 5.8 The Equilibrium Portfolio: Choice Between Risk and Yield

The risk on the portfolio (σ_p) is measured along the base axis. It depends on the credit risks on the individual securities in the portfolio and the proportions in which these two securities are included in the portfolio. In this particular case, the function linking the risks on the individual securities and the risk on the portfolio is simple. Since the credit risk on the government bond is zero $(\sigma_r = 0)$, given the risk on the corporate bond, the risk on the portfolio depends simply on the portion of the portfolio devoted to the relatively risky security. That is,

$$\sigma_p = a_r \, \sigma_r \qquad (5.3)$$

This is a very special case. In general, the relationship is not that simple.

The line YR describes the combinations of expected yield and risk available to the asset holder by varying the proportions in which he divides his portfolio between the government bond and the corporate bond. At point Y the entire portfolio is invested in the government bond. The risk is minimized ($\sigma_p = 0$), and the expected yield on the portfolio is minimized ($y_p = y_r$). As we move out along the line YR, the proportion of the relatively risky security in the portfolio increases, and as a result, so do the expected yield and the risk on the portfolio. In the extreme, at point R, the entire portfolio consists of the relatively risky and high-yielding corporate bond. At that point, both risk ($\sigma_p = \sigma_r$) and expected yield ($y_p = y_r$) are maximized.

Each point along the line YR, then, represents a different possible portfolio with different degrees of risk and different expected yields. Which of the alternatives available to him will the asset holder choose?

The general answer is that he will select the portfolio—the combination of risk and expected yield—that will provide him with the highest possible level of utility. We can identify that portfolio in a theoretical sense through an application of indifference curve analysis.[4]

The curves labeled PP′ in Figure 5.8 are indifference curves that describe the asset holders' preferences as between expected yield and risk. They incorporate our assumption of risk aversion. Any one curve, say P_2P_2', identifies alternative combinations of expected yield and risk that the asset holder finds equally acceptable. He is "indifferent" between portfolios lying along this curve. Thus, he would find nothing to choose between the two portfolios represented by points E and F. While portfolio F involves a higher degree of risk, the asset holder would feel that he was fully compensated for assuming that higher degree of risk by the higher expected yield also associated with portfolio F.

While the asset holder would thus be indifferent between portfolios E or F, he would prefer either of these to the portfolio represented by the point G. This portfolio has the same degree of risk as portfolio F, but it also has a lower expected yield. There is a whole set of portfolios that the asset holder would regard as equivalent to portfolio G, including portfolio H. They all lie along the indifference curve P_1P_1', which then describes portfolios that are inferior to those lying along P_2P_2'.

Similarly, the asset holder would prefer the portfolio represented by point J to either E or F. Portfolio J has the same risk as portfolio F but a higher expected yield. There is a whole set of portfolios that the asset holder would regard as equivalent to portfolio J, all lying along the higher indifference curve P_3P_3'.

If the asset holder is to maximize utility, he must select the portfolio available on the market (and hence lying along the line YR) that he prefers most. Thus, between portfolios E and H, both of which are available to him, he would always choose E. By an extension of the same logic, between portfolios E and K, both of which are available, he would always choose E. (Why?) By contrast, he would much prefer portfolio J to any of these, including E. However, portfolio J is not available in the market. That combination of risk and expected yield cannot be obtained, given the risk and expected yield on the two securities from which he must construct his portfolio.

Portfolio E, then, is the portfolio that would be selected. It is the *equilibrium portfolio*. It does not provide the maximum expected yield. Portfolio R would do that. It does not provide the minimum risk. Portfolio Y would do that. However, it is on the highest indifference curve between risk and expected yield that can be achieved by the asset holder, given the risk and expected yield on the financial instruments available in the market.

Conclusions: The Significance of Risk. The existence of risk and risk aversion means that financial instruments are not all perfect substitutes in the minds of asset holders. An increase in the yield on one security will lead to some substitution of the higher-yielding security for the lower-yielding security (it will induce asset holders to take on more risk), but it will not lead to total replacement of the low-yielding asset portfolios. Figure 5.9 duplicates the essential feature of Figure 5.8 but allows for an increase in the yield on the corporate bond with no change in the yield on the government bond or in the credit risk on the corporate bond. The portfolio opportunity line YR' thus becomes steeper. For any given degree of risk, the asset holder can now obtain a higher expected yield. The new equilibrium portfolio is now represented by point M on a higher indifference curve. The asset holder has assumed more risk and obtains a higher yield. As an exercise, the student should demonstrate what happens when:

1. The expected yield on the "safe" security is lowered.
2. The riskiness of the "risky" security increases.
3. The expected yields on both securities increase proportionately (remember: Risk might be an "inferior good").

If we know the size of the asset holder's portfolio at that point in time, we can derive his demand for each type of security. Given the riskiness of each security, the demand for the "risky" security will be an increasing function of the differential between the expected yield on the "risky" and the "safe" securities. The opposite is true of the "safe" security. At wider and wider differentials, the demand function probably becomes increasingly inelastic.

The market demand curve is the sum of individual asset holders' demand functions. The demand for risky securities, therefore, is presumably a function of the wealth of asset holders (and hence the size of portfolios) and the differential in yield between risky and safe securities.

LIQUIDITY

The third basic attribute of financial instruments for which a risk-avoiding asset holder is presumed to have a preference is liquidity. We pre-

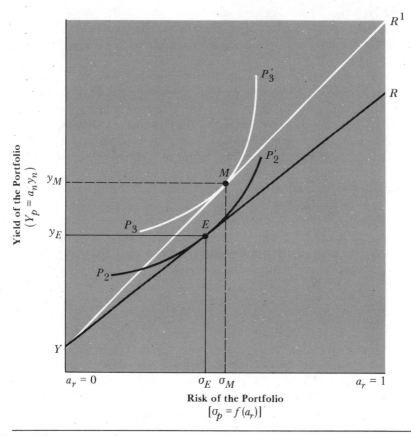

Figure 5.9 **The Equilibrium Portfolio: Choice Between Risk and Yield Under Conditions of Change in Yield**

sume that, other things being equal, an asset holder prefers more liquid assets to illiquid ones.

The Liquidity of a Portfolio. Like expected yield and credit risk, liquidity is a property of individual financial assets. It becomes a property of a portfolio through the inclusion of highly liquid assets in the portfolio. Therefore, by the liquidity of the portfolio we mean simply the portion of highly liquid assets in the portfolio, that is, the ratio of liquid assets (L) to total assets (A).

The decision on the degree of liquidity is inseparable from the decision on the expected yield and the risk on the portfolio. However, as we did in the case of risk, we can analyze the choice between liquidity and yield, holding other considerations constant. Such an analysis is presented in Figure 5.10.

The vertical axis on this chart measures the yield on the portfolio.

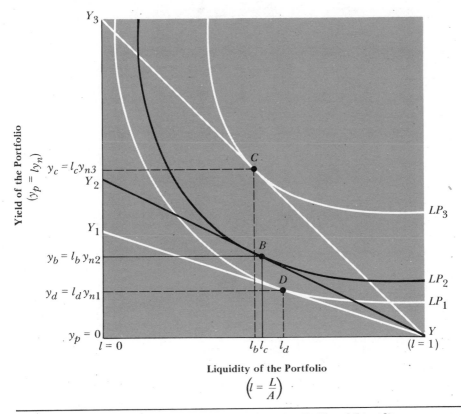

Figure 5.10 **The Equilibrium Portfolio: Choice Between Yield and Liquidity**

We assume that the portfolio consists only of a liquid asset (L) like money, which bears no interest, and an illiquid asset (N) like corporate stock, which has a positive expected yield (y_n). The expected yield on the portfolio depends simply on the portion of the portfolio devoted to the illiquid asset ($1 - 1$). That is,

$$y_r = (1 - 1) \, y_n$$

On the base axis we measure the liquidity of the portfolio, that is, the portion of the portfolio devoted to liquid assets (1). At point Y the entire portfolio is invested in liquid assets, and the expected yield on the portfolio is zero. At point Y_2 the entire portfolio is invested in illiquid assets, and the expected yield on the portfolio is y_{n2}, the expected yield on the illiquid asset. The line Y_2Y therefore traces the opportunities possible in the market. It shows the yield on alternative possible portfolios incorporating varying proportions of liquid and illiquid assets.

The lines labeled LP are indifference curves with respect to liquidity and expected yield. The determination of the equilibrium portfolio involves

105

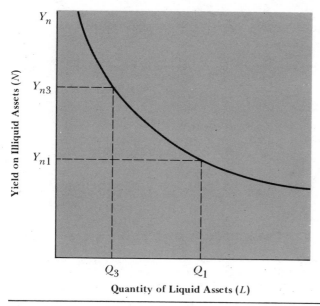

Figure 5.11 **Demand for Liquid Assets**

the same logic as that developed in the discussion of risk. The object is to achieve the highest possible indifference curve. If the expected yield on the illiquid asset is y_{n2}, then equilibrium will be achieved at point B on curve LP_2.

We can trace what happens when the expected yield on the illiquid asset increases or decreases. If the expected yield rises to y_{n3}, the new equilibrium portfolio will be at C, with a smaller portion devoted to liquid assets. Similarly, if the expected yield on the illiquid asset is reduced to y_{n1}, the new equilibruim will be at D, with a larger portion of the port-folio devoted to liquid assets. (As an exercise, the student should work out what would happen if the liquid asset had a positive expected yield.)

In other words, as the expected yield on illiquid assets changes, there is a general substitution between liquid and illiquid assets in asset holders' portfolios. Given the size of the total portfolio, then, we can trace the asset holder's demand curve for liquid assets. It would show an increase in the quantity demanded, from Q_3 to Q_1, where $Q_1 > Q_3$, and $Y_{n3} > Y_{n1}$, as the yield, Y_{n3}, on illiquid assets falls to Y_{n1}. Liquid and illiquid assets are imperfect substitutes for each other. (See Figure 5.11.)

OTHER DIMENSIONS OF PORTFOLIO SELECTIONS

This analysis of the selection of a portfolio has focused on two margins of choice, the expected yield-risk margin, and the expected yield-liquidity margin. Even if we limit ourselves to the three variables, expected yield, risk, and liquidity, we must remember that there is a third margin of choice, risk versus liquidity. We have not explored that margin because it does not make an important contribution to our analysis. However, the student should remember that the degree of riskiness chosen may well affect the position of the *LP* curves and hence may affect the choice of a degree of liquidity (the direction of the effect is not known).[5]

A second limitation of our analysis rests in the fact that we have dealt only with two-asset portfolios (including different assets when we discussed risk than when we discussed liquidity). This is necessary if we are to use geometrical constructions. The mathematics of multiple-asset portfolios becomes rather complex.

It should also be noted that we have implicitly assumed that the size of the portfolio does not affect preferences as between risk, liquidity, and yield. It is not obvious that this is a valid assumption; however, we do not know how the functions shift with increasing portfolio size.

In the same connection, we have assumed that the rate of return on assets does not depend on the size of the portfolio. For reasons that we will discuss in Chapter 8, this is not necessarily the case, particularly since there are "transactions costs" involved in purchases and sales of assets (and hence in all rearrangements of portfolios) that depend largely on the number rather than the value of transactions. To rearrange a large portfolio, where the value of each purchase or sale of a security is relatively large, will involve smaller transactions costs per dollar invested. For this reason, the return to the portfolio may be greater than for a small portfolio.

Finally, we have used the concept of expected yield in this discussion as yield to maturity, and we have ignored the effects of inflation. The earlier discussions of speculation and inflation should not be forgotten. There may be circumstances under which the yield for shorter holding periods is relevant, and all yields should be adjusted to a "real" basis (including the yield on money). Incorporating this in our analysis of the selection of a portfolio would make the whole matter impossibly complex.

THE DEMAND FOR FINANCIAL INSTRUMENTS IN A GENERAL EQUILIBRIUM CONTEXT

Developing the demand for financial instruments in the context of the selection of a portfolio makes it clear that all financial instruments are substitutes, albeit imperfect ones. This means that a rise in the expected yield on a short-term government bond does not confine repercussions to the government bond market. It will produce general substitution effects, altering the demand for other short-term securities but also reaching out in much diminished magnitude as far as the market for speculative corporate stocks. As a result of substitutions in portfolios, yields on all financial instruments should tend to increase. Furthermore (and this will be of vital importance when we come to study monetary theory), substitutions may not be limited to financial assets. We earlier excluded consideration of choice between financial and real (or capital) assets. This was done primarily for convenience. But the reader should be aware that the change in the expected yield of one particular asset (be it real or financial) will in turn affect the demands for it and all other assets. Thus, if we can change the yields on financial assets relative to the yields on real assets we can expect to affect the demand for real assets.

SUMMARY

The demand for wealth—the saving decision—is fundamental to household demands for financial assets. An individual must then choose the specific assets that will comprise his portfolio from a variety of financial assets. One factor that will weigh in the selection of particular assets is the expected yield. The demand for any particular financial instrument will be greater, the higher the expected yield on that asset. However, there is the possibility that the actual yield will be different from the expected yield. This is termed credit risk. The individual must then not only assess the expected yield on a particular asset but also weigh the credit risk attached to that asset.

We assume most asset holders are risk avoiders. To purchase a riskier security, they will require a higher expected yield than that obtained on a less risky security.

Another factor influencing the demand for particular assets is the relative liquidity of those assets. Earlier we defined money as the most liquid financial instrument because its price is fixed. A liquid asset, then, is one whose market price is relatively stable. By this definition a variable income security with a fluctuating market price could not be a liquid asset, nor could a fixed income security that is subject to substantial credit risk and hence fluctuating market price be a liquid asset. To be highly liquid, a financial instrument must be a low-risk claim to fixed future payments.

Because inflation reduces the real value of fixed payments, asset holders should respond to the risk of inflation and the expected rate of inflation in making their portfolio decisions.

All financial instruments are substitutes (imperfect) for each other. A change in the expected yield of one particular asset will affect the demand for it. Substitutions in portfolios will occur, affecting the demand for and the expected yield on other financial assets. In turn, changing yields on financial assets can affect the demand for real assets.

NOTES

1. In the first two sections of this chapter we have taken liberties with certain concepts that have more rigorous formulations in economic theory:

a. It will appear that we are defining the expected yield as the mode of the distribution of possible yields, when it is more common to define it as the mean or mathematical expectation of the distribution. When we come to a more rigorous definition (appendix, Chapter 8), we will adopt the standard convention. However, in introducing the subject theoretical precision is less important than conveying a general feeling for the concept.

b. Note also that the probability distributions that we use in the next few pages are all symmetrical (a circumstance that, incidentally, makes the distinction between mean and mode unimportant in fact, if not in principle). Clearly, if we had in mind only bonds, the probability distributions could not be symmetrical. For simplicity we are implicitly considering a wider range of securities.

c. We are ignoring the fact that different securities have different terms to maturity. This is not a factor in our analysis at this stage, but we will turn to it later.

d. In our discussion of expected yield and credit risk we are implicitly assuming that the asset holder plans to hold each security until maturity. We will turn later to the question of the significance of possible transactions in the open market, including the significance of changes in market price.

2. If the portfolio consisted of three assets with expected yields of 0, 0.05 and 0.10, then the expected yield on the portfolio would depend on the proportion of each in the portfolio. If the proportions were 10 percent, 30 percent, and 60 percent, respectively, then the expected yield on the portfolio would be

$$\bar{y}_p = \frac{.1 \times 0 + .3 \times .05 + .6 \times .1}{.1 + .3 + .6}$$

$$= \frac{.015 + .06}{1}$$

$$= .075$$

If, by contrast, the proportions were 60 percent, 30 percent, and 10 percent, respectively, the expected yield on the portfolio would be

$$\bar{y}_p = \frac{.6 \times 0 + .3 \times .05 + .1 \times .1}{1}$$

$$= \frac{.015 + .01}{1}$$

$$= .025$$

3. In fact, the relationship between the riskiness of the portfolio and the proportions of "risky" and "safe" assets in the portfolio is much more complicated than this. Full analysis of the topic—particularly if we admit the existence of a large number of different assets—requires relatively advanced mathematics. In a more advanced treatment of the subject it would be demonstrated that, up to a point, increasing the proportion of risky assets in the portfolio can reduce the riskiness of the portfolio as a whole. In other words, given the range of securities available in the market, there exists a combination of securities that is a minimum risk portfolio. In general (although there are exceptions), that portfolio is a diversified portfolio. It does not consist of only the safest asset. Indeed, a portfolio consisting of several relatively risky securities can be less risky than a portfolio consisting of one relatively safe security. The main exception is when there is some security that is absolutely safe; that is, there is no risk in holding it. Such a security might be money (although you should remember our discussion of the significance of inflation: If there is a risk of inflation, there is a risk of loss of real purchasing power—a risk of a negative yield—in holding money; perhaps in a more general framework, money

is not a riskless security). If there is such a security, then a portfolio consisting of only that security would be riskless and hence, by definition, would be the minimum risk portfolio.

These issues involve the theory of portfolio diversification, which is introduced in Chapter 8 and considered somewhat more systematically but still on an elementary level in the appendix to that chapter. In all of this discussion we are using the standard deviation of the yield on each asset and on the portfolio as the measure of risk.

4. Students not familiar with such analysis should consult a good textbook on the principles of economics.

5. In a more advanced analysis, liquidity preference would be developed as a special case of risk avoidance.

Appendix
to Chapter 5

Capital Value and Yield: Basic Concepts of Financial Markets

$\mathbf{T}$his appendix provides a more complete and systematic discussion of the relationship between prices and yields on financial instruments. We also require the concept of capital value (or present value). It is easiest to explore these concepts initially with respect to bonds. We will then turn to variable income securities.

CAPITAL VALUE AND YIELD ON A BILL

Consider first the simple type of bond that we previously called a bill. This is a financial instrument that calls for a single lump-sum payment at the end of a fixed period of time, which we will assume is one year. For simplicity we assume that the bill has no credit risk. There is no question but that the payment will be made.[1]

Capital Value of a Bill. The basic question facing the potential purchaser of a bill is how much he should offer to pay for it (we assume that if he purchases it he will hold it until maturity). As with most questions in economics, the answer can be given only in terms of the alternatives open to him. Suppose he has the alternative of depositing the funds in the bank for one year (another riskless financial instrument) at a fixed rate of interest. If he chooses this alternative, by the end of the year he will have accumulated an amount equal to the amount deposited plus one year's interest on that sum. Then, since they are both riskless instruments, we can say that he should pay no more for the bill than the sum of money he would have to deposit in the bank at the going rate of interest in order to accumulate, by the end of the year, an amount equal to the redemption value of the bill. That sum—the amount he would have to deposit with the bank at the going interest rate—is the *capital value* of the bill.

We can define the capital value of the bill more precisely with the assistance of some basic financial mathematics. Suppose the going interest rates in riskless one-year financial instruments is 100r percent per annum.[2] Then, $V lent now, at this interest rate, will accumulate to:

$$\begin{aligned} A_1 &= V + Vr \\ &= V(1 + r) \end{aligned} \tag{5A.1}$$

by the end of the year. In other words, in order to accumulate the sum A_1 by the end of the year we would have to invest $V at the going interest rate of 100r percent per annum. If A_1 is the redemption value of the bill, then $V must be its present value. In general:

$$V = A_1 \left(\frac{1}{1 + r} \right) \tag{5A.2}$$

Thus, if the bill called for a single payment of $1000 at the end of one year, and if the going rate of interest on riskless one-year loans were 4 percent per annum, the present value of the bill would be:

$$\begin{aligned} V &= 1000 \left(\frac{1}{1 + .04} \right) \\ &= 962 \end{aligned}$$

Yield on a Bill. Faced with the alternatives of a riskless bill and a riskless one-year bank deposit, an investor who has no other reason for preferring one instrument over the other should pay no more than $962 for the bill. If the market price of the bill (P) happened to be $962, a purchaser of the bill who held it to maturity and received the redemption payment of $1000 would effectively earn 4 percent per annum on his investment. The yield on the bill would be 4 percent per annum. If the market price exceeded $962, the yield would be less than 4 percent per annum. If the price were less than $962, the yield would exceed 4 percent per annum.

In interpreting these statements it must be remembered that we calculated the capital value of the bill using the rate of interest on a closely competitive financial instrument. Thus, what we mean by the yield on the bill is the interest rate that is implicit in the relationship between the market price of the bill and its redemption value. It is the interest rate at which the present value of the bill would be equal to its market price. Given that we know the market price (P) and the redemption value (A_1), we can find the yield by substituting these values in Equation 5A.2 and solving for the interest rate. For a one-year bill, the yield (y) will be:

$$y = \frac{A_1}{P} - 1 \qquad (5A.3)$$

If the market price of the $1000 bill were $966, the yield would be $3\frac{1}{2}$ percent per annum. If the market price were $957, the yield would be $4\frac{1}{2}$ percent per annum. Note that for a given future payment, market price and yield vary inversely.

Effect of Term to Maturity. We have assumed that the bill has a one-year term to maturity. This is clearly a special case, one that we have assumed for convenience.

Suppose, instead, that the bill had a two-year term to maturity. To find the present value we can ask what sum (V) we would have to invest in order to accumulate A_2 by the end of the second year, when the interest rate is 100r percent per annum.

From equation 5A.1 we know that V will accumulate to $A_1 = V(1 + r)$ by the end of the first year. If this sum is then invested for a second year at the same interest rate, by the end of the second year we will have accumulated:

$$\begin{aligned} A_2 &= A_1 + A_1 r \\ &= V(1 + r) + V(1 + r)r \\ &= V(1 + r)(1 + r) \\ &= V(1 + r)^2 \end{aligned} \qquad (5A.4)$$

Or, dividing through by $(1 + r)^2$:

$$V = \frac{A_2}{(1 + r)^2} \qquad (5A.5)$$

It can be shown that in general the present value of a single payment of A_n to be made at the end of n years, where the prevailing interest rate for loans of that duration is 100r percent per annum, is:

$$V = \frac{A_n}{(1 + r)^n} \qquad (5A.6)$$

The present value of a given payment thus varies inversely with the term to maturity. It also varies inversely with the interest rate, and there is a strong interaction between term to maturity and the interest rate. This is illustrated in Table 5A.1.

CAPITAL VALUE AND YIELD ON A BOND

Capital Value of a Bond. The bill is a particularly simple type of bond that involves but a single future payment. In general, a bond will involve a series of semiannual payments (the coupon payments) and a final lump-sum payment (the par value or redemption value). If we assume

113

Table 5A.1. **Present Value of a $1000 Bill**[a]

Term to Maturity (Years)	Interest Rate (Yield) (Percent per Annum and Dollars)				
	3%	4%	5%	6%	7%
$\frac{1}{4}$	$993	$990	$988	$985	$983
$\frac{1}{2}$	985	980	976	971	966
1	971	962	952	943	935
2	913	925	907	890	873
5	863	822	784	747	713
10	744	676	614	558	508
20	554	456	377	312	258
50	228	141	87	54	34
∞	0	0	0	0	0

[a]Rounded to the nearest dollar. The present values for maturities of $\frac{1}{4}$ year assume compounding four times per year; for $\frac{1}{2}$ year, compounding twice per year; and for all other maturities, compounding once per year.

for simplicity that the coupon payments are made once per year (rather than the usual twice per year), then what the purchaser is purchasing is a stream of payments of the order:

$$C_1 + C_2 + C_3 + \cdots + C_n + A_n$$

where $C_1 \ldots C_n$ are the annual coupons and A_n is the final payment, made at the end of the nth year. What is the present value of such a stream of payments?

To eliminate a difficult complication we will again assume that we are talking about a bond on which there is no credit risk, for example, a federal government bond. If we then assume that the interest rate is the same for riskless loans of all maturities, the present value of the stream of payments associated with the bond is simply the sum of the present values of each of its component parts. That is, the present value of the stream of payments is:

$$V = \frac{C_1}{(1 + r)} + \frac{C_2}{(1 + r)^2} + \frac{C_3}{(1 + r)^3} + \cdots + \frac{C_n}{(1 + r)^n} + \frac{A_n}{(1 + r)^n}$$

This equation can be simplified to:

$$V = \frac{A_n}{(1 + r)^n} + C\left[\frac{1}{r} - \frac{1}{r(1 + r)^n}\right] \tag{5A.7}$$

where

$$C_1 = C_2 = C_3 = \cdots = C_n$$

In the case of a consol, a bond with a fixed annual payment in perpetuity and hence no redemption value, the formula can be further simplified to:[3]

$$V = \frac{C}{r} \tag{5A.8}$$

114

Table 5A.2. Price and Yield[a] on a 5 Percent Bond

Term to Maturity (Years)	Yield				
	3%	4%	5%	6%	7%
1	$1020	$1010	$1000	$990	$981
2	1038	1019	1000	981	963
3	1057	1028	1000	973	947
5	1092	1045	1000	957	917
10	1172	1082	1000	926	858
15	1240	1112	1000	902	816
20	1299	1137	1000	884	786
25	1350	1157	1000	871	765
	1667	1250	1000	833	714

[a]Assuming twice annual compounding. Prices have been rounded to the nearest dollar.

The capital value of a bond thus depends in a rather complex fashion on the size of the annual coupon payments $(C_1, C_2 \ldots C_n)$, the redemption value (A_n), the term to maturity (n), and the going level of interest rates (r). The capital value varies directly with the size of the coupon and redemption value and, what is important for our analysis, inversely with the market interest rate.

Yield on a Bond. The concept of the yield on a bond is analogous to the yield on a bill in that it is the interest rate that is implicit in the relationship between the market price of a bond and the stream of coupon payments and the redemption value. The yield on a bond is the interest rate at which the present value of a bond would be equal to its market price. If the price of the bond is greater than present value calculated at the going market interest rate, then the yield is less than the interest rate. If the price is less than the capital value, then the yield is greater than the market interest rate.

We were able to offer a simple formula for the calculation of the yield on a one-year bill. No such simple formula can be derived for the more general case of the yield on a bond. However, comprehensive tables of bond prices and yields are published. For a bond with a given coupon and term to maturity, it is possible to read the yield off the table if you are given the price (or the price if you are given the yield).

In Table 5A.2 we have presented a small sample of prices and yields on a bond with annual interest coupons totaling $50 and a redemption value of $1000. From this table we can see, for example, that a 5-year bond selling for $957 will yield 6 percent per annum if held to maturity. Similarly, if it is to yield 6 percent per annum a 25-year bond must sell for $871 and a consol for $833.

The market price of a bond, then, can be regarded as the present value of the stream of coupon payments and the final redemption payment when the present value is calculated at a particular rate of interest, that is, the rate of interest that is the yield on the bond. This is a true interest rate. It is the rate a purchaser will earn on his investment if he buys the security at the market price. It is also the rate a new borrower would have to pay if he borrowed money by issuing a comparable security. Thus, when we are considering the determination of the market price of a bond we are simultaneously considering the determination of an interest rate. As the price falls, the interest rate rises. They are linked mathematically.

It was demonstrated in Chapter 5 that interest rates on all types of securities are related to each other. While they are not rigidly tied to each other, they do not move independently of each other either. A general rise in interest rates will be reflected in the yields on all securities.

THE YIELD ON VARIABLE INCOME SECURITIES

In principle the same concepts can be applied to variable income securities (or real assets, for that matter). That is, it should be possible to calculate the yield on such a security on the basis of the existing market price. However, a complication arises because, unlike a bond, a fixed stream of future payments is not specified in the contract of a variable income security. Both the size and the length of the stream of payments depend on future developments that can never be perfectly foreseen. As a result, we can only calculate the present value of a share of common stock, for example on the basis of some expected stream of dividend payments that by its very nature must be conjectural. Individuals may disagree sharply on the most probable stream of future dividends, and individual opinions may be revised drastically from time to time as new information is forthcoming.

Risk on Fixed Income Securities. In our discussion of the yield on fixed income securities we ignored the risk that the "fixed" interest and redemption payments will not be made. However, such risk of default exists with respect to most bonds. In this respect a high-risk bond has some of the characteristics of a variable income security. The actual payments may be less than those specified in the contract, or they may be delayed beyond the time specified in the contract (of course, they cannot be more than specified in the contract). This is something that should be taken into account in calculating yield.

Theoretical vs. Expected Yield. We can refer to the yield calculated from information in the contract between borrower and lender as the *theoretical yield*. It is calculated on the presumption that the payments specified in the contract will all be made in full and on time. In the case of variable income securities no theoretical yield can be calculated, and in the case of high-risk bonds the theoretical yield may not be the most likely yield. We thus need the concept of *expected yield* to refer to the most probable yield, based on the asset holder's expectations of the size and timing of future payments. In the case of a perfectly safe bond, expected yield and theoretical yield will be the same.

By analogy with a consol, another security with no fixed maturity, the theoretical yield on common stock is sometimes measured by the ratio of current dividends to market price. This, however, could be a valid calculation of the theoretical yield only if the current dividend payments were expected to continue unchanged in perpetuity. Unlike the consol, for which the annual interest payment is fixed in perpetuity, in general there is no reason to expect the current dividend on common stock to continue indefinitely. As a result, the calculated dividend price ratio is not directly analogous to the yield on a consol, and indeed its meaning is not obvious.

Inflation and Taxes. We would remind you of two points made in the text of the chapter. First, if the general level of commodity prices is expected to change, then it is important that "real" rather than "nominal" yields be calculated. The nominal yields calculated as discussed earlier should be adjusted for the expected rate of inflation. Second, it will generally be the after-tax yield that is relevant for investor decisions. Given the nature of our taxation system, the adjustment for expected taxes may affect not only the general level of yields but also the relationship between yields on different types of securities.

SUMMARY: CAPITAL VALUE, MARKET PRICE, AND EXPECTED YIELD

The concepts of capital value and expected yield are basic to all economic analysis involving intertemporal decisions, that is, decisions involving events that occur in more than one time period. These concepts are basic to the analysis of the determination of the market price of financial instruments because financial instruments are claims to payments to be made in future periods. We will encounter the concepts again in discussing capital expenditure decisions of business firms, since these are also decisions involving current expenditures (on plant and equipment) for the purpose of making profits in future periods. The student is advised to review and master the concepts.

The main purpose of this appendix has been to provide a more systematic definition of the concept of the expected yield on financial instruments and a more careful development of the relationship between expected yield and the market price of the instrument. The important points to keep in mind are:

1. If the stream of future payments is given, then the determination of the market price involves simultaneously the determination of the yield. Market price and yield are linked mathematically.
2. Yield and market price vary inversely for any given stream of future payments.
3. If the expected size of the future payments changes (as in a variable income security), then the price or the expected yield on that security must change in the same direction. Larger expected dividend pay-

ments on common stock in a corporation must mean either a higher price for the shares of stock or a higher expected yield on the stock (or both).

4. If the streams of payments on two financial instruments are different, then their market prices must be different if they are to give the same yield. Thus, if a 5 percent, 20-year bond ($50 annual coupon) and a 3 percent, 20-year bond ($30 annual coupon) are both to yield 4 percent, the price of the 5 percent bond must be $1137 and the price of the 3 percent bond $863.

This last point is important. It is the price of financial instruments that is determined in the marketplace. However, since the characteristics of financial instruments are so diverse, market price does not provide a useful basis for comparison of financial instruments. Expected yield is the most useful common denominator for purposes of comparison and decision making.

NOTES

1. This assumption is important. Toward the end of this appendix we will distinguish between the expected yield and the theoretical yield on financial instruments. The theoretical yield is calculated from information in the contract between the borrower and the lender. It presumes that all contractual payments will be made in full and on time. The expected yield allows for the possibility of partial or total default, or delays in payment. If there is complete certainty that payments will be made, there is no need to distinguish between these two concepts, and we can refer to either simply as the yield.

2. It may seem strange to quote interest rates at 100 percent per annum. The interest rate "4 percent per annum" can be written in ratio form as .04. If we want r to represent this ratio, that is, $r = .04$—then we must refer to the rate of interest at $100r$ percent per annum (i.e., $r = .04$).

3. A consol calls for annual payments through all future time, that is, $n = \infty$. But as n approaches ∞, $1/(1 + r)^n$ approaches 0. Hence, the terms $A_n/(1 + r)^n$ and $C/r(1 + r)^n$ both approach 0, and the capital value of the bond approaches C/r.

ELEMENTARY THEORY OF FINANCIAL MARKETS

Part 3: Supply and Market Equilibrium

Up to this point we have discussed the theory of financial markets from the viewpoint of asset holders, or the demand side of the market. We now turn our attention to the supply side and to the nature of equilibrium in financial markets.

STOCKS AND FLOWS: TWO CONCEPTS OF SUPPLY

The supply of financial instruments has its origins in acts of borrowing and lending—in the demands of deficit spending units for funds to finance their deficits. However, in discussing the supply side of the market it is important to make a sharp distinction between two different concepts of supply. One is the *stock* of financial instruments outstanding at a particular point in time, and the other is the *flow* of new borrowing over a particular period of time.

At any point in time there will be an outstanding stock of financial instruments already in the hands of asset holders. Both the size and the composition of this stock is a reflection of past history. It reflects previous borrowings by households, governments, and corporations. In our analysis of the financial system, this stock is something that must be taken as given—a predetermined variable.

The stock concept of supply is basic. However, we must recognize that over a period of time the outstanding stock is subject to change. Attempts of spending units to raise funds to finance deficits create a steady flow of new financial instruments onto the market that augment the basic stock. At the same time, partial or complete repayment of outstanding debts by some spending units work to reduce the outstanding stock. The difference between these two magnitudes—the flow of new borrowing and the flow of repayments—is the second concept of supply. It is supply as a net flow: an addition to or subtraction from the basic stock over a period of time.

Like the demand for financial instruments, the supply of financial instruments involves two fundamental decisions—a decision on the amount to be borrowed (the *borrowing decision*) and a decision on the types of financial instruments to be issued (the *liability balance decision*). A complete analysis of the supply of financial instruments must simultaneously explain both decisions.

THE BORROWING DECISION

One major conclusion that will follow from our analysis of the borrowing decisions of households, governments, and corporations will be that, with certain important exceptions (including the borrowings of financial intermediaries, which fall into a class by themselves and must be treated separately), the primary purpose of borrowing is to finance the purchase or construction of durable real assets. In the government sector these assets may consist of highways, schools, or sewage disposal plants; in the corporate sector, factory buildings, machinery, or equipment; and in the household sector, automobiles, household durables, or houses. The objects may be widely different, but they all have an extended life and have value to their purchasers because they are expected to provide services to be either consumed directly or sold during future periods. While the specific motivations of the individual sectors may differ widely, this aspect of the borrowing decision that all sectors have in common provides a convenient peg on which to hang our theoretical analysis.

THE CONSUMER SECTOR

Since we have already made an extensive examination of the asset demands of households, it is convenient to begin our analysis with this sector. A simple adaptation of the balance sheet and accumulation identities of Chapter 4 provide a useful framework for the consideration of household borrowing decisions.

The Basic Identities Again. Consider first the balance sheet identity, which we previously wrote as:

$$\text{Wealth} = \text{Assets} - \text{Liabilities} \tag{4.1}$$

By splitting assets into the two categories, financial assets and real assets, and rearranging the terms, we can rewrite this equation as:

$$\text{Liabilities} = \frac{\text{Real}}{\text{Assets}} + \frac{\text{Financial}}{\text{Assets}} - \text{Wealth} \qquad (6.1)$$

Or, expressing the same relationships in terms of flows over time:

$$\Delta \text{ Liabilities} = \Delta \frac{\text{Real}}{\text{Assets}} + \Delta \frac{\text{Financial}}{\text{Assets}} - \text{Saving} \qquad \mathbf{(6.2)}$$

(Remember, the symbol Δ means "the change in," and from Equation 4.3 saving $= \Delta$ wealth.)

Equations 6.1 and 6.2 simply state that the decision of a household to go into debt involves a desire to hold assets, real or financial, in excess of the household's wealth. We have assumed that each household is striving to maximize the utility it expects to derive from its lifetime income. Within the framework of the life cycle hypothesis, what reasons can we discover for household borrowing?

Categories of Borrowing. The first category might be called *transitory borrowing*. A chance illness to the head of the household, which both interrupts the flow of income and creates medical bills, might be the occasion of borrowing, particularly in the case of households that do not have many marketable assets. In terms of the concepts we developed earlier, this is a case in which income is temporarily depressed below its "permanent" level and consumption is raised above its "permanent" level. Borrowing is a response to transitory or random factors—an alternative to making more fundamental adjustments in the households "permanent" consumption plans.

In the second category we have borrowing that is part of a deliberate plan to redistribute consumption over time—a regular part of the life cycle of the household. A young family with good income prospects might borrow in order to support a level of present consumption in excess of its present income, planning to repay the accumulated debt out of its expected higher future income. This might well be the case of a married student paying his way through university with the assistance of loans.

While it is difficult to marshall statistical evidence to support the proposition, it is clear that these two purposes (transitory borrowing and redistributing income over time) account for a relatively small part of the total indebtedness of a typical household. The third category is of much greater importance. This category is borrowing to finance the acquisition of specific assets.

The typical household will presumably borrow to accumulate assets when the expected yield on those assets exceeds the expected interest cost on the debt. True, the desire for liquidity may be sufficiently strong that the household may borrow simply to create or maintain its stock of relatively liquid assets, even at some net interest cost to the household. However, the major rationale for borrowing will be the excess of expected yield on assets over the interest cost on liabilities.

In some cases these assets will be financial assets. Many households, particularly relatively high-income households, borrow funds to purchase corporate stock on which they expect to receive a relatively high return. Some of these funds will be borrowed from financial institutions, and some will be borrowed directly from stock brokerage firms. At the end of June 1973, customer indebtedness to stockbrokers amounted to $6.2 billion. Individuals also had debts of $1 billion to commercial banks secured by marketable securities, but a large portion of these loans had probably been used for purposes other than the purchase of securities. In any case, borrowing for the acquisition of financial assets accounts for a small portion of the total indebtedness of the typical household.

If we take mortgage debt and installment debt outstanding as a measure of household borrowing to acquire real assets, it is apparent from Table 6.1 that household borrowing to finance the acquisition of real assets is the dominant factor in household indebtedness. Over 75 percent of the debts of households included in the 1963 Survey for the Board of Governors of the Federal Reserve System were in these two categories. It is also interesting to note that the indebtedness of these households traces out a distinctive life cycle pattern, as described in Chapter 4. In the early years, the accumulation of household assets is accompanied by increasing indebtedness. In the later years, indebtedness falls off sharply.

The Expected Yield on Real Assets. A rational householder will only borrow to finance the purchase of real assets—a house or household durable goods such as furniture or appliances—if the expected yield on these assets is greater than the interest cost incurred by borrowing. It makes little sense to acquire an illiquid real asset expected to yield 2 percent per annum if to do so you have to borrow and pay an interest rate of 12 percent per annum. Are householders rational in their borrowing decisions?

This is a difficult question to answer empirically, since the yield on most household real assets is not monetary. Rather, it is in the form of a stream of services consumed directly by the household. There is a market for many of these services (automobile rentals, coin laundries, movie theaters, and frozen food lockers are some familiar examples), and two economists have taken advantage of this fact to estimate the actual rate of return on selected consumer durables, using the prices of equivalent services in the marketplace. They concluded that the implicit financial yield on the consumer durables owned by the typical household was very high indeed—frequently over 25 percent per annum. If one allows for intangible values such as convenience, independence, or security associated with owning rather than renting consumer durables, the true yield on such assets is impossible to measure. The point of relevance for us is that if households make some rough calculation of this sort, given the implicit yield on real assets, households should be

Table 6.1. The Life Cycle in Household Debt, December 31, 1962

Age: Head of Household	Total Debt	Secured by Home	Installment Debt		Other Debt	Total Equity in Assets	Equity in Home	Portfolio		
			Total	Auto				Total	Investments	Other
Under 35	$4,139	$2,988	$720	$474	$ 431	$ 6,304	$1,660	$ 1,393	$ 815	$3,252
35–44	5,481	3,904	678	443	899	16,068	4,939	5,134	3,514	5,996
45–54	5,122	3,332	565	359	1,226	22,521	7,358	8,331	5,761	6,892
55–64	2,717	1,502	233	145	899	32,527	8,134	16,445	12,212	7,948
65 and Over	1,323	582	114	53	621	30,838	6,895	19,463	14,506	4,481
Average All Households	3,834	2,529	478	306	827	20,982	5,693	9,688	7,013	5,641

SOURCE: Dorothy Projector, Survey of Financial Characteristics of Consumers (Washington, D.C.: Board of Governors of the Federal Reserve System, 1966), pp. 110, 130.

less willing to borrow at higher interest rates. That is, the supply of financial instruments from households should be an increasing function of the yield on consumer durable goods and a decreasing function of the level of interest rates in financial markets (i.e., of the yield on financial instruments).

Since the yield on consumer durables cannot be measured, this is a very difficult proposition to test. Numerous attempts have been made to identify the sensitivity of consumer borrowing to changes in the level of interest rates. The results of such tests are at best inconclusive. However, most economists feel that such a relationship does exist, although it may be relatively weak.

THE CORPORATE SECTOR

Most business firms are engaged in the production of goods and services for sale in the marketplace with the primary objective of making profit. The exceptions to the profit-seeking characterization of businesses are sufficiently unimportant that we can ignore them. Why should a profit-seeking business borrow funds?

Financing Real Capital Formation. As in the case of households, the primary, but not exclusive, purpose of borrowing by business firms is to finance the purchase or construction of real assets, capital goods to be used in the process of production (including inventories of raw materials, goods in process of production, and finished goods awaiting sale). The issuance of financial instruments, whether stocks or bonds, is not the only method of financing capital formation. A firm could also draw down holdings of financial assets accumulated in the past, or it could finance it out of business saving. By *business saving* we mean the portion of the gross revenue of the firm that is not used to pay out-of-pocket costs, such as wages, costs of raw materials purchased, interest on debts, and the like, or is not paid out to the stockholders in the form of dividends. It is, in other words, the firm's capital consumption allowances plus its retained profits.

In Figure 6.1 we have presented some data to show the relationship between business borrowing and business capital expenditures. It should be noted that business saving in fact provides by far the largest portion of the funds required by businesses. However, the point of importance to us is the relatively close correspondence between corporate capital expenditures and the issuance of new corporate debt securities. Also note that in the last few years corporate saving has fallen far short of capital financing requirements.

Interest Rates and the Yield on Capital Goods. Just as households cannot ignore the time dimension in planning consumption so as to maximize utility, business firms cannot take a static approach to the maximization of profits. The management must not only plan production with the production facilities at its disposal, it must also plan the expansion of those production facilities at a rate and in directions that will maximize the profits the firm expects to receive in the future. This means that the management of the profit-maximizing firm must be continually alert for opportunities for capital expansion in which the expected yield will exceed the interest cost

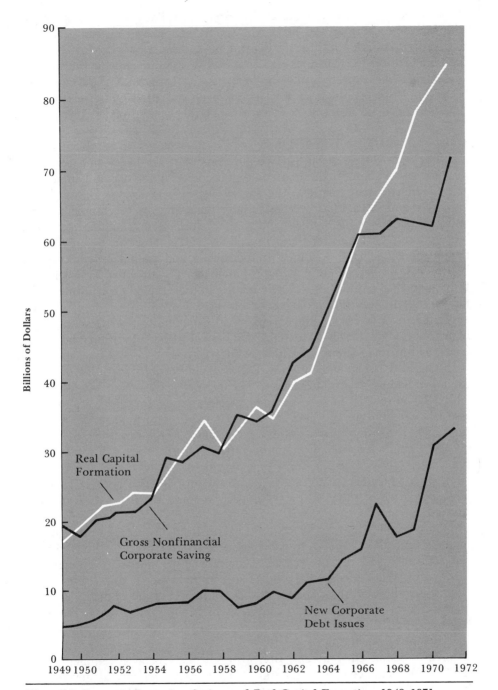

Figure 6.1 **Corporate Borrowing, Saving, and Real Capital Formation, 1949–1971**
SOURCE: New corporate debt data: U.S. Department of Commerce, Bureau of the Census, *Statistical Abstract of the United States* (Washington, D.C.), various issues; other data from flow-of-funds data in Federal Reserve *Bulletin*, various issues.

of the funds required to finance the expansion. Thus, the willingness of corporations to borrow, and hence the supply of financial instruments from corporations, should be directly dependent on the expected yield on real capital and inversely dependent on the level of interest rates in the market. The higher the expected yield on real assets, the greater the volume of borrowing to be expected; the higher the level of interest rates (or expected yields on financial instruments), the smaller the volume of borrowing.

THE GOVERNMENT SECTOR

The borrowing decisions in the government sector have some points of similarity with those in the household and corporate sectors, and some notable differences, particularly at the federal government level.

State and Local Borrowing. Consider borrowing by the municipal government bodies in the United States. The stock of outstanding state and local government bonds for the period 1940–1970 is shown in Figure 6.2 and the relationship between municipal borrowing and capital expenditures in Figures 6.3(A) and 6.3(B). It is apparent from the latter that borrowing by these municipal authorities is closely related to their capital expenditures. The market rise in the outstanding debt of these borrowers in the 1950s and 1960s reflects a corresponding sharp rise in expenditures for social capital— highways, bridges, hospitals, schools, facilities for higher education, and so on. The trend in these figures is quite startling.

Expected Yield and Interest Rates. It is possible to think of social capital providing a yield to society. The rational government official, then, will only borrow to finance a capital project when the yield on the real assets exceeds the interest cost of the funds required to finance the expenditure. As in the case of real assets in the consumer sector, however, the returns on social capital are mainly nonmonetary. Although there are some exceptions, the returns take the form of a stream of services, consumed collectively by the members of the society, with no (or perhaps a nominal) charge. The calculation of the yield on these assets requires the imputation of value to these services.

In principle, the supply of financial instruments from junior governments should be responsive to the level of interest rates. Like borrowing in the consumer and corporate sectors, borrowing by junior governments is mainly to provide durable real assets that can be expected to provide a yield to the members of the society. The borrowing decision should involve a comparison of yield and interest cost: The higher the interest rate, the fewer the projects that will provide a yield in excess of interest cost and the smaller the amount of borrowing.

The Federal Government. Borrowing by the federal government has a radically different character. Like all other sectors, the federal government borrows when its revenues fall short of its expenditures. However, as should be evident from Figure 6.3, there is no clearly definable relationship between

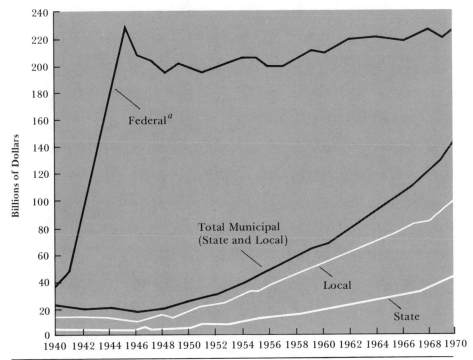

Figure 6.2 **The Stock of Government Bonds Outstanding, 1940–1970**
[a]Federal bonds outstanding net of federal bonds held by the Federal Reserve System and federal agencies.
SOURCE: U.S. Department of Commerce, Bureau of the Census, *Statistical Abstract of the United States* (Washington, D.C.), various issues.

federal capital expenditures and federal borrowing (indeed, if there is such a relationship it is inverse).

A glance at Figure 6.2 reveals that the net borrowing that accounts for most of the existing stock of federal government bonds occurred during the period 1940–1945. Additional increases have occurred during three other periods, 1951–1954, 1957–1959, and 1960–1962. The major increase of the first period was a result of wartime efforts to finance our involvement in World War II. The 1951–1954 period coincided with our involvement in the Korean conflict. The latter two periods were ones of economic recession in the U.S. economy. What Figure 6.2 does not reveal is the increase in federal government debt that has been absorbed by federal government agencies. This outlet was particularly important during the Vietnam conflict, when additional debt securities were issued but in large measure were bought by federal agencies.

If we omit exceptional events such as major wars, the bulk of the borrowing by the federal government is related to the general state of the

127

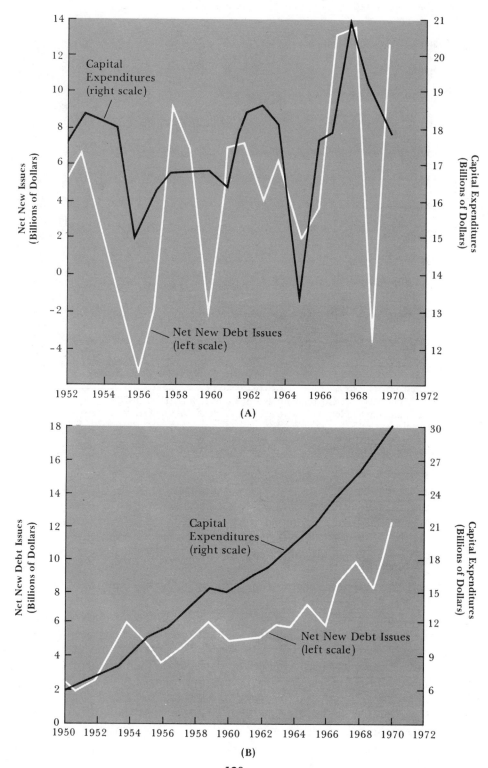

(A)

(B)

128

national economy. When unemployment is high, the government tends to run a deficit in its budget and hence must borrow. In periods of high levels of economic activity, the opposite is true. For reasons that are explored in any principles-of-economics course, this is not only an automatic response to fluctuations in economic activity, it is a desirable response. The federal borrowing decision should be related to economic conditions, not to capital expenditures by the federal government.

THE BORROWING DECISION: SUMMARY

In all but the federal government sector, the borrowing decision is primarily related to the decision to acquire real assets. Thus, the supply of financial instruments from the consumer, corporate, and municipal government sectors is closely related to capital expenditures by these sectors (including the purchase of household durables as capital expenditures).

The capital expenditure decision can be considered as a process of comparing the yield on real assets with the interest cost of borrowing funds, that is, with the expected yield on financial instruments. The higher the level of interest rates for any given level of expected yields on real assets, the less likely it is that any particular capital project will be undertaken. As a result, the supply of financial instruments from these sectors should be an inverse function of the level of interest rates.

The federal government is an exception to all of these generalizations. Peacetime borrowing by the federal government is more closely related to the level of economic activity than to the level of federal government capital expenditures.

THE LIABILITY BALANCE DECISION

Having decided to borrow, the household, corporation, or government agency must choose the type of financial instrument to be used. For the most part this is a question of whether to issue a long-term or a short-term bond, but in the case of a corporation there is also the question of whether to issue bonds or stocks.

This subject is far too complex for us to explore here. However, it should be clear that there is a parallel set of considerations to those that we dis-

Figure 6.3 (A) Net Federal Government Borrowing and Capital Expenditure, 1952–1970
Figure 6.3 (B) Net New State and Local Government Borrowing and Capital Expenditure, 1950–1970
SOURCE: Capital expenditure data: U.S. Department of Commerce, Bureau of the Census, *Statistical Abstract of the United States* (Washington, D.C.), various issues; debt data: Federal Reserve *Bulletin*, various issues.

cussed in connection with the portfolio balance decision on the demand side of the market.

Relative Yields. One consideration, clearly, must be the relative yields on financial instruments in the market. Other things being equal, the borrower will want to pay as low an effective interest rate as possible. As a result, he will be inclined to issue financial instruments with the lowest effective yield.

Liquidity. Relative interest costs are not the only consideration. Liquidity may also be important. However, from the point of view of the borrower, rather than being a desirable property of a financial instrument, liquidity will normally be an undesirable property. You will recall that liquid instruments are short-term instruments. A debtor with a major portion of his debt in liquid form faces the risk of having to redeem these securities on short notice. If his assets will only yield returns over a long period, this can cause severe financial difficulties.

There are exceptions, of course. Some of the assets financed through borrowing may yield their returns over a short period. This would be true of inventories, for example. Thus, a firm with a fluctuating level of inventories might find that short-term liabilities are the most appropriate types.

Speculation. There are other exceptions to the general undesirability of liquidity as well. In particular, when interest rates are relatively high, borrowers may wish to speculate on a fall in interest rates in the future. Rather than contracting for a long-term debt at relatively high interest rates, they may borrow on a short-term basis, planning to refinance the debt with long-term bonds when interest rates fall.

Borrower's Risk. Earlier, we discussed credit risk from the standpoint of the asset holder. The other side of credit risk or risk of default is *borrower's risk.* Borrowers also assume a risk in committing themselves to fixed future payments. The assets that they count on to provide the income to meet these payments may not return the expected yield. This will affect the choice between stocks and bonds as financial instruments to be issued. If the borrowing firm chooses common stock, inadequate returns on the asset will not force the firm into bankruptcy court (although if the venture is successful beyond expectations, the additional returns must be shared with the new stockholders).

Borrower's risk may also affect the borrowing decision. Any risk-avoiding borrower will demand an expected return on his capital investment substantially above the interest rate on borrowed funds to compensate for borrower's risk before he will undertake the venture.

Inflation and Taxation. Expectations of inflation and taxation will also affect the choice between types of instruments to be issued. The effects are the opposite of those discussed previously in connection with the demand for such instruments. For example, expectations of continued rapid inflation would induce borrowers to borrow on as long-term a basis as possible, since future fixed payments would be paid off in "cheap" inflated dollars.

A NOTE ON THE FEDERAL GOVERNMENT

As in the case of the borrowing decision, the federal government should be (but is not always) an exception to all that we have said about the liability balance decision. The considerations governing the structure of the federal debt should be related to the general state of economic conditions rather than the range of considerations entering into the liability balance decisions of other spending units. This is a topic that we will consider in Chapters 20 and 23.

THE LIABILITY BALANCE DECISION: CONCLUSIONS

Just as the asset holder must choose among alternative assets to be held, so the debtor must choose between alternative types of instruments to be issued. In general, the considerations entering into the debtor's choices are the same as those entering into the asset holder's choices, but they work in the opposite direction. Thus, debtors tend to prefer to issue low-yielding instruments (to them, the yield is a cost) and to avoid liquidity. Risk aversion would probably lead them to issue variable income rather than fixed income securities. The important point to note, however, is that just as all financial instruments are substitutes for each other in asset portfolios, so they are substitutes for each other as methods of borrowing funds. A change in the yield on one financial instrument will not only result in adjustments in the composition of asset portfolios, it will also lead to changes in methods used by borrowers to finance their current deficits.

MARKET EQUILIBRIUM

Until now, our discussion of the market for financial instruments has been primarily an analysis of the determinants of the behavior of the individual participants in the market—the households, business firms, and government agencies that are the ultimate lenders and borrowers. We examined how each participant might make decisions about the size and composition of his asset or liability portfolio by taking into account his reactions to liquidity and risk, and by taking the prices—or better, the expected yields—on the instruments as given. However, we cannot take prices and yields as given. They are determined in the marketplace through the interaction of the demand and supply forces that result from the portfolio selection decisions of all of the individual borrowers and lenders in the market. It is one aspect of the process by which the market allocates credit among all alternative uses.

EQUILIBRIUM PRICE

Equilibrium price is a familiar concept in economics: It is a price that under existing conditions of demand and supply has no tendency to change. Prices tend to rise under the pressure of excess demand and to fall under the pressure of excess supply. An equilibrium price, therefore, is a price at which there is neither excess demand nor excess supply—a price at which market demand and supply are in balance. In the context of financial markets, this means a set of expected yields on financial instruments such that there is neither an excess demand for nor an excess supply of any category of financial instrument.

In a more advanced textbook the concept of equilibrium in financial markets would be the subject of very careful and extensive analysis. It is a difficult concept because it involves two dimensions—stocks and flows. As we have seen, we can talk about supply both as a stock at a point in time (the stock of financial instruments outstanding) and as a flow over a period of time (the flow of net borrowing). Likewise, we can talk of the demand for financial instruments as a stock (the desired stock at a point in time) and a flow (the flow of net saving over a period of time). A thorough analysis of financial equilibrium, which is beyond the scope of the present discussion, would have to explore both dimensions and to examine the interrelationships between them. For now, certain elementary points should be kept in mind.

Stock Equilibrium. If we could stop the clock and look at financial markets at a point in time, we would be faced with a situation in which the quantities of financial instruments outstanding are given. Given time, new securities can be issued and existing securities retired. However, at any instant the quantities are fixed by the cumulative effects of past history. In the immediate past, transactions in the market established a set of prices (and hence expected yields) for those securities. For this set of prices to be an equilibrium set in a stock sense, asset holders must have no incentive to alter the composition of their portfolios. They must be content to hold the existing quantities of securities at the prevailing market prices for those securities. This is the condition for stock equilibrium.

Suppose this is not the case and that there is a group of asset holders who feel that the market price for some of the securities they are holding is too high (i.e., the expected yield is too low) relative to those on other assets (e.g., other securities, money, or physical assets). If we could somehow permit trading of securities without allowing time to pass (i.e., without changing the outstanding stocks of securities and other factors affecting demand and supply conditions), these asset holders would offer to sell what they consider overpriced securities and would submit bids for the underpriced securities. Since the quantities of these securities cannot change, the only effects of these transactions can be to rearrange portfolios (if the securities exist, some asset holder must have them in his portfolio) and to change prices.

The price of the overvalued securities will be bid down and the price of the underpriced security bid up, the adjustments presumably continuing until stock equilibrium is established.

In one case, which will assume major importance in our later analysis, it may be that asset holders in general have more money in their portfolios than is consistent with portfolio balance at existing prices and expected yields on securities. They will attempt to dispose of money in exchange for securities. This attempt at shifting portfolios will lead to a bidding up of the prices of all securities (a lowering of interest rates). Neither the stock of money nor the stock of securities can change (remember, we assumed them to be fixed in number), yet the level (and perhaps the structure) of interest rates will change.

It is this change in interest rates that allows the public to achieve portfolio balance with the given stock of money. The opposite adjustment would occur if there were an excess demand for money.

Flow Equilibrium. This analysis of the adjustment of prices and expected yields in the face of stock disequilibrium is highly artificial because it implies the passage of time without any changes in the external environment. However, time does pass, and as it does, the basic determinants of portfolio balance decisions change. The outlook for particular industries, the expected returns on outstanding securities, and the expected yield on new physical capital formation change. Physical capital can be created or depleted. Income is generated, and consumption and saving occur. Government policy can be implemented or changed. Commodity price levels may rise or fall, perhaps accompanied by changes in employment levels. Expectations with respect to any of a great variety of relevant developments—including future security prices—may change slightly or drastically.

All of these considerations come to bear on two vital flows. First, as time passes borrowers can issue new securities and retire outstanding issues. Both the size and the structure of the stock of financial instruments available to be held will probably change. Second, the flow of saving during the period increases the size of asset holdings, thus increasing the demand for financial instruments. Dissaving has the opposite effect. Over that period the prices (and hence expected yields) on financial instruments must adjust so that the increasing demands for financial instruments resulting from the flow of saving is just offset by the increasing stock of financial instruments resulting from borrowing to finance capital and other expenditures. (Remember, both the saving decision and the borrowing decision should be sensitive to the level of interest rates, although perhaps in varying degrees.) This, then, is the condition for flow equilibrium.

It should be evident from what has been said that what we mean by "flow" equilibrium is in fact "stock" equilibrium at successive points in time, with the basic determinants of equilibrium changing from instant to instant.

MARKET EQUILIBRIUM AND RESOURCE ALLOCATION

Most microeconomic theory focuses attention on the determination of relative prices in equilibrium. However, the underlying concern is always the allocation of scarce resources among alternative possible uses. Whether in the markets for bread and bicycles or the markets for financial instruments, the process of price determination takes on importance because it is at the core of the process by which production and employment decisions are made in a market economy.

What is being allocated in the market for financial instruments is credit. Thus, the price of financial instruments not only determines the yield to asset holders, it also determines the cost of funds to borrowers. The yield to asset holders should affect savings decisions, thus affecting the share of income devoted to consumption and the share available to finance capital formation. The interest cost to borrowers should affect their willingness to engage in deficit spending, whether for consumption or for capital formation. Thus, the determination of equilibrium prices in financial markets should influence choices between present and future consumption, as well as the pace and industrial composition of capital formation.

MARKET EQUILIBRIUM AND GOVERNMENT POLICY

There is also another aspect of equilibrium in financial markets that must be noted. We have seen that all financial instruments are more or less close substitutes, both as assets that might be held by asset holders and as liabilities that might be issued by debtors. This means that the markets for the various types of financial instruments cannot be considered separately. They are tightly interconnected, such that a disturbance to equilibrium in one market will also involve disturbances in others. But, as we have just noted, the prices of financial instruments also enter into decisions on consumption and public and private capital formation. This opens up the possibility that the government can engage in operations in the financial markets—altering the size of the outstanding stock of certain financial instruments (e.g., government debt, money)—for the purpose of altering the level of expenditures on consumer and capital goods. It creates the possibility of a monetary policy to regulate the level of aggregate demand for goods and services. This is the topic of the second half of this book.

A QUANTITATIVE PERSPECTIVE
ON AMERICAN FINANCIAL MARKETS

The past three chapters have been concerned primarily with theoretical abstractions. Perhaps it would be useful at this point to anchor the discussion in the real world by providing a brief overview of the flow of funds through the American financial system.

THE FLOW-OF-FUNDS ACCOUNTS

The American economy has had social accounting in the sense of national income and product accounts since the 1930s. These accounts were developed and are published today by the Department of Commerce. The national income and product accounts provide an aggregate measure of transactions in the current output of final goods and services. These accounts specifically exclude financial transactions such as borrowing and lending and transactions in the output of intermediate goods. They ignore the financial influences that operate on and affect the level of spending for final goods and services.

The Board of Governors of the Federal Reserve System has set up the flow of funds accounting structure to fill this void. This system is based on the research and work of Morris Copeland of Cornell University. In 1952 Copeland published his findings on financial flows for the period beginning in 1944. The flow-of-funds accounts are maintained and published quarterly by the Board of Governors of the Federal Reserve System.

The flow-of-funds accounts connect the effects of nonfinancial transactions on financial markets and the reciprocal effects of activity in the financial markets on the demand for goods and services.

SOURCES AND USES OF SAVING

Simply, the Federal Reserve flow of funds accounts provide detailed estimates of the financial transactions and the allocation of saving among the alternative uses and sectors of the economy. The national income and product estimates are used in order to arrive at the gross saving estimate. Flow of funds accounts are then developed to show the gross savings estimate for each sector. The accounts show the gross and net savings generated in each of several sectors of the economy and the corresponding gross real capital formation in each sector. The difference between saving and capital formation for any sector is its net lending or net borrowing—in our terminology, its financial surplus or financial deficit.

Sectors. In the flow of funds accounts each sector is composed of a group of economic units that share a similar function and institutional structure. They are the familiar groupings of spending units, consumers and nonprofit organizations, farm business, nonfarm business, corporations, federal government, state and local governments, commercial banking and monetary authorities, savings institutions (mutual savings banks, savings and loan associations, and credit unions), insurance companies and private pension plans, mutual funds, sales finance companies, security brokers and dealers, and the rest of the world. Data are collected on some 20 sectors but are consolidated into various larger groupings, depending on the type of information being presented. In constructing Table 6.2 we have consolidated these into 5 sectors.

Table 6.2. Savings and Capital Formation in the United States, 1970

	Households	Business	Government	Financial	Rest of the World	Total Sectors	Discrepancy	Total
1. Capital Consumption	$ 91.2	$ 71.9	—	$1.6	—	$164.7	—	—
2. Net Saving	69.3	10.5	−18.1	2.1	−0.7	63.1	—	—
3. Gross Saving (1 + 2)	160.5	82.4	−18.1	3.7	−0.7	227.8	—	227.8
4. Gross Real Capital Formation	113.4	109.9	—	1.9	—	225.2	—	—
5. Net Financial Investment	46.4	−30.3	−15.2	1.5	0.8	3.2	−3.2	—
6. Gross Investment (4 + 5)	159.8	79.6	−15.2	3.4	0.8	228.4	−0.6	227.8
7. Net Surplus (+) or Net Deficit (−) (3 + 4)	47.1	−27.5	−18.1	1.8	−0.7	2.6	−2.6	—
8. Discrepancy (3 − 6)	0.6	2.8	−2.9	0.3	1.5	—	−0.6	—

SOURCE: Federal Reserve Bulletin, November 1971, p. A70.

Table 6.3. Financial Surpluses in the Household
            Sector, 1960–1970 (Billions of Dollars)

Year	Surplus
1960	$ 4.3
1961	11.1
1962	10.7
1963	9.1
1964	15.8
1965	19.2
1966	24.4
1967	35.1
1968	32.7
1969	29.7
1970	47.1

SOURCE: Adapted from flow-of-funds data, Federal Reserve *Bulletin*, various issues.

Surplus Sectors. As is evident from Table 6.2, the major source of financial surpluses in the economy in 1970 was the saving of households. This has been consistently the case in recent years (Table 6.3). It should be remembered in this connection that purchases of consumer durables and the activity of owning houses are considered capital investment by the household sector. Contributions to life insurance and pension funds are forms of saving, and the claims households have on life insurance and pensions are considered assets.

In 1970 the financial sector was also a net source of a very small financial surplus. As we shall see in subsequent discussion, this small surplus does not accurately convey the importance of financial intermediaries in the flow of funds. The surplus does indicate, however, that this sector was more than able to finance its own capital formation from its gross savings. The sector is dominated by the commercial banking subsector and nonbank financial institutions. Data for the period 1960–1970 are presented in Table 6.4 on both subsectors.

Deficit Sectors. In 1970 the financial surpluses of the nation were absorbed on balance by the government sector and the business sector. Over the decade of the 1960s the government sector has, with two exceptions, been a deficit sector. State and local governments have consistently spent more than they saved (Table 6.5), while the federal government had surpluses in 1960 and 1969.

The business sector also was a deficit sector, with two exceptions, during the period 1960–1970. In Table 6.6 the business sector is divided into its two subsectors, (1) farm and nonfarm noncorporate business and (2) nonfinancial corporate business. The former subsector has consistently run deficits between $3 billion and $4.5 billion. The corporate subsector, however, generated surpluses early in the 1960s but toward the end of the decade experienced rapidly increasing deficits.

Table 6.4. Financial Surpluses and Deficits in the
Financial Sector, 1960–1970 (Billions of Dollars)

Year	Commercial Banks	Private Nonbank Finance[a]	Total
1960	$1.6	$1.5	$3.1
1961	1.3	1.6	2.9
1962	1.5	1.9	3.4
1963	1.7	1.2	2.9
1964	1.9	0.7	2.6
1965	2.1	1.0	3.1
1966	2.5	1.1	3.6
1967	2.3	0.7	3.0
1968	2.9	−0.9	2.0
1969	3.1	−1.1	2.0
1970	3.0	−0.3	2.7

[a]After subtracting expenditures for fixed investment by life insurance sector.
SOURCE: Adapted from flow-of-funds data, Federal Reserve *Bulletin*, various issues.

Table 6.5. Financial Deficits in the Government
Sector, 1960–1970 (Billions of Dollars)[a]

Year	State and Local	Federal	Total
1960	$2.1	$(2.5)	$(0.4)
1961	3.0	4.8	7.8
1962	1.6	4.9	6.5
1963	1.2	0.6	1.8
1964	1.1	4.4	5.5
1965	2.4	0.2	2.6
1966	2.7	1.6	4.3
1967	5.5	13.8	19.4
1968	5.7	7.5	13.2
1969	5.3	(7.7)	(2.4)
1970	4.9	13.2	18.1

[a]Surpluses are expressed in parentheses.
SOURCE: Adapted from flow-of-funds data, Federal Reserve *Bulletin*, various issues.

Table 6.6 Financial Surpluses and Deficits in the Nonfinancial
Business Sector, 1960–1970 (Billions of Dollars)

Year	Total	Farm and Nonfarm Noncorporate	Nonfinancial Corporate
1960	$− 1.0	$ 0.3	$− 1.6
1961	− 0.3	−0.7	0.4
1962	0.6	−2.0	2.5
1963	0.7	−3.2	2.7
1964	− 2.6	−4.0	4.3
1965	− 4.5	−4.4	1.7
1966	− 7.4	−3.0	− 1.5
1967	−11.3	−4.2	− 3.2
1968	−11.4	−3.9	− 7.3
1969	−21.4	−4.3	−16.9
1970	−23.9	−3.1	−20.8

SOURCE: Adapted from flow-of-funds data, Federal Reserve *Bulletin*, various issues.

Finally, the rest-of-the-world sector was a net supplier of funds in 1970. Over the decade this has only been the case in the second half. The magnitude of the deficit or surplus has been quite small in any year and, because of the netting out of total flows, understates the influence the rest of the world has on American financial markets and vice versa. We shall elaborate on this aspect in the following chapter and in our discussion of monetary policy later in the book.

Balancing the Table. If we reexamine Table 6.2 we see that gross saving for all sectors should equal gross investment (real plus financial) by all sectors. While each sector may, on net, be a surplus or deficit unit, the economy as a whole should absorb all the savings in real capital formation and net financial investment.

Errors arise in the flow of funds accounts themselves, giving rise to discrepancies between the sum of saving and investment estimates for the sector. No significant attempt is made to reconcile these accounts with the national income and product accounts because of certain statistical and methodological differences in collecting the data for the two accounts. One goal of users of both sets of data is that these differences be reconciled so that the two forms of social accounting will be integrated in the future.

FINANCIAL TRANSACTIONS AMONG SECTORS

The flow of funds accounts are more than a statement of the sources and uses of saving by sector. They are also a fairly detailed statement of the types of financial assets and liabilities acquired by each sector during the period in question. Thus, the flow of funds data provide insights into the asset and liability preferences of members of the various sectors and permit some analysis of the financial transactions among sectors.

Table 6.7 is a condensation of the financial transactions data for 1970.

Reading the Table. While it may appear somewhat formidable, Table 6.7 is actually quite simple.

The rows of the table (1–23) relate to the financial instruments listed at the left of the table. Each row shows the net change during the year 1970 in the value of the particular financial instrument held by the particular sector shown in the columns.

The columns of Table 6.7 relate to sectors. Again we have consolidated the sectors into five major groups. Each sector is represented by a column. Each column has two parts, one designated S, the other U. The symbol S means sources of funds and indicates from which financial instrument funds were raised by that sector. It also indicates a change in a particular category of liability for that sector. The symbol U indicates uses of funds raised either through saving or through changes in holdings of financial assets. Changes in U indicate net additions or diminuations of particular categories of assets held by that sector.

It is important to remember that the assets of one sector are the liabili-

Table 6.7. Financial Transactions Among Sectors, 1970ᵃ (Billions of Dollars)

	Households		Business		Government		Financial		Rest of the World		Total	
	Uses	Sources	Uses	Sources	Uses	Sources	Uses	Sources	Uses	Sources	Uses	Sources
1. Net Financial Investment	$46.4	—	$-30.3	—	$-15.2	—	$1.5	—	$0.8	—	$3.2	—
2. Financial Uses	66.8		23.8		12.8		107.8		6.1		217.4	
3. Financial Sources		$20.4		$54.1		$28.1		$106.3		$5.4		$214.2
4. Claims on Financial Intermediaries												
5. Demand Deposits	3.3		1.1		3.4		0.9	8.9	0.3		9.0	9.0
6. Time and Savings Deposits	34.5		12.8		9.3		0.7	55.4	-1.9		55.4	55.4
7. Life Insurance and Pension Reserves	22.4					2.4		20.0			22.4	22.4
8. Fixed Income Securities												
9. U.S. Government	-5.3		1.7		-3.0	12.7	18.6	7.6			20.4	20.4
10. State and Local	-1.5		0.4		0.3	11.8	12.7				11.9	11.8
11. Corporate and Foreign Bonds	12.6	14.0		21.3	0.2		11.3	2.1	0.5	1.1	24.6	24.6
12. Mortgages	2.5			10.6	0.3		22.4	0.6			25.2	25.2
13. Loans												
14. Consumer Credit		4.3	1.9				2.5				4.4	4.3
15. Bank Loans (not elsewhere classified)		0.3		0.9			0.6	-0.2		-0.4	0.6	0.6
16. Other Loans		2.7	-2.0	6.9	2.9	0.4	10.1	-0.7	0.5	2.2	11.5	11.5
17. Security Credit	-0.6	-1.8					0.4	1.5	-0.2	-0.1	-0.4	-0.4
18. Variable Income Securities												
19. Corporate Shares	-1.1			6.7			10.3	3.2	0.7		9.9	9.9
20. Equity in Noncorporate Business	-2.3	0.6		-2.3							-2.3	-2.3
21. Trade Credit			6.9	7.1	-0.7	-0.4	0.4		1.0	0.7	7.6	8.0
22. Gold, SDRs, and Official Foreign Exchange					-2.0		-1.4		0.8	-2.5	-2.6	-2.5
23. Miscellaneous Claims	2.5	0.4	1.1	2.9	2.1	1.1	18.4	7.9	-4.0	4.4	20.1	16.7

ᵃTotals may not add due to rounding.
Source: Federal Reserve Bulletin, March 1971, p. A70.

ties of some other sector or sectors. This fact imposes an accounting rule on the table. If we add, along a row, the change in the holdings of a particular financial asset by all sectors, the total should equal the change in the total value of all sectors' liabilities in that form.

With this interpretation of the table in mind, we can consider what it tells us about the pattern of financial activity in the United States in 1970. We will also allude to differences that occurred in 1970 compared with preceding years.

Household Sector. In 1970 the household sector had another net financial surplus. The household's financial behavior pattern was different in 1970 from that of the preceding two years in particular. In 1968 and 1969, this sector had accumulated, on net, federal and state and local government securities. In 1970, they reduced their holdings of these securities as well as corporate shares and moved into corporate bonds, which were being issued that year with historically high coupon rates. Households also added significant amounts to time and savings accounts. However, the amount of net new consumer credit was less than half the amount of consumer credit extended to the household sector in 1969.

Leaving these matters aside, the important point to note is the dominant role of financial intermediaries in the financial transactions of households. In 1970, as in most years, claims on financial intermediaries accounted for the largest part (90 percent) of the total increase in households' financial assets. Mortgages and loans extended to this sector by financial intermediaries dominated the increase in households' liabilities.

Business Sector. When we examine the business sector and note that it ran a financial deficit in 1970, we see that it is not so dependent on financial intermediaries. Half of its increase in liabilities was raised through issues of corporate shares (row 19) and corporate bonds (row 11). Transactions with financial intermediaries, particularly in the form of loans and mortgages, are not negligible, but they are far from dominant. Business also depends on others in the same sector to help finance its operations. While trade credit extended was $6.9 billion, credit received by the business sector was $7.1 billion, down significantly from the 1969 figure of $19 billion. The most startling figure is the $0.9 billion increase in bank loans (row 15). This was an abnormally small increase in this form of business liability. The other unusual pattern in 1970 for the business sector was the buildup of time deposits, for a net increase of $12.8 billion (row 6) from the year-earlier figure. Much of this increase came in the third quarter of 1970, when business acknowledged the signs of an impending liquidity crisis and sought to replenish its liquid reserves.

Government Sector. The pattern of government financial activity is complex. In 1970 both the state and local governments and the federal government ran deficits. Both obtained additional funds primarily by issuing their own debt securities (rows 9 and 10). State and local governments liquidated some of their holding of U.S. government securities (row 9) and added $9.3 billion to their time deposits. In fact, the government sector's increase in assets was almost entirely through increasing its claims on financial intermediaries. Financial intermediaries played almost no role in assisting this sector to raise additional funds directly but purchased most of the government securities that were available.

Rest-of-the-World Sector. In 1968, 1969, and 1970 the rest-of-the-world sector had been a source of funds on net. These figures, however, do not indicate the magnitude of U.S. influence in foreign financial markets and capital formation abroad. Nor do they indicate the volume of funds that have been invested directly by foreigners in the United States or vice versa. They do indicate some of the financial areas of foreign involvement in the United States.

In 1970 the foreign sector raised an additional $1.1 billion by selling bonds in the United States (row 10). This represented 4 percent of the total net new funds raised through bonds by all sectors that year. The rest-of-the-world sector obtained $1.7 billion in new loans (rows 15, 16, and 17). This same sector bought $8.4 billion of U.S. government securities. This represented an accumulation by one sector of 40 percent of the total net additions of U.S. government securities issued in 1970. Most of these securities were purchased by foreign official agencies rather than foreign private citizens. It was about the only way in which surplus dollars that they had accumulated could be productively invested in income-earning assets. By the first quarter of 1971, this sector was buying U.S. government securities at an annual rate of $26 billion, thereby providing the federal government with large infusions of new funds.

This brief survey of the characteristics of financial flows has not explored the significance of the international connection of our financial markets nor that of financial intermediaries in as much depth as is necessary to improve your understanding. Given their quantitative importance in financial flows, these two areas will be examined in detail in the next five chapters.

SUMMARY

With certain exceptions, the primary purpose of borrowing by households, governments, and business is to finance the purchase or construction of durable real assets. The supply of financial assets coming from these sectors reflects two fundamental decisions by the deficit spending units: a decision on the amount to be borrowed and a decision on the types of financial instruments to be issued.

With the exception of the federal government sector, the supply of financial instruments is closely related to capital expenditures by each sector. The capital expenditure decision can be considered as a process of comparing the yield on real assets with the interest costs of borrowed funds, that is, with the expected yields on financial instruments. The higher the level of interest rates for any given level of expected yields on real assets, the less likely it is that any particular capital project will be undertaken. Thus, the supply of financial instruments from these sectors should be an inverse function of the level of interest rates.

Federal government borrowing, on the other hand, occurs when tax receipts fall short of expenditures. Thus, peacetime borrowing by the federal government is more closely related to the level of economic activity than to the level of federal government capital expenditures or the level of interest rates.

In deciding what types of financial instruments to issue, each deficit spending unit must choose among the alternatives. In general, borrowers tend to prefer to offer low-yielding instruments and to avoid short-term issues. The debtor issuing short-term instruments is faced with the risk of having to redeem these issues on short notice. If his specific real assets will only yield returns over a long period, this can cause severe financial difficulties. Risk avoidance would often encourage borrowers to try to issue variable income securities rather than fixed income securities.

The price of financial instruments determines the yield to asset holders and the cost of funds to borrowers. The yield should affect saving decisions and thus affect the share of income devoted to current consumption and the share available to finance capital formation. Interest costs should influence the willingness of borrowers to engage in deficit spending. Just as the change in yield on one type of financial instrument initiates adjustments in the composition of asset holders' portfolios and substitutions between real assets and financial assets, so too does a change in yield lead to changes in the types of financial instruments issued by borrowers to finance their current deficits.

Because financial instruments are more or less close substitutes for each other, the markets for various types of financial instruments cannot be considered separately. They are closely interconnected, so that a change in equilibrium conditions in one market will affect other markets. The federal government can alter the size of the outstanding stock of certain financial instruments and, as a result, alter the level of expenditures on consumer and capital goods. Monetary policy can then be conducted through manipulation of certain financial markets to regulate the level of aggregate demand for goods and services.

NOTE

1. J. V. Poapost and W. R. Walters, "Rates of Return on Consumer Durables," *Journal of Finance* 1, no. 4 (December 1964), 673–677.

ELEMENTARY THEORY OF FINANCIAL MARKETS

Part 4: International Aspects of Market Equilibrium

Now let us broaden our analysis and examine what effect, if any, the international connections between financial institutions (to which we alluded in Chapter 3) and financial markets have on the determination of equilibrium in American and foreign financial markets.

WIDENING THE FIELDS OF CHOICE

One obvious implication of the international connection is that it broadens the range of alternatives open to both asset holders and borrowers in the United States and abroad. American asset holders have the option of holding claims on foreigners as well as on American residents. They can purchase stocks and bonds of foreign corporations and governments almost as easily as those of American corporations and governments. Similarly, American borrowers have the option of borrowing in financial markets throughout the world, as well as in American financial markets.

The widening of the field of choice for American asset holders and debtors is important in itself. It should permit a much closer matching of asset holdings with asset preferences than would be possible with a narrower range of choice.

INTERNATIONAL YIELD DIFFERENTIALS
AND MARKET EQUILIBRIUM

Given our earlier conclusion that expected yield is a major consideration in the selection of assets to be included in a portfolio, and the parallel conclusion on the liability side that interest cost is an important consideration in the borrowing decisions, it follows, in the absence of restrictions on capital movements, that both American asset holders and American borrowers should turn to foreign markets when there is a significant yield advantage to be gained in doing so. Indeed, if expected yield were the only consideration in portfolio management, American asset holders would switch from American to foreign securities whenever the expected yield on foreign securities exceeded that obtainable on comparable American securities. Similarly, American borrowers would borrow in foreign markets if the interest cost of doing so were less than that involved in borrowing at home. Presumably, foreign asset holders and borrowers would behave in a similar fashion. Higher yields in the United States would lead foreign asset holders to purchase American securities, and lower yields in the United States would induce foreign borrowers to raise funds in the American market.

Behavior of this sort by American and foreign asset holders and borrowers will tend to equalize yields on comparable securities in world markets. If foreign yields, for example, were relatively high, the combination of American asset holders purchasing foreign securities and foreigners borrowing here should depress yields abroad and raise yields in the United States. In this manner, American and foreign yields should be drawn together. Any departure of yields from equality should induce a shift of demand or supply between the markets, tending to reestablish equality.

The United States as Capital Exporter. The United States has been a net supplier of private and government long-term capital and grants to the rest of the world in every year since the end of World War II. Much of this capital has been in the form of *direct investment*, that is, the purchase of physical assets, real estate, and businesses abroad. Most significant has been the purchase by American firms of corporate branches and subsidiaries abroad. It is beyond the scope of this book to investigate the underlying "real" economic reasons for this type of investment. It is worthwhile to note that in 1971 the book value of American direct investments abroad amounted to $86 billion, or almost two-thirds of the total of privately held claims against foreigners.[1]

The effect of this volume of direct investment abroad by Americans on foreign and domestic financial markets is difficult to assess. In large measure, these funds have bypassed financial markets. Undoubtedly the accumulation of additional real (although foreign) assets has reduced the volume of funds available for purchasing real assets here and financial assets here and abroad. In the absence of this alternative, we could assume that American residents

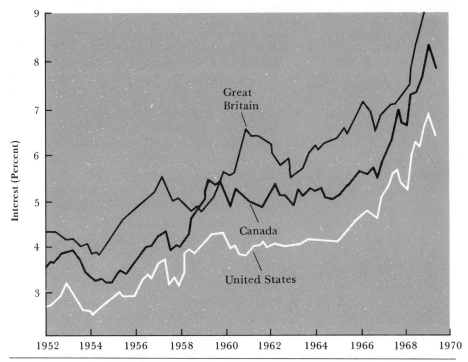

Figure 7.1 **Quarterly Yields on U.S., Canadian, and British Long-Term Federal Government Securities**
SOURCE: Federal Reserve *Bulletin*, various issues.

and corporations would have accumulated other forms of real assets or would have tried to accumulate additional financial assets. If these funds were channeled only into American financial markets, interest rates would have been pushed lower. However, the same volume of funds channeled through foreign financial markets would have had a greater effect on interest rates there because the volume of securities available in separate foreign financial markets is much smaller than in the United States.

In the period from 1960 through 1971, Americans invested directly $35 billion abroad. Income earned abroad on direct investments and returned to the United States in the form of cash assets, dividends, and interest amounted to more than $9 billion in 1971 alone.[2] Nonetheless, the federal government has tried to curb direct investment abroad and in 1965 imposed voluntary controls, which were made mandatory in 1968.

American residents have also supplied funds to long-term foreign borrowers on a large scale. Interest rates on long-term issues have generally been lower here than rates on comparable issues abroad. (See Figure 7.1.) The incentive to borrow at lower interest costs attracted foreign borrowers to

American financial markets. Bonds denominated in dollars were sold in American financial markets by foreign corporations and governments. The borrowers offered a slightly higher yield than similar American issues were bringing. In addition, the foreign borrowers assumed the risk that is peculiar to international transactions, the risk that the exchange rate would change in the course of the debt claim.[3]

Despite the risk of changing exchange rates and the need to pay a premium rate above the interest rate on competing American bond issues, the generally lower interest rate levels prevailing in the United States still attracted foreign borrowers until the U.S. government curtailed foreign borrowing in American financial markets in the early 1960s. In 1964, the government imposed the Interest Equalization Tax on the interest premium foreign borrowers were paying American asset holders above comparable yields on competing American securities. The tax did not apply to Canadian issues, nor to securities issued by developing countries.

If foreign borrowers are raising funds in American financial markets, then yields on these securities are tied directly to yields on comparable issues in the same markets here. However, if we wish to examine the pattern of long-term interest rates on securities issued in separate markets, assuming that capital funds can flow freely across boundaries, then we should look at similar issues denominated in the currency of the issuer. If foreign and American securities were perfect substitutes for each other in the minds of foreign and American asset holders, and hence if relative yields were the only basis for choosing among these securities, then by the process we described earlier the yields on foreign and American securities would tend to be equal.

SOME EVIDENCE: LONG-TERM GOVERNMENT BOND YIELDS

We have chosen for comparison long-term bonds issued by the Canadian government, the British government, and the U.S. government. In Figure 7.1 we have plotted the yields on these securities for the period 1952–1970. The evidence provided by Figure 7.1 is interesting. It shows quite clearly that while yields on these securities tend to move up and down together, they are far from equal to each other. In the period in question yields on long-term Canadian government bonds tended to remain roughly 25 percent higher than yields on U.S. government bonds. Yields on long-term British government bonds over the same period were as much as 50 percent higher than those on U.S. government bonds. While the yields on these securities are obviously closely related to each other, apparently the equilibrium relationship is not one of equality. The differential is too persistent for this to be the case. How can we explain this?

Comparability. Are these long-term bonds comparable? Undoubtedly, in the minds of asset holders these securities are not perfect substitutes for each other, although maturity and issuer are similar. In the minds of Amer-

147

ican asset holders there is a greater degree of credit risk in holding foreign government securities. In long-term issues there is some apparent risk of default that is not present in holding long-term U.S. government securities. American asset holders may fear that foreign issues will not be as marketable in foreign financial markets as they know U.S. government securities are here. As risk avoiders, American asset holders would require some premium yield in order to compensate for this additional risk.

These are some of the influences that should explain the higher equilibrium rates of interest that comparable foreign securities exhibit. Another part of the explanation lies in the existence of a type of risk that we have not yet discussed but to which we have alluded. This is a risk peculiar to international transactions. It arises because two different currencies are involved in either commercial or financial transactions across national boundaries—the currency of the buyer or lender and that of the seller or borrower. Because the rate of exchange between the two currencies (or the price of one currency in terms of the other) is not absolutely fixed, it may change during the life of the financial instrument or trade contract. The effect of a change in the rate of exchange affects the expected profitability of the investment and introduces another risk, which we call the *foreign exchange risk*.

Foreign exchange risk exists whenever an asset holder owns a financial instrument calling for fixed future payments in a foreign money or whenever a debtor has an obligation to make fixed future payments in a foreign money. The risk is that on the payment date the foreign exchange rate will be such that the fixed sum of foreign money to be received or paid will amount to a different sum of domestic money than was initially expected.

To understand the nature of foreign exchange risk it is necessary first to discuss foreign exchange, its nature, market, and price.

Foreign Exchange. Foreign exchange is important in any trade or financial activity beyond our boundaries. To simplify, we can say that the goods and services we sell to others (exports) provide us with the means (foreign moneys or exchange) to buy goods and services from abroad that we want (imports). Foreign exchange is thus obtained whenever American companies sell their goods abroad or when American borrowers obtain funds in foreign markets in exchange for financial claims on themselves. Foreign exchange is used to buy goods from other countries and when American asset holders obtain foreign financial claims (or lend money to foreign borrowers).

Foreign Exchange Market. As far as most Americans are concerned, since foreign moneys are not acceptable within the United States as a medium of exchange, they are just so many other financial instruments. Foreign exchange, like other financial instruments, is traded in a market. Foreign exchange markets exist in most leading financial centers in countries actively involved in trade. It is not necessary here to describe the organization and institutional arrangements of the foreign exchange market in the

148

Table 7.1. Foreign Exchange Rates, Selected
Countries, as of November 2, 1973

Country	Dollar Price of 1 Unit
Great Britain (Pound)	$2.4358
Canada (Dollar)	1.0048
Belgium (Franc)	0.027275
Switzerland (Franc)	0.3258
West Germany (Deutschmark)	0.4095
Mexico (Peso)	0.0801
Japan (Yen)	0.003675
Sweden (Krona)	0.2398

SOURCE: Wall Street Journal, November 6, 1973, p. 28.

United States. Suffice it to say that buyers of foreign exchange (i.e., businesses, investment houses, commercial banks, etc.) needing to make payments abroad and sellers of foreign exchange determine through their interaction a price at which dollars will be exchanged for the currency desired.

Foreign Exchange Rate. The prices established in the foreign exchange market by the buyers and sellers are called foreign exchange rates. Since we are discussing the international aspects from the American viewpoint, to us the *foreign exchange rate is the dollar price of one unit of foreign money.* There are as many rates at any one time as there are foreign moneys. Some recent exchange rates are listed in Table 7.1.

If we were writing from the German, British, Canadian, or Japanese viewpoint, the foreign exchange rate would be the number of deutschmarks it takes to buy one dollar (or the amount of Canadian dollars, English pounds, or Japanese yen). Mathematically, these prices are reciprocals of the American dollar price of one unit of their money.

These rates are termed *spot exchange rates.* They may best be described as today's price for today's foreign money. Through the interaction of buyers and sellers in the foreign exchange markets, spot exchange rates for dozens of national currencies are established each day. Since there is not a single one foreign exchange market for all currency transactions but rather a group of markets in leading international financial centers, the possibility exists that the spot exchange rate for francs in London, for example, may differ from the spot rate quoted for francs in New York. Astute foreign exchange traders will simultaneously buy foreign exchange in one market and sell it in the other in order to profit from the differences in the two rates. As a result of this type of *arbitrage,* exchange rates tend to be equal in different markets.

Forward Exchange. At any time there may be several prices in the foreign exchange market for the same foreign money, depending on the time of delivery. Whereas spot exchange involves immediate delivery, forward exchange involves delivery on some specified future date. A forward exchange contract is an agreement calling for the purchase or sale of a specified amount

Table 7.2. Currency Futures, November 2, 1973 (from International Monetary Market of Chicago Mercantile Exchange)

Country	Date	Dollar Price of 1 Unit
Great Britain (Pound)	December 1973	$2.424
	March 1974	2.399
Canada (Dollar)	No Sales	
West Germany (Deutschmark)	December 1973	0.409
	March 1974	0.4091
	June 1974	0.4096
	September 1974	0.412
Switzerland (Franc)	December 1973	0.3266
	March 1974	0.3275
	June 1974	0.3289
	September 1974	0.3296

SOURCE: Wall Street Journal, November 6, 1973, p. 28.

of foreign money on a specified future date at a price agreed upon at the time the contract is signed, regardless of the actual spot exchange rate prevailing in the market on that future date.

Contracts are usually confined to periods of 180 days or less. On a given day the foreign exchange market will give quotes on a set of forward exchange rates, that is, rates at which contracts can be negotiated for the purchase or sale of forward exchange 30 days, 60 days, 90 days, and so on, in the future.

A few examples of forward exchange quotations are given in Table 7.2.

By means of forward exchange contracts, firms can fix the exchange rate today at which the transaction will occur when there is a lag between the time the agreement for delivery of goods is signed and the time payment is to be made. A forward exchange contract serves to eliminate the foreign exchange risk for that transaction. Otherwise, a rise in the spot exchange rate would increase the cost of goods and services to the importer, and a fall in the spot exchange rate would reduce the returns from the sale of goods and services to the exporter.

Foreign exchange risk exists because spot exchange rates can vary over a given period. The degree to which spot exchange rates can vary is limited. Under the Bretton Woods Agreement of 1944, which helped establish an international monetary system, the degree to which the forces of supply and demand were permitted to operate on exchange rates was constrained. Fluctuations in exchange rates vis-à-vis the dollar were confined to a narrow band on either side of the officially designated par rate of exchange.

Recent experience has shown, however, that official exchange rate agreements are not sacred. From time to time official par rates of exchange have been altered. The French devalued the franc by 11 percent in 1969; the Germans appreciated the deutschmark by 9 percent in the same year. The

British devalued the pound by somewhat more than 14 percent in 1967. These were abrupt, major changes in the existing exchange rate structure.

At times countries have abandoned support of their currency at official par rates of exchange and permitted their currency to "float," that is, to find an equilibrium rate of exchange through the interaction of the private forces in the exchange markets. In 1970 Canada floated its dollar. In early 1971 Germany for a time permitted the mark to float. In August 1971 the United States ceased to redeem in gold any dollar liabilities and ended its informal intervention in foreign exchange markets on behalf of maintaining fixed rates of exchange with the dollar. These actions set free the exchange rates of major foreign currencies vis-à-vis the dollar. New pegged rates of exchange were reestablished by several of the industrialized countries, including the United States, at the end of 1971; but in late 1972 and 1973 several countries floated their currencies again, and the United States devalued the dollar.

MAJOR FLUCTUATIONS VS. MINOR ADJUSTMENTS

Changes in official par exchange rates are dramatic events. In part, the foreign exchange risk referred to earlier is that of a major change. Expected yields on financial assets are wiped out overnight. For example, if you had bought a British government bond in October 1967 for £100, or the equivalent of $280, and held it for a month, by the end of November 1967, if the bond could still be sold for £100, you would have received the equivalent of $240. Your wealth was reduced simply as a result of a change in the exchange rate.

Aside from the foreign exchange risk due to possible major exchange rate adjustments, foreign exchange risk exists when spot exchange rates can fluctuate even within the narrow bands agreed to under the Bretton Woods rules. This foreign exchange risk can have serious consequences for short-term investments in particular. This is the risk of small fluctuations of the exchange rate from day-to-day or week-to-week around the official par rate of exchange but within the prescribed limits. A drop in the exchange rate of as much as 1 percent can be catastrophic to the holder of 30-day or 90-day notes denominated in foreign currency.

We will not explore the mathematics of this proposition here, but perhaps an example will help clarify the point. For this purpose, consider the data set out as Example 7.1, in which we have assumed that on a particular day the yield on 91-day U.S. Treasury bills was 4 percent and on comparable 90-day British Treasury bills was 5 percent. If yield were the only consideration, an American asset holder would purchase the British bill in preference to the U.S. Treasury bill and obtain a yield that was 25 percent greater.

However, as Example 7.1 makes clear, this yield advantage will hold only if, as in Case 1, the spot exchange rate 90 days later is the same as on the

EXAMPLE 7.1   The Foreign Exchange Risk on Short-Term Foreign Investments

1. Assume the following British pound price of 90-day British government
   bill, yielding 5 percent per annum, par value £1000 (Table 5A.1)   £988
2. Spot exchange rate $2.40
3. U.S. dollar price of British Treasury bill [(1) × (2)] $2371

Case 1   *Spot exchange rate remains constant at $2.40*
4. Return at the end of 90 days (£1000 × $2.40) $2400
5. Gross gain [(4) − (3)] $29
         or: 1.2% for 90 days   = 4.8% per annum
6. Yield on 91-day U.S. Treasury bill   = 4.0% per annum
7. Net gain [(5) − (6)]   0.8% per annum

Case 2   *Spot exchange rate falls by 0.25% in 90 days, to $2.394*
8. Return at the end of 90 days (£1000 × $2.394) $2394
9. Gross gain [(8) − (3)] $23
         or: 1.0% for 90 days   = 4.0% per annum
10. Yield on U.S. Treasury bill   = 4.0% per annum
11. Net gain [(9) − (10)]   0% per annum

Case 3   *Spot exchange rate falls by 1.25% in 90 days, to $2.37*
12. Return at the end of 90 days (£1000 × $2.370) $2370
13. Gross gain [(12) − (3)] $−1
          or: 0% for 90 days   = 0% per annum
14. Yield on U.S. Treasury bill   = 4% per annum
15. Net loss [(13) − (14)]   −4% per annum

Case 4   *Spot exchange rate rises by 1.25% in 90 days, to $2.43*
16. Return at the end of 90 days (£1000 × $2.43) $2430
17. Gross gain [(16) − (3)] $51
          or: 2.1% for 90 days   = 8.4% per annum
18. Yield on U.S. Treasury bill   = 4.0% per annum
19. Net gain [(17) − (18)]   4.4% per annum

day the asset holder purchased the British bill. The yield advantage in investing in British Treasury bills is wiped out if the spot exchange rate falls
by one-fourth of 1 percent (Case 2). If, as in Case 3, the spot exchange rate
falls by as much as 1¼ percent, the asset holder buying British bills experiences a loss. On the other hand, if the spot exchange rate rises (Case 4),
additional gains accrue to the asset holder.

If we were talking about a 30-day security rather than a 90-day security,
the respective changes in the spot exchange rate could be even smaller to
wipe out anticipated yields. A drop of less than one-tenth of 1 percent would
eliminate the yield advantage, and a drop of four-tenths of 1 percent would
produce a negative yield. Thus, for short-term investments the consequences
of very small changes in spot exchange rates can be very great.

To the American holder of a foreign financial asset, the serious risk is
that the foreign exchange rate will fall. The fixed sum of foreign money he
will receive as interest and principal on his foreign asset will produce fewer

American dollars than expected, and the yield on the asset will be correspondingly less than expected. By contrast, to the American borrower the risk is that the exchange rate will rise. If this occurs, the fixed future payments of foreign money that he is obligated to make will cost him more American dollars than expected, and the actual interest cost of the loan will be correspondingly greater than expected. The investor, as distinct from the speculator, would try to reduce this foreign exchange risk in order to secure the expected rate of return.

FOREIGN EXCHANGE RISK AND MARKET EQUILIBRIUM

We have now seen how major fluctuations in exchange rates can wipe out gains on long-term and short-term securities denominated in a foreign currency. We have also examined the nature of the foreign exchange risk resulting from minor exchange rate fluctuations and the effect it has on anticipated gains on short-term investments. In the past American asset holders have supplied long-term capital funds to foreign borrowers primarily by acquiring dollar-denominated claims. In this way the foreign exchange risk has been borne more often by foreign borrowers than by American lenders.

Assuming that asset holders are risk avoiders, they would demand a higher yield before taking a relatively riskier security into their portfolios. Since American asset holders can supply the largest volume of long-term funds by comparison with any other single market, the long-term rates prevailing in other countries must necessarily be linked to American rates. If foreign borrowers want American asset holders to hold assets denominated in a foreign currency, then the yields on these assets must be high enough to compensate American asset holders for all risks, including foreign exchange risk.

Returning to Figure 7.1, we note the stable and relatively persistent divergence in long-term yields. It is said that other countries pay a premium to attract American funds, that they deliberately maintain high interest rates in order to persuade Americans to purchase their securities.

Are there techniques available for avoiding foreign exchange risk? Are they applicable to both long-term and short-term investments? The basic principle is called *hedging* and is quite straightforward. It simply involves the assumption of one risk to offset an equal and opposite risk.

To commercial traders, hedging is commonplace. An importer with a foreign currency liability to pay in the future runs the risk that the price of that currency will have increased by the time the liability falls due. He can enter a forward exchange contract with an intermediary today, agreeing to buy foreign currency in 90 days and to sell dollars at a price specified today. The importer has offset his foreign currency liability with a foreign currency asset of equal magnitude.

153

Covered Foreign Investments. International investors also seek ways of eliminating foreign exchange risk. We saw in Example 7.1 how even small fluctuations in the spot rate could not only eliminate the underlying yield advantage to investing in British bills but also turn a potential gain into an actual loss. An American asset holder can "cover" his investment in a foreign currency asset through the use of a forward exchange contract. For example, he wants to buy the British Treasury bill due in 90 days (Example 7.1) today. He buys the necessary £1000 today at the prevailing spot exchange rate, $2.40. If, at the same time, he enters into a forward exchange contract with an intermediary and agrees to sell the £1000 he will receive in 90 days for dollars at the forward exchange rate agreed upon now, the asset holder will have "covered" any potential foreign exchange risk. This technique is used mostly for short-term investments.

Note carefully that two foreign exchange transactions are involved. The American simultaneously purchased foreign exchange spot and sold foreign exchange forward. Such a pairing of spot and forward exchange transactions is commonly called a swap.

A covered foreign investment is one with no foreign exchange risk. Now the question is, Can such an investment be profitable? Obviously this depends not only on the level of yields between the two countries but also on the relationship between the forward and spot exchange rates.

The Yield on Covered Foreign Investments. Assume that funds invested in British bills are returned to the United States at the forward exchange rate prevailing now, at the time of purchase, rather than at the spot rate of exchange prevailing in 90 days. This makes the forward exchange rate a crucial factor in the decision regarding short-term investment. If the forward exchange rate is equal to the spot exchange rate, the asset holder will go ahead and purchase the British bill to take account of the 0.8 percent yield differential (Example 7.1, Case 1). If the forward exchange rate is as much as 0.25 percent lower than the spot exchange rate today (similar to Example 7.1, Case 2) the asset holder knows today that there is not going to be any additional gain from purchasing the British bill and covering his investment rather than buying the U.S. Treasury bill. If the forward exchange rate is above the spot exchange rate today (similar to Case 4) by as much as 1.25 percent, we see that the yield on a covered investment in British bills is more than double what it would be if the asset holder had bought U.S. Treasury bills. Funds should flow out of the market for U.S. Treasury bills and into the market for British bills. This movement in itself will have a depressing effect on short-term British interest rates and will push short-term U.S. Treasury bill rates slightly higher. There will also be an effect on the spot and forward exchange rates as more American asset holders buy pounds spot, raising the spot rate, and sell pounds forward, putting downward pressure on the forward exchange rate, thus reducing the 1.25 percent differential that had existed between the two rates.

If the forward exchange rate is significantly higher than the spot exchange rate, covered investments in foreign securities with even lower nominal or "raw" yields than prevail on comparable American securities may become profitable.

Determination of the Forward Exchange Rate: The Interest Parity Theory. We have skirted the question of how the forward exchange rate is set. Given the importance this rate has assumed in our analysis, we must now face this issue head-on.

Obviously, the forward exchange rate is a price; however, it is a rather unusual price, since it is negotiated now for a transaction that will occur sometime in the future. As a price it is determined by the interaction of the forces of supply and demand in the market.

We have already identified two major classes of demand and supply, what we might call on the one hand commercial demand and supply and on the other hand asset holder demand and supply (later we will have occasion to note the possibility of a speculative demand and supply as well). We have already identified commercial traders as the regular participants in the forward exchange market. The demand for forward exchange from this group is related to the flow of American imports, since it results from attempts by importers to fix the foreign exchange rate on future payments for imports that they are contracting to purchase today. Either because the level of the exchange rate will affect the demand for imports or because at relatively high forward exchange rates the importer may elect to "take the risk," we expect that this demand curve will slope downward and to the right. That is, the higher the forward exchange rate, the smaller the quantity of forward exchange that will be demanded for commercial reasons.

The commercial supply of forward exchange must be closely related to the flow of exports, since it reflects the attempts of exporters to fix the exchange rate on payments they expect to receive in the future for exports they are contracting to sell today. We would expect this supply curve to rise to the right, like a normal supply curve. In part this reflects the fact that exports will be more profitable at higher exchange rates (and hence more will be offered for sale), and in part it is due to the fact that at relatively low forward exchange rates the exporter may be inclined to "take the risk" of not selling his foreign exchange earnings in the forward market.

We thus expect that commercial demand and supply in the forward exchange market can be described by curves of the "normal" shape, but asset holders' demands and supplies are a different story. There is a critical level of the forward exchange rate above which it is profitable for American asset holders to rearrange their portfolios, selling short-term U.S. securities and acquiring fully covered foreign securities of similar maturity. Since this can be done without altering the riskiness or liquidity of their portfolios, asset holders should be prepared to move very substantial sums of money across national boundaries in response to such a yield incentive.

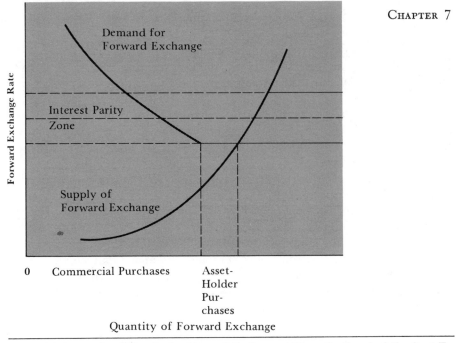

Figure 7.2 **Demand and Supply for Forward Exchange** (Given the Level of the Spot Exchange Rate and Short-Term Security Yields in Canada and the United States)

All such transactions create a supply of forward exchange, since American asset holders, for example, will be selling foreign moneys forward. At this point—determined by the level of the spot exchange rate and the difference between yields on short-term securities in the two markets—the supply curve for forward exchange should become virtually perfectly elastic. A small rise in the forward exchange rate above this point should induce large-scale readjustments in portfolios and hence large-scale supplies of forward exchange.

The asset holder demand curve for forward exchange is depicted in Figure 7.2 as having the shape normally associated with a demand curve through most of its length. However, it is shown as becoming perfectly elastic at some point and thus establishing a lower limit for the forward exchange rate. Similarly, the supply of forward exchange is depicted as having the shape normally associated with a supply curve through most of its length but becoming perfectly elastic at some point and thus establishing an upper limit for the forward exchange rate. It is perhaps paradoxical that, while the bulk of the transactions in the market are "commercial" transactions, the forward exchange rate will in effect be set by the possibly small flow of transactions on "asset holder" account. Regardless of the balance of supply and demand pressures in the forward market resulting from normal commercial transactions, the reactions of foreign and American asset holders should hold the forward exchange rate within narrow limits—limits that are

156

set by the level of short-term security yields in the two countries. The forward exchange rate is free to fluctuate, but only within these limits.

The range between the upper and the lower limits of the forward exchange rate might be called the *interest parity zone*. This range reflects the fact that asset holders incur costs in adjusting their portfolios and in buying or selling forward exchange. In part these are brokerage costs in the respective short-term money markets, and in part they constitute the "fee" that the bank charges for its services in the form of a spread between the buying price and the selling price for forward exchange (the bank sells forward exchange at a higher price than that at which it will buy it). In many expositions of the theory of forward exchange these transaction costs are neglected. As a result, the interest parity theory is presented as though it determined a precise forward exchange rate rather than upper and lower limits to the rate. If we made this assumption, the interest parity rate would be the midpoint of the interval. It is marked with a dotted line on Figure 7.2.

Impact on Financial Markets. Although some governments have been moderately successful in curbing direct investment in their countries and abroad and in imposing formal restrictions on holding foreign currency at different times, the buying and selling of short-term international assets is more difficult to impede. Short-term capital moves easily between international financial markets in response to interest rate differentials and expected exchange rate adjustments.

Commercial banks in the United States borrowed heavily in the Eurodollar market in 1969, when domestic sources of short-term funds had become scarce and domestic short-term rates were historically high. Since they were borrowing dollars, the commercial banks assumed no foreign exchange risk. Other American residents borrow in foreign currencies, but this type of borrowing is very limited. Multinational corporations borrow in several financial markets abroad and in several currencies. At the same time they try to insure themselves against the inherent foreign exchange risk or to profit from correct anticipation of exchange rate fluctuations.

Movement of short-term funds out of American securities and into foreign securities undoubtedly has a greater effect on markets and interest rates abroad than in the United States. This is the case because the volume and value of marketable financial assets in the United States is staggering. In 1970 it was estimated by the Federal Reserve that the market value of corporate stock held by Americans was over $900 billion. Sales of common stock on registered exchanges alone that year amounted to $130 billion. The value of short-term U.S. government securities outstanding is about $95 billion. If a small percentage of the funds invested in short-term money market instruments in the United States were shifted abroad, there would be little effect on the short-term interest rate structure here because of the enormous size, depth, and liquidity of the money market. The effect on international yields would be more significant, since the foreign financial markets are smaller and less integrated. It is therefore more likely that world market yields on comparable securities will be drawn to yields in the United States.

Thus, world market rates are linked to the prevailing rates on comparable securities in the United States. However, money market rates abroad are closely linked to each other. Since 1958, major European currencies have been convertible into each other. Foreign financial markets have developed rapidly since that time, and today short-term money flows easily across national boundaries, keeping interest rates in separate markets closely tied to each other.

Significance of the Forward Exchange Market for Equilibrium in the Financial Markets. Having explored the mechanics of forward exchange and of covered short-term foreign investments, we must ask the significance of all of this for the things in which we are interested and particularly for the determination of equilibrium in financial markets.

We had noted that as long as asset holders and borrowers are free to deal in either domestic or foreign financial markets, there should be a tendency for yields on comparable securities in separate markets to be pulled toward each other. However, because of the volume of funds the United States can make available for investment in foreign financial markets without significantly affecting the domestic markets, interest rates abroad tend to be pulled toward those prevailing in the United States. On long-term investments we noted that there is a persistent and relatively stable differential between security yields in Canada and Britain and those in the United States. We also noted that American holders of long-term claims against foreigners tended to hold more dollar-denominated claims, forcing the foreign borrowers to bear the foreign exchange risk. We also noted that covering investments and eliminating foreign exchange risk is used primarily for short-term investments.

On short-term investments American asset holders can move easily into foreign currency assets as well as dollar-denominated deposits abroad. However, we have now asserted that the forward exchange market provides an opportunity for asset holders to eliminate the foreign exchange risk on short-term investments. Thus, as far as an American asset holder is concerned, a covered investment in a British or Canadian Treasury bill, for example, should be, in all relevant respects, the same as an investment in a U.S. Treasury bill. In no case is there any foreign exchange risk. Moreover, they have the same term of maturity and thus have essentially the same degree of liquidity. They should be perfect substitutes for each other, and therefore forces in the marketplace should dictate that the yields on the instruments will be driven to equality with each other in equilibrium.

Note, however, that the yield relevant to this discussion is the foreign treasury bill yield adjusted for the cost or gain on forward exchange contracts (i.e., adjusted for the difference between the forward rate and the spot exchange rate). It is this adjusted yield that will be equated to the U.S. Treasury bill yield by market forces. Except in the case where the forward exchange rate and the spot exchange rate are equal, there is no reason why the "raw" yields on Treasury bills in two separate markets will be equal. Indeed, we can say that the forward exchange market drives a wedge between yields in the short-term securities markets abroad and in the United States. In principle, this wedge should permit the "raw" yields to move independently of each other, with the forward exchange rate adjusting to keep the "adjusted" yields equal to each other. If we allow for transactions costs, of course, perfect equality cannot be expected. Rather, as Figure 7.2 shows, fluctuations in the adjusted yields should be confined to relatively narrow limits.

Some Evidence: Canadian–U.S. Treasury Bill Yield Differentials and British–U.S. Treasury Bill Yield Differentials. Do these theoretical conclusions bear any relationship to the facts? Some evidence is presented in Figures 7.3 and 7.4, in which we have plotted the raw differential in yields on Canadian and U.S. Treasury bills and that differential adjusted for the difference between the forward and spot exchange rates. We have plotted similar data for yields on British Treasury and U.S. Treasury bills in Figure 7.4. In the lower sections we have also plotted the differential between the spot and forward exchange rates expressed in percent per annum.

Several conclusions seem to stand out from an examination of the charts:

1. The "raw" differential between yields on Canadian and U.S. Treasury bills and between those on British and U.S. Treasury bills has fluctuated over a relatively wide range in recent years.

2. In Figure 7.3 the fluctuations in the differential between the 90-day forward exchange rate and the spot exchange rate almost inversely parallels fluctuations in the raw yield differential on U.S. and Canadian securities.

    Although it is quite clear that the correlation between these two series shown in Figure 7.3 is less than perfect, a strong association is very evident. Remember that when the yield on Canadian Treasury bills is substantially above that on U.S. Treasury bills, American asset holders will attempt to buy Canadian securities. To cover the foreign exchange risk, they will sell Canadian dollars in the forward market. As a result, the forward exchange rate will be driven down to a deeper discount relative to the spot exchange rate, thus eliminating the advantage to Americans of investing in Canada on a covered (or riskless) basis.

3. As a result, fluctuations in covered yield differentials were generally confined to a much narrower range than fluctuations in the "raw" differentials.

    This is what the interest parity or interest arbitrage theory would

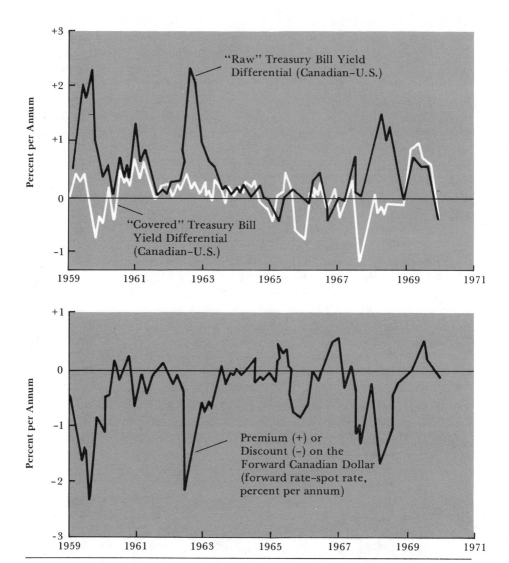

Figure 7.3 **Foreign Exchange Rates and the Yield on Foreign Investment: Canadian–U.S.**
SOURCE: Federal Reserve *Bulletin*, various issues.

predict. However, there were several occasions when fluctuations in the covered yield differential between Canadian and U.S. bills were outside the range that would seem reasonable under this theory. The winter of 1965–1966, the autumn of 1967, and mid-1969 are three obvious cases in point.

Similar conclusions apply to the data presented in Figure 7.4. Fluctuations in the "raw" Treasury bill differential on British and

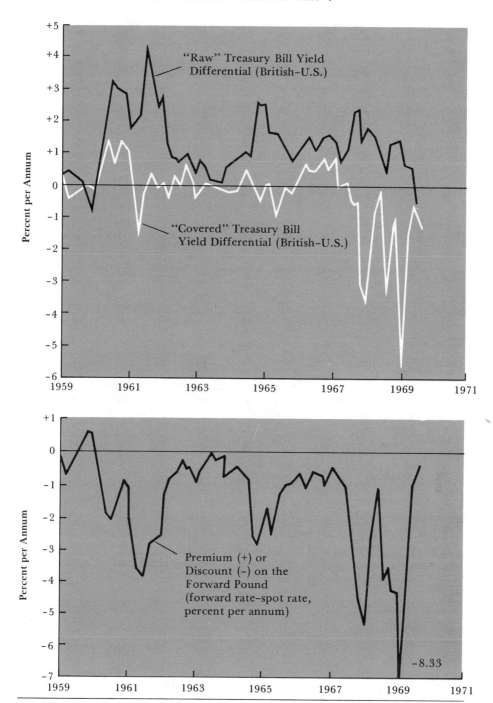

Figure 7.4 **Foreign Exchange Rates and the Yield on Foreign Investment:** British–U.S.
SOURCE: Federal Reserve *Bulletin*, various issues.

U.S. securities have been of greater magnitude than those between Canadian and U.S. securities. There have been wider fluctuations in short-term differentials than between the long-term British and American securities presented in Figure 7.1.

4. Fluctuations in the differential between 90-day forward and spot exchange rates also almost inversely parallel fluctuations in the "raw" Treasury bill differentials until 1968 and 1969. The covered Treasury bill differential between British and U.S. Treasury bills was also confined to a narrow range until 1968.

This evidence also supports the interest arbitrage theory. What, however, accounts for the divergence in 1968 and 1969? In November 1967 the British devalued the pound. International foreign exchange markets remained under speculative pressure in anticipation of devaluation of the dollar. The establishment of the two-tier gold market in March 1968 helped diffuse some of this speculative pressure, but the exchange value of the German mark and the French franc remained out of line. In 1969 the franc was devalued and the mark was revalued. The fluctuations in the difference between the pound forward exchange rate and the the spot exchange rate illustrated in the lower section of Figure 7.4 reflect the unsettled state of foreign exchange markets at that time.

The evidence presented in Figures 7.3 and 7.4 seems to suggest that the interest arbitrage theory of forward exchange rates is substantially correct. However, it cannot explain all of the significant developments in the forward exchange market. We may assume that in stable markets the interest arbitrage theory holds.

At other times, however, American asset holders are apparently less sensitive to risk-free international yield differentials than this theory assumes. In drawing Figure 7.2 we assumed that both the demand and the supply curves in the forward exchange market would become perfectly elastic at some point. Apparently this is not a valid assumption under all circumstances.

OTHER FACTORS IN FOREIGN INVESTMENT: PORTFOLIO DIVERSIFICATION AND SPECULATION

Our analysis of international investment transactions suggests that asset holders will purchase foreign securities when the expected yield on those securities is sufficiently higher than the expected yield on comparable American securities to compensate for the additional (foreign exchange) risk of having foreign securities in the portfolio. In the special case of short-term securities, this risk can be avoided through a forward exchange contract, but for such covered investments to be worthwhile the forward exchange rate has to be outside a particular limit. However, these two propositions are insufficient to explain all international transactions in financial instruments. There are at least two other considerations that we have not yet taken into account: portfolio diversification and speculation on the forward exchange rate.

PORTFOLIO DIVERSIFICATION

In Chapter 5, in our discussion of the economics of selecting a portfolio of assets, we noted that in general a diversified portfolio is less risky than a portfolio containing a single asset, a point that will be considered further in Chapter 8. This same motive may lead many asset holders to include some foreign currency assets in their portfolios.

SPECULATION

It should also be obvious that speculation on changes in the exchange rate may provide a strong inducement to some asset holders to buy or sell foreign currency assets from time to time. Thus, anticipations of a rise in the exchange rate will induce purchases of foreign currency assets—including speculative purchases of forward exchange. Correspondingly, anticipations of a drop in the foreign exchange rate will induce sales of foreign currency assets—including speculative sales of forward exchange. Widespread anticipation of a major devaluation can bring forth very large speculative pressures. However, there is also considerable scope for profitable speculation on changes in the exchange rate within the permissible limits around the official par rate of exchange.

SUMMARY

We have now completed a long but far from exhaustive discussion of some of the factors affecting international transactions in financial instruments. What is the upshot of this analysis?

You will recall that by "equilibrium in the financial markets" we mean a situation in which there is a set of yields on financial instruments at which there exists neither excess demand nor excess supply in the markets. In our discussion of equilibrium we emphasized the importance of including both stock and flow concepts of supply and demand in the analysis. It should be apparent from what we have just said about international capital flows that there is another dimension to equilibrium as well. Full equilibrium calls for a set of yields on financial instruments for which there is neither excess demand nor excess supply in the market, taking into account demand and supply from both domestic and international sources.

That is not to say that equilibrium is incompatible with international capital flows. It is the demand and supply from domestic and international sources combined that is relevant, which means that, in equilibrium, yields on foreign securities will be strongly influenced by yields on securities in American markets because the United States has been a major source of capital funds abroad. An increase in the supply of funds in the United States will tend to depress yields here, but the amount of the decline that actually occurs will be limited by the outflow of funds abroad. A widening of the differential in international yields may attract American asset holders to foreign securities (or induce foreign borrowers to approach American capital markets). Foreign yields are not tied rigidly to American yields. Attitudes toward foreign exchange risk permit a range of variations. At the short-term end of the capital market an additional margin of flexibility is permitted by adjustments in the forward exchange rate. However, all things considered, the existence of international capital markets and the significant role American funds play do affect the American capital market, and the interrelationship between American and foreign markets cannot be ignored.

NOTES

1. Federal Reserve *Bulletin*, March 1972.

2. U.S. Department of Commerce, *Survey of Current Business*, June 1972.

3. The borrower's risk, of course, is that the commitment to fixed dollar payments would cost more at maturity in local currency than he anticipated when issuing the claim. For example, a British firm borrows $100,000 by issuing dollar-denominated claims against itself due in 10 years. At the then existing relationship between dollars and pounds ($2.50 = £1), the borrower raises £40,000. If during the life of the bond the exchange rate changes to $2.25 = £1, then the British firm must raise £44,444 in order to repay the principal due of $100,000.

4. Figures 7.3 and 7.4 report international differentials in Treasury bill yields. Of course, there are other money market instruments. (See Chapter 3.) Of particular importance for international transactions are commercial paper, bankers' acceptances, and finance company paper. A major portion of the international arbitrage transactions are in these instruments rather than Treasury bills. While the behavior of Treasury bill yields will be substantially the same as the behavior of yields on these other instruments, the correlation will not be perfect. As a result, the picture of international covered-yield differentials would look marginally different for commercial and finance company paper as well as bankers' acceptances.

ELEMENTARY THEORY
OF FINANCIAL
INTERMEDIATION

$\mathbf{I}$n addition to the analysis of financial markets, the economics of the financial system is largely an analysis of the nature, operations, and impact of a group of business firms that we call financial intermediaries. They loom so large in the financial system that their activities can have a decisive impact on the effectiveness of the system as a mechanism for the allocation of credit, and hence they can have a significant effect on both the composition and the level of economic activity. It is also important to note that government monetary policy is largely effected through financial intermediaries. Their economic importance is pervasive.

In Chapter 1 we made passing reference to financial intermediaries, their nature, function, and importance. In this chapter we propose to examine them in greater detail, and in the process to develop an elementary theory of financial intermediation. In the following three chapters we will consider the specific characteristics of various types of financial intermediaries.

THE CONCEPT OF FINANCIAL INTERMEDIATION

A CONDUIT BETWEEN ULTIMATE LENDERS
AND ULTIMATE BORROWERS

In our earlier discussion of financial intermediaries we noted that they stand between the ultimate lenders (surplus spending units) and the ultimate borrowers (deficit spending units). They borrow from one group and lend to the other.

However, many economic units simultaneously borrow and lend: Indeed, we might go so far as to say that at some time or other most (if not all) economic units do so. Thus, if we adopted a catholic definition of a financial intermediary we would have to include other economic units in addition to those firms, such as banks, savings and loan associations, and insurance companies, which we normally consider financial intermediaries. Many individuals or families are simultaneously creditors and debtors. They hold such things as bank deposits and saving bonds while at the same time they have outstanding consumer loans or mortgage debt. Similarly, many corporations extend trade credit and make long-term investments in other corporations while at the same time they have outstanding bank loans or long-term debt. Moreover, and especially in the postwar period, many corporations have become increasingly aware of the opportunity costs (in terms of income forgone) of holding large amounts of cash for lengthy periods. Therefore, they frequently invest their funds for short periods in various money market instruments. Indeed, corporations have become major suppliers of funds to the money market. Should we consider all such individuals and corporations financial intermediaries?

A MORE SPECIALIZED CONCEPT

In one sense, all of these individuals and corporations are financial intermediaries. Perhaps we could call them ad hoc intermediaries. Their financial activities have an important place in the overall functioning of the financial system. Our concept of financial intermediation must be more specialized than this, however. We are concerned with a group of firms that make this type of financial activity their primary business. That is, their activities in simultaneously borrowing and lending are not an adjunct of some other activity but rather are the essential reason for their existence. They are continuously engaged in the business of borrowing and lending, not just on an ad hoc basis, and in general (with a few exceptions) they stand ready and willing to accept any and all funds placed with them at the posted interest rate.

Most financial intermediaries are private profit-seeking firms. There are exceptions; mutual savings banks and the rapidly growing credit unions are two. However, even these seek to make a return over and above costs, and in that sense they are profit-seeking institutions. Clearly, in order to earn profits financial intermediaries must be able to borrow at a lower rate of interest than that at which they lend. How can they do this? Why should any spending unit lend to a financial intermediary at a lower rate of interest than that at which he could lend to the ultimate borrower (and to whom the intermediary will in fact lend the same money)?

Transmutation of Assets. The answer must be that depositors regard claims on financial intermediaries as in some sense superior to claims on ultimate borrowers. This means that if given the choice between a claim on an ultimate borrower and a claim on a financial intermediary bearing the same effective yield, these wealth owners would always choose the claim on the intermediary and would only choose the claim on the ultimate borrower if it bore a significantly higher effective yield.

It is for this reason that many economists argue that the essence of financial intermediation is the transmutation of assets. Transmutation means literally the transformation of something from one nature, substance, or form into another. The financial intermediary accepts claims on ultimate borrowers that the ultimate lenders would not accept, and it issues claims to be held by the ultimate lenders with characteristics that the ultimate borrowers could not duplicate. The intermediary does not create real wealth but merely changes the form of the claims on real wealth held by the asset holders. In this act of transmutation the financial intermediary creates an asset form with unique characteristics.

The unique properties of claims on financial intermediaries are varied. Thus, some intermediaries provide financial instruments that can be used as payments money and are in demand for that reason. Some intermediaries provide claims that are highly liquid, even though they are not money. Others provide claims in the form of insurance policies, where the claim is payable only in the event of a specified contingency (a fire, a death, or an accident, for example). Still others provide an instrument whose price behaves like a broad average of stock prices.

Underlying all of these specific characteristics, however, is the central principle of *portfolio diversification*. A claim on a financial intermediary is in fact a claim on a diversified portfolio of assets and is but one claim in a diversified portfolio of liabilities. It is the fact of diversification—primarily on the asset side but also on the liability side—that permits the intermediary to create financial instruments with all of these specific and valuable properties.

THE THEORY OF PORTFOLIO DIVERSIFICATION

The essential effect of portfolio diversification is that it reduces risk. Diversification of asset holdings reduces the risk of loss of the total value of asset holdings (and also the "risk" of unexpected gains in the total value of asset holdings). Diversification on the liability side reduces the risk of having to make payment simultaneously on all liabilities (and also the "risk" of unexpected increases in liabilities).

DIVERSIFICATION OF ASSET HOLDINGS

A more precise statement of the theory of portfolio diversification is reserved for the appendix to this chapter. That exposition is necessarily

167

mathematical, since the fundamental proposition is basically mathematical, being derived from a primary proposition of probability theory. However, on an intuitive level, this basic principle underlying diversification of asset holdings can be succinctly stated in the old adage, "Don't put all of your eggs in one basket." In the present context it might better be restated, "Don't put all your wealth in one asset." In the case of the eggs in one basket, it takes only a single misstep, a single fall, to break them all. In the case of investing all your wealth in one asset, it takes the failure of only one debtor to bring about your complete financial ruin.

In Chapter 5 we defined risk as the probability of significant variations in the actual yield on an asset around the expected or more likely yield. We might now extend these concepts and talk about the yield and the risk on a portfolio of assets. The yield on the portfolio will be the average yield on the assets that make up the portfolio. The theory of portfolio diversification tells us, however, that the risk on the portfolio—the probability of significant variations in the actual yield about the expected or most likely yield on the portfolio—will be less than the average of the risks on the separate assets comprising the portfolio. Indeed, the risk on the portfolio will vary inversely with the number of independent assets that make up the portfolio. As the number of independent assets in the portfolio increases to a very large number (in the extreme, to infinity), the risk on the portfolio approaches zero. This is true even though each of the constituent assets of the portfolio has a significant risk attached to it.

This means that an asset holder faced with two assets equal in all relevant respects (i.e., same risk, same expected yield) should, if he has any aversion to risk at all, hold some of both rather than investing all of his funds in only one. By doing so he will have the same expected yield on his portfolio (the average of the two identical expected yields is the same as either of them) and at the same time a lower degree of risk.

The principle of diversification also means, however, that it may be highly rational for an individual to hold some assets with a high risk and some with a low risk. Suppose, for example, an individual wealth owner had only two alternatives to consider for investment, cash and shares of common stock in one particular corporation. He could choose to hold all his wealth in the form of cash. This alternative would offer some definite advantages. In addition to being perfectly liquid, the possibility of its becoming worthless (we ignore erosion of real purchasing power via price increases) is extremely remote under normal circumstances. There is a disadvantage associated with holding wealth in the form of currency, however: It earns no income, either in the form of interest or in the form of capital gains. Since our asset holder presumably desires to earn income as well as to avoid risk, a portfolio consisting only of cash is not optimal for him.

At the opposite extreme is a portfolio consisting only of shares of stock in a corporation. Unlike cash, common stock holds promise of a positive return in the form of either dividends or capital gains (or both). Stock, however, also has risk associated with it: The income of the corporation is far from certain, and fluctuations in the income of the corporation will be reflected in fluctuations in dividends paid and in the market value of the stock. In the extreme, the stock could become worthless (although, of course, it could increase in value, making the asset holder a very rich man indeed).

Should our wealth owner therefore hold all his wealth in cash, the possibility of loss is zero but so is the income, while on the other hand a portfolio consisting solely of stock will maximize his expected income but also maximize the risk of loss. If, as an alternative, the portfolio of the wealth owner consisted of some of both types of asset, then risk of loss would be reduced (should the corporation go bankrupt, the loss would be only the portion of wealth held in stock) but so would the total expected income (less would be invested in stock, thereby reducing expected income or capital gains).

In general, as was shown in Chapter 5, assets with high risks normally have high expected yields. As a result, diversification involving assets of high and low risk normally involves a reduction in the expected yield on the portfolio as a whole.

INDEPENDENT AND DEPENDENT ASSETS

There is one vitally important qualification that must be made with regard to these conclusions on portfolio diversification. In order to reduce risk, the assets in the portfolio must be at least partially *independent*. By an independent asset we mean one whose outcome is not directly associated with that of any other in the portfolio.

Under what conditions might assets be dependently related? Suppose that between two assets, A and B, there existed a relationship such that if A (for example, an automobile company) failed, then B (a steel plant selling its entire output to A) would fail, we would say they were *dependent* on each other. Holding a portfolio of dependently related assets would not reduce risk.[1]

Remember, however, that while in a micro sense investments may be independent (e.g., a loan to a shoe store and a provincial bond), in a macro sense most assets are mutually dependent. If some calamity struck the entire economy, such as a major depression, most ventures would incur losses and many would collapse, with corresponding declines in the market values of most financial assets. Even in the ordinary course of business fluctuations, most industries tend to prosper or falter together, and as a consequence their common stocks tend to rise and fall together. In this sense, then, there may be some limit to the reduction in risk that can be achieved through portfolio diversification.

DIVERSIFICATION OF LIABILITIES

Since financial intermediaries borrow as well as lend, the risk of fluctuations in asset values are not the only serious ones they face. They also face the possibility that their creditors may not extend their loans. That is, the holders of claims on financial intermediaries may all demand payment at the maturity of the loan. For easy reference we shall call this form of risk *banker's risk*. For financial intermediaries—particularly banks—this risk is acute because a substantial portion of their liabilities are payable on demand. Under extreme circumstances, virtually the entire set of claims against the intermediary could be presented for payment in cash simultaneously, forcing total liquidation of the intermediary. This is a contingency that the management of the intermediary cannot ignore. The probability of a mass withdrawal of funds (a "run" on the intermediary) may be extremely low, but certainly there is always a risk of significant withdrawals of funds in a short period of time.

With the advent of deposit insurance, runs on financial intermediaries have become rare. The Federal Deposit Insurance Corporation insures accounts of depositors to $20,000 for 98 percent of the nation's commercial banks. It, along with a state-operated insurance corporation, insures depositors' accounts at almost all mutual savings banks to the same $20,000 limit. The Federal Savings and Loan Insurance Corporation and two state-operated insurance corporations provide similar coverage for depositors at over 80 percent of all savings and loan associations. Recently a similar federal insurance corporation was established to insure accounts of credit unions. Insurance coverage has also been extended to accounts with stock brokerage firms.

Today most depositors need have no fear of losing their deposited funds in the event that the institution should fail. Yet, while runs may be a thing of the past, intermediaries cannot ignore the possibility of sizable fluctuations in the total level of their liabilities. As intermediaries gain experience with the changes in the levels of their liabilities, they are able to determine with some degree of certainty what a normal degree of variation will be. More important, they will be able to fix what portion of their total liabilities they can expect to have outstanding at all times. With the knowledge that, even though most or all of their liabilities are payable on demand, only a certain portion are likely to be canceled at one time, they can, in turn, invest a portion of their total portfolio in higher-yielding longer-term assets such as mortgages and government bonds. In effect, they can borrow for the short term and lend for the long term.

It is important to remember, however, that no intermediary will have complete certainty as to what portion of its liabilities will be outstanding at any given time. The fact that these calculations are approximate and not exact creates a problem. Should the intermediary invest a large portion of its portfolio in long-term assets and then suffer a larger-than-expected redemption of its liabilities, it may be forced to sell these assets at a loss in an effort to raise cash. Similarly, excessive pessimism about the possible cancelation of liabilities may lead the intermediary to hold large amounts of short-term, low-yielding assets when it might well increase its return to the portfolio by holding more long-term assets.

The primary determinants of banker's risk are very complicated and are only now beginning to be explored fully. Recent empirical work, concerned with the nature of bank liabilities in particular, found that the level of banker's risk varied directly with the average liquidity of the deposits. Thus, the greater the percentage of total deposits not subject to checking (i.e., payable on demand *de jure* or *de facto*), the larger was the portion of total deposits likely to remain with the firm at all times.

More important, given the risks of withdrawal by any one creditor of the intermediary, it is quite clear that the risk to the total portfolio is significantly reduced by diversification. Where there may be a significant risk that any one creditor will demand his money on any given day, the risk that all creditors will demand their funds at the same time is very small indeed.

But this proposition applies only if the creditors can be described as independent. Thus, if the depositors in a small bank in a small town are all employed in the same industry, the probability that they will all deposit and withdraw funds together may be very high indeed. They could not be described as independent. Similarly, if all creditors heard and believed the same rumor of impending failure of an intermediary, the probability that they would all attempt to withdraw their funds again is very high indeed. They could not be described as independent.

In summary, the essential point is obvious. The asset portfolio of the intermediary must be managed with an eye to the risks involved on the liability side as well as those involved in the case of a particular asset. As we will see in our discussion of specific types of intermediaries in later chapters, the risks assumed on the liability side leave a decided imprint on the asset portfolio of the institution.

ECONOMIES OF SCALE IN PORTFOLIO MANAGEMENT

The reduction of risk on asset holdings through portfolio diversification is a general phenomenon. What a financial intermediary does for him in this way, any individual could, in principle, do for himself. Moreover, by lending directly to the ultimate borrowers the individual could avoid the costs of intermediation. (Remember, financial intermediaries are profit-seeking firms. In order to cover their operating costs and make a profit they must pay to their creditors a lower rate of interest than they earn on their diversified portfolios of assets.) While portfolio diversification is fundamental to financial intermediation, by itself it does not seem sufficient to explain the fact that intermediaries both exist and flourish.

Part of the explanation is that in the long run financial intermediaries are able to earn a substantially higher net return on their assets than most individuals could by holding a similar range of financial assets. The essential difference between individual portfolio diversification and a claim on a financial intermediary is that the latter is a proportionate claim on a much larger total portfolio. The superior earnings position of the financial intermediary derives from the economies of large-scale operations.

The concept of economies of scale should be a familiar one to all students of economics. Where economies of scale exist (and they are neither universal nor continuous through all scales of operations), a firm can achieve a lower level of costs per unit of output by increasing the scale of its operations and making adjustments in techniques of production and organization appropriate to the larger scale.

All attempts to apply this concept to financial intermediaries have encountered the same problem: How do you identify and measure the output of financial intermediaries? The measurement of costs is relatively straightforward, but, as discussed in Chapter 1, the problem of measuring output in the sense of the value of the services performed by financial intermediaries has not been solved to the satisfaction of many economists. Without a fairly accurate measure of output, how can we measure and discuss variations in costs per unit of output as the level of output changes?

Fortunately, in the present context we can beg the question. We are not immediately interested in costs in relation to the level of output of the intermediary (unless we take the size of the intermediary's portfolio of assets as an indicator of output, as many studies have done),[2] but rather in the impact of costs on the net return per dollar invested in diversified portfolios of different sizes. It is in this unorthodox sense that we refer to economies of scale. The student should be aware that it is not exactly the same concept as that employed in the theory of the firm.

Why should there be economies of scale in portfolio management? We can divide the relevant considerations into three categories. In part, the economies arise because of indivisibilities in financial assets. Perhaps more obvious are economies that arise in connection with the decision-making processes relating to the management of the portfolio. To some extent economies also arise in connection with transactions in financial markets and hence are dependent only indirectly on the size of the asset portfolio.

INDIVISIBILITY OF FINANCIAL ASSETS

Not all financial assets are available in small denominations. For example, Treasury bills come only in multiples of $10,000, or IBM stock sells for more than $250 per share. These minimum unit sizes are beyond the financial capacity of many wealth owners, and because of this, the range of alternative investment forms is limited. Could an individual with total assets of $5,000 invest in a diversified portfolio including several mortgages on residential property? Obviously not. However, a deposit in a savings and loan association effectively buys him a share of a portfolio including many such mortgages. The financial intermediary is able to hold a broader range of assets, including some higher-yielding assets, simply because of the larger total size of its portfolio.

ECONOMIES IN MANAGEMENT

The management of an investment portfolio involves choices among alternatives. The essential inputs are prompt, accurate information on current and prospective developments in a broad range of economic activities, and technical expertise in interpreting the financial implications of these developments. Each potential investment (including those already in the portfolio) must be assessed in terms of probable return and risk, and its merits considered relative to all possible alternative uses of funds. A large investment portfolio will be able to support a group of individuals who will devote their full time to supervising the investment of funds. By working full time rather than part time on the problems of investment, they frequently become specialists in particular industries, regions, or groups of securities. They acquire an expertise and knowledge that frequently allows them to evaluate a particular investment opportunity quickly and shrewdly. It is almost impossible to imagine such expertise in a wide range of markets being possessed by any one individual.

It is true that such technical expertise is itself a marketable commodity. Individuals can hire the services of professional investment counselors, and indeed many brokerage houses offer advice of this sort as a part of their services to their customers. However, the fees of independent investment counselors tend to bear more heavily on small portfolios than on large ones. Thus, suppose the fee of an independent counselor is $100 per day or any fraction of a day. The larger the amount of wealth involved, the lower will be the cost per dollar of having this expert advice. For example, if the portfolio is worth $5000, the cost per dollar of assets for one day's advice would be 2¢, while if the portfolio is worth only $500, the cost would be 20¢ per dollar of assets. The larger portfolio is better able to combine expert, specialized advice with low cost per dollar of assets.

ECONOMIES IN MARKET TRANSACTIONS

The optimum portfolio for a wealth owner or an intermediary will normally not be constant in size and composition over time. As wealth increases or the yields and risks associated with various investment alternatives change, so will the composition or structure of the portfolio. But changes in the size and composition of the portfolio imply transactions in financial markets, and these transactions are far from costless. As we saw in Chapter 3, there are "transactions costs" in the form of fees and commissions of brokers and dealers as well as miscellaneous other costs involved in purchasing and selling securities in the market (and corresponding costs in making loans and handling deposit accounts). With few exceptions, transactions costs are stated either as a flat sum per transaction or as a declining percentage of the value of the transaction. As a consequence, in most transactions the larger the total amount involved, the lower will be the transaction cost per dollar exchanged.

Clearly, if two equally diversified portfolios, one large and one small, were to involve the same number of market transactions in a given period, the burden of transactions costs would be heavier on the smaller portfolio than on the larger one. As a result, the net return on the smaller portfolio would be less than on the larger one. The smaller one cannot get the benefits of the same degree of diversification, adapt to all market developments, and get the same return on the portfolio as can the larger one.

ECONOMIES OF SCALE AND THE ROLE
OF FINANCIAL INTERMEDIARIES

If we regard the primary characteristic of the financial intermediary as the provision of a claim on a diversified portfolio of financial assets, this analysis suggests on a priori grounds one reason why such intermediaries should exist and flourish. Economies of scale in the management of investment portfolios, including economies in market transactions, permit the intermediary to obtain a higher net return on a diversified portfolio for any given degree of risk than could an investor with a relatively small sum to invest. This also suggests that financial intermediaries should be relatively more important to investors with relatively small portfolios than to those with relatively large ones.

OTHER ASPECTS OF THE MARKET POSITION
OF FINANCIAL INTERMEDIARIES

Clearly, the analysis of portfolio diversification, including the analysis of economies of scale in portfolio management, is only a partial explanation of why financial intermediaries exist and flourish. We have neglected another minor element in the determination of the riskiness of claims on financial intermediaries. More important, we have not given due consideration to a point introduced earlier but not fully developed relating to the diversity of products offered by intermediaries.

THE CAPITAL ACCOUNTS AND THE RISKINESS
OF CLAIMS ON FINANCIAL INTERMEDIARIES

We should not forget that financial intermediaries are generally corporations, with stockholders who have subscribed capital to the corporation, which have normally retained earnings over a period of time so as to accumulate surpluses and reserves. We can group all of these items together as the

174

capital accounts of the intermediary. These accounts are in fact the excess of the value of the assets of the corporation over that of the fixed dollar claims against that corporation. This excess of the value of assets over liabilities provides an additional margin of safety to the depositors, since they have a prior claim to the earnings and assets of the corporation. That is, the claims of the depositors must be met before those of the stockholders can be considered. Some intermediaries will use their reserves to stabilize payments of interest to depositors in spite of fluctuations in earnings on the assets held by the intermediary.

PRODUCT DIFFERENTIATION

We must reemphasize, in explaining the growth of financial intermediaries, that they have succeeded in creating financial instruments with characteristics that could not be created by many ultimate borrowers. We need only think of the liquidity and convenience of demand deposits, the special features of insurance, or the diversified portfolio of stocks obtainable from a mutual fund to realize this.

As long as wealth owners, or surplus spending units as we called them in Chapter 1, cannot obtain directly or by personal diversification a particular type of asset that they desire, there exists the possibility of an intermediary being created to provide the missing form. This is one of the primary reasons why we have such wide diversity in the types of intermediaries operating in the United States.

In a very general sense, these institutions are basically similar in that they all perform the function of financial intermediation. Thus, the theoretical analysis of this chapter applies to all of them. However, in a more specific sense, each group plays a different role in the financial system. These differences are reflected in the types of liabilities they issue as they collect funds and in the types of assets they acquire as they allocate those funds among the many investment alternatives. The main point of the next three chapters is to bring out the unique characteristics of each group of institutions and hence to explore the role each plays in the financial system. It should not be surprising, therefore, that our analysis focuses on the institutions' assets and liabilities.

SUMMARY

In a narrow sense financial intermediaries are actively and continually engaged in the business of borrowing and lending as their primary purpose. For the most part they are private, profit-seeking firms. Financial intermediaries are willing to hold claims of ultimate borrowers in exchange for funds because intermediaries are able to issue claims on themselves that are more acceptable to ultimate lenders than those of ultimate borrowers. The claim on a financial intermediary is a claim on a diversified portfolio of assets and is but one claim in a diversified portfolio of liabilities. This diversification reduces risk.

We know that the yield on a portfolio of assets will be the average yield on the assets it comprises. The risk on the portfolio (i.e., the probability of significant variations in the actual yield about the expected yield on the portfolio) will be less than the average of the risk on the separate assets. Thus, the risk on a portfolio will vary inversely with the number of independent assets making the portfolio. A financial intermediary, by holding a large number of independent assets in its portfolio, significantly reduces the risk of fluctuation in expected asset yields.

A financial intermediary faces another type of risk, which we call banker's risk. This is the risk that holders of claims against the intermediary may all demand payment simultaneously. For some intermediaries, such as commercial banks, this risk is particularly acute. No intermediary has complete certainty regarding the portion of its liabilities that will be outstanding at any time. Misjudgments are costly. Hence, the composition of the asset portfolio must be managed with an eye to the risks involved on the liability side as well as those involved in particular assets.

Because of the size of funds at hand, financial intermediaries are able to take advantage of some economies of scale that arise because of indivisibilities in financial assets, economies in decision making and portfolio management, and economies in financial market transactions.

NOTES

1. There is one additional relationship that, for completeness, should be mentioned. Some assets might be inversely related: That is, if one is successful the other will fail by an equal amount. An example might involve two shipyards with only enough business to support one. Whichever yard gets to build the ship survives and flourishes; the other fails. Diversification with inversely dependent assets would reduce risk to 0 and also reduce income to 0.

2. For example, P. Horvitz, "Economies of Scale in Banking," in *Private Financial Institutions*, Commission on Money and Credit (Englewood Cliffs, N.J.: Prentice-Hall, 1963).

Appendix
to Chapter 8

Portfolio Diversification
and Risk

$\mathbf{T}$he concepts of expected yield and risk on an asset were introduced in Chapter 5. We noted that the yield on an asset is always uncertain. A number of alternative outcomes are possible, but some are less likely to occur than others. We represented this situation by a probability distribution of alternative possible yields, with the expected yield being the most likely of the alternative possible outcomes and the risk being represented by the standard deviation of the probability distribution of these outcomes.

Expected Yield. What we mean by the expected yield is what mathematicians refer to as the mathematical expectation of the probability distribution. It is simply the average of the alternative possible yields when each possible yield is weighted by the probability that it will occur. The formula for calculating the expected yield is:

$$y = \sum_{i=1}^{n} p_i y_i \tag{8A.1}$$

where n represents the number of alternative possible yields in the probability distribution, y_i represents each of the alternative possible yields, and p_i represents the probability that that particular yield (the ith yield) will

177

occur (remember that $\sum_{i=1}^{n} p_i = 1$).

Standard Deviation. The standard deviation, a complex measure of the distribution of the alternative possible yields around the expected yield, is a much more difficult concept. Its derivation and properties are explored in any basic textbook in statistics.[1] In brief, it is the square root of the average of the squared deviations of the alternative possible yields from the expected yield. The mathematical formula is:

$$\sigma = \sqrt{\frac{\sum_{i=1}^{n} (y_i - \bar{y})^2}{n}} \tag{8A.2}$$

where the symbol σ (the Greek letter sigma) represents the standard deviation.

In the discussion of these problems another concept, the variance of the distribution, is sometimes used. The variance is simply the standard deviation squared. That is:

$$V = \sigma^2 = \frac{\sum_{i=1}^{n} (y_i - \bar{y})^2}{n} \tag{8A.3}$$

EXPECTED YIELD AND RISK ON A PORTFOLIO

By a portfolio we mean a collection of assets. A portfolio is diversified if it includes more than one asset (provided that the assets are independent to some degree).

Expected Yield of a Portfolio. The expected yield of a portfolio is simply a weighted average of the expected yields of the individual assets that make up the portfolio. Thus:

$$\bar{y}_p = \sum_{i=1}^{m} x_i \bar{y}_i \tag{8A.4}$$

where m represents the number of assets in the portfolio, y_p the expected yield on the portfolio, y_i the expected yield on each asset in the portfolio, and x_i the portion of the portfolio represented by that asset $\sum x_i = 1$. Thus, for a portfolio consisting of two assets, A and B, the expected yield would be:[2]

$$\bar{y}_p = x_A \bar{y}_A + x_B \bar{y}_B \tag{8A.5}$$

Risk of a Portfolio. The risk of a portfolio is the standard deviation of a probability distribution of the alternative possible yields on that portfolio. The risk of the portfolio depends on the composition of the portfolio (the relative shares of each asset in the portfolio), the risk on each asset in the portfolio, and the relationship between the yields on the assets included in that portfolio. In the comparatively simple case of a two-asset portfolio, it can be shown that:

$$\sigma_p^2 = \chi_A^2\sigma_A^2 + \chi_B^2\sigma_B^2 + 2\chi_A\chi_B R\sigma_A\sigma_B \qquad (8A.6)$$

where σ_p is the standard deviation of the portfolio (σ_p^2 is the variance of the portfolio) and R is the coefficient of correlation between the yields on the two assets.

The coefficient of correlation is a new concept that requires brief explanation. (For a full exposition of its derivation and properties, the student is referred to any basic textbook in statistics.[3]) For our purposes, suffice it to say that it is a measure of the extent to which the yields on the two assets tend to move together. If $R = 1$, then every time the yield on asset A increased, the yield on asset B would also increase by a predictable amount. This is a case of perfect positive correlation. Similarly, if $R = -1$, then every time the yield on asset A increased, the yield on asset B would decrease by a predictable amount. In the terminology used in the chapter, the assets are inversely dependent. And there is perfect negative correlation between their yields. If $R = 0$, then the yields on the two assets move quite independently of each other. Knowing the yield on asset A does not permit you to say anything definite about the yield on asset B. Of course R can have any of these three polar values or some value in between. But let us examine the three polar cases in detail, leaving it to the reader to work out the conditions for other values.

1. Independent Asset

In the case of independent assets ($R = 0$), the term $2\chi_A\chi_B R\sigma_A\sigma_B$ in equation 8A.6 drops out. In this case, the variance of the portfolio is a weighted average of the variances on the individual assets. That is:

$$\sigma_p^2 = \chi_A^2\sigma_A^2 + \chi_B^2\sigma_B^2 \qquad (8A.7)$$

However, the risk on the portfolio, represented by the standard deviation, is:

$$\sigma_p = \sqrt{\chi_A^2\sigma_A^2 + \chi_B^2\sigma_B^2} < (\chi_A\sigma_A + \chi_B\sigma_B) \qquad (8A.8)$$

In other words, the risk on the portfolio is less than the weighted average of the risks on the two assets in the portfolio. (Remember, the expected yield on the portfolio is a weighted average of the expected yields on the individual assets in the portfolio. Diversification among independent assets thus reduces the risk for any given level of expected yield.)

2. Perfect Positive Correlation

If the yields on the individual assets are perfectly correlated ($R = 1$), then the variance of the portfolio becomes:

$$\sigma_p^2 = \chi_A^2\sigma_A^2 + \chi_B^2\sigma_B^2 + 2\chi_A\chi_B\sigma_A\sigma_B \qquad (8A.9)$$

This is a familiar quadratic equation.

179

If we take the square root of this equation to obtain the standard deviation of the distribution of possible yields on the portfolio, we find that:

$$\sigma_p = (\chi_A\sigma_A + \chi_B\sigma_B) \tag{8A.10}$$

The risk on the portfolio is the weighted average of the risks on the individual assets. Since the expected yield on the portfolio is also the weighted average of the expected yields on the portfolio, diversification does not reduce risk for any given level of expected yield.

3. Perfect Negative Correlation

Finally, in the case of perfect negative correlation ($R = -1$), Equation 8A.6 becomes:

$$\sigma_p^2 = \chi_A^2\sigma_A^2 + \chi_B^2\sigma_B^2 - 2\chi_A\chi_B\sigma_A\sigma_B \tag{8A.11}$$

Again, this is a familiar quadratic equation, the square root of which is:

$$\sigma_p = (\chi_A\sigma_A - \chi_B\sigma_B) \tag{8A.12}$$

The significant thing about this portfolio is that there is some combination of the two assets in the portfolio ($\chi_A/\chi_B = \sigma_B/\sigma_A$), in which the risk on the portfolio is zero.

CONCLUSIONS

The important results are those represented by Equations 8A.4 and 8A.6. They tell us that the expected yield on a portfolio is the weighted average of the expected yields on the assets that make up the portfolio. If it can be shown, however, that portfolios are wholly or partially independent of each other in a statistical sense ($-1 < R < 1$), then the risk on the portfolio will be less than the weighted average of the risks on the assets in that portfolio. The results of portfolio diversification have been explored for portfolios consisting of two assets; it can be shown that they apply to portfolios consisting of more than two assets. The analysis can also be extended to determine the composition of the portfolio that provides the minimum risk. In general (contrary to the example developed in Chapter 5), this is a portfolio that includes some of each asset, with the proportion of each asset inversely proportional to the variance of its yield.

Table 8A.1. **Probabilities of Different Rates of Return, Two Assets**

| Asset | Outcome | | | |
	Rate of Return	Estimated Probability	Expected Value	Standard Deviation
A	0.10 0.05 0.00	0.33 0.33 0.33	0.05	0.041
B	0.0605 −1.00	0.99 0.01	0.05	0.105

An Example. A simple example, for the case of a two-asset portfolio, can be developed using the data presented in Table 8A.1. If we assume $R = 0$ and the portion of the portfolio held in asset $A = 0.8$ and the portion held in asset $B = 0.2$:

The expected value of the portfolio equals:

$$.8 \times .05 + .2 \times .05 = .05$$

Similarly, the variance for such a portfolio is equal to:

$$(.8)^2(.041)^2 + (.2)^2(.105)^2 = .00152 = \sigma_p^2$$

Therefore the standard deviation of the portfolio equals .039.

Thus, the portfolio of 80 percent asset A and 20 percent asset B has the same expected yield as an entire portfolio of either A or B and yet has a lower standard deviation (risk) than either of these alternative portfolios. We therefore say that such a portfolio is a more *efficient* portfolio.

NOTES

1. See for example Taro Yamane, *Statistics, An Introductory Analysis*, 3rd ed. (New York: Harper & Row, 1973), pp. 63ff.

2. See for example Harry Markowitz, *Portfolio Selection*, Monograph 16 for the Cowles Foundation for Economic Analysis at Yale University (New York: Wiley, 1959), pp. 72–101.

3. Yamane, op. cit., pp. 456ff.

COMMERCIAL BANKS

The most familiar, most pervasive, and perhaps most important type of financial institution is the bank. It has been the subject of more theoretical speculations and empirical studies by economists than any other type of financial institution, and its name is enshrined in innumerable university courses and textbooks on money and banking. In basic economics textbooks it is identified as having unique, quasi-magical power to "create money." Perhaps as a result, it has been the principal target of monetary reformers, crank and otherwise, and certainly the banking industry is regulated and supervised to a more intense degree than almost any other class of business.

THE CONCEPT OF A BANK

Several definitions of a bank are possible. Indeed, in the most general sense all financial institutions that accept relatively short-term deposits from the general public might be classified as banks. All such institutions have some degree of what we called in Chapter 8 banker's risk. That is, they all face the possibility that a substantial portion of their liabilities may be presented for payment over a short period of time.

The "Commercial" Bank Concept. Economists customarily distinguish between *commercial* banks and *savings* banks, primarily because of differences in the nature of their deposit liabilities and corresponding differences in the characteristics of their assets. A "pure" commercial bank (if it ever existed) would have short-term, highly volatile deposit liabilities that would be used as money in the normal course of events. It would have a relatively high degree of banker's risk, and as a result it would hold mainly short-term assets, including large quantities of short-term "commercial loans" (i.e., loans to businesses for working capital purposes). By contrast, a "pure" savings bank would have longer-term, lower-volatility savings deposits and a correspondingly lower degree of banker's risk. As a result, it would mainly hold longer-term assets such as bonds, equities, and mortgages (and hence would be involved primarily in financing the formation of fixed capital, assets with a long working life calling for long-term financing). The unmodified term *bank* would normally be applied to commercial banks.

The Money/Money Substitutes Concept. Despite the merits of classifying pure types of banking institutions for theoretical analysis, it is impossible to apply this dichotomy in practice. The important existing banking institutions are hybrids. Thus, in our discussion of the payments system in Chapter 2 we saw that a number of intermediaries issue claims on themselves—liabilities—that are close substitutes for money as liquid assets. Remembering this similarity, let us examine the unique characteristic of one type of commercial bank liability.

Commercial banks historically have been identified with accepting deposits of specie (currency and coin of the government), but so have other intermediaries. Commercial banks, however, could redeem withdrawal requests with their own bank notes, a right that other intermediaries had not been granted by legislatures. Commercial banks also agreed to honor on demand written orders to pay in cash when presented by a party other than the depositor, provided that funds were in fact on deposit. The significance of honoring on demand facilitated the role that check transactions play in our economy today and set commercial banks apart from other intermediaries.

Note issue by individual commercial banks no longer exists; this power has been assumed by the Federal Reserve. Banks remain unique because their demand deposit liabilities form the major component of our payments money. The term *commercial bank* is applied only to institutions that accept deposits that are payable *de jure* and *de facto* on demand.

A Legal Status Concept. In addition to the distinction between commercial banks and other financial intermediaries on the basis of demand deposit liabilities, we can also rely on the essentially arbitrary categories established through the legislative treatment of financial institutions. A commercial bank is a legal entity. In general, a commercial bank is organized as a private corporation. Like other corporations and other financial institutions, it must have a charter in order to function. Unlike many commercial corporations, banks can be chartered by the state in which they will do business or by the federal government. Banking regulations of the states and the federal government specify what is meant by conducting the business of banking and enumerate what conditions must be met before the charter application will be considered.

COMMERCIAL BANKS IN THE FINANCIAL SYSTEM

Commercial banks' claim to primacy of treatment in any discussion of the American financial system is almost unquestionable on several counts.

THE MONEY-ISSUING FUNCTION

One of the primary reasons why economists take an intense interest in the activities of financial institutions is their underlying concern with the causes and implications of changes in the size of the money supply. Our discussion of the payments system in Chapter 2 showed that the demand deposit liabilities of commercial banks are of overwhelming importance in this regard. If the money supply is the focal point for our interest in financial intermediaries, then we must be interested primarily in commercial banks.

NATURE OF ASSET HOLDINGS

The money-issuing function of the banks is of vital importance, and that alone would be sufficient to demand that we pay close attention to them. However, financial intermediaries are also a vital part of the mechanism whereby the savings of society are allocated among alternative possible uses. The selection of assets by these intermediaries can have significant microeconomic consequences. The size and composition of their asset holdings— over \$600 billion—set the banks apart from other financial intermediaries. The next-largest concentration of assets is in the hands of life insurance companies, with \$244 billion.[1]

CONCENTRATION IN LENDING ACTIVITIES

The composition of the assets held by commercial banks is significant to financial markets and the economy as a whole. More than half (about \$392 billion at the end of December 1972) of commercial bank assets are in the form of loans.[2] Bank lending tends to be concentrated in a few categories, with the result that banks often dominate lending for certain purposes or to certain sectors of the economy. For example, more than \$134 billion in loans (34 percent of all loans and 19 percent of total bank assets) were outstanding to commercial and industrial borrowers at the end of 1972. Most of these were short- or intermediate-term loans with initial maturities rarely exceeding five years.

There are other sources of short-term funds open to commercial users, as we saw in Chapters 3 and 6. Commercial paper alone accounted for \$29 billion (part of which was purchased by banks and is included in the $134 billion figure), but these other sources are nowhere near as important as commercial bank loans.

Commercial banks are not exclusively commercial lenders in this narrow sense. They play a vital role in the financial market, having extended over $30 billion in loans to other banks and financial intermediaries in 1972 and having made an additional $26.7 billion available, primarily to other commercial banks through repurchase agreements and to the federal funds market. Banks also provided $15.8 billion in loans to brokers and dealers in securities and to individuals to purchase and carry securities.

In a general sense, most of these loans are business loans. Nonetheless, commercial banks, by virtue of their tremendous asset size, also constitute a significant lender to other sectors of the economy. They are a major source of consumer credit, having $88 billion outstanding to individuals, about one-third of which was for automobile purchases. At the end of 1972 banks held $99.3 billion in mortgages, almost 60 percent of which was held on one- to four-family residences. Mortgages represented the second-largest category of loans after commercial and industrial loans, that is, 24 percent of total bank loans and 13 percent of total bank assets. Furthermore, some portion of the commercial banks' holdings of state and local government securities must also be regarded as movement into longer-term loans to these debtors, especially to the extent that an active secondary market for some of these issues may not exist and banks acquire them in large blocks through direct negotiation with the issuer.

WHAT IS A COMMERCIAL BANK?

Commercial banks are not simply an example of a "pure" commercial bank. They are the department stores of the financial industry, not specialty shops. It is true that their lending activities are highly concentrated in short-term loans to business, financial institutions, governments, and consumers and that in each area the banks have a major and frequently a dominant share of the market. However, they also hold large portfolios of marketable securities, and they also engage in longer-term lending. We should make no mistake about it: From whatever vantage point one examines them these are very complex institutions. Since we cannot hope to capture the full scope of their activities, it is necessary to focus on a few essential features.

THE BALANCE SHEET OF THE COMMERCIAL BANKS

We have already encountered the concept of the balance sheet identity in Chapter 4. A balance sheet is simply an elaboration of that identity. It is a formal statement of the assets, liabilities, and net worth of a firm, household, or other institution as of a particular date. In a balance sheet the assets and

Table 9.1. Consolidated Balance Sheet, Commercial Banks,
December 31, 1972 (Billions of Dollars)

Total Assets	$746.1	Total Liabilities	$746.1
Cash		Demand Deposits	
Currency and Coin	8.7	IPC	222.1
Reserves with Federal		U.S. Government	11.0
Reserve Banks	26.1	State and Local Governments	18.8
Interbank Deposits	32.5	Interbank-Domestic	28.7
Cash Items in Process		Certified Checks, etc.	11.8
of Collection	45.5		292.4
	112.8		
		Time Deposits	
Liquid Assets		IPC	
U.S. Treasury Securities	65.1	Savings	124.5
Other Federal Agency		Other Time (including	
Securities	21.4	for loan repayment)	149.0
Trading Account Securities	5.2	U.S. Government	0.6
Federal Funds and Securities		State and Local Governments	37.4
Purchased Under Agree-		Interbank-Domestic	3.6
ment to Resell	26.7		315.1
Acceptances	3.6		
	122.0	Government and Banks	
		Foreign Deposits	12.3
Investments—Other		Mutual Savings	1.7
State and Local		Miscellaneous Liabilities	
Governments	87.9	Federal Funds and	
Other Securities	5.6	Securities Sold Under	
	93.5	Agreements to Repurchase	33.9
		Other Borrowed Funds,	
Loans		Including Eurodollars	4.4
Real Estate	99.3	Mortgages	1.2
Commercial and Industrial		Acceptances	3.7
(including commercial		Other Liabilities	21.6
paper)	134.1		64.8
Loans to Banks and Other			
Financial Institutions	30.2	Capital Accounts	
Loans to Brokers, Dealers,		Reserves on Loans	6.9
and Others to Purchase		Notes and Debentures	4.2
and Carry Securities	15.8	Equity	48.7
Loans to Farmers	14.3		59.8
Other Loans to Individuals	88.0		
Other Loans	10.3		
	92.0		
Other Assets	25.8		

SOURCE: Federal Deposit Insurance Corporation, Board of Governors of the Federal Reserve System, and Office of the Comptroller of the Currency, *Assets and Liabilities —Commercial and Mutual Savings Banks* (Washington, D.C., December 31, 1972), pp. 8–9.

liabilities will be shown in more or less detail, depending on the purpose of the balance sheet, and will be organized into categories thought to reveal important characteristics of the business.

Table 9.1 presents a "consolidated" balance sheet for the commercial banking industry as of December 31, 1972. Since it is a consolidation of the assets and liabilities of all of the nation's commercial banks, numbering 13,950, it of course conceals important differences between the many firms in the industry. Commercial banks in the United States may be chartered by the federal government or under the banking laws of fifty states; state-chartered banks may choose to insure their depositors' accounts with the Federal Deposit Insurance Corporation and may make a separate choice about joining the Federal Reserve System. Federally chartered national banks have no choice regarding these affiliations. In addition, all banks are subject to the branching regulations of the states, which vary from statewide branching in some states to maintaining only a single office in others. There is also great diversity in the size of commercial banks. A few banks have more than $20 billion in assets; at the other extreme, some banks have less than $1 million.

With these qualifications in mind, let us examine the structure of this balance sheet as though it were the balance sheet of a "typical" commercial bank.

The assets and liabilities in Table 9.1 are grouped into categories designed to highlight certain important features of the banking business. Note on the one hand the relative importance of deposits payable on demand among the liabilities and, on the other, the high degree of liquidity possessed by the asset portfolio. One of our major concerns will be to explore the relationship between these facts.

DOMESTIC INTERMEDIATION: COLLECTION OF FUNDS

We have defined a financial intermediary as a firm whose primary business involves simultaneously borrowing from one set of spending units and lending to another, normally at a profit to the intermediary. In our discussion of financial intermediation in Chapter 18 we argue that this poses a paradox. To make a profit the intermediary must lend at a higher interest rate than that at which it borrows. Why, then, do not the ultimate lenders and borrowers bypass the intermediary completely, with gains to both of them? From whom do the banks borrow? Why are asset holders willing to hold claims on the commercial banks rather than potentially higher-yielding claims on ultimate borrowers? What are the characteristics of claims on commercial banks that make them attractive to these asset holders?

THE INSTRUMENTS OF INTERMEDIATION: DEPOSITS

More than 80 percent of commercial bank assets have been raised through deposits, of which about half are payable de jure and de facto on demand. If we also include savings accounts, which are usually paid on demand, almost 70 percent of total bank assets are susceptible to immediate withdrawal. This suggests at least part of the answer to our question. To a large extent, banks raise funds by appealing to asset holders' demands for liquidity, one of the three basic factors that we identified in Chapter 5 as entering into the portfolio balance decision.

The liquidity of most bank liabilities is a basic reality that pervades all aspects of the banking business. Every bank must so manage its affairs that it is able to meet all demands for the withdrawal of funds from demand deposits, and it must always allow for the possibility of a very substantial withdrawal within a short period.

Liquidity is thus the key concept in exploring the place of banking liabilities in asset holders' portfolios. However, that is not the whole story. The banks do not simply offer asset holders a single type of deposit with a single uniform characteristic—a high degree of liquidity. Banks offer several types of deposits, each with particular and distinct characteristics designed to appeal to asset holders' multifarious asset preferences. While most commercial bank deposits are payable on demand, some can be withdrawn only at the end of a fixed term or after a specified period of notice. Some are transferable by check; others are not. Some pay no interest; others pay interest at substantially different annual rates. Why do banks offer so many different types of deposits?

Demand Deposits. As we saw in Chapter 2, *demand deposits* must be considered as money. They are almost perfect substitutes for currency in many uses, and indeed in some aspects of the payments process demand deposits must be regarded as superior to currency. Demand deposits are perfectly liquid, pay no interest, and are transferable by check. The regular checking account is designed primarily for the use of business firms or, more generally, for spending units that regularly make a large volume of payments. It is also available to consumers. On this type of account banks normally levy a fee for each check written and each deposit made and, in addition, charge a monthly fee for servicing the account. The total amount of these charges may be reduced or waived if the average minimum balance meets the individual bank's cutoff. This charge by banks is an attempt to cover the costs involved in servicing checking accounts. Estimates by the Federal Reserve Bank of Boston show that costs per checking account run between $25 and $35 per year. Little research has been done to show how much banks earn on demand deposit money by lending and investing these funds.[3]

Largely as a competitive device, some commercial banks offer checking accounts at no visible cost to the customer. The bank must recover the costs of servicing these accounts either by charging higher rates of interest on loans, paying lower rates of interest on time deposits, or reducing dividends to bank shareholders.

There is another form of demand deposit designed for the use of individuals who write only a few checks each month. This is called a special checking account, and banks levy a monthly service charge or a fee of 10¢ to 15¢ per check, or both.

Demand deposit accounts at commercial banks that are held by individuals, partnerships, and corporations, as distinct from deposits of other commercial banks (interbank deposits), state and local governments, and the federal government, amounted to $205 billion in mid-1973. Fifty-one percent of these demand deposits were owned by nonfinancial businesses, 32 percent by consumers, 9 percent by financial businesses, and 1 percent by foreigners (7 percent were not classified).[4]

Banks themselves hold demand deposits with other commercial banks. These interbank deposits amounted to $32.5 billion in 1972. They are one sign of the correspondent bank relationships that we discussed in Chapter 2. Although interbank deposits earn no interest for the depositing banks, they facilitate the credit-transfering and -allocating functions of the banking system.

State and local governments maintain demand deposit balances with commercial banks to facilitate payments by and receipts due these governments. These balances amounted to $18.8 billion in 1972. The federal government also maintains demand deposits with nearly all commercial banks to facilitate its payments to the public and receipts from the public with a minimum of disturbance to the money supply. The federal government earns no interest on these demand balances, but the commercial banks are free to invest a portion of them in income-earning assets. Total federal government balances with the commercial banking system vary widely throughout the year in response to tax payment dates and other regular expenditures of the federal government. We will discuss this account in more detail in Chapter 16.

The Demand for Demand Deposits. In providing this type of deposit, then, the banks are reacting to asset holders' demands for assets that can be stored cheaply and safely and can be transfered from person to person, often over long distances, quickly and at low cost. They are satisfying the demand for an efficient medium of exchange.

If the demand is primarily for a medium of exchange, then the demand for this type of deposit should depend on the flow of transactions in the economy and hence on the level of economic activity. Thus, as the value of the gross national product increases over time, the quantity of demand deposits demanded should similarly increase. If the rate of increase in the gross national product should falter, or indeed if the gross national product should fall, a corresponding change should occur in the demand for demand deposits.

However, recent developments in economic theory suggest that the relationship between the level of economic activity and the quantity of the medium of exchange demanded should be neither rigid nor simple. The validity of this conclusion should be obvious from the information plotted in Figures 9.1(A) and 9.1(B). Figure 9.1(A) shows the gross national product, the average stock of demand deposits, and the value of checks cashed against

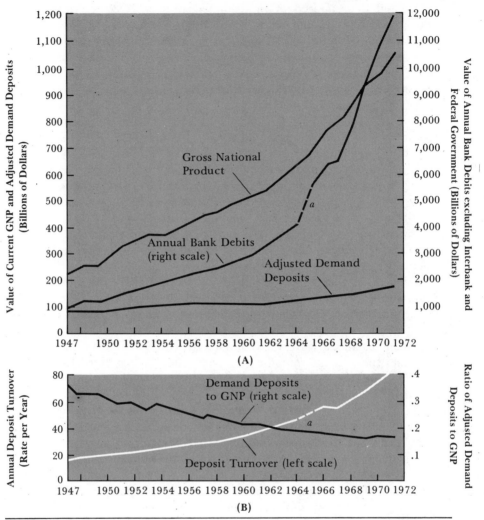

Figure 9.1 (A) Comparison of Gross National Product, Bank Debits, and Adjusted Demand Deposits, 1947–1971
(B) Comparison of Deposit Turnover Activity and the Ratio of Demand Deposits to Gross National Product, 1947–1971

ᵃChange in series.
SOURCE: Board of Governors of the Federal Reserve System, *Supplement to Banking and Monetary Statistics, Section 5* (Washington, D.C., 1966), pp. 6–18; *Federal Reserve Bulletin*, various issues; *Economic Report of the President* (Washington, D.C.), various issues.

demand deposits for the years 1947–1971. You should note the roughly parallel movements in the lines describing the behavior of the gross national product (which can be taken as a measure of the level of economic activity) and the value of checks cashed against demand deposits (which can be taken as a measure of the flow of expenditures effected using demand deposits). The behavior of the stock of demand deposits over this period was somewhat different. Although the stock of demand deposits, excluding interbank and federal government deposits, increased, the relationship was much less close, and in particular there was a much smaller relative increase in the stock of demand deposits than in either of the other two series. In Figure 9.1(B) we can see the result: The ratio of demand deposits to the gross national product declined substantially and almost continuously over this period, and the rate of turnover (or velocity of circulation—see Chapter 2) increased more than threefold.

We will have occasion to explore the demand for money in greater detail in Chapter 18. At this point we can conclude that a basic determinant is the value of transactions to be effected, or the level of economic activity. Over time, however, the spending units in the economy have found methods of economizing on their cash balances, so that the ratio of demand deposits to gross national product has been cut almost in half in a little over 20 years.

INTEREST-BEARING DEPOSITS

In addition to demand deposits, commercial banks also have a variety of interest-bearing deposits. These deposits are not transferable by check; therefore, they do not directly serve as a medium of exchange. Legally, to earn interest, funds must be left on deposit with a commercial bank for a minimum of 30 days. Whereas demand deposits must be honored by the commercial bank when presented, banks may require at least 30 days' notice prior to withdrawal of interest-bearing deposits. In addition, the maximum rate of interest that commercial banks that are members of the Federal Reserve System or insured by the Federal Deposit Insurance Corporation may pay on interest-bearing deposits is set by these federal authorities.

Savings Accounts. Perhaps the most familiar form of interest-bearing deposit is the savings account. Savings accounts are offered by most banks and are evidenced by a passbook. Only individuals and nonprofit organizations may hold funds in a savings account. Banks rarely exercise their legal right to require notice of intention to withdraw funds, so in effect these funds are payable on demand. One need only present the passbook in order to obtain a means of direct payment. Savings accounts earn a lower rate of interest than other types of interest-bearing accounts because they are readily withdrawn and typically are held in comparatively small denominations.

The demand for savings accounts is primarily, but not exclusively, a demand on the part of asset holders with relatively small portfolios for a safe, highly liquid asset bearing a modest but virtually guaranteed rate of

191

return. Savings accounts must be one of the most widely held types of financial assets, but in recent years other kinds of interest-bearing deposits offered by commercial banks and other financial institutions have grown more rapidly as asset holders have sought higher rates of return. In 1971 the University of Michigan's Survey of Consumer Finances estimated that 66 percent of the population had savings accounts, although it did not distinguish between savings accounts at commercial banks, savings and loan associations, or mutual savings banks. It estimated that 74 percent of the population held checking accounts with commercial banks.

Other Time Deposits. The variety of types of other time deposit accounts offered by commercial banks has increased dramatically in the last decade and has attracted large inflows of funds from depositors seeking safe, interest-yielding assets for excess cash balances. Other time deposits have grown more than tenfold since the end of 1961, when only $10 billion was held in these accounts. By the end of 1972 other time deposits held by individuals, partnerships, and corporations had risen to $149 billion, or almost 24 percent of total bank deposits, up from 4 percent of total bank deposits in 1961.

Banks have worked to make time deposit accounts attractive to more savers. They offer fixed maturity (one year or more), nonnegotiable certificates in comparatively small denominations ($500 or $1000) that pay a higher yield and turn over less frequently than passbook savings.

For larger investors, some banks offer negotiable, fixed maturity certificates. These certificates of deposit are issued in denominations of more than $100,000 and mature in less than one year. These large-denomination certificates are attractive investments for asset holders when the interest yield is in line with similar short-term money market instruments. However, in contrast to the free-market determination of money market instrument interest rates, rates paid on negotiable certificates of deposit, as on all interest-bearing deposits at member and insured banks, may be subject to a ceiling imposed by the federal authorities.

Another type of time deposit offered by most banks is multiple maturity, open-account time deposits. These are attractive to corporations and other organizations as a way of utilizing excess cash balances without becoming directly involved in the functioning of the money market and the secondary market for negotiable certificates. The depositor may place funds with a bank for at least 30 days in order to earn interest. The holder may renew the terms in 30-day multiples and may add to his open time account during the period. Notice of intention to withdraw any of these funds during the period must be given.

Banks usually pay significantly higher rates of interest on large blocks of funds committed for longer periods. The diversity of rates offered by commercial banks for interest-bearing deposits is reflected in Table 9.2.[5] Large-denomination, fixed maturity deposits for more than six months yield

COMMERCIAL BANKS

Table 9.2. Average Rates of Interest Paid on Interest-Bearing
      Deposits by Commercial Banks, July 31, 1973

Savings Deposits	4.7%
Open Time Accounts	5.8
Less than 1 year original maturity	5.4
1–2½ years original maturity	5.9
2½–4 years or more original maturity	6.3
Certificates of Deposit over $100,000	9.1

SOURCE: Federal Reserve *Bulletin*, October 1973, p. 729.

the depositor the highest return. Even large blocks of funds committed to open accounts may bring a high return if they mature in more than 90 days. Banks face strong competition for these funds from other financial institutions. The fact that rates paid on these accounts are relatively much higher than those paid on savings accounts or demand deposits does not necessarily mean that this other time deposit business is less profitable for the banks. The funds are attracted in large blocks, usually for a fixed term, which effectively lowers their administrative costs per dollar of deposit.

Large blocks of open-account time deposits and certificates of deposit do present issuing banks with a relatively high degree of banker's risk, even though each is for a fixed term and hence is relatively illiquid. Since each deposit is relatively large, the bank cannot achieve the same degree of diversification of its liabilities with these corporate notice deposits as it could, for example, with an equal value of savings deposits. When the accounts or certificates mature, there is no guarantee that those funds will be used to purchase new claims issued by that bank. Rather, as in 1969, large amounts may be invested in other, competing assets. As a result, corporate deposits tend to be more volatile in the aggregate than personal savings deposits.

TRENDS IN DEPOSIT LIABILITIES

It should be evident by now that the various types of deposits issued by commercial banks are close but not perfect substitutes for each other. At one end of the spectrum are demand deposits, which are highly liquid and non-interest-bearing, and on the opposite end are long-term deposit certificates, which are relatively illiquid and pay a premium interest rate.

In the period from 1959 to 1970, commercial bank assets grew at an annual rate of about 12 percent. Total demand deposits have experienced a growth of about 5 percent per annum over this period. This relatively slow rate of growth stands in contrast to the rapid growth rate of all interest-bearing deposits, which was about 27 percent per annum. Within this broad category we see that savings deposits have grown at about 9 percent per annum over the 20-year period. Since 1961, data have been collected separately on other time deposits, showing the tenfold increase we reported earlier. (See Figures 9.2 and 9.3.)[6]

193

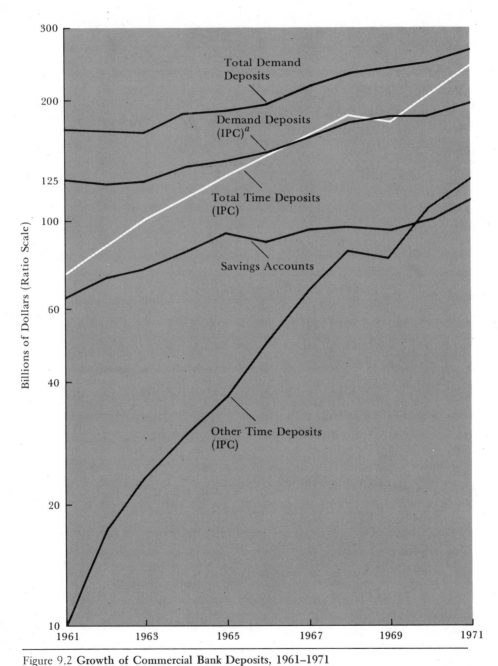

Figure 9.2 **Growth of Commercial Bank Deposits, 1961–1971**
[a]IPC refers to individuals, partnerships, and corporations.
SOURCE: Federal Deposit Insurance Corporation, *Annual Report* (Washington, D. C.),
various issues.

194

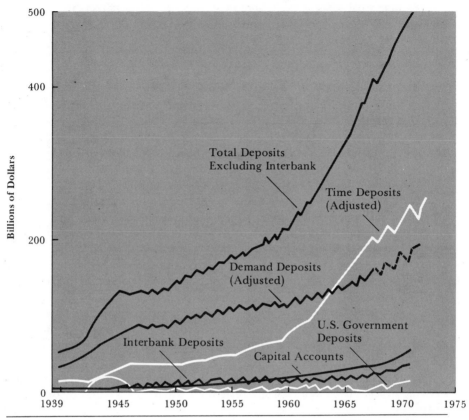

Figure 9.3 **Principal Liabilities and Capital Accounts of Commercial Banks, December 1939–June 1971**
SOURCE: Board of Governors of the Federal Reserve System, *Historical Chart Book, 1971* (Washington, D.C., 1972), p. 13.

Perhaps the crucial element in the new situation was the development of an active money market. Corporate treasurers became increasingly aware of opportunities for investing excess cash balances in short-term assets such as Treasury bills, finance company paper, and repurchase agreements with bond dealers. Holding large balances in demand accounts that paid no interest was, in terms of income forgone, an expensive proposition that offered few, if any, benefits.

Interest rate ceilings on savings and time deposits at member and insured commercial banks have been changed frequently by the regulatory agencies—the Federal Reserve and the Federal Deposit Insurance Corporation —since 1957. Banks have been able to offer rates that often were competitive with interest rates obtained on money market instruments. (See Table 17.2 for a record of the changes in Regulation Q.)

A somewhat similar situation developed in the market for personal savings deposits. In this case, competition from the near banks made large inroads into the relative position of commercial banks. (See Table 9.3.)

NONDEPOSIT SOURCES OF FUNDS

The balance sheet presented in Table 9.1 shows as nondeposit sources of funds for commercial banks several other categories of liabilities and the capital account.

Miscellaneous Liabilities. Miscellaneous liabilities, in addition to including such things as dividends payable but not yet collected by the shareholders, accrued tax liabilities, mortgages on bank properties, and other petty debts, also include *acceptances* and *liabilities for borrowed money*.

Acceptances. The account called Acceptances cannot really be described as a source of funds for bank operations. Unlike other entries on the balance sheet, this represents a "contingent" liability. Although there are several different types of items recorded in this account, in general the bank has simply undertaken to guarantee certain liabilities of some of its customers (and hence there is an offsetting asset account) in order to make those liabilities more acceptable in the marketplace. The bank could only be called upon to make payment in full out of its own resources if the customer failed to meet his obligation. In this sense it is a contingent liability. For this service the bank charges a fee, and as a result it is useful to include such items in the balance sheet.

Liabilities for Borrowed Money. This item includes advances from the Federal Reserve System and Eurodollar borrowings. *Advances* are short-term loans made by the central bank to its member banks. When a member bank, for reasons of a sudden and adverse clearing against it or because of a sudden deposit withdrawal, finds itself short of the legally required amounts of vault cash or deposits with the central bank, it can borrow the needed funds from the central bank for a short period. This loan or advance gives the member bank time to liquidate some of its assets and then use the proceeds to repay the loan from the central bank. Later in this chapter, when we consider the position of the banks in the money market, and again in Chapter 16, when we discuss the functions of the central bank, we shall discuss various aspects of these advances in greater detail.

Eurodollar Borrowings. They are discussed in more detail in Chapter 21. Here their importance to commercial banks is as another source of funds. Commercial banks are able to obtain additional funds through the Eurodollar market, which they may use in any manner. Over time the volume of Eurodollar borrowings by American banks varies widely. The Federal Reserve does require member banks to hold 8 percent in reserve against Eurodollar borrowings. At the end of 1972, Eurodollar borrowing by commercial banks amounted to $1.4 billion, which is included in the $4.4 billion item shown in Table 9.1.

Table 9.3. Growth in "Savings Deposits" at Financial Intermediaries, 1950–1972 (as of December 31; Billions of Dollars)

	1950		1955		1960		1965		1970		1972	
	Amount	Percent of Total	Amount	Percent of Total	Amount	Percent of Total	Amount	Percent of Total	Amount	Percent of Total	Amount	Percent of Total
Commercial Bank Savings Deposits	$35.2	50.0	$46.3	42.5	$67.1	39.3	$92.9	35.0	$99.1	29.8	$124.5	28.0
Credit Unions	0.9	1.4	2.4	2.2	5.0	2.9	9.2	3.1	15.4	4.6	21.7	4.8
Mutual Savings Banks	20.0	28.6	28.2	25.9	36.4	21.4	52.8	19.9	72.1	21.6	91.6	20.6
Savings and Loan Associations	14.0	20.0	32.1	29.4	62.1	30.4	110.4	43.0	146.7	44.0	207.3	46.6
	$70.1	100.0	$109.0	100.0	$170.6	100.0	$265.3	100.0	$333.3	100.0	$445.1	100.0

SOURCE: Data for commercial banks: Federal Deposit Insurance Corporation, Annual Report (Washington, D.C., various years); data on other intermediaries: U.S. Department of Commerce, Bureau of the Census, Statistical Abstract of the United States (Washington, D.C., 1971); data for 1972: Board of Governors of the Federal Reserve System, Annual Flow of Funds (Washington, D.C., August 1973).

The Capital Account. What we are calling the capital account of a bank is simply the difference between the reported values of the bank's assets and liabilities. The sums recorded in this account derive from three sources: the capital subscribed by the original purchasers of shares of the bank's stock, the funds raised through the sale of debentures or long-term debt obligations, and appropriations from the earnings of the bank over the years. Debentures and notes have been used by commercial banks only in recent times. A change in a national bank ruling in the early 1960s made the issuance of this type of debt more acceptable for commercial banks. The supposed advantage to banks of raising funds via debentures is their relatively long term (usually five years or more), coupled with their exemption from any reserve requirements.

The distinction between these components of the capital account is important to the accountant concerned with measuring the profitability of the bank or to the government concerned with assessing corporate income taxes (banks are allowed to make limited additions to reserves for losses in most years without treating these funds as taxable profits). However, from our present point of view the distinction is not important. The two components serve essentially the same function by providing a margin of safety for the bank's depositors and other creditors. This margin is provided by the fact that the value of assets exceeds the value of creditors' claims by the magnitude of the capital accounts and by the fact that the creditors' claims must be satisfied before any distribution of assets can be made to shareholders should the corporation go bankrupt. Thus, the capital accounts provide an estimate of the value of the residual claim of the shareholders to the assets of the bank: a claim that is legally "subordinated" to the claims of the bank's creditors, including depositors.

There has been a downward trend since the 1930s in the ratio of capital to total bank assets and in the ratio of capital to risk assets (excluding cash and U.S. government securities). At the end of 1972 the capital-to-total-assets ratio for all commercial banks was 0.072, and the capital-to-risk-assets ratio was 0.094.[7] The former figure was down from as high as 0.35 in 1875 and 0.10 in 1940. One major reason for the decline was the slow growth of capital funds. Further, while the capital account may provide a cushion in the event that the market value of bank assets declines significantly, there are other means available by which banks may meet such contingencies.

DOMESTIC INTERMEDIATION: ALLOCATION OF FUNDS

We have discovered that the liability side of a bank's balance sheet has a relatively unique structure but that in recent years that structure has been undergoing rather dramatic changes. The same things can be said about the asset side of the balance sheet. There is a standard, historical mold, but the pattern of bank involvement in the flow of credit to the economy has been changing significantly in recent years, and as a result the structure of banks' asset holdings has been changing too.

If we want to analyze banks' activities in the credit field, we must take account of four groups of factors: (1) the classic or historical pattern of bank activities, (2) the incentives to change created by attempts to maximize profits in a changing economy, (3) the ever-present necessity of coping with the high degree of banker's risk inherent in the structure of bank liabilities, and (4) a number of overriding legal constraints on what the banks are permitted to do.

THE ALLOCATION OF FUNDS: BANK LOANS

In addition to the legal definition of the business of banking mentioned earlier, H. P. Willis, one of the banking authorities of the early 1900s, wrote:

> . . . Their [commercial banks'] operations are limited by law to those classes of transactions that are obviously short-term in character. The restrictions placed upon the conditions under which the national banks may lend and the kind of security which they may accept, if rigidly observed, confine the banks to the commercial business of lending to persons who have live security and expect to pay at the end of thirty, sixty, ninety, or one hundred and twenty days.[8]

More recently, R. I. Robinson, a writer of a well-known exposition of the allocation of bank funds by commercial banks themselves, asserted that

> Once a bank has made itself safe, it should devote itself to the business for which it is best fitted. . . . Commercial banks are strategically located for lending. They know a great number of moderate-sized customers intimately; they can extend loan credit and collect where other lenders could not.[9]

These are the traditional views of the role of the banks in the flow of credit to the economy. The management of all other aspects of the banks' asset portfolios, including the banks' investment activities, must normally be subsidiary to the banks' lending activities. Is this a valid description of the contemporary activities of commercial banks?

We provided part of the answer to this question in the introduction to this chapter. Banks remain the primary source of short-term credit for business. But perhaps that should not be too surprising. The system developed over the years with the commercial lending function foremost in mind. The business of making loans involves face-to-face negotiations between the lender and the borrower. The organization of the banking system facilitates this process. The 14,000 commercial banks, many of which have been permitted to establish branches, have over 38,000 offices. These offices provide deposit collection facilities and administration points. They are also loan offices, often strategically located to service loan accounts.

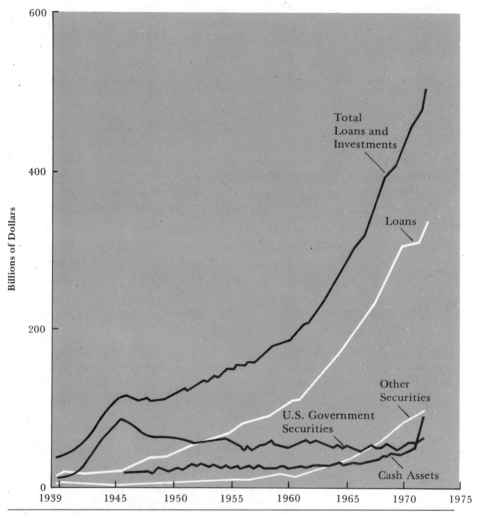

Figure 9.4 **Principal Assets of Commercial Banks, December 1939–June 1971**
SOURCE: Board of Governors of the Federal Reserve System, *Historical Chart Book,*
1971 (Washington, D.C., 1972), p. 12.

Loans vs. Securities. Figure 9.4 shows the growth of total loans and investments of commercial banks since 1940. Total loans and investments of commercial banks doubled between the end of 1943 and the end of 1960. They doubled again in the 1960s. Within the asset portfolio of commercial banks, the percentage of funds committed to loans has increased from 58 percent of the loan and investment portfolio at the end of 1961 to 68 percent at the end of 1972. The importance of loans among the assets of

200

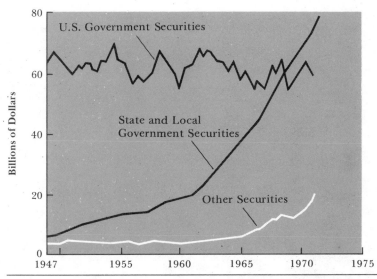

Figure 9.5 **Investments of Commercial Banks, June 1947–June 1971**
SOURCE: Board of Governors of the Federal Reserve System, *Historical Chart Book, 1971*
(Washington, D.C., 1972), p. 15.

commercial banks is now greater than it has been at any time since the
period before 1932.

Investments. Figure 9.5 shows clearly the changing composition of
banks' investment portfolios. Since the end of World War II, commercial
banks have held about $60 billion in U.S. government securities, although
there have been fluctuations in these holdings. Banks have increased their
holdings of securities issued by other federal agencies to $21 billion as these
securities have become more available. The real growth in investment holdings of commercial banks has been in state and local government issues.
These securities were discussed in Chapter 6 in some detail. Suffice it to say
that these securities are attractive investments for banks that desire income
that is exempt from federal income taxes.

Banks have also increased their holdings of other securities. In part,
this reflects renewed willingness on the part of commercial banks to hold
corporate debt issues. These issues were not always considered proper holdings for commercial banks. Legislation at the state and federal levels has at
times prohibited banks from holding corporate debt issues and at other times
severely limited bank holdings of these securities. During the Depression
commercial banks held what they thought to be marketable investment securities and found that the market for many corporate bond issues had
vanished and that they were left holding illiquid, nonmarketable, and often
worthless securities. It has taken a long time for banks to feel once again

201

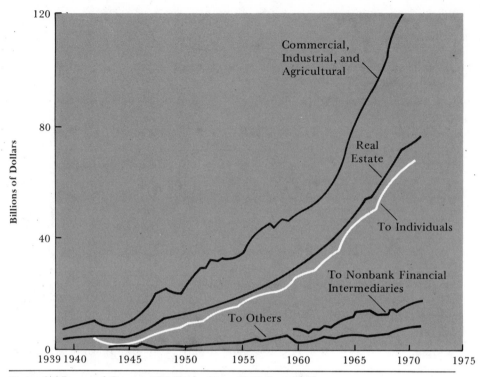

Figure 9.6 **Loans of Commercial Banks, June 1939–June 1971**
SOURCE: Board of Governors of the Federal Reserve System, *Historical Chart Book, 1971* (Washington, D.C., 1972), p. 15.

that corporate debt securities can play an appropriate role in their portfolios.

The Composition of the Loan Portfolio. In Figure 9.4 we see that the major credit activity of banks is lending money. Figure 9.6 shows more clearly that commercial and industrial loans have dominated bank lending activity. Both real estate loans and loans to individuals increased during the period 1939–1972 but maintained about the same relationship to each other. About one-fourth of the loan portfolio is in real estate loans and just over one-third in loans for commercial and industrial purposes. About another one-fourth is in loans to individuals.

Nonetheless, examining the consolidated balance sheet for all commercial banks conceals some of the differences that do exist between banks. The Federal Reserve Board made a study of the portfolio composition of banks on the basis of size. The findings showed that "small banks hold a larger portion of their earning assets in securities than do larger banks. . . ." The ratio of investments to total bank assets declines "from about 40 percent for the smallest banks to about 15 percent for the largest." State and local government securities are relatively more important in medium-sized banks' portfolios.

In terms of loans, broadly speaking, the larger the bank the higher the ratio of loans and discounts to total earning assets, rising from about "60 percent for the smallest size group . . . to about 75 percent" for the largest. Business loans show the closest association with bank size. Business loans assume an increasing position in the loan portfolio of a bank as the bank increases in size. This same relationship "is evident in the case of loans to financial institutions . . . and in loans to other investors for carrying securities." As might be expected, loans to farmers as a percentage of earning assets decline as bank size increases.[10]

Perhaps these findings confirm intuition. Large banks are better able to serve large commercial and industrial loan demands. They are also able to afford more sophisticated portfolio analysis and cash management. Smaller banks tend to be "country" banks, whose loan opportunities are confined to their customers, often dominated by farmers. Financial centers are located in large cities served by large banks. Demands for financing from this sector are met by those larger banks.

The Commercial Loan Theory of Banking. Early banking practices affirmed the principle that banks must be liquid. In order to be liquid, loans should be confined to financing the production and distribution of goods. In that way the loans would be safe because they were "supported continually during their currency by the existence of the goods," and the loans would be self-liquidating; that is, when the goods were sold, the means would be provided to repay the loans. Furthermore, it was argued that the volume of bank credit would automatically be adjusted to the needs of trade and therefore could be neither excessive nor deficient, and that the banks would never have liquidity problems because of the revolving short-term nature of their assets.

This is not the place to assess the merits of what has variously been called the "commercial loan" theory of banking or the "real bills" doctrine (commercial loans are "real bills" because they are backed by a corresponding value in real goods in the final stages of production). The theory proved deficient both from the point of view of safeguarding the liquidity of banks and from that of regulating the volume of credit. Indeed, institutional arrangements have been developed to supplant reliance on the commercial loan principle. As we will see, in contemporary banking practices reliance is placed on the central bank to regulate the overall volume of credit and on individual bank holdings of short-term financial instruments that can be sold in the money market. In addition, banks have the ability to borrow reserves from the central bank to safeguard the liquidity of the banking system.

Although some banks still cling to short-term commercial and industrial loans, most banks now extend an increasing portion of term loans to the commercial and industrial sectors. Rarely, however, do banks approve loans of this type for more than a five-year period. Personal loans have been extended in one form or another since the beginning of banking. Personal loans are generally backed by real goods as collateral and are extended for periods of up to 36 months. Bank loans to individuals are predominantly installment loans as opposed to single-payment loans.

Commercial lending remains the core of the loan portfolios of banks, although the commercial loan theory of banking has faded as economic conditions necessitated changes in banking laws and practices. Today commercial banks have diversified their lending activities to such a degree that they now deserve the sobriquet "the department stores of the financial system."

Interest Rate Charges on Bank Loans. Interest rate charges on bank loans vary as much as interest rates paid on time deposits. Generally, commercial and industrial short-term loans receive preferential rates. Rates are determined by the bank on the basis of the size of the loan, the prestige of the borrower, the term of the loan, and the collateral backing. Broadly, the larger the loan, the bigger the borrower, and the shorter the term, the lower the rate. Many of the larger commercial banks have established and publicized a *prime rate*. This is the rate of interest charged by that bank to its largest and best commercial and industrial borrowers. This is a base rate, with other loans being charged higher rates as the credit risk and/or term to maturity increases.

In 1971 several New York banks began to experiment with a fluctuating prime rate. Today some banks tie their prime rate to a money market instrument like commercial paper. Others use a formula weighting the rates prevailing on several short-term money market instruments. However, most banks still set their prime rate periodically to reflect prevailing money market conditions and loan demand.

In many states rates charged by banks on residential mortgages and consumer loans are subject to legal limitations. Many states have usury laws that prohibit money from being lent to individuals at rates above the usury limitations.

Usury laws in the United States are based on English usury laws. They have always been designed to protect the small, individual borrower, who is at a competitive disadvantage when he needs funds. In spite of the existence of usury laws, it became evident at the turn of this century that banks were charging individual borrowers more than the laws permitted or refusing to lend to small borrowers. These borrowers were forced to turn to illegal sources for funds if their demands were urgent. In reaction to these findings, the Russell Sage Foundation drafted a Uniform Small Loan Act in the early 1900s that was quickly adopted by many states. Under small loan legislation, borrowers of small amounts could legally be charged higher rates of interest than permitted under the state's usury laws. Enactment of this legislation stimulated the growth of consumer and sales finance companies and encouraged commercial banks to move into consumer lending in the 1920s.

Despite usury laws and small-loan legislation limiting the rate of interest that can be charged small individual borrowers, lenders can circumvent the legal limit. Banks per se are permitted to deduct interest costs in advance from the amount borrowed, reducing the amount available to the borrower. In addition, banks usually require that commercial borrowers maintain a demand deposit with the bank. This is known as a *compensating balance*. It effectively reduces the amount of borrowed funds available for use and raises the real cost of borrowing.

Lenders may add on the costs of credit investigation and legal and brokerage fees. Formerly they concealed the true costs of borrowing by stating interest costs only as a monthly charge, or they simply stated the rate charged as a rate applied to the full amount borrowed without accounting for the installment repayments over the entire period of the loan.

Recent passage of truth-in-lending legislation has forced disclosure of the actual annual rates of interest being charged for money borrowed. There has also been some pressure to raise the maximum interest rates permitted under usury laws when the general level of interest rates is rising, or to abandon the practice of setting ceiling rates. Advocates of the latter position argue that such ceilings inhibit the legal allocation of funds for such uses as mortgages when the general level of interest rates is high. They do not protect the small borrower from paying high rates. On the contrary, arbitrary ceilings cut off legal sources of funds because it is not in the lender's interest to make such loans. They force the small borrower into the hands of illegal lenders who may charge 20 percent per week on borrowed money.[11]

SAFEGUARDING THE LIQUIDITY OF BANKS

We must now turn our attention to an aspect of banks' management of their asset portfolios that we have so far glossed over: their techniques of coping with the banker's risk that is inherent in the structure of their liabilities. How are the banks able to guarantee payment of such an overwhelming portion of their liabilities on demand?

Cash Reserves. A bank is required to be continuously willing and able to pay out cash when cash is demanded by its depositors. To a limited extent normal cash drains will involve actual payments of currency over the counter in some or all of nearly 38,800 bank offices across the country. To meet these potential over-the-counter cash drains, each bank needs currency in the vaults of each of its offices. Primarily, however, cash drains will result from interbank settlements. One obvious solution to the problem posed by possible cash drains would be for each bank to keep on hand at all times sufficient cash to meet all conceivable short-term demands for funds by their depositors. As we have already pointed out, however, bankers know that under normal circumstances it is highly unlikely that a large portion of deposits will be called for payment within a short period. As a result, the cash they would have to hold to be "safe" would only be a fraction of their deposit liabilities—with the size of that fraction depending on the bankers' assessments of the probable volatility of their deposits and the degree of safety they desire.

An examination of Table 9.1 reveals that banks do in fact hold substantial amounts of cash in the form of currency in their vaults, reserve deposits with the Federal Reserve banks, and demand deposits with other banks. Is this, then, the banker's primary method of hedging against banker's risk?

The Cash Reserve Requirement and Bank Liquidity. We have to be very cautious in placing such a construction on the relatively large holdings of cash by banks. Banks do not hold all this cash voluntarily. The composition and size of a bank's cash reserves depend first on its regulatory status.

Regulatory Status. We referred earlier in the chapter to the two different legal means of entering the banking business, that is, meet individual state requirements, obtain a state charter, and adhere to that state's regulations, or meet federal requirements, obtain a national bank charter, and adhere to federal regulations.

State-chartered banks may join the Federal Reserve System and may insure their deposits with the Federal Deposit Insurance Corporation. In fact, almost all state banks insure their deposits with the FDIC. Only 1092, or 11 percent, of state-chartered banks are members of the Federal Reserve System and adhere to the Federal Reserve's regulations and requirements.

The more than 8000 state-chartered banks that remain outside the Federal Reserve System hold only 20 percent of the banking system's total deposits. These banks must adhere to the general banking regulations established in each of the 50 states. These requirements differ markedly from state to state, but in general the states' capital, cash reserve, and lending requirements are less stringent than the Federal Reserve's requirements for member banks.

Cash Reserve Requirements. State cash reserve requirements can generally be satisfied by cash in the bank's vault, deposits with other commercial banks, or in some states, holdings of state or federal government securities. The monetary liabilities of the federal government—what we will later call high-powered money—are a small part of the total cash reserves of nonmember banks. Correspondent balances are a much more important component.

The cash reserve requirement for member banks of the Federal Reserve System can be satisfied only by deposits with a Reserve bank and currency held in the member bank's vault. During the 1930s Congress relinquished some of its power over reserve requirements. Now it establishes a range within which the Board of Governors of the Federal Reserve System sets the specific cash reserve requirements on demand deposits and interest-bearing deposits for the two classes of member banks—reserve city and country banks.[12] The required reserve ratios in effect at the beginning of 1973 are presented in Table 9.4.

Table 9.4. **Member Bank Minimum Cash Reserve Ratios, November 1972**

Net Demand Deposits[a] (Millions of Dollars)	Reserve Percentage for All Member Banks
$2 or Less	8
$2–$10	10
$10–$100	12
$100–$400	13
Over $400	17.5

Interest-Bearing Deposits (Millions of Dollars)	Reserve Percentage for All Member Banks
All Savings Accounts	3
Other Time Deposits	
$5 and Under	3
Over $5	5

[a]Gross demand deposits less cash items in process of collections and less demand balances due from domestic banks.
SOURCE: Federal Reserve *Bulletin*, July 1972, p. 628.

As the terms imply, reserve requirements for member banks historically have been based on the bank's geographic location as well as its deposit size. Large banks in financial centers—so-called reserve city banks—were subject to higher cash reserve requirements against demand deposits than member banks elsewhere—the country banks. In 1972 the Federal Reserve redefined the terms *reserve city* and *country*. Banks with net demand deposits of less than $400 million would be "country" banks regardless of their geographic location. Member banks with net demand deposits in excess of $400 million would become "reserve city" banks. The Federal Reserve Board in explaining the change stated that the

> banking system has evolved to the point where basing reserve requirements on geographical considerations is no longer equitable. . . . Under the old system, for example, a few large active banks enjoyed country bank status, whereas some small banks bore the heavier burdens of a reserve city classification.[13]

It is interesting to note that on the average the actual cash reserves of nonmember banks are not significantly different from those of member banks (when expressed as a percentage of total deposits), as Table 9.5 shows. However, cash reserves are held in very different forms in the two groups of banks.

One might argue that if the banks are required to hold this cash to fulfill their legal obligations to regulatory authorities, then it cannot serve as a hedge against banker's risk because by definition the cash is not available to be paid out to depositors. Of course this is not true of any excess reserves of cash. Excess reserves are clearly available to be paid out to depositors. Data on excess reserves are available only for member banks of the Federal Reserve System. As Figure 9.7 demonstrates, total excess cash reserves of

Table 9.5.   Cash Reserves of Member Banks and Nonmember Banks, June 30, 1973

	Member Banks	Nonmember Banks	All Banks
	Billions of Dollars		
Deposits with Federal Reserve Banks	$ 25.14		$ 25.14
Vault Cash	5.75	$ 1.92	7.67
Total Federal Monetary Liabilities	$ 30.89	$ 1.92	$ 32.81
Balances with Domestic Banks	18.00	11.84	29.84
Total Cash	$ 48.89	$ 13.76	$ 62.65
Total Deposits	$486.77	$138.17	$624.94
	Percent of Total Deposits		
Deposits with Federal Reserve Banks	5.1		4.0
Vault Cash	1.2	1.4	1.2
Total Federal Monetary Liabilities	6.3	1.4	5.2
Balances with Domestic Banks	3.7	8.6	4.8
Total Cash	10.0	10.0	10.0

SOURCE: Federal Reserve *Bulletin*, October 1973, pp. A22, A23.

member banks tend to be very small. In the past 10 years they have rarely exceeded 0.3 percent of total member bank deposits in any month. Surely excess reserves of that magnitude do not give member banks a significant margin of safety. Furthermore, excess reserves are not evenly distributed

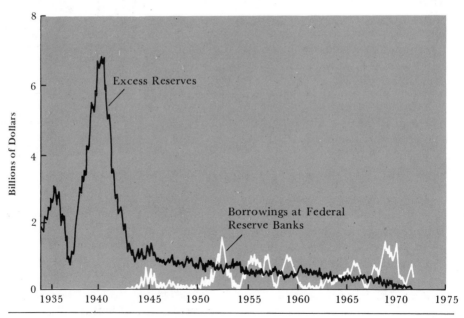

Figure 9.7 **Excess Reserves and Borrowing of Member Banks**
SOURCE: Board of Governors of the Federal Reserve System, *Historical Chart Book, 1970* (Washington, D.C., 1971), p. 6; Federal Reserve *Bulletin*, November 1971.

among all member banks. The large banks located in financial centers usually must borrow reserves from other banks that have excess reserves or from the Federal Reserve banks in order to meet their weekly legal reserve commitments.

However, the apparent conclusion that the bulk of banks' holdings of cash cannot be counted as a liquid asset must be modified somewhat because the legal cash reserve requirement for member banks is neither as simple nor as rigid as the preceding discussion implies. For example, the average cash reserve requirement for a member bank with $100 million in demand deposits and $5 million in savings accounts expressed as an equation would be as follows (millions of dollars):

$$\frac{\substack{\text{Required} \\ \text{Deposits at} \\ \text{Federal} \\ \text{Reserve} \\ \text{Bank}}}{\substack{\text{Daily} \\ \text{Average} \\ \text{of Current} \\ \text{Averaging} \\ \text{Period}}} = \frac{\substack{(\text{Reserves Held Against}) \\ (\text{Net Demand Deposits}) \quad\quad (\text{Savings})} \\ .08 \times \$2 + .10 \times \$8 + .12 \times \$90 + .03 \times \$5 - \text{vault cash}}{\substack{\text{Average Net Deposits of the Reserve Period Ending} \\ \text{2 Weeks Earlier}}}$$

Take particular note of the time periods involved. Only the required deposit at the Federal Reserve refers to the current reserve period. All other elements in the equation relate to an earlier period.

From the point of view of the liquidity of banks' cash holdings, there are two important elements of flexibility in the reserve requirement: (1) the fact that the reserve requirement need be satisfied only on a daily average over a set period and (2) the fact that the vault cash (currency) that is to be counted in calculating the cash reserve was that held by the bank two weeks ago.

The significance of the first point should be obvious. Since member banks do not have to satisfy the reserve requirement every business day, they can draw their reserve deposits below the required level on some days as long as they exceed the requirement on other days by an amount sufficient to provide a daily average that satisfies the requirement. This introduces an important element of flexibility, making banks' reserve deposits at the Federal Reserve more liquid than might appear at first glance.

Clearly, in assessing the liquidity of these deposits an important question is how far the member banks are willing to draw down their deposits below the required level on any given day. Since daily statistics are not published, we do not know. However, it undoubtedly depends in part on the length of the averaging period. The longer the averaging period, the easier it will be for a bank to make up reserve deficiencies and hence the less reluctant it will be to fall substantially below its requirement on any given day. In the United States the reserve averaging period had been one week for reserve city banks and two weeks for country banks. In 1968 all member banks were made subject to a weekly reserve period.

The significance of the second point—the fact that it is the vault cash held two weeks ago that enters the calculation of reserve holdings—may not be as obvious. However, it means that there is no legal impediment to a bank's paying out currency that it has in its vaults. The entire holdings of currency could, in principle, be paid out without affecting the bank's legal reserve position. It is true that it will affect the reserve deposit that the bank must hold at the Federal Reserve on a daily average for the weekly reserve period two weeks hence. However, paying out currency cannot create a reserve deficiency *this week*. For this reason, cash in the vaults of bank offices across the country can be regarded as a perfectly liquid asset, at least for meeting over-the-counter drains.

The Demand for Excess Cash Reserves. We can conclude that bank holdings of cash provide only a partial hedge against banker's risk. Vault cash is available to satisfy over-the-counter demands for currency, and adverse clearing balances can be satisfied out of excess reserves or out of very temporary reductions in reserve deposits below the legal requirement. Clearly, the magnitude of the excess cash reserve is a crucial determinant of liquidity. However, we have seen that banks in fact hold very small excess cash reserves. Given the banks' ever-present liquidity problem, is this not surprising? Should we not expect banks to have a strong demand for liquidity and hence to hold large sums of their most liquid asset, excess cash reserves?

An explanation for the low level of excess reserves among Federal Reserve member banks as shown in Figure 9.7 is simple. The banks require sufficient stocks of liquid assets to meet possible clearinghouse drains. However, these liquid assets need not be idle excess reserves. They can be any short-term asset that is virtually risk free and can be converted into cash on very short notice. While excess cash reserves do have the desirable property of immediate availability, they have the undesirable property of being sterile. Under the law the Federal Reserve cannot pay interest on member banks' reserve deposits. By contrast, other liquid assets that the banks might hold do bear interest. As a result, a profit-maximizing banker will attempt to keep his idle excess cash reserves to a minimum.

The large banks attempt to manage their portfolios more closely than smaller banks, balancing their liquidity needs against their earnings requirements and costs. As a result, there are many variations among banks in their holdings of excess reserves. Data on member banks indicate that the larger banks located in financial centers like New York and Chicago are consistently borrowing reserves to meet their Federal Reserve cash requirements, whereas smaller banks in rural settings usually hold more than their legal minimum reserve deposits and vault cash.

The growth of the federal funds market has enabled smaller member banks to lend their excess reserves, turning them into income-earning assets. It has also relieved the larger city banks from continually liquidating other short-term assets to obtain necessary reserves and has enabled them to conserve on their holdings of U.S. government securities, which usually yield less than other money market instruments, and avail themselves of the federal funds market when necessary.

Secondary Reserves. In addition to bank holdings of vault cash, reserves with the Federal Reserve banks, and demand deposits with other banks, member and nonmember commercial banks hold assets that are readily convertible into cash without significant loss. These assets are termed *secondary reserves.* This is not a legal concept, since banks are not required by state or federal regulations to hold certain amounts of certain types of assets. Rather, it is a useful way of classifying bank holdings of U.S. government securities, bankers' acceptances, commercial paper (although there is no functioning secondary market for this instrument), call loans (primarily to U.S. government securities dealers), and reserves lent as federal funds.

Holdings of these assets provide commercial banks with liquidity first and some yield or income second. Such holdings enable the banks to meet the unexpected large adverse clearings, loan demands, or cash withdrawals with a minimum of dislocation. Their substantial holdings of liquid assets serve as banks' primary hedge against banker's risk. This requires an active, stable money market on which banks can rely to guarantee the liquidity of their secondary reserves.

The Federal Reserve and Bank Liquidity. The Federal Reserve safeguards the liquidity of member banks and the banking system as a whole. In the first instance the Federal Reserve banks will make short-term advances to member banks. Such advances are usually for a period up to fifteen days and are made at a rate of interest called the *discount rate.* Historically this rate has usually been slightly higher than the Treasury bill rate. In contrast to the bill rate, which is determined by the forces of supply and demand in the money market, the discount rate is set by the Federal Reserve banks. The Federal Reserve discourages "continuous borrowing" and wants to be considered a "lender of last resort." Reserve borrowings by member banks tend to be quite small.

The Federal Reserve also assists the money market through loans to and repurchase agreements with bank and nonbank government security dealers. This facility is actively used by the Federal Reserve to alter or maintain credit conditions. Open-market operations are conducted to maintain stability in credit and economic conditions and to offset countervailing influences, as well as to dynamically alter those conditions.

The purpose of the reserve lending power and timely interventions of the Federal Reserve is to provide a broad, stable market on which the banking system can rely for reserve adjustments. Thus, banks with sizable cash drains have several options open to them: (1) They can temporarily draw down their cash reserves in the expectation of a reversal of the drain in the near future; (2) they can call loans to U.S. government security dealers, confident that the security dealers will always be able to pay on demand;

(3) they can sell into the money market any of a variety of short-term securities. Which technique they choose presumably depends on which one costs the least—in selling securities, which security produces the least income (yield). Similarly, banks with cash inflows have several adjustment techniques, and they will choose among the alternatives on the basis of maximizing their returns. In general, we can expect the large banks to be in the money market daily to adjust their cash holdings.

OTHER ASSETS

We have not specifically discussed several categories of assets that appear on the domestic portion of the banks' balance sheet (Table 9.1). The account called Items in Transit, or bank *float*, as it is sometimes called, includes such things as checks that have been deposited with a bank but not yet collected from the bank on which they were drawn. The Acceptances account is simply the asset counterpart of the contingent liability account of the same name that we discussed earlier. It appears as an asset because this is the liability of the banks' customers under the letters of credit or guarantees issued by the banks. All Other Assets is a grab bag of miscellaneous assets, including bank premises.

INTERNATIONAL INTERMEDIATION

In the United States there are a large number of independent commercial banks operating under a fragmented system of chartering, supervision, insurance, and regulations. The entire banking system, however, is interconnected through private correspondent bank relationships. These ties can connect even the smallest rural bank with a larger bank that can provide international financial services directly or through its correspondent bank.

As we have already seen, the large banks in the financial centers and main port cities provide part of the apparatus for the *international payments system*, that is, the foreign exchange market and an international network of correspondent relationships with foreign banks in leading financial centers throughout the world.

The rapid growth of world trade has increased the need for international banking services. With the entrance of more independent developing nations into the trade arena, more financial facilities are needed in more countries. It is estimated that the United States alone has more than 3000 corporations operating in 114 countries. At the end of 1971, direct investment abroad by Americans had a book value of $86 billion. At the same time there was $13 billion worth of direct investment by foreigners in this country. The growth of an economy that is international in scope spurs the need for additional banking services.

Foreign Branches. International banking demands of American business were handled by British banking concerns until the passage of the Federal

Reserve Act of 1913. From that time on, national banks with more than $1 million in capital and surplus were permitted to open foreign branches.

A few giant banks, notably First National City, Bank of America, and Chase Manhattan, established foreign branches and dominated the foreign banking field. Recently, however, there has been a rapid increase in the number of member banks setting up branches abroad. At the end of 1967, 15 member banks operated 292 branches in 54 countries. By the beginning of 1973, there were 107 member banks operating 627 branches in 73 countries. (This is still a small number but reflects the significant number of new entrants.)

There is other federal legislation that enables other banks to perform foreign banking and business functions abroad. Banks have formed subsidiaries, for example, to operate as agencies in New York City and perform foreign exchange operations for the parent bank as well as to assist its international lending and credit accommodation functions. Other banks have bought stock in foreign banks and foreign financial institutions to extend their financial domain beyond the normal domestic boundaries.

International Banking. In some countries U.S. bank branches provide commercial banking services for local consumers and businesses. Particularly in South America, American branches have helped establish a formal banking system. In other countries, branches of U.S. banks have concentrated on assisting American business interests, providing deposit facilities, and intermediating loan demands.

Commercial banks and their overseas branches now participate in financial markets throughout the world. They transact business in large multiples of funds for corporations, governments, and other banking and financial firms in markets that are truly international in scope. Funds borrowed in one country are loaned in others. The foreign branches of American banks as well as foreign banks themselves perform the role of international intermediary through a complex network of branches and correspondents throughout the world.

In so doing they have increased and helped redistribute the available pool of international funds. They have assisted in the growth of world trade and economic growth. They have undoubtedly speeded the development of a more efficient and unified international money market. These international intermediaries have been able to provide the ultimate lenders with a greater degree of diversification and consequent reduction in risk than they would enjoy if they could put their funds only with a single-purpose domestic intermediary.

SUMMARY

In their domestic operations commercial banks provide a classic stereotype of a financial intermediary. Commercial banks collect funds by appealing to asset holders' demands for highly liquid assets, including assets that can be used as a medium of exchange. Banks have become increasingly successful in developing different types of deposits to appeal to many different specific asset preferences. The most rapid growth of bank assets has been in various kinds of time deposits. On the other side of their operations, the use of funds collected, banks have been primarily short-term commercial lenders. This pattern of activities is also changing as commercial banks extend more term loans and consumer installment loans and acquire more conventional residential mortgages.

Commercial banks also hold sizable portfolios of marketable securities. A part of the investment portfolios is invested in long-term state and local government bonds. A small but growing portion of corporate bonds is also held. Short-term liquid securities, primarily Treasury bills, form an essential part of commercial banks' investment portfolios. As we have seen, the main purpose of these marketable securities is to provide a hedge against banker's risk and to transfer lending power over time. As a result, bank holdings of securities fluctuate fairly widely from day to day, week to week, month to month, and year to year.

We must not forget that commercial banks are not simply domestic financial intermediaries. Directly or indirectly, many commercial banks have vast international operations, not only serving American companies and individuals abroad but operating as true international intermediaries.

NOTES

1. Federal Reserve *Bulletin*, October 1973, p. A28.

2. In Chapter 3 we distinguished between loan transactions and investment transactions as follows: "In the former category we place all transactions involving face-to-face negotiations between borrowers and lenders. . . . In the second category we place all transactions in 'public issues,' financial instruments designed to be sold on an impersonal basis to any and all buyers."

3. J. Hazelton, "Bank Service Charges in New England," in Federal Reserve Bank of Boston, *New England Business Review*, May 1968.

4. Federal Reserve *Bulletin*, October 1973.

5. These are average rates. A closer examination would reveal significant diversity in rates, depending on the size of the bank, its location, and other bank and near-bank competition.

6. The vertical axis in Figure 9.2 is a logarithmic scale. As a result, equal changes on any of the lines on the chart represent equal percentage rates of change, not equal dollar rates of change.

7. Federal Deposit Insurance Corporation, *Annual Report*, 1971 (Washington D.C., 1972), p. 238.

8. H. P. Willis, *American Banking*, rev. ed. (Chicago: La Salle Extension University, 1923), p 12.

9. R. I. Robinson, *The Management of Bank Funds* (New York: McGraw-Hill, 1951), p. 16.

10. Statement by A. Brimmer to Subcommittee on Financial Institutions, reprinted in Federal Reserve *Bulletin*, April 1971, p. 312.

11. President's Commission on Financial Structure and Regulation, *Report* (Washington, D.C., 1971).

12. Member banks must also hold reserves against balances borrowed by domestic banks from its foreign branches and from other foreign banks. As of January 1971, 20 percent had to be held in reserve against these borrowings. Only a comparatively few banks are in a position to borrow from foreign branches and foreign banks.

13. These new reserve classifications were promulgated in July 1972 in that month's Federal Reserve *Bulletin*. Member banks, however, enjoined the Federal Reserve from actually putting the new requirements into practice. The courts upheld the Federal Reserve Board, and the new requirements became effective in November 1972.

10
NEAR BANKS AS FINANCIAL INTERMEDIARIES

$\mathbf{I}$n the previous chapter we considered a group of financial intermediaries that by any definition must be classified as banks. There are about 14,000 commercial banks in the United States. In their hands we find the largest concentration of assets and the most diversified portfolio held by any group of financial intermediaries in the United States. As we saw in Chapter 9, the relative position of commercial banks has been eroded by intense competition from a large number of generally smaller intermediaries. Although these intermediaries are different in certain respects from each other, they can be grouped together in the general category of near banks.

THE CONCEPT OF A NEAR BANK

Our definition of a near bank is quite simple. It is a financial intermediary that raises a major portion of its operating funds by issuing liabilities or claims on itself that are close, if not perfect, substitutes for the savings deposits issued by commercial banks. Like savings deposits of commercial banks, this type of liability must first be converted into currency or check before it can directly effect a transfer of real goods. Also like savings deposits of commercial banks, this type of claim is readily converted into a medium of exchange.

Near banks actively compete with commercial banks for the surpluses generated by the household sector of the economy (Chapter 6). They offer the household a liquid asset that is quite safe and on which interest is paid. Near banks confine their activities to the domestic economy. Most are essentially local, personal savings banks.

MUTUAL SAVINGS BANKS

Of all the groups of near banks we will examine in this chapter, mutual savings banks are the only ones chartered solely by the states. There is no federal law that directly regulates these institutions.

As their name implies, these banks are mutual associations managed by self-perpetuating boards of trustees. The designated purpose of mutual savings banks was to provide a place for the small saver, the working man, to place his meager savings with the assurance of safety and liquidity. The mutual savings banks were to be thrift institutions.

Massachusetts chartered the first mutual savings bank in 1816. Throughout the nineteenth century other mutual savings institutions were chartered by the industrializing states in the Northeast. Commercial banks did not oppose states' chartering this type of intermediary because they did not view mutual savings banks as competitors. Mutual savings banks could not issue their own bank notes and therefore did not threaten this profitable prerogative of commercial banks. By the end of the century, however, other types of intermediaries existed. Many states never passed legislation permitting mutual savings banks to be chartered. Today only eighteen states charter mutual savings banks.

Throughout their existence, mutual savings banks have had an excellent record of safety. Even during the Depression of the 1930s few of these institutions failed. Several states had their own insurance corporations for mutual savings bank deposits. Since 1933, mutual savings institutions have been free to insure their deposits with the Federal Deposit Insurance Corporation. About two-thirds of them do. The remaining third, chartered by Massachusetts, insure their deposits with a state-owned insurance company.

Many mutual savings banks limit the size of account any one depositor may hold to $25,000. It is felt that this policy prevents the institution from becoming too dependent on one depositor and further reduces the banker's risk attached to a large withdrawal by one asset holder. The deposit liabilities of mutual savings banks traditionally have had a very low turnover, also reducing banker's risk and the need for substantial cash holdings. As a result, mutual savings banks have held, on the average, only 1.5 percent of total assets in cash.

From Table 10.1 we see that real estate mortgages form 67 percent of mutual savings banks' asset portfolios in 1972. Home mortgages became an acceptable investment for mutual associations in 1893. Since that time, the list of legal investments for mutual savings banks has been broadened by

Table 10.1. Consolidated Balance Sheet, Mutual Savings
Banks, December 31, 1972 (Millions of Dollars)

Assets	$100,593	Liabilities	$100,593
Cash and Deposits	1,644	Deposits	91,613
Securities	25,393	Miscellaneous	2,024
U.S. Government	5,523	Surplus	6,956
State and Local			
Government	873		
Bonds and Notes	15,397		
Stock	3,600		
Loans	70,535		
Real Estate	67,556		
Personal	1,476		
Other	1,503		
Miscellaneous	3,021		

SOURCE: Board of Governors of the Federal Reserve System, *Flow of Funds Accounts,
1945–1973* (Washington, D.C., August 1973), p. 99.

several states. Today, in fact, mutual savings banks frequently have more liberal loan and investment powers than savings and loan associations operating in the same state. Mutual savings banks are permitted to hold corporate debt issues and, in some states, corporate equity issues. Twelve states permit mutual savings banks to make consumer loans, and six permit them to accept demand deposits.[1]

Today there are fewer than 500 mutual savings banks. At the end of 1972 they had combined assets of $100.6 billion. Although savings shares at these institutions have grown from $20 billion in 1950 to $91.6 billion at the end of 1972, the prospects for future growth and expansion are not as favorable as for other near banks. It is unlikely that other states will pass legislation permitting mutual savings banks to be chartered. Their growth, then, must come in the Northeast, the Middle Atlantic, and a few Western states. These states, however, have been slow to permit mutual savings banks to branch. This confines the banks to inner-city locations that have not experienced either the population or income growth of the suburbs. Mutual savings banks have been able to maintain their position with other financial intermediaries by adjusting their loan and investment policy to include some emphasis on earnings as well as safety and liquidity.

SAVINGS AND LOAN ASSOCIATIONS

Whereas the mutual savings banks were founded to provide safe repositories for the modest savings of the working man, savings and loan associations were founded to secure a large enough pool of funds to support home financing and home ownership.

The first, the Oxford Provident Building Association, was founded in 1831 and was similar to the building societies of England. There was a need

218

for building or savings and loan associations, since home mortgages were available only from state banks. National banks were prohibited from making mortgage loans, and mutual savings banks were not permitted to hold mortgages until 1893.

During the first two decades of the twentieth century, savings and loan associations grew rapidly, benefiting from rising economic prosperity and the growth of the middle class, who wished to own homes. Savings and loan associations developed the amortized mortgage loan, which enabled the borrower not only to pay regular interest payments over the period of the loan but also to repay a part of the principal with each payment as well. Previously, mortgage loans were extended for five years. At the end of the period the borrower either had to come up with the principal in full to pay off the loan or request the bank to renew the loan for another five-year period.

The Depression severely hurt the savings and loan industry. In 1931, deposit withdrawals increased and loan repayments slowed. More and more loans became delinquent, foreclosures increased, and savings and loan associations found themselves in the real estate business. Commercial bank failures compounded the problem as savings and loan associations found access to their primary liquid assets—demand deposits with commercial banks—closed.

In the 1930s a system of Federal Home Loan Banks was set up. Legislation was passed enabling federal charters to be granted to associations meeting federal capital and cash reserve requirements. Provision was made to establish the Federal Savings and Loan Insurance Corporation, where savings and loan associations' deposit accounts could be insured.

As a result of this legislation, savings and loan associations are subject to the same fragmentation of supervision, insurance, chartering, and examination that is present in the commercial banking system. At the end of 1970, 2,067 of the 5,738 existing associations were federally chartered and therefore insured with the FSLIC. Another 2,298 state-chartered associations had insured their depositors' accounts to $20,000 either with FSLIC or with state insurance corporations in Massachusetts and Connecticut.[2]

The Federal Home Loan Bank System, with twelve regional banks, is similar to the Federal Reserve System. The banks are owned by member associations, and they hold some reserve deposits for member associations. Primary power is centralized in a board of five people. Member savings and loan associations may borrow from the Home Loan Bank System in times of excessive requests for withdrawal of deposits. In contrast to commercial banks, savings and loan associations have not been reluctant to borrow, and as of December 31, 1972, $7.9 billion in member borrowings was outstanding.

Member associations are subject to cash and liquid asset reserve requirements set by the Federal Home Loan Bank Board. Liquidity requirements

Table 10.2. **Consolidated Balance Sheets, All Operating Savings and Loan Associations, December 30, 1972 (Millions of Dollars)**

Assets		Liabilities	
Assets	$243,571	Liabilities	$243,571
Cash	2,770	Savings	207,305
Investments—U.S.		Federal Home Loan	
Securities	21,778	Bank Advances and	
Mortgages	206,387	Borrowings	7,979
Consumer Credit	2,423	Loans in Process	6,225
Other Assets	10,213	Other Loans	1,887
		Reserves and Surplus	20,175

SOURCE: Board of Governors of the Federal Reserve System, *Flow of Funds Accounts, 1945–1973* (Washington, D.C., August 1973), p. 99.

went into effect in January 1972. They are based on the average of the preceding month's total share deposits and may be met by holding cash, demand deposits with insured commercial banks, U.S. government securities, acceptances, federal agency notes, or commercial bank negotiable certificates of deposit. These requirements are not so much an attempt at monetary control as an effort to protect associations from large net withdrawals that could impair their solvency.

Federally chartered or insured savings and loan associations have been subject to limitation on the rate of interest they can pay on deposits since 1966. As shown in Table 10.2, with 80 percent of their liabilities in a highly liquid claim against themselves, savings and loan associations have found themselves vulnerable to large deposit withdrawals when the general level of interest rates rises above the legal rate they can pay on such deposits. This occurred in 1966 and again in 1969. In a period of disintermediation, that is, when asset holders are not willing to hold the indirect claims of financial intermediaries but go into the market for the direct claims of borrowers, intermediaries like savings and loan associations are pinched. Their inclination is to offer higher and higher rates to attract depositors. These funds, however, must then be reloaned at even higher rates of interest, often to high-risk borrowers. In recent periods when this occurred, several associations failed and others had to merge with stronger associations when their loan defaults increased. Limitations on interest rates paid by associations curb speculative bidding for funds and the resulting need to make high-risk loans.

Almost 80 percent of savings and loan associations' total assets are in mortgages. As mentioned earlier, mortgage loans come under usury laws in some states. In periods of generally high interest rates it may not be profitable to make mortgage funds available. The particular sector—housing and home construction—in which savings and loan associations concentrate their lending will suffer from lack of funds. There has been some discussion of permitting frequent renegotiation of rates charged on mortgage loans to protect the borrower from getting locked into high rates and the lending institution from getting locked into low ones.

The Federal National Mortgage Association has given savings and loan associations some relief by purchasing Veterans Administration guaranteed mortgages, mortgages insured by the Federal Housing Authority, and, as of February 1972, conventional mortgages from these institutions. Savings and loan associations can now sell some of their long-term illiquid assets (mortgages) for cash.

Savings and loan associations have sought broader lending authority from state and federal authorities, but it has not been forthcoming. Only a few states, notably Texas, permit associations to make personal loans that are unsecured or secured by property other than real estate or savings. Lending is generally limited to mortgages within the state or within a 100-mile radius of the institution. Thus, funds raised in an area are generally lent within that area.

Savings and loan associations have grown in number and asset size. Savings deposits have increased from $14 billion in 1950 to $207 billion at the beginning of 1973. Their share of total savings at both commercial banks and near banks has also increased, from 20 percent in 1950 to about 45 percent by the beginning of 1973. Regulations have improved the financial soundness of the industry. The industry stands to benefit from the development of a new secondary market for mortgages. Increased lending powers would assist the industry in its attempts to further diversify its portfolio, but it is difficult to predict the effect on savings and loan associations' asset growth.

CREDIT UNIONS

The credit union movement began in Germany in 1848. By 1900 a credit union had been organized in Canada. The first credit union in the United States was chartered by Massachusetts in 1909.

Credit unions were formed to promote thrift among their members and to provide them with a source of credit. Charters are granted only to "qualified groups which share a strong common bond of occupation or association or place of residence." Generally they are organized as cooperatives. Since passage of the Federal Credit Union Act in 1934, credit unions may be chartered by the states or by the federal government. Most states permit credit unions, but more than 12,000 of the nation's 22,000 credit unions have federal charters. Those with federal charters must insure their members' deposits to $20,000 with the National Credit Union Administration under a law that became effective January 1, 1971. State-chartered unions may voluntarily insure their depositors' accounts. It is estimated that credit unions have about 22 million members, of which 12 million belong to federally chartered unions. The federal credit unions are required to hold cash and liquid assets in an amount equal to 10 percent of their outstanding loans and risk assets. In fact, these institutions held about 5.2 percent in

221

Table 10.3. Consolidated Balance Sheet, Credit Unions,
December 31, 1972 (Millions of Dollars)

Assets	$21,709	Liabilities	$21,709
Cash	990	Shares of Members	21,709
Deposits in S&Ls	709		
U.S. Government Securities	2,197		
Home Mortgages	900		
Consumer Credit	16,913		

SOURCE: Board of Governors of the Federal Reserve System, *Flow of Funds Accounts,
1945–1973* (Washington, D.C., August 1973), p. 99.

cash, 10.4 percent in U.S. government securities, and 2.7 percent in savings and loan shares.[3]

As is obvious from Table 10.3, almost 100 percent of credit union funds comes from members' deposits. The use of these funds is limited by charter to loans to members only, cash, and liquid assets. At the end of 1970, credit unions had assets of $17.9 billion, of which almost $14 billion was in loans to members. By December 1972, assets had grown to $21.7 billion, of which $17.8 billion was lent to members.

All credit unions are limited to charging a maximum rate of 1 percent per month on the unpaid loan balance, or 12 percent per annum. There are no fees or credit investigation charges, so this rate is effectively less than most retail store credit and also less than finance company charges, which can legally run as high as 42 percent per annum in some states. Generally, loans are short term, and about half are secured with collateral. Increasingly, credit unions are making automobile loans, remodeling loans, and now some mortgage loans with maturities to ten years.

The interest rate paid to depositors varies widely. Often it is below what the saver could get from a savings and loan association or even a commercial bank. However, many credit unions are competitive, cutting the costs of administration through the use of volunteer help and donated office space. In addition, savers are willing to accept a lower rate in return for the right to borrow.

While only a minor threat to commercial banks or the other near banks we have discussed, credit unions have experienced rapid growth. Today they provide more than 12 percent of the total consumer installment credit outstanding and are strong competitors of finance companies.

FEDERALLY SPONSORED SAVINGS

The last near bank we are going to consider is one aspect of the federal government's activities. While the federal government does not acquire a majority of its funds by issuing a claim that is a close, if not perfect, substitute for commercial bank savings deposits, the funds it raises are substantial.

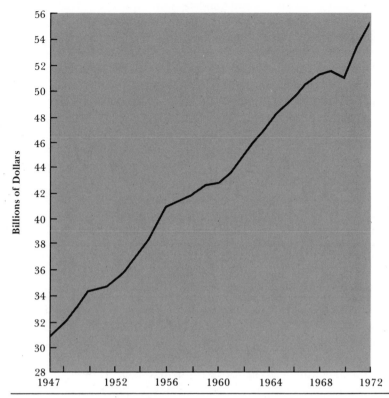

Figure 10.1 **Total Value Series E and Series H Savings Bonds Outstanding, 1947–1972** (Fiscal Year Ending June 30)
SOURCE: U.S. Department of the Treasury, *Annual Report, 1970* (Washington, D.C.); Federal Reserve *Bulletin*, September 1972, p. A44.

The savings bond program was begun in World War II as a method of mobilizing pools of idle savings and excess liquidity held by households to help finance the war effort. It has continued, although somewhat modified, to provide the asset holder with a risk-free claim that is guaranteed by the government and easily converted to cash at preestablished rates of interest depending on the length of time the bond is held.

These bonds are not negotiable, nor are they transferable except at death. Therefore, they are not marketable. However, in contrast to the other near-bank claims we have discussed, these bonds may be redeemed at most insured commercial banks and at many savings and loan associations.

Two types of savings bonds are still offered. The Series E bond is sold by the government at a discount. Currently, when held to maturity in five years and five months they yield the asset holder a 6 percent return. If a bond is redeemed prior to full maturity, the yield is somewhat less. From time to time the yield on these bonds has been increased by shortening the maturity. The Series E bonds come in denominations as small as $25. Series H bonds are also sold by the government. These are bought at par value in minimum denominations of $500, and the interest is paid to the holder semiannually.

Savings bonds have remained quite competitive with other saving deposit alternatives. Figure 10.1 shows the increase in total savings bonds outstanding that has occurred since 1947.

Savings bonds are a safe and, by virtue of their instant convertibility to cash throughout the United States, perfectly liquid asset offering a competitive rate of return. These bonds may be viewed as strong competitors with near-bank claims for funds from private depositors.

The federal government also offered a postal savings plan for the smaller saver beginning in 1910. Never acquiring large amounts of funds, the program ended in 1966, when the postal savings system's remaining $0.5 billion in liabilities was assumed by the U.S. Treasury.

BANKS AND NEAR BANKS

What we have chosen to call near banks is a diverse group of institutions. We have lumped them together here because their common feature is that they attract savings of consumers or individuals by offering claims that are close substitutes for each other and a close substitute for the savings deposit liabilities of commercial banks. Near banks have competed aggressively for households' savings. Since 1950, with the exception of mutual savings banks, they have increased their share of total savings deposits, largely at the expense of commercial banks. Today households hold more than $300 billion in liquid claims against these institutions, but even including savings bonds held by the public, their holdings against these institutions are only equal to half the total assets of commercial banks.

Historically, commercial banks almost ignored time deposit business. It fell to them as a matter of convenience. The near banks, in contrast, have sought consumer savings by offering more attractive interest rates on these deposits than commercial banks could pay. Near banks provided more convenient and flexible hours, locations, and banking services. Near banks often would give depositors preferential loan treatment when commercial banks and other intermediaries would have denied credit or charged much higher rates.

The composition of the share of total savings of households held in commercial banks, near banks, and federal savings bonds has changed since 1950. Many factors have contributed to this changing pattern. The rapid assumption of dominance by savings and loan associations came during the period when these institutions were not limited by interest rate ceilings and could pay premium rates. Throughout the period commercial banks have been subject to government-imposed ceilings, and at times this has limited their ability to compete for savings. The growth of savings and loan associations was also concurrent with the period of strong demand for housing. Savings bond sales have been constrained by the government's reluctance to change interest yields. Lagging interest rate changes have deterred households from increasing their holdings of savings bonds more rapidly.

Note that we do not include other time deposits of commercial banks, which showed phenomenal growth during the decade of the 1960s, because these deposits are not held exclusively by individuals. It is in this area that commercial banks have been able to attract a large volume of new funds from individuals and businesses. Commercial banks, furthermore, have a broader depositor and borrower constituency than near banks. As a result, they tailor their services to their corporate borrowers and depositors, while near banks have been able to cater to individuals and attract their savings.

SUMMARY

A near bank is a financial intermediary that raises a major portion of its funds by issuing claims on itself that are close, if not perfect, substitutes for the savings deposits issued by commercial banks. Near banks actively compete with commercial banks and each other for the surpluses generated by the household sector.

One group, mutual savings banks, is owned by the depositors. Because they are chartered only by eighteen states, their growth numerically and in asset size has been hindered. Real estate mortgages dominate the asset portfolios of mutual savings banks. Savings and loan associations may be chartered by the states or by the federal government. Some are capital stock companies, but most are mutual associations. Savings and loan associations have experienced rapid asset growth and have funneled most of the funds acquired into real estate mortgages. Credit unions are the third group of near banks. They, too, may be state or federally chartered. Although still small in asset size compared with either mutual savings banks or savings and loan associations, credit unions have been a strong force in providing credit to members for installment buying. Each of these near-bank groups can insure deposits (asset holders' claims) up to $20,000 each through various federal deposit insurance corporations.

Another close substitute for commercial bank savings deposits are U.S. savings bonds. Savings bonds have attracted more than $55 billion in funds from individuals. They offer asset holders a risk-free claim that is easily converted to cash.

Together, near-bank deposits plus U.S. savings bonds accounted at the end of 1970 for almost $285 billion, almost entirely from households.

NOTES

1. President's Commission on Financial Structure and Regulation, *Report* (Washington, D.C., 1971).

2. Federal Home Loan Bank Board, *Journal*, September 1971.

3. National Credit Union Administration, *Annual Report, 1970* (Washington, D.C., 1971).

11

OTHER FINANCIAL INTERMEDIARIES

 In the previous two chapters we examined financial institutions whose liabilities are either money or near substitutes for money. To round out our discussion of financial intermediaries we must now turn our attention to a heterogeneous collection of intermediaries whose liabilities do not have this characteristic. That is not to say that these institutions have little economic significance, for a major portion of the savings of society are channeled through them. They now hold assets of over $450 billion, and their relative importance in the financial system is continuing to increase. This pool of funds significantly affects the stock markets, corporate bond and state and local debt issues, and consumer lending.

The range of activities of firms in this residual group is extensive. At one extreme we have the mutual fund, a type of intermediary that simply provides portfolio diversification and professional selection of securities for the asset holder. The liabilities of the mutual funds do not have the same quality of liquidity as those of depository intermediaries, but they can be redeemed quite readily. At the other extreme are insurance companies, a set of institutions whose liabilities have very specialized characteristics whose nature makes it easy to omit these companies in a list of intermediaries.

One tends to forget that they borrow and lend and to regard them simply as firms selling a service, insurance.

Between these two extremes are several other more or less specialized intermediaries that seek out sources of funds to be borrowed on a wide variety of terms, lend for specialized purposes, and, by holding a diversified portfolio of securities, perform the essential function of risk spreading. These specialized intermediaries are so numerous and so varied that they almost defy systematic cataloging, and the list is continually changing as firms are established to take advantage of new opportunities for profitable intermediation.

PURE INTERMEDIATION: OPEN-END MUTUAL FUNDS

THE NATURE OF A MUTUAL FUND

The concept of a mutual fund or investment company is quite simple. As defined in the Investment Company Act of 1940, these corporations are in the business of investing, reinvesting, owning, holding, or trading in securities. More than 40 percent of their assets must be invested in securities other than U.S. government obligations and cash.

Both open-end and closed-end investment companies are commonly called mutual funds. We will discuss the closed-end fund in a later section of this chapter. In an open-end mutual fund, individuals contribute funds to a central pool by purchasing shares or "units" in the fund. The number of shares or units an open-ended fund may sell is unlimited. Thus, open-end funds are able to acquire additional funds for investment as long as they can sell additional shares.

Members' claims on the fund are proportionate to the number of units they own. Over time, the value of any given portfolio of securities will change as a result of changes in the market prices of the securities included in the portfolio. As a result, the value of each unit will change.

The cost of each new unit of an open-end fund will depend on the value of the portfolio of securities at the time the new unit is issued. This may be higher or lower than the cost of the original units, and earlier subscribers will correspondingly earn capital gains or capital losses on their units.

Open-end funds not only sell additional shares continuously at the current net asset value but also redeem (or cash in) members' units for the current net asset value by selling securities out of the portfolio if necessary.

With the pool of funds acquired from individuals in exchange for shares, mutual funds purchase a portfolio of securities. The portfolio is then adjusted in line with the investment objectives of the fund, expectations about its holdings, and infusions of additional funds.

In principle any group of individuals could organize an open-end fund. For example, you and nine other friends could decide to form a mutual

Table 11.1. Assets of Open-End Investment Companies
(Mutual Funds), December 31, 1972 (Millions of Dollars)

	Amount	Percent
Liquid Assets		
Cash and Demand Deposits	$ 913	1.5
Fixed Income Securities		
U.S. Government Securities	689	1.2
Corporate Bonds	5,068	8.5
Open-Market Paper	1,433	2.4
Variable Income Securities		
Corporate Shares	51,728	86.4
Total	$59,831	100.0

SOURCE: Board of Governors of the Federal Reserve System, *Flow of Funds Accounts,*
1945–1973 (Washington, D.C., August 1973), p. 102.

fund. You might decide that the value of the initial units will be $10. Each
purchases one unit, providing an investment fund of $100.

As the value of the assets purchased with the original subscribed capital
rises or falls, so does the value of the units. But since it is an open-end fund,
the number of units is not limited to the original number, and the value
of a unit is not fixed at the original value. Thus, if after one month the
value of the portfolio has increased so that the unit value is $12 (i.e., the
total fund is now worth $120), additional units would cost $12 each. Similarly, if in the following month, because of an adverse turn in the market,
the total portfolio falls in value so that the unit value is only 8, then additional units can be purchased at that price and existing units can be cashed
in for that price. Why? Because that is the value of the assets that must be
sold out of the fund so that a unit can be cashed in.

Such a mutual fund is more likely to be called an investment club.
Unlike a true mutual fund, it does not sell units to the general public but
confines its membership to a specified group of individuals. Such clubs are
quite common, and the arrangements normally call for fixed monthly sub-
scriptions by each member of the club. Given the small scale of the typical
club's investment portfolio, the opportunities for portfolio diversification are
limited, as are the possibilities for expert management (see the discussion
of economies of scale in financial intermediation in Chapter 8). People frequently join such clubs to learn about the stock market and to gain experience in making investment decisions while pooling the limited time each
one can devote to research on securities. On a small scale, the basic principle is the same as that involved in a true mutual fund (although the operations of true mutual funds are supervised by government agencies).

THE ASSET PORTFOLIOS OF OPEN-END MUTUAL FUNDS

A consolidated statement of the assets of open-end mutual funds is
shown in Table 11.1. The contrasts between the portfolio of this inter-

mediary and those of most of the other financial intermediaries we have examined so far are very pronounced.

Liquidity. You should note particularly the relatively small holdings of cash characteristic of the mutual funds. Like banks, their liabilities are payable on demand (the units can be cashed at any time). Unlike banks, the dollar value of the claims is not fixed but fluctuates in value with changes in the market value of the asset portfolio. Like depository intermediaries and commercial banks, mutual funds have a degree of banker's risk, but it is not as high as that faced by commercial banks. Theoretically, the mutual fund could sell its entire portfolio of securities in a short time and redeem all shares outstanding at the net asset value of each share. The fear many people express, however, is that if there were a "run" to redeem mutual fund shares, the industry would have to sell its holdings in large blocks, which would severely depress stock prices and panic other shareholders, largely individuals and pension funds.

Concentration of Equities. An equally important point to note in Table 11.1 is the overwhelming importance of equities among the assets of mutual funds. At the end of 1972, corporate shares accounted for over 85 percent of the market value of the assets of these reporting mutual funds. For many funds that are almost completely in corporate shares, this proportion would of course be much higher.

Growth Rate. Mutual funds first appeared in the United States in 1924. These were closed-end funds, which we shall discuss subsequently. Mutual funds fell from favor during the Depression and had great difficulty attracting much investor interest until after World War II.

In 1940 the Investment Company Act was passed, under which mutual funds were classified and required to register with the Securities Exchange Commission. Mutual funds must also adhere to SEC regulations that apply to publicly held corporations. In 1941 the SEC reported a total of 436 companies with total assets of $2.5 billion.

By 1965 the number of mutual funds operating had increased to 727, and the market value of their total assets was $44.6 billion. During much of this period stock market prices were rising. Clearly, fluctuations in the market value of securities has much to do with changes in mutual funds' total assets. For example, in 1969 mutual funds had assets of $72.5 billion, but by the end of 1970 their assets had dropped to $50 billion. What portion of the growth of mutual funds is due to rising stock market prices and what portion is due to increased purchases of fund shares by asset holders? From 1959 to 1970 the number of mutual funds doubled. Net sales of mutual fund shares (sales in excess of redemptions) brought an additional $23.3 billion to mutual funds. Capital gains accounted for an additional increase in asset value of $11.4 billion.[1]

What we see, then, is that mutual funds have grown in number and asset size, in part owing to infusions of new funds from individual investors and in part owing to the general rise in the level of stock prices. What accounted for this strong demand for mutual fund shares?

Risk Spreading and the Demand for Mutual Fund Shares. In Chapter 5 we analyzed the demand for financial instruments in terms of a choice at the margin between expected yield, risk, and liquidity, with inflation and taxation important considerations entering into the calculation of "real" yield. Although shares of mutual funds are more liquid than many assets, it is clear that, unlike banks and near banks, mutual funds do not appeal to asset holders' demands for liquidity. Rather, it is in the realm of risk and expected yield that we must find the answer to our question.

The essential characteristics of common stock as a financial instrument were discussed in Chapter 3. The point stressed was that these securities involved a residual claim to the potentially highly variable profits of a business enterprise. Considered individually, therefore, common stocks are relatively risky assets. Asset holders with a strong aversion to risk might be expected to eschew heavy investment in stocks unless their asset portfolios were large enough to permit substantial portfolio diversification and to generate sufficient income to permit the purchase of professional investment advice. A mutual fund, by pooling the funds of many small asset holders, can achieve the necessary scale of operations to afford professional selection of securities and to achieve substantial portfolio diversification.

You will recall from Chapter 8 that the expected yield on a diversified portfolio of securities is the weighted average of the yields on the individual securities included in the portfolio. In this sense, the mutual fund does not alter the yields available in the marketplace. What the fund does is reduce the risk associated with any given level of expected yield. Thus, the mutual fund effectively improves the trade-off between risk and expected yield available to asset holders, particularly to those with relatively small asset portfolios.

Are Mutual Fund Shares Riskless? It is worth noting that although a mutual fund effectively reduces risk through portfolio diversification, even a mutual fund that invests in a broad range of corporate stocks cannot render negligible the total risk to its shareholders. As noted in Chapter 8, portfolio diversification is effective in reducing risk only if the yields on the assets included in the portfolio are independent. To some extent this is true of the yields on common stocks. Individual companies may prosper or fail regardless of the fates of other companies. However, because of broad cyclical movements in the economy as a whole, the profits of all companies have a tendency to rise and fall together. Thus, the yields on common stocks are not completely independent but have some degree of positive correlation. Even the shares of a widely diversified mutual fund cannot be riskless.

Specialization Among Mutual Funds. The individual investor has a range of choice open to him. The degree of portfolio diversification varies widely among funds. There are funds that invest almost exclusively in chemi-

Table 11.2. Mutual Funds by Asset Size, 1970

Asset Size	Number of Funds	Percent of Total Mutual Fund Assets
More Than $1 Billion	10	32.7
$500 Million–$1 Billion	14	19.5
$300 Million–$500 Million	13	10.2
$100 Million–$300 Million	59	19.9
$50 Million–$100 Million	56	8.0
$10 Million–$50 Million	169	8.1
$1 Million–$10 Million	188	1.5
Less Than $1 Million	77	0.1

SOURCE: Wiesenberger Financial Services, *Investment Companies, 1971 Mutual Funds and Other Types* (New York), p. 44.

cal stocks, mining property stocks, insurance companies, or natural-resource-oriented companies. There are funds that invest exclusively in the securities of other mutual funds. The individual can find a range of management objectives as well. There are funds that hold only common stock and a small amount of liquid assets, funds that hold both equity and debt obligations of corporations as well as some liquid assets, and funds that hold preferred stock and debt issues. At the end of 1970, approximately 82 percent of total mutual fund assets were in diversified common stock funds, 13 percent in balanced funds that held both bonds and stock with the objective of income and some capital appreciation, and 5 percent in income funds. In recent years the industry has moved away from balanced funds to diversified common stock funds that emphasize capital appreciation of assets.

The individual investor can also choose among a wide range of funds by size. As shown in Table 11.2, 6 percent of the mutual funds control over 60 percent of total mutual fund assets. However, while a few funds may dominate the industry in terms of size, others may dominate performance, which varies from year to year.[2]

Finally, the individual may choose a mutual fund on the basis of whether it is a "load" fund or a "no-load" fund. If an investor chooses a "load" fund, shares are bought at the net asset value on that day. In addition, the buyer is charged a fee of 5 percent to 9 percent of his purchase to cover the cost of selling the fund's shares and managing its assets. Often this charge absorbs the first year's appreciation in value of the shares. For example, an individual wishes to invest $1000 in a "load" fund whose shares are selling at $10. The loading fee is 8 percent. Instead of buying 100 shares at $10 per share, he actually purchases only 92 shares at $10 per share, with the remaining $80 going to cover the administrative and selling costs of the fund. To break even on his investment, the holder would have to obtain $10.87 each for his 92 shares.

Shares of a "no-load" fund are also bought at net asset value but without any amount being used to pay sales fees. The "no-load" fund meets its administrative costs by paying an annual fee to its investment advisors. This fee is usually stated as a percentage of the average net asset value of the fund, that is, half of 1 percent of the average net asset value. If it were a $100 million fund, the management would receive $500,000, which is calculated daily and subtracted from the net asset value at which shares are sold and redeemed.

Many mutual stock funds are highly specialized, with consequent relatively high degrees of risk. Why should these mutual funds be such attractive investments, particularly since we have assumed that most investors are risk avoiders?

Inflation and Taxes. An important attribute of common stock (which we discussed at some length in Chapter 5) is that, unlike bonds and other fixed income securities, the real value of common stock is not necessarily eroded as a result of inflation and may even be enhanced by it. Through portfolio diversification, mutual funds consisting almost exclusively of common stock reduce some of the risk attached to such holdings. At the same time they provide a *hedge* against the risk of inflation. This appears to be a significant consideration leading to investment in mutual fund shares.

In Chapter 5 we also noted that the taxation system may affect choices among financial instruments. The particularly important consideration in this regard is the fact that capital gains are taxed at a lower rate than interest income on corporate debt securities. This makes specialized stock funds, with the possibilities of substantial capital gains, very attractive.

MUTUAL FUNDS: A PURE INTERMEDIARY

We can summarize the essential contribution of mutual funds to the structure of the financial system by saying that the mutual fund provides the individual asset holder with a better trade-off between risk and yield on corporate securities than he could obtain directly in the marketplace. In part this is accomplished by taking advantage of economies of scale in portfolio management: through professional appraisal, selection, and trading of securities. Mutual funds spread the risk of holding such securities at a comparatively low cost for the small investor. The fundamental principle through which the mutual fund alters the *risk-yield trade-off* is portfolio diversification. Through their large purchases of a number of different securities, mutual funds narrow the risk differential. By providing the small investor with an alternative to holding the fixed income securities that are typically open to the small asset holder, the mutual funds have raised the return to him.

On the other side, as an intermediary, mutual funds have increased the flow of funds and availability of funds in the capital markets. This increased flow has kept down the real costs of obtaining capital to finance expansion of plant and equipment. Whether mutual funds have improved the allocation of funds or greatly enhanced the efficiency with which the markets allocate money capital has not been the subject of study to any great extent. By comparison, several groups publish annual appraisals for asset holders as to funds' performances in the market. Increasingly, funds are important to the functioning of the capital markets. Along with pension funds, they hold large blocks of securities, thereby compounding the problems of an orderly functioning market.

Regulation of investment companies began in 1940, and amendments to the Investment Company Act of 1940 passed in 1970 strengthened some of the Securities Exchange Commission's regulatory practices. Here again we encounter the problems of protecting the individual. Management fees, load charges, and contractual plans have all been criticized. The rapid growth and proliferation of funds combined with recent declines in stock prices have brought demands for closer regulation and scrutiny.

PURE INTERMEDIATION: CLOSED-END INVESTMENT FUNDS

The mutual funds we have been discussing are open-end funds in that they involve unlimited provision for the issuance of new shares or units of the fund and will redeem outstanding shares in cash at the net asset value prevailing at that moment.

Closed-end funds differ from open-end funds in that they authorize a limited number of shares to be sold in order to acquire a pool of funds, which is then used to purchase a portfolio of securities. If additional funds are desired by the closed-end investment company, it must obtain permission from its shareholders, like other corporations, to make a secondary offering of shares.

The shareholder in a closed-end fund can sell his shares in the market only through a broker. There is no redemption privilege attached to closed-end fund shares. The price of a closed-end share is determined by market forces, the supply of shares outstanding, and the demand for those shares, rather than being tied directly to the current net asset value of the shares.

However, the basic principle on which both open-end and closed-end funds operate is the same—improving the trade-off between risk and yield for individual asset holders by spreading risks over a diversified portfolio of securities. Closed-end funds have virtually no banker's risk, since they have no obligation to redeem shares on demand. In periods when open-end funds experience net redemptions, this is a definite advantage.

Closed-end companies have found it more difficult than open-end funds to attract new pools of funds because of the limitation on shares. They have not been able to market dividend reinvestment, contractual share accumulation plans, and the like, devices that open-end funds have used successfully. Recently, several new closed-end investment companies have been formed that issue two types of shares, income and capital. Income shareholders receive payments out of the dividends the portfolio generates. Capital share-holders receive dividends to the extent that the fund sells shares that have appreciated in the marketplace. These dual-purpose funds have attracted new investor interest.

In June 1970 there were about 195 active closed-end funds. Only 24 are of significant size, with total assets of $6.1 billion. The largest closed-end fund reported total assets at the end of 1972 of almost $850 million.[3]

The first closed-end funds were established in the United States in 1924. In addition to selling an initial offering of shares, many closed-end funds borrowed heavily, offering their notes and debentures in exchange for funds. These funds were then invested in a portfolio of securities during a period of rising stock market prices. The funds' shareholders were delighted as the value of their shares rose even more rapidly than the level of stock market prices. If a closed-end fund, for example, sold 100,000 shares at $10 per share and then borrowed an additional $1 million, it could acquire a portfolio worth $2 million. If the value of the portfolio increased by 50 percent, to $3 million, the value of each share would be close to $20, an appreciation of 100 percent. However, if the portfolio declined in value from $2 million to $1 million the shares would be worthless, since the remaining assets would have to be used to pay the debts of the funds before any share-holder claims would be honored.

It was estimated that closed-end funds held some $7 billion in assets in 1929, before the stock market crash. Large losses were incurred by these funds when stock market prices fell rapidly, and closed-end funds fell from investor favor.

FINANCE COMPANIES: SPECIALIZED
LENDING TO HIGH-RISK BORROWERS

As we noted in Chapter 9, commercial banks have dramatically increased their lending to individuals since 1950. By 1973, banks had about $90 billion extended to consumers. There has also been an increase in consumer loan activity by credit unions as their assets have grown. Both banks and credit unions have aggressively competed with finance companies for this business. Finance companies, however, have also diversified their lending activities and moved into mobile home financing and commercial leasing, as well as into financing business receivables.

At one time finance companies could be divided into three broad groups on the basis of their primary lending activity. There were personal finance companies, sales finance companies, and business finance companies. Personal finance companies concentrated their activities in making cash loans to individuals. Sales finance companies, on the other hand, had little direct contact with consumers. Rather, they bought consumer installment sales contracts from automobile dealers and other retail merchants. Business finance companies remained outside the consumer credit arena and confined their lending activities to the business sector. They would buy accounts receivable or lend funds to a business against its accounts receivable for short periods. They also assisted businesses in financing new equipment and capital purchases.

Over time, however, finance companies have become more diversified in their lending activities, so that the traditional classification of companies by primary lending activity is no longer made. In 1970 the Federal Reserve surveyed finance companies, as it had done at five-year intervals since 1955.[4] It was evident from the responses that in the preceding five years finance companies had become more diversified in their lending activities and fewer in number. During the period there were a number of business failures and mergers in the industry. By 1970 there were only 3000 useful respondents to the survey compared to 4300 in 1965. In addition to the decline in the number of firms, there was also evidence that the portion of total business done by a few giant firms in the industry had increased. In 1970, 4.5 percent of the firms had gross receivables of over $25 million and held 93 percent of the industry's total gross receivables. In 1965, just under 3 percent of the finance companies had gross receivables of more than $25 million, and they held about 88 percent of the industry's total. It continues to be an industry in which a few giant firms account for an overwhelming portion of the business.

Lending Activities. The 1965 survey of finance companies showed that consumer receivables accounted for 65 percent of the industry's gross receivables. By 1970, consumer receivables accounted for 55 perecent of total gross receivables. Figure 11.1 illustrates the different types of lending by finance companies in 1965 and 1970. After personal cash loans, automobile financing directly to consumers was the next major lending activity to consumers. Finance companies also assisted automobile dealers by buying automobile paper from them. A major part of the $7.5 billion in wholesale business receivables held in 1970 was automobile paper. Leasing accounted for 16 percent of the total gross business receivables held by finance companies in mid-1970. This is an alternative method used by businesses to acquire capital equipment.

Sources of Funds. It had been evident from earlier surveys that each of the three types of finance companies had somewhat different sources of funds. Sales finance companies relied quite heavily on short-term debt, particularly commercial paper. Personal finance companies obtained a major portion of their lendable funds by issuing long-term debt, while business finance companies, generally smaller, relied heavily on bank loans.

The data presented by the Federal Reserve for 1970 are in consolidated form. However, it is evident that there was a shift to greater reliance on commercial paper and short-term debt for funds. In 1965, 53 percent of the total debt issued by finance companies was short term. This shift was un-

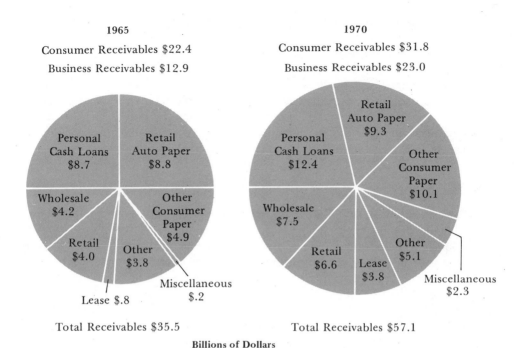

1965

Consumer Receivables $22.4

Business Receivables $12.9

Personal Cash Loans $8.7

Retail Auto Paper $8.8

Wholesale $4.2

Other Consumer Paper $4.9

Retail $4.0

Other $3.8

Lease $.8

Miscellaneous $.2

Total Receivables $35.5

1970

Consumer Receivables $31.8

Business Receivables $23.0

Retail Auto Paper $9.3

Personal Cash Loans $12.4

Other Consumer Paper $10.1

Wholesale $7.5

Retail $6.6

Lease $3.8

Other $5.1

Miscellaneous $2.3

Total Receivables $57.1

Billions of Dollars

Figure 11.1 Composition of Loan Portfolio: Finance Companies, 1965 and 1970
SOURCES "Survey of Finance Companies—1970," Federal Reserve *Bulletin*, November 1972, p. 967.

doubtedly a response to rising interest rates that began in 1966. Finance companies were reluctant to issue long-term debt obligations at high interest rates, and commercial paper became an increasingly popular method of raising short-term funds during this period. In 1965, commercial paper outstanding represented about 60 percent of finance companies' total short-term debt. By 1970, this figure had risen to almost 75 percent. The data on finance companies were collected for June 30, 1970, about the time the commercial paper market was undergoing its retrenchment (see Chapter 3).

Table 11.3. **Consolidated Balance Sheet, Finance Companies, December 31, 1972 (Millions of Dollars)**

Assets	$77,974	Liabilities	$77,974
Demand Deposits and Currency	3,208	Open-Market Paper	22,130
Home Mortgages	11,097	Bank Loans (not elsewhere classified)	16,377
Consumer Credit	37,529	Corporate Bonds	32,093
Other Loans to Business	26,140	Taxes Payable	298
		Other	7,076

SOURCE: Board of Governors of the Federal Reserve System, *Flow of Funds Accounts, 1945–1972* (Washington, D.C., August 1973), p. 105.

Finance companies have reduced their reliance on commercial paper as a source of funds since that time, as is evident in Table 11.3.

Consolidated figures obscure not only the differences between types of finance companies but also their variation in size. Only the largest and best-known finance companies can issue commercial paper. These firms dominate the industry. For companies with gross receivables above $25 million, bank loans accounted for about 11 percent of total liabilities and capital. For firms with less than $25 million in gross receivables outstanding in 1970, bank loans accounted for almost 35 percent of total liabilities and capital.

CONCLUSIONS

Finance companies have become more diversified lenders, but their loans are still significant to consumer buying. Loans are most often made directly or indirectly to higher-risk individuals and small businesses. Finance companies actively compete with each other and increasingly face competition for consumer loans from commercial banks and credit unions. However, finance companies have become more aggressive in pursuing business lending opportunities, particularly in the area of business leasing.

Finance companies are rather specialized intermediaries that have developed skills in intermediating a particular type of risk. In many cases these finance companies have serviced loan demands that other intermediaries have been unable or unwilling to accept.

SPECIALIZED INTERMEDIATION: INSURANCE COMPANIES

The combined assets of the 3000 general insurance companies (i.e., those specializing in insurance against fire, theft, automobile accidents, disability, etc.) and the 1800 life insurance companies in the United States totaled almost $300 billion at the beginning of 1973.[5] This represented the largest pool of funds administered by any single group of financial intermediaries aside from commercial banks. Clearly, the insurance companies represent a major concentration of financial resources. But is it legitimate to refer to them as financial intermediaries? Selling insurance seems to have little in common with commercial banking.

INSURANCE AS AN ASSET

Before attempting to answer this question we should explore the nature of insurance as an asset.

Pure Insurance. In its "pure" form, insurance simply involves a pooling of risks. Life insurance is probably the most familiar type of insurance; hence, an example involving life insurance may help make the point.

Imagine that you are among 100 people, all of the same age and sex, who decide to insure each others' lives for the forthcoming year. The agreement is that if any member of the group dies during the year his estate will be paid $1000. By consulting an actuary—a person trained, among other things, to derive probabilities of people of specified characteristics dying over a specified period on the basis of mortality tables (historical records of the incidence of death)—you discover that it is most probable that one of the people in the group will die during the course of the year. This means that each member of the group must expect to contribute $10 during the year. Of course, the incidence of death is uncertain. It may be greater or less than the most probable number, and the necessary individual contribution may be higher or lower than $10. However, actuarial estimates of the death rate are surprisingly accurate, at least for large groups. For a small group— and 100 is a small group—the risk to the insurers will be relatively great.

In order to avoid the risk that some member will not pay his share when called upon, you may agree to form a mutual insurance company, with each paying his contribution—his premium—in advance. In order to cover the expected claim payments from the fund during the year, each member's premium would have to be $10. The higher the probability of death within the specified period, or the larger the payment to be made upon death, the higher the premium would have to be. The insurance company must also recognize that the death rate may be higher than predicted, and it must make financial provision for such a contingency—it must maintain "reserves." In order to accumulate funds for this purpose and to cover the costs of administering the company (collecting the premiums, keeping the company's books, managing its funds, dealing with policyholders' claims, selling insurance, etc.), the premium will have to be substantially higher than $10—perhaps $12 to $15.

A life insurance policy is an asset to each policyholder and a claim on the insurance company. But it is a very unusual asset. Unlike a bond, for example, the date of future payment is not fixed, and indeed the fact of payment is not certain. Payment will only be made if a specified event (in this case a death) occurs during a specified period (the term of the policy, in this case the following year). If that event does not occur during that period, and it may not, then no payment at all will be made and the policyholder has no further legal claim on the insurance company.

The Present Value and Expected Yield on Pure Insurance. If pure life insurance is an asset that can be purchased in varying quantities in the marketplace, then rational choice presumably calls for a comparison of the present value of the insurance with its market price or a comparison of the expected yield on insurance with the yields on other assets that might be purchased with the same funds.

Consider again the earlier example of an insurance policy calling for a payment of $1000 should the insured die during the forthcoming year. Since the amount of the payment is uncertain—it may be either $1000 or $0—we can calculate the present value of the asset only on the basis of the expected value of the payment (i.e., taking account of the probability that a payment of $1000 will be made). In the present case, given that there are two possi-bilities—a payment of $1000, with a probability of .01, or a payment of $0, with a probability of .99—the present value of the insurance payment is:

$$v = (.01)(\$1000) + (.99)(0)$$
$$= \$10$$

In other words, the purchaser of this insurance policy must pay perhaps $15 for a claim to a possible future payment, when the present value of that claim is only $10! Clearly, the expected yield on such an asset is negative. The same basic principles can be applied to pure insurance policies written for contingencies other than death and, while the calculations are more complicated for terms longer than one year, always with the same result. If insurance companies are to cover all administrative and selling costs and to make a profit, the expected yield on pure term insurances must be negative.

There is always a wide variety of assets available in the marketplace having expected yields that are greater than zero. Why, then, would anyone purchase pure insurance as an asset?

The Demand for Pure Insurance. Our analysis of the problem of asset selection in Chapter 5 stressed that expected yield was not the sole criterion governing such choices. Rather, the problem is that of choice, at the margin, between expected yield, risk, and liquidity. Purchasers of pure insurance are acquiring an asset designed as a hedge against the risk of financial loss, and they are doing it at some expected net cost in the sense that the expected yield on the asset is negative. In general, insurance is purchased to hedge against the risk of destruction or impairment of other assets, such as the risk that fire may destroy a house or factory, or that illness or death of the major breadwinner might impair the future income of the household. However, it may also be taken out as a hedge against a great variety of other financial contingencies, including very commonly the risk of legal liability for auto-mobile accidents.

INSURANCE POLICIES AS A VEHICLE FOR SYSTEMATIC SAVING

Not all insurance policies sold by life insurance companies are of this pure or *term* variety. A pure insurance policy cannot be used as a vehicle for the accumulation of savings, since at the end of the specified term, if the event against which insurance was taken out (death, fire, accident) has not occurred, the policyholder has no further claim on the company. However, life insurance companies also offer a variety of policies that permit the sys-tematic accumulation of savings. The periodic "premiums" paid to the insur-ance company include the cost of insurance per se (plus the administration cost, of course) plus an additional sum that constitutes a periodic payment into a cumulating fund. At the end of a fixed term the policyholder has a claim to a specified lump sum payment from the company whether he dies within the period or not, and during its life the policy has a cumulating cash value that the policyholder can claim by surrendering his policy or borrow against. Such a policy involves the principle of coinsurance. In the early years of the policy the insurance is provided primarily by the insurance company, whereas in the later years of the policy the insurance element declines sharply, with protection provided primarily by the policyholder's own savings accumulated with the insurance company.

It is difficult to calculate the rate of return on such savings-type life insurance policies. However, most calculations that have been made suggest that the rate of return is generally low relative to yields available on alternative assets. Nonetheless, such insurance policies are very popular, with the result that life insurance provides a major vehicle for personal saving. Why is this such an attractive vehicle for savings?

In part, the answer may be that the policyholders do not know the rate of return on their savings accumulated with life insurance companies. In part they may be attracted by the very fact that insurance is combined with saving. They may also be impressed with the apparent safety of their funds with insurance companies. Also, policyholders are clearly attracted by the systematic nature of the saving process.

INSURANCE COMPANIES AS FINANCIAL INTERMEDIARIES

When we explored the concept of financial intermediation we saw that it has two important aspects. On the one hand, a financial intermediary issues financial instruments, or claims on itself, and uses the funds so collected to make loans and acquire a variety of financial assets. On the other hand, by holding a large, diversified portfolio of assets, a financial intermediary takes advantage of economies of scale and spreads risk, permitting it to offer a class of financial instruments with a better trade-off between risk, expected yield, and/or liquidity than would otherwise be available in the market.

Many economists would argue that, given this concept of a financial intermediary, insurance companies can be considered financial intermediaries only to the extent that they issue life insurance policies with a savings feature attached. Financial intermediation involves the holding of a diversified portfolio of assets in order to spread risks. Pure insurance is different. It simply involves a pooling of risks. For pure insurance there need be no necessary accumulation of assets and hence no lending activities. By this criterion, companies that do not issue savings-type life insurance policies (e.g., most general insurance companies) should not be classified as financial intermediaries.

However, the business of an insurance company does not simply involve its acting as an agent to effect a pooling of risks among its policyholders. The company stands as a true intermediary in the process. An insurance policy is a claim on the insurance company, just as a bank deposit is a claim on the bank. And just as the bank cannot know with certainty the portion of its deposits that will be called for payment in any given period, so an insurance company cannot know with certainty the number of claims for payment that will be made under outstanding policies during any given period. Accordingly, the insurance company, like the bank, must make provision for the possibility that its estimates are wrong. It must accumulate a pool of assets—contingency reserves—to guarantee its ability to make contractual payments. And the composition of the portfolio of assets must be adapted to the degree of risk the insurance company has assumed. While it is true that the major accumulation of funds administered by insurance companies is the savings of life insurance policyholders, there would seem to be little merit in the argument that general insurance companies (or life insurance companies with respect to their term insurance business) are not financial intermediaries. Moreover, as is apparent from Table 11.4, we are talking about a sizable concentration of financial assets.

The Deployment of Insurance Company Funds. The degree of risk assumed by general insurance companies is greater than that assumed by life insurance companies. The accidental destruction of real property like railroad rolling stock, a house, or an automobile is much less predictable than death or retirement. Since the requirements for funds to make payments on policies are correspondingly less predictable, general insurance companies find that they must keep relatively more liquid asset portfolios than do life insurance companies. This is illustrated in Table 11.4, which shows the assets held by both groups of companies.

You should note the small holdings of cash and U.S. government securities by life insurance companies. They also hold comparatively small amounts of corporate equity securities. Many states legally limit the proportion of corporate shares to total assets that life insurance companies may hold. This limitation is thought to protect policyholders over the long run. Note also the concentration of commercial mortgages and corporate debt securities held by life insurance companies. Life insurance companies are a major factor in the mortgage markets and a major source of long-term, external corporate debt financing.

In comparison, general insurance companies are not constrained from holding corporate equity issues and have found common stocks an attractive investment asset. State regulations, however, require general insurance companies to set aside adequate amounts in reserves against claims under investigation.

COMPETITION BETWEEN INSURANCE COMPANIES AND OTHER FINANCIAL INTERMEDIARIES

While insurance is clearly a rather unique type of financial instrument, we should not assume that insurance companies and other financial intermediaries do not compete for funds. The competition may be more remote

Table 11.4. Assets of Insurance Companies in the United States, December 31, 1972

	Life Insurance Companies		General Insurance Companies	
	Millions of Dollars	Percent	Millions of Dollars	Percent
Liquid Assets				
Demand Deposits and Currency	$ 1,893	0.8	$ 1,590	2.6
U.S. Government Securities	3,770	1.6	3,497	5.4
Fixed Income Securities				
State and Local Government Obligations	3,341	1.4	25,000	38.7
Corporate Bonds	86,804	37.4	8,800	13.6
Variable Income Securities				
Corporate Shares	26,375	11.5	20,500	31.7
Loans				
Mortgages	77,319	33.4	225	0.3
Other Loans, Including Policy Loans	21,205	9.1	—	—
Miscellaneous Assets	11,076	4.8	4,950	7.7
	$231,783	100.0	$64,562	100.0

SOURCE: Board of Governors of the Federal Reserve System, *Flow of Funds Accounts, 1945–1972* (Washington, D.C., August 1973), p. 102.

than that between banks and trust companies for term deposits, but it does exist, particularly in regard to life insurance with a savings feature.

During the past two decades there have been significant changes in the market for long-term consumer savings. Whereas life insurance was at one time virtually the only form of long-term contractual savings available, in recent years a number of substitutes have developed, the most important of which are mutual funds and pension funds. Life insurance companies also face renewed attacks from other longer-established forms of saving, such as time deposits with banks and savings and loan associations. Rates paid on these forms of saving rose steadily throughout the past two decades, and the low rates paid on life insurance savings served to reduce the relative appeal of this form of saving. Life insurance companies have responded to these competitive challenges in various ways. First, there has been a gradual increase in the rates paid on savings held by the life companies. Second, they have increased their efforts to sell combined packages of group term, health, and disability insurance along with pension fund administration. By this scheme an insurance company agrees to provide low-cost group term and other insurance and at the same time undertakes to administer the pension fund of the employer. Finally, insurance companies have attempted in recent years to increase the attractiveness to individual savers of their own insurance policies by embellishing them with additional services such as medical coverage and occasionally disability insurance.

At times the savings feature of life insurance provides an important source of funds to the policyholder. The ability to borrow against the cash value of his insurance policy at comparative low rates of interest has been an attractive feature in times of tight money. Some economists regard the total cash value of life insurance as near money, since it is quickly converted to a means of direct payment at stable prices.

SPECIALIZED INTERMEDIATION: PENSION FUNDS

Like insurance companies, we must consider pension funds as members of a group of financial intermediaries offering a highly specialized product— a pension. Recently it was estimated that all pension funds together held more than $300 billion in assets, so by sheer size they have become an important vehicle for individuals' long-term savings.

In our discussion of the demand for financial instruments in Chapter 4, we argued that the underlying demand for wealth reflected a desire to redistribute income and consumption over time. A pension plan does this explicitly. It collects a portion of each member's income during his working life and returns it (plus interest) in the form of an annual pension following retirement. Most pension plans involve an element of insurance as well. That is, members of the plan who live unusually long will continue to receive their pension in spite of the fact that their lifetime contributions by themselves would not have been adequate to purchase such a stream of retirement income.

In addition to the federal retirement plan commonly called social security, which we will discuss later, there are other pension plans. State and local governments have retirement programs for their employees with about $72 billion in assets at the beginning of 1973. Life insurance companies themselves administer pension funds for individuals and groups that as of the end of 1972 covered 11 million people and had $52 billion in reserves. These are called "insured" plans and usually guarantee a fixed income or annuity. These plans are administered in a manner consistent with the investment of the insurance companies' own life insurance reserves.[6]

A more rapidly growing group of pension funds are the private pension plans. These are administered by the company itself or turned over to commercial banks or specialized management firms for administration and investment. At the beginning of 1973 the assets of private pension funds totaled $152 billion.

Most private pension funds do not promise a fixed payment. Rather, they are invested for growth and capital appreciation. As a result, holdings of variable income securities by private pension funds are almost two times larger than holdings of fixed income securities. (See Table 11.5.)

Private pension funds have grown rapidly, increasing almost 300 percent since 1959. This rapid growth of private pension funds and the increased use of pension plans as a vehicle for individual saving has stimulated concern

Table 11.5. Assets of Private Pension Funds and State and Local Government Retirement Funds, December 31, 1972 (Millions of Dollars)

	Private Pension Funds	State and Local Government Plans
Cash	$ 1,810	$ 493
Fixed Income Securities		
U.S. Government Securities	3,690	5,056
Corporate and Foreign Bonds	27,425	43,416
State and Local Government Bonds		1,680
Variable Income Securities		
Corporate Shares	111,800	14,172
Mortgages	3,000	6,954
Miscellaneous Assets	4,580	
	$152,305	$71,771

SOURCE: Board of Governors of the Federal Reserve System, *Flow of Funds Accounts, 1945–1972* (Washington, D.C., August 1973), p. 102.

about the need for additional regulation of pension funds to protect and increase the rights of the beneficiaries. Legislation has been proposed to require full financial disclosure of funds' portfolios at regular intervals, some form of insurance of the funds to protect individuals who are anticipating certain retirement benefits, and earlier vesting of participants so that they will be able to obtain a share of a plan to which they contributed after a certain period, regardless of whether they remain with that company until retirement.

The federal government established a form of retirement insurance in its Old-Age, Survivors and Disability Insurance Program (social security). It covers most of the employed work force and their dependents today. It is funded by contributions from the employer and the employee. The level of benefits is tied to the length of time worked and the amount of a worker's contributions. Participants in this federal pension plan have no choice, nor do they have any firm information about what benefits they will receive 30 or 40 years later, when they reach retirement age. These are all determined by congressional action. It is estimated that 108 million people are fully covered by this program. In 1970, $34.7 billion was collected in taxes by OASDI and $31.9 billion paid in claims. Most of the funds are invested in U.S. government debt issues and cash.[7]

OTHER SPECIALIZED INTERMEDIARIES

In addition to the various types of intermediaries that we have already discussed, there exist many other firms that in one form or another provide specialized intermediation. For example, there are firms, frequently referred to as small-business investment corporations, that both lend and participate directly via equity holdings and/or management in smaller- and intermediate-size firms. To a large extent they provide venture capital to firms that cannot raise funds via bank loans or are too small or closely held to warrant bond and/or equity issues.

Indeed, close scrutiny of the system would probably turn up a number of intermediaries whose existence we do not even suspect. Unfortunately, data concerning the activities of all these "other" intermediaries are either nonexistent or sketchy at best. Many private intermediaries by their very nature prefer to be anonymous and thus are not anxious to provide information concerning their activities. We suspect, however, that if the data were available most of these unclassified intermediaries would be shown quantitatively to play only a very minor role in the total financial sector. This is not to say that they are either unimportant or irrelevant.

GOVERNMENT-SPONSORED FINANCIAL INTERMEDIARIES

There are a number of government-operated lending institutions designed to assist specific segments of the economy. Some federal agencies concentrate on supplying farm credit. The Rural Electrification Agency lends funds to increase the supply of public power to farms. The Farmers Home Administration makes loans to farmers who cannot find credit accommodation elsewhere. Loans to farmers for operating funds may run as long as 5 years; loans to purchase or improve farm property may run as long as 40 years. The Commodity Credit Corporation subsidizes farm products. It lends to the farmer directly or through the local bank on the basis of the farmer's production at the support price for that commodity. If the market price is below the support price, the farmer delivers the goods to the CCC in satisfaction of the loan. If the market price rises above the support price, the farmer sells the product, repays the loan, and keeps the difference.

The Federal Reserve banks can make working capital loans to businesses for five-year periods. However, there is little use of this provision of the amended Federal Reserve Act. The Small Business Administration lends to investment companies that have been chartered with the intention of supplying small businesses with long-term funds. The Export-Import Bank makes intermediate- or long-term loans to facilitate foreign trade and development. It guarantees some export credit and provides export credit insurance. The Veterans Administration guarantees veterans' business loans, usually not above $5000, and also guarantees mortgages obtained by veterans.

The Federal Housing Authority insures lenders of mortgage money and repair and modernization loan money against the risk of default. It was established in 1934 to encourage new residential construction and to encourage private financial intermediaries to commit funds to this sector. Recently the Government National Mortgage Association was set up to purchase from intermediaries riskier, nonconventional mortgages. Noncon-

Table 11.6. Consolidated Balance Sheet, Federally Sponsored Credit Agencies (FNMA, FHLB, COOP, FICB, FLBS), December 31, 1972 (Millions of Dollars)

Assets	$56,949	Liabilities	$56,949
Cash and Demand Deposits	199	Agency Issues	49,357
Credit Instruments		Miscellaneous Liabilities	6,393
U.S. Government		Other	1,199
Securities	1,282		
Loans			
Mortgages	36,602		
To Savings and Loan			
Associations	7,979		
To Farmers	6,096		
Other Loans to Coops	2,298		
Other Assets	2,493		

SOURCE: Board of Governors of the Federal Reserve System, *Flow of Funds Accounts, 1945–1972* (Washington, D.C., August 1973), p. 90.

ventional mortgages are those insured by the FHA or guaranteed by the Veterans Administration.

There are five other organizations that were originally part of the federal government. Today they are privately owned companies supervised by the federal government. The Federal Land Bank System was set up in 1916 to provide mortgage funds for farm properties. In 1923, the Federal Intermediate Credit Banks were established to extend short- and intermediate-term credit to farmers. In 1933, the federal government formed the Banks for Cooperatives, which make various types of loans to farmers' marketing, production, purchasing, and service organizations. Today these three intermediaries are owned by farmers, their associations, and their cooperatives. They obtain funds by issuing notes and debentures on themselves in the financial markets. They then channel those funds to a private institution, in many cases a bank, which in turn lends them to the farmers.

In the housing area, the Federal Home Loan Bank System was created in 1932 to assist savings and loan associations. Today the twelve banks are owned by the member savings and loan associations. In return, member associations may borrow on a short-term basis from the Federal Home Loan Banks when short of funds or in a liquidity squeeze.

The Federal National Mortgage Association was established in 1938. In recent years it has become a private corporation. It issues its own notes and debentures in the financial markets in order to obtain funds, which are used to purchase mortgages from intermediaries. Originally it confined its activity to nonconventional mortgages, but it has moved into purchasing conventional mortgages as well. In performing this function, FNMA and GNMA have reduced some of the risk involved in holding long-term assets, particularly for savings and loan associations, mutual savings banks, and other financial intermediaries. Through their activities they have created a secondary market for these instruments, which were once regarded as illiquid and non-marketable.

Table 11.6 is a consolidated statement for these five federal credit agencies. The largest today is the Federal National Mortgage Association, followed by the Federal Home Loan Bank System. The agricultural agencies operate within a smaller sector of the economy, hence the overwhelming dominance of mortgages and loans to savings and loan associations, as shown in Table 11.6.

SUMMARY

We have completed our survey of the major financial intermediaries. We have not discussed retail credit extended to consumers by stores, which then often turn to factors to purchase their accounts receivable. We have not discussed service and trade credit extended by doctors, dentists, utilities, and businesses to consumers and to each other. Nor have we made mention of pawnbrokers, loan sharks, and other informal credit sources.

We have tried to divide the intermediaries into groups or categories for purpose of description. While most of these groups have roots in federal or state laws, we also discovered that each had a rather distinctive pattern of assets and liabilities. On this basis we could say that each group represented firms engaged in a particular field of financial intermediation. However, it should also be obvious that from an economic point of view the various categories of financial intermediaries are largely—but not completely—arbitrary. The activities of firms in each group impinge directly on those of some, if not all, other groups.

Consider, for example, commercial banks. While banks are unique in that part of their liabilities constitutes a substantial portion of the money supply, they still face strong competition. Savings and loan associations, mutual savings banks, and credit unions all compete with banks for personal savings deposits. In assets, banks face competition from finance companies for consumer and business loans and from mutual savings banks, savings and loan associations, and life insurance companies for mortgages.

While banks are much less specialized in their intermediation than is the case with some other intermediaries, their example should make the major point: The activities of intermediaries do not fit into tight, specialized compartments. The patterns of overlapping activities among groups of intermediaries are both complex and quantitatively important. Moreover, as the discussion in the previous chapters suggests, these patterns are not static—they are continually changing.

These are points that should be kept in mind as we turn our attention to questions of public policy with respect to competition and soundness in the financial system.

NOTES

1. Securities Exchange Commission, *36th Annual Report, 1970* (Washington, D.C., 1970), p. 136.

2. Wiesenberger Financial Services, *Investment Companies 1973: Mutual Funds and Other Types* (New York, 1973).

3. Ibid.

4. "Survey of Finance Companies—1970," Federal Reserve *Bulletin*, November 1972, pp. 958–972.

5. U.S. Department of Commerce, Bureau of the Census, *Statistical Abstract of the United States, 1971* (Washington, D.C., 1971).

6. Institute of Life Insurance, *1973 Life Insurance Fact Book* (New York, 1973).

7. Ibid., p. 40.

12
THE DEVELOPMENT
OF THE AMERICAN
FINANCIAL SYSTEM

Our major concern in this chapter is with the evolution of financial intermediaries in the United States. From a relatively uncomplicated beginning in the colonies, the American economy has grown in size and complexity. Economic growth created demands for an infinite variety of specialized financial services and specialized forms for the accumulation of wealth. At the same time, changes in the structure and performance of the economy, including its proclivity to develop periodic crises, posed frequent challenges and tests for financial institutions and public authorities. Our present complex network of financial institutions and markets is an outgrowth of the continuously changing economic environment and competing political forces.

DOMINANT THEMES

The arrangements for the chartering, regulation, and supervision of financial institutions in the United States reflect a long and contentious history of interaction between state and federal governments, and between agencies within the federal government. Although it was granted authority under the Constitution "to coin money and regulate its value," it was contended that the federal government did not have additional powers over financial institutions that were not specifically granted by the Constitution. These powers were reserved by the states. There have been many arguments over this constitutional issue.

In addition, during the formative period in banking legislation in the United States, so-called populism was the dominant political force. Basic to this doctrine was the belief that local affairs (very broadly defined) should be locally controlled. This manifests itself partly in pressure for the decentralization of political authority (local authority vs. the state, states' rights vs. the federal government) and partly in a fear of centralization of economic power.

There was also an underlying concern with formulating appropriate policy and encouraging the development of institutions that would provide security and stability to the financial system. More recently public policy has been concerned with extending federal supervision to a broad range of financial institutions. Federal insurance of individual deposits at several types of financial institutions has been enacted. Individuals are protected against loss of their funds in the event that a specific institution should fail. More often than not, there is conflict between proposals for change that would enhance the public's safety and increase government regulation, and the industry's desire for freedom from present cumbersome restrictions. There is also conflict between the desire to broaden competition among financial institutions and the fear of excessive competition and resulting instability.

ORIGINS OF AMERICAN BANKING: COLONIAL TIMES TO 1832

Early U.S. irritation with Britain was in part over money and banking matters. Trade with Britain consistently left the colonies with an adverse trade balance. Specie earned in profitable trade with the West Indies had to be sent to Britain both to settle the colonies trade accounts and to enable them to purchase necessary imports from Europe. Circulating money, at that time generally confined to coin, was in scarce supply. Britain was in part responsible, since it forbade the coining of specie money by the colonies. To alleviate the shortage of money, some of the colonies printed and issued paper notes backed by goods or land and declared these notes to be legal tender for settlement of debts due within the colonies. However, the diversity of notes between the colonies inhibited their use in intercolony trade. In 1751, Britain tried to suppress the printing and circulation of these paper notes. Although the action met with relatively little success, it was a further irritant to the colonies.

In addition to lacking a uniform circulating medium of exchange like the paper bank notes, as well as an adequate supply of coin or specie money, the colonies also lacked a formal banking system of their own. The business of banking was conducted through British banks and by individuals, private, unincorporated concerns, and partnerships.

251

When the American Revolution began, the financial problems of the colonies were multiplied. Some loans of gold from abroad were obtained, but for the most part the Continental Congress relied on paper currency issues to finance the war. Overissue of notes resulted in rapid loss of value until the notes were "not worth a continental." Merchants and farmers were reluctant to supply clothing, matériel, and food in return for this paper.

THE FIRST BANK CHARTERS: STATE ISSUED

In the waning days of the American Revolution, Robert Morris secured a loan of $200,000 in gold from France. With this specie backing, he requested authority from Pennsylvania to formally conduct the business of banking. A charter was granted, and the first American bank—The Bank of North America—opened in 1782. This bank made loans to the federal government, issued paper notes backed in full by specie (i.e., they could be converted into gold on demand), and assisted in the reestablishment of business and commerce in the new nation. Merchants who made short-term loans to each other on an informal basis now hurried to incorporate other banks. Other states followed the lead of Pennsylvania in granting bank charters by legislative acts.

Thus, the first banks operating in the United States were state banks chartered by special legislative acts. These first state charters were general in nature, specifying little about bank structure and bank powers. The major restriction on the first state banks applied to specie backing for their paper bank notes. All paper bank notes were to be fully backed by specie. These notes were in no way to be construed as lawful money or legal tender; in the eighteenth century gold and silver were the accepted forms for legal money, and only the central government coined and issued it.

The first state banks accepted deposits, but their most profitable activity was making loans and issuing their own bank notes. These bank notes were a surrogate for lawful money (that is, specie), were convertible into specie on demand, and became the primary circulating medium of exchange.

THE ROOTS OF CENTRAL BANKING IN THE UNITED STATES

The First Bank of the United States. The first federally chartered bank did not open until 1792. At that time there were five state-chartered banks operating. The charter for the First Bank of the United States was drawn up by Alexander Hamilton, the first secretary of the Treasury, and was based on concepts of banking developed in Great Britain and particularly in Scotland. This charter was much more specific than those under which state banks had been chartered.

The First Bank of the United States opened in Philadelphia with a 20-year charter that gave it wide and specific powers. It could establish branches (it opened eight), and it could issue notes to the amount of its capital, a specific limitation. While these notes were legal tender only for payments to the government, they were a significant step toward a lawful paper currency. The bank was capitalized at $10 million, one-fifth of which was subscribed to by the federal government and paid for by loans to that government from the bank itself. The Bank made loans to the public but was limited to charging a maximum interest of 6 percent. Through its branches, it transfered funds rapidly around the country. In addition, it made other loans to the government and functioned as a depository for government funds.

The First Bank of the United States imposed indirect monetary controls on state banks. Through its branches it quickly redeemed state bank notes for specie. The Bank thus forced state banks to actually hold large amounts of specie as backing for their circulating bank notes in order to honor the continuing demand for conversion to gold. Through this procedure the amount of circulating bank notes was controlled, overissue of state bank notes was deterred, and the value of state bank notes was stabilized. As a result, paper bank notes became widely acceptable as a medium of exchange, and real economic growth was facilitated.

Opposition to the First Bank of the United States. There was strong opposition to the Bank, despite its success. Hamilton had envisioned the First Bank of the United States as an embryonic central bank that would regulate and bring order to the American banking and financial system. It would complement a strong central government and provide a pattern for the orderly future development of the financial industry. At the time it was chartered (1791), American banking institutions were a disparate collection of state-chartered banks and private, unincorporated banking concerns operating without specific guidelines or legal framework.

Many, however, feared the centralization of banking power in the hands of the federal government. To them the fight for freedom from Britain had been a fight for freedom from a strong central government. Opponents of the Bank contended that such a bank was unconstitutional, for although Congress reserved the "sole right to coin money," it did not have the explicit right under the Constitution to charter a bank. The Bank of the United States became an issue between those favoring federalism and those wishing to defer political and economic power to the states.

The Bank of the United States alienated both hard-currency and easy-money advocates. Hard-currency advocates objected to the designation, however limited, of the Bank's notes as legal tender. They contended that only hard money—specie—would avoid the pitfalls of overissue.

Easy-money advocates, representing primarily agricultural interests, wanted additional amounts of paper bank notes put into circulation, which would drive up commodity prices. They objected to the Bank's practice of converting state bank notes to specie, thereby limiting the amount of state bank notes in circulation. Agricultural interests were already resentful of

Hamilton. They felt that they had been duped when they first accepted Continental paper issue in exchange for food supplies and matériel during the Revolutionary War. At the end of the war, when the paper notes were almost worthless, farmers and merchants sold the paper notes at a fraction of their face value to speculators. Hamilton later redeemed these notes at full value as a gesture to reestablish the nation's credit abroad. In so doing he alienated agrarian interests at home.

Other Bank opponents objected to foreigners' owning some of the Bank's stock. After 20 years had elapsed, the charter was not renewed by Congress. From 1811 to 1816 only state banks were chartered.

The Second Bank of the United States. During the War of 1812 state banks suspended redemption of their bank notes for specie. By 1816 there was pressure in Congress to charter another federal bank. In that year the Second Bank of the United States was granted a 20-year charter. The bank was similar to the First Bank but had a larger capitalization ($35 million). Although inept management and a postwar recession discredited the early operation of the bank, by 1819 it was well run. The Second Bank of the United States opened 25 branches and became a significant part of the business and financial mechanism of the East and South. In the West, however, it was most unpopular. It, too, presented state bank notes promptly for redemption in specie and put a damper on overissue of state bank notes and speculation. If the state banks could issue notes far in excess of their specie holdings without any fear of having to redeem large amounts of them in gold, they could make more loans in paper notes and increase their profits. The temptation to overissue thus was very great.

Opposition to the Second Bank of the United States. Again easy-money advocates attacked the federally chartered bank because it limited state bank note issue. Others feared the increasing concentration of economic and federal power. State banks themselves objected to the unfair competitive advantage of the Bank of the United States. Despite an earlier Supreme Court ruling, some opponents continued to question the constitutionality of the Bank. In 1819 the Supreme Court upheld the right of Congress to charter a bank. In *McCulloch v. Maryland* the Supreme Court defended the constitutionality of the Bank against the State of Maryland, which had attempted to tax the Bank's branch in Baltimore.

There were strong political counterforces operating at the time. During two administrations the Hamiltonian Whigs had attempted to build a strong central government. During the next six administrations the Jeffersonian Democrats emphasized the rights of the states and attempted to confine the federal government by strictly interpreting the Constitution.

The election of 1828 of Andrew Jackson and his campaign for reelection in 1832 centered on the rechartering of this bank. When the bill to recharter passed by a narrow margin in Congress, Jackson vetoed it. Subsequently he withdrew government funds on deposit with the Bank and placed them with state banks. One historian has written, "Jackson's war on the bank was not wholly personal but an aspect of that fundamental hostility to monopoly and special privilege which the colonists had brought from England. . . ."[1]

After the demise of the Second Bank of the United States, the era of a quasi-central banking authority operating under a federal charter ended. It would be more than 25 years before the federal government would charter banks again, and 75 years would elapse before any central banking authority would be reinstituted.

THE 1830s TO THE CIVIL WAR:
STATES' RIGHTS AND POPULIST PRESSURES

The First and Second Banks of the United States had brought stability to the banking system. By virtue of their branches they enabled the payments system to function more smoothly. However, their existence heightened fears that the financial power would be concentrated in the hands of the federal, as opposed to the local or state, government. These banks ran against the feeling that each state and locality should have power over its banking business. Concentration of financial as well as political power was feared; indeed, no institution that centralized so much wealth could be totally acceptable to the diverse groups in the United States.

The Banks of the United States also served as focal points for agrarian discontent. The populists believed that the Banks were in league with other money interests in the financial centers of Philadelphia, New York, and Boston to exploit the rural areas. It was argued that conservative commercial banking principles discriminated against them—an allegation that had some substance, in that land or mortgages on land were not considered bankable assets in conservative, commercial banking principles based on the real-bills doctrine. Moreover, the instability of agricultural crops and markets made any loans to farmers risky assets and called for premium interest rates (if indeed credit was extended at all).

The Free-Banking Movement. The populists favored *free banking*; that is, they wanted general banking legislation that would make it easy to establish small banks under local control, using local funds and, most important, making local loans (primarily to farmers). The free-banking principle involved granting a bank charter by executive action, rather than legislative, to any group that met minimum requirements set out in state legislation.

The old procedure of requiring legislative action on each charter application had encouraged scandal, bribery, and payoffs for and against new bank charter applications. Existing banks tried to restrict entry and monopolize bank facilities within a given area.

Michigan and New York enacted free-banking laws in 1837 and 1838, respectively. Other states followed. In general, the minimum requirements and particularly the minimum amount of capital that had to be subscribed to the new bank were kept low for the express purpose of facilitating the entry of small banks. Restrictions were often placed on the opening of branch offices to encourage retention of local control.

Some state governments owned and operated banks themselves. In other states, a new bank, in return for a charter under free-banking laws, had to assist in financing local projects like canals and railroads. In still other states, any interested parties who raised necessary capital could be granted a charter, make loans, and conduct the business of banking within broad guidelines set down by that state. In general, state banks operated without supervision or examination by state authorities. A few states did constrain the banks by instituting specie cash reserve requirements against bank note issues and deposits, but most did not.

Many new banks suffered from inadequate capitalization. Capital was often obtained by lending stockholders money to purchase the bank's shares and by accepting bank notes of dubious value. Excessive dividend payments weakened the financial reserves of many other banks. Some banks made highly speculative loans or accepted a large portion of real estate loans, thus acquiring a portfolio of illiquid assets.

Bank note abuses were also prevalent. In the face of widespread counterfeiting, inadequate specie backing, and increasing numbers of bank failures, most bank notes were either totally unacceptable as a means of payment or universally discounted by the recipient beyond the issuing bank's immediate geographic area. In general, it would take more than a dollar's worth of bank notes to purchase a dollar's worth of real goods. The diversity and questionable value of most bank notes impaired their function as a medium of exchange, resulting in curtailment of production and real economic growth.

The State Banks and U.S. Government Funds. During this period, until the Civil War, state legislatures assumed dominant control of financial institutions. The responsibilities of the federal government were narrowly interpreted. Beginning with Andrew Jackson's administration, the federal government tried to have no concern with the functioning of commercial banks and bank note issues, which were now the sole responsibility of the states that had chartered them.

Jackson had withdrawn U.S. government deposits from the Bank of the United States and placed them with state banks. However, during the Panic of 1837 many state banks failed. Congress became concerned about the loss of government funds that these banks had on deposit. An independent treasury, or federal repository for U.S. government funds, was proposed. Such a scheme was unacceptable to the states, and enactment of the independent treasury system did not pass Congress until 1846. Under this legislation the Treasury was required to hold all funds in its own vaults in Washington or in subtreasuries established in leading cities.

Another move of considerable consequence was Jackson's "specie circular." From 1836 on, the federal government would accept only specie—gold or silver—in payment for land. In 1837, Congress passed more general legislation requiring the Treasury to make payments to the public only in specie and to accept all payment only in specie from the public. No regard was given to the effect on the banking system and the economy of large shifts in specie holdings from the Treasury to the public and vice versa. When payments were due the Treasury, specie was withdrawn from the commercial banks, forcing them to contract the total of their bank notes outstanding. Conversely, when the Treasury made large specie disbursements to the public, specie flowed into commercial banks, permitting them to expand their note issues.

This specie restriction on federal government disbursements and receipts would eventually constrict the government's ability to finance Civil War expenditures and force it to seek a new national currency and establish a national banking system that would issue the currency.

Conclusions. In the twenty-five years from the expiration of the federal charter of the Second Bank of the United States until the Civil War, the banking system suffered from lack of common guidelines and constraints. Confidence in banking institutions waned in the face of multiple bank failures. Currency abuses were commonplace, threatening survival of the payments mechanism. The Treasury and the federal government had not attempted to intercede but, rather, had withdrawn government funds from state banks and held cash balances in specie.

The populists had encouraged easy entry to banking. The free-banking principle was rooted in a concern for ready access to credit rather than a concern for the protection of depositors and bank note holders. The populists had forced rejection of any central stabilizing institution like the Bank of the United States. In its absence, the workings of the payments mechanism had been impaired and economic growth retarded by frequent severe "panics."

THE BEGINNINGS OF DIVERSIFIED
FINANCIAL INTERMEDIATION

Although commercial banks continued to dominate the financial system, various other types of financial intermediaries were being established during this period. Conservative banking practices emphasized short-term commercial loans. There was a need for other intermediaries specializing in longer-term—particularly mortgage—financing while at the same time providing safe repositories for the working man's modest savings. Mutual savings banks, which were established as early as 1816, expanded in part to fill this need. They opened offices in many eastern cities, obtaining charters through legislative acts of the states. Elsewhere, building societies, forerunners of the savings and loan associations, were established beginning in 1832. These first associations, in contrast to mutual savings banks, were voluntary organizations, unincorporated and unregulated. They were subject to dissolution each time someone left the group, but by the 1850s these provisions had been changed to provide continuity and greater organizational flexibility.

During this period the American economy was undergoing a rapid and profound transformation. Movement westward opened new lands. Canals were built, facilitating the shipment of goods to distant domestic markets. Railroads were begun. In the North, industrialization took hold. Towns grew up marked by the appearance of textile mills and factories. In the South, cotton was the dominant crop and land was increasingly brought under cultivation. From 1839 on, there was growth in real income per capita. Expanding markets at home and abroad for cotton resulted in a rise in farm wages in the South.

The rise in real income, rapid commercial and capital development, and labor force migrations to towns encouraged the growth of other financial intermediaries. With the increase in American exports and other economic changes within the country, fire and marine insurance companies began to emerge as important financial institutions. Life insurance companies also grew rapidly as people had more money to save and the urbanized population was more accessible for sales. For example, life insurance assets in New York State grew from $16 million in 1827 to $75 million in 1860. Life insurance companies, particularly in the North, took advantage of changing financing requirements of businesses in the area and shifted from large asset holdings of farm mortgages to textile loans with a term of one year or more.[2] Nonetheless, as Table 12.1 shows, commercial banks and mutual savings banks held about 85 percent of the total assets of financial intermediaries in 1860.

There was a shift in the composition of the money supply. In 1839 and 1849, currency in circulation was about two times larger than deposits at commercial banks. By 1860, as Table 12.1 shows, deposits at commercial banks had become the dominant component of the money supply.

THE CIVIL WAR TO 1913: REASSERTION OF FEDERAL INFLUENCE

The secession of the southern states beginning in 1860 can be viewed as the ultimate assertion of states' rights. Secession threatened the very existence of the nation. To suppress secession and preserve the nation would require strong action by the federal government.

The federal government turned first to its Treasury for funds to finance the war effort. Reserves, however, were inadequate. The government tried to sell its bonds to the public, but the state banks in particular were reluctant to give up precious specie for government bonds. Salmon P. Chase, Secretary of the Treasury, arranged a $150 million bank loan from several northern

Table 12.1. The American Financial System, 1860

I. *The Money Supply (1867)*

	Millions of Dollars	Percent
Currency (Held by the Public)	$ 585	44.5
Deposits at Commercial Banks	729	55.5
Total	$1314	100.0

II. *Assets of Financial Intermediaries*

	Millions of Dollars	Percent
Commercial Banks	$ 800	65.0
Mutual Savings Banks	240	20.0
Life Insurance Companies	24	2.0
Property Insurance Companies	96	8.0
Other Financial Intermediaries	60	5.0
	$1220	100.0

SOURCE: Money supply data: M. Friedman and A. Schwartz, *A Monetary History of the United States, 1867–1960* (copyright © 1963 by National Bureau of Economic Research), published by Princeton University Press, Princeton, N.J., Table A-1, p. 704. Reprinted by permission of Princeton University Press. Asset data: R. Goldsmith, *Financial Institutions* (New York: Random House, 1968), p. 158; U.S. Department of Commerce, Bureau of the Census, *Historical Statistics from Colonial Times* (Washington, D.C.).

banks but insisted that the loan be paid to the Treasury in specie, which since 1837 had been the only acceptable form of payment to the Treasury. This action by Chase forced the commercial banks to suspend specie payments in December 1861.

The war continued and specie was unobtainable. Obviously, if the government continued to refuse to accept state bank notes, some change in government policy would be necessary if adequate funds were to be raised to finance the war. Moreover, an efficient and stable payments system was essential to a war economy.

In 1862, Congress permitted the federal government to take the first of three proposed steps in a program of fiscal and monetary reform. For the first time since the American Revolution, the federal government itself issued paper currency and declared it legal tender. Known as greenbacks, this currency was inconvertible into specie. The government at the same time sought to levy additional taxes to raise another $150 million.

Third, Chase urged Congress to pass a national banking law that would provide a safe and uniform currency backed by federal bonds. The National Currency Act of 1863 and its amended version, the National Bank Act of 1864, encompassed Chase's proposal. "Supporters of the National Currency Act (1863) stressed two main deficiencies of the state banking system: a confusing variety of circulating notes making payment vexatious and inefficient, and a recurring tendency to overissue them that often ended in panic and ruinous deflation."[3] There was prolonged argument in Congress over the national bank legislation. Its most eloquent and persuasive supporter in Congress, John Sherman, relied heavily on the nationalistic attributes of the bill. He argued that it was important to establish federal sovereignty over currency issue and over the banking institutions that would provide the mechanism for issuing the new currency. The actual legislation also guaranteed a ready demand for federal government securities.

The National Bank Act followed the free-banking laws in that anyone meeting the general federal requirements could obtain a national bank charter. It enumerated the following requirements to obtain a national bank charter:

1. *Capital.* Minimum capital on the basis of population was required in an attempt to enhance bank safety. Fifty thousand dollars was required for banks operating in areas with populations of less than 6,000. One hundred thousand dollars was required if the population exceeded 6,000 but was less than 50,000, and a $200,000 minimum was necessary if the area had a population of more than 50,000.

2. *Supervision and examination.* The Act established the Office of Comptroller of the Currency to grant national bank charters and to receive periodic reports from the national banks. From this office bank examiners annually examine each national bank.

3. *Bank loans.* No longer was good judgment with regard to bank assets left solely to the banks' management. Real estate loans to national banks were prohibited. Other loans to one borrower were limited to a maximum of 10 percent of the paid-in capital and unimpaired surplus. Loans to bank officers were curtailed.

4. *Note issue.* Each national bank's notes were printed by the federal government to discourage counterfeiting. Each national bank could obtain its notes from the Comptroller by giving U.S. government bonds in exchange. This encouraged the development of a national bank market for these bonds and facilitated wartime finance efforts. Each bank could issue notes only in an amount equal to its paid-in capital and had to maintain a redemption fund for its notes. National banks were further required to accept each other's notes at par thereby limiting the widespread practice of discounting. To discourage state banks from issuing their own notes, a tax of first 2 percent and then 10 percent was levied on their face value. This tax severely curtailed the profitability of issuing state bank notes, and they soon ceased to exist.

5. *Reserve requirements against national bank notes and bank deposits.* Following the lead of certain state banking laws, the National Bank Act imposed cash reserve requirements to protect depositors and preserve national bank liquidity. The Act divided the national banks into three classes based on geographic location. Thus, it created a

formal system of correspondent banking relationships based on location. It also created a pyramid of credit.

National banks located in New York, Chicago, and St. Louis were designated *central reserve city* national banks. They became the acceptable depositories for the other national banks and usually the state banks as well. These banks were required to hold 25 percent in lawful money (specie, greenbacks, and silver and gold certificates) against their circulating notes and deposits. National banks in other cities were called *reserve city* national banks. They had to hold 25 percent in cash reserves against deposits and circulating notes, but half of these required reserves could be placed on deposit with central reserve city banks to earn interest. At the next level were the *country* national banks, which were obligated to hold 15 percent in cash reserves against their notes and deposits, but three-fifths of these cash reserves could be deposited with reserve city or central reserve city national banks. Thus, the actual cash reserve backing national bank notes and deposits in the system was less than the officially perceived backing.

An example may clarify the extent of the problem. If $100 million were deposited in country national banks, they were required to hold only $6 million in cash reserves in their vaults; the other $9 million in cash reserves could be deposited with reserve city national banks and earn interest. The reserve city national banks were to hold 25 percent in cash reserves against this deposit, but only half, or 12.5 percent, had to be held in the reserve city bank's own vaults. Thus, against the $9 million they held ($9 million × 0.125), or $1,125,000. The other $1,125,000 could be placed on deposit with central reserve city banks. They had to hold 25 percent in cash reserves against this deposit, or ($1,125,000 × 0.25) — $280,000. The total actual cash reserves being held by the national bank system against $100 million deposited with country national banks actually amounted to only $7.41 million instead of the apparent $15 million (15 percent of $100 million).

It was not solely the level of cash reserves that proved inadequate in times of severe economic disturbances. The National Bank Act prohibited national banks from making new loans and paying dividends if they were deficient in reserves. If the deficiency persisted, the Comptroller of the Currency, after 30 days' notice, could close and liquidate the bank. This threat of closure inhibited the banks from using their cash reserves and permitting reserves to fall below the required level. National banks in practice would rather refuse to make new loans, liquidate short-term assets like call loans, or in extreme emergencies, close their doors. During that interim, normal credit accommodation loans were not made and many businesses went bankrupt.

The reserve requirements of the National Bank Act were inflexible. Cash reserves held by national banks were sterile; in practice, they did not ensure that the banking system could withstand currency runs, as had been intended. There was no institution outside the banking system to hold cash reserves and make them available in times of need; there was no institution with the power to create reserves, if necessary, to bolster the banking system.

Dual Banking and Fragmentation. The federal government could not prohibit the chartering of banks by the states. It sought, however, to establish a national banking system that would be attractive enough to compel state banks to convert to national charters but, at the same time, stringent enough to restore the public's confidence in commercial banks and public acceptance of the new currency. The imagined competitive advantage to national bank charters was not strong enough to drive all state banks from the industry. The continuing struggle between federal and state governments was not laid to rest. The United States ended up with a "dual banking system" instead of the hoped-for federally chartered and regulated system.

Commercial Banking After the National Bank Act. In the period after the Civil War there was a need for new banking facilities to finance reconstruction. Expansion westward and the acquisition of new territory added to the need for credit facilities. Many existing banks, but not all, converted to national charters. By 1880 state banks had declined in number relative to national banks; there were about 2100 national banks and 650 state banks that year.

Table 12.2. **The American Financial System, 1890**

I. *The Money Supply*

	Millions of Dollars	Percent
Currency (Held by the Public)	$ 888	22.7
Deposits at Commercial Banks	3020	77.3
Total	$3908	100.0

II. *Assets of Financial Intermediaries*

	Billions of Dollars	Percent
Commercial Banks	$5.6	58.0
Mutual Savings Banks	1.7	18.0
Savings and Loan Associations	0.6	6.0
Life Insurance Companies	0.8	8.0
Property Insurance Company	0.4	4.0
Other Financial Intermediaries	0.6	6.0
	$9.6	100.0

SOURCE: Money supply data: M. Friedman and A. Schwartz, *A Monetary History of the United States, 1867–1960* (copyright © 1963 by National Bureau of Economic Research), published by Princeton University Press, Princeton, N.J., Table A-1, p. 705. Reprinted by permission of Princeton University Press. Asset data: R. Goldsmith, *Financial Institutions* (New York: Random House, 1968), p. 158; U.S. Department of Commerce, Bureau of the Census, *Historical Statistics from Colonial Times* (Washington, D.C.).

Table 12.3. The American Financial System, 1912

I. *The Money Supply*

	Millions of Dollars	Percent
Currency (Held by the Public)	$ 1,831	12.0
Deposits at Commercial Banks	13,553	88.0
Total	$15,384	100.0

II. *Assets of Financial Intermediaries*

	Billions of Dollars	Percent
Commercial Banks	$21.82	64.0
Mutual Savings Banks	2.01	12.0
Savings and Loan Associations	0.95	3.0
Life Insurance Companies	4.57	13.0
Property Insurance Companies	1.00	3.0
Pension Funds	0.01	0.0
Finance Companies	0.0	0.0
Federal Lending Agencies	0.01	0.0
Other Financial Intermediaries	1.40	5.0
	$33.77	100.0

SOURCE: Money supply data: M. Friedman and A. Schwartz, *A Monetary History of the United States, 1867–1960* (copyright © 1963 by National Bureau of Economic Research), published by Princeton University Press, Princeton, N.J., Table A-1, pp. 707–708. Reprinted by permission of Princeton University Press. Asset data: R. Goldsmith, "The Share of Financial Intermediaries in National Wealth and National Assets, 1900–1949," Occasional Paper no. 42, National Bureau of Economic Research (1954), pp. 26–27; R. Goldsmith, *Financial Institutions* (New York: Random House, 1968), p. 158. We have excluded assets held in personal trust accounts by commercial banks' trust departments and other intermediaries, following Goldsmith's format in *Financial Institutions*, op. cit., pp. 21–22.

Bank organizers in the West and South, however, were discouraged by the rigid national bank lending limitations and stringent capitalization requirements. States continued to charter banks that would finance real estate, make crop loans, and open banking facilities in rural areas. While national banks grew in deposit size, they lost their numerical dominance to state banks from the 1880s on. This condition prevails today. By 1900 there were 3700 national banks and 5000 state banks.

Changing Composition of the Money Supply. In addition to easier chartering requirements for state banks, which spurred their increase, the importance to bank profits of issuing bank notes diminished. Gradually during the post-Civil War period, more financial transactions were made by check rather than by specie or paper currency. By comparing Table 12.1 with Tables 12.2 and 12.3, we can see the dramatic change that occurred in the composition of the money supply. Currency in the hands of the public declined from 44 percent of the money supply in 1860 to 12 percent by 1912.

PROFILE OF THE FINANCIAL SYSTEM, 1890 AND 1912

The period from 1860 to 1912 was one of real economic growth. Building of railroads and highways was financed by state governments, financial intermediaries, English banks, and individuals. There was a significant increase in primary security issues and direct sales of securities to the public. With increased security issues came the rise of formal exchanges and the growth of underwriting. Urbanization proceeded at a rapid pace. There were increases in savings as a percentage of income, an increase in the wage share of total income, and an increase in the inequality of income distribution.

These economic changes provided fertile ground for the very rapid expansion of both bank and nonbank financial intermediaries. Taken together, their assets grew at an average annual rate of 6.5 percent until 1890. Life insurance companies grew faster, averaging an annual growth rate of 10.5 percent. As a result, life insurance companies increased their share of total financial assets from 2 percent in 1860 to 8 percent in 1890 and 13 percent in 1912, as shown in Tables 12.2 and 12.3. This phenomenal expansion was certainly aided by the rising level of real incomes and the urbanization of the population. Life insurance companies developed extensive sales forces and tailored policies to meet the insurance needs of people with small incomes.

Although accurate data are unavailable, the savings and loan industry probably experienced a rapid rate of growth like that of life insurance companies. However, it suffered a setback in the late 1890s, when many associations failed during the two economic downturns of that time.

THE SEARCH FOR STABILITY: THE CENTRAL BANK

If populist banking policies meant free entry to the banking industry and banks that were small, locally owned, and sensitive to local credit requirements, it all too often meant banks that had weak management and insufficiently diversified portfolios, which were peculiarly vulnerable to bankruptcy. The search for methods to eliminate this instability resulted in a reassertion of federal influence.

Shortcomings of the National Banking System. The National Bank Act had provided a uniform, minimum set of requirements for new banks. However, these requirements were too stringent to attract all who wished to form new banks. The Act established a uniform paper currency that became as acceptable to the public as specie. However, both the supply of paper currency and the supply of specie were inelastic. In times of economic disturbances the supply was inadequate to meet public demand.

The amount of coin in circulation in the short run was fixed. Silver and gold certificates were issued only in exchange for equivalent amounts of metal; greenbacks could be issued only to a specified statutory maximum set by Congress. National bank notes were put into circulation by the national banks. They had to deposit U.S. government bonds with the Comptroller of the Currency. For each $900 of national bank notes issued, the national bank had to deposit government bonds with a par value or market value of $1000, whichever was lower. Although the national bank continued notes depended on the cost of obtaining the federal bonds. When these to draw the interest on the bond, the profitability of issuing national bank securities could be bought at or just below par, there was a strong profit incentive to issue national bank notes.

After 1880 the Treasury ran budget surpluses and used these surpluses first to retire callable bonds and then to purchase other government bonds in the open market. Prices on government securities were driven up. For example, in January 1879, a government bond with a 4 percent coupon maturing in 1907 sold for $997.50 to yield about 4 percent. By January 1882, the same bond was selling for $1179.70, yielding around 3 percent. National banks lost the incentive to buy government bonds and deposit them with the Comptroller against national bank notes. Each bank could still issue only $900 in national bank notes against a bond with a par value of $1000, even if it had paid $1179 for it. As a result, new national bank note issues ceased and the paper component of the money supply failed to grow.

Finally, in the 1890s, premium prices on U.S. government bonds fell sharply and national bank notes began to be issued again. In 1900 the laws were amended and national banks could issue notes to 100 percent of par value of U.S. government bonds.

The supply of national bank notes was tied to the government bond market, which, in turn, was tied to federal budget surpluses and deficits. The supply was not responsive to seasonal demands for currency. The volume of national bank notes outstanding over the year remained rather stable. The supply was not responsive to secular growth demands. This limitation was not as significant, however, because of the rapid growth of demand deposit accounts during this period and the increasing use of checks for payment. Most important, the supply was not adequate to withstand periodic runs by the public. No institution stood ready to supply additional currency when needed to restore the public's confidence in the banking system.

Although the reserve system worked quite well in calm times, providing adequate liquidity to national and state banks, the national bank reserve requirements were inflexible. If an economic crisis impaired the reserves of the central reserve city banks, the national banking system had no alternative source from which it could borrow reserves to obtain currency so it could act to restore public confidence.

In addition, a central facility was needed that would speed check collections and enable the payments system to work more efficiently. At the turn of the twentieth century there were almost 9000 separate banks in the United States. Checks drawn on distant banks were cleared through a series of correspondent banks. Routing of checks was circuitous and time-consuming.

There was also widespread imposition of exchange charges. Banks on which checks were drawn would deduct an arbitrary fee from the face value of the check when presented for payment. This practice of nonpar clearance inhibited the acceptability of checks and interfered with the efficiency and neutrality of the payments system (see Chapter 1).

The passage of the National Bank Act in 1864 did not solve all the problems of the banking system. Recurring banking crises continued, with particularly severe panics in 1873, 1884, 1893, and 1907, revealing the limitations of the present dual banking system. Pressure mounted for even more fundamental reforms.

ESTABLISHMENT OF A CENTRAL BANK

After the panic of 1907 Congress set up a national monetary commission to study and bring forth suggestions on how to improve the stability of the financial system. Two features of the National Bank Act became focal points for revision: the provision for reserve requirements and the regulation of the supply of currency. This search for an institution to eliminate the instability in the financial system provided another theme in American public policy. Since it was inevitably centralizing in its effects, the search came into conflict with populist principles.

A Compromise with Populism. After extensive hearings the commission recommended the establishment of a central bank. Nelson Aldrich, chairman of the commission, introduced a bill in 1912 to establish a single, central bank. However, in that year Woodrow Wilson and a democratic majority were elected. Recalling Andrew Jackson's fight against the Second Bank of the United States, they viewed a single, central bank as an unacceptable concentration of economic power. The legislation that was finally passed as the Federal Reserve Act was a compromise with their populist feelings.

Organization. In its internal organization the Federal Reserve System was decentralized. It was not to be a monolithic central bank but a federation of twelve regional reserve banks. The individual Reserve banks were not to be owned by the federal government but by the member banks. Each member bank would buy stock in the Federal Reserve bank that served its geographical district. Elaborate controls were instituted to ensure that the boards of directors of each Reserve bank could not be dominated by the larger banks of that reserve district. Banks were grouped according to asset size, with each of the three groups electing two directors. The directors were also divided into groups to ensure that not only the banking interests but the public, industry, commerce, and agriculture were represented as well. The national body that was created, the Federal Reserve Board, was made up of individuals appointed by the President of the United States. The Board had little real power or authority. The economic power and influence was held by the Reserve bank presidents (at that time called governors).

Purpose. In principle a central bank should be able to underwrite the stability of the banking system. While it may not be able to prevent the failure of particular individual banks that may have been the victims of fraud, bad management, or an unfortunate combination of circumstances, it should be able to prevent the failure of some banks from bringing down others in their wake. The Federal Reserve System proved incapable, however, of performing this task during the 1929–1933 debacle.

Under the provisions of the original Federal Reserve Act of 1913, its purpose was "to furnish an elastic currency, to afford means of rediscounting commercial paper, to establish a more effective supervision of banking, . . ." and "to facilitate commerce and business." The Federal Reserve System was not given much discretionary power. In fact, its operations were to be automatic. It was a narrowly conceived system designed to provide some of the institutional needs to prevent future banking panics.

States' Rights Again. The preeminence of states' rights meant that membership in the Federal Reserve System could be made compulsory only for national banks. Membership was voluntary for state banks. On the eve of the crisis in 1929, two-thirds of the commercial banks in the United States (holding, however, only one-third of total bank assets) were not members of the Federal Reserve System. Even in mid-1971, over 58 percent of all commercial banks were nonmembers, although they held less than 20 percent of total bank assets. This voluntarism was a serious limitation to the extension of federal control over the banking system. It meant not only that most banks did not have access to the central bank as a lender of last resort but also that the Federal Reserve could not impose strict standards on its members without inducing many of them to forsake membership (including, perhaps, a national bank charter) for nonmembership.

Cash Reserves of Member Banks. Reserves of member banks were held by the regional Reserve banks. Minimum reserve requirements were set by the Federal Reserve with congressional approval. Following the national banking system, different requirements were imposed on different member banks, depending on their geographic location. Under the original Act neither vault cash nor correspondent bank deposits would be counted toward legal reserves, nor would Reserve banks pay interest on reserve deposits.

The original purpose of required reserves was to ensure that each member bank held adequate reserves against its deposit liabilities. By creating institutions separate from the commercial banking system to hold these reserves, it was believed that these reserves would always provide the necessary liquidity for the banking system.

Reserves would not be frozen, as they were under the national bank system. Member banks could obtain additional reserves from the central bank by borrowing against or selling eligible paper at a discount. Eligible paper consisted of short-term commercial paper, which commercial banks acquired as collateral against loans they made to commerce, industry, and agriculture. The paper usually matured within 90 days and conformed to the real-bills doctrine (Chapter 9). The Reserve banks would accept all eligible paper offered by member banks in exchange for additional reserve balances. The discount mechanism was the keystone of central bank activity at the beginning.

It was believed by the framers of the Federal Reserve System that these Reserve banks would respond to the initiatives and needs of member banks. In times of economic expansion member banks would turn more frequently to the central bank for additional reserves as loan demands increased. They would offer the Reserve banks eligible paper. With additional reserves, member banks could accommodate the needs of the economy for additional funds. In times of economic slowdown, member banks would permit their reserves balances to accumulate to repay their loans to the central bank and would not need additional reserves. The system would contract. It was emphasized that the central bank would passively and almost automatically accommodate member banks.

Currency. The Federal Reserve Act also provided for a new paper currency issued by the Federal Reserve banks. It was anticipated that in time these paper notes would replace national bank notes. The Federal Reserve notes were to be backed by eligible paper (to 60 percent) and by gold (at least 40 percent). With commercial paper as a backing it was alleged that these notes would possess the elasticity that national bank notes had lacked. Federal Reserve notes would expand and contract with economic activity, as reflected in member banks' needs for additional reserves.

Federal Reserve bank notes were also tied to gold. It was believed that, by requiring the central bank to hold at least 40 percent of the value of its notes outstanding in gold, it would increase the acceptability of Federal Reserve notes and prevent overissue. However, by tying a component of the money supply to gold, the framers of the Federal Reserve Act also imposed an internationally sensitive constraint on the monetary operations of the central bank. Changes in gold flows resulting from changes in trade balances would be transmitted to the domestic money supply. We will discuss the implications of these changes on the domestic economy in Chapters 20 and 21.

Borrowing Privileges. The Federal Reserve banks automatically accepted eligible paper offered by member banks in exchange for additional reserve balances. The Reserve banks were constrained from offering unlimited credit only by the requirement that they must also hold gold equal to 35 percent of their reserve deposit liabilities. Member banks borrowed reserves from the Federal Reserve banks against their promissory notes, which were backed by U.S. government securities as collateral. We shall discuss the discount mechanism and borrowing privileges as an instrument of monetary policy in Chapter 16.

DEFICIENCIES OF THE FEDERAL RESERVE SYSTEM

Monetary Management. Management of the money supply is an essential function of a central bank. Economic conditions may require expansion or contraction of the money supply and bank reserves to promote economic stability, real economic growth, and full employment. Under the terms of the original Federal Reserve Act, changes in the cash reserves of member banks were to be dictated largely by the needs of trade and at the initiative of the member banks, rather than by the central bank in response to broader economic considerations.

It was not until ten years after the establishment of the Federal Reserve System that the Reserve banks found that they could influence member bank reserves, interest rates, and general economic conditions when they bought and sold financial assets like acceptances and federal government bonds for their own portfolios. From 1923 on, the nascent open-market committee bought and sold securities for the Reserve banks. The committee was dominated by Benjamin Strong, head of the Federal Reserve Bank of New York. As a result, open-market operations more often accommodated New York bankers' needs than those of the economy at large.

The Federal Reserve Act introduced a new paper currency that was to have "elasticity." However, this currency was tied to supplies of eligible paper and gold, with no provision in the Act to suspend or broaden the backing requirements in the event of economic emergencies. This had been one of the shortcomings of the national bank notes.

During the Panic of 1907–1908, the Aldrich-Vreeland Act was passed, permitting national banks to issue notes backed only with commercial paper. This gave the currency some additional flexibility, broadened its backing temporarily, and enabled banks to accommodate unusual currency demands. It was emergency legislation that was applied successfully in 1914. When war broke out in Europe, the public here demanded currency immediately. National banks were able to meet the demand by issuing notes without U.S. government bond backing. The legislation expired in 1915, and no such emergency provision was made a part of the issuance of Federal Reserve notes. Hindsight tells us that such a provision might have helped turn the tide of bank failures in the 1930s.

Deposit Insurance. It was believed that the Federal Reserve System would eliminate future panics and banking crises. The version of the legislation that the Senate passed in 1913 contained a provision for deposit guarantees—part of the Federal Reserve banks' earnings would be set aside in a depositors' guaranty fund. This provision was deleted in the Senate-House conference committee.

Eight states established some form of deposit insurance between 1907 and 1917. However, with the increases in bank failures in the 1920s, all of these funds were insolvent by 1933.[4] The Comptroller of the Currency had recommended some form of deposit insurance for all national banks as early as 1917.[5] A variety of funding schemes were suggested, but none was established until June 1933. This lack of deposit insurance proved to be a major weakness of the original Federal Reserve Act.

The Federal Reserve System was grafted onto an existing banking structure that was already fragmented between state and federal control. The authority of the central bank was in fact decentralized. As an institution it was given little direct authority or opportunity for strong independent action. It formed an institutional framework within which some of the deficiencies of the commercial banking system could be remedied. It was not sufficient for the task, however, of handling the profound financial crisis of the 1930s.

PROFILE OF THE FINANCIAL SYSTEM IN 1929

The period from the end of World War I to 1929 is generally characterized as one of prosperity accompanied by rising real incomes. Financial intermediaries experienced rapid growth in total assets during this period. In fewer than twenty years, the total assets of financial intermediaries increased fourfold. Asset growth was accompanied by a proliferation of new, more specialized financial intermediaries such as credit unions, private and government-sponsored pension and retirement funds, consumer and sales finance companies, investment companies, federal postal savings, federal land banks, the Federal Reserve banks, and other federal lending agencies.

Savings and loan associations grew rapidly during the housing boom of the 1920s, aided by the growth of the suburbs, the increased mobility of the population (due in part to the automobile), and the ease with which new savings and loan associations could be formed. They attracted deposit funds from the public by offering higher interest rates than either commercial or mutual savings banks.

Life insurance companies maintained their share of total financial assets during this period, as shown in Table 12.4, despite strong competition from investment companies, which offered individuals another vehicle for investing their savings.

Rising stock market prices and broader ownership by the public of common stock resulted in an unprecedented rise in demand for credit to purchase securities. The role of security brokers and dealers as an intermediary expanded rapidly. "At the height of the movement in the fall of 1929, security brokers had raised $8.5 billion of funds—about as much as the total deposits that either mutual savings banks or savings and loan associations had accumulated over a half a century or more. . . ."[6] The Federal Reserve Board was concerned about the role commercial banks were playing in fueling the speculative frenzy. Aside from moral suasion, it had no weapon to force commercial banks to curtail their lending to security brokers and dealers and to bank customers who wished to use loan proceeds to purchase securities.

Table 12.4. The American Financial System, 1929

I. *The Money Supply*

	Millions of Dollars	Percent
Currency (Held by the Public)	$ 3,828	14.6
Demand Deposits at Commercial Banks	22,281	85.4
Total	$26,109	100.0

II. *Assets of Financial Intermediaries*

	Billions of Dollars	Percent
Federal Reserve Banks	$ 5.46	4.0
Commercial Banks	66.24	49.0
Mutual Savings Banks	9.87	7.0
Savings and Loan Associations	7.41	5.0
Finance Companies	2.40	2.0
Life Insurance Companies	18.33	13.0
Property Insurance Companies	4.71	4.0
Pension Funds[a]	1.98	2.0
Investment Companies	7.34	5.0
Federal Lending Agencies and Land Banks	2.23	1.0
Other Financial Intermediaries[b]	10.99	8.0
	$136.96	100.0

[a]Private trusteed and public funds.
[b]Including security brokers and dealers.
SOURCE: Money supply data: M. Friedman and A. Schwartz, *A Monetary History of the United States, 1867–1960* (copyright © 1963 by National Bureau of Economic Research), published by Princeton University Press, Princeton, N.J., p. 712. Reprinted by permission of Princeton University Press. Asset data: R. Goldsmith, *Financial Institutions* (New York: Random House, 1968), p. 158.

Despite the general economic expansion and stock market advances, there were signs of profound economic distress. The agricultural sector continued to lag the general economy. During World War I the entire economy had been stimulated by wartime deficit financing and large gold inflows from abroad. There had also been a sharp increase in demand for agricultural products from abroad. Commodity prices and farm land values soared. Then, in 1920 and 1921, economic activity declined as it readjusted to peace. Commodity prices collapsed, and the agricultural sector really did not recover during the 1920s. Several federal agencies and programs were established during this period specifically to assist the farm sector.

During this period, until 1929, total commercial bank assets grew rapidly. (Compare Tables 12.3 and 12.4.) However, from 1921 to 1929 about 5400 commercial banks were permanently closed. Many of these were rural banks that suffered when their agricultural constituency was unable to recover economically. These small rural banks had made mortgage and crop loans on the basis of inflated World War I farm land and crop values. When agricultural prices fell, these banks held loans at values far above that of the devalued collateral. Other banks suffered from the shifts in population that were occurring as better economic opportunities drew people from the farms into the labor force in the cities.

THE REFORM OF 1933–1934: MOVES TOWARD CENTRALIZATION

The commercial banking system was dealt a severe blow when the stock market crashed in 1929. A general and sharp decline in economic activity began, reaching a climax in 1932–1933. The central bank had inadequate powers to prevent the large-scale collapse of the commercial banking industry. In 1928, there were about 25,000 commercial banks in operation; by the end of 1933, only 14,000 were operating. During this period of spiraling bank failures, the public came to distrust even sound banks, demanding that their deposits be converted to currency and further undermining the asset stability of these banks. The Federal Reserve banks were hampered by limited gold supplies and eligible paper from putting additional amounts of currency into circulation to meet commercial bank demand. Thus, there was no remedy at hand to cure the loss of public confidence in banks. Finally, over the weekend before March 6, 1933, President Franklin Roosevelt moved to close all banks. The bank holiday of 1933 marked the final collapse of the banking system.

The collapse had both structural and economic roots. There had been a rapid increase in the number of new banks formed in the period from 1900 to 1920. Capital requirements for new national banks had been lowered, facilitating entry. Many of the new state bank facilities were small, tied to a limited local economy, and inadequately capitalized. When the population shifted or the local economy declined, many of these banks were not of an economically viable size to survive.

Legislation had been enacted to permit national banks to buy and sell investment securities other than stock and to hold corporate securities for investment purposes. Lending against real estate collateral was also liberalized. In general, there had been an easing of banking standards. When stock prices fell, real estate values declined, and agricultural production slowed, many commercial banks found that they had made unsound selections of loans and investments for their portfolios. Risky loan and investment assets were worthless; once-liquid security investments and sound real estate mortgages were nonmarketable and uncollectable. Many banks, it is alleged, were forced into acquiring high-yielding risky assets for their portfolios because of the speculative bidding for deposits that resulted in higher rates of interest being offered.

The banking crisis of 1933 produced a fundamental change in the banking industry and in the federal government's role in supervising and regulating that industry. The Banking Acts of 1933 and 1935, the Securities Act of 1933, and the Securities Exchange Act of 1934 imposed restrictions on commercial banks and forced disclosure of information about securities issues. Deposit insurance was established and extended to any commercial bank that wished to join the Federal Deposit Insurance Corporation. We shall discuss the implications of federal deposit insurance in a later section.

Restructuring the Federal Reserve. This crisis-oriented legislation also dramatically restructured the central bank. Although the appearance of a decentralized service organization for member banks was maintained, the substance of it was revoked. Two interrelated centralizing institutions were created. First, the weak Federal Reserve Board was reorganized and transformed into a strong Board of Governors of the Federal Reserve System. Each of the 7 governors would be appointed by the President of the United States for a 14-year term. The Comptroller of the Currency and the Secretary of the Treasury would no longer serve as Board members. Only the chairmanship of the Board of Governors would be a 4-year term coincident with the presidential elections. Thus, the Board was given statutory independence from political pressures.

Second, the ad hoc coordinating committee for open-market transactions in acceptances and U.S. government securities was restructured and given legislative status as the Federal Open Market Committee. It has 12 members, which include the 7 governors of the Board and the president of the Federal Reserve Bank of New York (in recognition of the importance this Reserve bank plays in the entire banking system). The 4 other seats are rotated among the other Federal Reserve bank presidents.

In addition to these centralizing institutional changes, the Board of Governors was given responsibility for management of the money supply. It was to devise and implement monetary policies that would promote economic stability and real economic growth.

The discount mechanism was altered. Loans of reserves to member banks were no longer made automatically by the central bank. Although advances of reserves to member banks could now be made against any sound financial asset, not just eligible paper, borrowing reserves from the central bank became a privilege of membership rather than a right. Quantitatively, discounts and advances declined to insignificance. Now, initiative to change member bank reserves was taken by the Federal Open Market Committee. Transactions in U.S. government securities rather than advances through the discount window became the primary vehicle for changing reserves available to the banking system and changing credit conditions.

The backing for Federal Reserve notes was broadened to include U.S. government securities as well as gold and eligible paper. This move gave the paper currency additional flexibility and elasticity, which it had lacked under the national banking system and the original Federal Reserve Act. Finally, the central bank's link to the real-bills doctrine was discarded.

As part of its new power, the Board of Governors was given authority to vary the cash reserve requirements for member banks within broad limits set by Congress. This is a powerful, albeit blunt, instrument of monetary control. (See Chapter 17.) The Board of Governors was also given authority to limit loans made by banks, brokers, and dealers backed by securities as collateral. These limits are called *margin requirements*. Under Regulation Q the Board of Governors was given the power to set the maximum rates of interest paid by member banks on time and savings deposits. At the same time, payment of interest on demand deposits was prohibited. Legislation also limited loans to bank officers, and dealings in investment securities were no longer deemed an appropriate bank activity.

Congress and the central bank moved to strengthen the financial system. Some requirements of Federal Reserve membership were eased to encourage the smaller rural banks to join the system. Some of the restraints that had been applied to national banks were eased to encourage them to remain part of the national bank system and the Federal Reserve. Increased federal supervision, regulation, and responsibility for all banks to prevent future bank failure resulted from the legislation passed from 1933 to 1935.

ESTABLISHMENT OF THE FEDERAL DEPOSIT INSURANCE CORPORATION

The transformation of the Federal Reserve System into a centralized agency for monetary policy was not the only significant change in government policy toward the banking and financial structure in the period 1933–1935. Perhaps equally important was the creation of the Federal Deposit Insurance Corporation.

The FDIC provides insurance to bank depositors, guaranteeing the safety of their deposits in insured banks.[7] Membership in this plan was made compulsory for all members of the Federal Reserve System but was also made available to nonmember banks who could qualify under the FDIC's strict standards. The plan proved immensely popular. By the end of its first year of operation, 85 percent of all nonmember banks had been admitted to the insurance plan, and as of December 31, 1972, 98 percent of all commercial banks (accounting for over 99 percent of commercial bank assets) were insured by the FDIC.

New Banking Policies. With federal deposit insurance virtually a *sine qua non* of banking, the federal government was placed in a strong position to impose new policies on the whole banking system. A new pattern of banking policies emerged, emphasizing the soundness of assets and management policies, limitations on "destructive competition," and avoidance of "overbanking."

In order to improve the quality of assets and management policies, federal supervision was extended to all state banks that joined the FDIC. This involved applying new, conservative criteria for the valuation of bank

Table 12.5. The American Financial System, 1939

I. *The Money Supply*

	Millions of Dollars	Percent
Currency (Held by the Public)	$ 5,682	17.9
Demand Deposits at Commercial Banks	25,986	82.1
Total	$31,668	100.0

II. *Assets of Financial Intermediaries*

	Billions of Dollars	Percent
Federal Reserve Banks	$ 19.03	12.0
Commercial Banks	66.31	40.0
Mutual Savings Banks	11.85	7.0
Savings and Loan Associations	5.20	3.0
Finance Companies	2.7	2.0
Investment Companies	3.14	2.0
Life Insurance Companies	30.47	18.0
Property Insurance Companies	4.88	3.0
Pension Funds[a]	7.28	4.0
Federal Lending Institutions	9.90	6.0
Other Financial Intermediaries[b]	3.92	2.0
	$164.68	100.0

[a]Private trusteed and public funds.
[b]Includes security brokers and dealers.
SOURCE: Money supply data: M. Friedman and A. Schwartz, *A Monetary History of the United States, 1867–1960* (copyright © 1963 by National Bureau of Economic Research), published by Princeton University Press, Princeton, N.J., pp. 715–716. Reprinted by permission of Princeton University Press. Asset data: R. Goldsmith, *Financial Institutions* (New York: Random House, 1968), p. 158.

assets, and regular inspection by federal officials. Federal bank examiners not only assess and report on the quality of the bank's assets but also evaluate the quality of the bank's management.

Although this was not the primary purpose of the plan, the establishment of the Federal Deposit Insurance Corporation made it possible for the federal government to exert considerable control over the subsequent evolution of the structure of the banking system.

PROFILE OF THE AMERICAN FINANCIAL SYSTEM IN 1939

Most private financial intermediaries were profoundly affected by the stock market collapse in 1929. We mentioned earlier the severe contraction experienced by the commercial banking industry. Between 1929 and 1934 almost 10,000 commercial banks closed their doors permanently.

The flight from commercial bank deposits went in part into currency. As shown in Table 12.5, by 1939 the currency component of the money supply had increased to almost 18 percent. Two types of financial intermediaries, mutual savings banks and life insurance companies, seemed to attract some of the funds withdrawn from commercial banks. By 1939 life insurance companies increased their total share of all financial assets to 18 percent. Mutual savings banks benefited from a very low failure rate, in sharp contrast to the relatively high failure rates of savings and loan associations and banks.

Federal lending agencies increased in number and in asset size during this period in an attempt to shore up specific sectors of the sagging economy. Many other financial intermediaries experienced either no growth or a net loss in financial assets during this ten-year period. As a result, the relationships between different financial intermediaries shifted. As shown in Table 12.5, in 1939 commercial banks held only 40 percent of total financial assets. Life insurance companies, Federal Reserve banks, and federal lending agencies had significantly increased their percentage share of total financial assets.

AVOIDANCE OF OVERBANKING: RESTRICTIONS ON ENTRY AND COMPETITION

Enactment of free-banking legislation had encouraged the formation of many small banks. By 1920 there were more than 30,000 separate banks. By the middle 1920s, however, the Comptroller of the Currency's office had begun to review new national bank charter applications more carefully. In light of increasing bank failures, the Comptroller started denying almost half of all new charter requests during this period.[8] The era of free banking was coming to an end.

After the Banking Acts of 1933 and 1935, entry to banking was regulated on all sides. It was believed that entry had to be closely controlled to prevent overbanking and to protect the liquidity and solvency of existing banks. A new bank not only had to obtain a charter from the state or national authorities but also had to obtain a certificate of insurance from the FDIC.[9] The Comptroller of the Currency in approving new bank charters and the FDIC in issuing new insurance certificates were required to consider the new bank's "future earnings prospects," "the general character of its management," and the "convenience and need of the community to be served." A bank wishing to open a branch or to increase its capital had to obtain approval from the federal authorities under the same criteria regarding public need, profitability, and competitive effects.

Competition for deposits among established banks was limited through the imposition of a ceiling on the rates of interest banks could pay on time and savings deposits. It was argued that free competition via interest rates had contributed to the instability of the banking system in the 1930s. Initially the prohibition of interest on demand deposits and the ceiling rates on time and savings deposits were accepted with enthusiasm by many bankers, but in recent years Regulation Q has become an object of controversy, and there has been considerable agitation to eliminate or modify it.[10]

Clearly, the legislation of the 1930s had centralized power over the banking industry in the hands of the federal government. It had transformed banking from a rather freely competitive industry into a fully regulated one. Free banking had ended; states deferred some of their authority over state-chartered banks to the FDIC. Federal authorities sought to eliminate bank failures and prevent a repetition of the 1933 collapse.

As a result of federal regulation, supervision, and insurance, bank failures became rare and losses to depositors even rarer. The basic industry was constrained by these regulations. The total number of commercial banks in operation from 1935 to 1973 declined from about 15,500 to 14,000. The number of bank facilities (home offices and branches) doubled during the same period. Looking more closely at the data, we find that until 1950 there was little change in the number of commercial banks and only a small increase in bank branches. Since 1950 there has been an increase in merger activity between existing banks. The effect of mergers has outweighed a rather stable annual rate of new bank charters.

One exception to the comparatively stable number of new bank charters occurred during the period 1962–1965. In these years the Comptroller of the Currency's office, under the leadership of James Saxon, approved many more new national bank charter applications. Saxon believed that there was a shortage of banking facilities and, further, that the restrictions on banking begun in the 1930s had limited the industry's ability to compete with other types of financial institutions. He believed it was time to modify the criteria of public need, competitive effects, and expectations of profit used to judge new bank charters and branch applications. The net increase in new national banks chartered was a temporary phenomenon; when Saxon left office, the federal authorities returned to the conservative pattern of restricting new bank entry.

Two other changes in bank structure have occurred. Bank facilities have increased in number, largely as a result of branching. The legal constraints on establishing branches are determined by state law; recently several states have liberalized their branching regulations. The federal authorities consider branch requests only if they are in accord with state law. The number of branches has increased from 4,700 in 1950 to 23,400 at the beginning of 1972.

Where branching is prohibited or severely curtailed by state law, we find that there have been more new banks chartered and greater merger activity between banks. The limits on branching have probably hampered existing banks from growing in size and resulted in more separate banks than would exist without these restraints.

PRESERVATION OF COMPETITION AS A POLICY OBJECTIVE

The reforms of the 1930s were designed to rationalize and stabilize the banking system, in part by restricting competitive forces. More recently, renewed emphasis has been placed on the preservation of competition in banking markets, particularly where it is believed that competition is threatened by a proliferation of bank mergers or bank holding companies.

Fearing increased economic concentration as a result of bank merger activity in the 1950s, Congress passed legislation to curtail this trend. Under the Bank Merger Act of 1960, all bank mergers involving banks under federal jurisdiction (national banks, member banks, or insured banks) require prior approval of the regulating authorities. Impact on competition is one of the factors that must be considered, along with the future prospects for existing and proposed institutions. The Attorney General of the United States is also required to submit a brief to the bank regulatory authorities offering his assessment of the competitive impact of the merger. Moreover, recent Supreme Court decisions have held that banks are subject to antitrust laws, which in effect make impact on competition the primary consideration in reviewing applications for mergers. The application of antitrust laws to a fully regulated industry that must obtain prior federal approval for merger is considered by some a questionable practice.

Under the Bank Holding Company Act of 1956, multibank holding companies are required to register with the Board of Governors of the Federal Reserve. The Board's approval is required for acquisition of banks by holding companies. The Act was amended in 1970 and now requires all one-bank holding companies to register with the Board of Governors as well. In 1970 it was estimated that there were 1200 one-bank holding companies.[11]

The Board of Governors was also given responsibility for issuing guidelines on what types of nonbanking activities are acceptable for one-bank holding companies. It had been feared by some that one-bank holding companies would use their new corporate form to unfair competitive advantage against other commercial banks.

Regulation of the banking industry is justified by many because of its tie to the payments mechanism and its credit-creating power. However, we must question how federal regulations and the interpretation of those regulations have affected the banking industry and the economy. We shall turn to these questions in the next chapter.

IMPLEMENTATION OF MONETARY POLICY SINCE THE 1930s: FROM DEFERENCE TO INDEPENDENCE

The banking legislation of the 1930s altered the structure and locus of power of the central bank. Out of the collapse of the banking system came a central bank responsible for affecting general economic conditions and protecting the banking system from failures.

The Federal Reserve used its new monetary policy tools cautiously. Commercial banks' excess reserves were quite large and increasing, and loan demand was sluggish. The commercial banks themselves now placed a much higher priority on liquidity than they had in the late 1920s. Gold inflows increased in response to the devaluation that had occurred and to political unrest in Europe. Commercial banks were reluctant to purchase U.S. government securities with their excess reserves because yields were very low, at times less than one-fourth of 1 percent. Although the Federal Open Market Committee did buy and sell long-term and short-term securities, its actions were not aimed specifically at affecting bank reserves. Rather, the FOMC was trying to influence yield patterns and maintain low interest rates to stimulate the economy.

The Board of Governors was concerned about the increasing volume of excess reserves. It feared that the existence of a substantial amount of excess reserves would inhibit its ability to quickly tighten bank credit and damp speculative and inflationary tendencies in the economy if it became necessary to do so. In three steps between 1936 and 1937, the Board used its discretionary authority over reserve requirements and doubled them. Economic recovery was set back by this move, obviously an unintentional effect. Its initial experiences with monetary controls thus were not very successful.

On the day after the bombing of Pearl Harbor, December 8, 1941, the Board of Governors announced its intention to ensure that an ample supply of funds would be available at all times for financing the war effort. The Federal Reserve deferred its responsibilities for credit conditions to the Treasury and its overwhelming financing needs. Credit policy would accommodate the Treasury's and the nation's war effort. Throughout the war the central bank provided ample supplies of bank reserves and bought all U.S. government securities not purchased by the public. It maintained low interest rates to keep debt costs to a minimum. It relied on selective credit controls to channel funds to industries directly engaged in the war effort and to ration funds available for nondefense purposes.

In the postwar period the Federal Reserve continued to serve the Treasury and support its refinancing efforts. The Fed guaranteed the yields on U.S. government securities by setting a bottom price and purchasing all securities offered at that price. Its policy of pegging bond prices prevented market forces from driving the prices on bonds below the established floor and limited the public's risk of capital loss. The Federal Reserve's commitment to maintain bond prices severely limited its ability to influence credit conditions and promote economic stability.

With the outbreak of the Korean War, the Federal Reserve had no flexibility in implementing a restrictive credit policy. It felt that it was further committed by the Employment Act of 1946 "to promote" the achievement and maintenance of "maximum employment, production, and purchasing power." By 1951, the central bank was no longer willing to be subservient to the Treasury. An accord was reached establishing once again the Federal Reserve's independence and responsibility for the conduct of monetary policy to achieve the goals outlined in the Employment Act of 1946.

Table 12.6. The American Financial System, 1970

I. *The Money Supply*

	Billions of Dollars	Percent
Currency (Held by the Public)	$ 48.6	22.7
Demand Deposits at Commercial Banks (Excluding Interbank and Federal Government Deposits)	165.7	77.3
Total	$ 214.6	100.0

II. *Assets of Financial Intermediaries*

	Billions of Dollars	Percent
Federal Reserve Banks	$ 85.1	5.9
Commercial Banks	503.3	34.7
Mutual Savings Banks	78.9	5.4
Savings and Loan Associations	176.6	12.2
Finance Companies	60.3	4.2
Investment Companies	47.6	3.3
Life Insurance Companies	199.1	13.7
Property Insurance Companies	51.7	3.6
Pension Funds[a]	162.6	11.2
Federal Lending Institutions	46.0	3.2
Other Financial Intermediaries	39.0	2.6
	$1450.2	100.0

[a]Private and state and local pension funds.
SOURCE: From flow-of-funds data, U.S. Department of Commerce, Bureau of the Census, *Statistical Abstract of the United States* (Washington, D.C., 1971), p. 429.

The period since the accord has been marked by increased use of monetary and fiscal policy to promote those goals. One of the major problems, however, has been the realization that policies that promote economic growth and full employment often conflict with policies designed to achieve price stability.

PROFILE OF THE AMERICAN FINANCIAL SYSTEM IN 1970

Table 12.6 illustrates the increasing complexity of the American financial system, as well as its growth, when compared with earlier tables. Total assets held by financial intermediaries have increased almost ninefold since 1939. In addition to this phenomenal growth, there has been a marked shift in the share of total assets held by various intermediaries. The most startling increases have been in holdings of assets by savings and loan associations and pension funds. We have discussed this trend in Chapters 10 and 11. During World War II, Federal Reserve banks' share of total financial assets increased to 13 percent as the central bank assisted the Treasury in its wartime financing. Since the end of the war, their share has returned to about 6 percent. Life insurance companies as a group have increased their assets in

280

absolute terms but have managed only to maintain their percentage share of total financial assets.

During the same period, currency as a portion of the money supply increased from 18 percent in 1939 to almost 23 percent in 1970. The total money supply, narrowly defined, has increased almost sevenfold.

The period from 1939 through 1970 has been one of almost continuous real economic growth. Real income per capita (in 1953 dollars) increased from $1500 in 1939 to $3500 in 1970. Rising real incomes enabled the population to save a greater share of its income. While the supply of lendable funds was increasing, we find business demand for such funds to finance plant expansion and capital asset acquisition also increasing. At one time business relied predominantly on internally generated funds to finance expansion. Today, a major share of those funds comes from external sources (see Chapter 6).

Financial intermediaries have responded to this climate of growth. They have devised different, more flexible financial instruments to attract household and corporate saving. They have moved across once traditional lending barriers and diversified their asset portfolios. Some intermediaries that have grown more rapidly than others, such as savings and loan associations, pension funds, and credit unions, have also had the advantage of preferential tax treatment.

SUMMARY

In this chapter we have tried to convey some of the political and economic conditions that have influenced and altered the structure of the American financial system. The growth and increasing complexity of the financial system are evident in Table 12.7, which summarizes the preceding tables. It should be clear that the system has evolved in response to economic needs and political constraints rather than by purposeful design.

The Great Depression had the most profound effect on the entire financial industry. Legislation passed during that crisis dramatically strengthened federal control over both state-chartered and federal institutions. In the name of stability and solvency, federal regulatory agencies were able to exert considerable control and direction over commercial banking, the securities industry, and other financial intermediaries.

It is difficult to assess whether the economic climate, the institutions themselves, or the new regulations inhibited the growth of commercial banks since the 1930s. During the same period, other financial institutions grew much more rapidly. However, since 1960 commercial banks have, through mergers, acquisitions, branching, and holding company arrangements, moved aggressively into bank-related activities, expanded their assets, and sought new ways to better serve their commercial and private deposit customers.

Table 12.7. **The American Financial System, 1860–1970 (Billions of Dollars)**

	1860	1890	1912	1929	1939	1970
The Money Supply						
Currency	$0.585	$0.888	$ 1.83	$ 3.83	$ 5.68	$ 48.6
Deposits	0.729	3.020	13.55	22.28	25.99	165.7
Total	$1.314	$3.908	$15.38	$ 26.11	$ 31.67	$ 214.6
Assets of Financial Intermediaries						
Federal Reserve Banks	—	—	—	$ 5.46	$ 19.03	$ 85.1
Commercial Banks	$0.800	$5.6	$21.82	66.24	66.31	503.3
Mutual Savings Banks	0.240	1.7	2.01	9.87	11.85	78.9
Life Insurance Companies	0.024	0.8	4.57	18.33	30.47	199.1
Property Insurance Companies	0.096	0.4	1.00	4.71	4.88	51.7
Savings and Loan Associations	—	0.6	0.95	7.41	5.20	176.6
Pension Funds	—	—	0.01	1.98	7.28	162.6
Finance Companies	—	—	0.0	2.40	2.7	60.3
Federal Lending Agencies	—	—	0.01	2.23	9.90	46.0
Investment Companies	—	—	—	7.34	3.14	47.6
Other Financial Institutions	0.060	0.6	1.40	10.99	3.92	39.0
	$1.220	$9.6	$33.77	$136.96	$164.68	$1450.2

SOURCE: Adapted and combined from Tables 12.1, 12.2, 12.3, 12.4, 12.5, and 12.6. (See individual tables for source for a particular year.)

The financial industry will continue to develop and change. It must do so in order to meet changing economic needs and political constraints. The financial system has emerged without an overall vision; it functions under diverse authority and myriad political and legal arrangements. It must be free to change and respond to the economy and its needs in the future: it is to be hoped that the system will become more efficient in obtaining and allocating scarce capital.

NOTES

1. S. E. Morison, *The Oxford History of the American People* (New York: Oxford University Press, 1965), p. 440.

2. A. Conrad, "Income Growth and Structural Change," in Seymour E. Harris, ed., *American Economic History* (New York: McGraw-Hill, 1961), p. 39.

3. P. Cagan, "The First Fifty Years of the National Banking System—An Historical Appraisal," in D. Carson, ed., *Banking and Monetary Studies* (Homewood, Ill.: Irwin, 1963), p. 17.

4. Federal Deposit Insurance Corporation, *Annual Report, 1950* (Washington, D.C., 1951), pp. 61–69.

5. Comptroller of the Currency, *Annual Report, 1917*, vol. 1 (Washington, D.C., 1918), p. 24.

6. R. Goldsmith, *Financial Institutions* (New York: Random House, 1968), p. 171.

7. The insurance policy is actually taken out by the bank on behalf of its customers, and the bank pays a premium based on its total deposits. Each account is insured up to $20,000, but since the FDIC can generally arrange to have a failing bank merged into a sound one (making appropriate financial adjustments to compensate for the shortfall of assets in the failing bank), losses to depositors have been small.

8. Comptroller of the Currency, *Annual Report, 1963* (Washington, D.C., 1964).

9. This was the normal procedure, unless, of course, it chose to operate without FDIC insurance. It has been reported, however, that many state banking authorities refused (and still do) to issue a charter unless the FDIC will issue a certificate of insurance. [See Comptroller of the Currency, *Annual Report, 1964* (Washington, D.C., 1965), p. 242.]

10. Regulation Q applies to member banks, but the FDIC adopts the same ceiling for nonmember banks. In 1966 a similar (but not equal) ceiling was imposed on rates paid by savings and loan associations; it is enforced by the Federal Home Loan Bank Board.

11. Board of Governors of the Federal Reserve System, *Annual Report, 1970* (Washington, D.C., 1971).

THE SOCIAL INTEREST IN THE STRUCTURE OF THE FINANCIAL SYSTEM

Issues in Microeconomic Policy

Our discussion of the microeconomics of the American financial system so far has been in positive terms. We have described some important features of the structure and history of the system and have developed an elementary analysis of the function of financial markets and financial intermediaries. However, in spite of our avowed concern with public policy, and with the exception of some matters relating to the payments mechanism, we have so far avoided the discussion of normative issues. The purpose of this chapter is to explore some of these issues. It is concerned with the objectives and content of public policy with respect to the structure and functioning of the financial system.

THE CONSTITUTIONAL PROBLEM

The United States is a federal state with a constitutional division of power between the federal and state governments. The Constitution outlines specific areas wherein the federal government has exclusive control. It guarantees the states authority over the areas that are not expressly prohibited to them under the Constitution. Thus, as we have seen, the chartering and regulation of financial institutions at the beginning of the republic was the sole prerogative of the states.

The Constitution did assign the federal government exclusive control over the coining of money and regulation of interstate commerce. It also admonished the federal government to provide for the general welfare. Using these powers, Congress has passed specific legislation regarding many aspects of the financial system and industry.

At no time, however, has federal regulation abrogated the states' right to enact their own legislation regarding financial institutions. As a result, federal and state governments continue to charter commercial banks, credit unions, and savings and loan associations. They both issue regulations regarding the operation of these institutions. Most of the other groups of financial intermediaries are chartered solely by the states, but must adhere to federal regulations where interstate business is concerned. Thus, there exists a "multisystem" of chartering, supervision, and regulation of most financial institutions. The result is apparent inefficiency in all three areas, as well as significant differences in legal and economic criteria that result in competitive disadvantages for similar institutions, depending on their source of incorporation and membership in federal systems.

This "multisystem" of authority places a major obstacle in the path of formulating a single, national financial policy. Obtaining such a policy would require cooperation between the federal government and various federal agencies as well as the 50 state governments.

The federal government has made substantial progress in asserting its supremacy over the regulation of financial institutions, primarily through deposit insurance and protection of the individual consumer. The adoption by the states of federal deposit insurance as a precondition to chartering new state banks has enabled the federal government to exert its control and supervision over more banks. Extension of federal deposit insurance to credit unions, savings and loan associations, and mutual savings banks chartered by the states has brought even more financial institutions under federal supervision.

There is little hope at present that a unified financial policy will be forthcoming or even that Congress will move to smooth the structure of supervision, regulation, taxation, and insurance of financial institutions at the federal level. Some argue that diversity in chartering and regulatory criteria stimulates innovation in the interpretation of the criteria and competition between similar institutions. Others argue that the "multisystem" discriminates unfairly between similar institutions and is destructive and inefficient.[1]

COMPETITION AS AN OBJECTIVE OF PUBLIC POLICY

Public policy with regard to competition among financial institutions has vacillated. At one time populist forces pressed for legislation that would encourage the formation of many independent institutions under local control, fearing concentration of economic and political power in the hands of a few.

The experience of the 1930s brought reforms that were designed to rationalize and stabilize the financial system, in part by restricting normal competitive forces and entry, thereby preventing overbanking.

Recent federal legislation has reemphasized preservation of competition in commercial banking and among financial institutions. Since the 1950s, for example, Congress has expressed increasing concern about the decline of competition among commercial banks. Several laws have been passed that constitute a change in attitude with respect to the structure of the financial system. One major objective of this legislation has been to maintain the existing numbers of various kinds of institutions, to continue their corporate independence from each other, and to try to increase the degree of effective competition in the financial system. Most of the legislation passed has been aimed specifically at commercial bank operations, so although the federal government does not have the power to regulate all financial institutions or all financial markets, it directly controls certain vitally important institutions, and federal policy, particularly with respect to commercial banks, can have wide repercussions on the entire financial system.

COMPETITION AS A POLICY OBJECTIVE

It is true that economists commonly advocate a high degree of competition as an objective of public policy toward most industries in the economy, but should we treat the financial system the same way we treat other industries? Is not the financial system different in an important sense that makes competition an inappropriate objective of public policy with respect to it?

Competition and Economic Efficiency. At the root of public policy designed to stimulate competition is a concern for *economic efficiency*—a concern that society obtain the maximum possible benefit from the limited real productive resources at its disposal. Economic efficiency has two basic dimensions. The first is that excessive resources should not be absorbed in the production of any product. That is, each good or service must be produced at the least attainable cost. If the quantity of output of every product were predetermined, that would be all that there was to economic efficiency. However, all resources have alternative possible uses. The range and quantity of products produced can be altered. Therefore, the second condition for economic efficiency is that all resources must be allocated to their most valuable uses. That is, the *optimum quantity* of each good or service must be produced. One of the important conclusions of elementary economic theory is that, if we accept the relative valuations of goods and services implicit in consumer demand curves, then, with certain exceptions, highly competitive markets provide the most reliable mechanism for achieving economic efficiency in both senses.

Competition and Efficiency in the Financial System. As was argued in Chapter 1, the financial system can be considered an industry—a collection of firms producing financial services. The production of these services absorbs part of the scarce resources of the economy. As in any other industry, then, it is important that the appropriate quantity of financial services be provided and that they be provided at the least attainable cost.

However, to rest the case for a high degree of competition in the financial system on such an analogy with other industries is to miss an important dimension of the matter. The significance of the financial system cannot be assessed simply in terms of the resources absorbed in producing financial services—in terms of value added in banking and finance. The financial system is, above all else, a mechanism for allocating credit to alternative possible uses and a mechanism for providing asset holders with convenient forms in which they may accumulate wealth. The allocation of credit affects the structure of economic activity: It determines, among other things, what lines of activity will expand and what new ventures will get off the ground. The range of financial instruments available, and the yield on each instrument, affects the welfare of all asset holders. The fundamental case for a policy of stimulating competition is in ensuring that credit is allocated to its most valuable uses (i.e., to the uses promising the highest rates of return) at the minimum attainable cost, and in ensuring that a broad range of financial instruments is made available to asset holders on the best possible terms (i.e., offering the most favorable combinations of risk, liquidity, and expected yield).

CONCENTRATION AND COMPETITION IN THE AMERICAN FINANCIAL SYSTEM

From our earlier discussion of financial markets it should be obvious that in one sense there are always a very large number of participants in the financial system, both as lenders and as borrowers. Virtually every household, business firm, nonprofit institution, and government agency in the United States, plus many foreigners, are involved in one side of the market or the other. Since a very large number of participants on both sides of a free market virtually guarantees a high degree of competition, does it not follow that the financial system is highly competitive?

Not necessarily. What we have to be concerned with is not the number of ultimate participants in financial markets—households, business firms, and so on—but the number of firms and the state of competition among firms that bring the ultimate borrowers and lenders together. We must be concerned with competition among firms acting as brokers and dealers in financial markets on the one hand and firms acting as financial intermediaries on the other. Although there are many households and firms on each side of the market, the market cannot be highly competitive unless the intermediaries in the marketing process are also competitive. What are the facts?

The financial industry is not homogeneous. Commercial banking operations differ substantially from mutual fund operations; this is obvious. However, within commercial banking, firms have disparate characteristics as well as common ones. The small rural bank differs drastically in its concerns, management objectives, portfolio policy, and personnel operations from the large money market bank. The same observations apply in many other sectors of the financial industry.

In some of these sectors there is evidence of a high degree of concentration of business in the hands of a few large firms. While a high degree of concentration is inimical to active price competition, it does not necessarily imply lack of competition. What must be kept in mind is that each sector of the financial industry usually markets many services and products. Firms may compete with each other vigorously, or they may dominate the local, regional, or national market for one or more services.

CONCENTRATION IN COMMERCIAL BANKING

The commercial banking industry is characterized by a large number of firms (over 14,000). This number is in sharp contrast with the commercial banking industry in countries like Canada, which has 9 commercial banks, and Great Britain, which has 12. Although the United States has a large number of independent banks, each bank facility serves on the average many more people. In the United States in 1970 there was one bank facility for every 5,800 people. This is the lowest number since 1932. In 1960 there was one bank facility for every 7,500 people. The rapid change has been the result of increased branching rather than an increase in the number of independent banks. In contrast, however, Canada has one bank facility for every 3,800 people.

The American banking system is dominated by independent unit banks. In part this is a result of the legal restraints against branch banking and stringent barriers to entry for new banks. Only about 4000 banks operate branch facilities, which now number over 24,800.

State law regulates whether commercial banks operating within that state may establish branches. Nineteen states and the District of Columbia permit statewide branching. Sixteen states limit branching to the county in which the head office is located or to contiguous counties. The remaining 15 states severely limit or prohibit branching entirely. As a result of these state laws, 70 percent of all branch offices are located in the same county as the head office of the bank, and 85 percent are situated in that same county or in contiguous counties. Statewide networks of branches of a single bank are relatively rare, and nationwide branches are prohibited.

Expansion Through Branch Banking. As can be seen from Figure 13.1, aside from a temporary aberration during 1962–1965, when the Comptroller

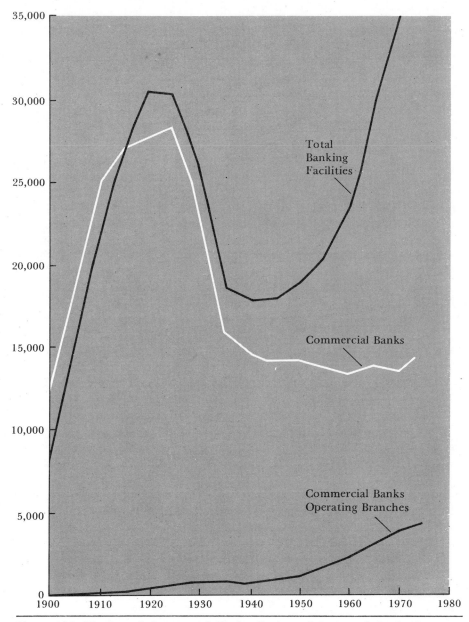

Figure 13.1 **Number of Commercial Banks, Banking Offices, and Banks Operating Branches in the United States, 1900–1972**
SOURCE: U.S. Department of Commerce, Bureau of the Census, *Historical Statistics of the United States, Colonial Times to 1957* (Washington, D.C.), pp. 631, 634, 635; Federal Reserve *Bulletin,* various issues.

of the Currency dramatically increased the number of national bank charters approved, there has been a steady, slow decline in the number of commercial banks in operation.[2] This is the net result of chartering about 100 new banks a year and the disappearance, primarily through mergers, of about 150 banks annually. Bank failures have been negligible.

It is clear that the present structure of the American banking system is not a result of free market entry and exit of firms but rather the direct result of government regulation. Two types of powerful market forces have been partially restrained by federal and state banking authorities.

The overall growth of the economy and increase in population, as well as movement of the population from the farm toward the cities, has produced a rapid increase in the demand for new banking facilities. The primary accommodation to this demand has been a sharp increase in branch banking offices (although such an adjustment is not possible in states that prohibit or severely restrict branch banking). It can be argued that the growth of banking facilities has not been rapid enough to remove the disparity between supply and demand in the market.

The second important force was internal to the banks. Changing technology and the extension of financial markets have produced new economies of scale in banking and created strong pressures to increase the size of banking firms. In some instances banks have grown by branching; in other cases they have merged with other banks and affiliated through holding company arrangements. However, state laws that limit branch banking and federal policy that curtails mergers and bank acquisitions have restricted the pace of these adjustments.

Size Distribution of Banks. One direct consequence of the populist philosophy coupled with restraints on concentration has been a proliferation of commercial banks with very small financial resources. At the beginning of 1971, almost 60 percent of the nation's banks had less than $10 million each in assets, and together they held less than 8 percent of total bank deposits. (See Table 13.1). These very small banks typically have only one office and solicit deposits and make loans in a very limited local market, usually a small town and the surrounding area. A high portion of their loans are for agricultural purposes, and they are little involved in commercial and industrial finance. They do not participate actively in the national money market, have almost no dealing in foreign exchange, and rely heavily on their city correspondents (Chapter 2) for assistance and advice and for the provision of specialized banking services for their customers.

Not all banks are small local institutions. There are many medium-sized institutions that carry on a normal range of commercial banking activities in cities throughout the nation. In addition, the large metropolitan areas contain some of the world's major banks, including the largest bank in the world, California-based Bank of America. The four next largest are also American banks.

Table 13.1. **Number of Commercial Banks and Total Deposits by Size of Bank, December 31, 1970**

	Number of Banks[a]		Total Deposits	
Size of Bank Deposits	Number	Cumulative Percentage	Amount (Millions of Dollars)	Cumulative Percentage
Less Than $1 Million	295	2.1	$ 170.3	0.0
$1–$2 Million	928	8.9	1,450.0	0.3
$2–$5 Million	3,296	32.9	11,271.4	2.6
$5–$10 Million	3,463	58.1	25,105.0	7.8
$10–$25 Million	3,400	82.9	52,553.0	18.6
$25–$50 Million	1,216	91.8	42,027.8	27.3
$50–$100 Million	546	95.8	37,777.2	35.1
$100–$500 Million	436	99.0	91,725.0	54.0
$500–$1 Billion	69	99.5	49,022.8	64.1
$1 Billion or More	56	100.0	$174,416.1	100.0

[a]Includes 194 noninsured banks and trust companies.
SOURCE: Federal Deposit Insurance Corporation, *Annual Report* (Washington, D.C., 1970) p. 189.

This means that there is an extreme range between large and small banks in the United States. While there are almost 300 banks with total assets of less than $1 million, there are 3 banks with total assets of over $20 billion and 13 with assets of $5 billion or more. In contrast to the tiny local banks, the giant institutions carry on banking activities that are national and international in scope. Most of them have representatives (but not branches) in major cities throughout the country in order to service their large industrial customers, and they generally have branches or agencies in the world's financial centers. Some of the major American banks also operate networks of branch offices carrying out a normal commercial banking business in other countries, particularly in South and Central America.

In terms of the magnitude of the financial resources at their disposal, the very large banks dominate the American banking system. As we can see from Table 13.1, the 125 banks with total deposits of $500 million or more hold almost half of all deposits. The largest bank alone holds over 5 percent of the entire banking system's deposits, and the 10 largest banks hold over 25 percent.[3]

Group and Chain Banking. The figure of 14,000 incorporated banks somewhat exaggerates the number of independent banking firms. Many banks belong to either banking groups or banking chains.

A banking group exists when two or more banks are controlled by a holding company. At the beginning of 1971 there were 111 different holding company groups owning 895 banks in 35 states and the District of Columbia. Most of these groups are relatively small and include only a few small unit banks in a single state. However, in 1968 there were 6 groups with aggregate deposits of over $3 billion, and the largest had deposits of $8.3 billion, making it in effect equivalent to one of the 6 or 7 largest banks in the nation.

Group banks account for 12 percent of the offices and 16.2 percent of the deposits in the United States. On a nationwide scale they do not have significant effect on the banking structure as yet. (At the end of 1970, one-bank and multibank holding companies held one-third of total commercial bank deposits.) Their impact in some states, however, is substantial. For example, Minnesota has strict limitations on branch banking, and as a result there are 730 unit banks in the state. Eight holding companies control 124 of these banks, which together hold 60 percent of all deposits in the state. Similarly, in Nevada, which permits statewide branch banking, one group controls 2 of the state's 8 commercial banks and 62.5 percent of all deposits in the state. In 13 states, commercial banks controlled by holding companies have more than 40 percent of all bank deposits in those states. In other states the picture is less extreme.[4]

Interstate branching by one bank is prohibited in the United States. Nonetheless, 4 holding companies own banks in different states. The largest multibank holding company, based in California, owns 23 banks with 680 offices in 11 western states.[5] Recent bank holding company legislation prohibits new bank holding companies from owning banks across state lines.

Chain banking differs from group banking only in that no holding company is involved. Rather, control of 2 or more banks is in the hands of an individual or a partnership. Unlike banking groups, chains do not have to register with the federal banking authorities, and hence there are no data on them. One study, which covered only banks that were members of the Federal Reserve System, identified 431 chains involving 1169 banks in 1962.[6] Most chains involved only 2 banks, but some involved more; one involved 21 banks. Chain banks are located mainly in small towns in states that prohibit branch banking.

Even taking chain and group banking organizations into account, there are 11,000–12,000 independent banking firms in the United States. Does this mean that the American banking industry approximates the economists' idealized concept of a purely competitive industry?

Banking Markets and Banking Competition. It would be a mistake to think that all 12,000 independent banking firms compete in the same market. Banks are multiproduct firms. They provide a variety of services for, accept deposits from, and extend credit to customers who differ greatly in their access to alternative sources, partly because of the cost and inconvenience involved in dealing with relatively remote banks (another case of the importance of transactions costs) and partly because of the importance of information on credit worthiness in the functioning of loan markets.[7] Thus, it is generally argued that the market for services provided to households (checking accounts, personal savings accounts, safety deposit boxes, mortgage credit, consumer credit, etc.) is largely local in scope. In the case of business firms, small, local firms in the distributive trades are dependent primarily on local banks; larger firms with more established regional reputations may have ready access, with little or no additional costs or inconvenience, to banks over a much wider area; and very large firms with established nation-wide reputations have access to the large banks in all parts of the country. Many of the very large firms have regular dealings with several banks, sometimes because of a provision in federal banking laws that limits the amount of credit that can be extended to any single borrower to 10 percent of the national bank's capital.

It is important to keep this hierarchy of markets in mind in interpreting the structure of the banking system. While the national banking market may be highly competitive in many respects, local banking markets are much more concentrated and apparently less competitive, particularly outside the larger urban areas and in spite of the fragmentation of the banking system into small unit banks. Thus, a 1959 study revealed that 55 percent of all unit banks were in towns with only one banking office and 92 percent were in communities with no more than two banking offices.[8] Including both branch banking and unit banking states, there were over 10,000 communities in the United States that had only one banking office and 15,400 that had no more than two offices. They were almost exclusively communities with fewer than 25,000 inhabitants, but among them they accounted for two-thirds of the banking offices in the United States. For these communities the fragmentation of the banking system does not mean the absence of monopoly in local banking markets.[9]

It has been argued that modern developments in transportation and communication reduce the significance of local banking monopolies defined in this geographic sense. Customers can now deal with banks in a broader area with little additional cost or inconvenience. However, several studies have produced evidence showing that concentration in this sense has a decided impact on interest rates charged and paid by banks. In general, interest rates on loans and service charges on accounts tend to be higher and interest rates paid on deposits lower, the higher the degree of concentration in the banking market.[10] The most competitive rates are those set in the national market for big business accounts.

The Importance of Entry. It is interesting to examine the change that occurs when a new bank or branch opens in an area previously served by only one bank. There is evidence of improved loan service, more price competition, reduction in service charges, and many more service-related innovations. If entry is restricted, the borrower continues to face a monopoly bank. There is no conclusive evidence, however, to show that the monopoly bank makes high returns. Studies show that bank returns are not correlated to monopolistic elements but more directly related to asset size and quality of management.

At one time in history, almost anyone meeting certain objective criteria could obtain a bank charter. In the 1920s, concern about overbanking led to more careful review of charter and branch applications. Fear of bank failures became an overriding concern of regulatory authorities. New administrative procedures erected effective barriers to bank entry.

Barriers to Entry. These are of several types. First, there is the *incorporation* barrier. In contrast to the securities industry, in which any form of organization is acceptable for a broker or dealer, banks must issue stock and obtain a corporate charter from the state or the Comptroller of the Currency. Any bank charter application is reviewed in terms of the need for additional bank services within the locality, the profit potential for the new bank, and the effect it will have on existing banks' profits. Review is also made of the bank management, since much of a bank's success depends on it.

In addition to these legal controls, there is a financial barrier in the form of a minimum capital requirement. National banks must adhere to requirements set by the Comptroller of the Currency. States have capital requirements that are usually less stringent than federal minima. Nonetheless, financial adequacy in the eyes of chartering authorities may be significantly higher than statutory minima. These minima are often too low for a new bank trying to attract business in areas where existing banks are large and well capitalized.[11]

These barriers are undoubtedly significant restrictions against new banks. But more fundamental barriers are those inherent in the market structure and the existence of substantial economies of scale in banking. Various aspects of the market structure are relevant. In its lending activities, a new bank must attract customers from existing banks and financial intermediaries if it is to establish itself as a commercial lender. If other banks are permitted to have branches, it may be difficult to provide the additional physical facilities at the outset to accommodate new customers. In attracting deposits, the new bank must find a place for itself in a market already filled with established banks and must somehow convince depositors that it is a sound institution. Clearly, federal deposit insurance is a major benefit in this respect.

Economies of Scale. Recent research suggests that banking is subject to certain economies of scale. The use of computers is one obvious area in which there are economies if the bank is large enough. New banks not only have an immediate problem in attempting to break into the market but, as long as they remain small, will probably suffer from an inherent cost disadvantage. Moreover, one discovery of recent research indicates that the behavior of costs depends not simply on the size of the bank but on the nature of the business done (strong scale economies were discovered in managing the securities portfolio and in "business development"; less pronounced economies were discovered in handling demand deposits, business loans, and administration; and no economies were found in handling time deposits) and on whether the bank is a unit bank or has a system of branch offices (on this the evidence is quite equivocal).[12]

The existence and extent of economies of scale and economies of branch banking are important issues in other ways as well. If such economies exist and are substantial, economic efficiency requires industrial concentration. That is, it requires large-scale branch organizations that can take advantage of scale economies. Currently, within parts of the banking community itself there are strong pressures for a more concentrated banking structure. Mergers and the establishment of new branches by existing banks are the two most effective methods of rapidly increasing bank size. However, both within and outside the banking industry there are countervailing pressures to maintain the status quo, to block mergers, deny charter applications, and continue state legislation against branch banking.

Public Policy. One objective of public regulation of commercial banking has been to prevent destructive competition among banks. Unfortunately, denying new bank charters limits the degree of competition within an area and reinforces existing spheres of influence. Existing banks are thus shielded from new institutions. The growth of banking facilities fails to keep pace with the demand for them, thus reducing economic efficiency.

On the other hand, public policy has increasingly been designed to protect competition, defined in a narrow sense. Legislation passed since the 1950s has been a reaction to the trend toward concentration of financial resources in the large branch bank organizations and bank holding companies.

Passage of the Bank Merger Act of 1960 gave regulatory authority to the three federal agencies (Federal Reserve, Comptroller of the Currency, and Federal Deposit Insurance Corporation). Depending on jurisdiction, the appropriate federal agency must give an opinion on the proposed merger's effect on competition. There is no consistent, rigid set of guidelines by which market effect may be judged. In general, the regulatory agencies as well as the courts have looked only at the effect a proposed merger will have on commercial banking services, particularly in terms of the small depositor. A concentration ratio is used that indicates the share of total deposits the new merged bank will hold in a given geographic area. Little or no weight is given to the presence of nonbank financial intermediaries.

Many economists and commissions have argued that nonbank financial intermediaries offer close substitutes for many of the services commercial banks offer. Others, and particularly the courts, have argued that commercial banks offer a unique package of services that are tied together and cannot be duplicated by other nonbank financial intermediaries.

Beginning in 1963, the Justice Department applied both the Clayton Act and the Sherman Antitrust Act to the banking industry. It attempted to block bank mergers that had been approved by federal regulators by showing that a proposed merger would result in a significant concentration of banking firms and would lessen competition and/or result in restraint of trade. The Justice Department did not confine itself to litigating mergers of very large banks like Manufacturers Trust and the Hanover Bank, both of New York, but also blocked a proposed merger of banks that were quite small.

The growth of bank holding companies was curbed by passage of legislation in 1956 and subsequent amendments. This legislation gave exclusive jurisdiction over bank holding companies to the Federal Reserve System. It also enumerated specific criteria by which proposed bank acquisitions could be judged. In addition to considering solvency, asset condition, and capital adequacy to protect bank depositors, the Federal Reserve was instructed to weigh the effect on the convenience and needs of the community and the competitive effect on other banks. In 1970 Congress amended the Bank Holding Company Act and extended the Federal Reserve's jurisdiction to include one-bank holding companies. The Federal Reserve was to define and approve acceptable, related activities in which one-bank holding companies could participate.[13]

Conclusions. Legislation and regulation undertaken in the name of maintaining competition has often reduced the efficiency with which credit resources are allocated. Denial of mergers in the name of protecting local bank competition has not given due weight to the increased economies of scale and the increased competition the merged bank may stimulate in other banking markets. Policy with regard to the commercial banking system has not even considered the submarkets in which banks compete with each other and other nonbank financial intermediaries.

Without sacrificing either the liquidity or the solvency of the banking system, policy must be formulated to ensure that all potential bank customers have adequate facilities that give them quality service at minimum cost. New banks as well as new branches of existing banks must be given room to penetrate new banking markets. If further research leads to the conclusion that branching is a means of providing banking facilities more efficiently, then Congress should pass legislation permitting branching by national banks regardless of state laws and allow national banks to set the standard model for bank structure, as they did in 1863.

CONCENTRATION IN OTHER BRANCHES
OF FINANCIAL INTERMEDIATION

In Chapters 10 and 11, for purposes of description, we grouped financial intermediaries into several categories based largely on legal distinctions but also reflecting differences in the composition of asset and liability portfolios. If we examine each of these categories we find differing degrees of concentration of economic assets.

For example, at the beginning of 1971 the five largest life insurance firms held 45 percent of the industry's total assets.[14] The five largest mutual funds held 22 percent of that industry's total assets,[15] the five largest mutual savings banks held 14 percent of total mutual savings bank deposits,[16] and the five largest federal credit unions held less than 3 percent of federal credit union assets.[17]

What conclusions can be drawn about concentration in these other sectors of the finance industry? It appears to be a mixed picture. The segments with the greatest degree of concentration are dominated by a few firms with nationwide branch organizations. In each sector the large, dominant nonbank financial intermediaries are surrounded by a sizable fringe of smaller firms. Many of these smaller firms carry on a highly specialized or localized business; however, many are in full and direct competition with the larger enterprises. There is also wide diversity in the number of firms in each sector. At the beginning of 1971 there were more than 2,900 finance companies, 1,800 life insurance companies, 400 reporting mutual funds, 500 mutual savings banks, and 12,000 federally chartered credit unions.

A Broader Concept of Competition. While concentration is inimical to active competition, to place exclusive emphasis on the apparently high degree of concentration in the asset holdings of some nonbank fianancial intermediaries is to miss certain essential elements in their competitive situation.

The measures of concentration that we have used are based on legal definitions of industries that do not always make economic sense. The concept of an industry is one of the most widely used ones in economics, but in a world in which the goods and services produced by different firms are seldom identical but frequently similar, this concept is somewhat vague, and the groupings of firms used for statistical analysis are generally quite arbitrary. This is clearly true in the case of financial intermediaries. For example, the operations in financial intermediation of many savings and loan associations and mutual savings banks are virtually indistinguishable, although they operate under different laws. They draw on the same sources of funds (time and savings deposits of households) and use those funds to acquire similar types of assets (primarily mortgages). Indeed, there are often sharper differences in operations among firms within each of the two categories than between "typical" firms in each category. What is true of these intermediaries is true of firms operating in other sectors. Near banks, narrowly viewed, offer unique services; from a broader viewpoint, however, they compete with each other for funds and for similar types of assets for their loan portfolios.

This suggests that in analyzing concentration and competition in financial intermediation we ought not to look at legal categories but should examine separately each line of financial activity (e.g., savings deposits, demand deposits, commercial lending, mortgage lending, consumer lending, etc.). Moreover, various studies show that frequently it is a mistake to think of a single national market. Many borrowers, particularly individuals and small firms, cannot compete for funds on a nationwide basis but are effectively confined to local lenders. A truly comprehensive analysis of concentration and competition ought to take this into account.

It is clear that the activities of financial intermediaries overlap in a very complex pattern, that competition has impinged in varying degrees and at various points on the activities of commercial banks, and that this has been a primary factor eroding the bank's dominant position in the financial system in recent years. Active competition among nonbank financial intermediaries and between these institutions and commercial banks has been a major dynamic force in the American financial system.

Public Policy. Unlike the situation in commercial banking, entry, branching, and until recently mergers by nonbank financial intermediaries are comparatively easy, with fewer restraints. The federal government is quite lenient in granting federal charters to savings and loan associations and credit unions. State governments apply minimal capital and competitive criteria in reviewing charter and branch applications. In fact, most states are anxious for new financial businesses. In general, states have more liberal branching regulations for nonbank intermediaries than for commercial banks. Furthermore, there is not the degree of reporting, supervision, or examination of these institutions that commercial banks face from both state and federal authorities.

In addition to ease of entry, many nonbank financial intermediaries have been aggressive and innovative in their approach to their business. They have provided service, quality, and reliability for customers. They have worked through state and federal legislators to broaden their financial powers and to compete for the business that has traditionally gone to commercial banks on both the liability and asset sides. This aggressive attitude by segments of the financial industry has provided a vital source of competitive pressure.

CONCENTRATION IN FINANCIAL MARKETS

As discussed earlier, there are a variety of financial markets for financial instruments. The number of participants dealing in the secondary market for U.S. government securities is very much smaller than the number of participants dealing in the market for IBM common stock.

The short-term money market as discussed in Chapter 3 is characterized by a few dealers making the market in each type of instrument. Despite the comparatively small numbers of participants as market makers (high degree of concentration), the short-term market is highly competitive. The professionalism of the buyers and sellers—large banks, corporate treasurers, and others—and the nature of the products (highly liquid, short-term instruments, usually of excellent quality and adequate quantity, that are easily substituted for each other in portfolios) increase the competitiveness of the market. Rates (prices) on these instruments tend to move together, and there is only a very narrow spread between them. We can conclude that, because of the short-term nature of the instruments, their liquidity and substitutability, and the professionalism of the participants, this market is competitive.

The longer-term bond market is more difficult to assess. The instruments are not as easily substituted for each other. The degree of marketability varies widely. Corporate bond issues may be privately placed or offered to the public at large. Dealer-brokers may specialize in private placements and underwriting. There is usually vigorous competition among underwriters to market a large new issue, and the underwriting of large corporate and municipal issues is dominated by the major New York dealer-brokers.

It is more difficult for small firms or municipalities to attract underwriters. Often the issuer must accept terms offered by only one underwriter or give up hope of floating a new issue. Hence, we conclude that in the longer-term new-issues market competition among underwriters varies greatly.

Once a stock or bond has been offered to the public, secondary trading can begin. Prices on stocks traded over the counter are negotiated between the potential buyer or seller and a dealer in that issue. Markets in some high-volume, over-the-counter issues are made by several dealers, and there is more opportunity for price competition between them with regard to the spread. The fewer the dealers in an issue, the easier it is for one dealer to control the market. He may reap substantial profits, but he bears greater risk of substantial loss.

Although the over-the-counter market is significant, in terms of shares traded and dollar volume most secondary trading occurs in listed stocks on registered exchanges, particularly the New York Stock Exchange. At one time more than 90 percent of all stock trading took place on the Exchange. In recent years this position has been eroded by regional exchanges, over-the-counter trading, and the development of the third market, that is, trading stock listed on the New York Exchange outside the Exchange's facilities. Nonetheless, member firms (about 500, or 10 percent of the industry) dominate the brokerage industry. They earn about 96 percent of the commissions paid for trading listed stock, do nearly 70 percent of the over-the-counter business and almost 80 percent of the underwriting of new issues, and earn 78 percent of the total revenue of the industry ($4.6 billion of the $5.9 billion revenue in 1969). The 17 largest brokerage firms in the United States are all members of the New York Stock Exchange.

One of the most notable features of the securities industry is the extent to which formal supervision and regulation is performed by the exchanges and trade associations rather than the federal government. The exchanges establish rules of conduct, minimum capital requirements, debt-to-capital limits, financial disclosure rules, and trading regulations. The National Association of Securities Dealers performs similar regulatory functions in the over-the-counter markets. For the most part, the Securities Exchange Commission oversees the self-regulation of the exchanges and the markets.

Recently, the Securities Exchange Commission and Congress, in response to public complaints, have suggested changes that would affect the entire industry. They have proposed wider financial disclosure, urged evenhanded treatment of individual and institutional customers, and suggested movement to a completely negotiated commission structure as well as the "unbundling" of charges for services performed by brokerages.

The New York Stock Exchange has opposed some of these and other suggestions for change. It has resisted the establishment of a truly national exchange with easier entry for broker-dealers, opposed price competition between member firms on commission rates, and prohibited member firms from trading listed stock outside the exchange's auspices (i.e., dealing in the third market). The NYSE argues that easier entry and rate competition will impair the financial soundness of member firms and increase the rate of failure. While there are inherent problems for investors, the securities industry, and the economy when a number of securities firms fail, the Securities Investment Protection Corporation now protects the individual customer against loss in the event that his firm should fail.[18]

The industry is changing, albeit slowly. With the advent of computer technology and stockholder protection, the industry could now concentrate on improving its efficiency in serving as an intermediary in allocating capital.

CONCLUSIONS: COMPETITION AND THE CONTENT OF CONTEMPORARY PUBLIC POLICY

Concern for economic efficiency provides a powerful argument for a public policy directed toward the stimulation of competition, particularly price competition, as long as increased competition does not preclude taking advantage of significant economies of scale. We have suggested that there is evidence of significant restraints on competition in some sectors of the financial system, as well as evidence of active competition in others.

The main thrust of contemporary public policy with respect to the financial system has been to protect the individual in the event of failure by an intermediary and to supervise and regulate the financial industry in such a way as to reduce the potential number of failures.

Some efforts have been made to increase competition in the financial industry. One-bank holding companies have been given rather liberal opportunities to enter bank-related businesses; broker-dealers may sell life insurance; in Rhode Island, credit unions chartered by the state are permitted to offer checking account services. Intermediaries themselves have sought new activities. However, these efforts are not carried to logical extremes. Restraints on entry into banking and branching are preserved; mergers are denied; most commissions on stock transactions are still fixed rather than negotiated.

There has been no concerted and combined overhaul of the federal or state legislation affecting the financial industry since the 1930s. Most changes have come in a piecemeal manner, despite a number of presidential commissions that have recommended sweeping changes in the industry.

The President's Commission on Financial Structure and Regulation argued in its report, submitted at the end of 1971, that financial intermediaries offered similar products and services, supporting the financial industry concept, and therefore should be treated equally under the law. Commercial banks, savings and loan associations, mutual savings banks, and credit unions should be allowed to offer a wider range of financial services and to actively and directly compete with one another. Moreover, the Commission held that each group of intermediaries should face similar supervision, regulation, insurance, tax treatment, interest rate restrictions, and reserve requirements. It believed that if existing regulatory differences were eliminated, a more homogeneous financial structure would result, increasing competition and improving the efficiency with which capital is mobilized in the various sectors and allocated to different uses.[19]

In spite of such sweeping proposals, many people express concern that wide-open competition may be inconsistent with the soundness of financial institutions and the belief that soundness must be a preeminent objective of public policy.

THE POLICY DILEMMA: ARE COMPETITION AND FINANCIAL STABILITY INCONSISTENT OBJECTIVES?

It should be obvious from this discussion that those charged with the formation and administration of public policy are faced with a fundamental issue. Both a high degree of competition and financial stability are objectives in which the general public has a very vital interest. Are they inconsistent objectives? Is it necessary to constrain competition in the general interests of financial stability?

In considering this matter, a distinction should be drawn between the stability of the financial system and the solvency of individual financial institutions. While financial instability involves the failure of many financial institutions, the failure of selected institutions need not imply general financial instability. The problem is to prevent the failure of one institution from setting off a chain reaction. For this purpose the government has two primary instruments: the central bank as lender of last resort and deposit insurance.

The Central Bank and Financial Stability. As we have seen, the Federal Reserve has essentially unlimited powers to issue legal tender. The central bank is therefore in a key position to facilitate financial stability. By acquiring assets from or extending loans to otherwise sound institutions, it can provide those institutions with as much liquidity as necessary to meet a panic-induced "run."

The Federal Reserve will extend loans directly to commercial banks and to nonbank government security dealers. The Federal Home Loan Bank Board provides similar assistance to the savings and loan industry. In addition, in the event of pressure on any large financial institution, the Federal

Reserve can support the securities market, protecting the institution that is forced to sell a large volume of its assets. The central bank can also make funds available to commercial banks that may wish to extend temporary credits to the institution. The Federal Reserve illustrated the importance of its indirect intervention in 1970, when the Penn Central bankruptcy threatened the commercial paper market and the financial industry at large. The Federal Reserve removed Regulation Q ceilings on certificates of deposit and increased bank liquidity through its open-market and discount window operations.

Nonetheless, the effectiveness of the Federal Reserve would be increased if all commercial banks and other institutions with highly liquid assets (e.g., all near banks) maintained reserve deposits with the Federal Reserve and, hence, had access to Federal Reserve advances.

Deposit Insurance and Financial Stability. The central bank works behind the scenes, providing liquidity as necessary. Deposit insurance has a more direct psychological effect. By guaranteeing the safety of deposits, it has the effect of heading off runs before they start. The extension of deposit insurance to mutual savings banks, savings and loan associations, credit unions, and brokerage customers has done much to protect the financial industry from panics and runs.

Should Financial Institutions Be Allowed to Go Bankrupt? Given that institutions for underwriting the stability of the financial system exist, the question is whether the government must create an environment in which it is virtually impossible for any financial institution to go bankrupt.

The possibility of bankruptcy performs an important economic function. It forces the owners and managers of a business to accept ultimate financial responsibility for their actions (although, given limited liability provisions, their responsibility is limited to the value of their investment). Such responsibility is presumably an incentive to efficiency, responsiveness to market developments, and competitive innovation.

Strong arguments can be made that banks and other financial institutions ought not to be an exception to the general rule that bad management produces either bankruptcy or takeover by other interests. It is clear, however, that this view is not widely accepted and is not adhered to by federal agencies charged with granting new financial charters and some branch applications, nor by the New York Stock Exchange, for example.

SUMMARY

In earlier chapters we alluded to the problems confronting financial institutions when both the states and the federal government charter, supervise, and regulate similar institutions in a dissimilar manner. Any proposals to revamp the financial system and place primary authority in the hands of the federal government confront the states' rights arguments all over again.

302

Nonetheless, commissions continue to be formed and to recommend changes in the industry. Enactment of any sweeping set of changes is unlikely, given this "multisystem" of authority, unless there is a profound financial crisis.

In addition to the problem of overlapping jurisdictional authority, there appears to be disparity even within the federal government in interpreting existing statutes. For example, the several federal agencies that have responsibility for federally chartered institutions have differing views on merger proposals, new bank chartering, branching, and appropriate asset holdings. Even when these agencies have concurred in a merger proposal, for example, the Justice Department has attempted to countermand their actions.

Public policy has long been concerned with protecting and encouraging competition in the name of economic efficiency. Proponents of a public policy designed to stimulate competition in the financial industry are also concerned with economic efficiency, that is, encouraging the allocation of credit to its most valuable uses at the minimum cost attainable and the provision of a broad range of financial instruments to asset holders on the best possible terms.

In fact, public policy seems to be of several minds regarding competition in the financial industry. Legal action is taken to block proposed mergers on the ground that increased concentration in certain markets will limit competition. At the same time, legal barriers inhibit entry of new banking firms that would increase competition in the area. Other legal barriers inhibit much of the price competition in commercial banking. Banks cannot pay interest on demand deposits, and ceilings are imposed on the rates they pay for time deposits. Banks and other intermediaries cannot charge individual customers more than state usury and small-loan legislation permits.

Much of the legislation passed and interpretation of existing statutes reflects an overriding concern that competition in the financial industry could be destructive and result in widespread failure of financial institutions. Deposit insurance and pension reform proposals are aimed at protecting the individual who has entrusted his savings to a financial institution in the event that it fails. At the same time, continuing restrictions on entry, branching, and mergers, and limiting price and service competition between sectors in the financial industry permit inefficient firms to remain in operation and inhibit competition and resulting economic efficiency.

NOTES

1. The former view was espoused by James Saxon, Comptroller of the Currency from 1961 to 1966. He believed that the multiple interpretations might temporarily give advantage to certain financial institutions but that in time others would catch up and the overall impact would be constructive. The latter view was recently espoused by the Hunt Commission (President's Commission on Financial Structure and Regulation). It sought uniform tax treatment for financial institutions, one deposit insurance organization, one regulatory agency for state-chartered institutions, and one for federally chartered institutions.

It viewed financial institutions as offering similar products and services within a broad industry.

2. The net increase in commercial bank charters was primarily from national banks. This can be directly attributed to the appointment of James Saxon as Comptroller of the Currency. As the federal officer directly responsible for the chartering and supervision of national banks, Saxon drastically altered existing policies governing the granting of national bank charters in the interest of stimulating competition, thus contradicting a basic tenet of post-Depression banking policy. The policy was short-lived. However, the increase in new bank charters during this period seems to indicate that a substantial number of potential bankers thought they saw profitable opportunities for new banks but were kept out of the market by restrictions on entry.

3. Moody's Investors Service, Moody's Bank & Finance Manual, 1972 (New York, 1972), p. a44.

4. Federal Reserve Bulletin, June 1971.

5. Moody's Investors Service, op. cit., p. a45.

6. J. C. Darnell, "Chain Banking," National Banking Review 3 (March 1966), 307–331.

7. The classic discussion of these issues is D. Aldaheff, Monopoly and Competition in Banking (Berkeley, Cal.: University of California Press, 1954). See also C. H. Kreps, Jr., "Characteristics of Local Banking Competition," in D. Carson, ed., Banking and Monetary Studies (Homewood, Ill.: Irwin, 1963), pp. 319–332; J. M. Guttentag and E. S. Herman, "Banking Structure and Performance," in The Bulletin, New York University, Graduate School of Business Administration, Institute of Finance, no. 41/43 (February 1967), 34–38.

8. Guttentag and Herman, op. cit., pp. 47–50. Similar data are reported in Kreps, Jr., op. cit., and "Changes in Banking Structure, 1953–1962," Federal Reserve Bulletin 49 (September 1963), 1191–1198.

9. The presence of group and chain banking also increases the degree of concentration in local banking markets. We noted some aspects of this in our discussion of group banks. There is little comparable information for chain banks, but the study referred to earlier found that in 1962 over half of all chains had their affiliated banks in one county, suggesting that chains increased concentration in certain local markets to a significant degree. Darnell, op. cit.

10. The relevant evidence is surveyed by Guttentag and Herman, op. cit., pp. 80–103.

11. The authorities can require more capital for a new bank, and in practice many state and federal authorities appear to do so. Thus, in a study of banking in Illinois, it was reported that "the statutory minima bear no relationship to recent practice. Both the State authorities and the F.D.I.C. regard the statutory capital requirements as far too low." I. Schweiger and J. S McGee, "Chicago Banking," The Journal of Business 34 (July 1961), 297.

12. Guttentag and Herman, op. cit., pp. 114–123, 181–196. F. W. Bell and N. B. Murphy, Costs in Commercial Banking: A Quantitative Analysis of Bank Behavior and Its Relation to Bank Regulation, Federal Reserve Bank of Boston, Research Report no. 41 (1968).

13. For an interesting statistical review of the types of businesses engaged in by one-bank holding companies, see "One-Bank Holding Companies Before the 1970 Amendments," Federal Reserve Bulletin, December 1972, pp. 999–1008.

14. Institute of Life Insurance, 1971 Life Insurance Fact Book (New York, 1971).

15. Weisberger Financial Services, Investment Companies 1971: Mutual Funds and Other Types (New York, 1971).

16. Moody's Investors Service, op. cit., p. a46.

17. National Credit Union Administration, Annual Report, 1970 (Washington, D.C., 1971).

18. The Securities Investor Protection Corporation was created in 1970. It is not a government agency, but it has standby authority to borrow from the U.S. Treasury if necessary. Its function is to provide funds to protect customers of an SPIC member firm in the event that the firm is liquidated. Up to $50,000 in securities and $20,000 in cash per customer are covered. The purpose of the corporation is to maintain public confidence in the securities industry and preclude the possibility of a "domino effect" in the event of one or several broker-dealer failures.

19. President's Commission on Financial Structure and Regulation, *Report* (Washington, D.C., 1971).

14

TRANSITION TO
MACROECONOMICS

$\mathbf{T}$he preceding sections of the book were concerned with the microeconomics of the financial system. We now turn to macroeconomic problems.

MACROECONOMICS VS. MICROECONOMICS

Microeconomics is concerned with the composition of economic activity. Applied to the financial system, it is an analysis of the behavior of individual decision-making units (households, firms, and governments in their roles as asset holders and debtors) and of the process by which their interaction in the marketplace determines a set of prices for financial instruments and the allocation of credit among alternative uses. By contrast, macroeconomics is concerned with issues relating to the stability of economic activity. The basic units of analysis are broad aggregates like the money supply, consumption, or investment, and the analysis focuses on such variables as the general level of prices or the general level of employment. Monetary theory, as a branch of macroeconomics, is concerned primarily with the implications of the size of the stock of money for economic stability.

THE HISTORICAL ROOTS OF MONETARY THEORY

Monetary theory has had a long and contentious history, including many diversions into the search for monetary panaceas for deep-seated social ills and for a monetary constitution appropriate to fundamental reform of the social structure. However, modern monetary theory can be regarded as having two primary roots in the history of economic analysis. The first, and in a sense the most fundamental, is the classical quantity theory of money. This theoretical analysis is familiar to students of introductory economics as a proposition that in a static, fully employed economy there is a direct and proportional relationship between the stock of money and the general level of prices. In some ways it is unfortunate that the hypothesized relationship between money and prices has become the center of attention in discussions of classical monetary theory. What is of greater significance in the present context is one of the building blocks of the classical analysis. That is the assumption that in general there is a stable demand for money function. As we will see, this is one of the two central propositions of monetary theory. Indeed, most of the heated debates in theoretical and empirical monetary economics in recent years have related to the nature of this function, its stability, the relevant variables in it, and the relative size of the various parameters.

The second major root of modern monetary theory is John Maynard Keynes' *General Theory of Employment, Interest and Money*. Published in 1936 in the midst of the most devastating depression the industrialized world had ever experienced, this book was an attempt to develop a consistent theoretical explanation of why the self-regulating mechanisms of a market economy are in general insufficient to guarantee continuous full employment of the nation's productive resources. As a theory of how an economy could be in stable equilibrium at less than full employment, the *General Theory* has been subjected to increasingly effective theoretical criticisms in the three decades since its publication. Nonetheless, it has had a profound and lasting impact on economics. While it would be stretching a point to say that it created modern macroeconomics, it did produce a reorientation of theoretical macroeconomics away from preoccupation with the general level of prices and the business cycle in favor of the determination of an equilibrium level of employment. The central analytical concept became the level of aggregate demand, and with it came a whole new set of theoretical concepts with which to explore macroeconomic problems. As one of the most effective critics of Keynesian theory noted recently, "in one sense, we are all Keynesians now; in another sense no one is a Keynesian any longer. We all use the Keynesian apparatus; none of us any longer accepts the initial Keynesian conclusions."[1]

The impact of Keynesianism on monetary economics is difficult to summarize. In part it was theoretical. Keynes took over the Classicists' concept

307

of the demand for money, explored and extended it, and drew conclusions that had profound new implications for the effectiveness of monetary policy in regulating the level of aggregate demand. For the most part, however, the impact was empirical. The controversies over the theoretical implications of Keynes' assumptions about the demand for money produced a spate of increasingly refined attempts to quantify the demand for money function. Similarly, Keynesian pessimism over the general effectiveness of monetary policy in influencing aggregate demand has produced many penetrating empirical studies of the impact of monetary variables on economic activity. Macroeconomic model building and testing have become major preoccupations of monetary economists.

THE TWO BASIC PROPOSITIONS OF MONETARY THEORY

We make no attempt in this book to explore all of the subtleties of post-Keynesian macroeconomic models. We want to focus on the impact of monetary variables on the level of aggregate demand and hence on certain crucial macroeconomic variables like the general level of prices and employment. However, one of the things that has been learned from the endless controversies over the Keynesian treatment of monetary factors is that they cannot be considered in isolation. We cannot avoid exploring general macroeconomic models. It is a question of emphasis. Since our primary concern is with monetary phenomena, we will concentrate mainly on the monetary sectors of such models.

Our development of monetary theory in the next few chapters is organized around two basic propositions:
1. The institutional arrangements are such that the government (the "monetary authorities") has the potential to control the supply of money.
2. There is a measurable, and normally relatively stable, demand for money function.

Monetary theory, in this sense, is simply an application of elementary demand and supply analysis to money. Monetary policy involves the deliberate creation of either an excess demand for money or an excess supply of money. As we will see, the controversial issues in monetary economics at present are how the economic system purges itself of such disequilibria in the financial system. How and to what degree does an excess supply of money increase the aggregate demand for real goods and services?

THE MICROECONOMIC FOUNDATIONS OF MONETARY THEORY

Microeconomics and macroeconomics appear to be very different. They are concerned with different ranges of problems, and as a result they employ different types of analytical concepts to explore different kinds of economic relationships. However, they must not be thought of as unrelated fields of study. In spite of their notable differences, they involve the study of the same behavior from different vantage points.

On a very general level the relationships between the two are quite obvious. The behavior studied in macroeconomics is simply an aggregation of the corresponding aspects of the behavior of decision-making units studied in microeconomics. While the points of emphasis may differ, macroeconomic theory should have its foundations in microeconomic theory.

The link between macroeconomic and microeconomic theory is one of the most difficult and least explored branches of economic theory. Economic theorists have had little success in deriving macroeconomic propositions from the common assumption of microeconomic theory that the decision-making units maximize something (be it utility or profits). As a result, most macroeconomic relationships must be regarded simply as "plausible" generalizations, perhaps with recognized empirical justification, rather than propositions derived in a consistent fashion from familiar propositions of microeconomic theory.

It follows that any observations we make on the microeconomic foundations of monetary theory must be of the most general sort. With that caveat, it is useful to draw together a few basic microeconomic propositions that we have already examined and that can be regarded as providing the foundations for the two basic propositions of monetary theory.

Consider first the question of the demand for money. We have already established that money is a financial instrument with certain peculiar characteristics. It is technically designed to be an efficient medium of exchange, and as a result, considered as an asset to be held in a portfolio, it has a very high degree of liquidity. Liquidity is a characteristic of assets that is highly prized by many asset holders. Indeed, we have demonstrated that under normal circumstances many asset holders are willing to pay a premium (in the form of potential interest income forgone) in order to hold assets that are highly liquid. That is, we have demonstrated that in a microeconomic context many individual asset holders will have a demand for liquid assets.

Money is not the only liquid asset. However, the macroeconomic theory of the demand for money—one of the two basic propositions of monetary theory—rests loosely on the microeconomic foundations we have established in our discussion of the portfolio balance decision. That is, it rests on the assumption that individual asset holders will choose to hold part of their wealth in the form of money, in part because of the technical qualities of money as a medium of exchange and in part because money is the most liquid of assets. Since money is not the only liquid asset, however, our microeconomic theorizing suggests that the aggregate demand for money should depend in part on the yield and availability of other highly liquid assets—close substitutes for money. Some of the major recent controversies in monetary theory have focused on the nature, extent, and strength of such substitution effects in the demand for money. Our microeconomic theory cannot provide answers to these questions, although it does suggest that, large or small, such effects should exist.

On the supply side, the relevant microeconomic propositions relate to the behavior of financial intermediaries. It was established in Chapter 2 that the money supply consists mainly of the liabilities of private, profit-seeking financial intermediaries, particularly commercial banks. Such institutions extend credit out of borrowed funds. But whenever they borrow money they create money. This seeming paradox arises because, as evidence of the debt created through the act of borrowing, the bank issues a financial instrument that is used as money. The process of money creation, then, is but an aspect of the process of financial intermediation, which we explored in several of the preceding chapters.

We will be concerned primarily with the ability of the monetary authorities to control the supply of money. Clearly, this is a matter of their ability to control the willingness or ability of the money-creating private financial intermediaries to borrow and lend. As we explore this question it will turn out that the central proposition in the analysis is one that we have already examined. That is the proposition that profit-maximizing bankers are generally unwilling to hold "excess" cash reserves and are not permitted to hold "deficient" cash reserves. As a result, through manipulation of the quantity of cash in bank vaults, the monetary authorities have substantial leverage over the banking system.

SUMMARY

As we turn our attention to the macroeconomic issues relating to the functioning of the financial system, you would be well advised to review quickly some of the basic elements of our microeconomic analysis of individual demands for wealth and of the behavior of financial intermediaries. They are the microeconomic foundations of monetary theory.

NOTE

1. M. Friedman, *Dollars and Deficits: Inflation, Monetary Policy and the Balance of Payments* (Englewood Cliffs, N.J.: Prentice-Hall, 1968), p. 15.

CONTROL OF THE MONEY SUPPLY

Part 1: Banks and Near Banks

Our first task in exploring the macro-economics of the financial system is to examine the mechanism by which the supply of money is expanded and contracted. As a preliminary step, we should remind ourselves of the nature and composition of the money supply.

THE MONEY SUPPLY

You will remember that our major conclusions in Chapter 2 about the money supply were that (1) the appropriate scope of the money concept is ambiguous, but (2) if we adopt a medium-of-payments concept of money, the money supply consists of currency in circulation and checkable deposits with commercial banks. Government-issued currency is legal tender, but checkable deposits are more important as a medium of exchange. They constitute the largest part of the total supply of payments money outstanding, and they account for an even larger share of the total flow of transactions in any given period.

THE PROCESS OF DEPOSIT CREATION

Clearly, our first task in the analysis of the supply of money must be to explain what controls the supply of demand deposits.

THE PRINCIPLE OF DEPOSIT EXPANSION

To set the basic mechanism controlling the supply of deposits in clear relief, let us assume that we have a financial system with only one commercial bank, that this bank issues only demand deposits, and that these demand deposits are the only type of money in circulation.

The basic principle by which this bank can expand the money supply follows directly from the concept of money and the nature of financial intermediation. You will recall from Chapter 8 that a financial intermediary finances its portfolio of earning assets by issuing liabilities, claims on itself, that have particular valued characteristics (liquidity, relatively low risk, etc.). Normally, in order to acquire more earning assets a financial intermediary must first sell its own liabilities. It must exchange its liabilities for money, offering them at a sufficiently attractive yield so that asset holders will be willing to take them into their portfolios. However, the liabilities of our financial intermediary, a bank, have the peculiar characteristic that they are money. Thus, when the bank wants to acquire earning assets it does not have to sell its liabilities for money first. Since its liabilities are money, it can exchange them directly for earning assets, adding to the stock of money outstanding in the process. In other words, by the very process of financial intermediation this bank creates money. This is the basic principle of deposit expansion. Deposit expansion occurs whenever banks make a net addition to their earning assets (loans or securities) that is not financed by capital subscribed by the banks' owners (or by nondeposit liabilities).

Credit Creation. It is important to keep in mind that both sides of the balance sheet are involved in this process. When a bank creates deposits, it simultaneously creates credit. Indeed, the creation of deposits is not the primary objective. Rather, it is to add to the portfolio of earning assets and thereby to increase the bank's profits (it follows that credit creation will occur only when a bank finds profitable loans or securities to add to its portfolio). The creation of deposits occurs as a by-product. It is the method by which the banks finance the net addition to the stock of credit extended directly or indirectly to businessmen, consumers, and governments.

Money Creation and Wealth. Note that the money created in this way will be an asset to whoever receives it, but in the aggregate it does not increase the wealth of the community directly. In the books of the bank there has been an equal increase in assets and in liabilities. The bank's net worth has not increased. Similarly, in the books of the community at large there has been an equal increase in assets (money) and in liabilities (debts to the bank). The public's net worth has not increased. In the technical jargon of the economist, money created in this way has come to be called "inside money." It is money offset by an equal value of private debt.

An Example. To make these points quite clear and explicit, consider Example 15.1. The structure of the initial balance sheet of the bank is quite simple. We have assumed that the assets consist of equal portions of loans

312

EXAMPLE 15.1   Deposit Expansion by a Monopoly Bank (Thousands of Dollars)

1. *Initial Balance Sheet of Monopoly Bank*

Assets		Liabilities	
Loans	$ 5,000	Demand Deposits	$ 9,000
Securities	5,000	Capital Accounts	1,000
	$10,000		$10,000

2. *Transaction:* The bank makes a loan to a businessman.

Bank				Businessman			
Loan	+10	Deposits		Deposits	+10	Loan	+10

3. *Closing Balance Sheet of Monopoly Bank*

Assets		Liabilities	
Loans	$ 5,010	Demand Deposits	$ 9,010
Securities	5,000	Capital Accounts	1,000
	$10,010		$10,010

4. *Net Change*

Money Supply	+10
Credit	+10

---

and securities and that the sources of funds are either demand deposits or capital subscribed by shareholders. You should note that this bank has no cash reserves among its assets. By assumption, there is no other type of money besides its demand deposits. There is nothing to hold as cash reserves, nor is there need for such reserves.

The bank makes a loan of $10,000 to a businessman, crediting the businessman's demand deposit with that sum of money. Up to this point the transaction is simply an exchange of assets and liabilities. The bank gains a claim on the businessman; the businessman gains a claim on the bank. Neither the net worth of the bank nor that of the businessman has changed; the assets and liabilities of both have increased by like amount. However, the businessman now has in his possession money that previously did not exist. The businessman is free to spend the funds he has borrowed to meet his payroll, purchase raw materials, pay for capital equipment, and the like. As he makes those payments, the money created by his act of borrowing from the bank enters into general circulation. The money supply has expanded by $10,000. When the loan is repaid, a corresponding contraction of the money supply will occur unless the bank replaces the loan with another of equal value.[1]

It should be obvious that the bank does not have to wait for someone to approach it for a loan in order to expand the money supply. If the bank enters the open market and purchases government bonds (or any securities), making payment by crediting the seller's demand deposit, the same effect will occur. The money supply will expand by an equal amount. Indeed, whenever the bank purchases any asset this will happen (or even whenever the bank pays for goods or services rendered to it).

313

CONSTRAINTS ON DEPOSIT CREATION

The context in which we have developed the basic principle of deposit creation is highly artificial. Given our unrealistic assumptions, there is no effective constraint on the ability of the bank to create money other than its ability to find acceptable assets to purchase. By relaxing these assumptions we can identify the constraints that actually exist.

CASH RESERVES AND "EXCESS RESERVES"

Banker's Risk. We have so far assumed that there is only one type of money: demand deposits. Relaxation of this assumption reveals an important constraint on the banks imposed by what we earlier called banker's risk.

It does not matter what we assume to be the other money, provided only that it is not issued by the bank itself. If we take a historical perspective, we might assume that it is gold or silver coin. However, in the contemporary world it is more likely to be inconvertible paper money, issued by a central bank or other governmental agency and endowed with legal tender status. The important point is that the bank is required to convert its deposit liabilities into legal tender at par and on demand. Therefore, the bank's portfolio must be managed with one eye on its ability to meet possible demands for payment in legal tender.

The Demand for Cash Reserves. This means that the banks will have a demand for legal tender to be held as cash reserves, and this demand will depend, among other things, on the size and potential instability of its deposit liabilities.[2] The smaller the bank's cash reserves relative to its deposits, the greater the risk that it will not be able to meet all depositors' demands for cash. However, it is highly unlikely that all, or even a large portion, of total deposit liabilities will be presented for payment within a short period. As a result, the bank does not have to hold cash equal in value to its deposit liabilities or even nearly equal in value. The bank must hold cash reserves, but these can be a fraction of total deposit liabilities.

The banker's problem in managing his cash reserve position is simply another example of the problem of portfolio selection, which we examined in some detail in a different context in Chapter 5. The banker is deciding on the composition of his portfolio as between earning assets (loans and securities) and nonearning, but highly liquid, assets (cash). The larger the proportion of reserves, the higher the degree of safety. But the larger the proportion of reserves, the smaller the interest income. Like any portfolio manager, the banker must balance these considerations at the margin.

It is commonly assumed that banks will hold reserves in a fixed percentage of deposit liabilities. However, if we view the decision as a problem of portfolio balance, it would be surprising if the banker chose the same proportion of cash reserves under all circumstances. A drop in the risk of cash withdrawals (as he perceives that risk) or a rise in interest rates (and hence in the opportunity cost of holding reserves) should induce him to reduce the cash reserve ratio. A decline in interest rates or a rise in the risk of withdrawals should have the opposite effect.

LEGAL RESERVE REQUIREMENTS

Legal reserve requirements in one form or another have been around since 1837. At that time state governments began to impose specified minimum acceptable ratios of cash reserves to currency and deposits. The National Bank Act of 1863 was the most far-reaching in terms of affecting more banks across the country. At times (e.g., the 1930s) the legal requirements have not been an effective constraint on the banks. Banks have chosen to hold cash reserves substantially above those required by law. At other times the cash reserve requirement has been effective. The minimum cash reserve ratio specified by law has been at least equal to and apparently substantially greater than that which the banks would have chosen to hold voluntarily. As a result, the cash reserve requirement introduced an important element of rigidity into the management of banks' asset portfolios, and the cash reserve ratio became more stable. In the period from 1963 to 1968, when there was no significant change in reserve requirements, commercial banks held about 16.5 percent of total assets in the form of cash reserves and items due from other banks. There was some slight variation in this ratio, and also between state member, national member, and nonmember banks. Undoubtedly one would also find variation among individual banks. However, it is appropriate to assume a rather fixed cash reserve ratio.

By making the assumption of a fixed cash reserve ratio plausible, the fact of an effective legal cash reserve ratio simplifies the analysis of banks' demands for cash reserves. It is important to remember, however, that while this assumption is in accord with recent experience, it is neither necessary nor representative of a longer run of historical experience.

An Example. This principle can best be explored through an example. For the purposes of Example 15.2 we have modified the initial balance sheet of the "monopoly bank" to allow for a 16 percent cash reserve requirement. At the outset the bank has no excess reserves. It is required to hold cash in the amount of 16 percent of deposits, and it chooses not to hold more.

In the next chapter we will explore the various ways in which the cash reserves of the banks may increase or decrease. In order to minimize the complications, we can assume that the government prints $10,000 of new currency, which it deposits in the bank (perhaps intending to spend it over a period of time). Total deposits and cash reserves increase in the same amount, but the required cash reserve increases by only 16 percent of that sum, that is, by $1600. The bank has excess reserves of $8400.

Given this excess cash reserve, on which it earns no interest income, the bank's asset portfolio is not in equilibrium. In order to achieve portfolio balance, the profit motive dictates the acquisition of more earning assets. In Example 15.2 we assume that the bank extends more loans, although it might well acquire additional securities, particularly short-term liquid securities. In either case, the proceeds are credited to someone's demand deposit, providing a net addition to the money supply.

EXAMPLE 15.2   Deposit Creation by a Monopoly Bank with a 16 Percent Reserve Ratio (Thousands of Dollars)

1. *Initial Balance Sheet of Monoply Bank*

Assets		Liabilities	
Cash Reserves	$ 1,440	Demand Deposits	$ 9,000
Loans	5,000	Capital Accounts	1,000
Securities	3,560		$10,000
	$10,000		

2. *Deposit Expansion, Stage I:* (A) The government deposits $10,000 of newly printed currency with the bank and (B) then makes equivalent payments by check to the general public.

Bank		Government		Public
A. Cash +10	Deposits	Deposits +10 ǀ Currency +10		ǀ
	Gov't +10			

B.	Deposits	Deposits −10 ǀ		Deposits +10 ǀ
	Gov't −10			
	Public +10			

Net Change

Bank	Government	Public
Cash +10 ǀ Deposits +10	ǀ	Currency +10 ǀ Deposit +10

Bank Reserve Position (end of Stage I)		The Money Supply (net change)	
Total Deposits	$9,010.00		Demand Deposits
Required Reserves	1,441.60	Stage I	+10
Actual Reserve	1,450.00	CUMULATIVE	+10
EXCESS RESERVES	8.40	(to end of Stage I)	

3. *Deposit Expansion, Stage II:* The bank makes loans in the amount of its excess cash reserves, crediting $8,400 to the deposits of businessmen.

Bank		Public
Loans +8.4	Deposits	Deposits +8.4 ǀ Loans +8.4
	Public +8.4	

Bank Reserve Position (end of Stage II)		The Money Supply (net change)	
Total Deposits	$9,018.40		Demand Deposits
Required Reserves	1,442.94	Stage I	+10.00
Actual Reserves	1,450.00	Stage II	+8.40
EXCESS RESERVES	7.06	CUMULATIVE	+18.40
		(to end of Stage II)	

316

EXAMPLE 15.2   (Continued)

4. *Deposit Expansion, Stage III:* The bank makes loans in the amount of its excess cash reserves, crediting $7,060 to the deposits of businessmen.

Bank			Public			
Loans +7.06	Deposits		Deposits +7.06	Loans +7.06		
	Public +7.06					

Bank Reserve Position (end of Stage III)		The Money Supply (net change)	
			Demand Deposits
Total Deposits	$9,025.46	Stage I	+10.00
Required Reserves	1,444.07	Stage II	+8.40
Actual Reserves	1,450.00	Stage III	+7.06
EXCESS RESERVES	5.93	CUMULATVE	25.46
		(to end of Stage III)	

5. *Final Balance Sheet of Monopoly Bank*

Assets		Liabilities	
Cash Reserves	$1,450.00	Demand Deposits	$ 9,062.50
Loans	5,052.50	Capital Accounts	1,000.00
Securities	3,560.00		$10,062.50
	$10,062.50		

Bank Reserve Position		The Money Supply	
Total Deposits	$9,062.50		Demand Deposits
Required Reserves	1,450.00	Stage I	+10.00
Actual Reserves	1,450.00	Stage II	+8.40
EXCESS RESERVES	0	Stage III	+7.06
		Stage IV	+5.93
		Stage n	0
		CUMULATIVE	62.50
		(to end of process)	

MULTIPLIER

Deposit Multiplier: $\dfrac{\Delta D}{\Delta R} = \dfrac{1}{r} = 6.25$

This is far from the end of the story, however. The extension of $8400 of loans will not reestablish portfolio balance, as is evident from the fact that excess reserves of $7060 remain at the end of Stage II in the example. Given the fractional reserve requirement, the increase in deposits has impounded as required reserves only a fraction of the excess reserve. Thus, when deposits increase by $8400, required reserves increase by only $1344, leaving excess reserves of $7060. Again, the profit motive dictates the extension of loans in the amount of the excess reserves, and an additional $7060 is credited to the public's deposits with the bank.

This process will go on until all excess reserves have been purged from the system. As is shown on the final balance sheet, that will be when total deposits have increased by $62,500, or 6.25 times the initial deposit of currency.

Algebraic Representation: A Simple Deposit Expansion Multiplier.
Using very elementary mathematics, it is possible to derive a general expression for the deposit expansion multiplier implied by our very simple assumptions. Let R represent cash reserves, D deposits, and r the reserve ratio (which has a value greater than 0 but less than 1).

For equilibrium in the bank's portfolio, there must be no excess reserves. Actual reserves must equal what the bank feels it is required to hold (to satisfy legal requirements plus any extra that it requires for safety). That is, in equilibrium:

$$R = rD \tag{15.1}$$

or

$$D - R(1/r) \tag{15.2}$$

It follows that if equilibrium is to be maintained in the face of an increase in cash reserves:

$$\Delta D = \Delta R(1/r) \tag{15.3}$$

That is, given an increase in reserves, to maintain equilibrium in the bank's portfolio deposits must expand by the factor $1/r$. We call this the deposit expansion multiplier. Given the reserve ratio of 0.16, the multiplier is 6.25. The higher the ratio, the smaller the multiplier. Thus, if the ratio were 0.04, the multiplier would be 25.

BASIC CONSTRAINTS IN PERSPECTIVE

The multiplier formulation provides a simple, explicit statement of the basic constraints on deposit creation in the banking system. These are (1) the quantity of cash reserves and (2) the effective reserve ratio.

Although the multiplier formulation suggests that the process of deposit creation is simple and mechanical, it is neither. Both the quantity of cash reserves in the banking system and the effective reserve ratio are affected by a complex of portfolio balance decisions made by the general public and other financial institutions, as well as by banks. Thus, the quantity of cash reserves is affected by decisions of the public about the form in which they will hold their cash balances—demand deposits or currency. The effective reserve ratio is affected by decisions of the public as to whether to hold time deposits or demand deposits and whether to hold time deposits in banks or in near banks. It is also affected by decisions made by near banks as to the level of their cash reserves and the form in which they will be held —cash in the vault or demand deposits with commercial banks. And, of course, the portfolio balance decisions of the public are conditioned by the incentives offered by banks and near banks in the form of interest payments on time deposits and other considerations. In the next several sections we explore some of these complications of the basic analysis.

CASH DRAIN

Our development of the deposit expansion multiplier ignores the effects of the public's demand for currency as opposed to demand deposits as a medium of exchange. However, in discussing the composition of the money supply in Chapter 2, we noted that currency was more efficient than demand deposits for certain types of transactions. As a result, as the money supply expands, the amount of currency in circulation is likely to rise as well.

This increase in currency in circulation is significant because every dollar of currency in circulation is a potential dollar of bank cash reserves, which, if it were lodged in the bank's vaults, would serve to support several dollars' worth of bank deposits (depending on the reserve ratio). In this sense, currency in circulation and bank cash reserves are both what some economists call *high-powered money*. Given a fixed total supply of high-powered money, an increase of currency in circulation will reduce bank reserves and will reduce the total money supply by a multiple of the cash drain. Correspondingly, a reverse drain from currency in circulation into bank reserves will expand the total money supply by a multiple of the increase in bank reserves.

In the example explored in the previous section we assumed an increase in bank reserves resulting from an increase in the total amount of high-powered money in existence. Clearly, if a drain of currency into circulation accompanies the expansion of the money supply, the total expansion will be less than that shown in Example 15.2. In order to see this, consider the following example.

An Example. In order to demonstrate the effects of the cash drain in Example 15.3 we assumed a currency-deposit ratio of 0.5. That is, we assume that in equilibrium currency is 50 percent of deposits. Otherwise the figures used in this example are the same as those in Example 15.2. As can be seen by comparing these examples, the effect of cash drain is to reduce the monetary expansion produced by the introduction of a given amount of new high-powered money into the financial system.

As a result of cash drain, some bank reserves are drawn out of the banks and into circulation as currency while deposit expansion proceeds. In the example, the money supply multiplier is reduced from 6.25 to 2.27 (the deposit expansion multiplier is reduced from 6.25 to 1.52). The larger the cash drain, the smaller the multiplier and the smaller the share of the banking system in the total monetary expansion. Thus, if the cash drain coefficient were 0.80, the money supply multiplier would be 1.88 and the deposit multiplier 1.05. By contrast, if the cash drain coefficient were 0.20, the money supply multiplier would be 3.33 and the deposit multiplier 2.78.

OTHER BANKS: CLEARINGHOUSE DRAIN

An additional source of artificiality in our analysis of the deposit expansion process is the assumption that there is only one bank with a monopoly of the demand deposit business when in fact there are more than 14,000.[3] Does this make a difference to the deposit expansion process? The presence of more than one bank alters the details of the deposit expansion process but not the basic principles.

EXAMPLE 15.3   Deposit Creation with Cash Drain—Monopoly Bank with a 16 Percent Cash Reserve Ratio (Thousands of Dollars)

1. *Initial Balance Sheet of Monopoly Bank*

Assets		Liabilities	
Cash Reserves	$ 1,440	Demand Deposits	$ 9,000
Loans	5,000	Capital Accounts	1,000
Securities	3,560		$10,000
	$10,000		

2. *Deposit Expansion, Stage I:* (A) Thé government deposits $10,000 of newly printed currency and (B) makes equivalent payments by check to the general public. The public's demand for currency can be described by the equation $C = 0.5D$. (C) The public divides its increased money holdings between currency and deposits on this basis, taking $3,330 in currency and holding $6,670 in deposits.

	Bank		Government		Public
A. Cash +10	Deposits Gov't +10	Deposits +10	High- Powered Money +10		
B.	Deposits Gov't −10 Public +10	Deposits −10		Deposits +10	
C. Cash −3.33	Deposits Public −3.33			Cash +3.33 Deposits −3.33	

Net Change

Cash +6.67 Deposits +6.67		High- Powered Money +10	Cash +3.33 Deposits +6.67	

Bank Reserve Position (end of Stage I)			*The Money Supply* (net change)		
Total Deposits	$9,006.67			Deposits	Currency Total
Required Reserves	1,441.07	Stage I		+6.67	+3.33 +10.00
Actual Reserves	1,446.67				
EXCESS RESERVES	5.60				

3. *Deposit Expansion, Stage II:* The bank makes loans in the amount of its excess reserves from Stage I ($5,600). The public takes the proceeds partly in currency ($1,870) and partly in deposits ($3,730), according to the demand for currency function.

Bank		Public	
Cash −1.87	Deposits	Cash +1.87	Loans +5.50
Loans +5.60	Public +3.73	Deposits +3.73	

Net Change

Assets +3.73	Deposits +3.73	Money +5.60	Loans +5.60

Bank Reserve Position (end of Stage II)			*The Money Supply* (net change)		
Total Deposits	$9,010.40			Deposits	Currency Total
Required Reserves	1,441.66	Stage I		+6.67	+3.33 +10.00
Actual Reserves	1,444.80	Stage II		+3.73	+1.87 +5.60
EXCESS RESERVES	3.14	CUMULATIVE (to end of Stage II)		+10.40	+5.20 +15.60

EXAMPLE 15.3 (Continued)

4. *Deposit Expansion, Stage III:* The bank makes loans in the amount of its excess reserves from Stage II ($3,140). The public takes the proceeds partly in currency $1,050) and partly in deposits ($2,090), according to the demand for currency function.

Bank				Public			
Cash	−1.05	Deposits	+2.09	Cash	+1.05	Loans	+3.14
Loans	+3.14			Deposits	+2.09		

Net Change

Assets	+2.09	Deposits	+2.09	Money	+3.14	Loans	+3.14

Bank Reserve Position (end of Stage III)	
Total Deposits	$9,012.49
Required Reserves	1,442.00
Actual Reserves	1,443.75
EXCESS RESERVES	1.75

The Money Supply (net change)

	Deposits	Currency	Total
Stage I	+6.67	+3.33	+10.00
Stage II	+3.73	+1.87	+5.60
Stage III	+2.09	+1.05	+3.14
CUMULATIVE (to end of Stage III)	12.49	6.25	18.74

5. *Final Balance Sheet of Monopoly Bank*

Assets		Liabilities	
Cash Reserves	$1,442.42	Demand Deposits	$ 9,015.15
Loans	5,012.73	Capital Accounts	1,000.00
Securities	3,560.00		$10,015.15
	$10,015.15		

Bank Reserve Position (end of process)	
Total Deposits	$9,015.15
Required Reserves	1,442.42
Actual Reserves	1,442.42
EXCESS RESERVES	0

The Money Supply (net change)

	Deposits	Currency	Total
Stage I	+6.67	+3.33	+10.00
Stage II	+3.73	+1.87	+5.60
Stage III	+2.09	+1.05	+3.14
Stage IV	+1.17	+0.58	+1.75
Stage n	0	0	0
CUMULATIVE (to end of process)	15.15	7.58	22.73

MULTIPLIERS (For derivation, see Appendix to Chapter 5, pp. 111–118.)
Deposit Multiplier: 1.515
Money Supply Multiplier: 2.272
NOTE: High-Powered Money Outstanding: +10.00
Currency in Circulation: +7.58
Bank Cash Reserves: +2.42

The complication that arises from the existence of other banks is that any bank engaging in monetary expansion is likely to experience a *clearing-house drain.* That is, as checks are written against its deposits and payments are made, some or all of the funds will be deposited in other banks in the system. Thus, a bank that makes loans in the amount of its excess reserves, creating an equal amount of new deposits, is exposed to the risk that the entire sum will be withdrawn and deposited in other banks. This forces the first bank to pay out an equal value of reserves. Its excess reserves disappear. The important point, however, is that, unlike a cash drain, the clearinghouse drain does not eliminate excess reserves from the banking system. It merely transfers them to other banks. These banks, impelled by the same profit motive, will make loans or purchase securities, initiating the second round of deposit expansion. They will also probably experience a clearinghouse drain, moving the reserves and the base of deposit expansion throughout the banking system. Eventually most banks will probably have had some share of the increased deposits. The process of expansion will stop when all excess reserves have been purged from the system. Unless the risk of clearinghouse drain induces banks to hold larger cash reserves than a monopoly bank would, the total expansion of deposits will be the same with many banks as with one bank.

Will the reserve ratio be higher in a banking system with several banks? On a priori grounds one would think so, although the development of an efficient, active short-term money market has reduced the need to hold cash reserves by making it possible to make reserve adjustments in the money market. Secondary reserves may substitute for cash reserves as a hedge against clearinghouse drains. In any case, it is clear that in recent years the required cash reserve ratio has been at least as high as that which the bank would hold voluntarily.

An Example. Deposit expansion with more than one bank (but ignoring the cash drain) is illustrated in Example 15.4. We have assumed a very simple pattern of clearinghouse drain. The initial deposit stays with the bank in each case, but any deposits created by the bank are withdrawn almost immediately and deposited in some other bank.

Even if the deposit-creating bank loses all of its excess reserves at each stage in the expansion process, those excess reserves immediately reappear in some other bank. For the system as a whole the total expansion of deposits through all stages is not affected by the presence of several banks. Each bank presumably shares proportionately in the total expansion.

SAVINGS AND TIME DEPOSITS

To this point in our analysis we have assumed, unrealistically, that banks issue only checkable deposits. But banks also issue noncheckable savings and time deposits. By our narrow definition of the money supply these deposits are not money, since they are not in a form that can be used as a medium of exchange. However, they are very liquid, and indeed a large portion of them are payable on demand. While they are not money, they are a very close substitute for money as a liquid reserve against contingencies. How do they affect the process of deposit creation?

This question is actually twofold: (1) How does the presence of time deposits affect the creation of monetary deposits, and (2) how does the presence of time deposits affect the creation of total deposits? Throughout, we take the level of cash reserves in the banking system as given, and to minimize complexities we ignore cash drain. However, we must allow for the possibility of different cash reserve requirements for time and demand deposits.

Time Deposits and Money Creation. Any bank depositor is free to choose whether he will hold his funds in a demand deposit, which yields no interest but is designed to be used as a medium of payment, or in a time deposit bearing a positive rate of interest but not designed to be used as a medium of payment. Although we have little empirical evidence on factors governing this choice, theoretical reasoning suggests that it will depend, among other things, on the level of interest rates paid on time deposits. In any case, we are interested at the moment in the effect of a transfer of funds from demand deposits to time deposits on the total supply of money and credit.

The immediate impact is obvious. If holders of demand deposits convert them into time deposits, there is an immediate reduction in the stock of demand deposits outstanding. The money supply is reduced. But how permanent is this reduction? Can the banks then make additional loans, creating new demand deposits to replace those that have been converted into time deposits?

The answer to this follows directly from our earlier analysis of the process of deposit creation. Additional deposits can be created only if the transfer to time deposits produces excess reserves in the banking system. If time deposits are subject to the same reserve requirements as demand deposits, no excess reserves will be created by the transfer. The restriction of the money supply will be "permanent" (i.e., will last as long as the funds are kept in time deposits or until more cash reserves are available), but the total deposits in and total credit extended by the banking system will be unchanged. However, if the time deposits are subject to a lower reserve requirement, the transfer will produce excess reserves. Additional deposits can be created. As long as the reserve requirement for time deposits is greater than 0, however, the demand deposits lost in the transfer cannot be fully replaced (some "permanent" reduction in the money supply will result). Nonetheless, total bank deposits will have increased, and with it total bank earning assets. If the reserve ratio behind time deposits is 0, no monetary restriction will occur, and total bank deposits will be greater by an amount equal to the amount of deposits transferred to time deposits.

An Example. These points are illustrated in Example 15.5, which considers three possible cases: where the reserve ratios for demand and time deposits are the same, where the reserve ratio for time deposits is less than that for demand deposits, and where the reserve ratio for time deposits is 0. The effects of a transfer of $10,000 from demand to time deposits is traced through for each case. When the reserve ratios are assumed to be the same (Case 1), total deposits are unchanged but demand deposits (the money

EXAMPLE 15.4 Deposit Creation with More Than One Bank, Each with 16 Percent Reserve Ratio (Thousands of Dollars)

1. Stage I: As in Example 15.2. (It is assumed that the deposits are initially held by Bank A).

Bank A		Bank B		Bank C		Public	
Cash +10	Deposits +10	Cash 0	Deposits 0	Cash 0	Deposits 0	Deposits +10	

Bank Reserve Positions
(cumulative change to end of Stage I)

	Deposits	Cash Reserves		
		Actual	Required	Excess
Bank A	+10	+10	+1.6	+8.4
Bank B	0	0	0	0
Bank C	0	0	0	0
System	+10	+10	+1.6	+8.4

The Money Supply
(cumulative change to end of Stage I)

	Deposits
Stage I	+10
CUMULATIVE	+10

2. Stage II: (A) Bank A makes loans in the amount of its excess reserves, crediting $8,400 to demand deposits. (B) These deposits are withdrawn almost immediately and deposited in accounts with Bank B.

A.

Bank A		Bank B		Bank C		Public	
Loans +8.4	Deposits +8.4					Deposits +8.4	Loans +8.4

B.

Bank A		Bank B		Bank C	
Cash −8.4	Deposits −8.4	Cash +8.4	Deposits +8.4		

Net Change

Bank A		Bank B		Bank C		Public	
Assets 0	Deposits 0	Cash +8.4	Deposits +8.4			Deposits +8.4	Loans +8.4

Bank Reserve Positions
(cumulative change to end of Stage II)

	Deposits	Cash Reserves		
		Actual	Required	Excess
Bank A	10.0	1.60	1.60	0
Bank B	8.4	8.40	1.34	7.06
Bank C	0	0	0	0
System	18.4	10.00	2.94	7.06

The Money Supply
(cumulative change to end of Stage II)

	Deposits
Stage I	+10.00
Stage II	+8.40
CUMULATIVE	+18.40

EXAMPLE 15.4 (Continued)

3. Stage III: (A) Bank B makes loans in the amount of its excess reserves, crediting $7,060 to demand deposits. (B) These deposits are almost immediately withdrawn and deposited in accounts with Bank C.

A.

Bank A	Bank B	Bank C	Public

B.

Bank B	Bank C	Public
Loans +7.06 | Deposits +7.06		Deposits +7.06 | Loans +7.06
	Cash +7.06 | Deposits +7.06	

Net Change

Bank B	Bank C	
Cash −7.06 | Deposits −7.06	Cash +7.06 | Deposits +7.06	

Bank A	Bank B	Bank C	Public
Assets 0 | Deposits 0	Deposits 0	Cash 7.06 | Deposits 7.06	Deposits 7.06 | Loans 7.06

Bank Reserve Positions
(cumulative change to end of Stage III)

	Deposits	Cash Reserves Actual	Cash Reserves Required	Excess
Bank A	+10.00	+1.60	+1.60	0
Bank B	+8.40	+1.34	+1.34	0
Bank C	+7.06	+7.06	+1.13	+5.93
System	+25.46	+10.00	+4.07	+5.93

The Money Supply
(cumulative change to end of Stage III)

	Deposits
Stage I	+10.00
Stage II	+8.40
Stage III	+7.06
CUMULATIVE	+25.46

4. Stage n: This process continues until excess reserves are exhausted.

Bank Reserve Positions
(cumulative change to end of Stage n)

	Deposits	Cash Reserves Actual	Cash Reserves Required	Excess
Bank A	+10.00	+1.60	+1.60	0
Bank B	+8.40	+1.34	+1.34	0
Bank C	+7.06	+1.13	+1.13	0
Bank D	+5.93	+0.95	+0.95	0
Bank n	0	0	0	0
System	+62.50	+10.00	+10.00	0

The Money Supply
(cumulative change to end of Stage n)

	Deposits
Stage I	+10.0
Stage II	+8.40
Stage III	+7.06
Stage IV	+5.93
Stage n	0
CUMULATIVE	+62.50

MULTIPLIER

Deposit Expansion Multiplier: $\dfrac{\Delta D}{\Delta R} = \dfrac{62.50}{10} = 6.25$

supply) fall by the amount of the transfer. When the reserve ratios are assumed to be 4 percent and 16 percent (Case 2), the bank is able to create deposits to replace three-fourths of the demand deposits that were trans-fered to time deposits. Total deposits expand by $7,500, and the net reduction in demand deposits is only $2,500. When it is assumed that no reserves are held against time deposits (Case 3), the bank is able to create deposits to replace all of the demand deposits transfered to time deposits. As a result, total deposits expand by the full $10,000.

In summary, as long as time deposits are subject to a lower reserve requirement than demand deposits, any transfer of funds to time deposits will lead to a net expansion of total deposits and total bank credit. The effective cash reserve ratio is reduced by such a transfer.

EXAMPLE 15.5   Time Deposits and Deposit Expansion (Thousands of Dollars)

CASE 1

Reserve Ratios: Demand Deposits   0.16
                  Time Deposits   0.16

$10,000 is transfered from demand deposits to time deposits.

Bank			Public		
Deposits			Deposits		
Demand	−10		Demand	−10	
Time	+10		Time	+10	

Bank Deposits

	Demand	Time	Total
Net Change	−10	+10	0

Bank Reserve Position (net change)

	Demand	Time	Total
Deposits	−10.0	+10.0	0
Reserves			
Actual			0
Required	−1.6	+1.6	0
EXCESS			0

CASE 2

Reserve Ratios: Demand Deposits   0.16
                  Time Deposits   0.04

Stage I: $10,000 is transfered from demand deposits to time deposits.

Bank			Public		
Deposits			Deposits		
Demand	+10		Demand	−10	
Time	+10		Time	+10	

Bank Deposits (net change)

	Demand	Time	Total
Stage I	−10.0	+10.0	0

Bank Reserve Position (cumulative change to end of Stage I)

	Demand	Time	Total
Deposits	−10.0	+10.0	0
Reserves			
Required	−1.6	+0.4	−1.2
EXCESS			+1.2

EXAMPLE 15.5   (Continued)

Stage II: The bank makes loans in the amount of its excess reserves from Stage I; $1200 is credited to demand deposits of the general public.

Bank			Public		
Loans +1.2	Deposits		Deposits	Loans +1.2	
	Demand +1.2		Demand +1.2		

	Bank Deposits (net change)				Bank Reserve Position (cumulative change to end of Stage II)		
	Demand	Time	Total		Demand	Time	Total
Stage I	−10.0	+10.0	0				
Stage II	+1.2	0	+1.2	Deposits	−8.8	+10.0	+1.2
CUMULATIVE	−8.8	10.0	+1.2	Reserves			
				Required	−1.4	+0.4	−1.0
				EXCESS			+1.0

Stage III: The bank makes loans in the amount of its excess reserves from Stage II; $1000 is credited to demand deposits of the general public.

Bank			Public		
Loans +1.0	Deposits		Deposits	Loans +1.0	
	Demand +1.0		Demand +1.0		

	Bank Deposits (net change)				Bank Reserve Position (cumulative to end of Stage III)		
	Demand	Time	Total		Demand	Time	Total
Stage I	−10.0	+10.0	0				
Stage II	+1.2	0	+1.2	Deposits	−7.80	+10.0	+2.20
Stage III	+1.0	0	+1.0	Reserves			
CUMULATIVE	−7.8	+10.0	+2.2	Required	−1.25	+0.4	−0.85
				EXCESS			+0.85

Stage n: The process continues until excess reserves are exhausted.

	Bank Deposits (net change)				Bank Reserve Position (cumulative to end of Stage n)		
	Demand	Time	Total		Demand	Time	Total
Stage I	−10.00	+10.0	0	Deposits	−2.50	+10.00	+7.5
Stage II	+1.20	0	+1.20	Reserves			
Stage III	+1.00	0	+1.00	Required	−0.40	+0.40	0
Stage IV	+0.85	0	+0.85	EXCESS			0
Stage n	0	0	0				
CUMULATIVE	−2.50	+10.0	+7.50				

The Limit to Deposit Creation with Time Deposits. This analysis makes it clear that any transfer of funds from demand to time deposits will increase the total deposits and earning assets of the bank. Other things being equal, such a transfer would appear to be profitable for the bank. If so, what limits such transfers? What restricts the expansion of credit through this mechanism?

We must remember that banks cannot reclassify accounts at will. To increase their time deposits they must induce people to give up demand

EXAMPLE 15.5   (*Continued*)

CASE 3
Reserve Ratios: Demand Deposits   0.16
                Time Deposits   0
Stage I: $10,000 is transfered from demand deposits to time deposits.

Bank		Public	
Deposits		Deposits	
Demand	−10	Demand	−10
Time	+10	Time	+10

<table>
<tr><td colspan="4" align="center">Bank Deposits
(net change)</td><td colspan="5" align="center">Bank Reserve Position
(cumulative change to end
of Stage I)</td></tr>
<tr><td></td><td>Demand</td><td>Time</td><td>Total</td><td></td><td></td><td>Demand</td><td>Time</td><td>Total</td></tr>
<tr><td>Stage I</td><td>−10</td><td>+10</td><td>0</td><td></td><td></td><td></td><td></td><td></td></tr>
<tr><td></td><td></td><td></td><td></td><td>Deposits</td><td></td><td>−10</td><td>+10</td><td>0</td></tr>
<tr><td></td><td></td><td></td><td></td><td>Reserves</td><td></td><td></td><td></td><td></td></tr>
<tr><td></td><td></td><td></td><td></td><td>Actual</td><td></td><td></td><td></td><td>0</td></tr>
<tr><td></td><td></td><td></td><td></td><td>Required</td><td></td><td>−1.6</td><td>0</td><td>−1.6</td></tr>
<tr><td></td><td></td><td></td><td></td><td>EXCESS</td><td></td><td></td><td></td><td>+1.6</td></tr>
</table>

Stage II: The bank makes loans in the amount of its excess reserves from Stage I; $1,600 is credited to demand deposits of the general public.

Bank		Public	
Loans +1.6	Deposits	Deposits	Loans +1.6
	Demand +1.6	Demand +1.6	

<table>
<tr><td colspan="4" align="center">Bank Deposits
(net change)</td><td colspan="5" align="center">Bank Reserve Position
(cumulative change to end
of Stage II)</td></tr>
<tr><td></td><td>Demand</td><td>Time</td><td>Total</td><td></td><td></td><td>Demand</td><td>Time</td><td>Total</td></tr>
<tr><td>Stage I</td><td>−10.0</td><td>+10.0</td><td>0</td><td></td><td></td><td></td><td></td><td></td></tr>
<tr><td>Stage II</td><td>+1.6</td><td>0</td><td>+1.6</td><td>Deposits</td><td></td><td>−8.40</td><td>+10.0</td><td>+1.60</td></tr>
<tr><td>CUMULATIVE</td><td>−8.4</td><td>+10.0</td><td>+1.6</td><td>Reserves</td><td></td><td></td><td></td><td></td></tr>
<tr><td>(to end of Stage II)</td><td></td><td></td><td></td><td>Required</td><td></td><td>−1.34</td><td>0</td><td>−1.34</td></tr>
<tr><td></td><td></td><td></td><td></td><td>EXCESS</td><td></td><td></td><td></td><td>+1.34</td></tr>
</table>

Stage n: The process continues until excess reserves are exhausted.

<table>
<tr><td colspan="4" align="center">Bank Deposits
(net change)</td><td colspan="5" align="center">Bank Reserve Position
(cumulative to end of
Stage n)</td></tr>
<tr><td></td><td>Demand</td><td>Time</td><td>Total</td><td></td><td></td><td>Demand</td><td>Time</td><td>Total</td></tr>
<tr><td>Stage I</td><td>−10.00</td><td>+10.0</td><td>0</td><td></td><td></td><td></td><td></td><td></td></tr>
<tr><td>Stage II</td><td>+1.60</td><td>0</td><td>+1.60</td><td>Deposits</td><td></td><td>0</td><td>+10</td><td>+10</td></tr>
<tr><td>Stage III</td><td>+1.34</td><td>0</td><td>+1.34</td><td>Reserves</td><td></td><td></td><td></td><td></td></tr>
<tr><td>Stage n</td><td>0</td><td>0</td><td>0</td><td>Required</td><td></td><td>0</td><td>0</td><td>0</td></tr>
<tr><td>CUMULATIVE</td><td>0</td><td>+10.0</td><td>+10.00</td><td>EXCESS</td><td></td><td></td><td></td><td>0</td></tr>
</table>

deposits in favor of time deposits. The primary incentive to do so is the rate of interest paid on time deposits.

This suggests the nature of the limiting mechanism. Additional time deposits can be gained only by offering higher interest rates on time deposits. This increases the opportunity cost (the interest forgone) of holding demand deposits and induces depositors to economize on their demand deposit balances, transferring a portion to time deposits. However, this cannot be done without limit or without inconvenience and cost to the depositor. Demand deposits are held mainly by business firms to facilitate the firms' transactions. They cannot be dispensed with readily. As a result, banks will find that to attract more time deposits they will have to pay higher interest rates and hence incur higher costs.[4]

Banks are business firms striving to maximize profits. As you will recall from your principles of economics course, if marginal revenue (the revenue derived from producing and selling an additional unit of output) exceeds marginal cost (the cost of producing an additional unit of output), the firm can increase its profits by increasing output. If marginal revenue is less than marginal cost, the firm can increase its profits by reducing output. Only when marginal revenue equals marginal cost will profits be maximized.

This rule can be applied to banks. Our assertions about the cost to the bank of attracting more time deposits can be interpreted to mean that time deposits are subject to rising marginal cost. The additional earning assets that can be acquired as a result of the increase in time deposits produce an increase in interest income (marginal revenue). It is only profitable, then, for the bank to strive for higher levels of time deposits if the expected marginal revenue exceeds anticipated marginal cost. With rising marginal cost and a given yield on new earning assets, this establishes a definite limit to the share of time deposits in the total deposits of the banking system.

In short, the limit to credit creation through the time deposit mechanism lies in the increasing cost of attracting additional time deposits. Attempts to expand time deposits beyond some point simply will not be profitable.

Time Deposits and the Money Multiplier. This analysis of the impact of time deposits on deposit creation assumed a single lump-sum transfer of funds from demand deposits to time deposits (perhaps in response to a change in interest rates; perhaps for a variety of other reasons). What if there is a systematic relationship between demand and time deposits? For example, what if, other things being equal, some fraction of any increase of demand deposits is normally transferred to time deposits?

It should be obvious from what has been said before that such a relationship between time and demand deposits will alter the size of the deposit multiplier. As long as time deposits are subject to reserve requirements, any transfer of funds from demand deposits to time deposits will reduce the amount of demand deposits that can be created on the basis of a given increase in bank reserves. The money supply multiplier will be reduced. At the same time, if the reserve ratio applied to time deposits is less than that applied to demand deposits, any such transfer will increase the total deposits in the banking system. What we might call the total deposit multiplier will be increased. The smaller the reserve ratio applied to time deposits, the larger the money supply multiplier and the total deposit multiplier. At the extreme, if the reserve ratio for time deposits is 0, the money supply multiplier will be the same as if time deposits did not exist. These points are explored in the appendix to this chapter.

NEAR BANKS AND DEPOSIT CREATION

One of the more contentious issues in the theory of the money supply is whether near banks can create deposits.

Many economists argue that only true commercial banks have deposit-creating powers. In this regard commercial banks are said to be unique among financial intermediaries. Near banks can increase their deposit liabilities by attracting deposits from commercial banks. They cannot "create" deposits.

Other economists disagree, denying the validity of the sharp dichotomy between banks and near banks, and asserting that any differences are just a matter of degree and that near banks participate actively along with banks in a complex process of deposit creation.

Near-Bank Liabilities and Bank Money. One factor in the debate is the monetary status of the liabilities of near banks. As we have seen, in the United States the liabilities of near banks are not transferable by check. By our definition they are not money. An example may help to clarify the issues and the interrelationships between banks and near banks.

An Example. In Example 15.6 we trace the effects of a transfer of $10,000 from a demand deposit with a commercial bank to a savings deposit with a savings and loan association. We are using the savings and loan association as a stereotype of a near bank. Several special assumptions are involved in the example; each is based on the characteristics of savings and loan associations and their role in the financial system, which we identified in Chapter 10. Two assumptions are particularly important.

The first crucial assumption is that savings and loan associations keep any addition to their cash reserves in the form of deposits with commercial banks. This is quite realistic. Currency in their vaults—the only other method of holding cash reserves—is typically a very small portion of total cash holdings of savings and loan associations. For the purposes of the example we have arbitrarily assumed a fixed reserve ratio of 4 percent for all S&L deposits, the same as the ratio we employed earlier for time deposits with commercial banks. Recent experience suggests that this is somewhat high.

The second basic assumption derives from our desire to consider the extreme case posed by American institutional arrangements. We assume that, since near-bank liabilities are not money, when the savings and loan association makes a mortgage loan or otherwise invests its funds, the proceeds are all deposited in demand deposits with banks, thus entering the general monetary circulation. There is no return flow into deposits with S&Ls.

EXAMPLE 15.6   Deposit Creation by Near Banks: Case I (Thousands of Dollars)

Stage I: $10,000 is transferred from demand deposits with commercial banks to time deposits with a savings and loan association. The savings and loan company deposits the funds in its demand deposit with its banker.

S&L		Bank		Public	
Reserves	Deposits +10	Deposits		Deposits	
Deposits +10		Public −10		Bank −10	
		S&L +10		S&L +10	

The S&L desires to maintain cash reserves in the form of correspondent balances with its banker in the amount of 4 percent of its deposit liabilities.

	Public Deposits (net change)				Reserve Position (cumulative change to end of Stage I)		
	S&L	Bank	Total		S&L	Bank	Total
Stage I	+10	−10	0	Total Deposits	+10.0	0	+10.0
				Reserves			
				Actual	+10.0		+10.0
				Desired	+0.4		+0.4
				EXCESS	+9.6		+9.6

Stage II: The S&L makes mortgage loans in the amount of its excess reserves. The $9,600 is deposited in demand deposits of the general public, entering general circulation.

S&L		Bank		Public	
Reserves		Deposits		Deposits	Loans +9.6
Deposits −9.6		S&L −9.6		Bank +9.6	
Loans +9.6		Public +9.6			

	Public Deposits (net change)				Reserve Position (cumulative change to end of Stage II)		
	S&L	Bank	Total		S&L	Bank	Total
Stage I	+10	−10.0	0	Total Deposits	+10.0	0	+10.0
Stage II	0	+9.6	+9.6	Reserves			
CUMULATIVE	+10	−0.4	+9.6	Actual	+0.4	0	+0.4
				Desired	+0.4	0	+0.4
				EXCESS	0	0	0

In Example 15.6, the immediate impact of the transfer of funds from banks to near banks is to increase the deposit liabilities of the near banks without reducing the deposit liabilities of the banks. It is true that the ownership of deposits in the banking system has changed significantly. S&Ls now own deposits that were previously owned by members of the general public, and by consequence the publicly owned money supply has fallen. However, since the banks have the same total deposits, their cash reserve position is unchanged (they have neither excess reserves nor deficit reserves), and they have no incentive to contract credit and deposits.

At the same time, S&Ls do have excess reserves. Their portfolios are in disequilibrium. The profit motive will dictate that they acquire more earning assets, and in making new loans or acquiring securities they will be adding to the total stock of credit available to the economy. In this sense, by attracting deposits from the banking system, the savings and loan associations are expanding the total supply of credit.

What happens to deposits and the money supply? As the savings and loan associations lend their excess reserves, they will lose those excess reserves in their entirety. Borrowers—probably house buyers—want money that can be spent. They do not want nonmonetary claims on near banks. As a result of the loan, then, savings and loan associations' reserve deposits with banks will be transfered to house buyers, and as the funds are spent they will enter the general monetary circulation. Thus, unlike the case of a normal cash drain (Example 15.3), there is no transfer of excess reserves among financial institutions. Because the excess reserves were in the form of deposits at a bank, they disappear once the loan is made. There is secondary credit and deposit expansion.

The upshot is that the interaction between near banks and the banking system has in fact "created" both credit and deposits. It is true that there is a small reduction in the publicly held money supply, narrowly defined, accounted for by the cash reserve that S&Ls hold in deposits with their correspondent banks against their increased deposit liabilities. The smaller the S&Ls' reserve ratio, the smaller this contraction will be. At the extreme, if the savings and loan associations do not increase their reserves with the increase in their deposits (i.e., their marginal reserve ratio is 0), no contraction of the money supply will occur. In any case, the overall effect is to increase the total of highly liquid deposits held by the general public.

Credit Creation and the Competition for Deposits. At first glance, the mechanism involved in this process of credit creation may appear to be different from that which we explored before. The availability of excess reserves of high-powered money proved to be the driving force behind the creation of credit by banks. In the present case, the competition for deposits between near banks and commercial banks appears to be at the heart of the process. In fact, however, the mechanism is exactly the same. The transfer of deposits to near banks leads to the creation of credit because it creates excess reserves of high-powered money in the financial system.

Excess reserves emerge because near banks hold their cash reserves in deposits with commercial banks. This economizes on high-powered money, since the only high-powered money involved in the reserves behind the deposits in near banks is that held by commercial banks as reserves behind the reserve deposits of the near banks. Reserves of high-powered money are a fraction of deposits in a near bank. Let us define the *equilibrium effective reserve ratio* as the ratio of high-powered money to total deposits (in banks and near banks) when no excess reserves remain in either banks or near banks (i.e., when the portfolios of both groups of institutions are in equilibrium). Then we can say that the transfer of deposits from banks to near banks creates credit because it reduces the equilibrium effective reserve ratio.

Moreover, as Example 15.7 makes clear, this expansion in deposits and credit will occur even if (as may be more likely) the funds that are attracted from the commercial banks come out of time deposits subject to the same nominal reserve requirement (in the example, 4 percent). The expansion occurs because the near bank holds its reserves in deposits with a commercial bank, thus reducing the equilibrium effective reserve ratio.

In order to consolidate your understanding of this point, it might be useful to do the following two exercises. First, trace what would happen if near banks held their cash reserves in the form of currency in their vaults. Second, trace what would happen if commercial banks held most of their cash reserves in the form of correspondent balances with each other. In assessing the relevance of the latter, remember that correspondent balances are an important part of domestic banking. Indeed, in some states state banks can count correspondent balances as part of their required cash reserves.

Limits on Near-Bank Credit Creation. This analysis demonstrates that any transfer of funds from banks to near banks will lead to an expansion of the supply of credit and the stock of liquid assets in the economy. We have seen that the amount of credit that can be created from any given transfer is strictly limited by the reserve ratios of banks and near banks. However, we have not established that there is any limit to the amount of funds that will be transfered. Will such transfers go on indefinitely? What limits the ability of near banks to attract deposits and expand credit?

The answer is exactly the same as the one we developed in the case of time deposits at commercial banks. It is a matter of profitability.

If a bank is to gain more deposits, it must persuade depositors to shift their accounts. To do this, it must offer terms that are sufficiently attractive to depositors to induce them to alter their banking habits. This may involve many factors in addition to interest rates paid on deposits, including such conditions as location of branches, business hours at branch offices, service charges on accounts, advertising, gifts for opening new accounts, and the like. To all of this, banks can be expected to respond in some degree. As a result, near banks can obtain more deposits only by being successful in a process of competitive bidding, and in doing so they will encounter rising costs. In brief, near-bank deposits are subject to rising marginal costs.

Given the yield that can be expected on new assets acquired by the near bank—marginal revenue—there is some point beyond which the competition for deposits is no longer profitable. Thus, competition for more deposits is no longer profitable. Thus, competition for more deposits will appear profitable only if expected marginal revenue exceeds marginal cost. When marginal revenue equals marginal cost, equilibrium will have been established, including an equilibrium distribution of deposits between banks and near banks.

EXAMPLE 15.7 Deposit Creation by Near Banks (Thousands of Dollars)

Stage I: $10,000 is transferred from time deposits with commercial banks to time deposits with a savings and loan company. The S&L deposits the funds in a demand deposit with its correspondent bank.

S&L

Reserves Deposits +10	Deposits +10

Bank

	Deposits
	Time −10
	Demand +10

Public

	Time Deposits
	Bank −10
	S&L +10

The S&L desires to maintain cash reserves in the form of correspondent balances with its banker in the amount of 4 percent of its deposit liabilities. The bank maintains as 4 percent reserve behind time deposits and 16 percent behind demand deposits.

Public Deposits (net change)
Time Deposits

	S&L	Bank
Stage I	+10	−10

	S&L	Demand Deposits	Total
Stage I		0	0

Reserve Position
(cumulative change to end of Stage I)

	S&L	Bank		
		Time	Demand	Total
Total Deposits	+10.0	−10.0	+10.0	+10.0
Reserves				
Actual	+10.0	0	0	+10.0
Desired	+0.4	−0.4	+1.6	+1.6
EXCESS	+9.6		} −1.2	+8.4

Stage II: The S&L makes mortgage loans in the amount of its excess reserves; $9,600 is transferred from S&L demand deposits with banker to public demand deposits in the banking system.

S&L

Loans +9.6	
Reserves −9.6	
Deposits −9.6	

Bank

	Demand Deposits
	S&L −9.6
	Public +9.6

Public

Demand Deposits +9.6	Loans +9.6

Public Deposits (net change)
Time Deposits

	S&L	Bank
Stage I	+10	−10
Stage II	0	0
CUMULATIVE	+10	−10

	S&L	Demand Deposits	Total
Stage I		0	0
Stage II		+9.6	+9.6
		+9.6	+9.6

Reserve Position
(cumulative change to end of Stage II)

	S&L	Bank		
		Time	Demand	Total
Total Deposits	+10.0	−10.0	+10.0	+10.0
Reserves				
Actual	+0.4	0	0	+0.4
Desired	+0.4	−0.4	+1.6	+1.6
EXCESS	0		} −1.2	−1.2

EXAMPLE 15.7 (Continued)

Stage III: Simultaneously the banks reduce their portfolios of earning assets, refusing to renew loans in the amount of their reserve deficiency.

S&L	Banks		Public	
	Loans −1.2	Demand Deposits Public −1.2	Demand Deposits −1.2	Loans −1.2

Public Deposits (net change)

	Time Deposits		Demand Deposits	Total
	S&L	Bank		
Stage I	+10	−10	0	0
Stage II	0	0	+9.6	+9.6
Stage III	0	0	−1.2	−1.2
CUMULATIVE	+10	−10	+8.4	+8.4

Reserve Position (cumulative to end of Stage III)

	S&L	Bank		
		Time	Demand	Total
Total Deposits	+10.0	−10.0	+8.8	+8.8
Reserves Actual	+0.4	0	0	+0.4
Desired	+0.4	−0.4	+1.4	1.4
EXCESS	0	} −1.0		−1.0

Stage n: This process of bank deposit contraction continues until the reserve deficiency is eliminated.

Public Deposits (net change)

	Time Deposits		Demand Deposits	Total
	S&L	Bank		
Stage I	+10	−10	0	0
Stage II	0	0	+9.6	+9.6
Stage III	0	0	−1.2	−1.2
Stage IV	0	0	−1.0	−1.0
Stage n	0	0	0	0
CUMULATIVE	+10	−10	+2.1	+2.1

Reserve Position (cumulative change to end of Stage n)

	S&L	Bank		
		Time	Demand	Total
Total Deposits	+10.0	−10.0	+2.5	+2.5
Reserves Actual	+0.4	0	0	+0.4
Desired	+0.4	−0.4	+0.4	+0.4
EXCESS	0	} 0		0

This, then, establishes the limit to credit creation by near banks. It is inherent in the profit motive.

SUMMARY

In this chapter we have explored the mechanics of the creation of deposits and credit in the private sector of the financial system. What have we established?

First, we have shown that the creation of deposits and the creation of credit are intimately connected. One is the obverse of the other. Thus, deposit expansion occurs as financial institutions make net additions to their total assets, that is, as they increase the volume of credit extended to the economy.

Second, we have demonstrated that, given the rules under which financial institutions must operate (e.g., legal reserve requirements) and the management policies of financial institutions, the quantity of high-powered money available in the financial system is the basic determinant of the stock of deposits and credit. Any increase in the quantity of high-powered money will lead to a multiple increase in deposits and credit.

Third, underlying all this and providing the driving force is the striving of financial intermediaries to maximize profits, subject to the constraints imposed on them by the monetary authorities (i.e., reserve requirements) and to the willingness of the public to hold various types of claims on financial intermediaries. The profit motive induces the banks to pare their excess cash reserves to the minimum consistent with legal requirements and prudent banking practices. This behavior is basic to the multiple expansion of deposits. The profit motive also determines the extent to which banks and near banks will compete for time deposits. When time deposits are subjected to lower effective reserve requirements—and particularly when near banks hold their reserves as deposits with banks—any increase in time deposits in banks or near banks will expand the supply of credit and deposits.

Under any given set of circumstances—given the quantity of high-powered money, individual preferences as between time and demand deposits, and the general level of interest rates and demand for credit—there will be a determinate level of credit and deposits at which the portfolios of all financial institutions will be in equilibrium. Change any of these determinants, and the equilibrium quantities will change.

The Supply of High-Powered Money. All of our analysis in this chapter has taken the supply of high-powered money as given. We have not explored the determinants of the quantity of high-powered money, although clearly this is a crucial consideration in determining the total supply of deposits and credit. That is the subject of the next two chapters. As we will see, even our implicit assumption in this chapter that the quantity of high-powered money is beyond influence by private financial institutions is not quite correct.

NOTES

1. It is logical to ask, But what about the interest on the loan? Since the businesssman must repay more than he has borrowed, will not the net effect of the extension and repayment of the loan be to reduce the money supply?

This is true to the extent that the bank makes a profit on the loan and does not distribute that profit as dividends to its shareholders. Any payment received by the bank tends to expand the money supply. The money supply will contract when the bank makes additions to its retained earnings. The bank's total assets remain the same; its liabilities contract, and its capital account expands by the amount of the retained profit.

2. These reserves may be held as deposits with the central bank and would be convertible into legal tender on demand.

3. Before dismissing the monopoly bank case, remember that the same principles apply to the Federal Reserve—the subject of the next chapter—which is in an important sense a monopoly bank with control over high-powered money.

4. The banker may feel that he is attempting to attract funds that would otherwise be invested in other financial instruments, such as stocks or bonds. However, if someone is to sell stocks or bonds to place the funds in a time deposit, he must find someone with money (demand deposits or currency or another time deposit to sell it to). If there is to be a net addition to time deposits, the funds must come out of demand deposits (or currency in circulation), directly or indirectly.

Appendix
to Chapter 15
Money Supply Multipliers

$\mathbf{I}$t is customary to develop the analysis of the creation of money by means of money supply multipliers of varying degrees of complexity. The purpose of this appendix is to review some basic multiplier models.

THE RELEVANCE OF MULTIPLER MODELS

It is possible to develop a great variety of multiplier models, each one more complex than the one before. The important question is, Do they have any relevance? Or are they just toys, designed to show off (very elementary) algebraic virtuosity?

Complex multipliers make an important point, although there is a major danger in using this approach to the analysis of the determination of the money supply.

The danger of the multiplier approach to the analysis of the supply of money and credit is that it seems to suggest that the expansion or contraction of the supplies of money and credit is a simple mechanical process. A complex multiplier, constructed from several ratios, regulates the relationship between changes in the quantity of high-powered money and changes in the supply of money and credit in the economy, just as the gears in an automobile regulate the relationship between the speed of the engine and that of the wheels. This mechanical analogy is unfortunate. It assumes constant things that are demonstrably not constant.

Each of the ratios involved in the more complex forms of the multipliers is in fact an assumption about the behavior of participants in the financial system. Thus, the reserve ratios are presumed to represent decisions made by banks with respect to the level of their cash reserves, and the cash drain and time deposit coefficients represent decisions made by members of the public as to the form in which they are going to hold liquid assets (currency, time deposits, or demand deposits). The complex multipliers make a very important point by emphasizing that the demands for currency and time deposits are relevant to the deposit expansion process. However, it is unreasonable to assume that these instruments are always held in portfolios in fixed proportions to each other, regardless of the level of interest rates and regardless of the level of income. Recent research suggests that portfolio balance decisions are much more complicated than that.

As a result, we can only take the multiplier model as a first approximation to a much more complicated model of portfolio selection, incorporating a great variety of other factors explaining the critical ratios.

THE BASIC MULTIPLIER

In the text we developed the formula for the basic deposit expansion multiplier, assuming only one type of deposit (demand deposits) and ignoring cash drain.

$$D = R(1/r) \qquad (15.2)$$

We developed this multiplier from the basic equilibrium condition that there should be no excess reserves in the banking system. It is sometimes developed in a different way, as the sum of a geometrical progression.

Deposit Expansion as a Geometrical Progression

STAGE 1

Currency is deposited in the banking system. Cash reserves (R) and deposits (D) increase by the same amount.

$$\Delta D_1 = \Delta R \qquad (15A.1)$$

Excess Reserves:

Required reserves (R_r) increase by a fraction (r) of the increase in deposits.

$$\begin{aligned} \Delta R_r &= r\Delta D_1 \\ &= r\Delta R \end{aligned} \qquad (15A.2)$$

Leaving excess reserves (R_e):

$$R_e(1) = \Delta R - r\Delta R \qquad (15A.3)$$

Stage 2

Loans are made, and deposits created, in the amount of excess reserves from Stage 1.

$$\Delta D_2 = \Delta R - r\Delta R \\ = \Delta R(1-r)$$
(15A.4)

Cumulative Expansion:

At the end of Stage 2, total deposits have increased:

$$\Delta D_1 + \Delta D_2 = \Delta R + \Delta R(1-r)$$
(15A.5)

Excess Reserves:

At the end of Stage 2, excess reserves remain in the amount of:

$$R_e(2) = R_e(2) - r[R_e(1)] \\ = \Delta R(1-r) - r[\Delta R(1-r)^2] \\ = \Delta R(1-r)^2$$
(15A.6)

Stage 3

Loans are made, and deposits created, in the amount of the excess reserves from Stage 2.

$$\Delta D_3 = \Delta R(1-r)^2$$
(15A.7)

Cumulative Expansion:

$$\Delta D_1 + \Delta D_2 + \Delta D_3 = \Delta R + \Delta R(1-r) + \Delta R(1-r)^2$$
(15A.8)

Excess Reserves:

$$R_e(3) = R_e(3) - r\ [R_e(2)] \\ = \Delta R(1-r)^2 - r[\Delta R(1-r)^2] \\ = \Delta R(1-r)^2(1-r) \\ = \Delta R(1-r)^3$$
(15A.9)

Stage n

Cumulative Expansion:

If we allow this process to continue for n periods, the cumulative expansion of deposits appears as the sum of a geometric progression, with first term ΔR and common ratio $(1-r)$. It is shown in elementary algebra that the sum of such a geometric series is:

$$\Delta D = \frac{\Delta R[1-(1-r)^n]}{1-(1-r)}$$
(15A.10)

Excess reserves will remain until n approaches infinity, and hence $(1-r)^n$ approaches 0. The expression for the cumulative expansion of deposits then becomes:

$$\Delta D = \Delta R \left[\frac{1}{1-(1-r)} \right] \\ = \Delta R(1/r)$$
(15A.11)

The deposit expansion multiplier is $(1/r)$.

THE MULTIPLIER WITH CASH DRAIN

The basic multiplier focuses attention on the cash of the banking system, on the assumption that these reserves are not drained out of the banks in the process of deposit expansion. However, bank reserves and currency in circulation are interchangeable. As the money supply expands, some bank reserves are likely to be drawn into circulation. The second deposit expansion multiplier takes such a cash drain into account.

While there are both long-term trends and short-term fluctuations in the relationship between currency and demand deposits, as a first approximation we can assume that there will normally be a fixed ratio (c) between currency (C) and demand deposits (D). That is, in equilibrium we assume:

$$C = cD \tag{15A.12}$$

From our definition of high-powered money (H), we know that:

$$\begin{aligned} H &= C + R \\ &= cD + R \end{aligned} \tag{15A.13}$$

Or:

$$R = H - cD \tag{15A.14}$$

But we also know that:

$$D = R(1/r) \tag{15.2}$$

Therefore:

$$D = (H - cD)1/r \tag{15A.15}$$

Reorganizing, we get:

$$D = H(1/r + c) \tag{15A.16}$$

In other words, in order to maintain equilibrium in the face of an increase in high-powered money (which may be used either for bank reserves or currency for circulation), total deposits must increase by a factor of $(1/r + c)$. This is a modified *deposit expansion multiplier*, allowing for an increase in currency in circulation as the money supply expands. Given the same reserve ratio, this multiplier is smaller than the basic multiplier.

It should be noted, however, that the total expansion of the money supply is somewhat greater than the expansion of deposits. The money supply (M) is composed of both deposits and currency in circulation. That is:

$$M = C + D \tag{15A.17}$$

On the assumption of proportionality between currency in circulation and demand deposits:

$$\begin{aligned} M &= cD + D \\ &= D(1 + c) \end{aligned} \tag{15A.18}$$

341

Substituting 15A.16 in 15A.18:

$$M = \left(\frac{H}{r+c}\right)(1+c)$$

$$= H\left[\frac{1+c}{r+c}\right]$$

(15A.19)

The expression in square brackets is the equilibrium *money supply expansion multiplier*, allowing for cash drain.

THE MULTIPLIER WITH TIME DEPOSITS

As we noted in the text, if a portion of any increase in demand deposits is automatically drawn into time deposits with a lower cash reserve ratio, it becomes necessary to distinguish between the money supply multiplier and the total deposit multiplier, and the relationship between demand and time deposits has a complicated effect on the size of these multipliers. For the purposes of the following analysis we are ignoring the complications introduced by cash drain and are assuming a simple proportional relationship between time deposits (T) and demand deposits (D).

That is:

$$T = tD$$

(15A.20)

Let the reserve ratio applicable to time deposits be r_t and that applicable to demand deposits be r_d, where:

$$0 < r_t < r_d < 1$$

(15A.21)

In equilibrium, total reserves (R) will be divided between demand and time deposits such that no excess reserves remain. That is:

$$R = r_d D + r_t T$$

(15A.22)

Substituting:

$$R = r_d D + r_t(tD)$$
$$= D[r_d + r_t t]$$

(15A.23)

or:

$$D = R\left[\frac{1}{r_d + r_t t}\right]$$

(15A.24)

The expression in square brackets is the *demand deposit multiplier*, allowing for time deposits. As long as $t > 0$, or $r_t > 0$, then:

$$\frac{1}{r_d} > \frac{1}{r_d + r_t t}$$

(15A.25)

That is, if positive cash reserves are maintained behind time deposits, the drain of funds into time deposits will reduce the demand deposit multiplier.

The total deposit multiplier will be greater than this. Total deposits are the sum of demand deposits and time deposits.

From 15A.24 and 15.A20:

$$D + T = R\left[\frac{1}{r_d + r_t t}\right] + tR\left[\frac{1}{r_d + r_t t}\right]$$

$$= R\left[\frac{1 + t}{r_d + r_t t}\right]$$

(15A.26)

The expression in square brackets is the *total deposit expansion multiplier*, allowing for time deposit drain. It can be shown quite easily that this will be greater than the basic multiplier if $r_d > r_t$.

THE MULTIPLIER WITH TIME DEPOSITS AND CASH DRAIN

Combining the analysis we can derive an even more complicated set of multipliers, allowing for all three effects: the applicable reserve ratios, the cash drain, and the time deposit drain.

From 15A.13 and 15A.22:

$$H = cD + r_d D + r_t T$$

(15A.27)

Substituting 15A.20 in 15A.27:

$$H = cD + r_d D + r_t tD$$
$$= D(c + r_d + r_t t)$$

or:

$$D = H\left[\frac{1}{c + r_d + r_t t}\right]$$

(15A.28)

The expression in square brackets is the *demand deposit multiplier*, allowing for both cash drain and the time deposit drain.

Substituting 15.A12 and 15A.28 in 15A.17:

$$M = C + D$$
$$= cD + D$$

(15A.29)

$$= H\left[\frac{1 + c}{c + r_d + r_t t}\right]$$

The expression in square brackets is the *money supply multiplier*, allowing for cash drain and time deposit drain.

We can also derive a total deposit multiplier by a similar process. The result is:

$$D + T = H\left[\frac{1 + t}{c + r_d + r_t t}\right]$$

(15A.30)

For additional models see J. Galbraith, "A Table of Banking System Multipliers," *Canadian Journal of Economics* 1, no. 4, 763–771.

16

CONTROL OF THE
MONEY SUPPLY

Part 2: The Federal Reserve
(Major Instruments)

In the previous chapter we analyzed the process by which money and credit are created and destroyed in the private sector of the financial system. We discovered several aspects of the behavior of banks, near banks, and the general public that affect the supply of money, but underlying all of this as the basic determinant is the supply of high-powered money.

THE CONCEPT OF HIGH-POWERED
MONEY: THE MONETARY BASE

We introduced the concept of high-powered money in the previous chapter, defining it as the sum of currency in circulation and bank cash reserves. This is sometimes (for obvious reasons) called the *monetary base*.

The concept of the monetary base implies an equivalence between currency in circulation and bank reserves. We have already seen that they are not equivalent in terms of their impact on the total supply of money. The composition of the monetary base is an important variable from this point of view, and one that cannot be controlled by the monetary authorities. However, currency in circulation and bank reserves are equivalent in another sense: They are directly convertible into each other. A dollar of currency when deposited in a bank becomes a dollar of bank reserves. And vice versa, a dollar taken out of the bank in the form of currency reduces bank reserves by a dollar.

The important point to note is that with the exception of subsidiary coinage (which we can ignore), the monetary base consists of liabilities of the Federal Reserve System. Currency takes the form of Federal Reserve notes (Chapter 2), and member bank reserves are either vault cash (predominantly Federal Reserve notes) or deposits with the Federal Reserve banks.

THE FEDERAL RESERVE

We have already encountered the Federal Reserve at several points in our analysis of the financial system. It is the United States' *central bank*. In brief, we can describe it as the bank for the financial system. It holds the bulk of the commercial member banks' cash reserves, handles the settlement of interbank clearing balances, makes advances to member banks and approved security dealers, manages the nation's central reserve of foreign exchange, and issues notes to be used as currency. In addition, the Federal Reserve acts as the fiscal agent of the federal government and also as the government's correspondent in dealings with foreign central banks. However, the aspect of the Federal Reserve that is of immediate concern to us is its function as manager of the money supply. When we ask what controls the size of the monetary base, one possible answer is the Federal Reserve. To see how, we must first analyze the Federal Reserve's balance sheet.

THE BALANCE SHEET OF THE FEDERAL RESERVE SYSTEM

The consolidated balance sheet for all twelve Federal Reserve District banks is set out in summary form in Table 16.1.

Assets. Compared to that of most of the other financial intermediaries we have examined, the composition of the asset portfolio of the Federal Reserve is quite simple. Indeed, from this vantage point the System appears to be little more than a warehouse for U.S. government securities. Interest earned on U.S. government securities is the major regular source of income for the Federal Reserve.

Another earning asset of the Federal Reserve is the account called Discounts and Advances to Banks. This account reflects the Federal Reserve's activities as lender of last resort for the banking system. You will recall from our earlier discussions that the Federal Reserve is empowered to make short-term advances to the member banks. It also enters into purchase and resale agreements with approved government securities dealers in the day-to-day conduct of its open-market operations (Chapter 3). (While resale agree-

345

Table 16.1. Consolidated Balance Sheet, Federal
Reserve System, March 31, 1972 (Millions of Dollars)

Assets	$92,137	Liabilities	$92,137
Gold Certificate Account	9,474	Federal Reserve Notes in	
U.S. Government Securities		Circulation	53,110
Bought Outright	69,255	Deposits	
Held Under Repurchase		Member Bank Reserves	27,746
Agreement	673	U.S. Government	1,293
Federal Agency Securities		Foreign	191
Bought Outright	810	Other	715
Held Under Repurchase		Deferred Availability	
Agreement	16	Cash Items	6,743
Acceptances		Other Liabilities	2,339
Bought Outright	82		
Held Under Repurchase			
Agreement	61		
Loans, Discounts, and			
Advances			
Member Bank Borrowings	255		
Cash Items in Process of			
Collection	9,905		
Foreign Currency	17		
Other Assets	1,588		

SOURCE: Federal Reserve *Bulletin*, April 1972, p. A12.

ments are not advances in form, they have the same effect and purpose and are designated in the balance sheet as Securities Held Under Repurchase Agreements.)

The Gold Certificate Account is also an asset for the Federal Reserve System. Gold certificates are issued by the Treasury against the actual gold stock it holds. Only the Federal Reserve System is authorized to hold gold certificates. At one time the Federal Reserve was required to back both Federal Reserve notes and member bank reserve accounts (the System's major liabilities) with a specific percentage of gold certificates. Over time, as the monetary gold stock dwindled and, correspondingly, the Federal Reserve's gold certificate account was reduced, both of those provisions for gold backing were rescinded.

The gold certificate account would change whenever the Treasury bought additional amounts of gold or sold large amounts of gold, or whenever the official price of gold changed. Since 1971 the Treasury has refused to sell gold to settle international payments accounts. The official price of gold was changed in 1971 and again in early 1973, resulting in an increase in the value of the Federal Reserve System's gold certificate account. (We will discuss these issues in Chapters 20 and 21.)

The Acceptances account is a small, income-earning asset for the Federal Reserve System. The Federal Reserve banks will buy banker's acceptances from commercial banks. Little use is made of this opportunity, however, by the banks.

The remainder of the Federal Reserve's assets have been grouped together into two accounts. The title of the first of these, Cash Items in the Process of Collection, is amply descriptive. Every day billions of dollars' worth of checks flow into the Federal Reserve District banks as part of their function of clearing and collecting checks. Time is required to credit the reserve accounts of the banks that are depositing them and to debit them from reserve balances of commercial banks on which the checks were drawn. Cash Items in the Process of Collection represents the value of checks held by Federal Reserve banks on a given day that have not been deducted from member bank reserves. A corresponding liability item, Deferred Availability Cash Items represents checks the Federal Reserve banks have received but have not yet credited to member banks by increasing their reserve accounts. Theoretically the two items should be equal, but in fact they are not.

Under procedures defined in Federal Reserve Regulation J, the Reserve banks increase member bank reserves (its liabilities) somewhat more rapidly than funds are actually collected from member banks (that is, deducted from reserve deposits). Thus, Deferred Availability Cash Items is always smaller than Cash Items in the Process of Collection. The difference between these two items is termed *float* and represents the amount by which reserve balances of member banks have been increased by the Federal Reserve System before collection. It constitutes Federal Reserve credit to member banks and is available as part of their reserves.

Float is affected by transfer delays between the Federal Reserve banks themselves and by administrative procedures. Mail and transportation delays can also significantly slow the collection process and result in an unintended, albeit temporary, increase in member bank reserves. The Federal Reserve is trying to speed the collection and clearing process that is under its control. In addition to building several automated check-clearing centers, it amended Regulation J in late 1972. Regulation J defines the procedures the Federal Reserve banks follow for requiring payment from banks when checks are presented for payment and for crediting checks to reserve balances although they are drawn on distant banks. The Federal Reserve amended Regulation J to require all banks using its check-clearing facilities to remit payment in immediately available funds on the day the checks are presented by the Reserve bank. Before this change was made, some banks could defer remittance and thus gain the use of reserve balances for an additional day or two. This move put all banks on an equal footing and will reduce both Cash Items and Deferred Availability. Preliminary data confirm this projection and indicate a slight reduction in float (the difference between the two).

Liabilities. The liabilities side of the Federal Reserve's consolidated balance sheet is also quite simple. The primary liability is Federal Reserve notes, which as we have seen are legal tender and account for the bulk of the supply of currency in the country. Most of the notes are in active circulation (93 percent), although some are held as cash reserves in bank vaults around the country.

The other liability of major consequence is the reserve deposits of the member banks. Along with coin and Federal Reserve notes held in their vaults, these deposits comprise the legal reserves of the banks in the Federal Reserve System, held to satisfy their legal requirements. Together, member bank reserve deposits with the Federal Reserve and Federal Reserve notes outstanding account for 88 percent of the total liabilities of the Federal Reserve banks.

The Federal Reserve also has other depositors. The federal government has an account with the Federal Reserve banks. Indeed, the management of the government's balances with the Federal Reserve and its demand accounts with more than 13,000 commercial banks raises some particular problems for the Federal Reserve, which we will have occasion to examine further in the next chapter. The other depositors are primarily nonmember banks, international organizations, other federal government agencies, and foreign central banks.

The liability item Deferred Availability Cash Items was discussed earlier. The Other Liabilities account is principally the capital account. It includes the capital paid in by member banks to acquire Federal Reserve bank stock, and the surplus item.

TWO IDENTITIES: THE MONETARY BASE EQUATION AND THE BANK RESERVE EQUATION

We are interested in the formal structure of the Federal Reserve System's consolidated balance sheet not for its own sake, but rather for what it can tell us about the mechanism by which the Federal Reserve can control the supply of money and credit.

As we have seen in earlier analysis, a balance sheet can be interpreted as an equation. Like other equations, the balance sheet identity can be manipulated algebraically to derive other analytically useful equations.

The Monetary Base Equation. We can transform the balance sheet identity into an equation that explains the monetary base in terms of other accounts in the balance sheet of the Federal Reserve System. The resulting equation is as follows:

$$\text{Monetary Base} = \text{Member Bank Reserve Deposits} + \text{Federal Reserve Notes in Circulation} + \text{Federal Reserve Notes in Banks}$$

The last two items are also identified as Federal Reserve notes outstanding. Now, using the balance sheet identity that assets = liabilities, and noting that the liabilities of the Federal Reserve include monetary liabilities (member bank reserve deposits and Federal Reserve notes outstanding) and non-

348

monetary base liabilities, by transposing we have:

		Millions of Dollars
Monetary Base =	+ Gold Certificates	9,475
	+ U.S. Government Securities[a]	70,065
	+ Discounts and Advances[a]	1,005
	+ Acceptances	82
	+ Float	3,162
	− Treasury Deposits	1,293
	− Other Deposits	906
	+ Other Assets (Net)	−734
		$80,856

[a]The figures above come from Table 16.1. Under U.S. Government Securities we have included obligations of federal agencies bought outright. The Discounts and Advances item also includes credit extended to securities dealers under repurchase agreements for U.S. government securities, federal agency securities, and acceptances, because they are functionally parallel in this analysis to discounts and advances.

The point of the equation is the demonstration that any change in the size of the monetary base must be reflected simultaneously in at least one other account in the balance sheet of the Federal Reserve. Or, turning the proposition around, a change in the magnitude of any of the Federal Reserve's asset or liability accounts, unless offset by an equal and opposite change in some other account on the right-hand side of the equation, will produce an equal change in the monetary base. Thus, an increase in any of the bank's assets—whether through the purchase of securities, the granting of an advance, or, indeed, the purchase of a new building—taken by itself, will involve an equal increase in the monetary base. Likewise, an increase in any of the bank's nonmonetary liabilities—perhaps an increase in federal government deposits or deposits of other central banks—taken alone, will involve an equal reduction in the monetary base. These principles should be familiar. They are exactly the same as those we encountered in Chapter 15 in the analysis of the expansion and contraction of the money supply by private financial institutions. The motives of the firms and the details and ultimate limits of the process may be very different. However, it is important to remember that the principles by which the central bank can create high-powered money are exactly the same as those by which commercial banks can create payments money. Thus, as when the commercial banks create money, the effective decision taken by the central bank in order to increase the money supply is a decision to increase its asset holdings.

The Bank Reserve Equation. The monetary base consists of currency in circulation and member bank reserves. However, as we have seen, a reduction in bank reserves will have a much more powerful impact on the supply of money and credit than will an equal increase in the amount of currency in circulation. Thus, the transfer of currency from bank reserve status to active circulation will actually lead to a contraction of the total money supply, other things being equal. For this reason it is frequently more important to examine changes in member bank reserves than in the monetary base per se.

By subtracting currency in circulation from each side, we can transform the monetary base equation into a bank reserve equation, as follows:

$$
\begin{array}{rl}
\text{Member Bank Reserves} = & \text{Monetary Base} - \text{Currency in Circulation} \\
(\$27,846) & (\$80,856) \qquad\quad (\$53,110) \\
& + \text{ Gold Certificate Account} \\
& + \text{ U.S. Government Securities} \\
& + \text{ Discounts and Advances} \\
& + \text{ Acceptances} \\
& + \text{ Float} \\
& - \text{ Treasury Deposits with Federal Reserve} \\
& - \text{ Other Deposits with Federal Reserve} \\
& + \text{ Other Assets (Net)} \\
& - \text{ Currency in Circulation}
\end{array}
$$

The Instruments of Monetary Control. These equations can be used to make a point of very considerable importance for our analysis. The previous chapter demonstrated the vital importance of the monetary base, particularly bank reserves, for the determination of the supply of money and credit. Control of the monetary base is an essential function of the central bank. However, the two preceding equations demonstrate that *not all of the determinants of the monetary base or of bank reserves are under the direct control of the central bank.* They are not all instruments of monetary control.

Consider first the monetary base equation above. As we will demonstrate more clearly in subsequent sections, normally the Federal Reserve can directly control only one of the terms of the equation—U.S. government securities. [The Federal Reserve controls foreign currency assets, included under Other Assets (Net), but this account is so small that its manipulation is of very limited use.]

Federal Reserve discounts and advances fall into a different category. The initiative for requesting and repaying such advances rests with the commercial member banks, not with the Federal Reserve. The same is true of the sale of acceptances to the Federal Reserve. They must be offered by the commercial banks. While the Federal Reserve can influence the level of discounts and advances outstanding through its open-market operations and the discount rate vis-à-vis other short-term interest rates, it cannot force banks to borrow at the discount window. Since it has only partial control, discounts and advances cannot be considered a positive instrument of monetary control.

Federal Reserve float is a phenomenon of the postal service and of the clearing system, as well as the crediting policy of the Federal Reserve. While the speed with which checks are cleared is influenced by the Federal Reserve, in general we must regard much of the behavior of float as beyond central bank control today. It is normally a small element in the monetary base equation, yet in the very short run it can fluctuate widely and have a significant impact on changes in the monetary base. Let us classify it as a technical factor in the equations.

The gold certificate account changes in response to external factors, such as discoveries of new gold that are sold to the U.S. Treasury, changes in gold flows resulting from the settlement of trade imbalances between the United States and other countries, and changes in the official international price of gold in terms of dollars. The Federal Reserve has no direct control over the size of this account. It is classified as an external factor.

We have grouped the other asset and liability account items together so as to consider them on a net basis. Again, with this residual we have a factor in the determination of the monetary base over which the central bank has little, if any, direct control. Some of the components in this sum involve longer-term arrangements (e.g., interest accrued on investments, or the value of bank premises), and others involve decisions made by outside agencies (e.g., the deposits of foreign central banks and others). Foreign currency assets are included here. Like float, Other Assets (Net) must be considered a *technical* or *external factor*. It cannot be considered an instrument of monetary control.

In order to summarize these propositions, we can rewrite the monetary base equation as follows:

$$
\begin{aligned}
\text{MONETARY BASE} = {}& \text{U.S. GOVERNMENT SECURITIES} \\
& \text{Federal Reserve Initiative} \\
+{}& \text{ADVANCES AND ACCEPTANCES} \\
& \text{Commercial Banks Initiative; Federal Reserve Influence} \\
-{}& \text{GOVERNMENT DEPOSITS} \\
& \text{Treasury Initiative; Federal Reserve Influence} \\
+{}& \text{GOLD CERTIFICATES} + \text{FLOAT} + \text{OTHER ASSETS (NET)} \\
& \text{Technical and External Factors}
\end{aligned}
$$

The Federal Reserve, then, does not control all of the determinants of the monetary base. Since the bank reserve equation derives from the monetary base equation, it follows that the Federal Reserve does not control all of the determinants of bank reserves. Indeed, as the bank reserve equation makes clear, the determination of member bank reserves involves an additional factor beyond the direct control of the central bank—the amount of currency in circulation. This is determined solely by members of the general public when they decide whether to hold their money balances in the form of currency or in the form of commercial bank deposits. The Federal Reserve and the commercial banks are passive agents in this process.

With this in mind, we can then rewrite the bank reserve equation, identifying the loci of control as follows:

351

MEMBER BANK RESERVES = U.S. GOVERNMENT SECURITIES
Federal Reserve Initiative
+ ADVANCES AND ACCEPTANCES
Commercial Bank Initiative; Federal Reserve Influence
− GOVERNMENT DEPOSITS
Treasury Initiative; Federal Reserve Influence
+ GOLD CERTIFICATES + FLOAT + OTHER ASSETS (NET)
Technical and External Factors
− CURRENCY IN CIRCULATION
Public Control and Initiative

Given that so many important factors in these equations are beyond the control of the central bank, can we really say—as is commonly alleged, and as we suggested at the outset of this chapter—that the Federal Reserve determines the size of the monetary base, the level of bank reserves, and hence the money supply?

Defensive vs. Dynamic Operations. The answer must be a qualified yes. It should be obvious that although some of the terms in the monetary base and bank reserve equations are beyond central bank control, this is not in itself sufficient to vitiate the proposition that the central bank can control the total amount of high-powered money outstanding and the size of bank reserves. The central bank can still achieve such control if it can anticipate and offset the effects of changes in the exogenous factors. Such operations have been called defensive operations—designed to defend a given monetary policy from extraneous influences—to distinguish them from the more familiar *dynamic operations* designed to change the money supply with a view to influencing the level of economic activity.[2] For example, the monetary effects of a reduction in float or in the deposits of other central banks could be offset by an equal increase in holdings of government securities. Or the effects on bank reserves of a decline in currency in circulation could be offset by a corresponding increase in Treasury deposits at the Federal Reserve. This suggests that in spite of its inability to control each and every item in the basic equations, the Federal Reserve can exert quite detailed control over the aggregate levels of the monetary base and bank reserves.

The Federal Reserve, primarily at the trading desk of the Federal Reserve Bank of New York, is continuously monitoring a constant flow of data. The manager of the Open Market Account must evaluate the data in light of the general directives given him by the Federal Open Market Committee. The manager knows the amount by which required reserves will change because they depend on changes in deposits of member banks two weeks previously (see Chapter 9). Estimates and projections are made regarding changes in float, currency in circulation, Treasury deposits, foreign central bank accounts, Federal Reserve foreign currency holdings, and all other factors. However, it is very difficult for the Federal Reserve to predict the exact timing and magnitude of changes in these factors. Seasonal factors are large and difficult to isolate. In addition, the behavior of financial institutions is influenced by dividend policy, tax due dates, Treasury financing, and external factors.

So the answer to the question of whether the Federal Reserve can control the monetary base and member bank reserves must be a qualified yes. It is even more difficult when the actions of the central bank indirectly induce a partially offsetting reaction in some other account; then the central bank's control is obviously weakened. Thus, for example, if the attempt to reduce the monetary base by sales of government securities produced an increase in central bank advances, the intentions of the central bank would be partially frustrated. However, this is a matter that requires further, more detailed investigation.

We can assume that under normal circumstances the Federal Reserve has sufficient power to control both the size of the monetary base and the level of bank reserves.

We now turn to a more detailed examination of the major tools of central bank control.

THE MECHANICS OF MONETARY CONTROL: OPEN-MARKET OPERATIONS

From the point of view of the implementation of monetary policy, the most important factor in the monetary base equation is the Federal Reserve's holdings of U.S. government securities. Not only is this the largest element in the equation but it also plays the central role in the implementation of changes in the supply of high-powered money.

TRANSACTIONS IN THE OPEN MARKET: THE LOCUS OF INITIATIVE

The Federal Reserve obtains government securities by purchasing outstanding issues in the government securities market. Likewise, the bank reduces its holdings either by not replacing maturing issues when they are redeemed by the government or by selling bonds out of its portfolio to other participants in the government securities market. Transactions in the government securities market—commonly called *open-market operations*—are particularly important in this respect because they permit the Federal Reserve to make frequent adjustments to the monetary base on its own initiative. As long as there is a broad, active market, with a large volume of transactions occurring every day, the Federal Reserve need only enter the market as a buyer or seller on the same basis as any other participant in order to effect the appropriate adjustments in the monetary base.

Given the importance of the government securities market in the analysis, it may be useful for you to review the discussion of the organization of financial markets presented in Chapter 3. You will recall that there is outstanding a very large stock of government bonds (about $340 billion in private hands at the end of March 1972), covering almost the entire range of possible maturities and held by a wide variety of asset holders, both in the

United States and abroad. These bonds are actively traded in the market—indeed, the secondary bond market is dominated by government bonds—through the intermediary of investment houses, which act as both dealers and brokers. The largest volume of continuous trading is in the short-term maturities, particularly Treasury bills. As with other participants in the market, when the Federal Reserve engages in open-market operations the System's account manager at the Federal Reserve Bank of New York submits bids and offers through the government security dealers.

An Example. The mechanics of the process by which the Federal Reserve can expand the monetary base by purchasing government bonds in the open market is illustrated in Example 16.1.

The monetary repercussions of the transaction follow from the method by which the Federal Reserve makes payment for the securities purchased. The Federal Reserve does not hold checkable deposits with commercial banks. Unlike a private purchaser, it does not make payment by writing checks ordering a commercial bank to make payment to the seller of the bonds. Rather, it draws a check on itself, and when that check is presented for payment by the seller's bank, an equal sum is credited to the bank's reserve deposit with the Federal Reserve. High-powered money has been created in the transaction, and the monetary base has been expanded. As we saw in the previous chapter, this lays the basis for a further (multiple) expansion of the supply of money and credit by private financial institutions.

Open-Market Operations and Interest Rates. We emphasized that in open-market operations the adjustment of the monetary base occurs at the initiative of the Federal Reserve, but we must qualify this proposition.

It is correct to say that in principle the initiative in open-market operations always rests with the central bank. However, open-market operations cannot be undertaken in any significant volume without affecting the market price and hence the yield on government bonds. Sale of bonds by the Federal Reserve will depress prices and hence raise yields. Conversely, purchase of bonds by the Federal Reserve will raise prices and hence reduce yields. Subsequent portfolio adjustments by private asset holders, coupled with the effects of changes in the supply of money and credit from private financial intermediaries induced by the change in the monetary base, will generalize the change in government bond yields to a change in the general level of interest rates. The Federal Reserve is free to take the initiative in open-market operations only if it is free to ignore the repercussions on interest rates.

There are two relevant aspects to this *caveat*. The first is that the Federal Reserve's open-market operations must not be guided by a profit motive. The Fed cannot be deterred from selling government bonds by the knowledge that in doing so it will incur substantial financial losses. Profits have no place in the policy decisions of a central bank.

Secondly, the Federal Reserve can have the freedom to initiate open-market operations only if the level of interest rates is not an independent

EXAMPLE 16.1   Open-Market Operations (Thousands of Dollars)
Purchase of government bonds in the open market
by the Federal Reserve

Stage I: The Federal Reserve purchases from government securities dealers government bonds worth $100,000. These bonds were previously held in the private sector of the economy and offered for sale to any buyer in the market. The Federal Reserve pays for the bonds with checks drawn on itself.

Federal Reserve			Securities Dealers	
Gov't. Bonds +100	Checks Outst. +100		Federal Reserve Checks +100	
			Gov't. Bonds −100	

Stage II: The government securities dealers deposit the checks in their accounts with commercial banks.

Securities Dealers		Commercial Banks	
Federal Reserve Checks −100		Federal Reserve Checks +100	Deposits +100
Bank Deposits +100			

Stage III: The outstanding Federal Reserve checks are cleared and collected, and the $100,000 is credited to commercial bank reserve deposits with the Federal Reserve.

Federal Reserve		Commercial Banks	
	Checks Outst. −100	Federal Reserve Checks −100	
	Deposits of Banks +100	Cash Reserves +100	

Net Change

Federal Reserve		Securities Dealers		Commercial Banks	
Gov't. Bonds +100	Deposits of Banks +100	Gov't. Bonds −100	Bank Deposits +100	Cash Reserves +100	Deposits +100

Notes:
1.   There has been no change in the society's wealth. The private sector of the economy has taken non-interest-bearing claims on the government in exchange for interest-bearing claims.
2.   The securities dealers will use their new bank deposits to purchase other securities (or to pay off other debts). The new deposits will go into general circulation.
3.   The deposit liabilities and the cash reserves of the commercial banks have increased by the same amount. The commercial banks will therefore have excess cash reserves and will further expand the supply of money and credit.
4.   The overall effects would have been the same if the Federal Reserve had purchased the bonds from members of the general public (other than the security dealers) or from commercial banks.

objective of government policy. Indeed, under the extreme circumstances in which the level of interest rates—or perhaps more precisely, the level of yields on government bonds—is pegged as a matter of government policy, the Federal Reserve may have to assume a completely passive attitude in open-market operations. It will have to respond to every initiative emanating from the market, buying bonds whenever private selling pressures would otherwise depress prices and raise yields. The central bank's open-market operations then become the vehicle for implementing a particular interest rate policy, and the size of the monetary base adjusts to whatever level is consistent with the chosen level of interest rates. (This policy was pursued during and after World War II. See Chapter 12.) The level of interest rates and the size of the monetary base cannot be chosen independently of each other.

THE MECHANICS OF MONETARY CONTROL: CENTRAL BANK ADVANCES

Central bank advances are an enigma. Quantitatively, they appear to be of minor importance in contemporary monetary systems. Even at times of peak central bank lending, advances account for only a minor fraction of total bank reserves, let alone the monetary base. Yet such advances have been the subject of a vigorous controversy among monetary economists in recent years. Defenders of the existing mechanisms argue that they perform a vital auxiliary function in the process of monetary control. They ameliorate the difficult situations created for individual banks from time to time, thus permitting more active pursuit of monetary controls. Some critics argue, by contrast, that the provision of central bank credit in this fashion weakens the central bank's control of the monetary base and hence that central bank lending ought to be abolished, or at least the arrangements for it significantly transformed. At the opposite extreme is a group of critics who find fault with the relegation of advances to an auxiliary role in monetary control. They argue that the mechanism for such advances ought to be rehabilitated to its classical position as the basic instrument of monetary policy.

Given the relatively small sums of money involved, the vehemence of the controversy surrounding this aspect of central banking is perhaps surprising. Our task in this section involves the exploration not only of how the mechanism works today but also of the issues underlying the controversy. For this purpose we must consider the role of central bank advances in classical theories of central banking, and the operations of the "discount window" of the Federal Reserve banks. But first we must review the relationship between central bank advances and the monetary base.

ADVANCES AND THE MONETARY BASE

Forms of Advances. For this discussion, there are two types of advances: rediscounts and loans secured by appropriate collateral. In addition, we include purchase and resale agreements because in this analysis they function like advances.

Rediscounting of commercial paper is the classic form of central bank advance. It involves purchase from a bank of the promissory notes of the bank's commercial customers. These notes have been endorsed by the bank so that they are simultaneously the liability of the bank and of the commercial customer. The notes are purchased by the central bank at a posted rate of discount from their face value. Such advances are rediscounts because the central bank is discounting the notes of a third party—notes that the commercial bank itself has previously "discounted." In the United States all central bank advances (except purchase and resale agreements) have come to be called *discounts*, the interest rate for all advances the *discount rate*, and the mechanism for such advances the *discount window*.

In contrast to rediscounts, direct loans by the central bank involve only the promissory note of the bank that is borrowing. However, the bank must normally pledge acceptable assets as security for the loan. The most common type of collateral is government bonds, although some central banks will accept other assets.

The *purchase and resale agreement* is the normal method by which a central bank makes advances to government security dealers. The central bank purchases securities from the dealer, but at the time of the purchase the dealer signs an agreement to repurchase the securities from the central bank on a particular date and at a specified price. The difference between the buying and selling prices determines the rate of interest on such advances. Short-term government bills are the most common type of security used in these arrangements, although some purchase and resale agreements are also made with bankers' acceptances.

Monetary Effects. As the monetary base equation makes clear, the extension of central bank advances expands the monetary base, and the repayment of these advances contracts it. The process is illustrated in more detail in Example 16.2. Central bank advances appear to be no different from open-market operations. The extension of advances has the same effects as the purchase of government bonds (or the acquisition of any asset), and the repayment of advances has the same effect as the sale of bonds.

Locus of Initiative. However, there are important qualitative differences. Unlike open-market operations, central bank advances involve direct, face-to-face negotiations between borrower and lender. They are not impersonal transactions in the securities of a third party that are traded actively in the open market.

The locus of initiative for the two types of central bank operations is correspondingly different. Open-market operations are normally entirely at the initiative of the central bank. Advances are at the initiative of the banks and securities dealers. The central bank establishes the line of credit available to each borrower, sets the conditions for advances, and posts the interest rates at which advances will be made. While it can make the terms for advances more or less favorable, for example by lowering or raising the relevant interest rates, the central bank must then sit back and await the decisions of possible borrowers. It can offer incentives but cannot initiate

EXAMPLE 16.2   Central Bank Advances (Thousands of Dollars)
A purchase and resale agreement between the Federal Reserve
and government securities dealers

Stage I: A government securities dealer enters into a purchase and resale agreement with the Federal Reserve. The Federal Reserve purchases $100,000 worth of government bills from the dealer, and the dealer simultaneously signs an agreement to repurchase the securities from the Federal Reserve in five days. The Federal Reserve pays for the securities with a check drawn on itself.

In the following accounts, in order to minimize complications, we treat this transaction as though it were a direct advance from the Federal Reserve to the dealer—which in effect it is.

Federal Reserve			Securities Dealer	
Advances +100	Checks		Federal Reserve	Advances from
	Outst. +100		Checks +100	Federal Reserve +100

Stage II: The dealer deposits the check with his bank.

Securities Dealer			Commercial Bank	
Federal Reserve			Federal Reserve	Deposits +100
Check −100			Checks +100	
Bank				
Deposits +100				

Stage III: The outstanding Federal Reserve check is cleared and collected, and the $100,000 is credited to commercial banks' cash reserves.

Federal Reserve		Commercial Bank	
	Checks	Federal Reserve	
	Outst. −100	Checks −100	
	Reserve	Cash	
	Deposits +100	Reserves +100	

Net Change

Federal Reserve			Securities Dealers	
Advances +100	Deposits of		Bank	Advances from
	Banks +100		Deposits +100	Federal Reserve +100

Commercial Banks	
Cash	Deposits +100
Reserves +100	

Notes:
1.   There has been a direct increase in the money supply of $100,000. It is now in the hands of the securities dealers, but they will use it to pay off other (private) debts or to purchase securities. The money will go into general circulation.
2.   The deposit liabilities and the cash reserves of the commercial banks have increased by the same amount. The banks now have excess cash reserves, which provide the base for a further expansion of the supply of money and credit.
3.   While the initial impact would have been different, the overall effect would have been the same if the Federal Reserve had made the advances directly to the commercial banks.
4.   Repayment: When the advance is repaid (i.e., the securities repurchased), exactly the opposite set of transactions will occur. The dealer will pay by check. When the check is cleared and collected, commercial bank reserves will be reduced, and credit contraction should ensue. You should note that, because of the interest charges involved, a larger sum will be repaid than was lent.

the advances that will change the quantity of high-powered money outstanding.

In the eyes of most contemporary economists, monetary policy is quantitative: It involves direct manipulation of the size of the monetary base and hence the money supply. Although central bank advances affect the size of the monetary base, since they cannot be sensitively adjusted at the initiative of the central bank they are not widely considered an effective positive instrument of monetary control. Rather, they are assigned a minor supporting role in monetary control.

This was not always the case. In one theory of central banking—we can call it the classical theory—the roles of the discount mechanism and open-market operations are reversed, with the former dominating and the latter assuming the supporting role.

THE ROLE OF CENTRAL BANK ADVANCES: CLASSICAL THEORY

The central bank of classical theory did not have the same modern quantitative preoccupation. It was not thought of primarily as an institution engaged in continuous, direct, and detailed regulation of the size and growth of the money supply. However, it would be a mistake to think that classical theory did not call for active intervention on the part of the central bank to attempt to direct financial developments. It was the method of intervention that was markedly different. The primary instrument of central bank intervention was the discount rate—the interest rate applicable to central bank advances. Open-market operations were considered a method that might be used from time to time to make an increase in the discount rate "effective."

Role of the Discount Rate. It was assumed that the banking system would normally be in debt to the central bank and that each commercial bank would regularly use its line of credit with the central bank in the management of its liquid asset position. It would borrow to obtain more cash, and repay debt as it became more liquid. Central bank credit would be sufficiently important to the banking system so that the banks would be highly sensitive to any change in the discount rate. A rise in the rate would lead to a reduction in commercial bank borrowing and therefore in total reserves. This, in turn, would cause a reduction in the total supply of money and credit, and hence a rise in market interest rates. A reduction in the rate would presumably have the opposite effect.

This meant that the discount rate was the pivotal rate in the money market. Indeed, because of the expectations it would create, a change in the discount rate could be expected to have direct repercussions on all other interest rates, even before true credit restraint set in.

Role of Open-Market Operations. To the extent that open-market operations had any function in this system of monetary control, it was in support of the discount mechanism. If banks were very liquid, the money market might not respond sensitively to a rise in the discount rate. In such circumstances, open-market operations might be used to "force the market into the bank." That is, by selling securities the central bank could absorb cash, forcing the banks to seek central bank advances and thus driving the market interest rates up with the discount rate.

THE ROLE OF THE DISCOUNT MECHANISM IN AMERICAN EXPERIENCE

These classical principles of central banking were largely developed in England and reflected practices evolved by the Bank of England—in many ways the quintessential central bank. In the United States, however, central banking developed along somewhat different lines.

From Automatic Credit to Credit for Unusual Circumstances. The Federal Reserve System was established initially on what might be construed as a version of classical principles. The original legislation envisioned that each Federal Reserve bank would automatically extend credit to its member banks on the security of promissory notes of the member bank's commercial customers. In this way the supply of Federal Reserve credit would always meet the "legitimate demands of business and commerce"—an interesting extension of the commercial loan theory to central banking. The eligible or commercial paper (short-term bills of exchange drawn for agricultural, industrial, or commercial purposes) was rediscounted by the Reserve banks at the discount rate. This rate was established by each Reserve bank with agreement from the Federal Reserve Board and was changed by the Reserve banks from time to time. The rate was to be set "with a view to accommodating commerce and business."

In the 1920s some experiments were conducted with the use of the discount rate as a regulating device, more or less in accordance with classical principles. Gradually, however, reliance came to be placed on open-market operations. With this change in emphasis, a new policy emerged with respect to the discount window. Continuous borrowing by member banks was discouraged, with the discount window to be used for "seasonal and temporary requirements of members" and particularly to meet "unusual circumstances," such as those caused by "adverse economic circumstances in their localities and among their customers."

In the early 1920s over 70 percent of the member banks had occasion to borrow from the reserve banks each year. The importance of the discount window as a source of bank reserves declined somewhat in the mid-1920s, but nonetheless extensive use of the facility continued until the early 1930s. From 1922 to 1929, borrowings averaged 30 percent of total reserves. Following the banking crisis and major revisions in the legislation governing the operations of the Federal Reserve System in the early 1930s, reliance on the discount window by member banks declined sharply.[3]

360

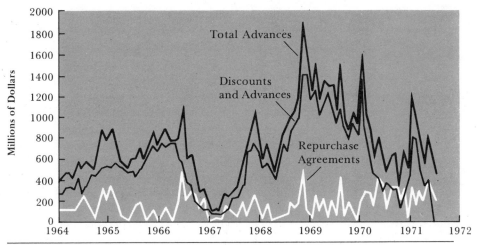

Figure 16.1 **Federal Reserve Advances to Member Banks and Security Dealers, 1964–1971**
SOURCE: Federal Reserve *Bulletin*, various issues.

From 1934 to 1942, sizable gold inflows buoyed bank reserves. At the same time, commercial banks wanted to hold large amounts of idle reserve balances. From 1942 until 1951, the Federal Reserve kept the member banks flush with reserves in order to assist Treasury war-financing programs. The Federal Reserve stood ready to purchase any amount of U.S. government securities at specified prices, so there was little need to use the discount window to adjust liquidity positions.

The volume of discounts remained insignificant until the early 1950s, by which time a new concept of the role of the discount window in policy formation was firmly established. With the Treasury-Federal Reserve Accord in 1951 (see Chapter 12), there was a need to restore the discount process as an adjustment mechanism to assist banks and the banking system when faced with temporary liquidity difficulties. The principles underlying access to the discount window have not changed significantly from those evolved in the 1920s and 1930s, yet a new controversy has developed. What is the debate all about?

Cyclical Behavior of Advances. The basic issues derive from the fact that Federal Reserve advances undergo systematic and relatively wide fluctuations. Periods of substantial increases in advances tend to be times when the Federal Reserve is pursuing a restrictive monetary policy, using the instruments of monetary control to restrict the growth of the monetary base relative to rising demands for money and credit (often with limited success). Periods of major declines in advances tend to be times when the Federal Reserve is pursuing an easier monetary policy, using the instruments of monetary control to actively expand the monetary base.

The behavior of Federal Reserve advances in recent years is shown in

Figure 16.1, including separate data on the two components, Discounts and Advances and Purchase and Resale Agreements. The cyclical behavior is obvious in this example, as is the fact that the fluctuations in the total are dominated by changes in advances to member banks, or Discounts and Advances. Advances to securities dealers in the form of purchase and resale agreements are relatively much less significant.

The important point is that the fluctuations in advances are closely related to changes in Federal Reserve monetary policies and appear to run counter to the intended actions of the Fed. As we have seen, an increase in central bank advances adds to the monetary base, whereas a reduction in such advances decreases the monetary base. For this reason, then, monetary policy and the discount window seem to work in opposition to each other. Critics argue that the discount window builds in "slippage," diminishing the rapidity with which the Federal Reserve can contract the monetary base.

Determinants of Central Bank Advances. Before examining the cyclical pattern of central bank advances, we must know why member banks seek loans from their Federal Reserve bank. What factors influence the magnitude of member bank borrowings?

To a banker, borrowing from the central bank is one technique of adjusting to a deficiency in his cash reserve position. Faced with legal minimum cash reserve ratios, prudent banking practice calls for immediate measures to correct any deficiency. In doing so, the banker is faced with several options. For example, he may call outstanding call loans; sell short-term liquid assets in the money market; borrow reserves from other banks through the federal funds market or, on occasion, through the Eurodollar market; compete vigorously for large blocks of corporate cash balances through the issuance of negotiable certificates of deposit; or borrow from his Federal Reserve bank. Various considerations will affect the choice, including the size of the bank (a small country bank is unlikely to enter the certificate of deposit, Eurodollar, or federal funds markets), the size and expected duration of the reserve deficiency, and the size of the bank's liquid asset holdings. One of the basic considerations is the relative cost of the alternative adjustment techniques. In the case of borrowing, the obvious cost is the interest that must be paid. In the case of selling short-term liquid assets, it is the opportunity cost of interest forgone. Borrowing from the Federal Reserve System should then be affected by the relationship between the discount rate and other money market interest rates.

Several studies have demonstrated that the differential between the discount rate and money market rates is an important determinant of member bank borrowing from the Federal Reserve System,[4] but how does this help explain the cyclical behavior of Federal Reserve advances and the opposition of open-market and discount window operations?

Determinants of the Cyclical Pattern of Advances. During a period of credit restraint, several forces will bear upon the commercial banking system

362

simultaneously. In general, the demand for loans will be strong and expanding rapidly, although this may not be true of all banks. The central bank will resist the credit and monetary expansion implicit in the rising loan demand by trying to restrict the monetary base. It should be noted that this need not imply a contraction of the monetary base. It may simply mean a lower rate of increase than that implicit in the expansion of economic activity. Our analysis in Chapter 15 demonstrated that restricted expansion of the monetary base means restricted expansion of total deposits in the banking system. As a result, collectively (there may be many individual exceptions) the banks will find increasing loan demand rapidly outrunning the increase in their resources.

The banks may respond to this situation in two ways. On the one hand, they may compete vigorously with each other for the available supply of deposits, particularly in the market for negotiable certificates of deposit. On the other hand, they may rearrange their asset portfolios, disposing of short-term liquid assets in the money market (and probably also some longer-term marketable bonds) in order to make room for additional loans. The liquidity of the banks' asset portfolios will be reduced, bond prices will be depressed, and, correspondingly, market interest rates will be bid up.

Cost Considerations. The discount rate is an administratively determined price. It is established by each of the 12 Federal Reserve banks with the concurrence and often at the suggestion of the Board of Governors. It is changed rather infrequently (rarely more than two or three times a year, although in 1971 it was changed six times, in 1972 not at all, and in 1973 almost a dozen). The changes that occur are usually rather large—that is, intervals of one-fourth or one-half of a percentage point. When the rate is changed, it of course affects the cost of borrowing from the Federal Reserve, but it also has an "announcement effect." Changes in the discount rate are viewed by the financial community at large as significant indicators of the Federal Reserve's appraisal of both the current credit conditions and the direction the Federal Reserve intends to move to influence future credit conditions. This announcement effect tends to be self-fulfilling and also triggers changes in the other free-market rates.

In between the discretionary changes in the discount rate, a gap or spread frequently widens between the discount rate and other continually adjusting, competitive money market rates. Figure 16.2 illustrates the more recent pattern beween the discount rate and money market rates. As you can see, the discount rate gives the appearance of a runner who makes occasional spurts to the fore but generally lags the pack.

In a period of generally rising interest rates this creates an obvious inducement for member banks to borrow from their Federal Reserve banks at the lower discount rate. For this reason alone, central bank advances can be expected to increase in periods of monetary restraint. In addition, the incidence of credit restraint among banks may be very uneven. Some banks

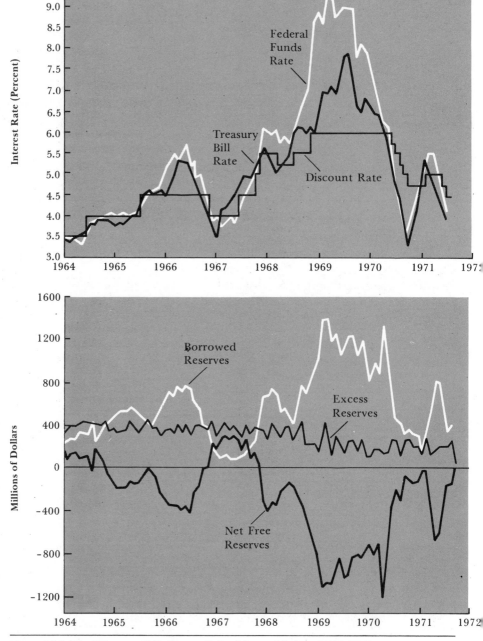

Figure 16.2 **The Discount Window and the Money Market, 1964–1971**
SOURCE: Federal Reserve *Bulletin*, various issues.

may experience severe cash drains and, given their reduced holdings of liquid assets, may find that they cannot cope with their cash deficiencies except by borrowing from their Federal Reserve banks. Such borrowing by certain member banks would occur even if the discount rate were continuously kept equal to short-term money market rates such as the Treasury bill rate.

In a period of monetary restraint more banks will be borrowing larger sums for longer periods. Federal Reserve advances will increase, providing additional high-powered money and thus offsetting at least some of the intended restriction of the monetary base.

Some such relationship seems fairly obvious in Figure 16.2, particularly if you focus attention on the gap between the federal funds rate and the discount rate of the Federal Reserve Bank of New York (the federal funds rate is a crucial money rate, and the New York discount rate can be taken as representative of the rates of all 12 Federal Reserve banks). As the whole level of interest rates increased from 1962 to 1969, the level of borrowing from Federal Reserve banks also increased. Particularly sharp increases in Federal Reserve advances occurred in 1966, 1968, and 1969, when the federal funds rate rose considerably above the discount rate. When the pressure on the federal funds market relaxed, the level of borrowing also fell off sharply. Since these were periods of restrictive monetary policy, this seems to provide evidence in support of the critics of the discount mechanism.

It should be remembered, however, that open-market operations are usually conducted with the intention of influencing the spread between the discount rate and the sensitive federal funds rate.

The "Free Reserve" Doctrine. The implication that the operations of the discount window partially frustrate the operations of monetary policy are vehemently denied by the Federal Reserve System and by many monetary economists.

One of the arguments advanced is that the discount window is an essential safety valve. By providing a reliable emergency source of funds, it cushions the impact of monetary restraint on individual banks that might otherwise be very adversely affected. It is argued that this permits the Federal Reserve System to ignore some of the harsher individual consequences of its monetary actions and to pursue a more vigorous policy than it would otherwise be able to do.

Proponents of this view argue that the purpose of monetary policy is to affect the cost and availability of credit, and particularly the availability of loans from commercial banks. Some argue that willingness of banks to extend new credit can be gauged by the level of *free reserves* in the banking system. A formal definition of free reserves is:

$$\text{Free Reserves} = \text{Excess Reserves} - \text{Borrowed Reserves}$$

Excess reserves are cash reserves over and above those required by law, and borrowed reserves are the outstanding advances from the Federal Reserve

System. When excess reserves of member banks exceed the aggregate borrowings from the Federal Reserve System, free reserves are positive. Conversely, when borrowings exceed aggregate excess reserves, free reserves are negative.

Although many different factors influence the level of free reserves at any one time, studies show that much of the variance in the level of free reserves results from changes in the level of indebtedness to the Federal Reserve System rather than from changes in the level of excess reserves (excess reserves tend to be relatively stable over time). It is argued that when banks have large amounts of free reserves they have excess cash and are not heavily in debt to the Federal Reserve System. Because they are not worried about a shortage of cash or under pressure to repay outstanding advances, it is assumed that they may be willing to extend more credit. By contrast, the argument continues, when free reserves are small, and particularly when they are negative (i.e., borrowings exceed cash reserves), the banks are under substantial pressure. They have pared down their cash somewhat and are heavily in debt. They must give top priority to repaying Federal Reserve advances and rebuilding their cash positions and hence are reluctant to extend more credit. In this way, it is argued, changes in the level of free reserves over time are a sensitive indicator of the availability of credit from the banking system and hence a sensitive indicator of the degree of tightness of monetary policy.

Figure 16.2 suggests that under relatively "easy" monetary conditions banks will have some excess cash reserves—perhaps $400 million to $500 million, spread across all 6000 member banks. At the same time, member bank indebtedness to the Federal Reserve System would normally amount to about $100 million, leaving net free reserves of $300 million to $400 million. Under tight money conditions the banks will reduce their excess cash reserves, but only slightly, and will borrow heavily from the Federal Reserve banks. Free reserves will become negative. Thus, in early 1968, a period of relatively tight monetary conditions, the free reserves of member banks amounted to –$400 million. In the extreme tightness of mid-1969 they fell to –$1 billion!

It is wrong, however, to use the level of free reserves as an exact indicator of the degree of tightness or ease in the monetary system. Free reserves may fluctuate widely within a very short period because of fluctuations in other factors that also influence the level of free reserves. These factors include Federal Reserve open-market operations, adjustments in commercial banks' investment portfolios and in their reserve positions, changes in bank deposits that affect the level of required reserves that banks must hold, and changes in bank lendings. These factors plus technical factors like changes in float affect free reserves.

Furthermore, the same level of free reserves may mean different things at different times. At one time, free reserves may only result in additional lending capacity being readily available at country banks while reserve city banks are heavily in debt to the Federal Reserve System. This condition would probably not result in rapid increases in system-wide bank lending. At another time, the same level of free reserves may be the result of more evenly distributed excess reserves between country banks and reserve city banks. This would provide a hospitable environment for a dramatic increase in bank credit within the entire banking system. Because of these many factors, critics of the free-reserve doctrine conclude that anyone relying solely on free reserves as the indicator of credit ease or restraint will be misled as to the actual intent of monetary policy on the one hand and the degree of ease or restraint in the banking system on the other.

There is another, quite different, point with regard to reserves. It is asserted that reserves that banks have borrowed from the Federal Reserve System are not really the same thing as those that the banks own outright. This follows because bankers are allegedly reluctant to be in debt to any other bank, including the central bank. Tradition has it that such indebtedness is a sign of poor bank management.

Like many similar traditions, the precise meaning of this is difficult to define. Bankers certainly do borrow from the central bank and from other banks when there is some advantage in doing so. However, the Federal Reserve System's regulations emphasize that borrowing is a "privilege" of membership in the Federal Reserve System, not a "right." Members may borrow only on a short-term basis and for "appropriate" purposes. Borrowing from the Federal Reserve is not to be a continuing source of funds to finance bank operations, and continuous or frequent borrowing is a matter for official concern and scrutiny. (Notice how radically different this approach is from the classical theory we discussed earlier.) Under these circumstances, it is argued, banks that are in debt to the Federal Reserve System will feel themselves under continuous pressure to restrict credit in order to repay their debt and to make a more fundamental adjustment in their deposit situation. The object of policy will be achieved, albeit gradually rather than abruptly. Bank borrowing from the Federal Reserve System does not offset the restrictive effects of open-market operations. It simply alters the way in which such effects are transmitted to the economy.

The discount mechanism has been subject to much criticism and examination by economists. Some of the critics of the discount window see it as building unnecessary and undesirable slippage into the execution of monetary restraint. Most acknowledge the need to provide temporary credit accommodation to the individual bank that may face liquidity difficulties, but critics see the discount window as extending that privilege to the system as a whole rather than selectively to specific banks. Others attack the method of determining the discount rate, the relatively infrequent changes, and the arbitrary announcement effects that accompany changes in the rate. There is a group of economists that argue for a "floating" discount rate. What, in brief, are the relative merits of a floating discount rate?

The Floating Discount Rate. A floating discount rate is one tied to free-market rates on short-term instruments. It could be pegged to be consistently less than, equal to, or more than a given money market instrument rate. If consistently higher than free money market rates, the discount rate would be a true penalty rate for being deficient in reserves. Such a penalty rate would deliberately avoid creating an incentive to borrow from the Federal Reserve, without at the same time imposing a serious burden on banks or dealers who were forced by circumstances to borrow. It would reinforce the Federal Reserve's philosophy of discouraging regular or continuous borrowing.

A floating discount rate would diminish the announcement effect. While movements in the floating discount rate would not be predictable from week to week, its relationship to certain other rates would be consistent and predictable. At present, a change in the discretionary discount rate is a deliberate, calculated act of intervention on the part of the central bank, dramatized through a public announcement. Invariably a change stimulates a spate of speculation in the financial papers. What does the rise in the discount rate mean? Does the central bank see storm clouds on the economic horizon? Or is it really an indication of continued economic expansion? Is the central bank simply adjusting to rising interest rates in the market? Or is it attempting to push the market to higher levels of interest rates? Is the country in for a period of tighter money and credit? The central bank normally finds it necessary to dispel uncertainty through a public statement of the purpose of the move (which sometimes provokes further speculation as the financial editors attempt to read between the lines to discover what the Federal Reserve "really" intends). By itself, the discount rate is an inefficient device for communicating complex information.

Paradoxically, critics of a floating discount rate attack its lack of announcement effect as its major disadvantage. A discretionary discount rate can be used to provide guidance to participants in the money market as to the level of short-term interest rates the central bank thinks is appropriate under the circumstances. By eliminating uncertainty about the central bank's intentions in this regard, the discount rate provides a clear focus for participants in the market without tying the market rigidly to any particular level or structure of rates. A discretionary rate is insulated from some of the shocks that free money market rates reflect that could be disruptive to some desired pattern of interest rates. Often the announcement effect of a change in the discount rate is an important means of signaling the central bank's concerns and intentions to our international partners.

CENTRAL BANK ADVANCES: OVERVIEW

Central bank advances should not be thought of as a positive instrument for monetary control. They provide a safety valve for individual member banks and securities dealers faced with severe but temporary cash deficiencies. Under some circumstances, however, these advances can have a perverse effect on the total supply of bank reserves in terms of the objectives of monetary policy. While the free-reserve doctrine holds that these fluctuations are simply part of the complex mechanism by which monetary policy is transmitted to the economy, many economists argue that they weaken the force of monetary policy and that for this reason the discount mechanism ought to be abolished. As long as the discount mechanism exists, however, a careful and flexible discount rate policy must be followed. This does not preclude the use of the discount rate as a money market signal, but it does suggest that the rate should be adjusted more frequently to introduce more flexibility and support of open-market operations.

SUMMARY

In the previous chapter we took the quantity of high-powered money as given. In this chapter we have illustrated the elements that influence and determine the quantity of high-powered money, or what is also called the monetary base. We have begun to examine the extent of the Federal Reserve's control over each of those elements. It may surprise some to find that the Federal Reserve has primary control and initiative over only one of the components that affect the level of member bank reserves.

In examining the Federal Reserve's balance sheet, we see that the asset side is dominated by holdings of U.S. government and federal agency securities. It is by changing its holdings of these securities that the Federal Reserve can take the initiative and manipulate the major element in the member bank reserve equation. Often the Fed must use its open-market operations defensively to offset changes in the other elements that influence member bank reserves—the elements it does not directly control. At other times it uses open-market operations dynamically to initiate a change in money and credit conditions that it is hoped will have the desired effect on the economy.

Today the primary instrument of monetary control is open-market operations. They are conducted continuously, bringing flexibility to monetary policy. Open-market operations are initiated by the Federal Reserve and affect member banks with a minimum lag.

The reliance on open-market operations represents a shift from classical central bank theory, in which the primary instrument of credit influence was the discount mechanism. Today, the discount window plays a secondary role in the implementation of monetary policy. Even in this secondary role, however, the discount mechanism has been the subject of much study and criticism. Many critics see it working to delay the effects of restrictive monetary policy by providing an "escape hatch" for banks that feel the pinch of tightening credit conditions. Statistical evidence shows that in recent times advances to member banks have increased when the monetary authorities were pursuing tight money policy. The Federal Reserve rejects this criticism of the discount window and stresses that advances through the discount window provide a "safety valve" for individual banks in need of temporary credit accommodation during the transition to restrictive monetary conditions.

NOTES

1. This statement requires qualification. Remember that we are ignoring coin in circulation and in bank vaults, which is part of the monetary base but not a liability of the Federal Reserve. However, this is a relatively small component of the monetary base ($7.8 billion, or 12 percent, on February 29, 1972). More important, since the volume of coin in circulation can be expected to adjust fairly systematically to the amount of other money in circulation, its existence as part of the monetary base does not impair the Federal Reserve's control over the monetary base.

2. The terminology is that of Robert Roosa, who was for many years an important officer of the Federal Reserve Bank of New York. His pamphlet *Federal Reserve Operations in the Money and Government Securities Markets* (New York: Federal Reserve Bank of New York, 1956) is one of the best available discussions of the inner workings of a central bank. As Roosa makes clear, most of the day-to-day operations of such a bank are defensive in nature.

3. Important among the changes were a broadening of the lending authority of the Federal Reserve banks (by eliminating the restrictive link to "eligible" commercial paper), the formalization of the institution of the open-market committee, and the introduction of variable cash reserve requirements. A brief history of discount window policy in the United States is contained in B. Shull, *Reappraisal of the Federal Reserve Discount Mechanism: Report on Research Undertaken in Connection with a System Study* (Washington, D.C.: Board of Governors of the Federal Reserve System, 1968).

4. Perhaps the best-known study is A. J. Meigs, *Free Reserves and the Money Supply* (Chicago: University of Chicago Press, 1962). Other studies are briefly reviewed in D. M. Jones, *A Review of Recent Academic Literature on the Discount Mechanism* (Washington, D.C.: Board of Governors of the Federal Reserve System, 1968), pp. 13–17.

CONTROL OF THE MONEY SUPPLY

Part 3: The Federal Reserve (Auxiliary Instruments)

While discount rate policy is an important dimension of central banking, in the modern context the primary instrument of monetary control is unquestionably open-market operations. Appropriate discount rate policy reinforces open-market operations; it does not supplant them. However, there are at least two other potential instruments of monetary control that can be used instead of or in conjunction with open-market operations. These are variations in the federal government's general account, which is held by the Federal Reserve banks, and variations in legal reserve requirements. Since they have restricted usability, we refer to them as auxiliary instruments.

GOVERNMENT DEPOSITS

The federal government uses the Federal Reserve banks as its fiscal agent and banker. Disbursements to the public for goods and services acquired, transfer payments, and redemption of U.S. government securities are made by the Treasury, drawing checks on its accounts with the 12 Federal Reserve banks. At any one time, however, the bulk of the federal government's cash balances rests in demand deposits with most of the nation's commercial banks, divided among them on the basis of a weighted formula by asset size.

371

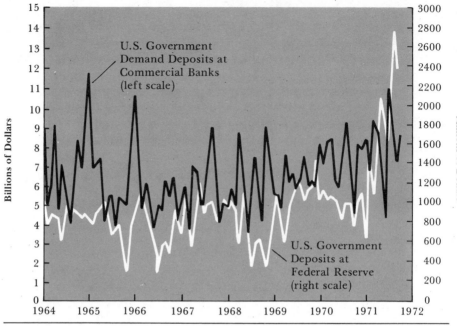

Figure 17.1 U.S. Government Deposits at Commercial Banks and Federal Reserve Banks, 1964–1971
SOURCE: Federal Reserve *Bulletin*, various issues.

In March 1972, for example, the U.S. government held $1.4 billion in its accounts with the Federal Reserve banks and $8.7 billion in demand deposits with commercial banks.

THE MANAGEMENT OF GOVERNMENT CASH

The division of the federal government's cash balances between the Federal Reserve and the commercial banks is a matter of deliberate Treasury policy. Because government receipts and expenditures do not balance during discrete periods of time, there are wide fluctuations in government balances from month to month. If the federal government held all of its cash balances with the Federal Reserve, these changes in government deposit balances would have a severe and undesirable impact on the monetary base.

Volatility of Government Deposits. Let us examine the volatility of government cash balances in order to understand the magnitude of the problem. Figure 17.1 illustrates the changes that have occurred in government cash balances held at the Federal Reserve banks and with commercial banks from 1964 to 1971. During the period covered, government deposits with commercial banks underwent wide swings. A change of $2 billion within a month was not unusual. There is also evidence of a strong seasonal movement in the balances with commercial banks, reflecting systematic differences

372

in the timing of tax collections and government expenditures. There are also irregular influences coinciding with the issuance and retirement of government securities.

Government Deposits and the Monetary Base. If the government held all of its cash balances at the Federal Reserve, the volatility indicated in Figure 17.1 would be concentrated there and would be troublesome for monetary management. Any change in government deposits at the Federal Reserve banks has an equal and opposite effect on the monetary base. An increase in government deposits at the Federal Reserve tends to reduce the monetary base by an equal amount; a reduction in these deposits tends to increase the monetary base. (Example 17.1 illustrates the effects on the monetary base of changes in federal government cash balances.) Since the monthly changes in government cash balances fluctuate widely, the Federal Reserve would have to engage in massive open-market operations just to offset the monetary repercussions of government transactions. Clearly, we are not talking about a minor complication.

The Two-Deposit Policy. These complications can be minimized (but not entirely avoided) by the simple expedient of a two-deposit policy. At present the federal government deposits its receipts from tax payments and sales of U.S. government securities to the public in its accounts with commercial banks (Example 17.1, Case 2). As a result, only the ownership of commercial bank deposits is transfered, without affecting the monetary base. All government expenditures are made out of the accounts with the Federal Reserve banks (Example 17.1, Case 3). Normally this would have an expansionary effect on the monetary base, since the funds would wind up as increases in bank deposits and reserves. However, by keeping the bulk of its cash balances with commercial banks and transfering funds to the general account with the Federal Reserve only as needed for expenditures (Example 17.1, Case 4), the government minimizes the repercussions of its expenditures on the monetary base.

GOVERNMENT DEPOSITS AS A POLICY INSTRUMENT

There is good reason, then, for the government to maintain bank accounts at both the Federal Reserve and commercial banks. The existence of two sets of accounts gives the Treasury a potentially powerful instrument for monetary control. The size of the monetary base can be adjusted just as effectively by a transfer of funds between the government's accounts with commercial banks and the Federal Reserve as it can by open-market operations. Indeed, the deposit transfer is a simpler and more direct method of changing bank reserves. In addition, it has no direct effect on short-term interest rates. However, it would be an error to assume that use of this tool by the government does not have any repercussions on short-term interest rates. If, to reduce the size of the monetary base, the government transferred cash balances held with commercial banks to the Federal Reserve banks, commercial banks would find their portfolios in disequilibrium. In order to acquire needed liquidity and additional reserves, the banks would sell short-term securities and borrow federal funds, driving up short-term interest rates.

Despite the potential of this tool, there is little evidence of vigorous or prolonged use of shifting government cash balances for monetary management. Normally the Treasury manages its cash balances in such a way as to minimize the inherent effects its receipts have on the monetary base.

At times the Treasury has pursued active manipulation of its cash balances to affect the monetary base. A recent example of Treasury use of its accounts to deliberately influence credit conditions occurred in 1972. A change in personal income tax withholding regulations resulted in overwithholding of personal income taxes in the first half of 1972. The Treasury's balances with commercial banks were substantially increased. The Treasury began to shift its balances between commercial banks and reserve banks to bring about desired changes in the monetary base. The Federal Reserve "all but shelved open-market operations" during the period.[1]

While the Treasury and the Federal Reserve generally cooperate in the implementation of monetary policy, it is unusual for the Treasury to be the primary agent. Continued reliance on the Treasury's ability to shift balances as a primary tool of monetary policy is unlikely. Long-term use of this instrument would require a substantial margin of cash in the hands of the Treasury in excess of its spending requirements. While such surpluses can be engineered through excess taxation or borrowing, this technique has significant effects on public spending patterns and would normally have little to commend it over direct open-market operations by the central bank.

VARIABLE RESERVE REQUIREMENTS

With the exception of some aspects of discount rate policy, the techniques of monetary management that we have discussed so far involve control of the size of the monetary base. In this task the central bank has a range of options open to it, particularly for shorter-term, temporary adjustments; but the main instrument of policy is undoubtedly open-market operations in government securities. To a very large extent, this is what central banking is all about.

Although we have focused on control of the monetary base, it is important that we not lose perspective on the purpose of central bank operations. Control of the monetary base is merely a means to an end—a method of regulating the supplies of money and credit in the economy. This is not the only possible technique by which the central bank can influence these variables. Two other types of measures have been used in certain situations: variation of minimum legal reserve requirements and direct or selective credit controls (including what is usually referred to as moral suasion).

EXAMPLE 17.1   The Effects of Government Deposits on the Monetary Base (Thousands of Dollars)

Case 1   Tax collections are deposited in U.S. government accounts with the Federal Reserve.

Stage I: Taxes are paid by members of the general public, with checks drawn on accounts at commercial banks. The Treasury deposits these checks in its general account with the Federal Reserve.

Federal Reserve

Checks on Commercial Banks +100	Treasury Deposits +100

Public

| | Tax Liability −100 |
| | Checks Outstanding +100 |

Stage II: When the outstanding checks are cleared and collected, member bank reserve deposits at the Federal Reserve are reduced by an equal amount.

Federal Reserve

| | Reserve Deposits of Banks −100 |
| | Treasury Deposits +100 |

Public

Bank Deposits −100	Tax Liability −100

Commercial Banks

Reserve Deposits −100	Public Deposits −100

Net Change

Federal Reserve

| | Reserve Deposits of Banks −100 |
| | Treasury Deposits +100 |

Public

Bank Deposits −100	Tax Liability −100

Commercial Banks

Reserve Deposits −100	Public Deposits −100

Notes
1. Public demand deposits have been reduced.
2. The money supply has been reduced by an equal amount.
3. Member bank reserves have also been reduced by an equal amount.
4. Assuming that the commercial banks had no excess reserves, they are now deficient in their reserve positions.
5. As a result of deficiency, multiple credit contraction will follow.

EXAMPLE 17.1 (Continued)

Case 2 Tax collections are deposited in U.S. government accounts with commercial banks.

Stage I: Taxes are paid by members of the general public, with checks drawn on accounts with commercial banks. The Treasury deposits these checks in its accounts with commercial banks.

Public

Bank Deposits −100	Tax Liability −100

Commercial Banks

	Deposits of Public −100
	Deposits of Gov't −100

Notes
1. Public demand deposits have been reduced.
2. The money supply has been reduced by an equal amount.
3. Government demand deposits at commercial banks have been increased by that amount.
4. Member bank reserves are unaffected since total deposit liabilities subject to reserve requirements are unchanged.
5. The monetary base is unchanged.

Case 3 Government makes expenditures from its account with the Federal Reserve.

Stage I: The Treasury redeems maturing securities held by the public with checks drawn on its general account with the Federal Reserve.

Federal Reserve

Treasury Deposits −100	
Checks Outstanding +100	

Public

Gov't Checks +100	
United States Securities −100	

Stage II: Checks are deposited in the public's demand deposit accounts with commercial banks and cleared through the Federal Reserve.

Federal Reserve

Treasury Deposits −100	
Bank Reserve Deposits +100	

Public

Bank Deposits +100	
Checks Outstanding −100	

Commercial Banks

Reserve Deposits +100	Public Deposits +100

EXAMPLE 17.1   (Continued)

Notes
1. Public demand deposits have increased.
2. The money supply has increased by an equal amount.
3. Member bank reserve deposits have also increased by an equivalent amount.
4. The commercial banks now have excess reserves.
5. Excess reserves induce a general expansion of credit.

Case 4   Transfer of Government Deposits.

Stage I: The government withdraws part of its cash balances with commercial banks and redeposits them with the Federal Reserve.

Federal Reserve		Commercial Banks	
Bank Reserve		Reserve	Deposits of
Deposits −100		Deposits −100	Gov't −100
Treasury			
Deposits +100			

Notes
1. The deposit liabilities of commercial banks are reduced.
2. There is no effect on the size of money supply since government demand deposits are not included in its measurement.
3. Member bank reserves are reduced.
4. Assuming that the commercial banks had no excess reserves, they are now deficient in their reserve positions.
5. As a result of this deficiency, multiple credit contraction will follow.
6. A transfer of deposits from the Federal Reserve account to commercial bank accounts by the Treasury would have the opposite effect, creating excess reserves and inducing a general expansion of credit.

377

DISCRETIONARY CASH RESERVE RATIOS

We demonstrated in Chapter 15 that the money supply can be related to the monetary base by a "multiplier," the value of which depends, among other things, on the cash reserve ratio maintained by the commercial banks. The higher the cash reserve ratio, the smaller the multiplier, and vice versa. Under normal circumstances banks will have little incentive to hold substantial excess cash reserves. This means that the size of the multiplier depends on the minimum cash reserve ratio required by law.

Provided that they have the authority to vary the required reserve ratio, this relationship gives the monetary authorities an additional instrument for monetary control. By lowering the required cash reserve ratio, the central bank can create excess cash reserves in every member bank simultaneously, inducing monetary expansion throughout the banking system. Similarly, by raising the required cash reserve ratio, the central bank can create deficient reserves in every member bank in the system, forcing monetary contraction. A variable cash reserve ratio, then, can be a powerful and pervasive instrument of policy that is independent of central bank operations in the open market.

Historical Experience. The Federal Reserve System was given the authority to vary the required cash reserve ratios of member banks within certain limits in 1935.[2] This power was used almost immediately, when the ratios were doubled in three stages in 1936 and 1937, raising them to their legal maximums. In subsequent years the power has been used on several occasions. (See Table 17.1.) Most recently, ratios were increased in January 1968 and again in April 1969 against demand deposits and reduced in October 1970 against time deposits.

In 1972 the Board of Governors altered the definition of country and reserve city banks for reserve requirement purposes. For the first time since enactment of the National Bank Act, country and reserve city bank designations (and hence reserve requirements) were based solely on deposit size rather than on deposit size and geographic location.

This change in classification represents a fundamental policy revision rather than a change in the required cash ratios for the purpose of monetary management. In fact, the shift was undertaken in two stages to minimize the effect on member bank reserves.

The Board of Governors of the Federal Reserve System has made it clear that it does not regard the variable cash reserve ratio as a normal tool of monetary policy but rather as one to be used in exceptional circumstances. This is particularly true of increases in the ratio, which the Board regards as a drastic move not to be taken without careful study and long deliberation. Thus, following the increase in the rates to their legal ceilings during the Korean War, the Federal Reserve System did not use its power to raise the ratios again for sixteen years, in spite of several periods of sharply restrictive monetary policy.

Table 17.1. The Variable Cash Reserve Requirement: Member Banks, 1935–1972

Effective Data[a]	Net Demand Deposits			Time Deposits, All Member Banks
	Central Reserve City Banks	Reserve City Banks	Country Banks	
December 1935	13.0	10.0	7.0	3.0
August 1936	19.5	15.0	10.5	4.5
May 1937	26.0	20.0	14.0	6.0
April 1938	22.75	17.5	12.0	5.0
November 1941	26.0	20.0	14.0	6.0
October 1942	20.0	20.0	14.0	6.0
September 1948	26.0	22.0	16.0	7.5
September 1949	22.0	18.0	12.0	5.0
February 1951	24.0	20.0	14.0	6.0
July 1953	22.0	19.0	13.0	5.0
August 1954	20.0	18.0	12.0	5.0
April 1958	18.0	16.5	11.0	5.0
December 1960	16.5	16.5	12.0	5.0
July 1962[b]	—	—	—	—

Effective Data[a]	Net Demand Deposits				Time and Savings Deposits		
	Reserve City Banks		Country Banks		Savings Deposits, All Banks	Deposits up to $5 Million	Deposits over $5 Million
	Deposits up to $5 Million	Deposits over $5 Million	Deposits up to $5 Million	Deposits over $5 Million			
July 1966	16.5	16.5	12.0	12.0	4.0	4.0	5.0
March 1967	16.5	16.5	12.0	12.0	3.0	3.0	6.0
January 1968	16.5	17.0	12.5	13.0	3.0	3.0	6.0
April 1969	17.0	17.5	12.5	13.0	3.0	3.0	6.0
October 1970	17.0	17.5	12.5	13.0	3.0	3.0	5.0

	Net Demand Deposits (Millions of Dollars)				
	Over $400	$100–$400	$10–$100	$2–$10	$2 or Less
November 1972	17.5	13.0	12.0	10.0	8.0

[a]High or low point of reserve ratios, except for 1968–1969.
[b]Authority of the Board of Governors to classify banks as central reserve city banks was terminated.
SOURCE: Federal Reserve Bulletin, various issues.

The Equivalence of Open-Market Operations and Variable Cash Reserve Ratios. The mechanical multiplier model of monetary expansion (see the appendix to Chapter 15) suggests that open-market operations and reserve ratio variations are equivalent methods of achieving a given objective, that is, a particular change in the size of the money supply. In other words, a desired increase in the money supply could be obtained either by holding the reserve ratio constant and increasing the monetary base or by holding the monetary base constant and reducing the reserve ratio. The opposite would be true for a desired reduction in the money supply. For this reason, it is sometimes suggested that open-market operations and cash reserve ratio variations are perfect substitutes as policy instruments and that the central bank should be indifferent as to which it uses in any particular circumstance.

Our brief survey of the use of cash reserve ratio variations in the United States indicates that the central bank does not regard these techniques as perfect substitutes. Rather, the Federal Reserve revealed a strong preference for open-market operations as the technique of policy under normal circumstances. Why?

There are important differences between open-market operations and cash reserve ratio variations considered as policy instruments. Open-market operations have much greater flexibility. They can be conducted in large or small amounts, and both the magnitude and the direction of the operations can be changed from day to day or week to week as necessary. This makes possible relatively delicate adjustments in the monetary base and permits a gradual approach to monetary restriction or monetary ease. Mistakes can be quickly and easily corrected.

By contrast, changes in cash reserve ratios are feasible only at distinct intervals. That is, changes must be made to coincide with the start of a new averaging period. Frequent changes in the continuous use of a variable reserve ratio as an instrument of policy is compatible only with very short reserve averaging periods.

In this connection it should be noted that the monetary repercussions of seemingly small changes in the required cash reserve ratio can in fact be quite large. An increase in reserve requirements affects all banks in that reserve requirement category. Banks with ample liquid assets have little difficulty adjusting to new reserve requirements. Other banks, however, whose liquidity positions are tighter, will have to make necessary portfolio adjustments, which may be more troublesome. Although the banking system at large may have excess reserves in the legal sense, we do not know what portion of these excess reserves is held by banks to fulfill self-defined requirements. We do know from Figure 16.2 that the banking system tends to maintain a fairly stable volume of excess reserves, even if it must increase its borrowings from the Federal Reserve to do so. We also know that excess reserves are not evenly distributed among all banks but tend to be held by banks outside the major financial centers. As a result, an increase in reserve ratios, while affecting all member banks, will not affect each bank equally.

Although the smallest increase in the cash reserve ratio in recent years was 0.5 percent, it is estimated that the increment, imposed in 1969, added $650 million to the required reserves of member banks. Usually the Federal Reserve softens the impact of increases in reserve requirements through off-setting open-market purchases.

It has been quite reasonably pointed out that the central bank is not constrained to reserve ratio changes in the traditional magnitudes of multiples of 0.5 percent. It could change the ratio by smaller fractional amounts, such as 0.1 percent. However, the possibility of frequent, though small, variations in the required reserve ratio introduces a new source of uncertainty for bankers, which cannot help but alter their management policies, and particularly to induce them to hold a larger share of their assets, on the average, in liquid form.

This reaction to uncertainty about the required cash reserve ratio is related to but conceptually different from the direct impact of higher reserve ratios on bank portfolio management policies. This points to what is perhaps the most significant difference between open-market operations and cash reserve ratio variations. While both can be used to change the size of banks' asset portfolios, changes in the reserve ratio also impose a constraint on the composition of banks' asset portfolios. An increase in the reserve ratio reduces the share of earning assets in bank operations. (Consider, for example, the implications of raising the cash reserve ratio to 100 percent.) It is not difficult to understand why commercial bankers are strongly opposed to increases in cash reserve ratios as a technique of monetary restraint (although they are generally quite happy to see cash reserve ratios reduced in periods of monetary ease). In general, varying cash reserve ratios has an unsettling effect on bank operations.

Finally, it is important to note that the cash reserve requirements cannot be changed without a public announcement, giving rise to speculation regarding the implications of the change. As in the case of discretionary changes in the discount rate, many economists argue that because their impact on economic activity is unreliable, such announcement effects should be avoided whenever possible.[3]

Use of Variable Cash Reserve Ratios. The general thrust of the points made in the previous section is critical of the use of variable cash reserve ratios as an instrument for monetary control. Not all economists agree that variable reserve ratios are of limited use in central banking.[4] Some would argue that the pervasive, dramatic, and rapid impact of reserve ratio changes is a positive attribute. All member banks are affected simultaneously and immediately, in contrast to open-market operations, which have their immediate impact at the financial centers and then gradually filter out to the rest of the banking system. It is argued that bankers will soon become accustomed to reserve ratio changes, that errors of magnitude can be adjusted through appropriate open-market operations, and that unfortunate effects on individual banks can be taken care of through the discount window.

DIRECT CREDIT CONTROLS

Another option that is sometimes open to central banks is the direct regulation of some of the activities of banks and other financial institutions. These regulations may have their roots in legislation that compels compliance and imposes formal legal penalties in proved cases of noncompliance, and they may be administered by an agency other than the central bank. Alternatively, the "controls" may be based on the moral authority of the central bank to command voluntary compliance. The latter type of control is commonly called moral suasion. All direct controls tend to have a selective impact on financial activity and hence are sometimes referred to as selective controls.

THE PURPOSE OF CREDIT CONTROLS

Direct controls restrain a specific type of financial activity that is felt to be producing undesirable pressures on the economy. Some examples may help clarify the point.

Margin Requirements. One area of financial activity in which there has been continuing direct control by the Federal Reserve is borrowing to purchase and carry securities listed on the national exchanges. Authority to regulate this type of borrowing came in the 1930s and has been in force ever since.

As mentioned in an earlier chapter, continuing speculation in the stock market during the late 1920s caused the monetary authorities a great deal of concern. They lacked instruments with which to control it, and efforts to persuade brokers and banks to curb their lending to potential investors went unheeded. The ease with which money could be borrowed to purchase securities fed the speculative demand and drove security prices higher and higher. With the crash in 1929, securities prices underwent a severe decline, adding to the general downturn in economic activity. When reforms were being considered by Congress, one concern was to prevent excessive borrowing to buy securities.

In 1934 the Securities Exchange Act was passed. One provision of this legislation was to give the Board of Governors of the Federal Reserve authority to regulate "the amount of credit that could be initially extended and subsequently maintained" for the purchase and carrying of listed stocks and bonds convertible into listed stock. This authority is covered in Federal Reserve margin requirements.

The margin is stated in terms of a percentage. It has two aspects. The "initial" margin is the percentage of the purchase price of a security that the buyer must put up himself to buy the stock. If the margin requirement is 70 percent and the buyer purchases a $50 stock, he must supply at least $35 of the $50 himself. The remaining $15 may be lent by his broker or bank, which takes the securities as collateral. The second dimension of margin is a "maintenance" provision designed to protect the creditor in the event that the prices of the securities it holds as collateral decline. The broker or bank must notify the borrower that additional cash or securities are needed to back the loan outstanding. The borrower receives a "margin call." If the $50 stock drops to $40, the broker or bank has now overextended credit to that borrower on the basis of the collateral's decreased value ($15 lent on each $40 share). The asset holder's interest in each share has decreased to $25, or only 62.5 percent instead of the required 70 percent. The asset holder must increase his equity, or the creditor may sell enough of the borrower's securities held as collateral to build the equity up to the required percentage.

The Federal Reserve can vary the margin requirements to discourage excessive use of credit to purchase securities or to encourage and restore confidence in stock market investments. The Federal Reserve has changed margin requirements only about a dozen times, however, since 1950. One side effect of margin requirements may be to reduce some of the fluctuations in securities prices.

Regulation Q. The Federal Reserve has had authority to limit the rates of interest paid by member banks on time deposits since 1933. The FDIC has similar authority with regard to insured nonmember banks. In practice, both agencies have enforced identical limits over time.[5]

For many years (1936–1957), there were no changes in the ceiling rates. In 1957, the Board of Governors increased rates payable on various types of time deposits but then made no further adjustment for another five years.

Since 1962, the Federal Reserve has changed rates payable under Regulation Q more frequently, as indicated in Table 17.2. Allegedly these changes have been made by the Federal Reserve to enable commercial banks to offer rates that are competitive with those available from other nonbank financial intermediaries and on short-term money market instruments, and at times to ease the liquidity squeeze commercial banks and other intermediaries were experiencing. Changes in Regulation Q can result in changes in the supply of money and credit and hence can be used as a countercyclical tool of monetary policy.

If the Federal Reserve changes Regulation Q, raising the ceiling rates commercial banks are permitted to pay on time deposits so that commercial banks attract funds currently on deposit with nonbank financial intermediaries, the effect on supply of payments money and credit is somewhat contractionary. On the other hand, the Federal Reserve can maintain the ceiling rates

Table 17.2. Maximum Rates of Interest Payable on Time Deposits

	Jan. 1, 1962	July 17, 1963	Nov. 24, 1964	Dec. 6, 1965
Savings Deposits				
12 Months or More	4.0%	4.0%	4.0%	4.0%
Less Than 12 Months	3.5	3.5	4.0	4.0
Other Time Deposits				
12 Months or More	4.0	4.0	4.5	5.5
6 Months–12 Months	3.5	4.0	4.5	5.5
90 Days–6 Months	2.5	4.0	4.5	5.5
Less Than 90 Days	1.0	1.0	4.0	5.5

	July 20, 1966	Sept. 26, 1966	April 19, 1968	Jan. 21, 1970	June 24, 1970
Savings Deposits	4.0%	4.0%	4.0%	4.5%	4.5%
Other Time Deposits					
Multiple Maturity					
30 Days–89 Days	4.0	4.0	4.0	4.5	4.5
90 Days–1 Year	5.0	5.0	5.0	5.0	5.0
1 Year–2 Years	5.0	5.0	5.0	5.5	5.5
2 Years and Over	5.0	5.0	5.0	5.75	5.75
Single Maturity					
Less Than $100,000					
30 Days–1 Year	5.5	5.0	5.0	5.0	5.0
1 Year–2 Years	5.5	5.0	5.0	5.5	5.5
2 Years and Over	5.5	5.0	5.0	5.75	5.75
$100,000 and Over					
30 Days–59 Days	5.5	5.5	5.5	6.25	[a]
60 Days–89 Days	5.5	5.5	5.75	6.5	[a]
90 Days–179 Days	5.5	5.5	6.0	6.75	6.75
180 Days–1 Year	5.5	5.5	6.25	7.0	7.0
1 Year and Over	5.5	5.5	6.25	7.25	7.25

[a]Maximum interest rates were suspended on these short-maturity, large-denomination deposits.
SOURCE: Federal Reserve Bulletin, April 1972, p. A11.

payable under Regulation Q unrealistically low compared with other money market rates. Some disintermediation will occur, and banks will experience withdrawal of time deposits, particularly short-term, large-denomination deposits that are quite sensitive to interest rates. When this occurs, both the demand deposit component of the money supply and total credit are expanded, despite the initial contraction that the banking system experiences. Examples 17.2 and 17.3 may help clarify these points.

EXAMPLE 17.2   The Effect of Shifting Funds in Reaction to Regulation Q (Thousands of Dollars)

Stage I: $10,000 is transferred from savings and loan associations to time deposits with commercial banks. The savings and loan associations hold cash reserves in the form of demand deposits with commercial banks.

S&L		Bank	Public
Reserve	Deposits −10	Demand	Deposits
Deposits −10		Deposits −10	S&L −10
		(S&L)	Time +10
		Time	
		Deposits +10	
		(Public)	

Effect on Savings and Loan Association.   It desires to keep cash reserves in the form of demand deposits with commercial banks equal to 4 percent of its deposit liabilities. It is now short of cash reserves as a result of the withdrawal of funds by the public. It must reduce its loans outstanding or sell securities equivalent to $9,600, in order to restore equilibrium to its portfolio.

Stage II: The S&L reduces its loans to the public by $9,600. It deposits the proceeds with the commercial bank.

S&L		Bank	Public	
Reserve		Deposits	Deposits	Loans −9.6
Deposits +9.6		Demand	Demand −9.6	
Loans −9.6		S&L +9.6		
		Public −9.6		

Effect of Transactions to This Point.   The S&L has reduced its credit outstanding by $9,600. Commercial banks have initially experienced a decrease in demand deposits (money) of $10,000 and an increase in time deposits of $10,000. Stage II did not affect commercial banks, since only the ownership of demand deposits was transfered. However, "public" demand deposits have been reduced, since the public has repaid the loan from the savings and loan association, thereby reducing total credit.

Stage III: The commercial bank, as a result of the shift in funds by the public from the S&L to the bank, finds that it has excess reserves. We can assume that the bank holds 16 percent in reserves against time deposits. The bank responds to this shift in funds in a manner similar to that outlined in Example 15.5, Case 2. The commercial bank now has excess reserves of $1,200 and responds by increasing loans and demand deposits by that amount.

385

Stage n: The banks in the system continue to respond to the excess reserves. The deposit expansion, credit creation process continues until there are no excess reserves in the banking system.

Effect of All Transactions. The commercial banking system extends credit and creates deposits in a multiple of its excess reserves. That multiple is $(1)/(r)$ or $(1)/(0.16) = 6.25$. The shift of funds created excess reserves of \$1,200. The banking system was able to expand credit and demand deposits by \$7,500. However, when coupled with the initial effect on the savings and loan association, we find that total demand deposits have been reduced by \$2,500 and that credit has been reduced by \$2,100.

EXAMPLE 17.3 The Effect of Shifting Funds in Response to Regulation Q and Money Market Rates: Disintermediation (Thousands of Dollars)

Stage I: \$10,000 is transferred from time deposits with commercial banks to money market instruments offered by corporations in response to higher interests rates on money market instruments.

Bank		Corporation		Public	
Deposits (Public)	Deposits	Securities +10		Deposits	
Time −10	Demand +10			Time −10	
Deposits (Corp.)				Securities +10	
· Demand +10					

Effect of Transactions to This Point. The public has exchanged \$10,000 of time deposits for securities. A corporation has been extended \$10,000 of credit by the public. It deposits its receipts from selling its securities with the bank as a demand deposit. Credit and the demand deposit component of the money supply have been increased by \$10,000.

Stage II: The commercial bank now finds that it is short of reserves, assuming that it was in equilibrium before the shift of funds. It must hold 16 percent in reserves against demand deposits and 4 percent in reserves against time deposits. It is short \$1,200 in reserves and moves to reduce its loan commitments and increase its reserve account by that amount. However, another bank, Bank B, loses demand deposits and reserves by \$1,200 and is now short of reserves.

Bank A		Bank B		Public	
Loans −1.2	Reserves −1.2	Deposits	Deposits	Loans	
Reserves +1.2		Demand	Demand −1.2	−1.2	
		−1.2			

Effect of Transactions to This Point. The initial increase in credit extended by the public to the corporation has been offset slightly by the bank's reaction to a shortage of reserves. The increase in the demand deposit component of the money supply has likewise been reduced. Bank B is now deficient in reserves by \$1,000 and must alter its portfolio.

Stage n: The commercial banking system continues to make adjustments in its loan and investment portfolios until it is no longer deficient in reserves. The banking system will undergo a multiple contraction of credit extended and a reduction in demand deposit liabilities of \$7,500. However, this contraction of credit and reduction of the demand deposit component of the money supply does not totally offset the initial \$10,000 expansion of credit and demand deposits.

Effect of All Transactions. The total effect of shifting funds from time deposits with commercial banks into money market instruments or direct securities has been slightly expansionary. Demand deposits have increased by $2,500, and total credit has been increased by an equivalent amount.

Consumer Credit. Consumer credit is a favorite target for direct controls, particularly in periods when strong consumer demand for durable goods is alleged to be producing inflationary pressures. The Federal Reserve was first given authority to regulate consumer credit in September 1941. This authority continued throughout World War II. It was then suspended but was reinstated from 1948 to 1949 in the face of postwar inflation. Consumer credit controls were imposed again during the Korean War to curtail inflationary pressures and excessive demand for consumer durables.

Consumer credit controls, in contrast to margin requirements, have been temporary and limited controls. The government, by requiring higher-than-normal down payments and shorter-than-normal repayment periods on installment credit, tries to restrict expenditures and curtail this type of consumer demand.

Real Estate Credit. Following the same reasoning as for controls on consumer credit, the Federal Reserve was granted authority during the Korean War to require a fixed percentage down payment and to set the maximum maturity for mortgage loans. In imposing these controls the Federal Reserve was trying to restrict housing activity in order to divert industrial production to the war effort. This control was not very successful and was allowed to lapse in 1953.

Moral Suasion. In general, moral suasion is designed to override the profit motive. It is used to restrain financial institutions from activities they would normally undertake or to induce them to undertake activities they would not do voluntarily. If the discrepancy between the dictates of the profit motive and the dictates of central bank "suggestions" is great, there is a strong incentive to evasion—an incentive that is accentuated if some firms suspect that others are evading or will evade the regulations. The central bank has the best chance of success if the financial institutions are vulnerable to central bank sanctions, if evasions can be detected easily, and if the financial institutions constitute a relatively small, closely knit, and hence self-policing group.

Examples of moral suasion are many. For example, in 1966 the Federal Reserve urged banks to curtail the rate of expansion of business loans and to maintain their portfolio investments in government securities rather than selling them in the market. The Federal Reserve has encouraged lending by banks to minority businesses, and it recently tried moral suasion as part of its program to improve the balance of payments. In 1973 it forced several giant banks to "roll back" or modify increases in their prime lending rate of interest.

SELECTIVE CONTROLS AND THE ALLOCATION OF CREDIT

It should be noted that even though direct controls are successful in achieving their proximate objective, such as the control of term loans by banks, they will not necessarily be effective in achieving their ultimate objective, the elimination of inflationary pressures on the economy. Selective controls attack the symptoms of the economic ailment, not the causes. If the problem is an excessive supply of money and credit, suppression of its expression in certain forms (e.g., particular types of credit or credit extended by particular types of firms) will result in its expression in other forms. Borrowers will seek out alternative sources of credit; lenders will find loopholes and disguised forms for extending the proscribed type of credit; pressures for the evasion of the regulations will build up, and "black markets" (and perhaps corruption) will be encouraged. There is evidence that selective controls can have the desired macroeconomic effects in the short run. In the face of sustained use, however, the market system is highly inventive, and the success of the controls is far less certain.

Perhaps the most serious aspect of moral suasion and other forms of selective controls is that if they are subject to comprehensive, sustained, and effective use, they introduce a new dimension to central banking. The central bank is no longer simply an arbiter of macroeconomic balance in the economy; it becomes an important arbiter of the allocation of credit and hence of resources. The collective judgment of "the market" as reflected in the interaction of supply and demand and the behavior of prices and profits is overruled by a centralized judgment as to the "national interest." If, as argued in Chapter 13, the competitive market is the most reliable mechanism for achieving an efficient allocation of resources in the economy, effective and sustained moral suasion is likely to produce serious distortions in resource allocation (unless it somehow compensates for distortions resulting from lack of effective competition). It is not surprising that vigorous advocates of the freely competitive market system denounce selective controls as harmful to the economy—and, indeed, argue that they do the least damage when they are evaded!

SUMMARY

Together, Chapters 16 and 17 suggest a few important conclusions. We saw in Chapter 15 that the supply of money and credit can be expanded and contracted by actions of private financial institutions. The important regulators are the supply of high-powered money and the cash reserve ratio.

Both of these variables can be subjected to central bank control. This provides the basis for central bank control of the supply of money and credit. The basic tool of central bank control is open-market operations in government securities. However, the central bank in fact has a wide range of other techniques at its disposal, particularly for temporary adjustments to the monetary base. Variations of the cash reserve ratio as a technique of policy suffers from inflexibility, and, like selective credit controls, it interferes unnecessarily with the operations of the banks.

NOTES

1. *Wall Street Journal*, May 25, 1972, p. 2.

2. A provision for increases in reserve ratios in a "national emergency" was introduced in 1933, but the Federal Reserve was not granted the authority to vary the ratios at its own discretion until 1935. At present the limits within which the ratios can be varied are:

> Demand Deposits
> at Country Banks   7–14%
> at Reserve City Banks 10–22%
>
> Time and Savings Deposits
> at All Member Banks 3–10%

3. Cf. M. Friedman, *A Program for Monetary Stability* (New York: Fordham University Press, 1960), pp. 45–50.

4. D. S. Ahearn, *Federal Reserve Policy Reappraised, 1951–1959* (New York: Columbia University Press, 1963), pp. 145–163.

5. Since February 1, 1936, the Federal Deposit Insurance Corporation has issued the same ceiling rates to nonmember insured commercial banks as those imposed by the Federal Reserve.

18

THE DEMAND FOR MONEY

We explored some aspects of the demand for money in Chapters 2 and 5. In those chapters we were concerned with the basic characteristics of money, its role in facilitating the flow of transactions in the economy, and its attributes as an asset that might be selected by an individual asset holder for inclusion in his portfolio. In the present chapter we change our focus. Instead of the individual asset holder's portfolio selection decisions, we are concerned with the aggregate demand for money in the economy as a whole. However, since the aggregate demand for money comprises the demands of individual asset holders, the earlier material provides the microeconomic foundations for our macroeconomic analysis. The reader may find it useful to review it briefly.

THE TRANSACTIONS DEMAND

Money is an asset designed to be used as a medium of payment. Under normal conditions money is the only generally accepted means by which purchasing power can be transfered from one spending unit to another, and the basic demand for it derives from this fact. It is a demand for money to facilitate transactions—to bridge the gap in time between successive receipts of income and hence to permit a continuing flow of expenditures. We can call this the *transactions demand for money.*

CLASSICAL THEORY OF THE TRANSACTIONS DEMAND FOR MONEY

It is frequently assumed that, given the institutional setting (the frequency with which payrolls are met, the pattern of payments flows among firms, the degree to which payments are made by check, the efficiency of the postal service, the speed with which checks are cleared and collected, etc.), the transactions demand for money depends only on the total value of transactions to be effected. Indeed, it is commonly assumed that the relationship between the quantity of money demanded for transactions purposes and the value of transactions to be effected is linear. That is, it is assumed that the demand function takes the form:

$$M_t = kT \tag{18.1}$$

In this equation, T is the total value of expenditures or transactions in the economy during a given period—a month or a year, perhaps. This is a *flow variable*. M_t is the quantity of money demanded for transactions purposes by all spending units in the economy. It is a *stock variable*. Thus, in a sense, the two variables are in different time dimensions, and to reconcile them M_t must be interpreted as the average quantity of money demanded at successive instants during the period over which T is measured. The coefficient k simply defines the relationship between the stock of money demanded and the flow of transactions. It is the reciprocal of the rate of turnover of the money supply.

We can refer to Equation 18.1 as the classical theory of the transactions demand for money. It is depicted graphically in Figure 18.1.

Sometimes what we have called the classical theory of the transactions demand for money is taken simply as an empirical observation, without any explicit theoretical justification. However, the usual theoretical defense is by analogy with the income-payments cycle of an individual household.

The Income-Payments Cycle and the Household's Demand for Transactions Balances. Consider a householder who receives a regular monthly salary of, say, $600, all of which is spent on goods and services during the month. For simplicity, suppose he deposits all of his salary into a current account with his bank on the first day of the month and spends it in equal daily installments of $20 during the month. The behavior of his bank balance is described by the stepwise line in Figure 18.2. On the first day of the month it will jump to $600 (the heavy vertical line); by the last day it will be zero. It is easy to demonstrate that the average daily cash balance during each month will be $300. Early in the month it will be greater; late in the month it will be less. However, if we define the householder's demand for money for transactions purposes as the average daily cash balance that he holds in anticipation of expenditures to be made before the next regular receipt of income, then it is $300, or half his monthly income.

If we can further assume that with a change in his income the householder will not alter the pattern of his expenditure within the month but

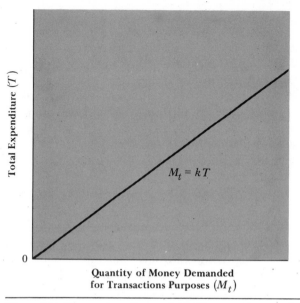

Figure 18.1 **Transactions Demand for Money: Classical Theory**

will change the amount of his daily expenditure proportionately (i.e., the "institutional setting" is given), then we can represent his personal transactions demand for money function by the equation:

$$m_t = \tfrac{1}{2} y_m \tag{18.2}$$

where m_t is the household's average daily cash balance during each month and t is the household's total monthly expenditure on goods and services.

The derivation of the equation is demonstrated in Figure 18.3. The

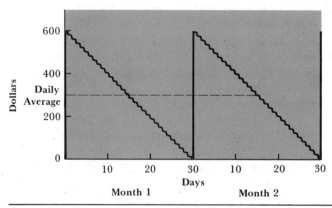

Figure 18.2 **The Income-Payments Cycle of a Household: Daily Cash Balances Assuming a Monthly Income of $600 and Daily Expenditures of $20**

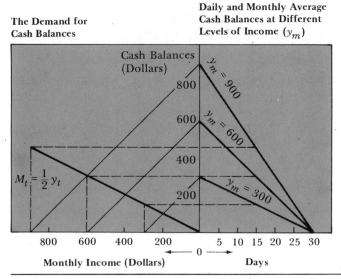

Figure 18.3 Derivation of a Household's Transactions Demand for Money Function: Classical Assumptions

right-hand panel duplicates Figure 18.2, with the daily steps straightened out and the daily level of cash balances shown for two other levels of monthly income (= expenditure), assuming the same pattern of expenditures during each month (i.e., equal daily expenditures of the entire monthly income). The heavy line to the left of the vertical axis relates the average cash balance during the month to the monthly income. This is the household's demand for transactions balances.[1] (Note that on the horizontal axis, monthly income increases to the left.)

Generalizing the Example. This formulation of an individual householder's transactions demand for money, although oversimplified, sets in clear relief the basic idea that money is held as a bridge between regular receipts of income, on the assumption that income and expected payments have different time patterns. The example could be made more complicated by modifying it to allow for part of the monthly salary being saved and invested in financial instruments rather than spent, and for more complex time patterns of income and expenditure. Although it is a bit more difficult, the basic concept could also be applied in the analysis of the demand for transactions balances on the part of business firms faced with differing time patterns of cash receipts from sales and cash expenditures. For both households and firms, transactions balances serve as a bridge in time, and as long as the basic pattern of income and expenditures does not change, the demand for transactions balances on the part of each spending unit will be a linear function of the total value of transactions.

The Aggregate Demand Function. Remember, however, that these are microeconomic examples relating to individual households and firms. The notion that the aggregate demand function derived by adding up all of the microeconomic demand functions will have similar properties may be intuitively appealing, but it is far from clear that this is the case. The shape of the aggregate demand function depends not only on the shape of the individual demand functions of individual firms and households but also on the distribution of transactions among spending units with differing individual demands. Since this information is unobtainable, we cannot be confident of the shape of the aggregate demand function. Nevertheless, the linear function of Figure 18.1 is very convenient, and it is a possible implication of the assumptions about household and firm behavior contained in the examples.

Why Hold Transactions Balances in Cash? The classical theory of the demand for transactions balances is plausible at first glance but, considered carefully, is really far from convincing as a theory of the transactions demand for money.

The classical theory demonstrates that a household or a firm with patterns of income and expenditure that are not coincident in time will have a demand for transactions balances in some form. This is not the same thing as a demand for money because money is not the only form in which transactions balances can be held; and it may not be the most desirable form, since it yields no interest income. Hence, why should the household of our example hold money, which it knows will not be spent till the end of the month, when it can invest the idle money in short-term, highly liquid assets, which yield interest income and can be sold at the very moment that expenditures are to be made? Indeed, why hold any cash at all? At the beginning of the month the householder can invest $580 (his salary minus the first day's expenditure) in a series of short-term $20 loans or securities, one to mature on each day during the month. This would provide him with cash as needed to meet anticipated expenditures and would put his money balances to work earning interest income. His demand for cash balances on a daily average during the month would be approximately zero. This possibility is not allowed for in the simple classical formulation.

TRANSFER COSTS AND THE TRANSACTIONS DEMAND FOR MONEY

If we lived in a "frictionless" world in which there were no costs involved in buying and selling financial instruments, the rational policy would indeed be to hold no money among transactions balances. As long as there were a positive rate of interest, people would hold money for only an instant before they made an expenditure, and the average cash balance of every spending unit would approach zero.

Thus, the crucial assumption implicit in the classical theory of the transactions demand for money is that transfer costs are so high that such transfers between money and nonmoney liquid assets are impracticable. It implies a world of extreme frictions. Although it is true that the real world is not frictionless, the implicit classical assumption of complete immobility between money and other assets is clearly not valid either.

Transfer Costs. The costs involved in transfers among asset forms were discussed in Chapter 8. These costs proved to be important in explaining the phenomenon of financial intermediation. They are also essential in explaining the nature of the transactions demand for money.

Some transfer costs are quite explicit, such as the fees and commissions of brokers, dealers, and investment advisers. Some, however, are implicit, such as the inconvenience of changing habitual arrangements, the time and bother involved in making the detailed calculations necessary for sophisticated decisions, or even the time involved in going to the bank to cash in a savings bond. Transfer costs are incurred both when assets are acquired and when they are sold. There is also the problem of indivisibilities. Thus, the wealth owner may find that minimum investment requirements force him to hold money until he has accumulated sufficient wealth to purchase a desired asset, such as Treasury bills with a minimum denomination of $10,000.

The important point is that, unlike interest income, these transfer costs normally do not depend directly on the value of the assets or the length of time they are held. Given the schedule of fees, they depend mainly on the number of transactions.

The Inventory Theoretic Model of the Transactions Demand for Money. Given the existence of different time patterns of cash expenditures, a positive interest rate on nonmoney assets, and transfer costs that depend on the number of transfers between money and other assets, how much money should an individual hold? Because of the interest rate, the classical conclusion that all transactions balances should be held in money is not likely to be optimal. Because of the transfer costs, the opposite conclusion—that all transactions balances should be held in nonmoney assets—is not likely to be optimal either. What division between money and nonmoney assets will maximize the net return on the transactions balances?

This problem in economic theory was explored independently in two pioneering articles by William Baumol[2] and James Tobin.[3] Because of its affinity to the problem faced by the retailer or manufacturer in deciding on the appropriate level of inventories to be held, their approach to the problem has been labeled the *inventory theoretic model* of the transactions demand for money. We will not explore its formal mathematics; however, the basic argument should be intuitively obvious.

It is assumed that a household with an income-payments cycle like the one examined in the earlier example seeks to maximize the net yield on its transactions balances. This depends on finding the optimum combination of money and earning assets in which to hold the transactions balances. If too much money is held, the loss of interest income will reduce the yield. If too little money is held, the transfer costs between earning assets and money will more than offset the additional interest income, thus reducing the net yield. It turns out that, given the level of transfer costs, the interest rate on earning assets, and the total value of transactions, there is a definite optimum level of cash balances. What is important, however, is that for an individual household or firm:

1. The optimum level of money balances increases with the total value of expenditures to be made during the period. However, the relationship is quite complex. The optimum level of cash balances for a household is a function of the square root of total expenditures.
2. The optimum level of money balances increases with the level of transfer costs between money and nonmoney assets.
3. The optimum level of money balances varies inversely with the level of interest rates on nonmoney assets.

The first of these three conclusions has a familiar ring. However, it should be noted that in the Baumol-Tobin analysis the optimum level of cash balances does not increase in proportion to the total value of expenditures as classical theory implies. Rather, it increases much less than proportionately, implying economies of scale in individual transactions demands for cash (i.e., a doubling of the level of income and expenditure for a household will not double the optimum level of cash balances).

The second and third conclusions, taken together, show that "when the yield disadvantage of cash is slight (i.e., when interest rates are low) the costs of frequent transactions will deter the holding of other assets, and average cash holdings will be large. However, when the yield disadvantage of cash is great, it is worthwhile to incur large transactions costs and keep average cash holdings low."[4] That is, the transactions demand for money on the part of individual households and firms—and hence the aggregate transactions demand for money—will display some interest elasticity. The higher the level of interest rates, the lower average cash holdings will be. However, the existence of transfer costs will induce people to hold some transactions balances, even at relatively high interest rates.

Baumol and Tobin both conclude that the advantages of such sophisticated management of cash holdings may be negligible for the average spending unit. We should not expect to find a high degree of interest elasticity with their cash holdings. However, for spending units with a large cash flow, such as corporations or municipal governments, the advantages from efficient cash management would be substantial. It is with their cash balances that we would expect to find substantial elasticity with respect to changes in interest rates.

The Interest Elasticity of the Aggregate Transactions Demand for Money. The Baumol-Tobin model, strictly speaking, applies to individual households and firms. What does it tell us about the nature of the aggregate demand for cash balances?

Again, consider the aggregation problem that we noted earlier in connection with the classical theory of the transactions demand for money. The information necessary to draw any firm conclusions about the aggregate demand for cash balances from such general microeconomic information is totally unobtainable.

However, one conclusion at least seems warranted. It is highly probable that the aggregate transactions demand for money has some negative interest elasticity.[5]

This suggests that we must revise our earlier formulation of the aggregate transactions demand for money. Using the common mathematical notation for a general functional relationship (i.e., a mathematical statement that one variable depends on another, without specifying the exact nature of this dependence), we can express the relationship between the transactions demand for money, the aggregate value of expenditures (T), and the level of interest rates (r), taking the level of transactions costs as given, as follows:

$$M_t = T(T, r) \qquad (18.3)$$

While we do not know the exact shape of the relationships (e.g., whether they are linear or not), we are confident that the demand for cash balances varies directly with the value of expenditures and inversely with the level of interest rates.

INCOME AND THE TRANSACTIONS DEMAND

The economic theory underlying both the classical and the inventory theoretic models relates the transactions demand for money to the value of total expenditures during a given period. However, in most modern formulations the aggregate transactions demand is related to the level of income rather than the value of total expenditures. Although the latter will normally be several times the former (remember all the double counting that has to be eliminated in deriving an estimate of national income from the flow of total expenditures), it is generally thought that this substitution is acceptable (to be perfect substitutes the relation between the two would have to be constant over time, and we cannot be certain of that). Most transactions occur in connection with the generation of income, that is, in the process of producing and distributing goods and services. Hence, the level of income should be highly correlated with the aggregate value of transactions. Either variable can be used as an index of the impact of the level of economic activity on the demand for money.

Moreover, the use of an income variable in the demand for money

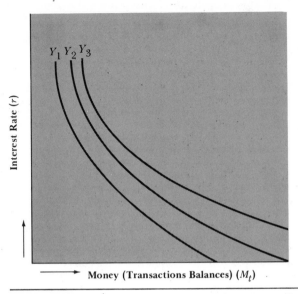

Figure 18.4 Transactions Demand for Money: Interest Rate and Income Effects

has a major advantage. A demand-for-money equation is seldom desired for its own sake. Whether in theoretical or empirical analysis, it is normally wanted as one equation in a macroeconomic model (a mathematical description of the economy in terms of the interaction among highly aggregative variables). Such a model may be relatively simple, involving only a few equations, or may be very detailed, involving 100 or more equations. In either case it is helpful to express the demand for money in terms of variables that are explained in the model. Income is normally such a variable; the aggregate value of transactions is not.

With this substitution in mind, we can rewrite our aggregate transactions demand for money function as follows:

$$M_t = T(Y, r) \tag{18.4}$$

where Y is an index of aggregate income, such as the gross national product.

These assumptions about the aggregate transactions demand for money are incorporated in Figure 18.4. The demand for money is shown to increase with the level of aggregate income and to vary inversely with the level of interest rates at each level of income. At any level of income there should be a maximum quantity of money demanded for transactions purposes (i.e., when the interest rate is so low that all transactions balances are held in money form), but the existence of transfer costs should guarantee that the demand for money will never be zero at "reasonable" levels of the interest rate.

ASSET DEMAND FOR MONEY

We introduced this chapter with the observation that money is an asset that has been specially designed as a medium of exchange. But this means that to its holders money must be the most liquid of assets. Our analysis of the portfolio balance decision in Chapter 5 demonstrated that asset holders have reasons for holding liquid assets in their portfolios in addition to the accommodation of specific expenditure plans in the near future (i.e., in addition to a generalized "transactions motive.") In particular, the provision of a hedge against uncertainty and speculation on changes in interest rates were suggested as important motives for holding liquid assets. But if money is the most liquid of assets, does this mean that there will be corresponding "precautionary" and "speculative" demands for money in addition to what we have called the transactions demand?

We will not repeat the analysis of uncertainty and speculation from Chapter 5. We take as proved the proposition that they can give rise to demands for liquid assets. Because of uncertainty about the future course of income and expenditures, each asset holder will want to hold part of his portfolio in liquid form. Likewise, in periods when interest rates are expected to rise, asset holders can be expected to shift out of long-term securities and into short-term instruments, giving rise to additional demands for liquid assets. Conversely, when interest rates are expected to fall, holdings of liquid assets will be abnormally reduced as asset holders shift into longer-term securities in anticipation of capital gains.

The Demand for Liquid Assets vs. the Demand for Money. In his famous book, *The General Theory of Employment, Interest and Money*, J. M. Keynes came to the conclusion that the very facts of uncertainty and speculation on interest rate changes were by themselves sufficient to explain the existence of asset demands for money.[6] However, Keynes derived this conclusion from a model in which the asset holder's range of choice is limited to two financial instruments, money and long-term bonds. Money is the only possible hedge against uncertainty, and money is the only possible vehicle for speculation on a rise in interest rates.

But again, we must remind ourselves that while money may be the most liquid of assets, it is not the only highly liquid asset. Normally the range of alternatives is wide, including short-term claims on governments, financial intermediaries, and private businesses, and including claims payable on demand or with little notice as one day. Given a wide range of non-money liquid assets, all of which yield interest income, we might well ask Keynes himself his famous question: "Why would anyone outside a lunatic asylum wish to use money as a store of wealth?"[7] Surely it is more attractive to hold precautionary balances in the form of earning assets than in the form of non-interest-bearing money, and surely it is attractive to supplement possible speculative capital gains with the interest earned on short-term investment of the speculative balances.

Transfer Costs. What the preceding discussion ignores is that the expected interest income must be sufficient to offset the probable costs of maintaining precautionary and speculative balances in nonmoney form for this to be worthwhile. If there are speculative or precautionary demands for money on the part of asset holders—particularly those with relatively large portfolios—they must be explained by these economic frictions.

Wealth, Interest Rates, and the Asset Demand for Money. If there is an asset demand for money, then it is positively related to total asset holdings (although the relationship may not be linear) and inversely related to the level of interest rates. That is:

$$M_a = A(A, r) \tag{18.5}$$

where M_a is the asset demand for money, A is the total value of asset holdings, and r is the level of interest rates.

The aggregate demand for money, then, is a combination of the transactions demand and the asset demands for money. That is:

$$M = M(A, Y, r) \tag{18.6}$$

However, the precise formulation of the aggregate demand function is a matter of controversy. While we have suggested that the asset demand for money is essentially a question of the composition of asset portfolios, at the aggregate level the asset demand is commonly related to wealth rather than total asset holdings. The central issue in the controversy is whether wealth, income, or both should be included in the demand function—with some advocates of the wealth formulation arguing that the interest rate variable should be omitted as of negligible importance.

We will return to these issues. However, our preference should be clear from earlier discussions. We regard the transactions demand for money as paramount and therefore conclude on a priori grounds that the income and interest rate variables are both essential. The importance of the wealth variable is moot. These are conclusions based on theoretical speculation. They may be wrong. Clearly, we have here issues that can be resolved only by subjecting the alternative theories to empirical tests. Unfortunately, the empirical tests to date are not conclusive.

In any case, in the short run we can take wealth or total asset holdings as given. The important point for our subsequent analysis is that there are sound theoretical reasons for believing that the aggregate demand for money has a positive association with the level of income and a negative association with the level of interest rates. In other words, taking wealth as given:

$$M = M(Y, r) \tag{18.7}$$

In this context, the main effect of including asset demand for money is to make the demand function somewhat more elastic with respect to the rate of interest, particularly at lower levels of the interest rate. Our

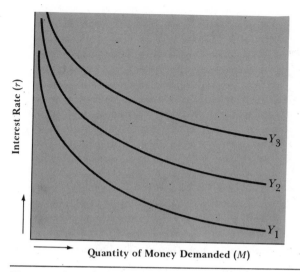

Figure 18.5 **The Demand for Money: Income and Interest Rate Effects**

assumptions regarding the aggregate demand for money are depicted in Figure 18.5, showing both the negative elasticity with respect to the interest rate and the positive elasticity with respect to the level of income.

Interest Elasticity of the Income Velocity of Circulation. We introduced the concept of the velocity of circulation of money earlier in the book (Chapter 2). One variant of this concept is the income velocity of circulation, a measure of the intensity with which money is used in the generation of income. We define the income velocity as the ratio of aggregate income to the stock of money:

$$V_r = \frac{Y}{M} \tag{18.8}$$

Our conclusions regarding the demand for money can be summarized succinctly using this concept.

If the demand for money depends on both the level of income and the level of interest rates, then the velocity of circulation—the ratio of income to money—will be directly related to the level of interest rates. At relatively high interest rates, households and firms economize on their money holdings, increasing the velocity of circulation of money. At relatively low levels of interest rates, the opportunity cost of holding money is less, and the velocity of circulation correspondingly falls. Is there any evidence in support of such a proposition?

Figure 18.6 is a "scatter diagram" showing the relationship between the income velocity of money and the yield on Treasury bills for each year from 1950 through 1970. Each point on the chart represents the velocity of circu-

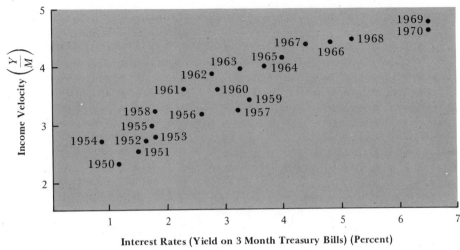

Interest Rates (Yield on 3 Month Treasury Bills) (Percent)

Money = M = Demand deposits adjusted + currency in circulation

Income = Y = Gross National Product

Figure 18.6 Interest Rates and the Income Velocity of Money, 1950–1970
SOURCE: Federal Reserve *Bulletin*, December 1970; *Economic Report of the President* (Washington, D.C.), various issues.

lation of money (vertical axis) and the yield on Treasury bills (horizontal axis) prevailing in the indicated years.[8]

While the correlation between the two variables is far from perfect, there is an obvious positive association between the interest rate and the velocity of circulation in this period. Years with high interest rates also had relatively high income velocities, and vice versa. While this is very crude evidence, it does provide some justification for our theoretical conclusion that the interest rate is a significant factor in the demand for money function.

PRICES AND THE DEMAND FOR MONEY

Up to this point we have discussed the demand for money on the implicit assumption that the general level of prices was stable. In the real world such an assumption is hardly reasonable. Inflation seems to be an ever-present phenomenon, and at times in some countries the rate of change of the price level has been so great as to merit the sobriquet hyperinflation. As we noted in Chapter 5, changes in the price level can be an important consideration in portfolio selection decisions. It follows that they should also affect the demand for money.

We must distinguish two different effects of the price level on the demand for money: the direct impact of a change in the price level and the impact of expectations of continuing price level changes.

Direct Impact. An increase in the general level of prices involves a decline in the real value of anything whose nominal value is fixed in terms of the unit of account. Money is such an item. For this reason, economists find it necessary to distinguish between the "nominal money supply" and the "real money supply." The former is simply the money supply as we would conventionally measure it—the number of dollars (currency plus checkable bank deposits) in circulation. The real money supply is the nominal money supply adjusted for changes in its real purchasing power. That is, we define the real money supply (M_r) as:

$$M_r = \frac{M}{P} \qquad (18.9)$$

where M is the nominal money supply and P is an index of the general level of prices.

As long as we made the implicit assumption of a stable price level, this distinction between real and nominal values was not revelant. However, when we allow for the possibility that the price level may change, it should be clear that the demand for money function, equation 18.8, should be written in real terms. That is, the aggregate demand for money should be:

$$\frac{M}{P} = M\left(\frac{Y}{P}, r\right) \qquad (18.10)$$

What, then, is the direct impact of a rise in the price level? At any given level of output and employment—that is, with the level of real income given—a rise in the price level, by increasing the nominal level of income, increases the nominal amount of money demanded at any given interest rate. The demand for real balances has not changed. However, because of the rise in the price level, proportionally more dollars are required to do the same work in the economy. In terms of the demand functions for nominal money balances plotted in Figure 18.5, the direct impact of a one-time rise in the price level is equivalent to that of a rise in income—except that the shift of the demand function will leave the ratio M/Y constant at any given level of the interest rate (something that is not necessarily true when the increase in income is entirely real).

The impact of expectations of continuing increases in the price level is somewhat different.

Expectations of Price Level Changes. As we saw in Chapter 5, expected increases in the price level in the future must be taken into account in assessing the probable yield on financial instruments and real assets. In this sense, the expected rate of inflation must be taken as an adjustment in the nominal yield in order to obtain the real yield. Applied to money, the expectation of inflation is equivalent to a negative interest rate on money balances. It should produce the same effect on the demand for money as an

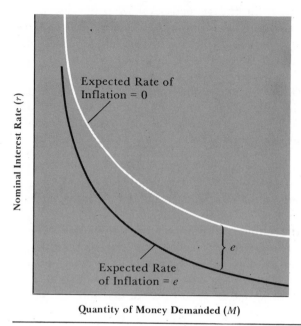

Figure 18.7 **The Demand for Money with Expectations of Inflation**

increase in interest rates by the amount of the expected rate of inflation. That is, it should reduce the quantity of money demanded at each nominal interest rate.

This effect is illustrated in Figure 18.7. The dotted line is the demand for money in the absence of expectation of inflation. The solid line is the demand for money when inflation is expected at the rate of 100 percent per annum.

Clearly, the expectation of a very high rate of inflation would shift the demand curve very far to the left—virtually driving money out of circulation. Such is the common observation in periods of hyperinflation. Studies of the demand for money under conditions of hyperinflation have shown that the rate of change of the price level is an important explanatory variable, although little success has been achieved in finding such an effect under conditions in which the changes in the price level were more gentle.[9]

SOME UNRESOLVED ISSUES

Although we have hinted at the existence of some points of controversy, we have presented a theory of the demand for money as though there remained few really serious points of disagreement among economists on this matter. Such an implication is far from the truth. While we cannot attempt to explore every nuance of every debate, it is important that students of monetary economics at least have their attention drawn to the major points of controversy.

EMPIRICAL RESEARCH ON THE DEMAND FOR MONEY

Like most controversies in economics today, the basic issues are empirical. They can be settled only by confronting theory with fact—by attempting to measure each proposed demand for money function statistically and then subjecting the competing theories to a quantitative test of their relative predictive ability.

Empirical work in this field requires the application of sophisticated analysis, using either cross-sectional or time series data to estimate the demand for money function. To report in detail on each of the various pieces of empirical research that has been undertaken would require a capsule course in econometric techniques, which is not the function of a text on money and banking. Accordingly, we can do little more than note our interpretation of the conclusions to be drawn from the various tests that have been undertaken and what further controversies remain to be explored.

Before doing so, it is important to note that not all statistical studies define money in the same way. Some of the studies use the concept of money the way we have; that is, money is narrowly defined as payments money. In other studies, money is defined more broadly to include some near moneys, most commonly time deposits at commercial banks. In a few studies money is defined very broadly indeed, to include virtually all short-term, highly liquid assets.

It should not be surprising, therefore, that the results are often contradictory. The broader the definition of money, the more interest rate substitutions between payments money and other liquid assets will be obscured.

IS THE DEMAND FOR MONEY INTEREST ELASTIC?

We have tried to present cogent reasons why we would expect the demand for money to have some degree of elasticity with respect to the level of interest rates. As we shall see, this is an important issue when it comes to identifying how changes in the money supply affect the level of economic activity. It is at the center of the major debates in monetary economics today.

A distinct negative relationship between aggregate holdings of cash balances and an interest rate was found in the earliest modern statistical studies of the demand for money, such as those by Tobin and Latané.[10] In subsequent more sophisticated and more detailed studies, using different forms for the demand functions, different types of data, and different definitions of money, this relationship has been fairly consistently confirmed.

The major critic is Professor Milton Friedman of the University of

Chicago. He has questioned the validity of these findings, contending that using observed interest rates and observed money holdings was improper because the behavior of both of these variables was in turn explained by other more basic factors. Using a long series of historical data and using cyclical average rather than observed values for the money supply, he found that the interest rate was not an important variable in explaining the demand for money. Rather, he found that "permanent income" was almost the only significant variable.[11] Recent work by Brunner and Meltzer and by Laidler,[12] using Friedman's data and various measures of interest rates, found opposite results; that is, the inclusion of the interest rate did improve the predictive ability of Friedman's demand function. We will examine Friedman's studies further later in this chapter.

Aside from the contrary results obtained by Friedman, the evidence appears to be strong that the interest rate is an important determinant in the demand for money. Indeed, one leading student in this field has gone so far as to state that "of all of the issues in monetary economics, this is the one that appears to have been settled most decisively."[13]

IS THERE A LIQUIDITY TRAP?

The division of the demand for money into transactions demand, precautionary demand, and speculative demand is due to J. M. Keynes, whose work in this field has already been noted. Whereas we have pushed the transactions demand to the fore, Keynes argued that the asset demand, and particularly the speculative demand, had the more potent impact on the economy. In this connection it must be remembered that Keynes was particularly concerned with the behavior of the demand for money at very low interest rates, such as those prevailing during a severe depression.

In the two-asset world of Keynes' model, interest rates that were widely believed to be abnormally low would give rise to strong speculative demands for money. This was the main Keynesian explanation of the negative interest elasticity of the demand for money. However, in the Keynesian literature the proposition has been pushed farther. It is argued that as the interest rate falls, the elasticity of the demand for money will increase. Indeed, some followers of Keynes argued that at some low rate of interest the demand for money would become infinite, and when this occurred we would be in what was called the liquidity trap. Interest rates would not decline further, since all wealth owners would prefer to hold money rather than alternative assets. The use of monetary expansion to lower interest rates and stimulate economic activity would be useless. Monetary policy would be paralyzed as an instrument of economic policy. Such a demand for money function is depicted in Figure 18.8.

The Keynesian liquidity trap hypothesis has been attacked on various grounds, both theoretical and empirical. We have already noted that in a multiasset world a strong speculative demand for money is unlikely to

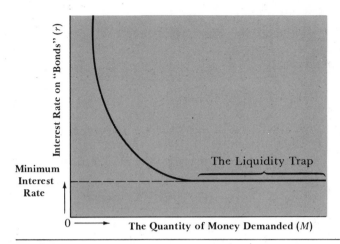

Figure 18.8 **The Keynesian Liquidity Trap**

exist at any positive interest rate on short-term securities. This would not necessarily be true, of course, if speculation or general economic conditions led to a sharp reduction in the supply of short-term instruments, reducing the short-term interest rate to near zero (e.g., at some time during the depression of the 1930s banks were reported to be refusing to accept corporate time deposits, and the yield on Treasury bills declined to less than 0.25 percent per annum). Under these extreme circumstances, money might be virtually the only highly liquid asset.

However, critics have also argued that the expectational assumptions of the liquidity trap hypothesis are implausible: that a prolonged period of low interest rates would lead to expectations that such low rates were "normal." Widespread expectations of a rise in rates would not exist.

Most economists would regard the question of the existence or nonexistence of a liquidity trap one to be resolved by confronting theory with fact. Several empirical studies have done just that, notably those by Bronfenbrenner and Mayer, Laidler, and Brunner and Meltzer.[14] While their results were consistent with the proposition that there is a negative relationship between the level of interest rates and the demand for money, their attempts to establish that the elasticity of the demand for money increases at low levels of interest rates generally produced negative results. Most of these tests used historical data for various periods in the twentieth century. It was anticipated that in the depths of the depression of the 1930s, when interest rates reached all-time lows, the liquidity trap would be found. Yet in various tests that were undertaken, no matter how money was defined—whether interest rates used were long or short term and whether wealth or income was included in the function—the existence of a liquidity trap in this sense could not be clearly established. It is always very difficult to prove

407

a negative proposition like "the liquidity trap does not exist," and many economists remain unconvinced by the evidence. However, we must accept that the available studies cast significant doubt on the importance of the Keynesian liquidity trap concept.

IS WEALTH OR INCOME THE APPROPRIATE VARIABLE IN THE DEMAND FUNCTION?

At various points in our discussion of the demand for money, we have mentioned the work of Professor Milton Friedman. Friedman's analysis plays such a prominent role in contemporary controversies in monetary economics that it merits a somewhat fuller exposition.[15]

The starting point of Friedman's analysis is essentially the same as ours. That is, he starts with the proposition that money is an asset, a form in which wealth may be held. To the business firm it is a capital good, a source of productive services that add to the productivity of the enterprise. The holding of money yields utility directly to the household. Thus, to the household, money is a durable consumer good, a source of implicit income in the form of consumable services. The nature of the service yielded by money to both households and firms is that which we have already identified. It permits the separation in time of expenditures from the receipt of income.

Where, then, does Friedman's analysis differ from the one we have presented? In brief, Friedman employs a broader concept of money, minimizes the importance of interest-rate-induced substitution effects and of the current income variable in the demand function, and places particular stress on a very general concept of wealth as the main explanatory variable for the demand for money.

Friedman chooses a broader definition of money than our "payments money" concept on the empirical ground that better statistical results are obtained with a definition that includes noncheckable time deposits at commercial banks (but does not include comparable deposits at other financial intermediaries or other highly liquid assets.) He notes, however, that the appropriate definition is not a point of major importance. He finds almost as good results with a narrower definition.

Consider first the demand by households for money. The household's wealth, to Friedman, is the present value of all expected future income, regardless of the source or form of the income (i.e., whether it is received in money or in the form of intangible services). Thus, his analysis includes human as well as nonhuman sources of income. Each source of wealth is an asset, with a measurable yield, and to maximize the utility derived from its portfolio each household must so arrange the composition of its portfolio as to equate the expected yields at the margin. In the process, each household elects to hold some portion of its wealth in the form of money. Firms, for whom money is a capital good, will engage in a similar balancing process, equating the marginal productivity of all factors of production, including money, at the margin.

A crucial problem in the empirical application of this approach is the measurement of wealth. Friedman surmounts this problem by substituting a summary measure of the stream of expected future income from which the concept of wealth is derived, that is, the concept of permanent income that we encountered in Chapter 4 in our discussion of the saving decision. Assuming that people's expectations are heavily influenced by developments in the recent past, Friedman estimates permanent income on the basis of a weighted average of past incomes, with most recent income weighted most heavily. This measure is used in the demand for money function as a proxy for wealth.

On the basis of a large body of empirical research, Friedman concludes that permanent income is the single most important determinant of the aggregate demand for money. Current income is significant only as one of the components of permanent income. While he does not deny that interest rates may play some role in the demand function—as we have seen, his theoretical formulation involves the balancing of rates of return on all assets at the margin—he argues that the interest elasticity of the demand for money is sufficiently low that this factor can be virtually ignored. Cyclical fluctuations in the velocity of money circulation are not explained by the influence of interest rates. Rather, they are explained by fluctuations of current income around permanent income. For example, in periods of boom, income tends to rise relative to the stock of money. However, this rise in the income velocity of money, conventionally measured as the ratio Y/M, does not reflect interest-rate-induced substitutions of other liquid assets for money in asset portfolios. Rather, it simply reflects the fact that current income has risen relative to permanent income. The quantity of money demanded is relatively stable, not because interest rates have increased but because permanent income is relatively stable. Indeed, the main conclusion Friedman draws from his work is that, provided that the price level is relatively stable, the demand for money is a relatively stable function of permanent income. This proposition, together with the theoretical analysis underlying it, is commonly known as the *new quantity theory of money*. We will return to it in the next chapter.

Figure 18.9 describes this relationship graphically in a simplified way. Y represents current income, which is increasing over time but at a fluctuating rate. Y_p represents permanent income, whose rate of growth is relatively more stable. Since the quantity of money demanded (M_d) is a constant function of permanent income, it follows a growth path like that of permanent income. Parenthetically, we might note that Friedman finds that money is a luxury good. That is, the demand for money increases somewhat more rapidly than permanent income.

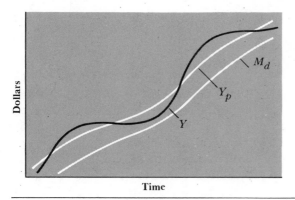

Figure 18.9 **Income, Permanent Income, and the Demand for Money**

Friedman's analysis thus has similar roots to ours but comes to rather different conclusions. In part this is because of a different definition of money, but in part it also reflects a different interpretation of the evidence. Unfortunately, the evidence is far from conclusive either way. There is substantial evidence that Friedman has underestimated the importance of interest rates in the demand for money function—even on his own formulation of that function. However, there is also some evidence that wealth or permanent income performs better in statistical demand functions than does the current-income variable that we stress. This is an area of continuing research, and we can only refer the serious student to the ever-expanding literature.

SUMMARY

In this chapter we have looked at the aggregate demand for money by the economy as a whole. We have used microeconomic analyses again to isolate the various motives behind holding money. We have also developed some of the differing theoretical expositions.

Money is an asset useful as a medium of exchange. Using this definition we can isolate two aspects of the demand for money by the economy as a whole. First, the demand for money to facilitate transactions is termed the *transactions demand for money*. The classical model, in brief, demonstrates that the demand for money for transactions is a function of expenditures over time. It fails to account for the fact that transactions balances can be held in forms other than money and that often it may be desirable to do so. Holding all transactions balances in money form forces the asset holder to forgo interest income. This approach to the transactions demand for money is called the inventory theoretic approach. In this model the individual is restrained from holding all his transactions balances in nonmoney, interest-yielding forms because of the transfer costs involved in exchanging the income-yielding asset into cash.

Although both the classical and inventory theoretic models relate the transactions demand for money to total expenditures in a given period, modern formulation uses the level of income as a variable instead of total expenditures. The demand for money for transactions balances is a function of income and interest rates, varying directly with income and inversely with interest rates.

The other dimension to the demand for money is the fact that money is an asset. Individuals hold money as a hedge against uncertainty and also for speculative reasons against changing interest rates. There is significant controversy surrounding the appropriate formulation of the asset demand for money and hence the total aggregate demand for money. The controversy revolves around whether wealth or income is the appropriate variable, or both, and what importance interest rates should play in the formulation.

The demand for money is the basic concept of monetary economics, but, as we have tried to make clear, this is not an area in economics in which there is a universally accepted doctrine. It is a field in turmoil, stirred by the theoretical disputes and contradictory empirical results.

We have attempted to present a perspective on the demand for money that emphasizes the role of money as a medium of exchange and directs attention to the role of transfer costs in explaining the otherwise apparently irrational habit of holding money as an asset.

Our approach seems to stand in opposition to those that stress that the demand for money reflects a process of choosing the form in which wealth is to be held. That is far from our intention. In fact we agree that this is the nature of the demand for money. The point at issue is, What objective factors bear on the decision on the portion of wealth that will be held in the form of money? We argue that it depends on the value of transactions to be effected with money and the relationship betweeen the interest rate (adjusted for expectations of price level changes) and transfer costs, while others argue that the ratio of money to wealth is relatively constant (meaning that wealth itself is the main determinant of the demand for money), modified only slightly by such factors as interest rates. Still others, notably Friedman, argue that wealth is the principal determinant and that money is a luxury good.

All agree, however, that the concept of a demand for money is meaningful: It can be measured statistically, appears to be relatively stable over time, and, as we shall see in the next chapter, has powerful economic implications.

NOTES

· 1. In this equation we have used small letters to signify that it relates to an individual rather than the aggregate.

If we substitute the householder's annual income for his monthly income in equation 18.2, it becomes:

$$m_t = 1/24y_a$$

This assumes that the salary continues to be paid in monthly installments and that expenditures are made on exactly the same pattern. Then the average daily cash balance is unchanged; the only change is that the income variable is inflated by a factor of 12.

It can be readily seen that if several large payments are made early in the month, the average cash balance will be less than $\frac{1}{2}y_m$. In the extreme, if the entire monthly income is paid out in a single lump-sum payment during the first day, the average cash balance will approximate 0. Likewise, if few payments are made early in the month, with the bulk spent in several large payments late in the month, the average cash balance will be greater than $\frac{1}{2}y_m$. In the extreme, if only one large lump-sum payment were made at the end of the month, the average cash balance would approximate y_m.

2. W. J. Baumol, "The Transactions Demand for Cash: An Inventory Theoretic Approach," Quarterly Journal of Economics 56 (November 1952), 545–556.

3. J. Tobin, "The Interest Elasticity of Transactions Demand for Cash," Review of Economics and Statistics 37 (August 1956), 241–247.

4. Tobin, op. cit., 242.

5. The macroeconomic implications of the square root rule are particularly hard to interpret. The usual problem of relating to the distribution of income and expenditures among households arises, of course. However, even ignoring that, we cannot tell whether the fact that the optimum level of cash balances for each household varies with the square root of the household's expenditures also implies that the aggregate demand for cash balances varies with the square root of total expenditures. Clearly, if the increase in total expenditures is spread over a larger number of firms and households (with no individual household's expenditures increasing), the square root rule would not apply. Without solid empirical evidence to the contrary, perhaps the classical linear assumption is most useful at the aggregate level.

6. J. M. Keynes, The General Theory of Employment, Interest and Money (London: Macmillan, 1936), p. 168.

7. Ibid., p. 216.

8. In constructing this chart we have chosen a narrow definition of money, that is, demand deposits (adjusted for bank float) plus currency in circulation outside banks. This corresponds to a payments money concept, including the forms of money that are most actively used in making payments. A broader definition of money would yield similar conclusions, as is shown, for example, in A. Breton, "A Stable Velocity Function for Canada?" Economica, N.S., 35 (November 1968), 451–453. We have used gross national product as the measure of aggregate income.

9. The most widely quoted study is P. Cagan, "The Monetary Dynamics of Hyperinflation," in M. Friedman, ed., Studies in the Quantity Theory of Money (Chicago: University of Chicago Press, 1956), 25–120. The literature is reviewed in D. Laidler, The Demand for Money: Theories and Evidence (Scranton, Pa.: International Textbook, 1969), pp.104–106.

10. J. Tobin, "Liquidity Preference and Monetary Policy," Review of Economic Statistics 29 (May 1974), 124–131; H. A. Latané, "Cash Balances and the Interest Rate—A Pragmatic Approach," Review of Economics and Statistics 36 (November 1954), 456–460.

11. Friedman in fact tested the importance of interest rates in an indirect way. He hypothesized that the demand for money was a function of a calculated figure for permanent income (see Chapter 4). He then compared the residual—that is, the difference between observed and predicted values for the demand for money—with various interest rates. On the basis of a visual correlation of the residuals and the various measures for interest rates, he could find no consistent pattern and therefore concluded that interest rates were not a primary determinant of the demand for money. See M. Friedman, "The Demand for Money: Some Theoretical and Empirical Results," Journal of Political Economy 67 (August 1959), 327–351.

12. K. Brunner and A. H. Meltzer, "Predicting Velocity: Implications for Theory and Policy," *Journal of Finance* 18 (May 1963), 319–354; D. Laidler, "The Rate of Interest and the Demand for Money—Some Empirical Evidence," *Journal of Political Economy* 74 (December 1966), 545–555.

13. Laidler, *The Demand for Money*, op. cit., p. 97.

14. M. Bronfenbrenner and T. Mayer, "Liquidity Functions in the American Economy," *Econometrica* 28 (October 1960), 810–834; D. Laidler, "The Rate of Interest and the Demand for Money," op. cit., 545–555; Brunner and Meltzer, op. cit.

15. Some of Professor Friedman's basic works in this field have been collected in the volume, M. Friedman, *The Optimum Quantity of Money and Other Essays* (Chicago: Aldine, 1969). The essays, "The Quantity Theory of Money: A Restatement" (pp. 51–68), "The Demand for Money: Some Theoretical and Empirical Results" (pp. 111–140), and "Interest Rates and the Demand for Money" (pp. 141–156) are particularly important.

19

THE THEORY OF
MONETARY POLICY

Monetary policy involves the manip-
ulation of the supplies of money and credit by the central bank with the
objective of influencing certain macroeconomic results of economic activity.
Various objectives are important from time to time, but two will figure most
prominently in our discussion: the level of income and employment and the
general level of prices. This chapter attempts to discover the channels
through which the monetary actions of the central bank may affect economic
activity and hence influence the levels of income, employment, and prices.
In the next chapter we will explore the international dimensions of monetary policy, and in Chapter 22 we will review several studies of the quantitative impact of monetary actions. It is important to keep this program in
mind as you read this chapter. We are concerned only with the direction of
the impact of monetary actions, not with their magnitude.

We saw in the last chapter that at any point in time there is a definable
demand for money that depends, *inter alia*, on the level of income and the
level of interest rates. In Chapters 15 and 16 we saw how the central bank
could manipulate the money supply—primarily through open-market operations that change the size of the monetary base. The question before us,
then, is: Given the demand for money, what happens when the central
bank changes the supply?

414

We can divide the repercussions into two interrelated categories: financial adjustments and real adjustments. By *financial adjustments* we mean the changes that occur in portfolios of financial instruments held by all types of asset holders. By *real adjustments* we mean changes that occur in the level of aggregate demand for goods and services and hence in the general levels of production, employment, and perhaps prices. The link between financial adjustments and real adjustments, whose nature is a subject of controversy among monetary economists, is a major concern of monetary theory.

FINANCIAL ADJUSTMENTS

The direct impact of central bank monetary actions is to produce disequilibrium in asset portfolios throughout the economy. The repercussions that follow result from asset holders' adjustments in the face of portfolio disequilibrium.

PORTFOLIO DISEQUILIBRIUM WITHIN THE BANKING SYSTEM

Consider first the financial repercussions of central bank measures to expand the money supply. As you will recall, such actions would normally take the form of purchases of government securities in the open market, although a variety of other expansionary techniques are also available to a central bank.

Bond Prices and Yields. The central bank cannot purchase government securities in the open market without raising their prices and hence somewhat depressing their yields. But we will leave that aspect of the matter aside for the moment. As we shall see, the direct impact of the central bank on government bond yields becomes swallowed up in the larger effects resulting from private portfolio adjustments.

Excess Bank Reserves. The major initial impact of the central bank's open-market purchases is to produce disequilibrium in the asset portfolios of commercial banks. The banks have a larger proportion of cash reserves among their assets than they would like, given the existing levels of interest rates. As we saw in Chapter 15, in this situation the profit motive will induce the banks to acquire additional earning assets. This has three important financial repercussions.

First, to some extent the banks will satisfy their demand for earning assets by purchasing securities, probably short-term government bonds, in the open market. Like the initial purchase by the central bank, this will tend to raise the price and hence lower the yield on government securities. Second, the banks will probably demonstrate increased willingness to extend loans. That is, at any given level of interest rates they will be willing to extend more credit. The supply curve for bank loans shifts outward. Depending on the competitive environment, this should lead to some reduction of interest rates and an easing of other terms for bank loans. In the jargon of central banking, there will follow a reduction in the cost and an increase in the "availability" of bank credit. Third, on the other side of the balance sheet, the increase in the banks' earning assets will be matched by an increase in the money supply.

These are all familiar propositions, developed in detail in Chapter 15. What happens outside the banking system?

PORTFOLIO DISEQUILIBRIUM AMONG OTHER ASSET HOLDERS

We now have three developments that combine to produce disequilibrium conditions within the portfolios of private asset holders other than banks: They are holding a larger than normal amount of money; the yields on government bonds have declined somewhat; and bank credit is available on more favorable terms. Together, these factors will induce private asset holders to rearrange their portfolios.

Excess Supply of Money. Perhaps the most important effect, and certainly the one most stressed in traditional monetary theory, is the increase in private holdings of money. This money was put into the hands of individuals when they responded to offers from the central bank or commercial banks for securities in their possession at marginally favorable prices or through the extension of loans by the commercial banks. In general, for private asset holders the new money is a temporary repository of purchasing power between the sale of one asset and the purchase of another. Given the levels of income and interest rates, they have no reason to hold the additional money itself. The new assets that they seek to acquire may be securities, or—and this is important as a link to the "real" side of the adjustment process—they may be real assets, capital goods or consumer durables.

The Level of Interest Rates. We can leave aside the effects on demand for real assets for the moment. In the market for securities, the attempts of private asset holders to purchase securities in exchange for the money they do not want to hold will add to the upward pressure on securities prices and hence to the decline in yields initiated by the central bank and aggravated by the portfolio adjustments of the commercial banks. Note also that through private portfolio adjustments the decline of government bond yields will be generalized to securities of all types and maturities. Asset holders will attempt to dispose of any securities whose yield has been abnormally depressed and attempt to purchase securities that still have relatively favorable yields. Given that the supply of each security is temporarily fixed, all that can happen as a result of such trading is a change in relative prices. Through the market adjustment, yields will tend to be equalized (allowing for risk and liquidity, of course) at new, lower levels. In other words, the end result is a decline in the general level of interest rates. Indeed, if there were no real adjustments, the level of interest rates would have to fall until private asset holders were content to hold the enlarged money supply. (Remember, as we demonstrated in Chapter 15, there is no way private asset holders can reduce the size of the money supply. They can only pass the unwanted money among themselves until interest rates are bid down sufficiently that some asset holders are willing to hold the money in their portfolios.)

This is an important *if*. There may be repercussions on real economic activity, and, as we shall see, these real repercussions also serve to adjust the demand for money to the expanded supply of money.

LINKAGES TO AGGREGATE DEMAND

The Real Balance Effect. We have already identified one direct link between monetary expansion and aggregate demand. The simple fact that people are holding more money than they desire at the existing levels of income, interest rates, and prices means that they now have more real assets than before the open-market purchase. With increased real money balances they will be inclined to purchase other assets, including, perhaps, real assets. This direct effect of the increase of money holdings on demands for goods and services is called the *real balance effect*. It plays a central role in some monetary theories.

Substitution Effects. The reduction of the general level of interest rates (and the associated increase in the availability of bank credit) also induces *substitution effects*. Remember that, while the yields on financial instruments have fallen as a result of the expansion of the monetary base, yields on fixed capital assets have not changed. Thus, lower yields on financial assets will increase the relative attractiveness of real assets. Rational asset holders will attempt to increase the share of real assets in their portfolios, some of them simply adjusting the composition of their existing asset portfolios, selling financial assets to acquire capital goods or consumer durables, while others, motivated by the lower cost and increased availability of credit, borrow funds to acquire additional real capital. The overall result is an increase in the demand for goods and services.

This is the major link to aggregate demand that we have been seeking. Monetary expansion, by reducing the yield on financial instruments relative to that on real capital, creates an incentive to invest in real assets, thus tending to increase the aggregate demand for goods and services.

The Yield on Real Assets. A crucial concept in this analysis is the yield, or rate of return, on real assets. Is this a meaningful concept?

We have already examined the concept of yield in some depth in Chapter 5 and its appendix. We discovered that it is simply the rate of interest implicit in the relationship between the market price of an asset and the stream of future income produced by that asset. We can apply the same concept to any piece of capital equipment. The stream of future income is the net addition to the revenues of the firm resulting from the employment of that piece of equipment (net after allowing for the cost of all cooperating factors). This stream may have a long or a short life, and it may be relatively certain or very uncertain. The market price of the asset is simply the cost of acquiring and installing the capital goods, whether they are purchased from another firm or constructed on the spot. Given a stream of future income with a finite length, and a market price for the asset producing the income, we can calculate the expected yield in the manner discussed in the appendix to Chapter 5. The yield on new real capital goods is commonly called the *marginal efficiency of capital.*

For industrial equipment and buildings, then, the concept of yield has a clear meaning. What about consumer durables?

Consumer durables can be thought of as producing a stream of future income—not in a financial sense but in "real" terms, as a flow of intangible services that yield utility directly to the consumer and have an implicit market value. In principle, then, we can also calculate the yield on durable consumer goods. While such calculations are difficult in practice, the yield on consumer durables is a meaningful concept for theoretical analysis.

The Saving Decision. There is also another type of substitution effect that might be induced by the general decline in the level of interest rates— a substitution of present consumption for future consumption. We discussed the saving decision at some length in Chapter 4 and noted that the division of income between current consumption and saving might be influenced by, among other things, the yield on financial assets. Although the direction of the effect is not absolutely certain, it is generally assumed that lower interest rates will induce more consumption and less saving. If so, we have another link between monetary expansion and the aggregate demand for goods and services.

Summary. In short, the linkages between financial adjustments and aggregate demand are complex. They involve in part the substitution of real assets for financial assets in portfolios, borrowing to finance the expansion of some portfolios, and the substitution of current for future consumption. Many individual decisions will be involved as each asset holder reassesses his portfolio in light of the new set of relative yields. As a result, the links may be highly diffused and perhaps difficult to identify. They are not necessarily confined to the market for industrial capital goods. They may involve the market for consumer durable goods and indeed the market for nondurable consumer goods and services.

REACTION TO MONETARY RESTRICTION

All of our discussion of the financial repercussions of monetary policy has been in terms of the responses of asset holders to an expansion of the monetary base. Their reactions to a restriction would simply be the reverse of those we have discussed. However, perhaps we should briefly outline these reactions before proceeding with our analysis of the real impact of monetary policy on income, employment, and price levels.

A restriction of the monetary base, as we know, is effected by the sale of government bonds by the central bank. This will create some upward pressure on bond yields and, by creating a cash reserve deficiency in the banking system, will lead to higher cost and restricted availability of bank credit. As the banks seek to deal with their reserve deficiency, further upward pressure on bond yields will occur, and this, coupled with the restriction of bank credit, will induce portfolio adjustments on the part of private asset holders. The rise in bond yields will be generalized to a rise in the level of interest rates, reducing incentives to invest in real assets. Through the various substitution effects we have already discussed, the incentives for businesses to purchase capital equipment and for households to purchase consumer durables will be reduced, and there may be some incentive to increase the rate of saving out of current income. All considered, there should be a restriction in the aggregate demand for goods and services.

MONETARY POLICY AND DEBT MANAGEMENT POLICY

Monetary Policy as Debt Management. Our discussion of monetary policy has focused on changes in the monetary base and hence in the money supply. However, as noted earlier, the monetary base is but one form of government debt. It has peculiar characteristics as debt in that it can be used as a medium of exchange, has the shortest possible term to maturity (payable on demand), and is non-interest-bearing. However, the very fact that it is government debt suggests an alternative perspective on monetary policy. It can be regarded as an aspect of debt management policy, that is, governmental policy with respect to the composition, and particularly the term structure, of the outstanding government debt.

In this context, an expansion of the monetary base through open-market purchases of government securities by the central bank can be considered as a reduction in the average term to maturity of the public debt, without any change in the size of the debt. The central bank has issued demand debt to replace debt in public hands that has a longer term to maturity. Similarly, a contraction of the monetary base through open-market sales of bonds by the central bank increases the average term to maturity of the public debt without altering the size of the debt. The central bank issues longer-term securities to replace demand debt in the hands of the general public.

"Conventional" Debt Management. Is the average term to maturity of the public debt itself an important macroeconomic variable? If it is, this provides the government with an additional instrument for stabilization policy because the government, or the central bank, can always engage in other types of operations in the open market to change the average term to maturity of the public debt. For example, the central bank can purchase long-term bonds from the general public, issuing Treasury bills rather than money in their place, thus reducing the average term to maturity. Alternatively, the bank can issue long-term bonds, retiring Treasury bills rather than money, thus increasing the average term to maturity. We can call such operations, involving a change in the term structure of the interest-bearing public debt with no change in either the monetary base or the aggregate size of the public debt, "conventional" debt management operations.

Monetary Effects of Conventional Debt Management. Many economists argue that conventional debt management operations have macroeconomic effects similar to those of monetary policy.

The principles underlying this argument are those that we developed earlier in our discussion of the demand for financial instruments and equilibrium in financial markets (Chapters 5 and 6). Consider the case of debt management operations to reduce the average term to maturity of the public debt. In order to achieve this objective, the government must disturb the preexisting equilibrium in financial markets. It must sell short-term securities (perhaps Treasury bills) that private asset holders do not want to hold at existing interest rates, and purchase long-term bonds that private asset holders do not want to sell at existing interest rates. In other words, the government must bid down the price, and hence increase the yield, of Treasury bills, while it simultaneously bids up the price, and hence lowers the yield, of long-term bonds.

A complex of portfolio adjustments should follow as private asset holders and borrowers respond to the new structure of interest rates. While we cannot trace these adjustments in any detail, two probable results are of interest.

First, the general public is holding more Treasury bills (a highly liquid substitute for money in some asset portfolios), which should reduce the demand for money. The outstanding stock of money is unchanged. As a result, there will be more money in the economy than the public wants to hold under the existing circumstances. As we saw earlier, the existence of this excess supply of money should lead, directly or indirectly, to an increase in the demand for goods and services. In this sense, the debt management operation is the equivalent of an expansionary monetary policy.

Second, the relative decline in the yield on long-term government bonds might induce other *substitution effects*, which would tend to expand aggregate demand. Because of this change in the yield on long-term government bonds, other, less liquid assets, including real assets (and perhaps current consumption), will become somewhat more attractive to private asset holders. They should make some marginal adjustments in their portfolios, leading to some expansion of aggregate demand. Thus, the substitution effects reinforce the effects of the reduction of the demand for money.

A lengthening of the average term to maturity of the government debt would presumably have opposite effects, increasing the demand for money and increasing the attractiveness of long-term government bonds as opposed to real assets for inclusion in private asset portfolios. The combined effect should be a contraction of aggregate demand for goods and services.

Monetary Policy vs. Debt Management Policy. While conventional debt management operations can have similar effects to those of monetary policy, there is an important difference. We saw in Chapter 15 that an expansion of the monetary base through the purchase of government bonds by the central bank would induce an absolute expansion of the size of the asset holdings of private financial institutions (particularly banks and near banks) several times as great as the expansion of the monetary base. Given present institutional arrangements, equivalent conventional debt management operations (e.g., an increase in Treasury bills outstanding equal to the postulated increase of the monetary base, offset by an equal reduction in long-term bonds outstanding) would not produce corresponding multiplier effects because the monetary base is not affected by the debt management operation. It seems likely, therefore, that the impact of conventional debt management operations on aggregate demand would be smaller than that of equivalent monetary operations.

Stabilization vs. Interest Cost. While the strength and reliability of the effects can be questioned (we will consider some evidence in Chapter 22), the arguments we have just reviewed provide an a priori case for the assertion that the term structure of the public debt is an important macroeconomic variable influencing the level of aggregate demand, and hence that conventional debt management operations can play a useful role in stabilization policy. However, it should be noted that the use of debt management operations for this purpose requires that the federal government not behave like the profit-maximizing debtors discussed in Chapter 6. That is, in general, the objective of debt management operations cannot be to minimize the effective interest cost of the public debt.

A moment's reflection should convince you of the potential conflict in debt management operations between the dictates of stabilization policy and those of interest cost minimization. Given the size of the public debt, interest cost minimization requires that the debt be funded into longer-term securities when interest rates are relatively low. By issuing long-term bonds when rates are low, the government can keep its interest payments low, even though interest rates rise in the future (if the debt was largely short term, it would mature and have to be refunded at the higher interest rates). However, as we have just seen, an increase of the average term to maturity tends to depress aggregate demand—and periods of low interest rates are likely to be precisely the times when the government is seeking to increase aggregate demand.

Exactly the opposite arguments apply to periods of high interest rates. At those times, interest cost minimization dictates that any new securities issued be short-term bonds. If long-term bonds are issued, the high interest rates will be built into the public debt, even though interest rates subsequently fall. However, periods of high interest rates are usually periods when the government wants to retard aggregate demand—and, according to the arguments developed earlier, this calls for a lengthening of the average term to maturity of the debt when interest rates are high.

The Conduct of Monetary Policy. It follows from this line of analysis that in the implementation of monetary policy attention should be paid not only to the magnitude of the change of the monetary base but also to the method by which the change is effected. An increase of the monetary base resulting from central bank purchases of Treasury bills will presumably have a marginally different impact on aggregate demand than will the same increase resulting from central bank purchases of long-term bonds. Unfortunately, however, although there has been considerable criticism of central bankers' preferences for dealing in short-term securities almost exclusively (the so called "bills only" doctrine),[1] there is little factual evidence that the form of the open-market operations makes a significant difference. It remains an interesting theoretical proposition.

Conclusion. Although we have barely scratched the surface in our discussion of the management of the public debt, we cannot pursue the topic further here. We will now return to our analysis of the transmission of monetary policy, viewing monetary policy in the traditional framework. However, it is important to realize that we are exploring only one aspect—although a particularly important one—of a much broader problem of the management of the public debt.

REAL ADJUSTMENTS: QUANTITY THEORY

We now turn to the consideration of what happens on the "real" side of the economy as a result of the financial adjustments induced by monetary policy. Again we start by considering the case of monetary expansion. As we have seen, incentives are created for business firms and households to purchase more goods and services. What are the implications of these incentives in terms of the objectives we specified for macroeconomic policy—income, employment, and the price level?

There are two radically different hypotheses to be considered, each of which contains an important message. We can call the first of these the *quantity theory* and the second the *Keynesian theory*.

THE CLASSICAL QUANTITY THEORY

A famous economist of the early part of the century, Irving Fisher, declared in his renowned book, *The Purchasing Power of Money*, that "one of the normal effects of an increase in the quantity of money is an exactly proportional increase in the general level of prices."[2]

This is the simplest and most forceful statement of the classical quantity theory of money. What type of model of the economy leads to this conclusion?

Long-Run Full Employment. In the first place, this statement is a proposition about the long run. The fundamental assumption underlying the classical quantity theory is that in the long run the economy tends to full employment of its productive resources, and particularly of the labor force. This means that in the long run the level of output and employment does not depend on the size of the money supply. In Fisher's words,

> An inflation of the currency cannot increase the product of farms and factories, nor the speed of freight trains or ships. The stream of business depends on natural resources and technical conditions, not on the quantity of money. The whole machinery of production, transportation, and sale is a matter of physical capacities and techniques, none of which depend on the quantity of money.[3]

This proposition should not be interpreted as an assumption of continuous full employment. Indeed, Fisher recognized that changes in the quantity of money might have temporary, "transitional" effects on levels of output and employment,[4] but these transitional effects are not of primary concern. Rather, attention is directed to the long run, when all of the economic forces inherent in the situation have worked themselves out. The mechanism that guarantees full employment as the "normal" equilibrium state of the economy is the general flexibility of prices. Unemployment implies an excess supply of labor at existing wage rates. Given time and price flexibility, the relative price of labor (the *real* wage rate) will fall sufficiently that the excess supply will be absorbed into productive employments. Inevitably, full employment will be reestablished.

Thus, in Fisher's model, "The price level is normally the one *absolutely passive* element. . . ."[5]

The Demand for Money. We have already discussed the second fundamental assumption of the classical quantity theory of money in Chapter 18. It is that the demand for money is a stable function of the level of income.

We can express this assumption in terms of the income velocity of money, a concept that we introduced in our discussion of the demand for money in Chapter 18. Remember, the income velocity of money (v) is defined as the ratio of aggregate income (Y) to the average stock of money (M), that is:

$$v = \frac{Y}{M} \tag{19.1}$$

For Fisher's statement of the quantity theory with which we introduced this section to be literally true, the velocity of money would have to be constant. Indeed, the classical quantity theory has frequently been interpreted in this way. However, this was not quite the proposition intended by the classical quantity theorists. They were asserting that, aside from temporary "transitional" effects, the velocity of circulation was determined by factors that were independent of the supply of money. Velocity had a long-run equilibrium value determined by relatively slow-changing technical and institutional factors, by the requirements for money to facilitate the flow of transactions in the economy. Thus, as long as the basic institutional and technical determinants of the demand for money were given, the quantity of money demanded in the economy in the long run would depend directly on the level of income. That is:

$$M_d = \left(\frac{1}{v}\right) Y \qquad (19.2)$$

where M_d is the quantity of money demanded and v is the long-run (equilibrium) velocity of money.

The Mechanics of the Quantity Theory. In order to explore the economic process involved in the quantity theory, let us trace the effects of a sizable increase in the supply of money.

As we have already seen, given the demand for money and given the existing levels of prices and incomes, the initial impact of an increase in the stock of money would be to create an excess supply of money. There would be more money in the economy than was demanded (or required?) under the existing circumstances. Remember, the stock of money is determined primarily by the government and the banking system. While each individual can dispose of money he does not want to hold by purchasing goods, services, or securities, he does so by passing the money on to someone else. Collectively, they cannot reduce the total stock of money. Moreover, under the classical assumption of full employment, the aggregate quantity of goods and services available cannot expand to satisfy the increased demands for goods and services on the part of those holding the excess money. All that can happen is that the general level of prices ·of goods and services is bid up.

We must now reintroduce the distinction between nominal values and real values. The classical assumption of full employment is equivalent to the assumption that real income is fixed. The increase in the general level of prices implies an increase of income in nominal terms. The price level must rise, then, until the level of nominal income is such that the excess supply of money is entirely absorbed. That is, the price level must rise until:

$$M_s = M_d = \left(\frac{1}{v}\right) Y \qquad (19.3)$$

The same proposition is sometimes stated in another way, focusing attention on the real money supply. Let us divide Equation 19.2 through by P, the general level of prices, in order to put it in real terms:

$$\left(\frac{M}{P}\right) d = \left(\frac{1}{v}\right) \frac{Y}{P} \qquad (19.4)$$

where $(M/P)d$ is the quantity of real money demanded and Y/P the level of real income. This is the demand for money expressed in real terms.

424

At the initial price level, the increase in the stock of nominal money has the temporary effect of increasing the supply of real money. However, given the basic institutional and technical determinants of velocity, and given the full-employment level of real income, Equation 19.4 tells us that the demand for real money will not have changed. Thus it follows: Given an increase in the nominal money supply, equilibrium between demand and supply will be reestablished only when the price level rises sufficiently that the real money supply is reduced to its original level. This means that the price level must eventually rise in proportion to the initial increase in the nominal money supply. You should take careful note of the fact that in this model the price level is the one and only variable that adjusts to maintain long-run equilibrium between the demand for and the supply of real money.

Implications for Monetary Policy. In the simplest possible terms, this is the classical quantity theory of money. It is fundamentally a theory of the demand for money, set in the context of an economy that has an automatic tendency toward full employment. It is a long-run theory—a set of propositions about ultimate equilibrium conditions—in which the price level is a variable but the levels of income and employment are not.

The implications for monetary policy are quite straightforward. Among our policy objectives, aside from transitional influences, only the general level of prices is amenable to control by the monetary authorities. Stability of the price level can be achieved only if the authorities maintain the stock of money that is demanded at the full employment level of income.

But perhaps we should set this conclusion in the context of a growing economy. In this context, stability of the price level, in the long run, depends simply on the choice of an appropriate rate of growth for the money supply. The growth rate of the nominal money supply should be the rate at which the availability of productive resources and technical advance will permit aggregate output to grow—adjusted, of course, for any changes in the institutional and technical conditions underlying the demand for money function.

THE MODERN QUANTITY THEORY

We have used the adjective *classical* to identify an early version of the quantity theory of money, which has a very long history in the literature of economics and achieved perhaps its most perfect exposition in the writings of Irving Fisher. As we shall see, this theory was abruptly discarded by the majority of economists in the 1930s and 1940s in favor of the macroeconomic theories derived from the works of J. M. Keynes. However, in recent years a new version of the quantity theory has emerged, primarily from the work of Milton Friedman. The modern quantity theory is more subtle and flexible than its classical counterpart and has provided a major stimulus to theoretical and empirical work in monetary economics.

The Demand for Money. The major departure of this theory is a

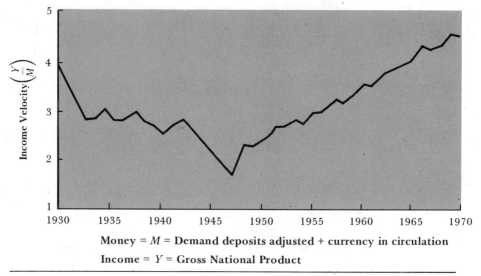

Money = M = Demand deposits adjusted + currency in circulation

Income = Y = Gross National Product

Figure 19.1 Income Velocity of Money in the United States, 1929–1970
SOURCE: Federal Reserve *Bulletin*, December 1970; *Economic Report of the President* (Washington, D.C.), various issues.

more general formulation of the demand for money function. We discussed Friedman's analysis of the demand for money as an asset in Chapter 18, and the major conclusions, you will recall, were that the demand for money was directly related to wealth rather than income and that for empirical work wealth could be approximated by a variable called permanent income. Other variables may enter the demand for money function, including the rates of return on other assets. However, the dominant variable is always permanent income. Thus, the fundamental assumption of the modern quantity theory of money is that the demand for money is a stable function of permanent income.

Stability of Velocity. This proposition permits a reinterpretation of the classical statement that in the long run the velocity of money is relatively stable.

One of the commonest criticisms of the classical quantity theory is that in fact the velocity of money is not a constant. This is evident in Figure 19.1, which describes the behavior of the income velocity of money. During this period velocity underwent wide fluctuations. As noted earlier, such criticisms tend to involve a misinterpretation of the classical theory. It was not argued that velocity was a constant but that in the long run velocity was independent of the money supply. Nonetheless, if velocity is not at least reasonably stable over periods that are not so long as to be irrelevant for policy purposes, the classical theory loses much of its potential interest. It may not be wrong, but it may be irrelevant.

In this context, the modern quantity theorist argues that it is important to distinguish between *measured velocity* and *permanent velocity*. Measured velocity, the ratio of current income to the stock of money, is subject to short-term fluctuations. *Permanent velocity*, the ratio of permanent income to the stock of money, is relatively stable. Measured velocity (v_m) depends not only on the underlying determinants of the demand for money (i.e., the determinants of permanent velocity, v_p) but also on the relationship between measured income (Y_m) and permanent income (Y_p). That is:[6]

$$v_m = v_p \left(\frac{Y_m}{Y_p} \right) \tag{19.5}$$

The fluctuations that we observe in the velocity of money, for example in Figure 19.1, are misleading. They do not reflect instability of permanent velocity, and hence of the underlying demand for money, but rather fluctuations of measured income around permanent income. They are a product of the transitory component of measured income. (See Chapter 4.)

Time Lags. It follows, as in the classical theory, that an increase in the supply of money will have a direct and powerful effect on the demand for goods and services. Moreover, in an economy that in the long run tends to full employment, the ultimate adjustment will be in the general level of prices. The price level must rise until the real money supply is again reduced to the quantity appropriate to the existing level of permanent income.[7]

In these respects the real adjustment process involved in the modern quantity theory is to all intents and purposes the same as that involved in the classical theory. However, the modern exponents pay much more attention to frictions and lags in the process of adjustment. In particular, they stress that the lags are both long, on the average, and highly variable. On the basis of past experience it has been argued that on the average 12 to 16 months must pass before the maximum effects of a change in the money supply will be felt, but that this period may be as short as 6 months or as long as 18 months.[8]

Policy Implications. According to this analysis, manipulation of the money supply can be a powerful weapon of economic policy, although the length and variability of the time lags involved also render it a potentially dangerous weapon. The problem is that since the effects of a change in the money supply will not be fully felt until some time in the future, present actions should be geared not to present developments in the economy but to future developments. However, even presuming adequate predictive abilities, if the time lag is highly variable, what is the relevant period in the future to which actions should be geared?

Exponents of the modern quantity theory argue that past attempts to stabilize the economy by manipulating the money supply have actually had a destabilizing effect. For example, monetary actions taken in response to recession have had their major impact on the economy when the recession was passed and the problem was excessive aggregate demand. That is, the major impact was felt when the opposite policies were called for, and in this way monetary policy tended to be a major disturbance to the level of economic activity. Indeed, it has been argued that the attempts of central banks to use their discretionary control over the money supply to counter short-term fluctuations in economic activity are inherently destabilizing—they will almost inevitably have a perverse effect. Under these circumstances, the modern quantity theorists argue that it would be much better if the monetary authorities simply followed the classical rule and increased the money supply at approximately the rate of growth of the potential output of the economy. Such a policy would remove the central bank as a major source of disturbances in the economy and would provide the maximum contribution to economic stability of which monetary management is capable.

REAL ADJUSTMENTS: KEYNESIAN THEORY

To many economists of the 1930s and 1940s, the classical quantity theory of money, with its assumption of long-run tendencies to full employment, seemed either wrong or utterly irrelevant. Indeed, in the face of massive and prolonged unemployment there was considerable speculation about whether the chronic unemployment of a high portion of the labor force rather than full employment was the normal equilibrium state of the economy. In this context, the Keynesian model, which focused on the level of employment, swept the field in macroeconomic analysis.

The classical quantity theory of money was a theory of long-run equilibrium, in which the price level is the central variable. The economics of "transitional" periods between one long-run equilibrium and another, including the possibility of prolonged, large-scale, involuntary unemployment, received little attention. To Keynes, by contrast, the analysis of this period contained the essence of the macroeconomic policy problem—a point that is underlined by the famous Keynesian aphorism, "In the long run we all are dead." The Keynesian theory is a theory about the short run in which output and employment are the central variables. Indeed, in the extreme version of the Keynesian theory, the price level is presumed to be fixed by institutional rigidities. Let us briefly explore this extreme model.

SOME BASIC IDENTITIES

The central concept in the Keynesian model is aggregate demand. This is a concept that we have used on several occasions. We must now consider it more carefully.

Aggregate Demand. By aggregate demand we mean the aggregate expenditures from all sources during a given period for the purchase of goods and services newly produced by factors of production. Note that aggregate demand has a time dimension. It is a flow concept.

428

Depending on the purpose of the analysis, aggregate demand can be broken down into many categories of expenditure. For most purposes, at least four sources of demand must be recognized: household expenditures for all types of consumer goods and services (commonly called *consumption* and represented by the symbol C); business expenditures for new capital goods, machinery, equipment, buildings, and inventories (*investment—I*); government expenditures for all types of goods and services, but excluding purely transfer payments, like unemployment insurance compensation, which are not payments for goods or services rendered (*government expenditure— G*); and the expenditures of nonresidents of the United States to purchase American goods or the services of American productive factors (*exports—X*). Mention of the foreign sector should remind us that not all expenditures by American households, business firms, and governments constitute demand for the services of domestic productive factors. Part of this demand is for the importation of foreign goods or the services of foreign productive services (*imports—Im*). In measuring aggregate demand we must deduct this part of the aggregate expenditures of American spending units.

By this definition:

$$\text{Aggregate Demand} = D = C + I + G + X - Im \qquad (19.6)$$

Aggregate Income. Another concept that we have used on several occasions is *aggregate income*. By this we mean the total income of all types (wages, rent, interest, profits) earned by factors of production owned by residents of the United States during a given period. Like aggregate demand, it is a flow concept.

The owners of factors of production earn income because of the participation of their factors in the production process. Indeed, because we have included profits in the category of income, it should be obvious that if it were not for problems relating to certain taxes, subsidy payments, and depreciation accounting,[9] the sum of all incomes earned should equal the value of output produced. All income payments besides profit show on the books of business firms as costs. But the difference between the value of output and costs measured in this sense is profit. Hence, if we add profit to factor costs, we should have a measure of both the value of output (*gross national product*, or GNP) and the value of aggregate income (Y).[10]

Thus:

$$\text{Aggregate Income} = Y = GNP = \text{Aggregate Output} \qquad (19.7)$$

We also know, however, that the value of aggregate output is the same thing as the value of aggregate expenditures. These two concepts are merely two sides of the same set of market transactions. GNP is the value of what has been produced and sold; D is the value of what has been purchased.

It follows then, that:

$$\text{Aggregate Income} = Y = C + I + G + X - Im = \text{Aggregate Output} \qquad (19.8)$$

What we have in the middle of this expression is aggregate demand.

Output and Employment. Remember, we are assuming that the price level is fixed. Since we can think of gross national product as the price level multiplied by the quantity of output produced, the assumption of a fixed price level means that any change in aggregate demand must involve a proportional change in output.

But in the short run, given the established techniques of production and existing productive equipment, any change in output will be reflected in a change in the level of employment. For various reasons, the change in employment may not be proportional to the change in aggregate demand, but it will be in the same direction. Thus, a decline in aggregate demand means a drop in the level of output, and it means unemployed labor and idle machinery and factories.

A Simplified Framework. Striving for closer and closer approximations of reality, modern Keynesian models recognize many more subcategories of aggregate demand. However, our interest in the Keynesian model is very general. We only want to identify the basic principles of how monetary policy is supposed to influence the level of income and employment. We can simplify rather than complicate the model by delaying consideration of the government sector and the international sector.

The simplified framework that we will consider is as follows:

$$\text{Aggregate Demand} = C + I = Y = \text{GNP} \qquad (19.9)$$

This equation is an identity. It provides a framework for analysis but tells us nothing about the economic processes that determine the levels of income and employment. For this we need assumptions about the behavior of the relevant macroeconomic variables. So far we have made two important assumptions: that the price level is fixed and that the level of employment depends directly on the level of output. What are the other essential assumptions of the Keynesian theory?

The basic distinction between the two categories of aggregate demand in Equation 19.9 is between the types of expenditures that are presumed to be directly affected by the current level of income (typified by consumption) and those that are largely independent of the current level of income (typified by investment). While the terminology is not fully appropriate, the latter are someimes called autonomous expenditures. We will consider this category first.

Behavioral Assumptions: The Investment Decision. Investment in the Keynesian model implies a decision to install new capital goods (factories, machinery, equipment) or to increase inventories of goods in process of production or distribution.

The relevant considerations in such a decision are the expected yield on the new capital goods (the marginal efficiency of capital) and the market yields on financial instruments (the level of interest rates). Of these the expected yield on new capital goods must be the dominant, dynamic factor. It involves a projection of earnings into the more or less remote future, an exercise that by its very nature must be speculative, subject to all kinds of psychological influences, and surrounded by uncertainty. For this reason it should not be surprising that among all of the categories of aggregate expenditure, investment is the one econometricians find most difficult to "explain" statistically. That is, they find it difficult to establish clear, stable relationships between investment expenditures and other macroeconomic variables.

Interest Rates and Investment Demand. The theoretical role of the yield on financial instruments in the investment decision has already been alluded to. On the one hand, interest rates represent the opportunity cost of using the firm's funds for real investment, and on the other hand (and probably much more important) they represent the cost of borrowing the funds required to finance the purchase and installation of the capital goods. Elementary economic theory tells us that when interest rates are high, business firms will attempt to economize on capital, choosing less capital intense techniques of production. At high interest rates many potential investment projects will not be undertaken because they do not offer a sufficiently high yield. But as the cost of borrowing falls, more and more projects become feasible. As just one elementary example, consider the feasibility of constructing a new subway in a large metropolitan area, a highly capital intensive project. One question that arises is how far the line should be extended into the suburbs. The lines in the center of the city, with high population density and correspondingly heavy traffic, can be expected to generate large revenues per mile of track. They offer a high yield. However, the farther the lines are pushed into the low-population-density suburbs, the smaller the revenue per mile of track, and correspondingly the lower the yield on the investment. Considered simply as a commercial venture, the extent of suburban penetration will depend on the level of interest rates. At very high interest rates, only the central city will appear to be a profitable location for a new subway. At very low interest rates, extension into the suburbs will appear profitable. The amount of subway investment, in other words, varies inversely with the interest rate.

The Investment Demand Function. In general, then, the higher the level of market interest rates, the lower the level of investment expenditures. This assumption is represented graphically in Figure 19.2, with the flow of investment expenditures planned by firms measured along the base axis and the level of interest rates along the vertical axis. This is the investment demand function for any given "state of expectations" relating to the yields of potential new capital projects. Among other things, a change in the economic outlook will shift the function—a buoyant outlook shifting it

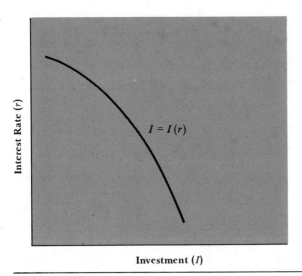

Figure 19.2 **The Investment Demand Function**

to the right and pessimistic expectations shifting it to the left. Similarly, a significant technological revolution might suddenly increase the amount of investment that would be worthwhile at various rates.

BEHAVIORAL ASSUMPTIONS: THE CONSUMPTION FUNCTION

We discussed the Keynesian postulate with respect to consumption in Chapter 4. In brief, Keynes asserted that the dominant factor determining the level of consumption expenditures is the level of income but that consumption increases less than proportionately with the level of income. That is, what he called the marginal propensity to consume has a magnitude less than 1. In linear form, the Keynesian consumption function is:

$$C = C_o + cY \tag{19.10}$$

where C_o is a constant (the part of consumption that is independent of the level of income—"autonomous" consumption) and c is the marginal propensity to consume, the slope of the consumption function in the top section of Figure 19.3.

A Saving Function. Applying an identity we developed in Chapter 4, we also know that:

$$Y = C + S \tag{19.11}$$

where S is aggregate saving. It follows, then, that:

$$\begin{aligned} S &= Y - C \\ &= Y - (C_o + cY) \\ &= Y (1 - c) - C_o \end{aligned} \tag{19.12}$$

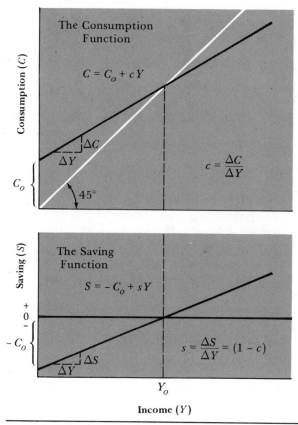

Figure 19.3 **Keynesian Consumption and Saving Functions**

In our simplified model, which ignores the government sector and external trade, this is the saving function. If we let s represent the marginal propensity to save, such that:

$$s = (1 - c) \qquad (19.13)$$

we can rewrite Equation 19.12:

$$S = C_o + sY \qquad (19.14)$$

The saving function is thus derived directly from the consumption function, as shown in Figure 19.3.[11]

EQUILIBRIUM IN THE "COMMODITY MARKET"

An equilibrium level of income is one that does not have an inherent tendency to change. We know from Equation 19.9 that aggregate income is the sum of consumption and investment expenditures, and we know from the preceding discussion that these two components are determined

433

independently. Consumption depends on the level of income, and investment depends on the state of expectations and the level of interest rates. However, for any given level of income to be an equilibrium level, it must be true that the level of investment expenditures that businesses want to undertake is exactly equal to the level of savings that households want to make.

A moment's thought should convince you of the validity of this proposition. If businesses want to invest more than households want to save at the given level of income, the sum of planned consumption and planned investment will have to exceed that level of income. Income will, of necessity, rise. The opposite is true if investment falls short of the planned savings of households.

Thus, we have the equilibrium condition in what we will call the commodity market. An equilibrium level of income is one at which the planned investment of businesses equals the planned saving of households.

Indeterminacy of Equilibrium Income. If the level of investment depends on the rate of interest, then there must be many different equilibrium levels of income that are consistent with any given investment and saving functions. Indeed, since there will be a different equilibrium level of income for each possible level of interest rates, we cannot identify a unique equilibrium level of income unless we have determined the level of interest rates. At best, we can draw a curve that shows all of the possible equilibrium levels of income, one for each level of interest rates. Such a curve is commonly called an *IS* curve because it shows all of the combinations of interest rates and income levels at which planned investment equals planned saving.

Derivation of the *IS* Curve. One method of deriving the *IS* curve is illustrated in Figure 19.4. This involves what is at first glance a rather complicated geometrical construction, a four-quandrant diagram, with the origin at the center (O) and with the scales on each axis increasing as you move away from the origin. (Note that this is in contrast to the usual four-quandrant diagram of elementary algebra, in which movements downward and to the left from the origin have a negative sign.) However, it is basically a simple construct, designed to demonstrate graphically the necessity for equilibrium interest rates and income levels to simultaneously satisfy both the investment demand function and the savings function.

Equilibrium requires that $I = S$. For any selected interest rate, say r_1, the investment demand function in Quandrant II tells us the associated level of investment, that is, I_1. Projecting this into Quadrant III, the saving function tells us the only level of income at which saving will equal this level of investment: Y_1. This is the equilibrium level of income for r_1. We can similarly find the equilibrium level of income for all other possible interest rates. In Figure 19.4 we have done this for two other levels of interest rates, r_2 and r_3.

The line in Quadrant IV is simply a geometrical device to project the

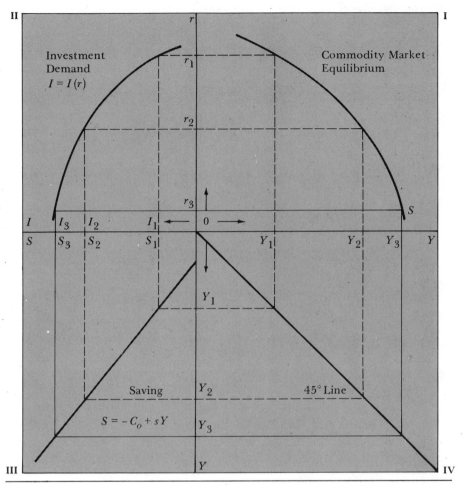

Figure 19.4 **Derivation of the IS Curve**

equilibrium incomes to the base axis of Quadrant I. This line makes a 45° angle with each of the two axes, so that the distance OY_1 in Quadrant I is the same as the distance OY_1 in Quadrant III. The resulting curve in Quadrant I, then, identifies the equilibrium level of income associated with each possible level of interest rates. It is the *IS* curve. At any point above the *IS* curve, saving will exceed investment and income will have to fall. Likewise, at any point below the *IS* curve investment will exceed saving and income will have to rise. (To demonstrate your understanding of the analysis, you should be able to explain why these statements are true.) The *IS* curve is the locus of equilibrium points in the commodity market.

Position and Shape of the *IS* Curve. The position of the *IS* curve depends on the positions of the investment demand and saving functions (and on the size of the marginal propensity to save). An increase in investment demand will shift *IS* function to the right. By contrast, an increase in the demand for saving, in the sense of an increase in saving at every level of income, will shift the *IS* function to the left.[12] You should be able to demonstrate these propositions.

Likewise, the shape of the *IS* function depends on the shapes of the investment demand and the saving functions. If investment were very inelastic with respect to the rate of interest (if the *I* function were very steep), the *IS* function would likewise be very inelastic. The increase in income for any given drop of the interest rate would be relatively small. Correspondingly, the smaller the marginal propensity to save (the closer the *S* function is to the axis), the more elastic the *IS* function will be. The increase in income for any given drop of the interest rate will be relatively large.

EQUILIBRIUM IN THE MONEY MARKET

This analysis of equilibrium in the commodity market makes clear the central variable in the Keynesian model: the level of interest rates. Without specification of the level of interest rates, the equilibrium levels of income and employment are indeterminate. But what determines the level of interest rates?

We cannot answer this question until we have explored the financial side of the Keynesian model. In particular, we have to establish the conditions for equilibrium between the demand for and supply of money. We call this "equilibrium in the money market."

The Demand for Money. As we stated in Chapter 18, Keynes accepted the classical argument that the demand for money depended on the level of income but argued that the level of interest rates was also a major factor in the demand function. Moreover, Keynes argued that at low interest rates the demand for money would become highly elastic with respect to the interest rate. Indeed, some of Keynes' followers hypothesized, there may be some low interest rate at which the demand for money becomes perfectly elastic: what we have called the liquidity trap. Such a demand for money function, at a given level of income, was depicted in Figure 18.8.

Indeterminacy of Equilibrium. In what follows, we take the supply of money as given by the central bank. If the demand for money depends on both the level of income and the level of interest rates, equilibrium in the money market depends on finding combinations of income and interest rates at which the demand for money equals the supply of money. As in the commodity market, we cannot identify a unique equilibrium in the money market considered alone. The best we can do is to draw a curve similar in concept to the *IS* curve, which describes all possible combinations of income and interest rates that will produce equilibrium in the money market. Such a curve is normally called an *LM* curve.[13]

Derivation of the *LM* Curve. One method of deriving the *LM* curve

436

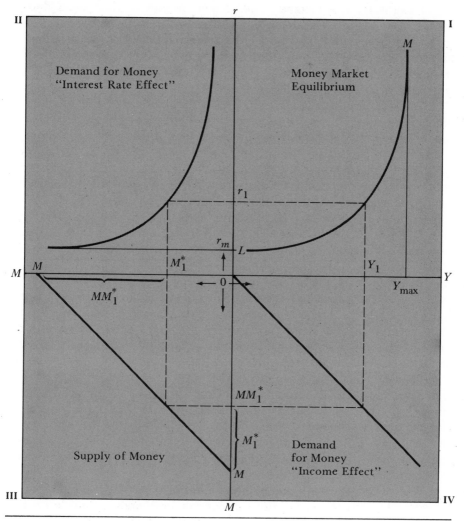

Figure 19.5 **Derivation of the LM Curve**

is presented in Figure 19.5. The graphic technique is similar to that employed in Figure 19.4.

For the purposes of this exercise, it is assumed that the Keynesian demand for money function takes a particular form, that is, that the interest rate and income effects on the quantity of money demanded are independent of each other and hence separable. In other words, it is assumed that the impact of a given interest rate on the quantity of money demanded is the same regardless of the level of income, and vice versa. This makes it possible to draw a curve showing the interest rate effect (as in Quadrant II) without regard to the level of income[14] and to add the interest rate effect directly to the income effect (Quadrant IV) to obtain the total quantity of money demanded. We also make the "classical" assumption that the relationship between income and the quantity of money demanded is linear. It must be emphasized that these are very special assumptions, adopted to make the graphic analysis manageable.

Consider Quadrant II first. If the interest rate is r_1, the quantity of money demanded because of the interest rate effect alone is M_1^*. The total supply of money made available by the central bank is M. Therefore, if equilibrium is to exist in the money market in the sense that the demand for money equals the supply of money, the quantity of money demanded because of the level of income must be MM_1^*. The problem is to identify the level of income that will produce this demand for money.

Quadrant III, labeled The Supply of Money, is the only part of Figure 19.5 that should require special explanation. Again, this contains a special construct making use of elementary geometry. The line MM makes a 45° angle with each of the axes of Quadrant III. It links the points indicating the total money supply as measured from the origin along each of these axes. It also serves to reflect the two components of the demand for money from the horizontal axis to the vertical axis of Quadrant III. Thus, because the line MM makes a 45° angle with the vertical axis, the distance from the point M to the point (MM_1^*) represents the quantity of money demanded because the level of interest rates is r_1. The remainder of the distance to the origin $Q - (MM_1^*)$ represents the quantity of money that has to be demanded because of the income effect if equilibrium is to prevail. From the curve in Quadrant IV, which shows the relationship between income alone and the quantity of money demanded, we can identify the level of income that will induce this demand for money. This level of income, Y_1, is indicated on the horizontal axis of Quadrants I and IV. Y_1 is the equilibrium level of income, given the interest rate r_1.

This provides us with one point on the LM curve. By the same process we could find other combinations of interest rates and income levels that would permit equilibrium in the money market. The end result would be a curve like that labeled LM in Quadrant I.

In order to demonstrate your understanding of the construction of the LM curve, you should be able to show that any point above the LM curve (i.e., to the left of the curve) implies a combination of income and interest rates at which the quantity of money demanded is less than the available money supply. It cannot be an equilibrium situation. Similarly, you should be able to demonstrate that any point below the LM curve implies a combination of income and interest rates at which the quantity of money demanded exceeds the quantity supplied by the central bank. The LM curve describes the locus of equilibrium points in the money market.

The LM Curve and the Money Supply. Note particularly the shape of the *LM* curve. It slopes upward to the right, with a virtually horizontal portion at very low interest rates and a virtually vertical portion at high interest rates. The flat portion of the curve reflects the Keynesian assumption of a liquidity trap. It implies that there is a minimum level of interest rates. The vertical portion implies that there is a maximum level of income for any given money supply.

You should also remember that the *LM* curve is drawn for a given money supply. If the money supply is increased (the *MM* curve of Quadrant III shifts to the left), the *LM* curve will shift to the right. The minimum interest rate may not change (why not?), but the maximum income level will increase. Similarly, a reduction in the money supply will shift the *LM* curve to the left.

The *LM* Curve and the Price Level. Remember, the Keynesian model assumes a fixed price level. What happens, however, if the price level changes?

In Chapter 18 we noted two different effects of a change in the price level. We can use Figure 19.5 to illustrate the differences between them.

Consider first the impact of a once-and-forever rise in the price level— what we called in Chapter 18 the direct impact of a rise in prices. For this purpose we should interpret all of the curves in Figure 19.5 as showing the relationships between real magnitudes. That is, the money supply is the real money supply and the income level is real income. Then, with the nominal supply of money fixed by the central bank, a rise in the general level of prices would imply a reduction in the real money supply. The *MM* curve in Quadrant III would shift to the right, implying higher interest rates and lower real incomes. Neither of the demands for money functions, expressed in real terms, would shift.

By contrast, consider the effects of a general expectation of a continuing rise of the price level in the future. The opportunity cost of holding money at any given level of market interest rates has increased by the expected rate of inflation. As a result, the demand curve in Quadrant II will shift to the right. That is, at any given market interest rate a smaller quantity of money would be demanded. The end result would be a higher level of income and a higher level of interest rates. The mere expectation of inflation can have powerful economic effects. (What would be the impact of the expectation of deflation?)

MACROECONOMIC EQUILIBRIUM IN THE KEYNESIAN SYSTEM

Macroeconomic equilibrium requires equilibrium simultaneously in both the money market and the commodity market. If one of the markets is in disequilibrium, at least one of the variables in the system, income or the level of interest rates, will change; and when it changes, the equilibrium in the other market will be disturbed. Therefore, full equilibrium requires a combination of income and interest rates that simultaneously satisfies both the *IS* function and the *LM* function, that is, the combination identified

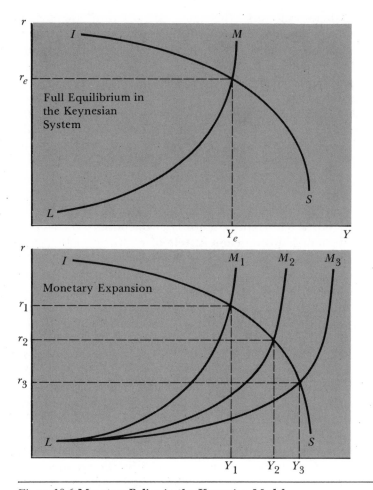

Figure 19.6 **Monetary Policy in the Keynesian Model**

by the intersection of the two curves. Thus, in the upper section of Figure 19.6 the equilibrium income and interest levels are Y_e and r_e, respectively.

MONETARY POLICY IN THE KEYNESIAN SYSTEM

We are now in a position to use the analytical apparatus of the IS and LM curves to examine the effects of monetary policy in the Keynesian model. In particular, let us consider the effects of an expansion of the money supply by the central bank.

We start with the economic system in equilibrium at income level Y_1 in the lower section of Figure 19.6. An increase in the money supply shifts the LM curve outward, from LM_1 to LM_2. At the preexisting levels of income and interest rate, the money market is now in disequilibrium. Asset holders are holding more money than they want to.

In the usual expositions of the Keynesian model, the complex of portfolio adjustments that we discussed in the first section of this chapter are much circumscribed. The only action asset holders are permitted to take is to attempt to purchase more "bonds." The excess supply of money does not directly induce them to acquire real assets—there is no real balance effect in either the consumption function or the investment demand function. With the stock of bonds given, all that can happen initially is that the price of bonds is bid up and hence interest rates reduced. This is the key element in the Keynesian analysis. It is the level of interest rates that provides the link between the financial sector and the real sector.

As interest rates fall, the quantity of money demanded increases (Quadrant II, Figure 19.5) and the level of investment expenditures rises (Quadrant II, Figure 19.4). As Figure 19.4 shows, an increase in investment expenditure produces an increase in income. Again, remember that in this model the price level is fixed. The increase of income means an increase in employment.

The system will gravitate toward a new equilibrium, with the levels of income and interest rates at Y_2 and r_2, respectively, in the lower section of Figure 19.6. A further increase of the money supply would produce a further adjustment in the same direction, perhaps to Y_3, r_3. Of course, a reduction in the money supply would shift the LM function and hence the equilibrium point in the opposite direction.

The economics of the Keynesian model, with its assumption of a fixed price level, is the economics of an underemployment economy. The problem is to increase the level of income from one that involves substantial unemployment to one that implies full employment of the labor force. Is monetary policy always capable of achieving this objective?

Impotent Monetary Policy: The Liquidity Trap. The upper section of Figure 19.7 illustrates one situation in which monetary policy is impotent. This is the Keynesian liquidity trap case. Interest rates are at their minimum level, so further expansion of the money supply does not increase the level of income.

This diagram also illustrates in an extreme form the Keynesian explanation for short-term fluctuations in the velocity of money, such as those described on Figure 19.1. Because of the interest elasticity of the demand for money, variations in income are not proportional to variations in the money supply. Not only will velocity change, but, contrary to the classical quantity theory argument, these variations in velocity are induced by changes in the money supply. Indeed, they serve to offset at least part of the impact of monetary policy, since velocity falls as the money supply expands and rises as the money supply contracts. In the extreme case of an economy caught in the liquidity trap, the money supply can change with no effect on income. In these circumstances, according to the Keynesian model, there is no limit to the velocity of money. Indeed, the very concept of velocity is meaningless.

441

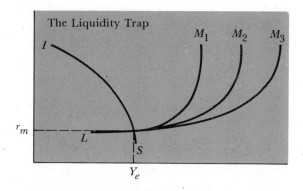

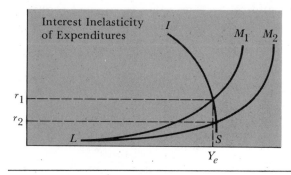

Figure 19.7 **Impotent Monetary Policy**

For this reason, it should not be surprising that the Keynesian concept of the liquidity trap has stirred up more controversy than any other concept in the recent history of monetary policy, nor that it has come under particular attack from advocates of the modern quantity theory of money.

As noted in Chapter 18, empirical studies of the demand for money tend to confirm the hypothesis that the demand for money is sensitive to the interest rate, but cast doubt on the extreme elasticity implied by the liquidity trap. Beyond this, many monetary theorists have invoked the concept of a *real balance effect* to argue that even with a liquidity trap there still exists a mechanism for monetary policy to increase income and employment. Although interest rates are fixed at a minimum level by the liquidity trap, eliminating interest-rate-induced substitution effects, further increases in the money supply will have a direct impact on expenditures. That is, it is argued that the size of the money supply itself is a factor affecting investment and consumption. However, there is little evidence that such a real balance effect caused by a decline in prices or by expansion of the money supply, if it exists, has any great quantitative importance.[15]

Impotent Monetary Policy: Interest Inelasticity of Expenditures. A more important possible reason for the impotence of monetary policy (particularly in the context of attempts to use it to restrict aggregate demand) is interest inelasticity of expenditures. This problem is illustrated in the lower section of Figure 19.7. In this case, because of the steepness of the IS curve, an increase in the money supply, shifting the LM curve from LM_1 to LM_2, lowers the level of interest rates but does not significantly increase the level of investment or income.

Again, there will be a change in velocity. If the increase in the money supply is not accompanied by an increase in income, by definition velocity falls. The converse would be true for a reduction in the money supply in the same range of the IS curve—for example, a shift of the LM curve from LM_2 to LM_1.

Clearly, the interest elasticity of expenditures is a crucial consideration in assessing the efficacy of monetary policy. We will review some of the evidence on this matter in Chapter 22.

THE FISCAL POLICY ALTERNATIVE

Our discussion of the Keynesian model to this point has focused exclusively on its implications for monetary policy to the neglect of its broader insights into the economics of stabilization policy. Nonetheless, we have discovered one important conclusion: Since there is a significant risk that monetary policy will be impotent in periods of large-scale unemployment, the achievement and maintenance of full employment may require other policy measures. Historically, the important result of the Keynesian monetary analysis was to thrust *fiscal policy* to the fore as the primary regulator of economic activity.

The economics of fiscal policy is subject enough for a book in itself. However, since many of the current controversies in monetary economics relate to the relative effectiveness of monetary and fiscal actions, it is important that we review the rudiments of the Keynesian analysis of fiscal policy.

The Nature of Fiscal Policy. By fiscal policy we mean decisions with respect to the levels of revenues and expenditures of the government sector of the economy. It is argued that by varying government expenditures or the level of taxation (or both), the government can have a direct and powerful impact on aggregate demand and hence, in the short run (i.e., with a given price level), on production and employment.

Government Expenditures and Aggregate Demand. The impact on aggregate demand of changes in the level of government expenditures for goods and services should be obvious from the aggregate demand equation (19.6). If the government increases its expenditures without doing anything that would induce private spenders to reduce their expenditures (whether consumption, investment, or exports), then aggregate demand must increase. Indeed, as the early Keynesians emphasized, the resulting increase of income and output might well induce further increases of private expenditures, particularly consumption expenditures, which are assumed to depend directly on income, thus reinforcing the initial increase of aggregate demand. This is the familiar "multiplier" process noted earlier in discussing the shape of the *IS* function. A reduction of government expenditures on goods and services would have the opposite effect; that is, it would reduce the levels of aggregate demand, production, and employment.

Taxes, Transfer Payments, and Aggregate Demand. The impact on aggregate demand of changes in the level of taxation is only slightly more complicated. Taxes do not appear directly in the aggregate demand equation, but changes in tax rates should have an indirect effect on aggregate demand because of their impact on expenditures by private spenders (households and firms). Taxes limit the share of earned income that private spenders have available to support their expenditures. A reduction of tax rates thus increases the funds available for other purposes and hence should stimulate private spending. By contrast, an increase in tax rates restricts the funds available in the private sector and hence should restrict private spending.

There are a great variety of taxes and many possible combinations of changes in tax rates, all of which may have different effects on private expenditures and hence on aggregate demand. The implications of an increase in customs tariffs might be quite different from those of an increase in the corporation income tax. However, the analysis is usually couched in terms of the personal income tax, with consumption expenditures the relevant component of aggregate demand that is to be regulated by fiscal policy. An increase in personal income tax rates, by reducing the disposable income of households, is expected to reduce consumption expenditures and aggregate demand. A reduction of personal income tax rates, by increasing disposable income, should increase consumption expenditures.

In this context it is important to distinguish between government expenditures on goods and services and government transfer payments. Transfer payments are typified by family allowances or unemployment compensation. They are payments by the government that are not payments for goods or services rendered to the government. In this sense they are negative taxes. They do not add directly to the aggregate demand for productive services, but they do add to the disposable incomes of private spenders and hence should stimulate private demand for goods and services. In the rest of our analysis we will not consider transfer payments explicitly. Rather, we will assume that they are deducted from taxes to obtain "net taxes."

Government Expenditure and Tax Functions. There is an important asymmetry in the treatment of government expenditures and tax revenues as instruments of stabilization policy in the standard exposition of the elementary Keynesian model.

It is usually assumed that the level of government expenditures on goods and services is a policy variable with respect to which decisions can be made independently of government tax revenues and of such other

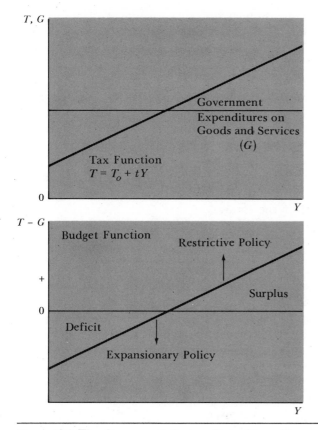

Figure 19.8 **The Government Sector: Expenditure, Tax, and Budget Functions**

economic variables as the level of income or the level of interest rates. This is not to deny that many categories of government expenditures are substantially affected by economic developments. The government is not a monolithic sector in which a single set of consistent decisions is made, controlling all expenditures at all levels of government in all parts of the country. The United States is, after all, a federal state. However, it is not necessary for all government expenditures to be a policy instrument. All that is necessary is that the central government have the potential to control the total of government expenditures—perhaps partly by varying its own expenditures on goods and services and perhaps partly by influencing expenditures at other levels of government through intergovernmental transfers (grants-in-aid, etc.).

Therefore, in drawing the government expenditure function as a horizontal line in Figure 19.8 we are assuming that the central government has the potential to control the level of aggregate government expenditures on goods and services as an instrument of fiscal policy.[16]

By contrast, it is generally assumed that the instrument of government policy is not the level of tax revenues but the rate of taxation of national income—in other words, that the government establishes a schedule of tax rates as a matter of policy, with the level of tax revenues then depending on variations in the level of income.

The relationship between tax collections and income can be quite complex. It depends on the mix of taxes established by the government (e.g., the relative importance of sales and excise taxes, property taxes, corporation income taxes, personal income taxes, etc.), on changes in the composition of economic activity and income (e.g., relative changes in retail sales or corporation profits), and on the progression of tax rates with income in the personal income tax. For simplicity, we have assumed a familiar linear tax function in Figure 19.8 of the form:

$$T = T_o + tY \tag{19.15}$$

where $T =$ tax collections and $Y =$ gross national product. The coefficient t is a constant marginal tax rate, the slope of the tax function in Figure 19.8.

A particular fiscal policy, then, implies a decision on both the level of government expenditures and the position and shape of the tax function.

Budgetary Surpluses and Deficits. Figure 19.8 summarizes our assumptions about the government sector, including the balance on the government's budget (lower section). It is important to note that active use of fiscal measures for economic stabilization implies that the government cannot be concerned with maintaining an exact balance of expenditures and tax revenues. As the lower section of Figure 19.8 demonstrates, the balance on the government's budget for any given fiscal policy (level of expenditures and tax function) depends on the level of income. At high levels of income, high tax revenues will produce a budget surplus. At low levels of income, low tax revenues will produce a budget deficit. An expansionary policy can be implemented either by increasing government expenditures or by shifting the tax function downward. The effect is to increase the budget deficit or decrease the budget surplus at each level of national income or, alternatively, to increase the level of income at which the government's budget is balanced. A restrictive policy can be implemented either by reducing government expenditures or by shifting the tax function upward. The effect is to reduce the budget deficit or increase the surplus at each level of national income or, alternatively, to reduce the level of national income at which the government's budget is balanced.

In this sense, the size of the surplus or deficit in the government budget is the central consideration in fiscal policy. The strong functional relationship between the balance on the government's budget and the level of national income should be noted. This means that the government sector tends to be an automatic stabilizer of economic aggregate demand. A decline in aggregate demand from private sources tends to be cushioned by the combination of stable government expenditures and declining tax collections, and hence by the emergence of a deficit in the government's budget. Similarly, an upsurge of aggregate demand tends to be restrained by the emergence of a budget surplus.

The sensitivity of the balance on the government's budget to changes in the level of national income also means that the actual magnitude of the budget deficit or surplus is not an adequate measure of the degree of ease or restrictiveness in fiscal policy. Since a deficit, for example, may emerge from a drop in national income with a given set to fiscal policy (i.e., given government expenditures, given tax schedules), it cannot be evidence of an expansionary policy. An expansionary policy would require a larger deficit than that which would emerge automatically as a result of the level of aggregate demand and income. It is frequently argued that a suitable summary measure of the degree of ease or restrictiveness of fiscal policy is the estimated balance on the budget with present expenditures and tax schedules if the economy were at full employment. This concept is called the *full employment deficit or surplus*.[17]

The Government Sector and the IS Functions. To carry through with the analytical technique we developed earlier, we must introduce a government sector into the *IS/LM* model. The important result of doing this is to change the shape of the *IS* curve. This is illustrated in Figure 19.9.

In constructing Figure 19.9 we have simply taken government expenditure and tax functions, such as those discussed earlier, and superimposed them on the basic *IS* model of the commodity market developed in Figure 19.4. In Quadrant II of Figure 19.9, we have added a fixed amount of government expenditures (G) to the original investment demand function. The result is a new investment and government expenditure function (I + G), which lies to the left of the original investment demand function. In Quadrant III, the tax function has been added to the savings function to obtain a new tax-plus-saving function.[18] The new equilibrium condition is that the level of investment plus government expenditures must equal the level of tax collections plus savings (you should be able to demonstrate why this is the new equilibrium condition). In Quadrant IV, we have the familiar 45° line, which reflects the equilibrium income levels to the base axis in Quadrant I. The *IS* curve, as before, shows the combinations of interest rates and income levels at which equilibrium can be achieved in the commodity market, taking account of both government expenditures and taxes.

As a reference base, we have also plotted the original *IS* curve from Figure 19.4 in Quadrant I of Figure 19.9 (the line I_oS_o). The change in shape as a result of the introduction of the government sector should be obvious. At relatively low levels of income, the new *IS* curve lies outside the old curve. Because of the assumed shape of the tax function, the income-generating effects of the given level of government expenditures outweigh

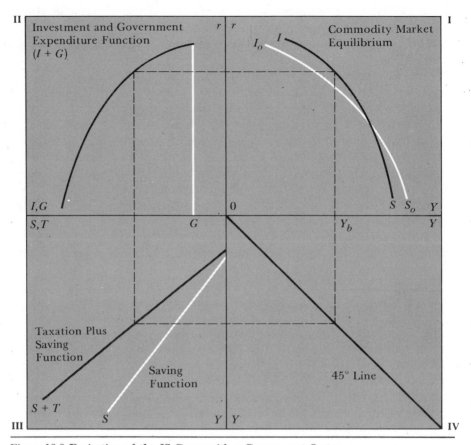

Figure 19.9 **Derivation of the IS Curve with a Government Sector**

the restrictive effects of taxation. As a result, the effect of government fiscal operations is to raise the equilibrium level of income associated with each possible level of interest rates in this range.

As we move down the IS curve, the restrictive effects of increasing tax revenues eventually offset and overwhelm the expansionary effects of the given level of government expenditures (this phenomenon has come to be known as fiscal drag). At relatively high levels of income, the new IS curve lies inside the old curve. In this range, the effect of government fiscal operations is to lower the equilibrium level of income associated with each possible level of interest rates.

The basic conclusion, then, is that the introduction of the government sector makes the IS curve steeper. The equilibrium level of income is less sensitive to changes in interest rates or, in other words, to shifts in the LM curve.

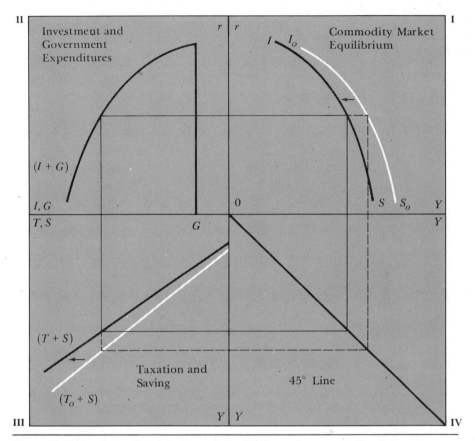

Figure 19.10 **Restrictive Fiscal Policy and the IS Curve: Increase in Tax Rates**

The level of income at which the government sector's budget is balanced (tax collections = government expenditures) is indicated at Y_b by the broken line. It is interesting to note that at this level of income the new IS curve lies outside the old one. A balanced budget in the government sector is not neutral with respect to the level of income. It has a slight net expansionary effect.[19]

Fiscal Policy. In this framework, fiscal policy—whether implemented through government expenditures or through tax rates—involves a deliberate shift of the IS function. Figure 19.10 illustrates the impact of a restrictive fiscal policy implemented through an increase in tax rates. In Quadrant III, the original tax-plus-savings function (broken line, $T_o + S$) has been shifted to the left, with an increased slope. The effect is to shift the IS function inward (from $I_o S_o$) and to make it steeper. At each possible level of interest rates, the equilibrium level of income has decreased.

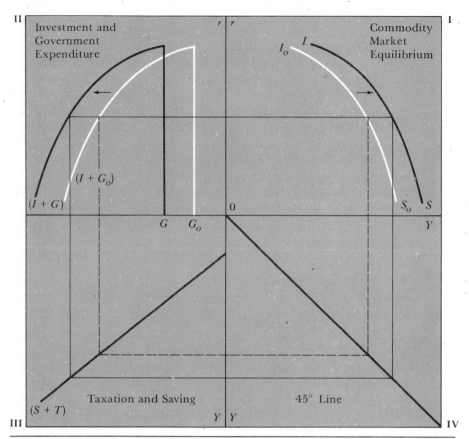

Figure 19.11 **Expansionary Fiscal Policy and the *IS* Curve: Increase in Government Expenditures on Goods and Services**

Figure 19.11 illustrates an expansionary fiscal policy implemented through an increase in government expenditures. The investment-plus-government-expenditures function in Quadrant I has been shifted to the left by the amount of the increased expenditures, with the result that the *IS* curve is shifted outward. At each possible level of interest rates, the equilibrium level of income has increased.

The possibilities for an expansionary fiscal policy in a situation in which monetary policy is impotent—what many economists would call the pure Keynesian case, involving a liquidity trap—are illustrated in Figure 19.12. We saw in Figure 19.7 that in this situation, with a horizontal *LM* function, monetary expansion could not lower interest rates below the minimum level, r_m, and therefore could not raise the level of income toward full employment. The analysis of Figure 19.12 demonstrates that by shifting the *IS* function an expansionary fiscal policy can raise the level of income (in this case from

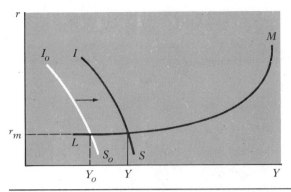

Figure 19.12 **Expansionary Fiscal Policy When Monetary Policy Is Impotent: The Case of the Liquidity Trap**

Y_o to Y), even though interest rates are frozen at some minimum level, r_m, by the operation of the liquidity trap. The same analysis applies for the case in which investment expenditures are sufficiently insensitive to interest rates as to make monetary expansion impotent.

Coordination of Monetary and Fiscal Policies. Normally, both monetary and fiscal policies, used independently, will have some impact on aggregate demand. Coordinated monetary and fiscal actions will have an even more powerful impact on aggregate demand than either instrument used (in the same degree) independently. This point is illustrated in Figure 19.13.

In this figure we have drawn IS and LM curves with enough elasticity so that both monetary and fiscal policies would be individually effective in raising national income. Starting with the initial curves, I_oS_o and L_oM_o,

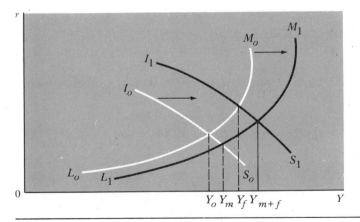

Figure 19.13 **Coordinated Monetary and Fiscal Policies**

451

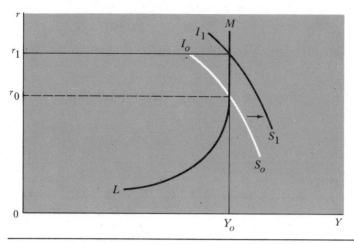

Figure 19.14 Impotent Fiscal Policy

and with the initial equilibrium level of national income, Y_0, we can trace the independent effects of monetary expansion (shifting the *LM* curve to L_1M_1) and fiscal expansion (shifting the *IS* curve to I_1S_1). Monetary expansion alone will raise income from Y_0 to Y_m. Fiscal expansion alone will raise income from Y_0 to Y_f. The combination of the same monetary expansion and the same fiscal expansion, however, will raise income to Y_{m+f}. This is the traditional argument for the coordination of monetary and fiscal policies. By parallel analysis, you should be able to show how conflicting monetary and fiscal policies can neutralize each other.

Impotent Fiscal Policy. There is one other situation that merits brief attention. The Keynesian model suggests one case in which fiscal policy would be impotent; this is illustrated in Figure 19.14.

In this case, fiscal expansion is incapable of raising the level of national income, output, and employment because at the existing level of income the *LM* curve is perfectly inelastic with respect to the level of interest rates. An expansionary fiscal policy could drive up the interest rate only until private investment expenditures are reduced sufficiently to make room for the additional government expenditures (or for the additional consumption made possible by tax cuts).

Such an extreme situation could arise only if there was no interest elasticity in the demand for money. There could be no substitutes for money as an asset. Indeed, money would have to be perfectly complementary to economic activity, such that any increase in income and output would absolutely require an expansion of the money supply. For this reason, this is generally referred to as the pure classical case. It should be noted, however, that if the *IS* curve is also highly interest inelastic, monetary expansion will not be sufficient to increase the level of income. Although monetary expansion is necessary, both monetary and fiscal expansion would be required.

In general, neither the extreme Keynesian case (liquidity trap) nor the extreme classical case seems likely to be a common occurrence. However, in some degree the lesson of the classical case is important. Fiscal expansion may be largely reflected in interest rates rather than income growth unless it is supported by appropriate monetary policies.

Financing the Deficit. In our discussion of fiscal policy we have studiously avoided discussing the methods to be used to finance any government budgetary deficit (or, alternatively, to discuss what would be done with a budgetary surplus). But as we have seen, an expansionary fiscal policy implies a budgetary deficit, an excess of government expenditures over revenues, and that deficit must somehow be financed. Our elementary accounting identities tell us that the net government debt, in one form or another, must expand. Correspondingly, a restrictive fiscal policy implies a surplus in the government's budget, an excess of revenues over expenditures. The net government debt must contract. We have considered only the impact of government revenues and expenditures on aggregate demand. Must we not also take into account the separate effects of changes in the government debt outstanding? If so, will this not seriously alter our basic conclusions on the impact of fiscal policy?

Such an argument has been advanced vigorously by some advocates of the new quantity theory of money.[20] In particular, it has been argued that, used independently (i.e., without coordinated monetary policy), fiscal policy is almost always ineffective. The financing of a government deficit will absorb funds that would otherwise be available to finance the investment expenditures of firms. Private expenditures will be depressed sufficiently to offset the impact of increased government expenditures or of reduced taxation. Correspondingly, a government surplus, involving the retirement of government debt, will indirectly provide funds to finance private expenditures, and these expenditures will expand sufficiently to offset the restrictive effects of reduced government expenditures or increased taxation.

There is one possible technique of financing the government deficit that we can dispose of quickly. It is always possible to provide the required funds to the government by expanding the money supply. For example, the central bank could make advances directly to the government, or it could purchase government bonds in the open market, thus "making room" for new issues of government bonds. However, this does not answer the quantity theorists' argument. This is not a case of "pure fiscal policy." It is precisely the case depicted in Figure 19.13—that of coordinated monetary and fiscal expansion. Rather than offsetting the impact of fiscal policy, this method of financing the deficit reinforces the impact of fiscal policy. Financing the deficit by creating money ensures the maximum possible impact from an expansionary fiscal policy, and conversely, using the funds generated by a budgetary surplus to retire part of the money supply ensures the maximum possible contractive effect from a restrictive fiscal policy.

But the case tells us nothing about the basic proposition that fiscal policy alone is ineffective. What about the case in which there is a budgetary deficit and no monetary expansion? Then, the government must sell bonds to finance the deficit, and private asset holders must be persuaded to purchase those bonds. Will it not require higher interest rates on government bonds to induce private asset holders to purchase them, and will not interest rates on other bonds rise correspondingly as the private asset holders sell them to make room for more government bonds? And will not the higher interest rates, in turn, restrict private spending?

The Keynesian answer is that this argument assumes that private asset portfolios are fixed in size. To the contrary, it is argued, an expansionary fiscal policy will generate additional income, which will, in turn, induce more saving, thus providing the required additional demand for government bonds to be held as financial assets. Remember the earlier discussion of the consumption function and the saving function. A rise in income implies higher levels of both consumption and saving. Remember, also, one of the lessons of Chapter 4: Saving is a demand for wealth and, in this context, a demand for financial instruments. As income and savings expand, private asset portfolios expand, thus creating the demand for the bonds that the government must issue in order to finance its deficit.[21] Indeed, one way to state the condition for a new equilibrium to be established in the commodity market is that income must rise to the point at which sufficient savings are forthcoming to absorb the increases in the government debt.

In other words, in the pure Keynesian case the problem of financing the deficit is not a limitation on the effectiveness of fiscal policy. If a constraint arises, it is because asset holders demand to hold part of their expanding asset portfolios in the form of the one asset that is in absolutely limited supply—money—and the restriction will be greater the less willing asset holders are to substitute other financial assets for money. That is, it will be the interest elasticity of the demand for money function and hence the LM function that limits the effectiveness of fiscal policy in raising aggregate demand and income. We are right back where we started. Taking into account the problem of financing the government's deficit does not suggest any new conclusions; it simply provides a different perspective on the same analysis.[22]

Exactly the same analysis applies in reverse to the problem of disposing of the surplus created by a restrictive fiscal policy. We will leave it to you to trace the analysis yourself.

Conclusions. Keynesian theory suggests that fiscal policy is a powerful instrument for economic stabilization, even when monetary policy is rendered impotent by a liquidity trap or the insensitivity of private expenditures to monetary variables. In general, the analysis suggests that monetary and fiscal measures should be used in combination. Coordinated monetary and fiscal policies are much more powerful than either policy used alone.[23]

THE KEYNESIAN MODEL OF THE ECONOMY
VS. THE QUANTITY THEORY MODEL

Perhaps it would be useful, before we go on, to briefly highlight the essential differences we see between the two leading models of the response of the economy to monetary policy.

The fundamental issue is quite simple. How is a central-bank-contrived disequilibrium between the demand for and supply of money resolved? We have distinguished between financial adjustments and real adjustments. Let us consider the financial adjustments first.

In terms of financial responses to monetary policy, there is very little difference between the two theories on the level of general principles. Underlying both theories is the notion that private asset holders strive to reestablish "balance" in their portfolios. However, to insist on this general similarity between the theories is to miss the essential issue. In both cases the discussion of portfolio adjustments is greatly simplified, such that only the demand for money function receives careful, explicit attention. The Keynesian theory stresses the interest elasticity of the demand for money, with the elasticity increasing at low interest rates and producing the "liquidity trap." The quantity theory minimizes the importance of interest rates in the demand for money, stressing instead the stability of the relationship between the demand for money and (permanent) income.

There are corresponding differences in the assumed links between the financial adjustments and real economic activity. The Keynesian theory emphasizes the role of interest rates in regulating capital expenditures and, between the interest elasticity of the demand for money and possible interest insensitivity of capital expenditures, admits the possibility of little or no real response to monetary policy. The quantity theory envisions the linkage as much more complex, involving many types of expenditure and direct real balance effects. There may be long and variable time lags, but the eventual impact of monetary policy on aggregate demand is powerful and certain.

It is in terms of the real adjustments themselves that the contrasts between the theories are most sharply drawn. The Keynesian theory takes the price level as determined independently in the short run by institutional factors. If there are any real repercussions from monetary policy (which it is argued, there may not be), it is real income and employment that must adjust. By contrast, the quantity theory assumes price flexibility. Since it is assumed that the economy automatically tends to full employment (at least if the money supply is managed properly, that is, is kept from being a source of frequent, erratic disturbances) and the demand for money is a stable function of income, the only factor that can adjust to eliminate the monetary disequilibrium is the price level. Indeed, without the assumption of price level flexibility, the quantity theory differs from the Keynesian analysis only in terms of the financial responses to monetary policy and hence in its prediction of the strength and certainty of the impact of monetary policy on aggregate demand.

In the analysis of real adjustments in the economy there is, predictably, a middle ground between the two extreme theories. Many economists—and much empirical evidence—would argue that the assumptions of neither theory, with respect to the essential issue of price flexibility, are "reasonable." A third view has emerged, which is perhaps closer to Keynes than to the classicists. It does not take the price level as given but does accept that prices are "sticky." For reasons that will become obvious, we label this the trade-off theory.

REAL ADJUSTMENTS: TRADE-OFF THEORY

A literal interpretation of the Keynesian assumption of a fixed price level is, of course, untenable. Price levels do change, and at times rather dramatically. The appropriate interpretation of the Keynesian price level assumption is that the price level does not change in the short run in response to changes in aggregate demand. However, even in this less rigid form the assumption seems to be in conflict with the evidence.

THE PHILLIPS CURVE AND THE PRICE LEVEL–EMPLOYMENT TRADE-OFF FUNCTION

The extreme version of the Keynesian model that we developed earlier obviously could apply only to an economy operating at less than full employment. When full employment is reached, output and employment cannot expand, and hence any further increases in aggregate demand must result in proportional increases in the price level. Ignoring differences in the financial sector, the Keynesian theory merges with the quantity theory.

But this implies a dramatic break in the macroeconomic performance of the economy at some magic point called full employment. The trade-off theory is based on empirical analysis of this transition. It has been demonstrated that instead of an abrupt shift from a regime in which output is the sole adjuster to one in which the price level is the sole adjuster, what actually happens is a gradual transition from a regime in which output is the primary but not exclusive adjuster to one in which the price level is the primary but not exclusive adjuster. That is, empirical research has discovered a negative relationship between the level of unemployment and the rate of change of wage rates, a particularly crucial set of prices. This relationship is apparently relatively stable and, at least over the limited range of unemployment levels observed in the 1950s and 1960s, is continuous. A curve describing this relationship is called a Phillips curve because of the pioneering contribution of an Australian economist, A. W. Phillips.[24]

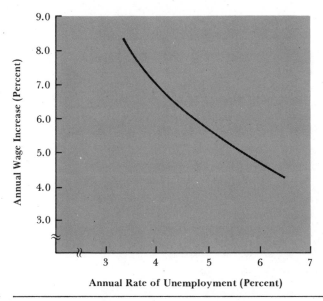

Figure 19.15 **Estimate of a Phillips Curve for the United States, 1969**
Source: George L. Perry, "Inflation Versus Unemployment: The Worsening Trade-Off,"
  Monthly Labor Review (Washington, D.C.: U.S. Department of Labor, Bureau of
  Labor Statistics), February 1971, 71.

One estimate of a Phillips curve for the United States is presented in Figure 19.15.[25] George Perry's estimates are based on his weighting of each age-sex group within the labor force and the relevant wages and hours worked. His study contrasts findings for 1969 with his earlier work for the mid-1950s. (See Figure 19.16, which presents Perry's earlier findings as a trade-off function assuming a 3 percent annual increase in labor productivity.) Findings presented in the later study suggest that the Phillips curve for the United States had shifted to the right, indicating a more difficult policy dilemma. A corresponding curve showing the relationship between the level of unemployment and the rate of change of the level of prices of consumable goods and services can be called the price level–employment trade-off function, or simply the trade-off function. While there is not a one-to-one relationship between rates of change of wages and prices, the Phillips curve and the trade-off function have broadly similar characteristics. A trade-off function using historical data for the United States is presented in Figure 19.17 for comparison.

THE THEORY OF THE TRADE-OFF FUNCTION
In terms of the nature of the real adjustments in the face of changes in aggregate demand, the trade-off function provides a middle ground between the extreme version of the quantity theory and the extreme version of the Keynesian theory. It is based on strong, although not undisputed, empirical

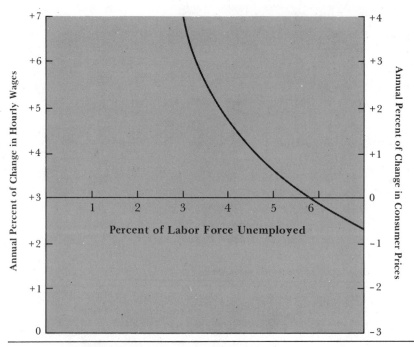

Figure 19.16 **Trade-Off Function for the United States**
SOURCE: Adapted from George L. Perry, *Unemployment, Money Wage Rates, and Inflation* (Cambridge, Mass.: M.I.T. Press, 1966).

evidence for many countries and many periods.[26] Unfortunately, it does not have an equally clear and consistent theoretical explanation. Rather, theories of the trade-off function tend to be based on ad hoc assumptions about the nature of the pricing mechanism in imperfect markets. The first problem is to explain the Phillips curve, since the trade-off function is derived from it.

The Phillips Curve. The common rationale for the existence of a Phillips curve is based on institutional information about price setting and price adjustments in labor markets. The theory of markets and price formation developed in most elementary economics courses is equilibrium theory. It asks the question, At what price will the quantity demanded equal the quantity supplied? Or, What is the new equilibrium price, given a change in demand or a change in supply? The common theory of the Phillips curve, by contrast, focuses attention on the situation when demand does not equal supply—when markets are in disequilibrium. In this sense, the theory underlying the Phillips curve is *disequilibrium theory*.

In the classical analysis of markets, as presented in most elementary textbooks, no constraints are placed on the adjustability of prices. When markets are in disequilibrium, prices change rapidly, thereby adjusting the quantity

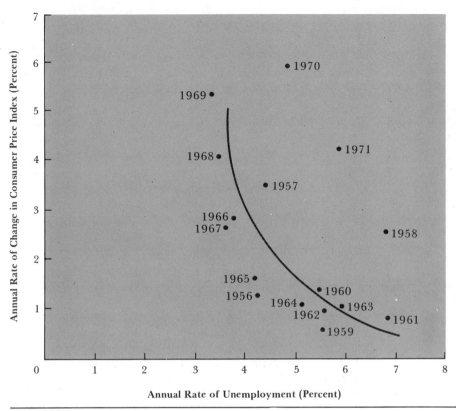

Figure 19.17 **Estimate of a Historical Trade-Off Function for the United States, 1956–1971**
SOURCE: *Economic Report of the President*, February 1971 (Washington, D.C.), pp. 222–223; *Monthly Labor Review* (Washington, D.C.: U.S. Department of Labor, Bureau of Labor Statistics), July 1972, 88.

supplied and the quantity demanded until a new equilibrium price is established. Observers of labor markets note, however, that wage rates are not that flexible. Wage rates are established in a process of collective bargaining and are subject to contracts of varying length. Thus, underlying the market is a pricing process that occurs at discrete intervals, not continuously. This does not mean that effective wage rates cannot change between contract dates. Contracts are sometimes opened for renegotiation; special bonuses are sometimes permitted; workers may be reclassified into different wage categories (even though the tasks performed do not change); and variable amounts of overtime work at premium wage rates will introduce variability into hourly earnings, even with a fixed scale of wage rates. The essential point is, however, that the institutions of the market make the wage rate "sticky." It does not adjust quickly or smoothly in the face of excess demand or excess supply in the labor market. As Keynesian theory suggests, a change of demand is likely to be reflected initially in a change in the level of employment rather than a change in the wage rate.

However, this does not mean that wage rates are established arbitrarily or that they do not respond to market forces. Rather, it is argued that the adjustment of wage rates to new market conditions takes time and that the speed of the adjustment is a variable that also depends on market conditions. Very strong excess demand for labor will induce rapid wage rate increases. Modest excess demand will induce slow wage adjustments. Thus, it is argued, the rate of change in the wage rate depends on the degree of excess demand (+ or −) in labor markets.

In this argument, the level of unemployment is taken as a measure of the degree of excess demand in labor markets in the aggregate. However, the relationship between the level of unemployment and the level of excess demand is not clear. Since there is always some "frictional" unemployment (workers who are between jobs) and some "unemployables" in the labor force, full employment in the sense of zero excess demand for labor cannot mean literally 100 percent of the labor force employed. Moreover, all individual labor markets are not subject to exactly the same conditions of excess demand at the same point in time. As a result, there may be some unemployment that is a product of structural imbalance in labor demand and supply. For these reasons, it is argued, substantial upward pressure on wage rates may exist even though employment is less than 100 percent of the measured labor force.

The Trade-Off Function. Given the Phillips curve, the trade-off function follows because of the importance of wage rates in total costs of production. In competitive markets, higher wage rates mean higher marginal costs and hence higher prices. In oligopolistic markets, where markup pricing is common, higher wage rates mean higher average costs and hence higher prices. In either case a relationship between unemployment and the rate of change in wage rates implies a relationship between unemployment and the rate of change in prices.

The exact relationship between wage rates and costs of production depends on the rate of change in labor productivity. However, studies show that while the rate of productivity advance has a slight cyclical pattern, it depends primarily on longer-term considerations and can be reasonably represented by a steady long-run trend. Under these circumstances, the unemployment/wage rate relationship provides the main short-run domestic explanation for the rate of the price level advance.

CONTROVERSY ABOUT THE NATURE
OF THE LONG-RUN TRADE-OFF FUNCTION

As with the evolving theory about the short-run determinants of the Phillips curve, economists are by no means united on the long-run relationship between changes in the price level and the rate of unemployment. Some contend that the long-run relationship is similar but more pronounced in shape than the short-run trade-off function. That is, the rate of change in the level of prices is a continuous and decreasing function of the unemployment rate. Another group of economists (many from the monetarist school) contends, however, that no long-run relationship exists between the rate of change in the price level and the rate of unemployment. Milton Friedman, for one, argues that there is some "natural" level of unemployment that is consistent with a stable structure of real wage rates and a stable price level (i.e., the rate of change in prices = zero). Any attempt to permanently reduce the "actual" or "market" level of unemployment below the "natural" rate by expanding monetary growth will have a temporary effect in line with the trade-off function but in the long run will result in an accelerating rate of inflation until that rate approaches infinity. Friedman concludes that "there is always a temporary trade-off between inflation and unemployment; there is no permanent trade-off."[27]

Many of the economists following this line of reasoning rely on an expectations theory of price determination. If the actual or market rate of unemployment is pegged below the natural rate of unemployment by means of monetary growth, in the short run there is some trade-off. That is, there would be some increase in the number of people employed, thereby reducing the unemployment rate. There would also be increased income and resulting increases in the selling prices of goods. Individuals would react to these price increases and anticipate or expect price increases. They would try to avoid changes in their real income by increasing their nominal income. They would bid for increases in nominal wage rates that could not be maintained over time unless monetary growth continued at an accelerating rate until the rate of change in the price level approached infinity. Sustained inflation, these economists conclude, is not a long-run solution.

This criticism of the existence or nonexistence of a long-run trade-off function draws heavily on the classical quantity theory of full employment. That theory relies on adjustments in money wage rates and the price level to move the economy back into equilibrium after a disturbance like an increase in the supply of money or the supply of labor. Money wage rates respond to unemployment, and the price level responds to changes in output.

Lucas and Rapping used data from the period between 1904 and 1965 to test the hypothesis that there was a long-run Phillips curve. They used the expectational theory to explain the behavior of labor. They found that there was enough statistical evidence to validate the existence of trade-off functions and of short-run Phillips curves over the period. These short-run curves, however, exhibited a great deal of instability. The evidence on the presence of a long-run Phillips curve was mixed. During the period 1930–1945 there was evidence of a long-run curve. For the other two periods, 1904–1929 and 1946–1965, there was no indication of a long-run curve.[28]

461

POLICY IMPLICATIONS

The trade-off theory is clearly much closer to the Keynesian theory than to the classical quantity theory. Indeed, one might characterize it as an important variation on the basic Keynesian model. The significant point is that it suggests that manipulation of aggregate demand through monetary policy (or fiscal policy) can normally be expected to have both price level and employment effects. Without additional policy instruments capable of shifting the Phillips curve or of changing its shape, the authorities cannot decide on price level and employment objectives separately. They must think in terms of combinations of objectives, trading off price level stability against employment to achieve the preferred combination. The downward-sloping trade-off function hypothesis suggests two dimensions of concern for policy makers: first, that of choosing an economic policy that acknowledges the dilemma between high levels of employment and price stability, and second, that of designing a policy that will shift and alter the shape of the Phillips curve so as to improve the trade-off between unemployment and inflation for the national economy in the long run.

One policy goal is to relieve some of the economic bottlenecks by training manpower for skills that are needed, where and when they may be best utilized. Programs to improve the allocation of unemployed manpower and to increase labor mobility must be undertaken.

Further, elimination of discrimination in labor markets would allow for more efficient use of labor inputs and would lower the rate of increase in wage rates, shifting the trade-off function to the left.[29] Other bottlenecks also inhibit market forces. It may be appropriate to examine market power and its traditional measures and limitations in light of an open, international economy with the knowledge that increased competition can also shift the trade-off function to the left. Government policies and expenditures at all three levels should be reviewed for anticompetitive elements that encourage higher levels of unemployment and inflation.

SUMMARY

We can briefly summarize the discussion in this chapter by posing and answering two questions:

1. Monetary policy implies manipulation of the money supply in order to affect real economic activity. If the central bank creates an excess supply of money, does this necessarily create an excess demand for goods and services? According to the Keynesian model, the answer is "not necessarily." The total impact may be absorbed in the financial system. According to the quantity theory, the answer is unquestionably yes. The impact of monetary policy may filter out through many devious channels and with long and variable time lags, but it is reliable and strong.

2. Presuming that there is some impact on the aggregate demand for goods and services, does this imply a change in the volume of output and employment? of the price level? or both? According to the Keynesian model, output and employment are affected. According to the quantity theory, the price level is affected "in the long run." According to the trade-off theory, both will be affected in some degree, depending on the existing level of unemployment.

You should note the key role the demand for money plays in the analysis. If monetary policy is to be a useful tool of policy, there must be a stable demand for money function such that the effects of a change of the money supply can be predicted with reasonable certainty. You should also note that the major issues in controversies among monetary economists are empirical. In principle they are answerable by reference to "the facts." Unfortunately, as we have seen in Chapter 18 with respect to the demand for money and as we shall see again in Chapter 22 in a broader context, the facts are not always certain.

NOTES

1. The "bills only" doctrine is explained and defended in W. Reifler, "Open Market Operations in Long-Term Securities," Federal Reserve *Bulletin* 44 (November 1958), 1260–1274. For a critical analysis see D. Luckett, " 'Bills Only': A Critical Appraisal," *Review of Economics and Statistics* 42 (August 1960), 301–306.

2. Irving Fisher, *The Purchasing Power of Money* (New York: Macmillan, 1911), p. 183.

3. Ibid., p. 155.

4. Ibid., pp 55–73, 159–161.

5. Ibid., p. 172.

6. Current or measured income (Y_m) is defined as the sum of permanent income (Y_p) and transitory income (Y_t). That is:

$$Y_m = Y_p + Y_t \qquad \text{(a)}$$

The two concepts of velocity are then:

$$\text{(permanent velocity)} \quad v_p = \frac{Y_p}{M} \qquad \text{(b)}$$

and

$$\text{(measured velocity)} \quad v_m = \frac{Y_m}{M}$$

$$= \frac{Y_p + Y_t}{M} = v_p + \frac{Y_t}{M} \qquad \text{(c)}$$

Using (a), we can rewrite (c):

$$v_m = v_p + \frac{Y_m - Y_p}{M} \qquad \text{(d)}$$

From (b), we know that:

$$M = \frac{Y_p}{v_p} \qquad\qquad\text{(e)}$$

Substituting (e) in (d):

$$v_m = v_p + \frac{(Y_m - Y_p) v_p}{Y_p}$$

$$= v_p + \frac{Y_p}{Y_m} \qquad\qquad\text{(f)}$$

7. Perhaps because of the danger of misinterpretation, the modern quantity theorists seldom make the strong theoretical assertion of proportionality between money and the price level that was the hallmark of the classical quantity theory. More common is a guarded, empirically based statement of the type: "To my knowledge there is no instance in which a substantial change in the stock of money per unit of output has occurred without a substantial change in the level of prices in the same direction. Conversely, I know of no instance in which there has been a substantial change in the stock of money per unit of output in the same direction." M. Friedman, "The Supply of Money and Changes in Prices and Output," reprinted in *The Optimum Quantity of Money* (Chicago: Aldine, 1969), p. 173.

8. Ibid., pp. 180–181.

9. The student who is not familiar with elementary national income accounting should review the relevant section of any standard principles-of-economics textbook.

The problem arises because in the conventional methods of accounting there are certain "costs" involved in the production of output that do not directly accrue as income to any factor of production. Primary among these is the capital consumption or depreciation allowance. It is because it is included in the measure of output that this measure is called the "gross" national product. Indirect taxes have the same effect. To the business firm they are costs, but they do not accrue as income to any factor of production. (Note that income taxes are different. As long as we measure income received before income tax is paid, the same problem does not arise.) Government subsidies to businesses are in effect negative indirect taxes.

It must also be remembered in this context that interfirm sales of semiprocessed goods net out in measuring aggregate income. That is, only the value added at each stage is included in the measure of aggregate output, and it is this figure that is equal to aggregate income (measured gross of depreciation and indirect taxes).

10. Again, remember, both income and output must be measured in the same way: either net or gross of depreciation, indirect taxes, and subsidies.

11. The dotted line in the upper section is drawn at a 45° angle to the base axis. Where this line crosses the consumption function, income and consumption are equal and savings are zero. This point has been projected onto the lower section. At all levels of income lower than Y_o, consumption exceeds income and saving is negative. Householders are drawing on their accumulated savings or are borrowing to finance consumption in excess of their income. At all income levels higher than Y_o, consumption is less than income and saving is positive. The saving function measures the vertical distance between the consumption function and the 45° line.

12. A larger marginal propensity to save will also shift the IS curve to the left, and a smaller marginal propensity to save will shift it to the right. Why? (Hint: Review the discussion of the investment-income multiplier, usually just called the multiplier, from your principles-of-economics course.)

13. Keynes called his demand for money function the liquidity preference function. Thus, the LM function connects points at which (L)iquidity preference = the (M)oney supply.

14. This point is tricky. Remember that the direct effect of income on the demand for

464

money is otherwise allowed for. What is depicted in Quadrant II is the effect of the interest rate pure and simple. It is to be added to the effect of income.

If our assumption did not hold, we would have to draw a different curve in Quadrant II for each level of income. Curves for successively higher levels of income might lie inside or outside the given curve and might have a different shape. This would complicate the analysis unnecessarily.

15. The real balance effect is usually invoked as an argument to explain why a decline in the price level in an economy stuck in the liquidity trap would stimulate the level of income and employment. Remember, a decline in the price level—provided that it does not provoke expectations of a continuing decline—is the equivalent of an increase in the money supply. It produces an increase in the relevant magnitude, the real money supply.

In assessing the significance of the real balance effect with a fixed price level, remember that in acquiring the new money each asset holder has either sold securities that he previously held or has borrowed from the bank. As a result, the increase in the money supply does not increase any asset holder's wealth. It seems unlikely that the change in the composition of his portfolio alone will create a powerful incentive to acquire real assets.

Where the real balance effect arises because of a drop in the price level, the situation is not fundamentally different. Not only is the real value of the money supply increased; so is the real value of all debts. In the aggregate these effects offset each other such that aggregate real wealth does not change (except, perhaps, for claims on outsiders—which many economists take to include the government on the ground that no one thinks of the public debt as his personal liability—subject to repayment in dollars with higher real value).

16. In some macroeconomic models of the economy, total government expenditures are considered an exogenous policy instrument. In some other macroeconomic models, the expenditures of junior governments are endogenous. Separate equations are included to "explain" their behavior. Only the expenditures of the central government are considered an exogenous policy instrument. Cf. F. de Leeuw and E. Gramlich, "The Federal Reserve —M.I.T. Econometric Model," Federal Reserve Bulletin 54 (January 1968), 11–40.

17. The concept of the full-employment budget as the guide to fiscal policy has been developed and applied by the Council of Economic Advisers in the United States. A relevant excerpt from their 1962 Annual Report is reprinted in W. L. Smith and R. L. Teigen, Readings in Money, National Income and Stabilization Policy (Homewood, Ill.: Irwin, 1965), pp. 281–284.

18. The savings function in Figure 19.9 is different from that in Figure 19.4. In constructing Figure 19.4 it was not necessary to distinguish between earned income and disposable (or after-tax) income. There was no government sector to collect taxes. In constructing Figure 19.9, however, this distinction is essential. We assume that the income concept that is relevant for private saving and consumption decisions is disposable income. Thus, if there is a linear consumption function such as that developed in Figure 19.3, it is a relationship between consumption and disposable income. The income concept in Figure 19.9 is gross national income. Disposable income is less than national income. The savings function in Quadrant III, then, shows the effects of both the relationship between disposable income and national income, and the saving decision out of disposable income. We assume that the existence of government reduces the level of private saving at each level of gross national income. The saving function in Figure 19.9 is closer to the vertical axis than that in Figure 19.4.

19. This is the proposition commonly called the balanced budget multiplier. The mathematics of it are developed in most textbooks on macroeconomic theory. The common sense of the argument is as follows: There is a systematic quantitative difference in the immediate impact of government expenditures and tax collections on aggregate demand. Government expenditures have a direct, dollar-for-dollar impact, increasing aggregate demand. Taxation has the opposite direct dollar-for-dollar impact on disposable income.

However, people react to the reduction of their disposable income partly by reducing consumption expenditures and partly by reducing saving. The impact on aggregate demand (via reduced consumption expenditures) is less than the total amount of the tax collections. Therefore, a balanced budget, in which government expenditures equal tax collections, has a net expansionary effect on aggregate demand. The reduction in consumption is less than the increase in government expenditures.

20. Perhaps the clearest and most explicit statement is that of M. Friedman in M. Friedman and W. Heller, *Monetary and Fiscal Policy: A Dialogue* (New York: Norton, 1969), pp. 43–62, 71–80.

21. Changes in the relative supply of government bonds (increased) and private bonds (unchanged) may well have some effect on relative interest rates on the securities. Thus, the government may find that interest rates on the public debt have risen relative to rates on private debt.

22. We have ignored the problem of time lags in this discussion of fiscal policy. If there are very long time lags in the effects of fiscal measures on aggregate income, then the initial effects of a deficit in the government budget may fall heavily on interest rates. The total effect, then, is very complex, depending as it will on the time lags in the impact of interest rates on private spending as well as the time lags in the impact of fiscal measures on aggregate demand.

23. It is sometimes argued that monetary and fiscal measures should not be coordinated in this sense; that is, they should not be used to achieve the same objective. From time to time economists have argued that monetary policy should be geared to keeping interest rates low in order to stimulate investment and economic growth, with fiscal policy used to stabilize aggregate demand in the short run. Similarly, it is sometimes argued that monetary policy should be used to maintain equilibrium in the balance of international payments, while fiscal measures are used for domestic stabilization. We will return to the latter argument in the next chapter.

24. A. W. Phillips, "The Relation Between Unemployment and the Rate of Change of Money Wage Rates in the United Kingdom, 1861–1957," *Economica*, N.S., 25 (November 1958), 283–299.

25. G. L. Perry, "Inflation Versus Unemployment: The Worsening Trade-off," *Monthly Labor Review*, February 1971, 71. Also see R. J. Flanagan, "The U.S. Phillips Curve and International Unemployment Rate Differentials," *American Economic Review*, March 1973, 114–131 and R. Bodkin, E. Bond, G. Reuber, and T. R. Robinson, *Price Stability and High Employment: The Options for Canadian Economic Policy, An Econometric Study* (Ottawa, Canada: Queen's Printer, 1966).

26. R. Bodkin, et al., op cit.

27. Particularly, M. Friedman, "The Role of Monetary Policy," *American Economic Review*, March 1968, 1–17; E. S. Phelps, "Phillips Curves, Expectations of Inflation and Optimal Unemployment Over Time," *Economica* 34 (August 1967), 254–281; and E. S. Phelps, et al., *Microeconomic Foundations of Employment and Inflation Theory* (New York: Norton, 1970).

28. R. E. Lucas, Jr., and L. A. Rapping, "Price Expectations and the Phillips Curve," *American Economic Review*, June 1969, 342–350.

29. A particularly powerful statement of this argument is presented in M. Friedman, "What Price Guideposts," in G. Shultz and R. Ailber, *Guidelines, Informal Controls and the Market Place* (Chicago: University of Chicago Press, 1966).

THE INTERNATIONAL CONSTRAINT ON MONETARY POLICY

Part 1: The Balance of International Payments and Macroeconomic Equilibrium

Our discussion of the theory of monetary policy in Chapter 19 assumed that the central bank had complete freedom to manipulate the money supply. Such freedom implies no significant constraints on the level of interest rates other than those imposed in the market by the behavior of asset holders. This is not always the case in practice.

For example, in discussing the theory of central bank control of the supply of money (Chapter 16) we referred briefly to the period during and immediately after World War II, when the Federal Reserve stabilized government bond yields at low levels. The Federal Reserve guaranteed holders of government bonds that the price of those securities would not change significantly. Under postwar inflationary conditions, the policy of pegging interest rates was inconsistent with the vigorous use of monetary policy to restrain aggregate demand. The Federal Reserve was virtually powerless to use open-market operations to restrain those inflationary pressures.

In the contemporary context, there are other powerful "external" constraints on independent monetary action by the central bank that have arisen from the rapid increase in trade between countries, persistent balance-of-payments disequilibria, and the increasing mobility of capital flows across national boundaries in a world that has adhered to fixed exchange rates. These international constraints on monetary policy are the subject of this chapter.

Like other parts of our macroeconomic analysis, the foundations for the analysis of this chapter were laid earlier in the book. In Chapter 7 we explored the international connections of financial markets, focusing on the international dimensions of the portfolio selection decisions of individual asset holders and on their implications for equilibrium in American and world financial markets. The task now is to extract certain implications for macroeconomic policy from that analysis.

THE INTERNATIONAL MONETARY CONSTITUTION

As will become evident, the nature of the interaction between domestic stabilization policy and international financial markets depends on the process by which the foreign exchange rate is determined. In this sense, the foreign exchange rate is the central variable in our analysis in this and the following chapter.

THE FOREIGN EXCHANGE RATE

You will recall from Chapter 7 that the foreign exchange rate is simply a price—the dollar price of one unit of foreign currency. Of course, there are many foreign currencies and in this sense many foreign exchange rates.

Although it is simply a price, in most respects just like the price of any other financial instrument determined in the marketplace by the interaction of supply and demand forces, foreign exchange rates have one rather unusual and, for our purposes, crucial characteristic. They have been the central concern of international negotiations, agreements, and tensions for several decades. In 1944 an international treaty, the Articles of Agreement of the International Monetary Fund (commonly called the Bretton Woods Agreement) was signed. It was supposed to resolve all financial problems between countries by creating a constitution for a stable international monetary system. The key concept was that of stable exchange rates, adjusted from time to time in an orderly, mutually agreed upon fashion. Nations were not to resort to competitive devaluations of their currency in order to achieve a balance-of-payments surplus or to correct temporary balance-of-payments disequilibria. An international monetary fund was created to oversee the monetary system and to make loans of foreign exchange reserves from time to time to assist in maintaining the fixed exchange rates. The emphasis of the Agreement was on promoting the exchange of goods and services—freer trade. Little was mentioned about freedom of capital movements. In fact, controls on international capital flows by individual countries were permitted. Gradually, barriers to international capital flows were relaxed by many of the industrialized nations.

The basic obligation assumed by the governments under the Bretton Woods international monetary constitution was to declare an official "par" rate of exchange and to ensure that the actual foreign exchange rate at which transactions were consummated in the spot foreign exchange markets did not depart from a narrow band around that official par rate.

The United States' obligation was to maintain convertibility between dollars and gold. The value of the dollar was fixed in terms of gold ($35 per ounce of gold); other national currencies were also fixed in terms of gold.[1] Those nations, however, maintained convertibility of their currencies into dollars (or, in a few cases, pounds sterling) rather than gold.

The Bretton Woods rules were not inviolable. Naturally, most national governments were unwilling to surrender control of their monetary sovereignty and become unquestioning adherents to these rules. Domestic policy considerations, often at odds with fixed exchange rates, necessitated unilateral action. Most countries made major or minor violations from time to time. From World War II to mid-1971, only 2 countries—the United States and Japan—out of 21 developed, industrialized countries did not change the official par value of their currency.

Despite the frequent violations of the Bretton Woods Agreement, this international monetary system served its members and world trade well until the mid-1960s. Since that time monetary crises were more frequent, which suggests that the Bretton Woods rules did not fit contemporary international conditions. By 1973, Bretton Woods rules had been abandoned for all practical purposes and the major industrialized nations were seeking a new international monetary constitution. Gold had been partially demonetized, and its price fluctuated widely in free international markets. Many major countries had flexible exchange rates while international conferences were convened to seek a new, more suitable set of rules; new monetary agreements are not written quickly. Such activity takes time, cooperative and creative effort, and a great deal of compromise.

Let us examine how the Bretton Woods system of fixed exchange rates constrained monetary policy, for although there were frequent and often serious violations of the Bretton Woods rules, that in itself should not be taken as evidence that those rules were irrelevant. Rather, the violations are evidence that rigid application of such rules gave rise from time to time to serious stresses and strains within the international financial system.

From our point of view, the underlying problem was that the Bretton Woods rules imposed severe constraints on domestic stabilization policies for many countries. Indeed, the policies required by the international rules of the game occasionally stood in stark conflict with those required to achieve important domestic objectives. Our task in this and the following chapter is to examine the economics of monetary and fiscal policies in the context of an international financial system operating according to the Bretton Woods rules. Only then will we be able to understand the nature of the problems that gave rise to urgent proposals for reform of the international financial system.

What were the most important rules of the game under Bretton Woods?

THE PEGGED EXCHANGE RATE

Under Bretton Woods rules, each government was obliged to ensure that the forces of supply and demand in the foreign exchange market did not drive its foreign exchange rate beyond the narrow band around the official par rate of exchange. (The band was set by the members of the International Monetary Fund and for many years was 1 percent on either side of the official par value. In 1971 the band was widened to 2.25 percent.) A flexible exchange rate that, in response to demand and supply pressures, fluctuated over a wider range than the official band on either side of par was a clear violation of the letter and spirit of the monetary constitution. Member countries could impose narrower bands and intervene when foreign exchange rates exceeded these self-imposed limits. The United States had a slightly different obligation under Bretton Woods. It guaranteed to maintain the dollar convertible into gold at a fixed price. It was willing to buy and sell gold at prices within a similar narrow band around the official price of $35 per ounce. The American central bank was not obligated to intervene in spot foreign exchange markets to maintain the official par value of a particular foreign currency in terms of the dollar; that was the responsibility of the foreign central banks. Its commitment was to maintain the price of the dollar in terms of gold. Since 1961, however, the Federal Reserve has intervened in both the spot and forward exchange markets from time to time to maintain exchange rates. The United States should be viewed as a country that normally did not intervene.

Adjustable Peg. Adjustments in the official par rate of exchange were not ruled out, although such changes were to be infrequent, subject to international consultation and approval, and only in response to exceptional and intractable balance-of-payments pressures. No criteria were made explicit by which official par exchange rate disequilibria could be judged as either temporary or fundamental. This hampered the timely adjustment of official exchange rates and permitted pressure on domestic economies and exchange rates to accumulate.

As we shall see, the requirement of a pegged exchange rate imposes severe international constraints on the freedom of national monetary authorities. Under certain circumstances the stability of the foreign exchange rate must be the overriding concern of central bank policy. The independent use of monetary controls to help achieve domestic price level or employment objectives may be rendered impossible.

AVOIDANCE OF DIRECT CONTROLS

There is frequently an easy way out of the dilemma posed by a conflict between the domestic and external objectives of monetary policy through the use of direct foreign exchange controls. Thus, for example, when the problem is excess demand for foreign exchange at the maximum permitted foreign exchange rate, it is possible to maintain stability of the foreign exchange rate by substituting official rationing of the restricted supply of foreign exchange in place of rationing by the price mechanism. By giving itself the power to approve or disapprove applications for foreign exchange, the government adds another weapon to its policy armory, making it possible to keep the foreign exchange market in a continuous state of disequilibrium (i.e., with demand in excess of supply at the pegged exchange rate). Since it is then unnecessary to use monetary policy to maintain equilibrium in the foreign exchange market, monetary policy is freed from the international constraint, at least in the short run.

Several countries have resorted to direct exchange controls from time to time. In order to control foreign currencies the government usually must license firms exporting and importing goods. The government must control the purchase of foreign assets by its residents, investments made abroad by its residents, and the amount of funds it permits individuals to take out of the country. As we saw in Chapter 16, direct controls involve arbitrary interference with the allocation of resources in the economy. In general, they impair microeconomic efficiency. In any case, aside from exceptional circumstances, direct foreign exchange controls with regard to trade of goods and services were to be avoided under the Bretton Woods rules.

In the event of excessive demand or supply pressures in the foreign exchange market, the government has two courses of action open to it if it is to maintain the stability of the foreign exchange rate without resort to direct foreign exchange controls. We can call these *direct intervention* and *indirect intervention*.

DIRECT INTERVENTION

The government can intervene directly in the foreign exchange market, buying foreign exchange when there is an excess supply at the minimum permitted exchange rate and selling it when there is excess demand at the maximum permitted foreign exchange rate. For this purpose the government requires a stock of foreign exchange that can be augmented or drawn upon as necessary to permit direct intervention in the market.

INDIRECT INTERVENTION

Alternatively, the government can attempt to regulate the underlying private demands for or supplies of foreign exchange. Thus, for example, if the problem is excess demand for foreign exchange, the government can attempt to reduce private demands for foreign exchange or to increase the flow of foreign exchange from private sources onto the foreign exchange market. Part of our problem is to show how the government can do this, and particularly how monetary policy can be used to regulate the demand for and supply of foreign exchange.

The main concern of this chapter is the analysis of these two modes of governmental intervention in the foreign exchange market. However, before turning to this analysis it is useful to have before us a brief sketch of the foreign exchange market.

THE FOREIGN EXCHANGE MARKET

The term *foreign exchange market* is used in a broad sense to encompass all transactions involving the exchange of foreign currencies against dollars, and in a narrow sense to refer to a highly organized component of the broad market, the interbank market in foreign exchange. In what follows we use the term in the broader sense, which encompasses all transactions in which foreign exchange is exchanged against dollars, whether those transactions occur in the United States or abroad. It should also be noted that the definition encompasses both spot and forward exchange transactions. However, since they are normally closely related to each other (see Chapter 7), throughout most of the discussion we will not distinguish between the spot and forward exchange rates.

The foreign exchange market in the United States is not an organized exchange with a specific physical location but is similar to the market for money market instruments. Its participants are linked by telephone and telex communication to each other here in the United States and to institutions performing similar functions in financial centers around the world. Several New York banks handle the bulk of trading in the United States, although some trading occurs in other cities. If these New York banks are to satisfy the requirements of their customers immediately and without question, they must hold an inventory of foreign exchange. To this end, they hold some foreign currency in their vaults and maintain deposit balances with foreign banks. These are the banks' "working balances." The banks buy and sell foreign exchange to meet the needs of thir customers, be they businesses, households, governments, or other domestic banks. Foreign exchange purchased is added to these working balances; foreign exchange sold is drawn out.

However, both profit maximization and the ever-present foreign exchange risk dictate that working balances should be no larger than necessary for efficiency in foreign exchange operations. This means that the banks must have an efficient mechanism for the quick disposal of excess foreign exchange and for the quick acquisition of foreign exchange to replenish working balances should they be inadequate. Such a mechanism is provided by the interbank market.

THE INTERBANK MARKET

The interbank market is made in New York among those dealing in foreign exchange—dealers and brokers in foreign exchange, agents of foreign banks, some securities firms, and the Federal Reserve Bank of New York acting on behalf of the Federal Reserve System and the Treasury. Secondary

472

markets for foreign exchange exist in places like San Francisco, Boston, Chicago, Philadelphia, and Detroit, but most participants have representatives in the New York interbank market as well.

International Arbitrage. The foreign exchange rate determined in the interbank market in New York is influenced by interbank foreign exchange markets in other financial centers throughout the world. In these other markets dollars as well as other currencies are bought and sold. If the rate in one market is out of line with that in another, an arbitrager will place an order for immediate execution to buy in one market and resell in the other. While the margin of profit in arbitraging is small (from which transactions costs must be deducted), on a large volume of funds this could be an attractive proposition. Arbitrage may involve more than two foreign exchange markets, and it may be conducted by professional arbitragers, who are alert to "disorderly cross-rates" of exchange, or by the normal participants in the market. Perhaps most important as a continuing force in the market are the banks buying the foreign exchange they require in the cheapest market and selling their excess foreign exchange in the dearest market. The banks are well organized to do this, being in instantaneous contact with their agencies in other major international financial centers.

An International Market. The important point is that arbitrage will occur as long as the rates in other markets are out of line with each other, and this arbitrage will have the effect of bringing the rates into line. In this way, arbitrage ties the foreign exchange markets in all countries together into a single international foreign exchange market.

SUPPLY AND DEMAND IN THE FOREIGN EXCHANGE MARKET

So much for the institutions of the foreign exchange market. They simply provide the framework within which the forces of supply and demand work themselves out. If we are to understand the policy dilemmas posed by a policy of pegging the foreign exchange rate, we must look beyond the institutions of the market and examine the nature of the underlying supply and demand forces themselves.

Demands to exchange dollars for foreign currencies can originate either inside the United States or abroad and can be for many different purposes, including a simple desire to hold foreign money in place of American money as an asset, perhaps speculating that there will be significant changes in the exchange rate.

However, in a general way we can think of the demand for foreign exchange as arising out of the desires of residents to make payments abroad— for the purchase of goods and services from nonresidents, to make gifts, to purchase equities and bonds from nonresidents, or to make other investments abroad. Similarly, the supply of foreign exchange arises out of the desires of foreigners to make purchases in the United States of American goods and services, equities and bonds, or other types of direct investments.

The analysis of supply and demand in the foreign exchange market must start with these flows of international payments—with the balance of international payments of the United States.

Table 20.1.   U.S. Balance of Payments, 1971 (Billions of Dollars)

Current Account			
Receipts		**Payments**	
Merchandise Exports	+$42.8	Merchandise Imports	$45.6
Nonmerchandise Exports		Nonmerchandise Imports	
Travel and Transportation	+6.1	Travel and Transportation	8.4
Investment Income	+12.7	Interest and Dividends	4.8
Military Sales	+1.9	Other Services	1.6
Other Services	+2.4	Military Expenditures	4.8
	+$65.9		$65.2
International Transfers			
Gifts, Remittances, Inheritances, Pensions			$ 1.5
U.S. Government Grants, Excluding Military			2.0
Total Current Receipts	$65.9	Total Current Payments	$68.7
Net Balance on Current Account			−$ 2.8

Capital Account			
Receipts		**Payments**	
U.S. Government Capital Flows (Net)			
Foreign Currency and Other		Loans and Other Long-Term	
Short-Term Assets	$0.2	Assets	$4.0
Repayments on Credits	2.0	Nonliquid Liabilities of	
		U.S. Government to Other	
		than Foreign Official	
		Reserve Agencies	0.5
Private Nonliquid Capital Flows (Net)			
Direct Investment by		Direct Investment by	
Foreigners in U.S.	−0.2	Americans Abroad	4.5
Portfolio—Long-Term		Portfolio—Long-Term	
U.S. Securities Other		Foreign Securities	0.9
than Treasury Issues	2.2	Other	0.6
Other	−0.1	Portfolio—Short-Term	
Portfolio—Short-Term,		Nonliquid	2.4
Nonliquid	−0.1		
Private Liquid Capital Flows (Net)			
		Liquid Liabilities to Foreign	
		Banks, Intern'l Organiza-	
		tions, and Other Foreigners	6.7
		Liquid Claims on Foreigners	
		Reported by U.S. Banking	
		and Nonbanking Concerns	1.1
Net Balance on Capital Account			−$16.7

Balance of Payments 1971	
Errors and Omissions	−10.9
Total Official Reserve Transactions Balance	−$30.5

Table 20.1.   (Continued)
Reconciliation—U.S. Government

Receipts		Payments	
Liquid Liabilities to Foreign Official Reserve Agencies	$27.6	Nonliquid Liabilities to Foreign Official Reserve Agencies	$0.2
Official Reserve Asset Transactions			
Gold	$ 0.9		
SDRs	−0.2		
Convertible Currencies	0.4		
Gold Tranche Position in IMF	1.3		
Allocation of Additional SDRs	0.7		
Total Reserve Asset Transactions	$ 3.1		

SOURCE: Federal Reserve *Bulletin*, April 1972, pp. A74, A75; U.S. Department of Commerce, *Survey of Current Business* (Washington, D.C., March 1972), p. 44.

THE BALANCE OF INTERNATIONAL PAYMENTS

The balance of international payments is a statistical summary of the actual flow of economic transactions between U.S. residents and residents of the rest of the world during a given period. Statistics on the balance of international payments for 1971 are presented in Table 20.1.

THE ACCOUNTS

For the purposes of balance-of-payments accounting, international transactions are divided into two major categories. Transactions involving payments for goods and services and recurring international gifts are recorded in the *current account*. Transactions involving payments for equities, bonds, or other types of international investments are recorded in the *capital account*.

Current Account. In statistics of the current account of the balance of international payments it is customary to distinguish between the value of commodities traded and the value of services. This distinction has been incorporated into the presentation of the current account in Table 20.1. It should be noted that, while new foreign investments by private Americans abroad are recorded in the capital account, interest and dividend payments for the use of American-owned capital employed abroad are recorded in the current account receipts.

It is also useful to distinguish between the commercial transactions recorded in the current account and the relatively small value of public and private gifts, which are also reported in the current account. While in principle they are different from regular commodity trade—they involve international "transfer payments"—they are customarily recorded in the current account because of their regular, recurring nature.

In examining the current account balance of the United States over time, excluding government grants, we find that the United States typically has had a surplus. Further, excluding remittances, the United States has had a merchandise surplus every year from 1893 until 1971. In 1971 and 1972 it ran a deficit in its merchandise account. In 1973, however, it again had a surplus.

The current account surplus (current receipts exceeding current payments) has consisted of a dwindling surplus in the merchandise account and a large surplus in receipts of investment income from abroad, which overwhelmed the deficit incurred in tourist expenditures, for example, and other current transactions. However, the overall current account balance has been far from stable. Fluctuations in the current account have important implications for the macroeconomic performance of the economy, a matter that we will examine later.

If we ignore the small amount of international transfer payments recorded in the current account, current account transactions involve demands for and disposition of *aggregate output*. Thus, as we saw in Chapter 19, what we call here the current account also appears as "exports" and "imports" in the national income accounts and in the aggregate demand equation.

The analysis of the macrobehavior of the current account is therefore an aspect of the analysis of aggregate demand, income, and employment. By contrast, transactions recorded in the capital account involve the purchase and sale of *financial assets*. The analysis of the behavior of the capital account, therefore, must involve analysis of the accumulation of wealth and portfolio balance decisions.

Capital Account. The capital account reports the flow of international transactions to financial instruments during a given period (in Table 20.1 the period is one year, 1971). This should not be confused with the stock of international indebtedness outstanding at any point in time. The two magnitudes are related, of course, in the same way that saving and wealth are related. The capital account of the balance of international payments shows the international transactions that produce a change in the size and composition of the stock of international indebtedness.[2] It should not be surprising that the annual capital flows are small relative to the total stock of international debt outstanding. For purposes of comparison, the United States' international investment position as of December 1971 is presented in Table 20.2.

International investment transactions can be classified in many different ways. In Table 20.1 we have chosen to highlight the differences between direct and portfolio investment, and within the category of portfolio investment between investments in long-term securities and short-term securities.

Direct Investment is associated with control of the corporations of one country by the residents of another country. For example, Americans invest funds in businesses abroad and obtain ownership rights and control of the operations of that company. In 1971 the value of total U.S. direct invest-

Table 20.2. **International Investment Position of the United States, December 31, 1971 (Estimated) (Billions of Dollars)**

1. U.S. Assets and Investments Abroad		
Private		
Direct Investments	$86.0	
Foreign Securities	22.3	
Banking Claims and Others	7.6	
Short-Term—Total	18.9	
Total		$134.9
U.S. Government Credits and Claims		$ 34.0
U.S. Monetary Reserve Assets		
Monetary Gold	10.2	
Other	1.9	
Total		$ 12.1
Total Assets		$181.0
2. Liabilities (Foreign Assets and Investments in U.S.)		
Private		
Direct Investments in U.S.	$13.4	
Corporate Securities	30.4	
Other Long-Term Liabilities	5.9	
Short-Term Liabilities—Nonliquid	3.6	
Liquid Liabilities	15.9	
Total		$ 69.2
Foreign Official Accounts		
On U.S. Banks	$ 7.4	
On U.S. Government	44.4	
On U.S. Government—Nonreserve[a]	1.4	
Total		$ 53.2
Total Liabilities		$122.5
3. Net Assets		$ 58.5

[a]Includes small amounts of nonreserve claims held by private foreigners.
SOURCE: Federal Reserve *Bulletin*, March 1972, p. 337.

ment abroad was estimated at $86 billion, while the value of direct investment by nonresidents in the United States was estimated at $13.4 billion.

Portfolio Investment, by contrast, implies international investment in securities without any implication of foreign control. It may involve transactions in equities or bonds, including securities issued by business firms, financial intermediaries, local and national governments, and international organizations. The gross flow of funds includes the placement of new issues of securities, the retirement of outstanding issues, and the secondary trading of securities in the open market. Transactions in short-term securities include such transactions as the placement of funds in foreign currency bank accounts, the purchase or sale of money market instruments, bank loans, and changes in international accounts receivable and payable (which are included in the account Other Short-Term Capital Movements).

When residents of the United States acquire foreign securities, dollars flow out of the United States; this is a *capital outflow*, or payment. When the federal government or American resident tries to reduce liabilities against

477

itself held by foreigners, it must pay dollars in order to obtain the claim again. This, too, is a capital outflow. From Table 20.1 we see that residents increased their holdings of foreign liquid securities by $1.1 billion (net) and reduced liabilities held by foreigners by $6.7 billion (net). Together, these two activities required a net capital outflow of $7.8 billion. Residents increased their holdings of external assets and reduced their external liabilities.

You may recall from our discussion in Chapter 7 that portfolio investments can be denominated either in dollars or in another currency. If the U.S. resident wishes to acquire securities denominated in a foreign currency, he bears the foreign exchange risk associated with holding such an asset. On the other hand, the American resident can often acquire the liability of a foreign corporation or government denominated in dollars. In that case, the nonresident issuer bears the foreign exchange risk.

Errors and Omissions. Certain international transactions go improperly or totally unrecorded. This item, Errors and Omissions, is a residual figure used to fill out and balance the accounts. It is generally assumed that much of the flow noted here is from underreporting of actual tourist expenditures and short-term capital flows that have not otherwise been recorded. During periods of international monetary disturbances this figure tends to increase. The fluctuation in Errors and Omissions, then, is often a reflection of instability in foreign exchange markets and the increased flow of funds from the United States into foreign money market instruments and foreign currency abroad.

Official Reserve Transactions. We have not yet mentioned one major account in the balance of international payments, what is called in Table 20.1 Reconciliation and Official U.S. Reserve Asset Transactions. In 1971 the total Official Reserve Transactions deficit amounted to $30.5 billion. (Total receipts fell short of total payments.) The U.S. government had to offset this deficit by increasing its external liabilities—Treasury securities sold to foreign official reserve agencies—and reducing its external assets—in this case official reserve assets like gold, Special Drawing Rights (SDRs—a creation of the International Monetary Fund functioning as a reserve asset similar to convertible currencies) and convertible currencies that it exchanged for dollars. Both activities resulted in capital inflows. Changes in official reserve assets exert a special pressure on the foreign exchange market and relate also to governmental intervention to stabilize the foreign exchange rate. For this reason we segregate them from the rest of the international capital flows.

THE BALANCE-OF-PAYMENTS IDENTITY

A basic principle of balance-of-payments accounting is that the sum of the net balance on current account and the net balance on capital account must equal the net change in official reserves. We can express this as an identity:

$$\begin{bmatrix} \text{Exports of} & & \text{Imports of} \\ \text{Goods and} & - & \text{Goods and} \\ \text{Services} & & \text{Services} \end{bmatrix} + \begin{bmatrix} \text{Capital Imports} - \text{Capital Exports} \end{bmatrix}$$
$$= \text{Net Changes in Official Reserves}$$

In this equation *capital imports* refers to the inflow of funds in payment for securities sold to foreigners (including the inflow of funds from direct investment in the United States). A capital import involves either an increase in the United States' external liabilities or a reduction in the United States' external assets. Similarly, the expression *capital exports* refers to the outflow of funds in payment for securities purchased from nonresidents. A capital export involves either a reduction in the United States' external liabilities or an increase in the United States' external assets.

The validity of the balance-of-payments identity should be intuitively obvious. To demonstrate the point, assume that there is a negative balance of $100,000 in the current account. Imports of goods and services have exceeded exports of goods and services by $100,000. How do we pay for these extra imported goods and services? One way of looking at the current account is to say that the export of goods and services provides the foreign exchange to finance the import of goods and services. In the present case the exports will not pay for the full value of the imports. How is this deficit to be financed?

There are a limited number of possibilities. They include reducing previously held foreign securities, reducing previously accumulated holdings of gold or other official reserve assets, or reducing accumulated holdings of foreign currencies (all of which reduce external assets), or borrowing foreign currency through international organizations or persuading foreign governments to increase their holdings of dollar claims against the United States (both of which increase external liabilities).

For example, it is possible that U.S. residents will sell holdings of foreign securities, providing foreign exchange through the foreign exchange markets to importers and thus permitting them to pay for the extra $100,000 worth of goods and services. But this reduces the United States' external assets. The current account deficit is financed by a capital import, and the balance-of-payments identity holds.

Alternatively, the foreign exporters could extend credit for a short period, or foreigners might decide to purchase U.S. securities or indeed increase their holdings of dollars, thus making the necessary foreign exchange available through the foreign exchange market. However, any of these occurrences implies an increase in the United States' external liabilities and hence a capital import. Again the current account deficit is financed by a capital import and the balance-of-payment identity holds.

All of these examples of capital account transactions depend on a fortuitous coincidence of circumstances.[3] Suppose that under the existing conditions in American and foreign financial markets no American holder of foreign currency assets chooses to dispose of part of his holdings, and no foreign asset holder is willing to take additional dollar assets into his portfolio. Then, either the government must provide the foreign exchange out of its holdings or persuade other governments to increase their holdings of dollar claims and provide the foreign exchange, or the current account deficits cannot occur. There are no other possibilities. A current account deficit must be financed by either a private capital inflow or an official capital inflow.

Exactly the opposite propositions hold true for a current account surplus.

The Policy Alternatives Again. The balance-of-payments identity thus provides another, more explicit, statement of the policy alternatives set out earlier. That is, if the free choices of American and foreign asset holders do not provide international capital flows consistent with the net current account imbalance, the authorities have only two alternatives if they are to maintain the stability of the foreign exchange rate without resort to direct controls. On the one hand, they may finance any net deficit by drawing down official reserves, or absorb any net surplus by building up official reserves. This is what we called direct intervention. Alternatively, they may change the basic conditions that govern the flows of international payments on current or capital accounts. This is what we called indirect intervention.

Posing the possibility of indirect intervention raises several obvious questions. What are the major determinants of the flow of payments on current account? Can the authorities intervene to regulate these flows (without resort to direct controls, of course)? What are the major determinants of the flow of payments on capital account? Can the authorities intervene to regulate these flows? What is the significance of all of this for monetary policy?

THE CURRENT ACCOUNT IN THE KEYNESIAN MODEL

A major concern of the pure theory of international trade is to explain the level and composition of imports and exports in the long run in a fully employed economy. The analysis usually assumes national economies that have different endowments with respect to factors of production, and explains mutually advantageous trade flows between these economies in terms of the principle of comparative advantage. However, this is a long-run theory that deals with a range of analytical problems that do not concern us in the present context. We will take the structure of comparative advantage as given and will focus exclusively on short-run fluctuations in the aggregate levels of imports and exports in an economy that is not necessarily at full employment. For this purpose, the appropriate framework is the theory of aggregate demand, income, employment, and price levels set out in Chapter 19.

Remember, we are assuming the foreign exchange rate to be fixed within very narrow limits. Moreover, as in our discussion of the basic Keynesian model, we take the level of prices, in the United States and abroad, as given. We will also revert to the terminology employed in respect to international trade in the discussion of aggregate demand in Chapter 19: The term *exports* will refer to all current account receipts from the sale of goods and services abroad, and the term *imports* will refer to all current account payments for the purchase of goods and services from abroad. In each case we are implicitly omitting international transfer payments from the current account.

IMPORTS, EXPORTS, AND AGGREGATE DEMAND

We saw in Chapter 19 that exports add to aggregate demand, whereas imports are a leakage from aggregate demand. Ignoring the government sector again, we can write the basic aggregate demand identity:

$$\text{Aggregate Income} = D = C + I + (X - Im) = Y = \text{Aggregate Demand} \quad (20.1)$$

This identity provides a framework for our analysis. We carry over the assumption we made earlier regarding the behavior of investment, consumption, and saving. What we need now are assumptions about the short-run behavior of aggregate imports and aggregate exports.

The Import Demand Function. Our basic assumption is that in the short run, other things being equal (i.e., the level of prices, the foreign exchange rate, and the long-run determinants of the structure of comparative advantage), the level of imports, and hence the demand for foreign exchange on current account, depends directly on the level of aggregate demand. As aggregate demand rises, the demand for imports rises. As aggregate demand falls, the demand for imports falls.

The demand for imports depends not only on the level of aggregate demand but also on the composition of aggregate demand. For example, a rise in the level of investment expenditures may have a stronger impact on the demand for imports than a corresponding increase in government expenditures.

We can incorporate both of these assumptions into an import demand function distinguishing between imports that depend on investment expenditures (Im_1) and those that depend on consumption expenditures (Im_2).[4] That is:

$$Im = Im_1 + Im_2 \quad (20.2)$$

For simplicity we will assume that in each case imports are proportional to the relevant expenditures:

$$Im = m_1 I + m_2 C \quad (20.3)$$

The coefficients m_1 and m_2 are not necessarily equal.

Equation 20.3, then, is our import demand function. It tells us that imports depend on the level of consumption expenditures and the level of investment expenditures.

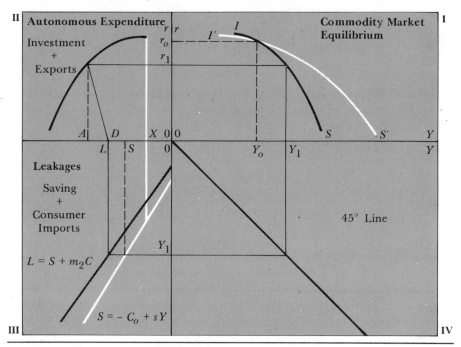

Figure 20.1 **Commodity Market Equilibrium with International Trade**

Exports as "Autonomous" Expenditures. When we first constructed the *IS* curve in Figure 19.4, we had only one category of expenditures that we assumed to be independent of the level of income—investment expenditures. In the present case we have two types of "autonomous" expenditures—investment and exports. Moreover, exports, unlike investment, are independent of the level of interest rates.

In Quadrant II of Figure 20.1, the given value of exports is indicated ·by the distance OX. In deriving what we might call the "autonomous expenditure function" (A) of that quadrant, we have simply added the given magnitude of exports to investment (derived from the original investment demand function of Figure 19.4) at each level of interest rates. That is:

$$A = I + X \qquad (20.4)$$

The effect on conditions for commodity market equilibrium is the same as if investment expenditures had increased at every level of interest rates. That is, the *IS* curve will be shifted to the right. The effect of including exogenous exports in the Keynesian model is simply to increase the equilibrium level of income at each possible level of interest rates.

The Demand for Imports as "External Leakage." The effects of adding an import demand function of the type we have specified to the Keynesian model is somewhat more complex. In general, the effect of imports is the opposite of the effect of exports. They reduce the equilibrium level of income for each level of interest rates, shifting the *IS* curve to the left. However, the fact that imports vary directly with investment and consumption expenditures also has an important effect on the shape of the *IS* curve. By limiting the increase in domestic consumption expenditures consequent on any given increase of investment expenditures, imports reduce the interest elasticity of the *IS* function.

One part of the impact of imports on the *IS* curve arises because the portion of investment expenditures that is devoted to the purchase of imports is irrelevant to the process of income generation in the United States. The import content of investment ($m_1 I$) is an "external leakage" that must be deducted from income-generating "autonomous" expenditures. In Quadrant II of Figure 20.1 we show the effect of this adjustment for the arbitrarily selected level of interest rates, r_1. At this level of interest rates, autonomous expenditures $(X + I)$ would be OA. However, from this must be deducted the import content of investment expenditures, leaving OD as the domestic component of autonomous expenditures. It is this magnitude—the sum of exports and the *domestic component* of investment expenditures—that is projected into Quadrant III at each level of interest rates.[5]

The second part of the import demand function, the import content of consumption expenditures ($m_2 C$), has the same effect on the *IS* curve as would an increase in the marginal propensity to save. It increases the share of any increment to income that is diverted away from income-generating consumption expenditures and thus limits the total increase of income that can result from a given increase of autonomous expenditures. Accordingly, in Quadrant III we have added the import content of consumption ($m_2 C$) to the original saving function from Figure 19.4 (the broken line in Quadrant III) to obtain the total leakage function:

$$L = S + m_2 C \qquad (20.5)$$

This function is represented by the solid line in Quadrant III.

Exports. In the same way that U.S. imports depend on the level of aggregate demand in the United States, its exports depend on the level of aggregate demand in the rest of the world. It is evident that for the United States and other countries there is no intrinsic reason for exports to equal imports. Exports help determine the level of income and employment in the United States, but they are not, in turn, determined by the levels of income and employment in the United States. Thus, although the absolute magnitude of exports is significant to the U.S. economy, it is the difference between exports and imports, which must be offset by private and official capital flows, that imposes constraints on monetary policy. Returning to the assumptions of the Keynesian model, then, exports are an exogenous variable—a variable whose magnitude is determined by external factors. In our analysis we simply take the value of exports as given.

THE CURRENT ACCOUNT AND THE *IS* CURVE

The addition of an exogenous export variable and an import demand function such as Equation 20.3 makes no difference in principle to the "real" side of the basic Keynesian model. In terms of the concepts we developed in the previous chapter, they simply alter the position and elasticity of the *IS* function. Figure 20.1 is a demonstration of this, using the now-familiar four-quadrant diagram.

In discussing the significance of external trade for macroeconomic equilibrium it is useful to distinguish between the effects of autonomous exports and the effects of the import demand function.

Equilibrium in the Commodity Market with International Trade. You will recall from Chapter 19 that equilibrium in the commodity market at any level of interest rates requires a level of income such that the (income-depressing) planned savings of households exactly offset the (income-generating) planned investment expenditures of business firms. With the introduction of international trade we have to redefine the conditions for equilibrium. Investment can exceed saving without pushing up income, provided that the excess of investment over saving is just offset by net inflow of goods from abroad (imports). The income-generating effects of excess investment are just offset by the net leakage of aggregate demand through the current account. The opposite is also true. That is, an excess of saving over investment is also consistent with equilibrium in the commodity market, provided that it is offset by an excess of exports over imports. The income-depressing effects of excess saving are just offset by the income-generating effects of excess exports.

We can state our new equilibrium conditions as:

$$X + I = Im + S$$
$$= m_2C + m_1I + S \tag{20.6}$$

Rearranging the terms:

$$X + I - m_1I = m_2C + S \tag{20.7}$$

or

$$A - m_1I = m_2C + S \tag{20.9}$$

In Quadrant III we see that the equilibrium level of income, given interest rate r_1, is Y_1. At this level of income, leakages ($S + m_2 = OL$) equal the domestic component of autonomous expenditures ($A - m_1I = OD$). By a similar process we could find equilibrium levels of income for all other possible levels of interest rates.

The *IS* Curve. The line in Quadrant IV is the now-familiar 45° line, used to reflect equilibrium levels of income from the vertical axis of Quadrant III to the horizontal axis of Quadrant I. Since investment depends on the levels of interest rates, there will be a different equilibrium level of income for each possible level of interest rates. As usual, the *IS* curve, the solid line in Quadrant I, is the locus of all combinations of interest rates and income levels that are consistent with equilibrium in the commodity market.

The broken line, IS, in Quadrant I is the original IS curve from Figure 19.4, drawn on the assumption of the same investment and saving functions but no international trade. It provides a convenient reference base for identifying the effects of introducing international trade into the Keynesian model.

The two IS curves have one point in common: the combination of interest rate (I_o) and income (Y_o) at which imports equal exports. This tells us that international trade makes no difference to the macroeconomic equilibrium in the economy if the current account is in balance. In our model, the level of income at which the current account is in balance depends on the level of exports. The larger the value of exports, the higher the level of income at which exports will equal imports and the farther to the right the intersection of the two IS curves.

In general, however, imports and exports are not equal, and whenever the current account is not in balance the presence of international trade affects the combinations of interest rates and income levels at which the commodity market will be in equilibrium. Thus, to the left of the intersection of the two IS curves in Quadrant I exports exceed imports. Because of this fillip to income, the new IS curve lies above the old. International trade will limit the decline of income and employment that would be the normal consequence of a rise in the level of interest rates. To the right of the point of intersection, the new IS curve lies below the old. Imports exceed exports. Because of the import content of both investment and consumption expenditures, international trade limits the increase of income and employment that would be the normal consequence of a reduction in interest rates.

The LM Curve. In Figure 19.5 we derived the LM curve for the economy. In that context the LM curve described all possible combinations of income and interest rates that produce equilibrium in the money market with a given money supply.

Now, expanding our analysis to an open economy, particularly in the context of the U.S. economy, we should note that part of the aggregate demand for money (dollars) comes from nonresident individuals and governments. This element in the derivation of the LM curve is significant in a model of the American economy because the dollar is widely held by nonresidents. The dollar is held by foreign individuals, businesses, and governments because it is a major *working* currency—a widely accepted international medium of exchange in which a large portion of international trade is denominated—and a *reserve* currency—a major component of officially held stocks of foreign exchange assets. Because of these two characteristics, as well as the fact that short-term dollar claims have been liquid, low-risk investments, foreigners have been willing to accumulate a large stock of dollar claims (about $90 billion in dollar claims was held by foreigners in 1973) and bear the foreign exchange risk inherent in holding an asset denominated in a currency other than their own. During the same period, however, foreign financial markets have expanded and become more efficient. Alternative foreign financial assets have been introduced that are safe, stable, liquid, and of low risk, and these now compete with dollar claims. Particularly with regard to a model of the American economy, nonresident demand for money (dollars) affects the position and elasticity of the *LM* curve.

Implications for Monetary Policy. These conclusions on the significance of international trade for macroeconomic equilibrium (with fixed prices and a fixed exchange rate) do not introduce any new principles into our analysis of monetary policy. However, they do provide additional reasons for thinking that the *IS* curve may be relatively interest inelastic, and this is an important matter. As we saw in Chapter 19, the lower the elasticity of the *IS* function, the lower the likelihood of a strong macroeconomic response to monetary policy.

There is another dimension to the macroeconomic implications of international trade that we have glossed over. One conclusion that can be drawn from our analysis is that, given the level of exports, the behavior of imports tends to stabilize the level of income and employment. It tends to damp any increase in income and to limit any decline in income consequent on any given change of autonomous expenditures. Any change in exports will shift the *IS* function in the same direction and hence will alter the equilibrium levels of income and employment. To the extent that exports depend on aggregate demand in the rest of the world, this provides a significant link between domestic income level and employment and economic activity abroad.

THE CAPITAL ACCOUNT IN THE KEYNESIAN MODEL

In our analysis of the role of international trade in the Keynesian macroeconomic model, we imposed no constraints on the current account balance. We implicitly assumed that there was no limit to the magnitude of the current account deficit or surplus that could be induced by a rise or fall in the level of aggregate demand. However, our earlier discussion of the balance-of-payments identity revealed that a current account deficit must be matched by an equal surplus in the capital account, or else official reserve assets must be drawn down. Similarly, any current account surplus must be matched by an equal capital account deficit, or else official reserve assets must increase. Do these facts not affect the extent to which current account deficits or surpluses can be incurred?

The answer is yes. As a result, in analyzing the conditions for macroeconomic equilibrium in the economy, we cannot consider the current account in isolation. We must consider it in relation to international capital flows and possible changes in official reserve assets.

486

The role of official foreign exchange reserves in this context poses special problems that are better deferred for separate treatment. What regulates private international capital flows?

THE DETERMINANTS OF INTERNATIONAL CAPITAL FLOWS

We have already considered the international investment decision in some detail in Chapter 7. There is no need to repeat that discussion here. If we regard international capital flows of all types—direct investment as well as portfolio investment—simply as international transactions in financial instruments (in the broad way in which we have defined the concept of a financial instrument), then what is involved in international capital flows are the portfolio balance decisions of American and foreign asset holders and debtors. Thus, private capital outflows result when American asset holders choose to take foreign securities into their portfolios, when foreign asset holders choose to reduce their holdings of American securities, or when American debtors decide to retire foreign-held debts. Similarly, private capital inflows result when foreign asset holders choose to take American securities into their portfolios, when asset holders here choose to reduce their holdings of foreign securities, or when foreign debtors decide to retire debts of theirs that are held by Americans.

Many types of financial instruments, many different asset holders and debtors, and hence many individual decisions are involved in the aggregate of international capital flows in any given year. Each decision calls for the weighing of a variety of considerations, some economic, some political; some long term, some short term. However, the central consideration in most of these decisions—whether they relate to direct investment or portfolio investment—must be the expected yield on the investment (considered relative to risk and liquidity, of course). Foreign capital will be attracted to the United States by relatively high expected yields on American investments. American capital will be attracted abroad by relatively high expected yields on foreign investments.

Interest Rates and Capital Flows. This line of argument suggests that there should be a direct link between monetary policy and international capital flows. A tight-money policy, as we have seen, implies increasing interest rates in the United States. Given the interest rates prevailing abroad, this should induce foreign asset holders to purchase relatively higher-yielding American securities and should induce American borrowers to raise more funds abroad from foreign banks and financial intermediaries. The net result should be an enlarged inflow of capital to the United States.

Similarly, an easy-money policy implies lower interest rates, at least initially, in the United States. Given the interest rates prevailing abroad, this should reduce the incentive for American borrowers to raise funds abroad. Indeed, a sufficient reduction of U.S. interest rates could induce substantial foreign borrowing in the United States.

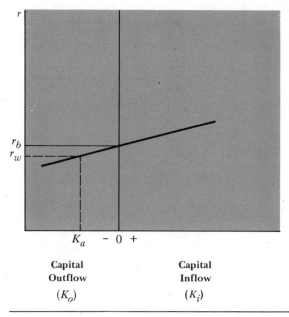

Figure 20.2 **The Net Capital Flow Function**

However, not all international capital flows are highly sensitive to international interest rate differentials. For example, empirical researchers have found little statistical evidence of a strong response of direct investment to interest rates. However, there is substantial evidence of high interest elasticity of portfolio investment, in both long-term and short-term forms.[6]

The Net Capital Flow Function. These basic assumptions about the dependence of international capital flows on the level of interest rates are incorporated into the net capital flow function presented in Figure 20.2.

We assume that international capital flows are highly sensitive to international interest rate differentials, and hence we have drawn the line with a relatively low slope. However, we have not adopted the extreme assumption of perfect international capital mobility that is sometimes employed in the analysis of this problem. Such an assumption would produce a perfectly horizontal line at the world interest rate (or perhaps at the world rate plus a small "risk premium"). Moreover, we have drawn the net capital flow function as a straight line purely for convenience.

The level of interest rates in the United States (r) is measured along the vertical axis and the net international flow of capital along the horizontal axis. At interest rate r_w, the level of interest rates in the United States is the same as that in the rest of the world. That is, the international differential between yields on comparable securities is zero. We have assumed that at this level of interest rates there is a net outflow of capital from the United

States (K_a). We might call this the autonomous capital outflow. It may take the form largely of direct investment abroad.

At higher levels of interest rates in the United States, a smaller net outflow of capital will occur, until at interest rates higher than r_b a capital inflow will result.

BALANCE-OF-PAYMENTS EQUILIBRIUM

The important new concept, *balance-of-payments equilibrium under pegged exchange rates*, can be defined as a condition in which normal market forces tend to keep the foreign exchange rate within the permitted range about the official par rate, without direct controls and without direct intervention by the government. Balance-of-payments equilibrium requires that the international capital flows resulting from the free choices of American and foreign asset holders and debtors are just sufficient to offset the net balance on current account at the pegged rate of exchange. No change in official reserves is required to achieve a balance of international payments.

The conditions for balance-of-payments equilibrium thus depend partly on the behavior of the capital account and partly on the behavior of the current account. We have a function, the *net capital flow function*, that describes the behavior of international capital flows in response to American interest rates. What we require to complete our analysis is a companion function describing the behavior of the current account.

The Current Account Balance Function. The required *current account balance function* can be derived from our earlier analysis of the determinants of imports and exports, and particularly from Figure 20.1. You will recall that we assumed that the value of exports was exogenous, determined by factors external to the United States, and that the value of imports depended separately on the levels of investment expenditures and consumption expenditures in the United States. From these assumptions, the current account balance depends on the level of income in the United States in the manner indicated in Figure 20.3.[7]

At one particular level of income, Y_0, imports will equal exports and the current account will balance. At higher levels of income, imports will be larger, and hence there will be a negative balance in the current account. At lower levels of income, imports will be smaller, producing a surplus in the current account.

The BK Function. Balance-of-payments equilibrium, then, must depend on the level of interest rates and the level of income. At any given level of income, there will be a unique level of interest rates that will induce a capital inflow equal to the current account deficit associated with that level of income (or a capital outflow equal to the current account surplus). Thus, balance-of-payments equilibrium requires a different level of interest rates for each possible level of income, and we can derive a function, similar in concept to the *IS* and *LM* functions, that identifies all possible combinations of

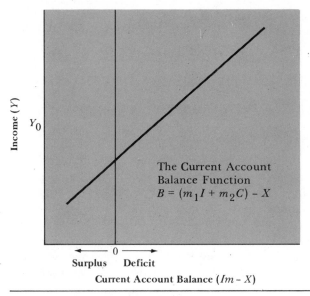

Figure 20.3 **The Current Account Balance Function**

interest rates and income levels consistent with balance-of-payments (or foreign exchange market) equilibrium. We call such a curve a *BK* function.[8]

The derivation of the *BK* curve from the net capital flow function of Figure 20.2 and the current account balance function of Figure 20.3 is demonstrated in Figure 20.4. The technique is the same as that employed earlier and should require no explanation. The net capital flow function is in Quadrant II, with the net international flow of capital measured along the base axis and interest rates along the vertical axis. The current account balance function is in Quadrant III, with the current account balance measured along the base axis and the level of income measured in a downward direction along the vertical axis. We can use these two curves to find combinations of interest rates and income at which the net capital flow and the current account balance are equal. Equilibrium income levels for each level of interest rates are projected from the vertical axis of Quadrant III to the base axis of Quadrant I, using the 45° line of Quadrant IV. The result is the balance-of-payments equilibrium line, *BK*, described by the solid line in Quadrant I.

At points above the *BK* function the level of interest rates is too high relative to the level of income. The net inflow of capital from abroad will exceed the current account deficit (to demonstrate your understanding of the *BK* function you should be able to show that this is the case). Excess supply in the foreign exchange market will put downward pressure on the foreign exchange rate. If such a condition is to exist, in the absence of direct controls

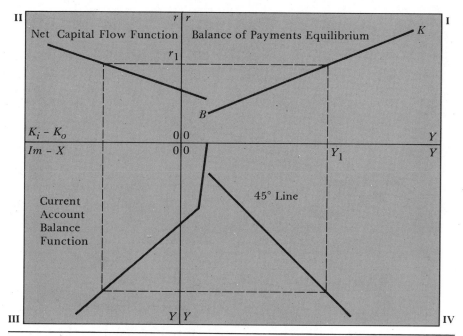

Figure 20.4 **Derivation of the Balance-of-Payments Equilibrium Function (BK)**

and without a change in the foreign exchange rate, the excess supply must be absorbed by an increase of official foreign exchange reserves.

At points below the BK function the level of interest rates is too low relative to the level of income. The net inflow of capital will fall short of the current account deficit, and excess demand in the foreign exchange market will put upward pressure on the foreign exchange rate. If such a condition is to exist, official foreign exchange reserves must be drawn down to satisfy the excess demand at the maximum permitted foreign exchange rate.

You should note that, according to our assumptions, at higher levels of income balance-of-payments equilibrium requires higher levels of interest rates. The more sensitive international capital flows are to interest rate differentials, the flatter this line will be. In the extreme case of perfect international capital mobility, the BK line will be horizontal at the world level of interest rates, I_w.

MACROECONOMIC EQUILIBRIUM WITH INTERNATIONAL TRADE AND INTERNATIONAL CAPITAL FLOWS

We are now in a position to incorporate international trade in goods and services and international capital flows into our analysis of macroeconomic equilibrium.

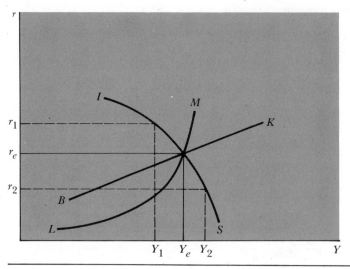

Figure 20.5 **Full Macroeconomic Equilibrium in an Open Economy**

MACROEONOMIC EQUILIBRIUM

We discovered in Chapter 19 that full macroeconomic equilibrium in a *closed economy* requires that equilibrium be achieved simultaneously in the money market and the commodity market. In an *open economy* we add a third condition: Equilibrium must be achieved simultaneously not only in the commodity and money markets but also in the balance of international payments. That is, full macroeconomic equilibrium in an open economy requires a combination of interest rates and income levels that will simultaneously satisfy the *IS* function, the *LM* function, and the *BK* function.

A state of full macroeconomic equilibrium is illustrated in Figure 20.5. At any combination of income and interest rates other than Y_e and r_e at least two of the three markets must be in disequilibrium (and with many conceivable combinations, all three markets will be in disequilibrium). For example, at the levels of interest rates and income indicated by r_1 and Y_1, equilibrium would be achieved in the commodity market. However, given the money supply, the money market would not be in equilibrium (the supply of money would exceed the demand, creating downward pressure on interest rates), and given the foreign exchange rate and foreign interest rates, the balance of payments would not be in equilibrium (the inflow of capital would exceed the current account deficit, creating downward pressure on the foreign exchange rate). At levels of interest rates and income represented by r_2 and Y_2 the commodity market would again be in equilibrium, but there would be excess demand in both the money market and the foreign exchange market. Full macroeconomic equilibrium would not exist. (To demonstrate your understanding of this discussion you should be able to explain the nature of the disequilibrium conditions represented by other combinations of interest rates and income.)

In the conditions depicted in Figure 20.5, full macroeconomic equilibrium is possible. Indeed, any departure from equilibrium income and interest rates would eventually be corrected. Thus, at points like $r_1 Y_1$, downward pressure on interest rates resulting from the excess supply of money and the excess capital inflows would increase investment, income, and imports, and would tend to move the system toward equilibrium at $r_e Y_e$. Similarly, at points like $r_2 Y_2$, upward pressure on interest rates would move the system toward equilibrium at $r_e Y_e$.

THE IMPOSSIBILITY OF EQUILIBRIUM

However, the tendency of the economy toward general macroeconomic equilibrium as depicted in Figure 20.5 is an accident—a product of the way in which we have drawn the three curves. Given the underlying behavioral functions (i.e., the demand for money function, the investment function, the import demand function, etc.), and given any arbitrarily selected money supply and foreign exchange rate, general macroeconomic equilibrium may be impossible. That is, given the money supply and the foreign exchange rate, there may be no combination of interest rates and income that will simultaneously satisfy the IS function, the LM function, and the BK function.

An example of a situation in which general macroeconomic equilibrium is impossible is depicted in Figure 20.6. The three functions do not have a common point of intersection. In this situation, with interest rates and income at r_1 and Y_1, respectively, the money and commodity markets will be in equilibrium but the balance of international payments will be in surplus. The economy can be maintained in this condition only if official foreign exchange reserves increase in each period by the amount of the balance-of-payments surplus (which we have ruled out by our definition of equilibrium).

The opposite situation is depicted in Figure 20.7. At the level of interest rates and income (r_2, Y_2) that produces equilibrium in the commodity and money markets, the balance of payments is in deficit. The economy can be maintained in this condition only if official foreign exchange reserves are drawn down in each period by the amount of the balance-of-payments deficit (ruled out by our definition of equilibrium).

It should also be noted that if macroeconomic equilibrium is achieved, as in Figure 20.5, it will be a fragile condition. Underlying each of the functions in Figure 20.5 is a great variety of variables and behavior patterns, some domestic and some external, each of which is subject to substantial change over short periods. A significant change in any major macroeconomic variable will disturb the equilibrium. Thus, for example, a rise in investment demand will shift the IS function; a decline in exports will shift the BK function; and an increase in the demand for money will shift the LM function. Moreover, a shift in any one of these functions will convert a

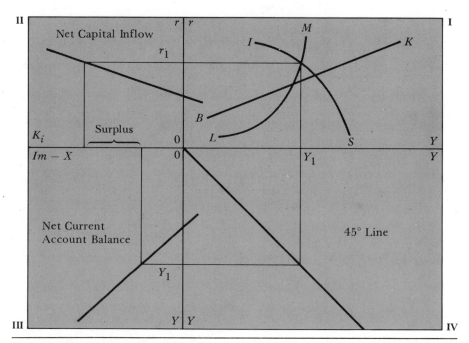

Figure 20.6 **Macroeconomic Equilibrium Impossible—Domestic Equilibrium: Balance-of-Payments Surplus**

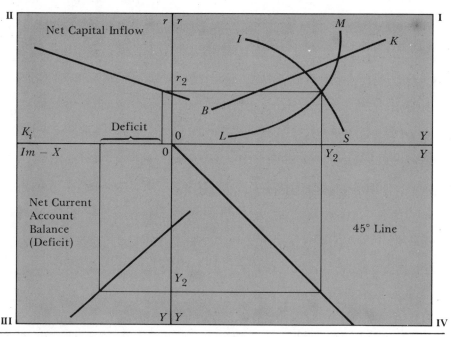

Figure 20.7 **Macroeconomic Equilibrium Impossible—Domestic Equilibrium: Balance-of-Payments Deficit**

condition of full equilibrium into a condition (such as Figures 20.6 and 20.7) in which equilibrium may be impossible without further intervention on the part of the government.

IMPLICATIONS FOR MONETARY POLICY

Let us continue our earlier assumption that the level of official foreign exchange reserves must not change significantly (as we shall see in the next section, this is not an unreasonable assumption). What, then, are the implications of this analysis for monetary policy?

Governmental Policy and Macroeconomic Equilibrium. The important point to be derived from this analysis is not that under certain plausible conditions macroeconomic equilibrium may be impossible in an open economy but rather that achievement of equilibrium may require a particular set of governmental policies. In this regard, we must remember that the position of the LM curve is a matter of governmental policy. It depends on the size of the money supply. Thus, in a situation typified by Figure 20.6, full equilibrium is impossible only if the government insists on restricting the money supply to the level that produces the indicated LM curve. Full macroeconomic equilibrium can always be achieved in this situation through monetary expansion, shifting the LM curve to the right until it intersects the IS and BK curves. There is some money supply that is compatible with full macroeconomic equilibrium—but that money supply implies a lower level of interest rates and a higher level of aggregate demand in the economy.

Similarly, in situations like that depicted in Figure 20.7, full equilibrium can always be obtained by the appropriate monetary policy. In this case, the money supply must be restricted, shifting the LM curve to the left until it intersects with the IS and BK curves. Full equilibrium implies a higher level of interest rates and a lower level of aggregate demand.

In principle, macroeconomic equilibrium can also be achieved through fiscal policies designed to shift the IS curve. However, for short-run adjustments this is seldom a practical alternative. The very flexibility of monetary policy normally throws the bulk of the shorter-term adjustments onto it. Nonetheless, the potential use of fiscal policy for this purpose—and particularly for the solution of longer-term problems—should not be overlooked.

This discussion suggests an important conclusion. In an economy with a pegged exchange rate and with official foreign exchange reserves (reserve assets) that cannot undergo major fluctuations, the central bank is constrained by balance-of-payments considerations in its use of monetary policy to alter conditions in the domestic economy. The central bank may find that monetary policy is dictated by the necessity of finding a money supply that is compatible with equilibrium in both the commodity market (the IS curve) and the balance of payments (the BK curve). Indeed, the very purpose of monetary policy ceases to be the regulation of domestic aggregate demand in the interest of achieving full-employment goals and price level stabilization. Rather, monetary policy becomes a tool for correcting balance-

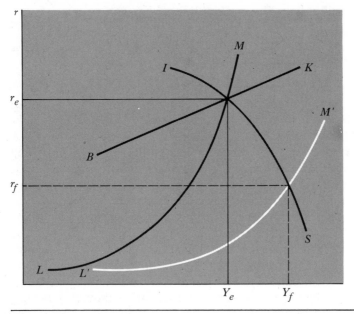

Figure 20.8 **Conflicts Between Policy Objectives—Balance-of-Payments Deficit and Un-employment**

of-payments disequilibria in order to achieve the harmonization of the balance of payments and domestic aggregate demand in the interest of macroeconomic equilibrium.

Conflicts Between Domestic and External Policy. This new perspective on monetary policy has another important implication. In Chapter 19 we discovered several reasons, within the Keynesian framework, why monetary policy might be relatively impotent as a tool for achieving domestic macroeconomic objectives like full employment and price level stability. The balance of international payments obviously imposes another constraint on the effectiveness of monetary policy for domestic economic stabilization, when the authorities must maintain a pegged rate of exchange.

Two important cases must be considered. The first is represented in Figure 20.8. In this situation the equilibrium level of income (Y_e) falls short of the level required to maintain full employment in the economy (Y_f). (Remember, we are dealing with a Keynesian economy, in which the price level is fixed.) Domestic considerations call for monetary expansion, shifting the LM curve to $L'M'$, inducing lower interest rates and increased credit availability and higher levels of investment, income, and employment. Balance-of-payments considerations curtail this. Equilibrium can be maintained in the foreign exchange market only at the pegged exchange rate with high interest rates. There is a clear conflict between the use of monetary

496

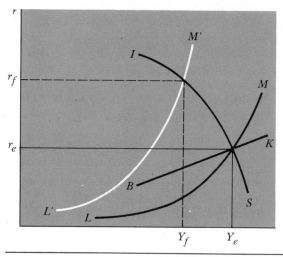

Figure 20.9 **Conflicts Between Policy Objectives—Balance-of-Payments Surplus and Inflation**

policy for domestic objectives and for external objectives. Overriding balance-of-payments considerations can render monetary policy perverse from a domestic point of view.

That is not to say that full employment and balance-of-payments equilibrium cannot be achieved simultaneously in this situation. As noted earlier, fiscal policy can be used to move the IS curve. What would be required in this situation would be expansionary fiscal policy (lower taxes, higher government expenditures) to move the economy toward full employment, coupled with a restrictive monetary policy to maintain balance-of-payments equilibrium.

Another case of conflict in the use of monetary policy is illustrated in Figure 20.9. The equilibrium level of income (Y_e) is greater than the full-employment level of income (Y_f). Full equilibrium calls for a larger money supply (LM) than that required for full employment ($L'M'$), and the lower interest rates and larger level of aggregate demand are inconsistent with price level stability. The monetary policy required to maintain stability of the foreign exchange rate in the absence of substantial increases in official foreign exchange reserves is an inflationary monetary policy.

Again, harmonization of the domestic and external objectives is possible in principle through the combined use of monetary and fiscal policies. As in the previous case, monetary and fiscal policies must be used in the opposite directions.

Conflicts between external and internal objectives are not inevitable, of course. In the case illustrated by Figure 20.10, at the existing level of income (Y), there is neither full employment nor full macroeconomic

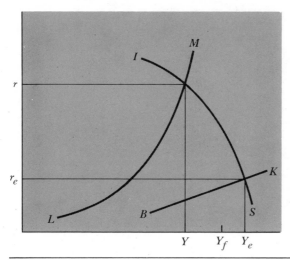

Figure 20.10 Conflicts Between Policy Objectives—Agreement on Direction of Policy: Conflict on Intensity of Expansion

equilibrium (the combination BY lies above the BK function, and hence the balance of payments is in surplus). The achievement of full employment and macroeconomic equilibrium both call for monetary expansion. There is no conflict on the direction of policy.

It should be noted, however, that in such a situation, the degree of monetary expansion appropriate to each objective may be different. This is also illustrated in Figure 20.10. Thus, once full employment is achieved (Y), further monetary expansion is still called for to eliminate the balance of payments surplus. The conflict between internal and external objectives re-emerges at full employment.

Obviously, examples of this sort can be multiplied *ad nauseam*. However, the manipulation of graphs is useful only if it produces important conclusions about the functioning of the economy. Have we discovered anything of significance?

An Important Conclusion. The results of our analysis to this point are important. They demonstrate again that in an open economy the scope for vigorous, independent monetary policy designed to regulate domestic aggregate demand is severely limited if the foreign exchange rate is pegged and if official foreign exchange reserves cannot undergo short-term fluctuations.

Surely this is a powerful conclusion, at least, if we accept the two caveats. The first suggests one of the major flaws in the Bretton Woods System that led to its demise. But what about official foreign exchange reserves? Can they not be used to reconcile the domestic and external objectives of monetary policy? That is, can official foreign exchange reserves not be increased to absorb any surplus, or drawn down to finance any deficit, in the foreign exchange market resulting from the use of monetary policy for purely domestic purposes? What is the function of official foreign exchange reserves in the financial system?

OFFICIAL FOREIGN EXCHANGE RESERVES

Official foreign exchange reserves are a pool of foreign exchange and other foreign currency assets that can be readily converted into foreign exchange in the hands of the government and its agencies, and are available to finance direct intervention by that government in the foreign exchange market. Reserves can be held in various forms, and the nature and composition of foreign exchange reserves raise a number of interesting and important economic issues. (We will sketch some of the major points in Chapter 21). Here we must be concerned with the role of foreign exchange reserves in ameliorating the potential conflict between domestic and external objectives of monetary policy, and for this purpose it is the overall size rather than the composition of foreign exchange reserves that is the vital concern.

FOREIGN EXCHANGE RESERVES
AND BALANCE-OF-PAYMENTS DEFICITS

Let us first consider the case illustrated by Figure 20.8. This is a situation in which less than full employment calls for monetary expansion, but monetary expansion implies excess demand for foreign exchange at the maximum permissible foreign exchange rate (again assuming a system of pegged rates). There is a clear conflict between the domestic and external objectives of policy. Full employment implies a balance-of-payments deficit.

Foreign Exchange Reserves as a Buffer Stock. The conflict is more apparent than real if the implied balance-of-payments deficit can be financed readily by drawing down official foreign exchange reserves. You will recall our discussion of obligations under Bretton Woods. To maintain pegged exchange rates, a member country was to intervene in foreign exchange markets whenever the band limits around the official rate were approached. In the case of balance-of-payments deficits, the member country would find the price of its currency depreciating from the official par value. It had to intervene, selling foreign exchange assets and buying its own currency. In this sense, official foreign exchange reserves can serve as a buffer stock, absorbing the balance-of-payments consequences of domestic economic policies (or, alternatively, shielding domestic policy from adverse developments in the balance of payments). Indeed, this is the economic function of official foreign exchange reserves. They are supposed to make the government's commitment to maintain the pegged exchange rate credible, without imposing continuous tyranny by the balance of payments over domestic monetary and fiscal policies.

If foreign exchange reserves are to perform this function, they must be large relative to potential balance-of-payments deficits. Remember that at any point in time, official foreign exchange reserves are a stock of finite magnitude. A balance-of-payments deficit (a flow) during any period will reduce the level of reserves available to finance a deficit in the following period. A continuing deficit will deplete the stock of reserves more or less rapidly, depending on the size of the deficit relative to the stock of reserves.

FOREIGN EXCHANGE RESERVES AND THE U.S. EXPERIENCE

The United States was not as restrained by a fixed stock of foreign currency assets during the existence of the Bretton Woods Agreement as the preceding analysis would imply. It continued to pursue conflicting domestic and external policy objectives, despite prolonged balance-of-payments deficits. What other alternatives did the United States have, and why?

The United States was able to rely on official capital flows to offset much of the balance-of-payments deficit that occurred as a result of autonomous trade and capital flows. It was able to persuade nonresidents to accumulate holdings of dollar claims.

Dollar claims were stable, safe, low-risk, liquid, income-earning assets for nonresidents. In addition, the dollar was in demand because it was a "working currency" used to denominate most trade transactions; a "vehicle currency" under Bretton Woods rules, wherein member nations used dollars to intervene directly in foreign exchange markets to maintain the official par value of their currencies; and a "reserve currency" and proxy for gold backing the domestic monetary base of many countries.

As long as the demand for dollars and short-term dollar claims by nonresidents was strong, the United States did not have to rely solely on its stock of foreign reserve assets (particularly gold) to finance its persistent deficits. It could create dollar claims against itself, which were then acquired by nonresidents. As a result, the United States was able to remain in a balance-of-payments disequilibrium longer without changing the official par value of its currency or resorting to domestically unacceptible monetary and fiscal policy that would restrain the domestic economy and without imposing severe exchange and trade controls.

Implications. These arguments seem to imply that the independence of domestic monetary and fiscal policy from the balance-of-payments constraint is simply a matter of being a reserve currency country or having adequate foreign exchange reserves. The greater the demand for the reserve currency or the larger the stock of reserves, the greater the scope for independent action in pursuit of domestic full employment, unhampered by concern about potential balance-of-payments deficits. The demand for a reserve currency is influenced by the stock of gold the reserve currency country holds relative to the outstanding stock of reserve currency claims ultimately redeemable in gold and alternative foreign exchange assets that can be used to finance direct intervention in the foreign exchange markets. The ability of a reserve currency country to continue to persuade the rest of the world to accept its currency instead of its stock of foreign reserves (gold) is influenced by the world's judgment regarding the continued stability in price and safety of that reserve currency.

Large stocks of foreign currency assets will finance larger or more prolonged deficits than will small stocks of reserves. Large stocks of gold will permit a reserve currency country to finance prolonged deficits by issuing reserve currency claims because others view the reserve currency as fixed in price relative to gold and redeemable in gold at that price. However, the degree of independence provided by even large reserves can be illusory.

A simple comparison of the size of the reserves with the size of probable deficits that will result from vigorous pursuit of a domestic full-employment policy neglects the effect of the vital force of speculation.

Speculation in the Foreign Exchange Market. We referred briefly in Chapter 7 to the possibility of speculative demands for foreign exchange in anticipation of a rise in the foreign exchange rate. From time to time in recent years, such speculation has proved to be a powerful, and at times decisive, force in foreign exchange markets. We cannot discuss the role of official foreign exchange reserves as a buffer stock between the balance of payments and domestic policy without considering the possibility that a drop in foreign exchange reserves will incite speculative activity.

The recent foreign exchange rate system was peculiarly vulnerable to speculative activity. While exchange rates were pegged, unlike the situation under the classical gold standard, they were not sacrosanct. Periodic adjustments were permissible and occurred with frequency in recent years, even for major currencies. However, with few exceptions (Canada in 1950; Germany in 1969), such changes occurred in sudden, discrete jumps of relatively large magnitude (e.g., 10 percent to 15 percent). The basis for speculation was not removed by gradual, continuous adjustments of the exchange rate such as might have occurred if it were a flexible price.

In this environment, with the exchange rate pressed against the ceiling and foreign exchange reserves falling, speculators may see a possibility for large gains with virtually no risk of a major loss. If a rise in the par rate of exchange occurred, they stood to make a substantial gain. Under the circumstances there was virtually no possibility that the par rate of exchange would be reduced. As a result, the worst they could expect was a small decline in the market rate away from the ceiling. Given the very one-sided risk, this was a speculation that might appeal even to "risk avoiders." Indeed, much speculative activity (in the sense of a transfer of funds in anticipation of a change in the exchange rate) was undertaken by conservative corporate treasurers who argued that they were not seeking speculative gains but were seeking to protect the financial position of the corporation. It should not be surprising, therefore, that a country that is losing foreign exchange reserves with the exchange rate pressed against the ceiling should find its currency under intense speculative attack.

The important point is that the government must make available all the foreign exchange the speculators demand if it is to prevent the exchange rate from rising above the ceiling. In other words, speculation induced by a drop in the level of official foreign exchange reserves will accelerate the decline of those reserves—and further declines will intensify the speculative activity. From the point of view of the monetary authorities, it is a vicious circle.

The U.S. Dollar. Speculation against the dollar under Bretton Woods rules appeared to be more of a problem for other central banks than for the United States. The member nations had to intervene in the foreign exchange market to stabilize the value of their currency at the official rate of exchange. If all member nations were maintaining the pegged rates of exchange in the markets, the United States was normally freed from direct intervention.

Speculation against the dollar and in favor of another currency reflected expectation that the dollar would have to be devalued against that currency, that the official price between the two would have to be changed. Speculators would dump dollars and buy that currency, driving the official rate to its limits. The foreign central bank would have to buy dollars, accumulating them until the wave of speculation abated or the official par rate of exchange was changed. We discuss the effect of accumulating foreign exchange reserves in a later section. The crucial question here is: How long would the foreign central bank continue to accumulate dollars? What would it do with the additional dollar claims? Would it hold them and continue to extend credit to the United States as a method of financing its deficits, or would it find its own portfolio in disequilibrium and try to exchange dollars for foreign reserve assets held by the United States? Finally, would it abandon the pegged exchange rate and revalue its currency in terms of the dollar?

Foreign central banks' willingness to accumulate dollars was influenced by internal policies, institutional arrangements, and a continuing appraisal of the safety and stability of the dollar in terms of gold. An increasing stock of dollar claims held by foreigners against a dwindling U.S. gold stock increased the risk of holding dollars as a fixed price claim against that gold. The growing risk and uncertainty stimulated shifts in asset preferences. The same large stock of foreign dollar claims made the U.S. dollar and other currencies particularly vulnerable to even small shifts in asset preferences as between dollars and other currencies or dollars and gold.

Speculation that the official price of gold would be changed was one-sided. There was no limit on how far the United States could go to offset downward pressure on the price of gold. It could create dollars in any amount to buy all the gold offered in the market. The limit was on its ability to offset pressure to change the price of gold upward. Until the late 1950s the United States held more than half of the world's monetary gold stock.

There was little reason to believe it could not maintain the price of gold at $35 per ounce. However, persistent balance-of-payments deficits had to be accommodated by drawing down its stock of gold and through increasing its external liabilities—short-term dollar claims held by nonresidents and official foreign agencies. As these claims increased quite rapidly, demand for dollar claims became saturated, finally resulting in the existence of supply exceeding demand at a fixed price. Speculative activity accelerated. Speculators concluded that when the U.S. stock of gold and foreign currency assets was depleted, it would no longer sell gold to maintain the official price of gold and gold would be revalued upward.

It is not necessary that the speculative attack culminate in a change in the par rate of exchange for it to be relevant and important. Whether or not it alters the exchange rate, in the face of intense speculation the government will be forced to adjust domestic monetary and fiscal policies to take the pressure off the balance of payments if it is to avoid resorting to direct foreign exchange controls. Indeed, the balance-of-payments crisis may dictate temporarily more severe domestic restraint than would have been necessary otherwise.

Intervention in the Forward Exchange Market. It is unlikely that speculation will be confined to the spot exchange market. Anticipations of a rise in the foreign exchange rate are also likely to lead to speculative demands for forward exchange (Chapter 7). Indeed, from the point of view of the speculator, forward exchange has an advantage over spot exchange as a vehicle for speculation in that it does not call for immediate payment. Payment will not occur until the contract expires and the actual delivery of foreign exchange occurs (at which time the speculator will presumably immediately sell the foreign exchange, taking his gains or losses). Because it involves no immediate payment, speculation in forward exchange might seem irrelevant to the problem of maintaining adequate foreign exchange reserves. If there is no immediate delivery of spot exchange, speculation in forward exchange cannot directly constitute a drain on the official foreign exchange reserves.

However, speculation in forward exchange will put upward pressure on the forward exchange rate, and this has two important consequences. First, by providing a clear signal that "the market" expects the spot rate to rise in the near future, a significant rise in the forward rate might intensify speculation in the spot market. Second, as we saw in Chapter 7, given the levels of short-term interest rates in the United States and abroad, a rise in the forward exchange rate will create an incentive to move funds out of the United States on a covered interest arbitrage basis. Thus, speculation in forward exchange will indirectly induce a capital outflow, add to the balance-of-payments deficit, and accelerate the drain of foreign exchange reserves.

For these reasons the government will probably find it expedient to intervene in the forward exchange market as well as in the spot market. Although it was not obliged to do so, the Federal Reserve and the Treasury acting through the Federal Reserve Bank of New York have participated in foreign exchange markets—both spot and forward—from time to time since 1961. It will offer to "sell" forward exchange in order to stabilize the forward exchange rate. That is, the Federal Reserve will enter into contracts to deliver foreign exchange at some specified date in the future at a price agreed upon now.

Intercentral Bank Credits: Another Buffer. To complete the discussion of governmental measures to stabilize the foreign exchange rate in the face of a balance-of-payments deficit, we must relax the assumption that at any point in time official foreign exchange reserves are absolutely fixed in amount. In addition to its explicit reserves in the form of gold, foreign exchange, and drawing rights at the International Monetary Fund available for immediate use at any time, the United States has a second line of defense implicit in the Federal Reserves close cooperation with the central banks of other industrialized nations, and in its membership in the International Monetary Fund. In effect, the United States belongs to an international mutual assistance society of central bankers and, like other members, can normally rely on substantial credits being extended by the International Monetary Fund, the Bank for International Settlements,[11] and other central banks in time of emergency, providing additional foreign currency assets to support the government's intervention in the foreign exchange market.

Credits that are potentially available in this way are commonly called *conditional reserves* because the extension of credit is conditional on the lenders' being convinced that the borrowing government will implement effective monetary and fiscal policies that assign top priority to correction of the balance-of-payments problem. While conditional reserves have proved to be a valuable and flexible device for combatting waves of speculation and stabilizing exchange rates, they are not designed to liberate domestic monetary and fiscal policy from the discipline of the balance of payments.

Conclusions: The Significance of Speculation. Speculation, whether in the spot or forward market, is a powerful force that cannot be ignored in assessing the adequacy of foreign exchange reserves as a buffer between domestic monetary and fiscal policy and the balance of international payments. An "adjustable peg" system of foreign exchange rates is peculiarly vulnerable to speculation, and periodic speculative attacks on one currency or another have become almost commonplace in international finance. From our point of view, the important point is not that speculative attacks occasionally forced a change in par rates of exchange. Rather, it is that speculation, or the threat of speculation, forces monetary and fiscal authorities to assign a higher priority to the balance of payments in deciding policy than might seem desirable on other grounds or might seem necessary given the magnitude of the buffer stock apparently provided by official holdings of foreign exchange. The presence of conditional reserves eases the problem of coping with a speculative attack, but it does little to modify the primacy that must be assigned to balance-of-payments equilibrium in policy deliberations.

Of course, it would be a mistake to imply that all speculative activity is initiated by attempts to pursue domestic policies that are inconsistent with balance-of-payments equilibrium at the pegged exchange rate. Any development that can be interpreted as a threat to the stability of the exchange rate is capable of inducing speculation, whether it be the nature of domestic monetary and fiscal policies, adverse developments in major export markets, political uncertainty, threats of war, or natural disasters.

FOREIGN EXCHANGE RESERVES
AND BALANCE-OF-PAYMENTS SURPLUS

So far, our discussion of the role of foreign exchange reserves as a buffer between domestic policy and the balance of international payments has been cast in terms of coping with balance-of-payments deficits in a period of less than full employment. Before we leave the subject, however, we must refer briefly to the opposite case, in which the balance of payments is in surplus when the economy is at full employment.[12] This is the situation depicted in Figure 20.9. Monetary expansion would eliminate the balance-of-payments surplus but would be inflationary.

Foreign Exchange Reserves as a Buffer Stock. Again, foreign exchange reserves appear in the role of a buffer stock. The balance-of-payments surplus can, in principle, be added to the official foreign exchange reserves and stored up to be used in times of balance-of-payments deficit.

However, accumulation of foreign exchange reserves is not without problems. In this case, the problem is to finance the acquisition of reserves in a manner consistent with domestic policy objectives.

With regard to the United States, its persistent deficits have had surplus counterparts abroad. Germany, particularly, has had a persistent balance-of-trade surplus, and the mark has come under waves of speculative buying in exchange for dollars in the expectation that it would be revalued vis-à-vis the dollar; that is, the dollar would be devalued. The problems of a balance-of-payments surplus to be described here are similar to problems faced by Germany, for example.

If there is a sustained surplus in the balance of payments, the government can avoid monetary expansion only if it can generate a budgetary surplus (by raising taxes or reducing other government expenditures) or borrow the required funds in the capital market. What has to happen is a diversion of part of the income of the nation from the acquisition of consumer and capital goods to the acquisition of gold and foreign exchange. The nation must be induced to accumulate wealth in the form of official foreign exchange reserves (although it is far from evident that the yield on official foreign exchange reserves is sufficiently great to justify the diversion of resources from alternative uses, whether in consumption or in real capital formation). If it borrows heavily, the government may force up interest rates on government bonds and, indeed, may aggravate the balance-of-payments surplus by attracting more foreign capital. If it raises taxes to finance the accumulation of foreign exchange reserves, the government may meet strong political resistance. In principle, it should be possible to finance the accumulation of foreign exchange reserves in a noninflationary manner; in fact, the technical and political problems of doing so may be very great. The problem of coping with a balance-of-payments surplus in a fully employed economy will obviously be aggravated if there is a wave of speculation that the exchange rate will have to be reduced.

A country that is running a balance-of-payments surplus may find that in accumulating foreign exchange assets and selling its currency to maintain a pegged rate of exchange it directly acquires a reserve currency that it uses to back its money supply. Obviously, expansionary pressure will be transmitted to the money supply as a result of the rapid increase in an important element in its monetary base. This would be difficult to neutralize or handle in some other noninflationary manner.

SUMMARY

In this chapter a number of topics have been explored that are linked to one another in a rather tangential manner. We looked at institutional arrangements that have existed until quite recently. We developed a theoretical construct of macroeconomic equilibrium under conditions of international trade in goods and services and international capital flows. To do this, we introduced the balance-of-payments accounts for the United States; which is a statistical summary of the actual flow of economic transactions during a given period.

From our rather restrictive Keynesian assumptions regarding the price level and the tenet of a pegged exchange rate, we saw that the use of monetary policy is constrained by balance-of-payments considerations. Monetary policy may be relatively impotent as a tool for achieving domestic policy objectives like full employment and price level stability at such times.

We saw that official foreign exchange reserves, if large enough, can act as a buffer between balance-of-payments considerations and domestic policy considerations. With a fixed foreign exchange rate, the independence of monetary policy depends on the existence of foreign exchange reserves as a buffer stock between domestic policy and the balance of payments. Large foreign exchange reserves are important, but it should be obvious from our discussion of speculation that the independence of domestic monetary and fiscal policies does not depend on the size of reserves alone. The essential question is whether the government can tolerate wide swings in the level of reserves within a short period of time.

If sharp changes in exchange reserves engender strong speculation, foreign exchange reserves are more likely to be useful in financing relatively small balance-of-payments deficits of relatively short duration, rather than relatively large, persistent deficits. This is surely a slim reed to which to tie the independence of domestic monetary policy.

NOTES

1. In principle, members of the International Monetary Fund declare their par values in terms of gold, since the U.S. *gold dollar* of 1944 is specified in the Articles of Agreement as the unit of account for the International Monetary Fund. In practice, however, this means that par values are declared and maintained in terms of the U.S. dollar (whose legal "gold content" has been changed only twice since 1944).

2. However, the capital account of the balance of international payments excludes an important factor in the change in international indebtedness—the reinvestment of retained earnings by U.S. controlled corporations abroad. Many economists would argue that reinvestment of profits ought to be recorded in the balance of payments, both as an additional inflow of dividends in the current account and as an outflow of capital in the capital account. While in a sense this creates two artificial transactions, it does serve to remind us of the understatement of the investment of U.S.-owned funds abroad during any given year.

3. In the long run, the coincidence of capital imports and current account deficits is not fortuitous. There are a complex of adjustment mechanisms that tend to produce this equality. They are analyzed in books on international economics under the general heading "the transfer problem." We will not explore them here.

4. For simplicity we are again ignoring the government sector, and we are implicitly assuming that exported goods and services have no import content.

5. Remember, we are ignoring the fact that exports may also have some import content. OX in Figure 2.1 should be interpreted as exports net of the value of any imported materials or component parts used in the production of those exports.

6. Some of the evidence is reviewed in R. E. Caves and G. L. Reuber, *Canadian Economic Policy and the Impact of International Capital Flows* (Toronto: University of Toronto Press for the Private Planning Association of Canada, 1969), pp. 11–18.

7. Our assumptions also imply that the current account balance will depend on the composition of aggregate demand, since the import content of investment and consumption expenditures, in general, will be different. However, with given investment demand and consumption functions, the composition of aggregate demand is also given for any particular level of income. For this reason, we can ignore this complication to the analysis.

8. It shows combinations of interest rates and income at which the Current Account (B)alance equals the Net (K)apital Inflow.

9. The student with some algebra will note that the basic problem is that we have only two variables but three equations that must be solved simultaneously. It is only by accident that a solution will be found.

10. Speculation occurs whenever someone takes an "open" position in foreign exchange (see Chapter 7) or covers what would otherwise have been an open position because he anticipates a rise in the exchange rate. Thus, a corporate treasurer who purchases foreign exchange now, whether spot or forward, knowing that the corporation will need it in the future and anticipating a rise in the exchange rate, is speculating. Similarly, a corporate treasurer who buys forward exchange to cover short-term foreign currency liabilities, when he would not normally do so, is speculating. In each case the treasurer would argue that

he is merely protecting the financial position of the corporation against a reasonably foreseeable risk, and in this argument he is correct. Nonetheless, he has the same impact on the foreign exchange market as a professional speculator. To say that the corporation is speculating in foreign exchange is not to say that it is doing anything illegal or immoral.

11. We will discuss the International Monetary Fund and the Bank for International Settlements further in the next chapter.

12. Remember that there is no conflict when there is unemployment and the balance of payments is in surplus, or when there are inflationary pressures and the balance of payments is in deficit. In either case, the direction of the policies required to achieve domestic objectives and balance-of-payments equilibrium is the same. As we noted earlier, however, the degree of ease or restriction called for by domestic and external considerations may be different. At some point conflict may reemerge.

THE INTERNATIONAL
CONSTRAINT ON
MONETARY POLICY

Part 2: Price Levels, Exchange Rates, and the International Liquidity Problem

In the preceding chapter we explored the theoretical relationships between monetary policy and the balance of payments within a strict Keynesian framework. That is, we assumed not only that the exchange rate was pegged but also that the price level was fixed. However, in our earlier analysis of the economics of monetary policy we discovered that the assumption of a fixed price level was at best only a crude approximation to reality. Fluctuations in aggregate demand, whether induced by exogenous developments or by monetary and fiscal policies, will normally have an impact on the price level as well as on income and employment. What are the implications of this fact for our analysis of macroeconomic equilibrium in an open economy?

THE PRICE LEVEL AND THE BALANCE OF PAYMENTS

One of the basic propositions of elementary economic theory is that a change in relative prices will induce substitution effects among the goods in question. Exactly the same thing will happen if the prices of American goods and services change relative to those of goods and services produced in the rest of the world. A rise in the American price level will induce international substitution effects.

These effects will show up in various ways. Domestic consumers will be induced to purchase more imported goods as substitutes for the relatively more expensive goods produced in the United States. Domestic producers of very close substitutes for imported goods will find that they cannot raise prices without losing many customers—but with rising costs they will find it much less profitable to produce these goods for sale at the given world prices. Their output will fall as imports take over a larger share of the market. Similarly, domestic producers of goods for export, faced with higher labor costs, will find it less profitable to produce for sale in world markets at the given world prices. Their exports will fall. Indeed, even exporters who are not price takers (i.e., who have some monopoly power in world markets, either individually or collectively) will find that at higher prices their sales will be reduced.

The extent of the impact on the flow of international trade will depend on the magnitude of the change in prices and the relevant elasticities of demand and supply. However, the general effect of a rise in American costs and prices relative to world prices will be some decline in exports and some rise in imports, reducing a surplus or increasing a deficit in the current account of the balance of payments. A decline in American prices relative to world prices would have the opposite effects. That is, it would tend to increase exports and reduce imports, increasing a surplus or reducing a deficit in the current account of the balance of payments.

This effect of changes in the price level on international trade introduces an important new consideration into our analysis of the relationship between domestic monetary and fiscal policies and the balance of international payments.

The Price Level, Domestic Policy Objectives, and the Balance-of-Payments Constraint. Earlier we explored the relationship between domestic monetary and fiscal policies and the balance of international payments on the assumption that the domestic objective of policy was very simple: the achievement of the unique level of aggregate demand that would provide full employment without inflation. If, instead of a unique full-employment level of income, the authorities are faced with a trade-off function, a negative association between the level of unemployment and the rate of change of the price level, the objective of domestic policy is necessarily more complicated. The choice of an objective involves an important subjective consideration. The government must balance the undesirable consequences of higher rates of inflation against the undesirable consequences of higher levels of unemployment in order to find what they consider to be the socially least undesirable combination of unemployment and inflation. The objective of domestic policy, then, is the point on the trade-off function that the government considers most preferable. It is not necessarily a point of full employment, nor is it necessarily a point of price stability. Let us briefly reconsider the problem of reconciling the domestic and external objectives of monetary and fiscal policies in this context.

The Trade-Off Function and Policy Conflicts. In our previous analysis we considered the domestic and external objectives of policy to have been achieved simultaneously if the balance of payments was in equilibrium at full employment. When we introduce the trade-off function, the comparable condition might seem to be that the balance of payments be in equilibrium at the point on the trade-off function selected by the government, that is, at the combination of inflation and unemployment preferred on domestic social and political grounds.

Unfortunately, the equilibrium of the balance of payments may be fleeting. The rate of price level change selected by the government may have continuing effects on the balance of payments that will eventually disrupt the equilibrium.

For example, suppose that the rate of inflation chosen by the government for domestic reasons is higher than that prevailing in the rest of the world. Even though the balance of payments is initially in equilibrium,[1] if prices here rise more rapidly than prices in the rest of the world, international substitution effects will gradually worsen the current account balance, and a deficit will emerge in the balance of payments. Under pegged exchange rates the exchange rate will be driven to the ceiling, and exchange reserves will begin to fall, with all of the attendant problems discussed in the previous chapter. What appeared initially to be a condition of harmony between the domestic and external objectives of policy will be turned into a condition of conflict.

Something has to give. There are only two possibilities (unless the government resorts to direct controls): the exchange rate or the domestic policy objectives. If the exchange rate is to remain pegged at its original par, the balance of payments must be brought into equilibrium, and that means domestic policy will have to be modified in order to accept a lower rate of inflation and a higher level of unemployment than the government would otherwise find most desirable on social grounds. In effect, domestic policy formation is faced with a price level constraint. If the balance of payments is to be kept in equilibrium, the country will have to move toward the same rate of inflation as that prevailing in the rest of the world.

The problems that arise because of balance-of-payments deficits are always dramatic. However, as we have already seen, continuous balance-of-payments surpluses can also be troublesome to a nation determined to maintain a pegged exchange rate.

With this in mind, consider what happens if the government chooses a rate of inflation lower than that prevailing in the rest of the world. In this case, international substitution effects will tend to produce an improvement in the current account, and although the balance of payments is initially in equilibrium, a balance-of-payments surplus will eventually emerge.[2] The exchange rate will fall, and the government will be forced to accumulate foreign exchange reserves to maintain the pegged rate.

Again, something will have to give. The government cannot go on accumulating foreign exchange reserves indefinitely. Even if the financial problems associated with the accumulation of reserves do not directly produce inflationary pressures, the government will eventually have to modify its domestic objectives and accept the higher world rate of inflation if it is going to maintain the pegged exchange rate.

Conclusion: The Price Level Constraint. The conclusion of this analysis is important. While there is always some room for maneuver inherent in the imperfect operations of markets and in time lags in the adjustment of production, consumption, and trade, with a pegged exchange rate a government cannot choose any rate of inflation it desires, even though that rate of inflation may initially be consistent with balance-of-payments equilibrium. There is a price level constraint on domestic policy. Although this constraint is not instantaneous, that government will be forced eventually to modify its policies to the world rate of inflation—accepting the implications of the trade-off function for the domestic level of unemployment. Attempts to achieve any other combination of inflation and unemployment will mean a chronic balance-of-payments problem.

But all this presumes that the exchange rate is pegged. What happens if we make the ultimate relaxation of our assumptions and allow the exchange rate to vary? Can the world economy and the world financial system function with flexible exchange rates?

THE ECONOMICS OF FLEXIBLE EXCHANGE RATES

A change in American prices relative to prices in the rest of the world can have a powerful impact on the U.S. balance of international payments. However, it is not necessary to change the price level to produce these effects. They could be achieved in theory equally well by changing the foreign exchange rate.

CHANGES IN THE EXCHANGE RATE
VS. CHANGES IN PRICE LEVELS

A rise in the price of foreign exchange (= a fall in the external value of the dollar) raises the delivered price of foreign goods to American buyers just as effectively as a rise in the foreign price level itself. Thus, it will tend to restrict American imports. Similarly, the rise in the foreign exchange rate lowers the delivered price of American goods to foreign markets just as effectively as a decline in the U.S. price level. It will tend to increase American exports. Taking the two effects together, a rise in the foreign exchange rate will improve the current account balance and hence will tend to increase a balance-of-payments surplus or reduce a balance-of-payments deficit. In terms of its impact on the balance of payments, a rise in the foreign exchange rate is a substitute for a fall in the American price level or for a rise in the world price level.

The opposite arguments hold for a fall in the foreign exchange rate (= a rise in the external value of the dollar). By making American goods more expensive for foreign buyers, it would tend to restrict exports. By making foreign goods less expensive by comparison for American buyers, it would tend to increase imports. Thus, a fall in the foreign exchange rate will tend to worsen the balance on current account and hence will tend to reduce a balance-of-payments surplus or increase a balance-of-payments deficit even more. In terms of its impact on the balance of payments, a fall in the foreign exchange rate is a substitute for a rise in the American price level or a fall in the world price level.

The Exchange Rate and Contradictions Among Policy Objectives. It follows that changes in the exchange rate could be used to resolve balance-of-payments problems that would otherwise force a drastic change in domestic monetary and fiscal policies if they were permitted under a new international monetary constitution. A balance-of-payments deficit (whatever its cause), we have seen, can be removed by an appropriate drop in the foreign exchange rate.

However, these are one-time changes. If domestic policy involves a rate of price level change that is different from the rate prevailing in the rest of the world, balance-of-payments equilibrium will require continual adjustment of the exchange rate. A more rapid rate of inflation than the rest of the world is experiencing is consistent with balance-of-payments equilibrium only if the exchange rate continuously rises. A slower rate of inflation than in the rest of the world would call for a continuous fall in the exchange rate. In other words, the independence of domestic policy from external constraints is possible only if the exchange rate can be continually adjusted to changing pressures in the foreign exchange market.

Flexible Exchange Rates. As we noted earlier, the foreign exchange rate is simply a price—the price of foreign money—and as such is determined by the interaction of supply and demand in the foreign exchange market. However, under the pegged exchange rate system, that price is allowed to vary only within very narrow limits around the official par rate (unless, of course, a decision is taken to alter the par rate). With a flexible exchange rate, there is no such constraint on the movement of the exchange rate.[3] A flexible exchange rate is free to adjust continually to changing pressures of supply and demand in the foreign exchange market.

FLEXIBLE EXCHANGE RATES AND MONETARY POLICY

Flexibility of the exchange rate creates a fundamentally different environment for monetary and fiscal policy from that provided by the Bretton

Woods international monetary constitution. We examined the implications of the Bretton Woods rules for domestic stabilization policy in the previous chapter. Let us now briefly explore some of the implications of a flexible exchange rate system.

The Exchange Rate and Balance-of-Payments Equilibrium. The crucial difference between the fixed and the flexible exchange rate systems is the mechanism for establishing equilibrium in the balance of international payments.

As we saw in Chapter 20, with a fixed exchange rate the maintenance of equilibrium in the balance of payments must be the responsibility of government policy, particularly monetary policy. Unless there is considerable flexibility in the levels of wages and prices, there is no automatic mechanism to ensure the equilibration of demand and supply forces in the foreign exchange market in the short run. With a flexible exchange rate, by contrast, the foreign exchange rate can be expected to adjust automatically to maintain equilibrium in the balance of payments.

Consider the case in which the balance of payments is in deficit, perhaps because the deficit on current account is greater than the surplus on capital account. There will be excess demand for foreign exchange at the existing exchange rate. It is this pressure of excess demand that will tend to increase the foreign exchange rate, and in the absence of an official constraint on the rate it will rise.

Will the increase of the exchange rate tend to eliminate the balance-of-payments deficit?

The Current Account. As noted previously, a rise in the foreign exchange rate is equivalent to a rise in the world price level relative to prices and wage rates in the United States. As a result, there should be substitution effects in the current account of the balance of payments. Exports, which are now relatively cheaper to the rest of the world, should increase, and imports, which are now relatively more expensive to Americans, should fall. The current account should adjust so as to eliminate the excess demand for foreign exchange.

The Capital Account. The behavior of the capital account is more problematic. As we saw in Chapter 7, the level of the foreign exchange rate per se should not be relevant to international portfolio investment decisions. As long as the investor expects to bring his funds back at the same exchange rate at which he takes them out of the country, the level of the foreign exchange rate will not be a factor in his calculations. This should be obvious from the examples explored in Chapter 7 (e.g., Example 7.1). If the investor expects the exchange rate to be the same when he brings his funds home as when he sends them out, the exchange rates applicable to the two foreign exchange transactions simply cancel each other out. All that is relevant to the calculation of the expected net return is the difference in interest rates (although the risk of change in the exchange rate will be relevant to the investment decision, of course).

It is different if the investor has reason to expect a change in the foreign exchange rate. Any increase in the foreign exchange rate will give an added premium to American investments in securities denominated in foreign currencies and will impose a penalty on nonresidents' investments in American securities.

To know what will happen in the capital account as the exchange rate rises, then, we must know what happens to investors' expectations about the future course of the exchange rates. If they expect a continuing rise in exchange rates, there will be an incentive for more American investment abroad and less foreign investment in the United States. Capital outflows should be increased or capital inflows reduced. However, if investors feel that the rise is temporary and that the rate will eventually subside, there will be an incentive for less American investment abroad and more foreign investment in the United States. Capital inflows should be increased or capital outflows curtailed. If, by contrast, they expect the exchange rate to be unchanged at any particular level established at any particular time, then capital inflows and outflows will be unaffected by the change in the exchange rate. In other words, if the net capital inflow does not increase or decrease it will stay the same!

The crucial consideration is that of investors' expectations of future changes in the exchange rate, not the present level of the exchange rate. Unfortunately, we know very little about the determinants of these expectations. With this in mind, perhaps it is best to first consider the case in which we can ignore expectations. That is, we will assume that investors take the existing exchange rate to be the best estimate of what future exchange rates will be, regardless of the present level or the past history of the exchange rate. In this case, the entire adjustment in the balance of payments occurs in the current account. The net capital inflow will be unaffected by the rise in the exchange rate: Imports must fall and exports rise until the current account deficit is tailored to the net capital inflow. Exactly the opposite arguments would apply if we had chosen a case of balance-of-payments surplus. What are the implications of these balance-of-payments adjustments for monetary policy?

To explore this matter, we return again to the *IS-LM* model of the open economy developed in Chapter 20. What modifications have to be introduced to allow for the flexibility of exchange rates?

The Balance-of-Payments Constraint on Monetary Policy. The first important point is that the *BK* curve (the locus of combinations of interest rates and income levels that are consistent with equilibrium in the balance of payments) is no longer a useful concept. Balance-of-payments equilibrium will be maintained through continual adjustments in the foreign exchange rate.

To see this, consider again how we constructed the *BK* curve. We started with the *net capital flow function* (Figure 20.3), reflecting the sensitivity of international capital flows to international differences in interest rates. If we can ignore expectations of future changes in the exchange rate, this function will be unchanged under a regime of flexible exchange rates.

The second component of the *BK* curve was the *current account balance function*, which we built up on the assumption that exports were given and imports depended on the levels of investment and consumption expenditures. However, with a flexible exchange rate, both imports and exports depend directly on the level of the foreign exchange rate. Moreover, since the foreign exchange rate will always rise when there is an excess demand for foreign exchange (e.g., the current account deficit exceeds the capital account surplus) and fall when there is an excess supply of foreign exchange (e.g., the current account deficit is less than the capital account surplus), the exchange rate will always adjust until the current account balance is equal in size and opposite in direction to the capital account balance.

It should be emphasized that this could require wide fluctuations in the exchange rate from time to time, depending on the sensitivity of import and export demands to changes in the exchange rate.

With a flexible exchange rate, the current account balance is a residual, determined by the capital account balance. The current account balance function is the mirror image of the net capital flow function. The sole determinant of the aggregate current account balance will be the level of interest rates in the United States relative to world interest rates.

This is illustrated in Figure 21.1. In this figure, the net capital flow function (K) is the same as that developed earlier (Figure 20.1). However, the current account balance function (B_f) is based on the assumption that the flexible exchange rate will adjust until the current account balance is just equal in size and opposite in direction to the capital account balance. At high levels of interest rates in the United States (r_1), there will be a net capital inflow. However, as a result of the automatic adjustment of the exchange rate, the surplus in the capital account will be exactly offset by an equal deficit in the current account. At low levels of interest rates in the United States (r_2), there will be a net capital outflow. However, as a result of the automatic adjustment of the exchange rate, the deficit in the capital account will be exactly offset by an equal surplus in the current account. The net balance-of-payments surplus or deficit (lower section) will always be zero, regardless of the level of interest rates (and hence, by implication, regardless of the level of income and output). A flexible exchange rate will ensure that the balance of payments is always in equilibrium.

This points to our first important conclusion. If the government is willing and able to ignore wide fluctuations in the foreign exchange rate, a flexible exchange rate frees domestic monetary policy from the balance-of-payments constraint.

This is not the only implication of flexibility in the foreign exchange rate, however. A flexible exchange rate, coupled with highly interest elastic international capital flows, will reinforce the impact of monetary policy on domestic income and output.

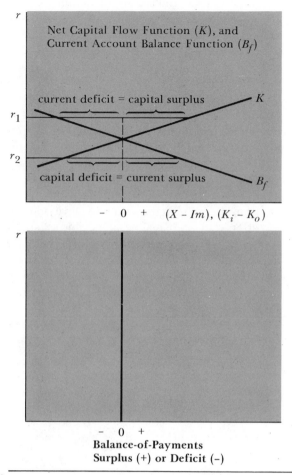

Figure 21.1 The Current Account, the Capital Account, and the Balance of Payments with Flexible Exchange Rates

Effectiveness of Monetary Policy. The implications of flexible exchange rates for the domestic impact of monetary policy should be obvious if you keep in mind that both exports and imports are factors determining the level of aggregate demand.

We have seen that restrictive monetary policy, which raises American interest rates relative to interest rates in the rest of the world, will induce capital inflows and thus, by creating an excess supply of foreign exchange, depress the foreign exchange rate. The exchange rate will have to fall until the combination of increased imports and reduced exports produces a current account deficit large enough to offset the capital inflow. But remember, both the increase in imports and the reduction in exports depress aggregate demand. These exchange-rate-induced effects on aggregate demand are in addi-

517

tion to any effects that might result from the direct impact of tight money on investment expenditures. In other words, the flexibility of the exchange rate, coupled with the sensitivity of international capital flows to interest rates, has strengthened the restrictive impact of a tight money policy.

You should be able to trace a similar analysis for the case of an expansionary monetary policy under a regime of flexible exchange rates. The conclusion is the same: Flexibility of exchange rates reinforces the impact of an expansionary monetary policy.

The *IS-LM* Model Again. These arguments are illustrated in Figure 21.2, which is another adaptation of the much-used four-quadrant diagram. First consider Quadrant II. The investment demand function, the broken line I_0I_0, is the same as that used in the diagrams of Chapters 19 and 20. In the present analysis, however, instead of showing the individual components of the current account balance, as in Figure 20.1, we have adopted the conclusion of the previous section that, in a regime of flexible exchange rates, the current account balance will be determined simply by the net capital inflow. Accordingly, we have deducted the current account balance function of Figure 21.1 from the investment demand function in Quadrant II to obtain what might be called the *investment-trade balance function* (*IT*).

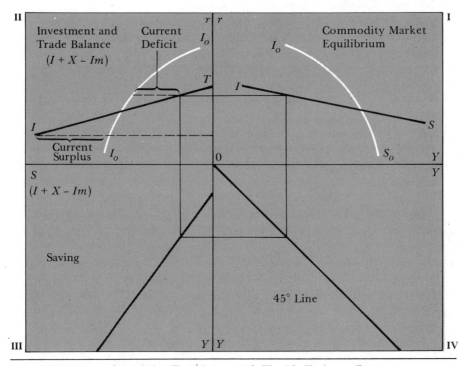

Figure 21.2 **Commodity Market Equilibrium with Flexible Exchange Rates**

518

It plays the same role in the analysis as the autonomous expenditure function of Figure 20.1.

The construction of the *IT* curve should be obvious. At high levels of interest rates there will be heavy capital inflows. As a result, exports must fall and imports must rise, producing a negative trade balance. This negative trade balance is a deduction from aggregate demand, and accordingly we have deducted it from the investment function to obtain the relevant point on the *IT* curve. By contrast, at very low levels of interest rates there will be strong capital outflows. Exports will have to rise and imports fall until there is an equally large trade surplus. This trade surplus is an addition to aggregate demand, and accordingly it has to be added to the investment demand function to obtain the relevant point on the *IT* curve.

In Quadrant III we now have only the saving function of our earlier analysis. We do not have to include induced imports in this quadrant, as we did in Figure 20.2, since total imports are allowed for in the construction of the *IT* curve.

The new equilibrium condition is that the level of investment expenditures plus the net trade balance (= the net capital flow) must equal gross saving. (You should be able to explain why this is the equilibrium condition.) In Quadrant IV we have the 45° line used to reflect the equilibrium levels of income to the base axis of Quadrant I. Taking these together with the associated interest rates, we can trace the *IS* curve for the flexible exchange rate case.

We have also plotted the original *IS* curve for the fixed exchange rate case (broken line, I_0S_0) in Quadrant I as a reference base. The important point to note is that in the flexible exchange rate case the *IS* curve is much more elastic with respect to the interest rate. A given increase in the money supply, shifting the *LM* curve, will have a much more powerful impact on income and employment than in the fixed exchange rate case.

A flexible exchange rate not only frees monetary policy from the international constraint but also increases the effectiveness of monetary policy as an instrument for manipulating domestic aggregate demand.

A Classical Case. The elasticity of the *IS* function in the flexible exchange rate case depends directly on the elasticity of the net capital flow function. In the extreme, we might conceive of a net capital flow function that is perfectly elastic with respect to American interest rates. That is, any deviation of American interest rates from some given level (world interest rates, or world interest rates plus a risk premium) would induce a massive movement of capital either into or out of the country. In such a situation, the level of interest rates here would be rigidly tied to the world level of interest rates, and the *IS* curve would also be perfectly interest elastic at this level of interest rates.

In this case, the level of income depends simply on the demand for and supply of money (i.e., on the position of the *LM* function). Monetary policy would be all-powerful, while fiscal policy would have absolutely no impact. An increase in government expenditures, for example, would tend to increase income. But with a given money supply this would imply higher interest rates. The resulting flood of capital flowing into the country would prevent interest rates from rising, but it would induce a drop in the foreign exchange rate. The result would be an offsetting deficit in the current account of the balance of payments. There could be no net change in the level of income and output unless there was a sympathetic increase in the money supply. With a perfectly elastic net capital flow function and flexible exchange rates, we are back in the world envisioned by the classical quantity theorists.

Exchange Rate Expectations. In this analysis of the economics of flexible exchange rates we have ignored what we said earlier was a crucial consideration in international capital flows—investors' expectations of future changes in the exchange rate. What modifications of the analysis are necessary if we drop the assumption that investors always expect the existing exchange rate to continue into the relevant future?

Let us consider the case in which an expansionary monetary policy initiates a rise in the flexible exchange rate. Aside from the assumption about exchange rate expectations that we have already explored, there are two possibilities. Either the rate is expected to continue to rise, or it is expected to fall back toward a more "normal" level.

Expectations of future rises in the exchange rate will induce speculative capital movements. Capital outflows will increase and capital inflows will be retarded. The net capital flow function of Figure 21.1 will shift outward to the right (larger capital outflows or smaller capital inflows at each possible level of interest rates), and the current account will have to respond. The *IT* curve of Quadrant II, Figure 21.2, will shift to the right, inducing a similar shift in the *IS* curve of Quadrant I. The impact of the expansionary monetary policy that initiated the whole process will be accentuated.

This is not the end of the story, however. If rises in the exchange rate induce expectations of further rises, the whole process could become cumulative. Exploration of the possible interactions between expectations and adjustments in the exchange rate requires a class of dynamic models that are well beyond the scope of an elementary money and banking textbook. It should be clear, however, that if a rise in the exchange rate induces strong expectations of a continuing rise in the future, there is a serious danger of severe instability in the foreign exchange market.

Expectations of a continuing rise in the exchange rate will reinforce the impact of monetary policy in a regime of flexible exchange rates. The opposite is true if the rate is expected to fall back to "normal" in the near future.

If a rise in the exchange rate induces expectations of a return to a lower, more "normal" level, the effects will be the opposite of those discussed earlier. The net capital flow function will be shifted to the left (smaller capital outflows or larger capital inflows at each possible level of interest rates) as speculators seek to avoid losses on holdings of foreign currency assets. As a result, the *IT* curve and the *IS* curve will also be shifted to the left. The rise of the exchange rate will be damped, and the overall effectiveness of the expansionary monetary policy will be reduced.

THE CONTROVERSY OVER FLEXIBLE EXCHANGE RATE

Considered from the point of view of the effectiveness of domestic monetary policy, flexible exchange rates appear to have a major advantage over pegged exchange rates. Yet flexible exchange rates are anathema to most central bankers (who are charged with the implementation of monetary policy) and to many economists who specialize in international financial economics. As a result, proposals for the adoption of a system of flexible exchange rates are surrounded by sharp controversy.[4] Two main charges are commonly directed against flexible exchange rates.

Instability and Uncertainty. It is argued that flexible exchange rates are inherently highly unstable. This amounts to an assumption that the dominant pattern of expectations is of the first type discussed earlier: that a change in the exchange rate will generate expectations of future changes in the same direction. Flexibility of the exchange rate, it is argued, provides excessive scope for speculators, and their activities may generate wide and purposeless fluctuations in exchange rates. The experience of the 1920s and 1930s is commonly cited as evidence that this is a real and serious problem.[5]

Promotion of Nationalist Economic Policies. The second argument is the primary argument in favor of flexible exchange rates, converted into an argument against flexibility.

Again, the experience of the 1920s and 1930s is invoked in support of an argument that flexible exchange rates promote nationalist economic policies rather than internationalist policies. Manipulation of a flexible exchange rate can be used instead of tariffs to protect domestic industries and, more particularly, to promote production in periods of recession. Thus, a country may use the flexible exchange rate to "export" its own unemployment problems.

We have seen that a pegged exchange rate can impose severe constraints on domestic monetary policy as long as the government is determined to maintain the par rate. The choice of a price level objective is particularly circumscribed. It is increasingly argued that in the contemporary context worldwide inflation is a serious threat, and that pegged exchange rates are an essential source of "financial discipline" on inflation-prone national governments. Flexible exchange rates would remove that discipline. Thus, it is argued, the adoption of flexible exchange rates would result in an accentuation of inflationary pressures throughout the world. In effect, this is an argument that national governments cannot be trusted with responsibility for the formulation of monetary and fiscal policies in the international—and, indeed, the national—interest.

521

The Case for Flexibility.[6] The case for flexibility is largely an assertion of national sovereignty in the formulation and implementation of monetary and fiscal policies—including the right to make disastrous mistakes—and the denial of the relevance or validity of each of the preceding points. Far from disrupting the international economy, it is argued, flexible exchange rates would further international development by providing an automatic solution to the international liquidity crises that have periodically beset, at times with devastating effect, the pegged exchange rate system.

First, the relevance of evidence drawn from the experiences of several countries with flexible exchange rates in the 1920s and 1930s is disputed, largely on grounds of the peculiar economic and political environment of that time. Indeed, most of the evils commonly ascribed to flexible exchange rates are asserted to have been a result of attempts to maintain or establish inappropriate par rates of exchange, or of the social, political, and economic turmoil of the time. They could hardly be blamed on the flexibility of exchange rates. The Canadian experience from 1950 to 1962 is commonly cited as evidence that, in an otherwise stable environment, expectations may tend to stabilize the exchange rate rather than inducing pointless fluctuations (thus somewhat reducing the effectiveness of a flexible exchange rate as a tool of nationalistic economic policies). During this period, the Canadian exchange rate was not a harbinger of inflation and, while flexible, was remarkably stable.[7] Furthermore, there is no evidence to suggest that by floating its currency Canada restricted its trade.

Indeed, it is argued that proponents of the former international monetary constitution with fixed exchange rates have the economics of speculation backwards. We have already seen that the adjustable peg system not only is peculiarly vulnerable to speculation but also tends to incite speculation. Speculation is turned into a one-way gamble, and as a result the official limits to exchange rate fluctuations become dams behind which tremendous speculative pressures can build up. With a flexible exchange rate, by contrast, speculators are faced with greater risks, and adjustments of the exchange rate in response to small amounts of speculative activity will quickly remove the basis for continued speculation. Speculation could actually be less intense than it was under the Bretton Woods system, and such speculation as did occur would perform the desirable economic function of speeding adjustment to new, more appropriate levels of the exchange rate. Thus, it is argued, speculation is a problem in attempting to maintain stability under an adjustable peg system, not under a flexible exchange rate system.

The associated proposition that flexible exchange rates increase the uncertainty surrounding all international investment decisions has also been disputed by proponents of flexibility. With respect to decisions on longer-term projects, there can be no certainty regarding the level of the exchange rate, even under the Bretton Woods type of system. Major realignments of par rates of exchange occur under that system. A flexible rate system would simply make the transition to new levels easier. With respect to short-term uncertainty, the forward exchange mechanism is capable of providing fully adequate hedges against the relevant risks.

Furthermore, it is argued, the pegged exchange rate system was not successful in preventing countries from pursuing inflationary financial policies if they so chose. All it did was to associate such policies with periodic financial crises or with direct controls. More fundamentally, attempts to impose "financial discipline" from outside are a significant infringement on national sovereignty. It is a denial of the right of a national government to choose its own policy objectives.

Thus, proponents of flexible exchange rates argue that a pegged exchange rate system is the worst of all possible worlds. It does not provide the certainty and the pressure for the international integration of economic and financial policies that would follow from immutable exchange rates, nor does it provide the freedom in domestic policy formation that is associated with flexible exchange rates. Indeed, it is calculated to maximize policy conflicts and purposeless speculation.

Conclusions. The economics of flexible exchange rates is a broad topic requiring historical as well as theoretical and statistical analysis. We have barely scratched the surface. However, the important point has been made: Flexible exchange rates provide a type of flexibility in domestic policy formation that is absent with a pegged exchange rate system. There is good reason to believe that flexible exchange rates are viable, but there is strong opinion to the contrary. In any case, there is little likelihood that a completely flexible exchange rate system will be adopted. Participating countries are sharply divided at present between returning to an adjustable pegged exchange rate system and institutionalizing the interim system of flexible exchange rates.

THE INTERNATIONAL LIQUIDITY PROBLEM UNDER A PEGGED EXCHANGE RATE SYSTEM

It should be obvious from what has gone before that official foreign exchange reserves played a key role in the functioning of the former international system, in which there was a commitment to maintain fixed exchange rates and avoid direct controls over international trade and payments.

How large of a stock of official reserves was needed? Was there a problem of inadequate international liquidity under the Bretton Woods system? If so, what solution can be found if there should be agreement to return to a modified system of pegged exchange rates? What rate of growth in foreign exchange reserves would be adequate?

This is an urgent question, which calls for a quantitative answer. Unfortunately, it is also a very complicated question to which no convincing quantitative answer has yet been given. Over the past two decades there have been many qualitative judgments that the stock of foreign exchange reserves was inadequate, but no one has produced an acceptable measure of the deficiency. Indeed, the expanding literature on the topic reveals that economists are not even agreed on how to define an optimum stock of foreign exchange reserves in theory, let alone how to measure it.[8] The best we can do is to suggest some relevant considerations.

To begin with, it is useful to distinguish between two interrelated concepts: the demand for foreign exchange reserves on the part of a single national government and the optimum stock (or rate of growth) of foreign exchange reserves in the world as a whole.

THE NATION'S DEMAND FOR FOREIGN EXCHANGE RESERVES

The Benefits. We have seen that from any government's point of view the attraction of large foreign exchange reserves is that they provide a buffer between domestic macroeconomic policies and the balance of payments under fixed exchange rates. With this in mind, one can think of a variety of factors that ought to enter into deliberations about the "target" level of reserves. Clearly, the government ought to be concerned with the risk that its domestic policy objectives will require policies inimicable to balance-of-payments equilibrium. But it should be equally concerned with the risks of balance-of-payments deficits resulting from internal or external developments over which it has no control: such things as sudden shifts in "autonomous" capital flows, unanticipated demands for imports, adverse developments in major export markets, changes in the economic policies of other governments, crop failures, civil strife, war, or natural disasters. The exchange market repercussions of any such developments could force sharp deflationary monetary and fiscal policies or else the need to resort to direct controls, unless the government has sufficient foreign exchange reserves to finance large-scale direct intervention in the market.

The Cost. Risk aversion might seem to dictate a very high target level of reserves. However, it must also be recognized that from the nation's point of view the accumulation of foreign exchange reserves has opportunity costs against which benefits must be weighed. Foreign exchange reserves involve a national investment in idle international purchasing power —an investment that could easily be used for other purposes.[9] The rate of return on alternative investments ought to enter the calculation of the optimum level of reserves.

Presumably, the government should also take into account the availability and cost of reserves on short notice from other sources. This includes not only the possibility of borrowing reserves from other governments and international institutions but also the possibilities for attracting short-term capital through the international capital market with moderate interest rate or forward exchange rate inducements.

The Problem of Quantification. The preparation of such a list of factors that might be relevant to decisions on a target level of foreign exchange reserves is not a difficult exercise. However, it is merely a preliminary to the real analysis of the problem. It is a long step from there to the discovery of a technique for quantifying the various considerations listed, and another long step to their use in calculating the optimum level of reserve holdings for a particular country at a particular time. Without these steps, the listing of considerations is almost trivial. These steps have not been taken. Economics has yet to make a significant contribution to the government's problem of actually choosing a target level of foreign exchange reserves.

Preferences Among Adjustment Techniques. Moreover, if we consider foreign exchange reserves as a buffer between domestic policy and the balance of payments, then the nation's demand for foreign exchange must depend not only on such objective factors as the risk of balance-of-payments deficits but also on such subjective considerations as the intensity of the government's aversion to risks and its willingness to resort to domestic deflation, exchange controls, or a change in the fixed exchange rate in times of balance-of-payments pressure. If the government has a firm commitment to full employment, free international payments, and the existing exchange rate, it should have a strong preference for large foreign exchange reserves. If the government has few compunctions about invoking direct controls, changing the exchange rate, or deflating the domestic economy at the first sign of a deficit, it will probably have little demand for foreign exchange reserves, even though its balance of payments is vulnerable.

Inevitably, the government's target level of foreign exchange reserves must be a matter of judgment and practical experience. Perhaps, as Fritz Machlup has argued, governments' demands for foreign exchange reserves cannot be explained by economic analysis, since they are based on a mixture of "rational theories, irrational myths, and traditional principles."[10] Perhaps this explains the bewildering differences in reserve policies among nations, which seem to defy explanation in terms of the usual economic variables.[11]

THE INTERNATIONAL OPTIMUM

Although each nation's demand for foreign exchange reserves may not be explainable in terms of rational economic principles, the fact that they exist is sufficient to raise another question: Is the supply of reserve assets in the world as a whole sufficient to meet the demands of all national governments? As we shall see, the crucial issue is a judgment on what macroeconomic policies national governments ought to pursue.

Real vs. Nominal Reserves. By analogy with the demand for money, we can assume that governments are concerned with the level of their foreign exchange reserves in real terms rather than in nominal terms. A doubling of the world price level, with nominal foreign exchange reserves given, will impair a nation's foreign exchange reserve position just as effectively as the loss of half of its reserves at a given price level. But it can be argued that in the long run the quantity of real foreign exchange reserves supplied will always adjust automatically to the quantity of real foreign exchange reserves demanded, regardless of what happens to the nominal quantity of reserves. This is suggested by an extension of the quantity theory of money: Equilibrium will be maintained in the long run through adjustment of the world price level.

A Quantity Theory Adjustment. Suppose, for example, that the stock of foreign exchange reserves in the hands of national governments was frozen at its present level but that aggregate demand for reserves continued to grow. Faced with a shortfall of reserves, governments would tend to pursue restrictive policies, either tight domestic monetary and fiscal policies or direct restrictions on international trade and capital flows. For one country considered in isolation, these are effective policies for accumulating foreign exchange reserves. They serve to redistribute the available stock of reserves among nations. However, when all (or most) countries pursue the same policies, the ultimate effect will be a depression of demand, income, and price levels throughout the world. But given the nominal stock of reserves, a reduction in the world price level means a larger stock of real foreign exchange reserves. Ultimately, the supply of real reserves will be equated to the demand.

It also follows from this line of argument that a very rapid rate of growth of foreign exchange reserves could be inflationary. If an international agency existed that could create new supplies of reserve assets, to be distributed freely to national governments, it could expand the stock of reserves at a faster rate than the aggregate of demands for reserves to be held. Attempts of all nations simultaneously to reduce the level of their reserves would create upward pressures on the world price level, and the rise in the price level would adjust the real quantity of reserve assets to the quantity demanded.

Central Bankers' Need for Reserves. The volume or rate of growth of foreign exchange reserves appropriate to any country defies economic precision. No quantifiable relationship appears to exist between the volume of trade, exchange rates, previous trade surpluses or deficits, and the appropriate level of reserves. They are adequate in each country if "large enough or growing fast enough to forestall anxiety over them."[12]

Anxiety also afflicts central bankers and may prompt them to enforce restrictive trade policies. Machlup has described the central bankers' noneconomic need for reserve holdings as follows:

> I conclude that the "need" for reserves is determined by the ambitions of the monetary authorities. I submit we ought to see to it that they get foreign reserves in amounts sufficient to be happy and satisfied; in amounts, that is, that will keep them from urging or condoning policies restricting imports or capital movements.[13]

In other words, the problem with inadequate growth of (nominal) foreign exchange reserves is not that desired levels of real reserves cannot be achieved in the long run by some combination of policies. Rather, it is that the alternatives to adequate growth of nominal reserves—worldwide deflation and widespread restrictions of trade and capital flows—are unpalatable. They imply unemployment, reduced levels of economic efficiency and hence of real income, and lower rates of economic growth. The excessive growth of foreign exchange reserves, on the other hand, creates danger of worldwide inflation.

The Problem of Adequate Reserve Growth. The optimum rate of growth of the world's foreign exchange reserves is an elusive concept. We know very little about the determinants of national demands for foreign exchange reserves. However, even if we did understand these completely, to define the optimum rate of growth we would still be left with the question, What macroeconomic policies should national governments pursue? What degree of independence should they have from balance-of-payments constraints in formulating their domestic policies?

Although we cannot explain the nature of national demands for foreign exchange reserves, they seem certain to grow in the future. If the supply of reserve assets does not grow accordingly, governments may pursue unfortunate, restrictive policies. If we are concerned with avoiding such policies, we must be concerned with the rate of growth of the supply of reserve assets. The informed judgment of most people in this field is that the growth rate has not been adequate in this sense in recent years. Why? What controls the rate of growth of reserve assets?

THE NATURE AND COMPOSITION OF FOREIGN EXCHANGE RESERVES

As a first step in the analysis of the control of the supply of foreign exchange reserves, we must be clear about their nature and composition. Summary data on the reserve holdings of all countries other than China, the USSR, and the countries of eastern Europe (for which no data are available) at the end of 1971 are shown in Table 21.1. The postwar evolution of the present composition of reserve holdngs is shown in Figure 21.3.

Gold. Gold has traditionally been the most important reserve asset of nations. Historically, gold once accounted for over 90 percent of reserve assets. By 1949, this ratio had declined to 70 percent, and the United States held about two-thirds of that monetary gold stock.[14] Over time, world trade

Table 21.1. **The Composition of Official Foreign Exchange Reserves, January 1, 1972 (Millions of U.S. Dollars)**

All Countries[a]	Dollars	Percent
Gold	$ 39,205	32
U.S. Dollars	50,569	41
Other Convertible Currencies	26,746	22
Drawing Rights at IMF	6,378	5
Total	$122,898	100

[a]Excluding China, USSR, and Eastern Europe.
SOURCE: International Monetary Fund, *International Financial Statistics* 25, no. 2 (February 1972).

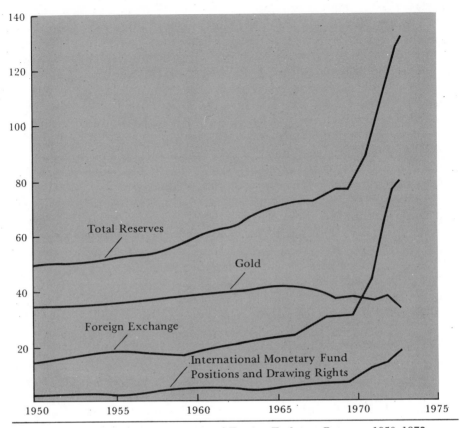

Figure 21.3 **The Changing Composition of Foreign Exchange Reserves, 1950–1972**
SOURCE: International Monetary Fund, *International Financial Statistics* (Washington,
D.C.), various issues.

has expanded more rapidly than the world's monetary gold reserves. The
increase in the output of gold has been modest. As a result, alternative
reserve assets have assumed a larger and larger portion of total monetary
reserves to accommodate expanding world trade. By early 1972, gold
accounted for only one-third of the world's foreign exchange reserve assets.

Foreign Exchange. As the importance of gold has declined, that of
foreign currency assets has increased. In principle, reserves could be held in
any convertible currency, that is, any currency for which there is an active,
unrestricted, international market. In practice, however, two currencies dominated as reserve assets before the dissolution of the Bretton Woods Agreement. These were the pound sterling and the U.S. dollar.

In the nineteenth and early twentieth centuries London was the world's
financial and banking center, and the pound sterling was the dominant

currency in international finance. As New York replaced London as the center of the world's financial system, the relative importance of the pound declined and the importance of the dollar increased. Since World War II, use of the pound in international payments and as a reserve asset has been virtually confined to the so-called Sterling Area, a group of countries with close historical and economic ties to the United Kingdom that effectively peg their exchange rates to the pound sterling.[15]

Outside the Sterling Area and a similar but smaller Franc Area,[16] the U.S. dollar dominated the scene. The U.S. dollar became the "working currency" of international trade and finance, and, since all currencies were effectively pegged to the U.S. dollar, it was the "vehicle currency" in which all countries conducted direct intervention in the foreign exchange market to maintain the pegged exchange rate. While gold retained its traditional status as an international reserve asset, all countries held and still hold at least working balances in U.S. dollars, and some countries hold a much larger portion of their reserves in this form.

Dollar claims and dollars have been accumulated by foreign official agencies because of the functions they performed in domestic and international economic trade. The rapid increase in officially held dollar claims as foreign exchange reserve assets in part reflects the movements out of dollars into gold and other stronger currencies in the exchange markets, as well as the accelerating balance-of-payments deficits of the United States in recent years. In addition to dollars, there has been rapid growth in other currencies, particularly the mark and the yen, held as foreign exchange reserve assets.

IMF Drawing Rights. Unconditional drawing rights at the International Monetary Fund account for a small but growing share of aggregate reserves. Moreover, the fact that such drawing rights accounted for only 5 percent of aggregate reserves at the beginning of 1972 significantly understates the importance of the International Monetary Fund in the international monetary system.

Conditional Reserves. Our measure of foreign exchange reserves does not include conditional reserves, such as credits extended by the IMF beyond the basic, unconditional drawing right. Such reserves are significant, although there is no effective way to measure the aggregate sum potentially available. We will return to a discussion of the IMF later.

THE STRUCTURE OF THE INTERNATIONAL MONETARY SYSTEM

The international monetary system now accommodates itself to the present. Member nations have abandoned most of the rules of Bretton Woods. However, these nations have not found any new set of rules to which they can all agree. Gold, U.S. dollars, several other currencies, and IMF drawing rights are now the basic reserve assets. To understand the mechanism regulating their supply, we must understand the historical roots of the institutional structure of the Bretton Woods international monetary system. It is particularly important to establish the role of gold in this system.

In this section we confine our attention to the system as it existed until early 1968. We will turn to the forces that produced the subsequent crises and changes in institutional arrangements later.

The Classical Gold Standard.[17] Historically, gold was money par excellence. Indeed, during the nineteenth century most industrial countries were formally on the gold standard. Gold coinage was in active circulation, and gold was the "standard money" into which other types of money were convertible on demand for both domestic and international payments.

The necessity for convertibility into gold imposed severe constraints on the management of the domestic money supply. Although the ratio of gold to the domestic money supply was not rigid, any substantial loss of gold through the settlement of international payments necessarily implied domestic monetary contraction, and any substantial inflow of gold generally implied domestic monetary expansion. There was no real question of a conflict between domestic and external objectives of monetary policy. In principle they were the same: convertibility into gold at a fixed exchange rate. Since excessive domestic monetary and credit expansion would result in a balance-of-payments deficit and an outflow of gold, governments could not pursue widely divergent monetary policies without precipitating a crisis. Thus, the very fear of gold drains was sufficient to maintain monetary discipline (except on the peripheries of the world economy, such as in North and South America, where suspensions of gold convertibility were not uncommon).

The classical gold standard was suspended during World War I, but the economic reconstruction of the postwar period included a painful, if short-lived, return to gold. In the economic disruptions of the Great Depression and World War II, the direct link between gold and domestic monetary management was again severed as country after country abandoned the gold standard and restricted the rights of its citizens to own or trade in gold. Gold stocks in the hands of private citizens and commercial banks were expropriated and turned over to central banks or exchange stabilization funds. For varying periods, the world's major currencies were allowed to float freely in the foreign exchange markets, but eventually new pegged rates were established. There was an alignment of nations into "currency blocks" and widespread resort to exchange controls, made very rigid during World War II. However, while it had lost its domestic monetary functions and could not be traded legally among private citizens, gold was still universally recognized as "international money," at least for official settlement purposes. As it turned out, the gold standard had not been abandoned. Through the nationalization of the gold stock, it had merely been transformed.

Remnants of the Gold Standard. New gold standard principles were formally incorporated into the reconstruction of international monetary arrangements agreed to at the Bretton Woods Conference of 1944. On the symbolic level, the 1944 gold dollar became the unit of account for the new International Monetary Fund, and all members were required to declare a par rate of exchange in terms of this gold dollar. Part of each country's initial subscription to the Fund had to be in gold or in currencies convertible into gold. The IMF accumulated a large stock of gold, and members were obliged to exchange their currencies for gold in the hands of the Fund, if necessary, at the par rate of exchange. As is evident in Figure 21.3, although the U.S. dollar emerged as the practical currency for international payments, central banks continued to accumulate a major portion of their foreign exchange reserves in gold.

The keystone of the Bretton Woods financial structure was the relationship between the U.S. dollar and gold. Although the U.S. government had terminated its formal obligation to convert private holdings of U.S. dollars into gold in the early 1930s (and residents of the United States were prohibited from owning or trading in gold, other than for artistic, industrial, and numismatic purposes), the government continued to guarantee the convertibility of dollars in the hands of foreign governments "for legitimate monetary purposes" and to purchase all gold offered to it at the official price of $35 per ounce.[18] The U.S. gold stock, which at the end of World War II amounted to almost three quarters of the gold in monetary reserves in the Western world, became in effect the central gold reserve for the world monetary system.

The London Gold Market.[19] Although not a part of the formal structure of the monetary system agreed to at Bretton Woods, a set of institutions that had a vital impact on the functioning of that system was an international network of gold markets, which after 1954 had the London gold market as its hub.

As noted earlier, many countries imposed severe restrictions on the ownership and trading of gold before and during World War II. In an environment of monetary instability and rampant inflation, black markets for gold, a traditional and relatively durable international store of value, flourished nonetheless. Although there were some important exceptions (notably the United States and the United Kingdom), most countries relaxed or abolished restrictions on gold ownership and trading in the early 1950s, and even countries that maintained rigid controls found it almost impossible to eliminate large-scale illegal transactions. In 1954, after a period of stability in free gold markets, the London gold market was opened for trading among nonresidents through the intermediary of British brokers (British citizens were still prohibited from owning or trading gold). It quickly became the dominant wholesale market.

The basic stock in trade of the London gold market and its satellite markets throughout the world was the annual output of the Western world's gold mines, which ranged between $1 billion and $1.5 billion in the late 1950s and the 1960s, augmented by periodic Russian gold sales, which reached $550 million in 1965. (See Figure 21.7.) From time to time various central banks also sold gold in the free market to gain foreign exchange. As long as the free-market price was above the U.S. Treasury's buying price ($34.9125 per ounce), suppliers of gold would offer it for sale in the market. If the price dropped below this, gold would flow into the United States' stock. As a result, the U.S. Treasury's buying price set an effective floor under the free-market price.

On the demand side, the market serviced a regular flow of private demands, amounting to approximately $500 million in the mid-1950s and rising to much higher levels in later years. Some of this demand was for normal artistic and industrial purposes. However, there was a continuing undercurrent of demand for private hoarding and, particularly in later years, for short-term speculation on the price of gold. The latter, as we shall see, eventually became a decisive factor disrupting the system.

European central banks also satisfied a large part of their demands for gold through purchases in the London gold market. Because they had the option of dealing directly with the U.S. Treasury, these central banks provided a bridge between the gold market and the U.S. gold reserve. If they could satisfy their demands for gold in the open market at a price less than the U.S. Treasury's selling price ($35.0875), they would do so. If the open-market price rose above this, they would switch their demands to the U.S. Treasury. This put an effective ceiling on the market price—unless private demands exceeded the flow of gold onto the market.[20]

In October 1961 this happened for the first time since the London gold market opened in 1954. Private speculation drove the market price to over $40 per ounce. Fearing that price instability would aggravate speculative pressures, the U.S. government intervened, supplying gold to the market through the Bank of England to stabilize the price close to the official price. In 1961 and 1962, in a series of agreements with major European central banks,[21] the Federal Reserve System organized joint intervention as necessary to keep the market price close to the official price. The United States agreed to provide half the gold required by the so-called Gold Pool, but of course the U.S. commitment to supply gold to central banks meant that in the long run a drain out of the Gold Pool was a drain out of the U.S. reserve.

In this way, given the flow of gold onto the market, private demands for gold determined the rate of growth of the aggregate stock of official gold reserves; and the sum of private demands and the demands of other central banks determined the rate of change of the U.S. gold stock. This proved to be a vulnerable situation that eventually rendered the entire monetary structure unstable. We will return to the analysis of this problem when we have completed our sketch of the structure of the international monetary system.

The International Monetary Fund. One of the important financial institutions to be established as a result of the Bretton Woods Conference was the International Monetary Fund. In a sense it was to be a central bank for the international monetary system, but initially it was denied the basic power of a central bank. It could not issue liabilities that would be accepted as international money.

From a financial point of view, the International Monetary Fund is simply a pool of gold and national currencies. When the Fund was established, each member was assigned a quota, of which 25 percent had to be subscribed in gold (the so-called gold tranche) and the balance in its own currency. As a result of new members joining the Fund and across-the-board increases of all quotas in 1959, 1966, and 1970, the aggregate value of all quotas increased from U.S. $8.8 billion in 1947 to U.S. $29.3 billion at the beginning of 1972. The Fund can augment its holding of currencies by borrowing directly from members. Under the General Arrangements to Borrow, the Fund had formal lines of credit with 10 members totaling $6 billion at the beginning of 1972 (and at that time, under the GAB and other arrangements, the Fund had outstanding borrowings from these 10 members of almost U.S. $1 billion).

Each member's rights and obligations vis-à-vis the Fund depend on the Fund's holdings of that member's currency relative to its quota. Members are permitted to purchase foreign exchange from the Fund in exchange for their own currency (such transactions are usually called drawings) under certain specified conditions. Each member has the right to draw foreign exchange from the Fund virtually without question, provided that the drawing does not increase the Fund's holding of the member's currency above its quota. This sum is the unconditional drawing right that we have included in our measure of foreign exchange reserves.

Drawings that will increase the Fund's holdings of the member's currency above its quota are "conditional." That is, they are governed by a complicated set of rules limiting both the amount that can be borrowed and the timing of the drawings (all of which can be waived by the Fund), and they require "substantial justification" on the part of the member to make a formal "declaration of intent" regarding domestic policies that will be undertaken to solve the balance-of-payments problem. Given an acceptable declaration of intent, the Fund will frequently make a standby arrangement, permitting virtually automatic drawings as necessary up to a specified sum within a specified period. Such an arrangement is sometimes a powerful psychological weapon to counter speculative pressures.

Each drawing from the Fund simultaneously reduces the Fund's holdings of other currencies (thus increasing other members' drawing rights from the Fund) and increases the Fund's holdings of the drawing member's currency. Drawings that increase the Fund's holdings of the member's currency above 75 percent of its quota create an obligation to repurchase. The amount and timing of the repurchase is governed by another complicated set of rules, but all repurchases must be made with gold or convertible foreign exchange. Interest is charged on the Fund's excess holdings of a member's currency as an inducement to early repayment, the interest rate increasing with both the magnitude of the excess and the time that it is outstanding. Thus, drawings on the Fund are appropriately regarded as short-term loans.

The IMF and International Credit Creation. In the International Monetary Fund, member governments have established an international agency with authority to create intergovernmental credit under fairly carefully defined circumstances and in strictly limited amounts. When a member draws on its gold tranche, it is drawing gold and foreign exchange that it had previously accumulated through its own national efforts and subscribed to the Fund. Thus, the gold tranche is simply the nation's gold reserves held in a different form. However, when a member draws foreign exchange in excess of this—in what are called the "credit tranches"—new reserves are created. The drawing member comes into possession of foreign exchange that was previously not counted as part of any nation's foreign exchange reserves, and it is free to use this foreign exchange. Other members have in effect extended credit in their own currencies through the intermediary of the IMF, and thus they temporarily help finance the drawing member's balance-of-payments deficit. In this way, the existence of the Fund makes a net addition to international liquidity.

How much credit can the International Monetary Fund extend to members? At first glance, the answer might seem to be the sum of all members' quotas and the Fund's lines of credit under the General Agreements to Borrow, less the gold tranche. At the end of 1971 this was over U.S. $21 billion, a net addition of 19 percent to the explicit reserves of the Western world. However, such a calculation implies that all currencies in the IMF pool are equally useful, which is not the case.

Members draw from the Fund in order to obtain currencies that they can use for direct intervention in the foreign exchange market. For this purpose they normally require U.S. dollars. This does not mean that they will draw only U.S. dollars from the Fund. However, it does mean that any currencies drawn from the Fund will normally be converted into U.S. dollars, usually in a direct transaction with the foreign exchange authorities of the country whose currency is drawn. This means at present that the usable currencies in the International Monetary Fund are those of only a few member countries with relatively strong foreign exchange reserve positions.

This is reflected in the pattern of drawings from the IMF. From 1947 through 1960, some 87 percent of all drawings from the Fund were in one currency, the U.S. dollar. With the economic recovery of Western Europe, more currencies became convertible and hence potentially useful to the Fund. However, the pattern of drawings from the Fund remained highly concentrated. Thus, from 1961 through 1971 the currencies of five industrialized countries[22] accounted for 68 percent of all drawings. By adding five more industrialized nations to the list[23] we can account for 93 percent of all drawings. Yet at the end of 1971 almost 29 percent of the Fund's holdings of gold and national currencies took the form of currencies of less developed nations and smaller developed nations, most of which were not convertible.

The contribution of the International Monetary Fund to international liquidity is thus greater than the gold tranche but much less than the sum of all quotas and lines of credit under the General Agreements to Borrow.

Intercentral Bank Credit. The International Monetary Fund is not the only source of international credit to supplement foreign exchange reserves. The central banks of major industrialized nations extend credit directly to each other in time of need. Each serious foreign exchange crisis has involved close consultation among the central banks, frequently leading to a large "package" of assistance. For example, during the currency crises in 1968 several nations borrowed extensively through this ad hoc network. At the end of 1968, outstanding ad hoc lines of credit of this sort totaled U.S. $9.3 billion. By 1970 foreign exchange markets were more stable and such ad hoc borrowings amounted to $4.7 billion, of which $3.1 billion was borrowed to support the British pound.

The major participants in this reciprocal credit network are the central banks of the ten countries participating in the General Arrangements to Borrow (the "Group of Ten") and Switzerland, which is not an IMF member. Thus, membership in the reciprocal credit network interlocks with the International Monetary Fund, but the arrangements were deliberately made outside the framework of the IMF.[24] A general increase of IMF quotas, a possible alternative, would have increased credit facilities on a global basis. The reciprocal credit network, by contrast, could be confined to industrialized nations. It is argued that the liquidity problem among industrialized nations is of a different order than the chronic reserve problems of less developed nations. The latter is, in fact, a problem of capital deficiency for economic development and should be handled as such. Moreover, it is argued, the rapid evolution of international financial problems among industrialized nations requires a much more flexible instrument of policy than that provided by the International Monetary Fund. The end result, however, is an exclusive—some would say unseemly—rich nations' monetary club.

In addition, the Federal Reserve System has developed an extensive network of explicit reciprocal lines of credit with other central banks. By March 1972 this "swap network" involved 14 central banks and the Bank for International Settlements, and amounted to U.S. $11.7 billion, an amount $1\frac{1}{2}$ times the U.S. quota at the IMF. The swap network has been used extensively by both the United States and the other participants.

The Bank for International Settlements. At the center of the reciprocal credit network, administering and effectively presiding over it, is another increasingly important but little-known international financial institution, the Bank for International Settlements.

This bank, with headquarters in Basel, Switzerland, is controlled by a group of Western European central banks. It was established in 1930 to handle the collection and distribution of reparations payments from Germany under the ill-fated Young Plan of 1929. This function was short-lived, but the bank proved to be a convenient and flexible vehicle for intercentral bank consultations and cooperation, and hence it survived the quick demise of its initial rationale. In the period after World War II it found a useful role administering various Western European financial arrangements, including the European Payments Union and its successor, the European Monetary Agreement (a sort of Western European clearinghouse). The bank does not do a regular banking business with the general public. Its funds are derived primarily from the deposits of central banks and are invested primarily in government securities and time deposits with banks (much of the latter in the Eurodollar market).

From our present point of view, the important thing about the Bank for International Settlements is that it has provided the forum for consultations, negotiations, and agreements among the central banks of industrialized nations, particularly following what has been called the Basel Agreement of 1961, under which central banks agreed to cooperate in the mutual defense of their currencies from speculative attacks in the foreign exchange market.[25] Consultations are almost continuous in that all members of the Group of Ten regularly attend the monthly meetings of the Board of Directors of the BIS, even though not all are on the Board. From time to time they are joined by representatives of other central banks.

Since the Basel Agreement, the Bank for International Settlements and the network of intercentral bank credits surrounding it have grown rapidly. The result is an international credit system rivaling the International Monetary Fund in size but oriented specifically to the international liquidity problems of the industrialized nations of the world. It is impossible to put a number on the magnitude of intercentral bank credits that could be negotiated in a crisis. However, some idea of the relative importance of the IMF and the Basel network may be gained from Table 21.2.

The flexibility of the Bank for International Settlements has also permitted it to take on other functions of importance for the stability of the international monetary system. For example, from time to time it has intervened in the gold market, and in recent years it has become a sort of central banker to the Eurodollar market.

The Eurodollar Market. We encountered the Eurodollar market very briefly in our analysis of commercial banks and international intermediation. (See Chapter 9.) The Eurocurrency market, to use the broader term, is an informal international market for borrowing and lending deposits denomi-

Table 21.2. **International Liquidity (Millions of U.S. Dollars)**

	1961	1964	1968	1971
	International Monetary Fund			
Aggregate Quotas	$15,043	$15,850	$21,198	$28,808
	The Basel Network			
General Arrangements to Borrow	—	$ 6,200	$ 6,057	$ 6,056
Federal Reserve Swap Network	$ 575	2,350	10,505	11,730
Ad Hoc Credit Facilities	1,132	4,380	9,263	4,736[a]
	$ 1,707	$12,930	$25,825	$22,522
	The Bank for International Settlements			
Total Assets	$ 1,295	$ 1,890	$ 3,940	$ 7,783

[a]As of December 1970.
SOURCE: International Monetary Fund, *Annual Report of the Executive Directors for the Fiscal Year Ended April 30, 1971* (Washington, D.C.), p. 30; International Monetary Fund, *International Financial Statistics* (Washington, D.C.), various issues; The Bank for International Settlements, *Forty-First Annual Report, 1 April 1970–31 March 1971* (Basel, 1971), pp. 170–172.

nated in several currencies. The major instrument, however, is dollar claims on American banks (primarily New York City banks).

A Eurodollar deposit originates when the ownership of a demand deposit balance with a American bank is transfered to a foreign bank or to the foreign branch of an American bank. For example, assume that a Belgian exporter has received payment for goods sold in the form of a dollar check, which he deposits in his checking account with a New York bank so that his balance is increased. He does not wish to spend the dollars immediately nor to convert them into his own currency. He cannot obtain interest on the deposit unless he leaves it with the New York bank for at least thirty days. He can obtain a return, however, by transfering ownership of the deposit in the New York bank to a European bank. In effect he is lending the Eurobank the title to his dollar deposit for a specific, usually very short, period.

The New York bank feels no effect, since only the ownership of the demand deposit has changed. There is no direct effect on the domestic monetary base here because demand deposits remain constant. The Eurobank accepts the title to the dollar deposit—an asset—and creates a dollar deposit claim against itself in the name of the Belgian. It pays the Belgian interest for the use of the title to the dollar claim.

The Eurobank, in order to make a profit, must find a borrower who needs dollars that are immediately available from the New York bank, and make the loan. A fraction of dollar assets are held in reserve by the Eurobank against its Eurodollar liabilities, which may be presented for payment. The interest rate charged the borrower may be only a fraction higher than that paid the depositer; but because of a large volume of transactions and the size of each transaction, the costs of intermediation per dollar of transaction are very low and the revenue can be substantial. Borrowers are internationally known and offer unsecured promissory notes as collateral, so the credit risk is very low. The Eurobank has acted as an intermediary between the ultimate lender of funds (those with dollar deposits in American banks that are not needed immediately) and the ultimate borrower who needs immediately available dollars.

Eurocurrencies are commonly borrowed for short periods, typically one to six months. However, the term may be as short as "call" or as long as a year or more. Typically they are borrowed to finance trade or to intervene in foreign exchange markets, either speculatively or in order to follow interest rate differentials between capital markets.

The Eurocurrency market was begun after currency restrictions were removed and European currencies were made convertible into each other. This encouraged foreign banks to accept deposits denominated in several currencies and to lend in different markets. The real impetus to the development of the Eurodollar portion of the market came when the United States imposed restrictions on capital outflows. It established the interest equalization tax, which curbed American purchases of foreign securities (particularly foreign bonds), restricted lending abroad by domestic banks, and curtailed direct investment abroad by American companies. These activities encouraged borrowers to tap non-American institutions and markets for needed funds. The incentive to keep funds in time deposits here was also curbed by the relatively low ceiling rates permitted under Regulation Q. Thus, owners of demand deposits were anxious to accept a Eurodollar deposit in return for higher interest rates.

The Eurocurrency market has facilitated international capital mobility between capital and money markets and foreign exchange markets. It was estimated that at the beginning of 1973 there was about $100 billion in gross Eurocurrency deposits. In 1965, there was $9.5 billion in Eurodollars in the market; by mid-1972, there was $68 billion (83 percent of total gross Eurocurrency deposits). Moving a small portion of these funds for speculative reasons can be disturbing to foreign exchange markets. The disturbance is magnified in fixed exchange rate markets where pegged exchange rates are different from what market forces would produce. Paradoxically, it is the smooth functioning of the market that has been attacked by critics, who feel that the ease and rapidity with which short-term funds can be moved in and out of currencies and money markets disturb those markets and make them particularly prone to crisis. Many proposals have been advanced to limit and contain the Eurocurrency market and inhibit short-term capital flows.

The Structure of the International Monetary System Under Bretton Woods Rules: An Overview. This, then, was the basic institutional monetary structure before the changes introduced in 1968, 1969, 1971, and 1973. It is perhaps useful to pull the main points together in a brief summary before we go on to consider the process of reserve asset creation.

The foundation of the Bretton Woods system was firmly planted in the stock of monetary gold. Gold was one of the two major reserve assets; the other, the U.S. dollar, was fully convertible into gold at a fixed price for official holders. The explicit reserve holdings of national governments were supplanted by an elaborate network of intergovernmental lines of credit. In part, these went through the intermediary of the International Monetary Fund, but for the most part they bypassed the Fund and were organized around the Bank for International Settlements.

This system proved to be unstable in the long run. Inevitable crises occurred in 1967, 1968, 1971, and 1973, making reform of the system imperative. What was the root of the problem?

THE INSTABILITY OF THE INTERNATIONAL
MONETARY STRUCTURE

The important point to keep in mind is that there were two types of international reserve money, gold and U.S. dollars, which were convertible into each other on demand at a fixed price but were not regarded as perfect substitutes by the world's central bankers and had very different aggregate supply conditions. In this combination of circumstances lay the inherent instability of the international monetary system.

International Financial Intermediation. The role of the United States in the world financial system has been compared to that of an international financial intermediary. At the same time that the United States was issuing monetary liabilities to the rest of the world—that is, borrowing on short-term liquid claims—it was acquiring less liquid short-term and long-term claims on the rest of the world. (It was also exporting capital in the form of official gifts.) This pattern is evident in the balance-of-payments data presented in Figure 21.4. Through the 1950s and 1960s the United States ran a substantial merchandise surplus and a significant but declining current account surplus. It was exporting capital on a massive scale on both public and private account. Part of the capital outflow was offset by foreign short-term borrowing and through the export of gold and issuance of liquid U.S. dollar liabilities by the government.

As we saw in Chapters 9 to 11, borrowing on short-term liquid instruments and lending on long-term and less liquid instruments is the classic pattern of a bank type of financial intermediary. In general, there is no reason to think that such an arrangement would be impractical in the long run, provided that the world's central bankers were willing to accept the U.S. dollar as the exclusive international money. Indeed, the adoption of an international "dollar standard," with the U.S. dollar as the exclusive, inconvertible international money, has many proponents.[26]

However, the Bretton Woods system had two types of international ·

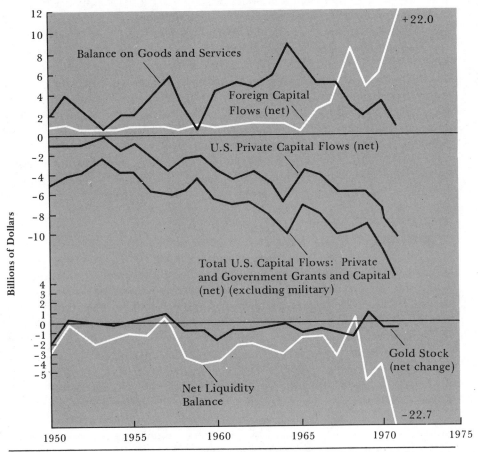

Figure 21.4 **The U.S. Balance of International Payments and the International Liquidity Drain, 1950–1971**
SOURCE: *Economic Report of the President, February 1971* (Washington, D.C.), pp. 298–299; U.S. Department of Commerce, *Survey of Current Business* (Washington, D.C., March 1972), p. 44.

money—U.S. dollars and gold. This proved to be a fatal flaw. Some central bankers displayed a strong preference for gold among their foreign exchange reserves. Given the rate of growth of foreign exchange reserves in the rest of the world, the required gold could be provided only by drawing down the U.S. gold stock. Eventually, the United States was placed in the position of a banker faced with a precipitous decline in its cash reserves. And the U.S. responded as a banker would, by restricting the extension of credit. Traditional monetary policies to curb the capital outflow were supplemented by various types of direct controls over capital exports.[27] However, as long as the U.S. dollar was the basic international money, measures that seemed necessary to the Americans to protect their own international liquidity position could be effective only if they curbed the rate of growth of reserves in the rest of the world and, hence, aggravated the international liquidity problem of the rest of the world.

International Redistribution of Gold Reserves. In the immediate postwar period the role of the United States as banker to the new international gold standard seemed quite viable. As noted earlier, the United States had emerged from World War II with almost three-quarters of the world's stock of monetary gold, more than ample to guarantee the convertibility of dollar balances in foreign official hands (in 1950 the U.S. gold stock was over $24 billion, while U.S. liquid liabilities held abroad were only $8.4 billion, of which $4.9 billion was in official hands). Moreover, the economic disruptions produced by the war had left Europe with a seemingly chronic balance of-payments deficit vis-à-vis the United States. Even under the tightly controlled conditions that prevailed, official foreign exchange reserves increased only very slowly.

By the mid-1950s, however, the situation began to change. With economic recovery and, in some cases, important monetary reforms, the balance of payments of continental western European countries improved dramatically. This was accompanied by large-scale accumulations of foreign exchange reserves, almost two-thirds of which were held in gold, with the balance largely in U.S. dollars. From 1950 through 1966 the accumulation of gold in the foreign exchange reserves of the industrialized countries of Western Europe alone was almost double the increase in the Western world's total reserves of monetary gold. (See Figure 21.5.) Other developed countries (principally Spain, Portugal, Canada, South Africa, and Japan) also accumulated gold, although in much smaller amounts. The overall effect was a vast redistribution of gold from the two reserve centers, and particularly from the United States, to other developed nations. As the reserves of the rest of the world increased, those of the United States declined (Figure 21.6), setting the scene for the gold crisis of 1967–1968.

Only a much more rapid rate of increase in the supply of monetary gold could have staved off the crisis by permitting the European central banks to increase their gold reserves without impairing the reserve position of the United States. What governed the rate of increase of the aggregate stock of monetary gold?

Gold Production. Gold mining is a peculiar industry. The price of gold has been fixed at U.S. $35 per ounce since 1934, but costs of production increased inexorably, partly as a result of the general rise in prices and wage rates and partly as a result of the exhaustion of the richest and most accessible deposits of ore. The implications for the profitability of gold mining are obvious. In spite of subsidies to gold mining in several countries, the production of new gold outside South Africa has been declining steadily over the past two decades.

In South Africa, the situation was different, but only by accident. Major new gold fields were brought into production beginning in 1953, and as a

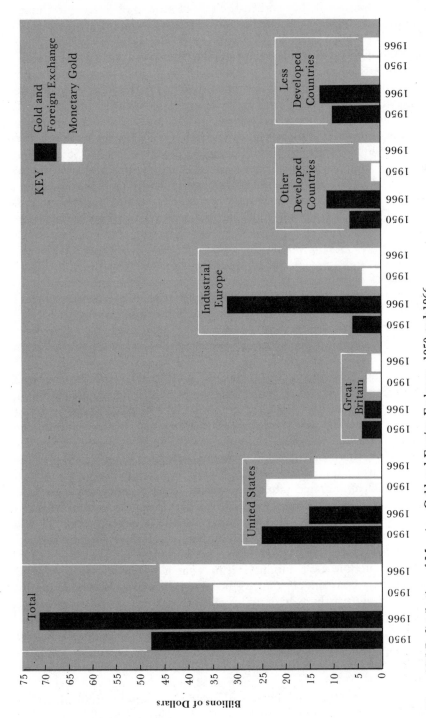

Figure 21.5 **Redistribution of Monetary Gold and Foreign Exchange, 1950 and 1966**
SOURCE: International Monetary Fund, *International Financial Statistics* (Washington, D.C.), various issues.

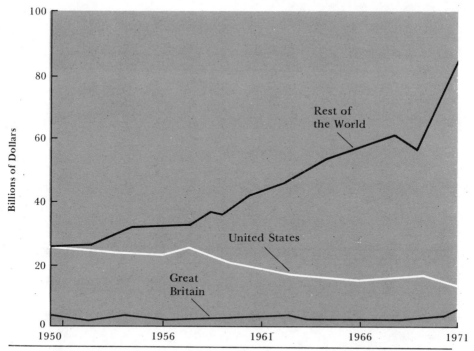

Figure 21.6 **Redistribution of Foreign Exchange Reserves Between the United States, Britain, and the Rest of the World, 1950–1971**
SOURCE: International Monetary Fund, *International Financial Statistics* (Washington, D.C.), various issues.

result total South African output increased substantially for several years. Whereas in 1953 South African mines accounted for half the world's output of new gold, by the mid-1960s they were producing three-quarters of the total. However, the entire increase in output in this period occurred in the new mine fields. Output from the old fields fell off as rapidly as in the rest of the world. By 1966 the output from the new fields began to level off also. Apparently this fillip to the base of the world's monetary system had run its course, and the underlying long-run retardation of gold production had reasserted itself.

Russian Sales and Private Demand. Although the production of new gold increased steadily from 1950 to 1966, net additions to the world's monetary stock were much more erratic. (See Figure 21.7.) On the one hand, new production was augmented by periodic Russian sales of gold (partly to finance purchases of Canadian wheat), and on the other hand the supply available to the monetary authorities was reduced by highly variable private demands for gold.

Although modest in amount at the outset, from their inception in 1953 through 1965 Rusian gold sales accounted for almost half the increase in the

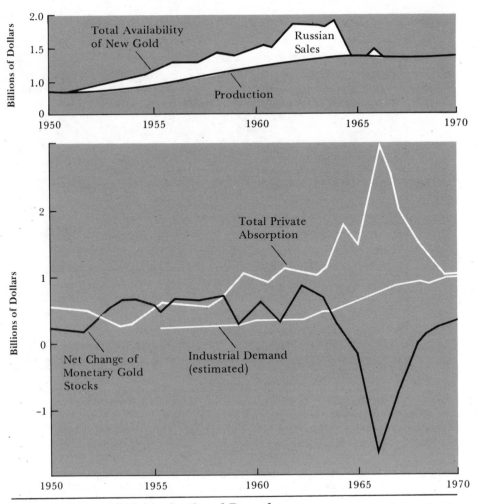

Figure 21.7 **The Gold Market: Supply and Demand**
Source: Internationl Monetary Fund, *Annual Report, 1971* (Washington, D.C.), p. 146.

monetary gold stocks of the West. In the last three years of this period alone, Russian sales amounted to over 85 percent of the total increase in official gold holdings. The abrupt termination of these sales in 1965 produced a radical change in the supply situation. (In 1967 $15 million of gold was sold by the Russians.)

Private demand was even less stable than Russian sales. As noted earlier, part of the private demand for gold was for normal industrial and artistic purposes. While there are no very good statistics on the purpose of gold for these purposes, available estimates suggest a steady increase in demand, from around 25 percent of annual output in the late 1950s to between 40 percent and 50 percent in recent years (Figure 21.7). Part of the acceleration of purchases by industrial users in 1967 and 1968, however, reflected hedging against a possible rise in the price of gold and hence should be counted as speculation.

Private hoarding of gold was a highly volatile factor in the total demand for gold. There had been a continuing demand for gold to be held as a store of value throughout the postwar period, presumably on the part of individuals who did not have confidence in their domestic money. The crucial factor in later years was shorter-term speculation on a rise in the price of gold. The continuing decline of the U.S. gold stock, coupled with the continuing rise in U.S. liquid international liabilities and the lack of agreement among central banks on the nature of appropriate reforms in the international monetary system, raised serious doubts that the existing gold price could be maintained. As is evident in Figure 21.7, from 1960 through 1967 successive waves of speculation increased in intensity until they overwhelmed the market. In 1967, for the first time in the postwar period, total monetary stocks of gold experienced a major decline. The vulnerability of an international monetary system tied to gold was laid bare for all to see. Reform was urgent.

REFORM OF THE INTERNATIONAL MONETARY STRUCTURE

Proposals for the reform of the international monetary system are legion. They range from proposals to create a true international central bank, with power to create an international fiat money, to proposals to return to a more classical version of the gold standard. These proposals have been surveyed in several excellent and readily accessible publications.[28] It is important to briefly review here the reforms implemented in 1968 and 1969. These involved two interrelated measures: a sharp distinction between private gold and official gold, and the introduction of a new international reserve credit facility, Special Drawing Rights at the International Monetary Fund.

Bifurcation of the Gold Stock. The initial response of the members of the Gold Pool to the crisis in the gold market following the devaluation of the pound sterling in the fall of 1967 was a vigorous reaffirmation of the two policies of pegged exchange rates and a fixed price for gold. However, the steady drain of gold from the Pool under continuing speculative pressure led to an emergency meeting of the seven members of the Pool in March 1968, after which a new gold policy was announced.[29] It introduced a sharp distinction between private gold and monetary gold.

The basic decision was to cease the de facto pegging of the price of gold in the free market. The members of the Pool announced that they would no longer sell gold to the free market nor buy it from the free market, and that they would not supply gold to other central banks to replace gold sold in private markets. At the same time, gold then in the hands of central banks would continue to be treated as a reserve asset. The United States would still buy and sell gold "for legitimate monetary purposes" at $35 per ounce, and all would feel free to use gold for official international settlements. Other central banks were invited to subscribe to the new principles, and most, but not all, did so.

Under the new "two-tier" policy for gold, the existing monetary stock of gold became, in effect, expensive yellow tokens with a fixed nominal value of $35 per ounce, usable only for intercentral bank clearings. Private gold could be traded freely in the open market at a price determined by the interaction of supply and demand. The initial response of the free market was a sharp rise in the price of gold. However, if the agreement were rigidly adhered to, a significant decline of the price of gold seemed probable. This is evident from the supply and demand forces in the market at the pegged price of $35 (Figure 21.7). Thus, in 1964, the last reasonably "normal" year before the climactic speculative outbreak, industrial purchases of gold were only half the annual output. Even allowing for some continuing private hoarding, a substantial expansion in industrial demand would be required to clear the market. This implied lower prices.

For some time, the price of gold was maintained by South Africa's withholding gold from the market. Thus, in the year following the March 1968 announcement, South Africa sold less than half its output of gold, and part of that was to other central banks.[30] South Africa could not continue this policy indefinitely, and, as gold sales accelerated in the second half of 1969, the price of gold fell in the free market; by year-end it was below the official price of $35 per ounce.[31]

The world market price of gold continued to fluctuate, reflecting industrial and speculative demands for gold. In late 1972 the price in London was quoted at over $60 per ounce, and in early 1974 the market price had risen to over $150 per ounce.

The March 1968 agreement did not solve the long-run problem of international liquidity. If adhered to literally by all central banks, it would have frozen the stock of monetary gold, but because of the nonadherence of some central banks and the role of the IMF in the gold market, it probably simply retarded the growth of the stock of monetary gold. Gold was not demonetized. Given deep-seated central bank traditions regarding the share of foreign exchange reserves that should be held in gold, continued growth of world foreign exchange reserves could set up renewed demands for gold among the world's central banks, and, in spite of the frequent assertions after the 1968 meeting that existing monetary gold stock was fully adequate, uncertainty and doubt about the adequacy of the United States' gold reserve position continued.

The March 1968 agreement contained a clear implication that further increases in aggregate foreign exchange reserves would be neither in gold nor in U.S. dollars, but in a new reserve asset, Special Drawing Rights.

Special Drawing Rights. A 1969 amendment to the Articles of Agreement introduced a new principle into the operations of the International Monetary Fund. It permitted the Fund to create a new reserve asset to be held by members in addition to their foreign exchange reserves, without requiring the members to subscribe either gold or their own currencies to the Fund. The first Special Drawing Rights were allocated in January 1970, with further allocations made in each of the succeeding two years. Total allocations over the initial three-year period were equivalent to $9.5 billion.

Special Drawing Rights (SDRs) are simply entries in a new set of books maintained by the IMF. They are intended to be used in the same way as foreign exchange reserves to finance temporary balance-of-payments deficits and hence to avoid exchange controls, unnecessary domestic deflation, or a change in the exchange rate. To this end, participating members may transfer their SDRs to other members designated to receive them by the IMF in exchange for convertible foreign currencies. The designated members are obligated to accept the SDRs and thus to extend reserve credit to the deficit country. However, there are built-in safeguards. No member may be required to accept additional SDRs in excess of twice his allocation, and all members are required to maintain their holdings of SDRs at 30 percent of their allocation on the average over a five-year period. The latter provision means that a member drawing down his allocation of SDRs is obliged to reconstitute his position through purchases of SDRs with convertible currency from other members or from the IMF itself. This ensures that SDRs will not become a large-scale chronic source of credit from one set of members to another.

Interest is paid on holdings and charged on allocations of SDRs at the same nominal rate of $1\frac{1}{2}$ percent per annum. Thus, a member who holds precisely what he is allocated will break even. Members who draw down their holdings will pay interest to the Fund, and members who are required to accept additional SDRs will receive interest from the Fund. All charges and interest are payable in SDRs. The rate is so low as to be ineffective as a serious incentive, however.

The provision for annual allocations of SDRs was designed to allow for the continuing growth of reserves on a global basis. The whole arrangement was to be reviewed at the end of the initial three-year period, when new allocations were to be decided. New allocations have to be accepted by members having 85 percent of the voting rights in the IMF, permitting a veto by the larger nations with large quotas. Thus, the rate of growth of reserves through the SDR mechanism is not a matter for impartial technical decisions within an international central bank. Rather, it is in the arena of international politics. Since there can be no guarantee of unanimity of opinion on the appropriate rate of growth of reserves in the future, there can be no guarantee that the rate of growth of SDRs will be in any sense "adequate."

The Demise of the Bretton Woods System. The establishment of the two-tier gold market and the introduction of an additional reserve asset in SDRs did not solve the problems inherent in the Bretton Woods system. The U.S. balance-of-payments deficits continued and grew larger. In 1971 and 1972, the United States ran deficits in its current account, triggering speculative attacks against the dollar. The drain of U.S. foreign currency reserves and gold accelerated.

On August 15, 1971, the United States unilaterally declared that it would no longer honor its commitment to redeem dollars for gold when presented by official foreign agencies, nor would it intervene in foreign exchange markets to maintain the price of the dollar vis-à-vis other currencies. In closing the gold window, the United States set the dollar afloat and effectively unpegged all other official rates. It believed that if the dollar were allowed to float, new and more realistic exchange rates could be established by free-market forces. By closing the gold window, it removed the link of the dollar to gold and hoped to force other nations to consider the need for a new reserve asset. Through its actions the United States had undermined the tenets of the Bretton Woods monetary constitution. Domestically, wages and prices were frozen and a surcharge was imposed on imports.

Foreign exchange and securities markets abroad remained closed for a week. When they reopened, the participants confronted an international monetary system that was in disarray. Each nation tried to adjust to the dramatic change in the rules of the game. Many nations were not willing to permit market forces alone to dictate new exchange rates that could be disadvantageous for their trade. They intervened in exchange markets, curtailing the free-market adjustment process. Controls on international financial transactions were selectively imposed. In the ensuing months there were threats of restrictive trade and tariff action aimed at American goods, and political friction increased.

The Smithsonian Agreement. In December 1971 the major industrial nations met with the United States at the Smithsonian Institution in Washington, D.C. These nations were concerned with realigning exchange rates and returning to the system of pegged rates. No attempt was made to deal with the structural weaknesses that pervaded the Bretton Woods agreement. The United States agreed formally to devalue the dollar in terms of gold, provided that other nations would also realign their currency in terms of the dollar. The price of an ounce of gold was changed from $35 to $38, an official devaluation of 8.5 percent. Several other countries revalued their currencies upward in terms of the dollar so that on the average the dollar was devalued 12 percent against other major currencies. Pegged exchange rates were reestablished, but the band around the official par value was widened to ±2.25 percent. The United States refused to reestablish convertibility of the dollar into gold. The gold window remained closed.

The Smithsonian Agreement only patched up the Bretton Woods system. The Board of Governors of the Federal Reserve System commented that:

The new economic program recognized the need for sizable and broadly based revaluation of foreign currencies vis-à-vis the dollar to help restore the international competitiveness of U.S.-produced goods. But in addition the new program was intended to encourage *improvements* in the Bretton Woods Agreements. . . .[32] (italics added)

548

Such comments lead critics to believe that even the United States was not quite ready for a profound overhaul of the international monetary system.

The Smithsonian Agreement did not address the fundamental problems of adjustment under pegged exchange rates nor the conflict between two reserve currency assets—gold and the U.S. dollar. Currency crises continued, and in mid-1972 Britain set the pound afloat. Several countries imposed additional restrictions on short-term capital flows that were designed to curb dollar inflows. Those countries did not want to be put in the position of having to buy inconvertible dollars in the exchange markets to support the pegged exchange rates.

In early 1973 another wave of speculation hit foreign exchange markets in a broad-based attack on the dollar. The official price of gold in terms of the dollar was increased 10 percent, to more than $42 per ounce. This did not quiet the exchange markets. Finally most of the major industrialized countries set their currencies to float against the dollar and against each other. Flexible exchange rates were agreed to in the absence of any agreement on alternatives.

How long will the system of flexible exchange rates last? There is broad agreement that exchange rates must be more flexible than under the old Bretton Woods system but also must be stable. It is probable that some major changes will be made in the near future.

Proposals for Reform. These are varied. Some countries undoubtedly would prefer to return to fixed exchange rates and narrow bands. A few others probably prefer the other extreme—completely flexible exchange rates determined in the market without any intervention. More consensus could be found for some form of flexibility with government intervention from time to time. There appears to be wide support for an "adjustable peg," wherein adjustments would be made in official parities only after a long-run balance-of-payments disequilibrium. The band, however, would be wider to permit short-run fluctuations without central bank intervention. There is also support for a "crawling peg" or a system of "gliding parities." Under this system official rates of exchange would be adjusted frequently in small increments in response to changes in some objective indicator of its balance-of-payments situation. One indicator that has been suggested by the United States is changes in foreign exchange reserves. Under the gliding parities, surplus nations and deficit nations would have their exchange rates adjusted automatically. This proposal has the virtue of symmetry, objectivity, and more flexibility.

Finding an appropriate world reserve asset may be a stickier problem. In early 1973 foreign monetary authorities held about $60 billion in liquid dollar claims. The process by which these holdings can be transformed into some other acceptable asset short of gold has no simple formula. Undoubtedly, SDRs will play a stronger role in any new international monetary system, but most experts feel that SDRs will not be an intervention currency. There will still be some demand for foreign exchange assets. Some asset, however, is needed that will permit the expansion of world trade and whose supply is not so limited in production as gold or tied to speculative forces and strong industrial demand.[33]

Although it still operates without many specific rules, the international monetary system is no longer in disarray. There is more flexibility than existed under the Bretton Woods System. International trade and investment continue; goods and investment capital continue to flow. The IMF and the Bank for International Settlements have adjusted to the changed world. For the interim, the ad hoc international monetary arrangements seem to work and may provide nations with an experience that in retrospect will be seen as essential when a new international monetary order is finally agreed upon.

SUMMARY

The main objective of the last two chapters was to explore the interrelationships between monetary policy and the balance of international payments. We discovered that with international capital movements highly sensitive to changes in interest rates, monetary policy has a powerful impact on the balance of payments. Under a regime of fixed exchange rates, this has two implications. On the one hand, the central bank cannot implement monetary policy without concern for its balance-of-payments implications, and on the other hand, exogenous developments in the balance of payments may dictate the course of monetary policy. Large foreign exchange reserves are a necessary condition for domestic monetary policy to have any degree of independence but given the power of speculation to move large sums of money across national boundaries within a short period, large foreign exchange reserves may not be sufficient to guarantee independence. Perhaps nothing short of greater flexibility of exchange rates can do that.

All of this implies growing demand for foreign exchange reserves in every country involved in world trade. With international monetary mechanism tied to a gold base, a reliable mechanism to provide for the growth of aggregate reserves did not exist. The natural mechanism, U.S. financial intermediation, was viewed with suspicion in many parts of the world and was constrained finally by a decline in the U.S. gold stock and a saturation of demand for liquid dollar claims abroad. The system proved unstable and faced increasingly severe trials.

Establishment of a two-tier gold system, introduction of SDRs, two devaluations of the dollar, and cessation of dollar convertibility were inadequate measures. In 1973 central banks began a period of temporary flexible exchange rates. Floating became the solution when all other alternative solutions were too difficult.

The need for reform is apparent. It is hoped that whatever system is drawn up will be able to foster expanding world trade and economic expansion and provide a climate for reducing restrictions on trade and capital movements. However, the creation of a new international monetary system takes time, adherence to the spirit and the letter of international cooperation, a great deal of restraint on economic and political nationalist forces, and an awareness of growing interdependence.

NOTES

1. If the balance of payments is not in equilibrium at the preferred combination of inflation and unemployment, then one of two situations must exist.

a. The balance of payments is in surplus. In this case, international substitution effects will move the balance of payments toward equilibrium, reducing exports and in-increasing imports, and hence reducing the surplus. However, if the same domestic policy continues to be pursued, the analysis in the text will begin to apply at this point; that is, the balance of payments will move right through equilibrium and into an ever-increasing deficit.

b. The balance of payments is in deficit. In this case, the substitution effects will aggravate the deficit, forcing a more rapid reappraisal of the domestic policy.

2. If the balance of payments is not in equilibrium at the preferred combination of inflation and unemployment, then one of two situations must exist.

a. The balance of payments is in deficit. In this case, international substitution effects will move the balance of payments toward equilibrium, increasing exports and reducing imports, and hence reducing the deficit. However, if the same domestic policy is continued, the balance of payments will move right through equilibrium into an ever-increasing surplus.

b. The balance of payments is in surplus. In this case, the substitution effects will aggravate the surplus, forcing a more rapid reappraisal of domestic policy.

3. A distinction is sometimes made between a freely fluctuating exchange rate, such as that implied in the text, and a floating exchange rate. In the latter, the government intervenes to modulate sharp movements of the rate. The Canadian experiment of 1950–1962 was of the latter type.

4. The case against exchange rate flexibility has been concisely stated in the International Monetary Fund, *Annual Report*, 1962, pp. 58–67.

5. The classic analysis of this period, including a powerful and influential statement of the case for the adjustable peg exchange rate system, is R. Nurkse, *International Currency Experience: Lessons of the Inter-War Period* (Geneva: League of Nations, 1944).

6. A short, vigorous statement of the case for flexible exchange rates is presented by H. G. Johnson, "The Case for Flexible Exchange Rates, 1969," in Federal Reserve Bank of St. Louis *Review* 51 (June 1969), 12–24. A classic statement is that of M. Friedman, "The Case for Flexible Exchange Rates," in *Essays in Positive Economics* (Chicago: University of Chicago Press, 1953), pp. 157–201.

7. The Canadian case has been discussed in many places, including Royal Commission on Banking and Finance, *Report* (Ottawa, 1964), pp. 479–488; and P. Wonnacott, *The Canadian Dollar 1948–1962* (Toronto: University of Toronto Press, 1965).

8. A review of some of the conceptual problems is presented by R. Clower and R. Lipsey, "The Present State of International Liquidity Theory," in *American Economic Review* 58 (May 1968), 586–595.

9. Note: The rate of return on foreign exchange reserves is not necessarily zero but, rather, depends on the composition of the reserve assets held. Gold bears a negative rate of return in that it is expensive to handle and store. Foreign money per se has a zero return, but typically it is held in relatively small quantities (i.e., working balance). Most "foreign exchange" is held in the form of interest-bearing bank deposits or U.S. government securities.

10. F. Machlup, "The Need for Monetary Reserves," in Banca Nazionale del Lavoro *Quarterly Review*, no. 78 (September 1966). This is more readily available as *Reprint*

No. 5, Reprints in International Finance, International Finance Section, Princeton University. Professor Machlup's view is also developed in F. Machlup, *International Payments, Debts and Gold* (New York: Scribner, 1964), chap. 13.

11. Machlup, "The Need for Monetary Reserves," op. cit., pp. 4–26.

12. L. B. Yeager, *The International Monetary Mechanism* (New York: Holt, Rinehart and Winston, 1968), pp. 114–115.

13. Machlup, "The Need for Monetary Reserves," op. cit., p. 27.

14. R. Triffin, *The Evolution of the International Monetary System: Historical Reappraisal and Future Perspectives,* Princeton Studies in International Finance, no. 12 (Princeton, N.J.: Princeton University Press, 1964), pp. 27–29, 66–71.

15. The Sterling Area emerged in 1931 when the United Kingdom abandoned the gold standard and a number of countries tied their currencies to the new floating pound. It became consolidated in the exchange controls imposed during and after World War II, which made a significant distinction between transactions with Sterling Area countries and transactions with the rest of the world (particularly the dollar area). Remnants of such restrictions still apply to international investment transactions. Sterling Area countries hold a major part of their reserves in pounds, use the pound as the normal means of international settlement, and look to the London capital market for finance. Although Sterling Area countries have their own stocks of gold and dollars, the British gold reserve is in effect a central reserve for the whole sterling area.

16. The Franc Area consists of 14 former French colonies: Cameroon, Central African Republic, Chad, Congo (Brazzaville), and Gabon (members of the Monetary Union of Cameroon and the Equatorial African States); Dahomey, Ivory Coast, Mauritania, Niger, Senegal, Togo, and Upper Volta (members of the West African Monetary Union); and the Malagasy Republic. At the end of 1968 the total foreign exchange reserves of the Franc Area, almost all held in French francs, amounted to U.S. $271 million.

17. This stylized description hardly does justice to the nature and history of the gold standard. Interesting reinterpretations are presented by A. I. Bloomfield, *Monetary Policy Under the International Gold Standard, 1880–1914* (Federal Reserve Bank of New York, 1959); and Triffin, op. cit.

18. The U.S. Treasury would actually buy at $34.9125 per ounce and sell at $35.0875.

19. The authoritative description of the London market is "The London Gold Market," in Bank of England *Quarterly Bulletin* 4 (March 1964), 16–21.

20. The willingness of central banks to purchase in the open market also depended on the location of the depository in which they wished to hold the gold. It has been estimated that the cost of transporting gold from New York to London was in the neighborhood of $0.08 per ounce. Thus, if the gold was to be held in Europe, they would buy in the London market at any price below the range $35.16–$35.20. The latter is generally taken as the ceiling price in the market and was formally made so by the activities of the Gold Pool, referred to in the next paragraph. Almost half the gold owned by countries other than the United States is actually held in New York.

21. The central banks of England, Belgium, France, Germany, Italy, the Netherlands, and Switzerland, and the Bank for International Settlements.

22. Germany, the United States, Italy, France, Canada.

23. The Netherlands, the United Kingdom, Belgium, Japan, Sweden.

24. The General Arrangements to Borrow have the same exclusiveness about them and in a sense are outside the framework of the IMF (in spirit, if not in administration). The IMF cannot borrow under this arrangement to supplement its resources for general use—only to extend credits to other members of the Group of Ten. Also, while Switzerland is not a member of the IMF, it participates indirectly in the General Arrangements to Borrow through reciprocal bilateral lines of credit with each member of the Group of Ten. Taken together, these eleven countries are commonly called the Paris Club.

25. The occasion for the Basel Agreement was the first serious bout of speculation

threatening the stability of the international monetary system, which also produced the Gold Pool, in whose operations the BIS was intimately involved. It has been emphasized that there was no written agreement at Basel, just a recognition of mutual interests in international monetary stability. See F. Hirsch, *Money International* (London: Penguin Press, 1969), chap. 12. This is an admirably readable book on the whole subject of international finance.

26. For example, R. I. McKinnon, *Private and Official International Money: The Case for the Dollar*, Princeton University International Finance Section, Essays in International Finance, no. 74 (Princeton, N.J., 1969).

27. The important measures included the interest equalization tax of 1963 and restrictive "guidelines" for banks and nonbank financial institutions extending credit to nonresidents and to firms making direct investments abroad. It was an intensification of such measures that produced the Canadian foreign exchange crisis in 1968.

28. R. Hawkins, "A Critical Survey of Plans for International Monetary Reform," in *The Bulletin*, New York University, Graduate School of Business Administration, Institute of Finance, no. 36 (New York, 1966); R. Hawkins, "Compendium of Plans for International Monetary Reform," op. cit., no. 37–38 (New York, 1966); F. Machlup, *Plans for the Reform of the International Monetary System*, Special Papers in International Economics, no. 3 (Princeton, N.J.: International Finance Section, Princeton University, 1962).

29. "New Procedures in the Gold Market," in *International Financial News Survey* (March 22, 1968). France had withdrawn from the Gold Pool in July 1967, reducing the membership from eight to seven. This was taken as further evidence of the rift between France and the United States on international monetary affairs. France's attitudes toward monetary reform stood in sharp contrast to those of the United States and most other countries. France distrusted any departure from gold, excessive reliance on the U.S. dollar as international money, and schemes for credit-based reserve creation, particularly on a global basis. From 1959 through 1966 France alone increased its gold holdings by $3,948 million, 46 percent of the total increase of gold reserves in industrial Europe (excluding the United Kingdom). France's holdings of foreign exchange were virtually the same in 1966 as in 1959.

France opposed a generalized form of the General Arrangements to Borrow that would have permitted the IMF to use the borrowed funds in its general operations. It also opposed proposals for large-scale increases of IMF quotas, and the implementation of the Special Drawing Rights proposal. On French attitudes toward international financial problems see Hirsch, op. cit., chap. 14.

30. South African gold was purchased by some central banks which did not subscribe to the 1968 gold policy (e.g., Portugal). In addition, some countries had drawn South African rands from the IMF. As it is entitled to do under the Articles of Agreement, South Africa paid gold rather than convertible currencies when these rands were presented for conversion. See U.S. Congress, Joint Economic Committee, *The Pedigreed Gold System: A Good System—Why Spoil It?* (Washington, D.C., 1969).

31. See the "Statement" of the Governor for the Fund from South Africa in the *Proceedings* of the annual meeting of the International Monetary Fund, 1969.

32. Board of Governors of the Federal Reserve System, *Fifty-eighth Annual Report* (Washington, D.C., 1972), p. 7.

33. W. Fellner, "The Dollar's Place in the International System: Suggested Criteria for the Appraisal of Emerging Views," *Journal of Economic Literature*, September 1972, 735–756.

THE EFFECTIVENESS
OF MONETARY POLICY

Our theoretical analysis of the impact of monetary policy was inconclusive. The purpose of monetary policy is to regulate aggregate demand in order to stabilize income, employment, and price levels. However, we were able to demonstrate cases in which, in theory, monetary policy would have no significant real repercussions, and cases in which monetary policy would have a powerful impact. Theory may suggest what we should look for, but theory alone cannot tell us which of the many possible cases is the relevant one. What, in fact, is the impact of monetary policy on economic activity? That is an empirical question. Economists' attempts to answer it provide the substance for this chapter.

THE EVIDENCE AND THE ISSUES

One of the frustrations of contemporary monetary economics is that, while most of the important controversies can be resolved only by empirical research, empirical studies seldom provide conclusive answers. No important issue is ever completely closed. The availability of new data, new analytical techniques, or new theoretical insights evokes new studies and hence an almost unending stream of new evidence to be digested, evaluated, and weighed against previous work. In many cases the evidence from different studies on any given point is conflicting, without being conclusive one way or the other (we saw examples of this in our discussion of the demand for money in Chapter 1). Occasionally, the same evidence is subject to diametrically opposed interpretations by different investigators.

For these reasons, we cannot hope to provide definitive empirical answers to the question we have posed. At best we can hope to provide a coherent overview of the evidence, some insights into its limitations, and guidance so that interested students can pursue the relevant literature on their own. In the footnotes we provide a selective guide to the literature. The student should be warned, however, that much of the literature in this field is highly technical, involving advanced techniques of statistical analysis. In fact, the controversy surrounding any given study frequently relates as much to the techniques of analysis employed as to the results obtained.

THE ISSUES

In this discussion we intend to focus attention on three issues, which we can summarize as three questions:

1. Is the money supply the appropriate variable for the monetary authorities to control, or does our model of monetary policy take too narrow a perspective on the process?
2. How sensitive are expenditures to monetary variables, including the level of interest rates?
3. How long and how stable are the time lags involved in the operation of monetary policy?

IS THE MONEY SUPPLY THE APPROPRIATE CONTROL VARIABLE?

The central variable in the theory of monetary policy developed in the preceding chapters is the "money supply," and the central institutions are the central bank and commercial banks. Thus, as depicted, the process of monetary control is based on the manipulation of the monetary base by the central bank. Commercial banks respond to changes in their cash reserves by expanding or contracting their total assets and liabilities, producing a change in the stock of money in the hands of the general public. Given a stable demand for money fluctuation, there will follow, through various channels, sympathetic changes in the levels of interest rates, aggregate expenditures, income, employment, and prices.

It has been argued that this is an inappropriate conceptual framework for the analysis of monetary policy because of the almost exclusive emphasis it gives to the money supply. In fact, this proposition is the starting point for two different types of criticism. According to one school of thought—which we will call the "credit conditions" school—the basic flaw is that the theoretical framework involves stock variables rather than flow variables. It is argued that the monetary authorities must be concerned with the flow of

555

credit to finance capital expenditures by businesses, governments, and households, not the stock of money in the hands of those businesses, governments, and households. The second school—which we will call the "total liquidity" school—accepts the basic analytical approach that emphasizes stock variables and adjustments in the composition of asset portfolios, but argues that the "money supply" as we have defined it is not the appropriate stock variable for monetary control. In defining money, it is argued, we have arbitrarily selected a particular group of highly liquid assets from a more general set of highly liquid assets, all of which are very close substitutes for each other. The real variable the central bank should be concerned with is the total liquidity of the economy.

Let us briefly consider these arguments.

THE CREDIT CONDITIONS SCHOOL

An approach to monetary policy that thrusts the flow of credit into the pivotal role bears the authoritative stamp of practitioners of the art of central banking. It has been argued forcefully by central bankers in the United States, Canada, and Great Britain, and has been endorsed by major commissions on monetary policy and banking institutions.

In the United States, emphasis on credit conditions has been part of the Federal Reserve's concerns for two decades, at times occupying the primary place and at other times a supporting concern.

Particular importance is placed on the "availability" of funds for would-be borrowers, as opposed to the "cost" of funds. This implies a rationing of loans by financial institutions on other than a strictly price basis. Because of standards of credit worthiness, collateral requirements, and various other qualitative aspects of the loan transaction, the funds may not always go to the highest bidder and because of variations in credit standards, a tightening of credit conditions may not be fully reflected in observed rises in interest rates.

This emphasis on availability was formally enunciated by Robert V. Roosa, then vice president of the Federal Reserve Bank of New York, in 1951.[1] The Federal Reserve Board publicly affirmed its commitment to the availability doctrine in testimony the following year before a congressional committee. From its statement, the Board held that

> A general tightening of credit results from a reduction in the availability of credit relative to the demand for it . . . banks cannot count with as much certainty on the ready availability of additional reserve funds and will therefore tend to be more restrictive in their lending practices and standards. . . . Applications for loans, particularly inventory loans, will be more carefully screened.[2]

A decade later, the Commission on Money and Credit concluded that "the direct effects of a restrictive monetary policy appear to work mainly through the availability of funds to would-be borrowers."[3] The Commission on Money and Credit was established in 1957 as a private committee to study the American financial system. It was the first formal review of the financial system and the operation of monetary policy since the Aldrich Commission in 1912. (See Chapter 12.)

From 1951 to 1966 the Federal Reserve's conduct of monetary policy was directed primarily at influencing the cost and availability of credit. The Federal Reserve looked to changes in interest rates as a signpost of its policy.

It is still agreed that changes in the level of interest rates are an essential aspect of the monetary process. At a minimum, changes in interest rates tend to parallel changes in credit availability, even though they may not fully reflect changes in the intensity of credit rationing. At a maximum, changes in interest rates play a vital role in affecting financial institutions' willingness to lend, a point much emphasized by the Federal Reserve System. Indeed, because of such indirect effects on the lending behavior of financial institutions and their reliance on interest rates, a British monetary commission— the Radcliffe Committee—concluded that "the authorities . . . have to regard the structure of interest rates rather than the supply of money as the centerpiece of monetary action."[4]

Money Creation vs. Credit Creation. We have seen in Chapter 15 that banks necessarily create credit at the same time that they create money, since bank assets (credit) and bank liabilities (money) expand (or contract) together. Control of the money supply also implies control of aggregate bank credit.

Moreover, according to the theory of monetary policy that we developed in Chapter 19, given a stable demand for money function, the supply of money and the level of interest rates are closely related. By manipulating the money supply, the central bank creates disequilibria in private asset portfolios, thereby inducing substitution among assets, lowering the yield on financial instruments, and making investments in real assets relatively more attractive. In this framework, interest rates (the cost of credit) provide the essential link between monetary policy and the real sector of the economy.

Does it not follow, therefore, that apart from a question of what aspect of the process is emphasized, an approach to monetary policy that focuses on the control of the stock of money and an approach that focuses on the flow of credit are for all practical purposes identical?

There is an important element of truth in such a proposition. Indeed, in many respects the true antithesis of the "credit" position is the strong monetarist position of the modern quantity theorists (which we will consider later) rather than the modified Keynesian theory of monetary policy that we developed in Chapters 18 and 19. Yet there are some issues of substance involved in the differential emphasis on money and credit.

Stability of the Demand for Money. One basic empirical issue on which the two approaches differ is the stability of the demand for money function. Confidence in the efficacy of management of the money supply must rest on the belief that money is an asset with unique characteristics for which there is a relatively stable demand function. Only then will changes in the money supply have predictable effects. The credit conditions approach rests on the assumption that the demand for money is not stable—and in particular that the relationship between money and the level of income is not predictable.

We referred to some of the empirical literature on the demand for money in Chapter 18 and will not repeat that discussion here. Suffice it to note that this is a field in which there is an extensive empirical literature and in which there is a large volume of research activity going forward, partly breaking new ground and partly reassessing old conclusions. There is general agreement among empirical researchers that there is a relatively stable demand for money, but there is an extremely wide range of opinion as to the nature of that demand function. Thus, although a policy of more conscious management of the money supply per se is attractive on theoretical grounds, it is difficult to argue that the empirical basis for such a policy is well established.

A Question of Tactics? This conclusion suggests that the credit conditions approach to monetary policy represents an ad hoc accommodation by central bankers in the face of uncertainty about the underlying demand for money. However, there are also at issue more fundamental questions about the tactics of monetary management.

One of the important points of the credit conditions approach is that it admits to a wide range of credit control policies. In addition to management of total bank credit, it relies on selective credit controls to bring about an efficacious allocation of that credit among the various sectors of the economy. These credit control policies are asserted to be appropriate additions to, or alternatives for, management of bank credit and regulation of the level of aggregate demand.

Adherents to the credit conditions approach place considerable emphasis on debt management as a technique of policy, where debt management is broadly defined as all operations by the government or the central bank to change the composition (not the size) of the government debt in the hands of the general public. Debt management is an important theme in the total liquidity school's analysis, and we will return to it again in that context. However, it has not been adopted as a major policy tool. It is sufficient to note that some groups, including the Commission on Money and Credit, have argued for greater use of debt management in conjunction with monetary policy. The CMC favored "broadening the range of discretionary debt management,"[5] pointing out that a more flexible, countercyclical debt management policy when used in conjunction with appropriate monetary adjustments would spread the effects of monetary policy quickly. The CMC acknowledged the parallels in impact on the economy of the two techniques, stating that "monetary policy and debt management both influence the level and structure of interest rates, the availability of loanable funds, and, through liquidity and asset changes, the velocity of money."[6]

It should be noted that the credit conditions analysis assigns particular importance to loans and advances by financial intermediaries as opposed to purchases of securities that are actively traded in the open market. It follows that a change in the composition of the asset portfolios of banks and other financial institutions is ascribed important effects, even though the total size of asset holdings (and hence the size of liabilities) does not change. In particular, an increase in bank loans, financed by sales of short-term securities in the open market, is assumed to have an expansionary effect on aggregate demand, even though the total money supply has not increased.

In one sense, then, the difference between credit conditions analysis and the money supply analysis is simply a difference of perspective toward which variables should be controlled directly and which should be treated as a residual. On the one hand, the money supply model argues that the money supply should be controlled, with the structure of interest rates and other aspects of "credit conditions" determined by market factors. On the other hand, the extreme version of the credit model argues that various dimensions of "credit conditions" ought to be controlled by whatever means necessary, leaving the money supply to be determined in the market at whatever quantity is demanded at the established set of "credit conditions."

Nonbank Financial Intermediaries. Finally, it is important to note that the credit conditions approach implies that the lending activities of a broader range of financial institutions than money-creating commercial banks are of direct concern to the central bank. The model provides an a priori case for the extension of formal central bank controls (such as compulsory cash reserve requirements) to such institutions, although it has been argued on empirical grounds that such controls are not necessary. We will return to this point later.

THE "TOTAL LIQUIDITY" SCHOOL

What we will call the total liquidity school has certain points in common with the credit conditions school, particularly concern about the implications of the operations of nonbank financial intermediaries, and emphasis on the role of debt management as an instrument of stabilization policy. However, whereas the credit conditions analysis focuses attention on the lending behavior of financial institutions, the liquidity model stresses the portfolio balance decisions of asset holders and the liability side of the balance sheets of financial institutions. In this sense, then, it is simply a more generalized version of the analysis that we developed in Chapters 18 and 19, but it takes explicit account of, and explores more completely, the implications of the existence and creation of close substitutes for money.

Near Money and Near Banks. The problem of distinguishing between money and near money has arisen at various places in our analysis. If we employ a narrow payments definition of money, then all short-term financial assets that are readily convertible into money on short notice and at a certain or almost certain price can be considered near money. This includes short-term, nonmonetary claims on banks and other financial intermediaries, and various types of money market instruments, particularly short-term claims on the government and some commercial and finance paper. As noted earlier, some economists employ broader definitions of money, in which case the definition of near money must be adjusted correspondingly.

Most, but far from all, of the stock of near money takes the form of liabilities of near banks. One of the striking features in the development of the financial system in the years since World War II has been the much more rapid rate of growth in the stock of near money than in the stock of money. Thus, as we saw in Chapter 9, within the banking system proper, personal savings deposits and time deposits have increased much more rapidly than have demand deposits, and near banks have grown much more rapidly than banks. (See also Chapter 10.) The implications of these facts for the effectiveness of monetary policy are the primary concern of the liquidity school.

Near Banks and the Effectiveness of Monetary Policy. In Chapter 19 we explored various cases in which monetary policy would be relatively ineffective. One of these was the case in which the demand for money was highly interest elastic, with the Keynesian liquidity trap representing the extreme situation. The basic hypothesis of the liquidity school is that the growth of near banks as suppliers of near money has increased the interest elasticity of the demand for money sufficiently to seriously impair the effectiveness of control over the money supply as a technique for regulating aggregate demand.

This hypothesis rests on two basic propositions (1) that there is a very high degree of substitutability between money and near money in asset portfolios, such that near moneys are much closer substitutes for money than are other financial or real assets, and (2) that there is a high elasticity of supply of near moneys. With respect to the second proposition, much emphasis is placed on the activities of near banks.

It is argued that the rise in interest rates associated with a restrictive monetary policy will increase the profitability of financial intermediation. Unhampered by high, legally enforced cash reserve requirements but subject to official limits on maximum rates of interest payable, near banks will be induced to compete more aggressively for deposits. As we saw in Chapter 19, an expansion of deposits at near banks can occur without any loss of deposits by banks, and the net effect will be an expansion of the total stock of highly liquid deposits. Banks themselves may respond, offering more attractive rates on savings and time deposits and hence participating in the growth of the stock of near money. Savings and time deposits at member banks are subject to cash reserve requirements and to limits on the interest rates they pay on these deposits, both factors that limit the extent to which banks could profitably meet the competition of near banks. In any case, a restrictive monetary policy should make near money a more attractive liquid asset than (non-interest-bearing) money. The stock of near money should expand relative to the stock of money, and near banks should expand relative to banks.

Thus, it is argued that the creation of near money makes it possible for asset holders to economize on holdings of money without seriously impairing the liquidity of their portfolios. The higher rates of interest earned on near money overcome the inconvenience and transactions costs associated with smaller money balances. The effect will be to increase the velocity of circulation of money. Money previously held idle as an asset is replaced by near money, and the money is placed in active circulation through the lending operations of banks and near banks. A larger flow of transactions and hence higher levels of expenditures, income, employment, and prices can be achieved with the same stock of money. To this extent the impact of restrictive monetary policy has been muted.[7]

This hypothesis can also be interpreted in terms of the credit conditions framework. An increase in deposits at near banks simultaneously increases their lending capacity. To the extent that any reduction in the flow of credit from banks is offset by an increased flow of credit from near banks, the aggregate effects of restrictive monetary policy will be weakened.

Implications for Policy. An extreme version of the liquidity hypothesis is evident in the assertion that there is no limit to the velocity of circulation of money. This implies that asset holders regard money and near money as perfect substitutes and that there is no constraint on the ability of near banks to expand their asset and liability holdings. In such circumstances, control of the money supply is futile, since money is but a part of a homogeneous mass of liquid assets. Trying to limit the money supply is like squeezing a balloon: Air (liquidity) that is forced out of one area of the balloon reappears elsewhere. The entire impact of the restriction of the money supply is absorbed within the financial system. Monetary policy is useless. What is required is a policy of regulating the aggregate stock of liquid assets.

In a less extreme version of the liquidity hypothesis, money and near money are very close, but less than perfect substitutes: A restriction of the money supply will be only partially offset by expansion of the supply of near money. This suggests that the creation of near moneys increases the intensity with which monetary restraint must be imposed to achieve any given real effects. However, in either case the efficiency of monetary policy would be improved by controlling the stock of liquid assets rather than the money supply. This means that near banks should be brought within the same framework of central bank controls (e.g., cash reserve requirements) as the banks. It also means that debt management operations may be an effective complementary instrument of stabilization policy.

We defined debt management operations as transactions to alter the composition (as opposed to the size) of the government debt in the hands of the general public—for example, swapping longer-term bonds for short-term securities. Such operations can be conducted by the Treasury, issuing new securities and retiring outstanding issues, or by the central bank, simultaneously buying and selling securities out of its portfolio. As we pointed out earlier, monetary policy is simply an aspect of debt management, at least when it is effected through open-market operations. The central bank simply exchanges non-interest-bearing, demand debts of the government (currency or bank reserves) for longer-term interest-bearing debt. Remember, however, that the expression "debt management" is usually used in the narrower sense to refer to changes in the composition of the interest-bearing (i.e., non-monetary) government debt.

Short-term government securities rank high among the important liquid assets in the economy. It is argued, therefore, that the overall liquidity of the economy will be reduced if the government increases the average term to maturity of the public debt, selling long-term securities and retiring short-term securities, and that this will have a restrictive effect on the level of economic activity. Similarly, the liquidity of the economy can be increased by reducing the average term to maturity of the public debt (increasing the portion of the debt that is in short-term forms) and that this will have a stimulating effect on economic activity.[8]

The liquidity model suggests that debt management operations can have a powerful impact on aggregate demand and on economic activity, and hence that debt management operations ought to be coordinated with traditional monetary policies in an overall policy to regulate the liquidity of the economy.

Clearly, the liquidity model is an important hypothesis that merits careful empirical investigation.

Empirical Evidence. As in other aspects of the empirical evidence we have surveyed, the evidence on this point is mixed and uncertain.

We have already seen (Chapter 19) that the velocity of money has displayed a pronounced cyclical pattern, rising in periods of rising economic activity and restrictive monetary policy, and falling in periods of declining activity and easier monetary policy. As is evident in Figure 19.1, this pattern is superimposed on an apparent upward trend in velocity in recent years.

However, to what extent are these changes in velocity a result of the activities of near banks and to what extent are they a result of more general portfolio adjustments, of which the substitution of money for near money is only one aspect? There have been two types of relevant studies. Some investigators have attempted to estimate directly the degree of substitutability between money and near money, and others to examine the responses of near banks to changes in monetary policy. The degree of substitutability between money and near money can be measured by the elasticity of the demand for money with respect to the rate of interest on near money.

We saw in Chapter 18 that there is fairly strong evidence that the demand for money has some sensitivity to interest rates. The relevant questions, then, are: Is there any empirical evidence that near moneys are closer substitutes for money than are other financial assets, and if so, is the indicated elasticity of demand for money sufficiently great to provide substantial justification for the liquidity school's concerns?

On the first point the evidence is contradictory. A well-known study by M. J. Hamburger showed that yields on near money had no greater effect on household's demands for money than did yields on other financial instruments.[9] By contrast, studies by T. H. Lee came to exactly the opposite conclusion.[10] That is, they showed a significantly higher elasticity of demand for money with respect to interest rates on near money than on any other class of financial instruments. A subsequent interchange between Hamburger and Lee did not fully resolve the issue, although it did suggest a balance of present evidence in Lee's favor.[11]

However, and this is a vitally important point, even if we accept Lee's conclusion that near moneys are better substitutes for money than are other financial assets, the indicated interest elasticity of demand is not so high as to come anywhere near supporting the extreme liquidity school position. It is true that money and near money are substitutes, but they are clearly not perfect substitutes. Far from approximating infinity, the cross-elasticity of demand suggested by Lee's study is in the neighborhood of -0.6.[12]

The second group of studies focused attention on the cyclical characteristics of the flow of funds to near banks. Studies by I. Friend[13] and A. R. Benavie[14] found no evidence that near banks gained funds systematically and significantly at the expense of banks in periods of monetary restraint. Indeed, Benavie found evidence that in periods of monetary restraint near banks lost deposits, thus reinforcing the impact of monetary policy, not weakening it. The President's Commission on Financial Structure and Regulation (the Hunt Commission) recently recommended that near banks be subject to similar reserve requirements as commercial banks. The Commission justified its recommendation on grounds not only of equity but also of increased certainty of the impact of monetary policy.

By and large, the impact of debt management operations on aggregate demand remains a matter of theoretical speculation. Little empirical work has been done that would justify some of the extreme claims for the power of changes in the average term to maturity of the public debt.

Beginning in 1961, a notable experiment in the use of debt management techniques was conducted in the United States. Commonly called *Operation Twist*, this was an attempt to "twist" the term structure of interest rates to help reconcile the domestic and international objectives of policy. It was thought that higher short-term interest rates would attract foreign capital and thus help solve the balance-of-payments problem, whereas lower long-term interest rates were necessary to achieve appropriate domestic economic expansion.

Two attempts to evaluate the impact on interest rates arrived at contradictory conclusions. A study by Modigliani and Sutch found that the behavior of the term structure of interest rates at this time could be adequately explained by developments other than Operation Twist.[15] However, in another econometric study, using a different specification of the equations that determine the levels of long-term and short-term interest rates, T. Holland found evidence that "Operation Twist had in fact raised the short-term rate without lowering the long-term rate, thus partially achieving the immediate objective of the policy.[16] Holland did not explore the ultimate impact on either the balance of payments or domestic expenditures.

These bits of evidence are far too sketchy to make a conclusive case. Perhaps all we can safely conclude is that there is limited empirical support for some aspects of a moderate version of the total liquidity hypothesis, but that much more research is necessary before we can place much confidence in the theoretical speculations of extreme versions of this position.

HOW SENSITIVE IS AGGREGATE DEMAND TO MONETARY VARIABLES?

Our theoretical analysis in Chapter 19 suggested a second dimension to the determinants of the effectiveness of monetary policy—the sensitivity of real expenditures to monetary variables, whether these variables be defined as the money supply, the total liquidity position of the economy, the level of interest rates, or credit conditions. As we shall see, studies of the real impact of monetary policy fall into two groups, those in the Keynesian tradition, which attempt to measure the impact on specific categories of expenditure, and those in the quantity theory tradition, which attempt to measure a much more general impact on economic activity. Both sets of studies have been concerned with two closely related but separable aspects of the real impact of monetary policy, magnitude and timing. In this section we will be concerned with the question of magnitudes. In the next section we will review the evidence on time lags.

NATURE OF THE EVIDENCE

The evidence relating to the sensitivity of expenditures to changes in monetary variables is of three basic types: surveys of decision makers, partial econometric studies of the determinants of expenditures, and complete econometric models of the economy.

Surveys. The basic approach of the survey technique is to ask decision makers, in a written questionnaire or, preferably, in an interview, about the factors affecting their expenditure decisions, and particularly about the role of such monetary variables as interest rates and the availability of credit. Such surveys have been used to study both consumption and investment decisions, but it is the investment studies that have received most attention in the literature on monetary policy.

Surveys have been criticized on various grounds, some highly specific to the survey in question (the nature of the sample selected, the framing of the questions, failure to follow up nonresponses to mail questionnaires, etc.) and some relating to the technique in general.[17] It is argued that in a large, complex firm there is always a problem of finding the man or men actually responsible for making the relevant decision. In addition, investment decisions are always very complex, and affected by so many considerations, that respondents have difficulty isolating the specific effects of one variable, like interest rates. Moreover, answers to hypothetical quesions ("What would you do if . . .?") are inherently unreliable. Answers to questions about actual decisions suffer from the fact that the relevant events are always in the past and memories fade quickly, so that the "facts" of the decisions get distorted. Respondents are busy, have undoubtedly filled out numerous required forms, and may fear that the information may be used in a way that is inimicable to the firm. Finally, the impact of monetary policy on customers and hence on the demand for the product and investment decisions may not be understood by the respondents themselves. All things considered, it is widely argued that such surveys tend to be biased in the direction of finding little response to monetary policy.

Partial Econometric Studies. Econometric studies approach the problem through the application of advanced statistical techniques in an attempt to find the equation that best "explains" the behavior of some economic variable like investment or consumption in terms of a set of explanatory variables like interest rates or national income. What we call "partial" studies focus on one category of expenditures (the "dependent variable") in isolation from all others, taking the explanatory variables in the equation as "predetermined" or "exogenous" for the problem at hand.

Econometrics involves the joint application of statistical methods and economic theory.[18] Thus, while such studies typically test various combinations of explanatory variables to find the combination that explains the largest part of the observed variation of the dependent variable (a statistical procedure), the variables selected for testing in this way are those suggested by economic theory. Moreover, for a variable to be included in the final version of the equation, its coefficient must pass two tests, one statistical and one theoretical.

The statistical test is that the coefficient of the variable must be "statistically significant." Statistical methods of estimating equations involve the application of probability theory. Thus, the coefficients estimated by econometric procedures are taken as probabilistic estimates of the true coefficient. The true magnitude of the coefficient may be different from the estimated magnitude. Indeed, even though the equation provides an estimate of the coefficient, the true magnitude of that coefficient may be zero (indicating that that variable plays no role in explaining the behavior of the dependent variable). However, the statistical procedure also assigns probabilities to possible variations of the true magnitude from the estimated magnitude. If a coefficient is statistically significant, the estimated probability that the true value is in fact zero must be so low that the investigator feels he can safely ignore that possibility.

If a coefficient is statistically significant, it must also satisfy a theoretical test before it can be accepted as an estimate of the effects of the variable in question. It must have the "right sign" ($+$ or $-$). That is, the direction of the effect of the variable must be that predicted by economic theory in cases where theory provides an unambiguous prediction of the direction of the effect. For example, it frequently happens that interest rates are statistically significant in equations explaining investment behavior, but the coefficient has a positive sign (investment expenditures increase if interest rates rise) rather than the negative sign predicted by theory. In such circumstances the investigator usually concludes that something is wrong with the equation, that for some reason the statistical procedure is assigning to interest rates the effects of other, unknown variables that have not been included in the equation. In these circumstances the estimate is usually rejected.

Like surveys, partial econometric studies also suffer from faults that are specific to the individual studies (e.g., failure to use the best data, inappropriate specification of the equation, etc.) and from problems that are endemic to the type of analysis. Lack of fully appropriate data is a common complaint. Econometric studies usually have to make do with statistics describing the historical record and recorded for many diverse other purposes. Thus, the econometrician has to take his observations as given by recorded history: He cannot experiment like the scientist in his laboratory, and he cannot go back to correct the errors of those who initially recorded the "facts." This gives rise to a common technical problem, the inability of the statistical method to distinguish between the effects of two variables that are highly correlated with each other in the historical record (a condition technically known as multicollinearity). This problem commonly plagues monetary variables like interest rates, making it particularly difficult to isolate the impact of monetary policy.

Perhaps an even more fundamental problem, however, is inherent in the fact that the studies in question are partial analyses: They focus on a single quotation in isolation. To do so, the econometrician must take as "given" variables that are in fact partially determined by the process he is studying. Thus, in attempting to estimate the effects of interest rates on the level of investment expenditures, he takes the record of interest rate changes as an independent determinant of investment decisions and assumes that the line of causation runs simply from interest rates to investment. In fact, however, the behavior of investment expenditures will, directly or indirectly, partly determine the behavior of interest rates (as is evident from the theoretical discussion in Chapter 19). Thus, an increase in investment as a result of other developments will produce a rise in interest rates, which will then be detected by the statistical procedure as partly determining the rise in investment.

This problem—commonly called the simultaneous-equation bias—plagues single-equation studies in varying degrees. In general, it is suspected that simultaneous-equation bias tends to produce underestimates of the impact of monetary variables like interest rates. The advantage of complete econometric models is that, at least in principle, they provide a method of surmounting this particular problem.

Econometric Models. An *econometric model* is a description of an economy, or part of an economy, in terms of a set of equations. Unlike partial econometric studies, a complete econometric model allows for the complex pattern of interdependencies among variables in the economic system. Thus, to take a simple example, interest rates are allowed to influence investment and investment to influence interest rates, and the coefficients in the various equations are estimated so as to allow for both types of effects simultaneously. In principle, this should make it possible to identify each of the effects separately and hence to assess the impact of monetary policy more accurately.

A complete econometric model describes the structure of an economic system. It is then possible to take the set of structural equations, change a single variable like the money supply, and trace its effects through the system. In general, the effects will be very complex, but we can focus attention on the few key variables like gross national product, employment, prices, or the state of the balance of payments in which we have particular interest. Such exercises are called *simulation experiments*. Using this technique, we can not only assess the impact of monetary policy but also assess the effects of alternative policy instruments, including the differential effects of monetary and fiscal policy.

Economic model building is also plagued by problems of faulty data and multicollinearity of variables. In addition, it should be noted that the estimation of econometric models is a very expensive and time-consuming process. The computational problems alone are staggering, particularly when many different estimations have to be attempted to find the "best fit." The whole procedure would be impossible without large-capacity, high-speed electronic computers.

In addition to the technical problems of estimation with faulty data, the basic problem with econometric models is a product of their chief virtue— the explicit recognition of interdependence in the economic system. Because of the complex pattern of interdependence among the equations of the model, errors in any single equation can have magnified effects throughout the model.

Almost every model has perplexing, sometimes anomalous, results in some equations. The danger exists that these will seriously bias the results of simulation experiments. Again, because of the very high degree of interdependence between monetary variables and other sectors of the economy, the monetary relationships in which we are interested may be particularly vulnerable to this risk.

A Word of Warning. In this section we have tried to emphasize the general limitations of the available evidence on the impact of monetary policy. All of the findings to date must be regarded as tentative. However, it is important that the results not be dismissed out of hand because of the very obvious difficulties in the research procedures. As time passes, and as the evidence of many careful studies accumulates, a reliable picture of the impact of monetary policy is emerging. The faults of earlier studies should be taken as a challenge, not as a basis for rejection of all research in the area.

THE EMPIRICAL EVIDENCE

Early Studies: Monetary Pessimism. The tone of professional opinion on the impact of monetary policy for two decades was set by a survey of business investment decision making by a team of economists at Oxford University in the mid-1930s.[19] They discovered that, contrary to received theory, interest rates appeared to play a minor role in investment decisions, and they concluded that investment expenditures would be insensitive to monetary policy actions.

This early study was criticized, partly on technical grounds relating to the composition of the sample, the importance of nonrespondents, and the interpretation of the responses, and partly because it reflected decisions taken in the abnormal circumstances of the Great Depression, with interest rates pegged at low levels. However, postwar studies, both surveys and econometric studies, seemed to confirm the Oxford results and, indeed, to generalize them to include expenditures by consumers and by state and local governments as well as business capital expenditures and investments in inventories. That is not to say that the studies were unanimous. Indications of some response to monetary variables were found in some studies, but the indicated response was usually weak and was frequently contradicted in other studies using somewhat different specifications for the equations or somewhat different data. The results, therefore, were inconsistent and inconclusive. The only category of expenditures for which strong monetary effects were found consistently was residential construction—and in this case the response was usually attributed to governmental controls over interest rates (which induced financial institutions to restrict the availability of mortgage funds in times of rising interest rates) rather than to decisions of house buyers.[20]

THE QUANTITY THEORY TRADITION: STRONG MONETARISM

Throughout most of the postwar period, nagging criticisms of this pessimistic empirical position were advanced by the few economists who persisted in the quantity theory tradition. Early empirical observations in this vein tended to be rather casual, such as the statement quoted earlier that "to my knowledge there is no instance in which a substantial change in the stock of money per unit of output has occurred without a substantial change in the level of prices in the same direction."[21] However, in 1963 two major studies were published that were designed to provide empirical substance to the quantity theory position. One of these was a monumental monetary history of the United States by Friedman and Schwartz,[22] and the other an econometric study by Friedman and Meiselman, designed to demonstrate that a simple quantity theory model produced better predictions of changes in the level of economic activity than did a simple Keynesian model.[23]

The Friedman-Meiselman study has been sharply critized on a number of grounds, some related to the statistical methodology employed and some to the specifications of the models to be tested.[24] However, the study has been immensely influential in reviving faith in the power of monetary policy, and it has stimulated a spate of other empirical studies. Some of the strongest empirical work by monetarists is coming from the St. Louis Federal Reserve Bank. Michael Keran adapted the Friedman-Meiselman formulations into a forecasting model in 1967.[25] Andersen and Jordan, also of the St. Louis Federal Reserve, attracted a great deal of attention in the following years with a model that used methodology very similar to that of Friedman and Meiselman. We shall discuss their model in more detail later.[26]

One of the strong points made by the modern quantity theory school is that the impact of monetary policy on individual sectors of the economy may be relatively small and hence difficult to identify with standard statistical tools, but the effects on individual sectors may add up to a substantial aggregate effect on economic activity. If so, sector-by-sector studies such as those referred to earlier, may seriously underestimate the overall impact of monetary policy. It is argued, therefore, that it is necessary to seek the impact of monetary actions on a much more general level.

Many of the correlations presented by the new quantity theory school are impressive, and the power of their theoretical arguments is frequently persuasive. However, their empirical formulations are quite simple and deal primarily with aggregates. Hence, it is difficult to argue that these essentially simple formulations have really captured the subtleties of the interaction of complex economic forces. As in the partial econometric studies referred to earlier, an essential assumption of the analytical methods of the quantity theory models is that the monetary variable, in this case the money supply, is truly an independent variable. If, as seems likely, the growth of the money supply is partly the reaction of the authorities to the growth of the economy, the Friedman method will grossly exaggerate the impact of monetary changes. It will attribute to money the responsibility for increases in economic activity that have resulted from other developments and have, in fact, induced the expansion of the money supply.

Recent Econometric Models: Renewed Optimism? The strong conclusions of the modern quantity theory school on the effectiveness of monetary policy have begun to receive tentative support from recent attempts to construct elaborate econometric models of whole economies and to use them for simulation experiments tracing the effects of changes in key monetary variables. Econometric model building is not a new art. Several models were developed in the late 1950s and early 1960s, some of which achieved quite remarkable success in economic forecasting. However, the early models were relatively small, did not have well-developed financial sectors (indeed, they frequently omitted financial variables), and by and large did not demonstrate substantial monetary effects.[27]

Improvements in both computing facilities and the application of statistical and mathematical techniques to economics have facilitated the design, development, and testing of increasingly larger and more complex econometric models in recent years. Each model is an attempt by its designers to quantify a theory of how the economy operates. Each model may propose different variables, weights, and linkages and may contain differing degrees of disaggregation.

Some models reflect a Keynesian view of the economy while others are more in line with the new quantity theory approach. Others attempt to meld the two in an eclectic theoretical approach to the economy.

Many of these models, such as the Wharton Mark III, the Data Resources model, the University of Pennsylvania model, and the Bureau of Economic Analysis model, have been reported elsewhere. We will discuss only three in any detail here—the Brookings model, the FRB-MIT model, and the Federal Reserve Bank of St. Louis Model.

The Brookings model, with over 400 equations, is the largest-scale effort of its kind yet to be attempted.[28] Work is continuing to correct certain defects in the model, but interesting simulation experiments have been conducted using a condensed version (176 equations) of the preliminary model. The model (influenced by Keynesian theory) has identified significant interest rate effects on housing and business investment, and the simulations suggest that, given time, "monetary policy is powerful."[29] Indeed, it would appear that the level of gross national product is more sensitive to changes in the monetary base than to equiproportionate changes in the level of either government expenditures or personal income taxes.

The FRB-MIT model is considerably smaller than the Brookings model, but it involves a much more intensive exploration of the financial sector of the economy and of the links between financial variables and real economic activity. Simulation experiments using a version of this model show even stronger fiscal and monetary effects than those detected by the Brookings model and also suggest that the monetary effects are stronger than the fiscal effects. A preliminary version used 200 variables in over 100 equations.[30]

The monetarist model of the St. Louis Federal Reserve is much smaller by comparison. It relies on only eight equations and primarily describes changes in aggregate dollar income as a function of changes in present and past monetary and fiscal policy. The model is largely the work of Andersen and Jordan, two economists at the St. Louis Federal Reserve. Their analysis uses methodology very similar to that of Meiselman and Friedman. Andersen and Jordan have concluded from their findings that quarterly changes in nominal GNP is correlated with current and lagged differences in the money stock and the monetary base. This quarter's change in GNP is heavily influenced by the previous quarter's change in the money stock and is affected somewhat less by the previous quarter's change in the money stock. "The response of economic activity to monetary actions compared with that of fiscal action is (I) larger, (II) more predictable, and (III) faster."[31]

Simulation experiments by deLeeuw and Gramlich, using an earlier version of the FRB-MIT model, illustrate the dynamic effects of changes in monetary and fiscal policy. The model simulated results for 16 quarters, beginning in 1964. The results of the simulation are shown in Table 22.1. Policy A indicates an increase in unborrowed reserves of $1.0 billion; policy B, an increase in real federal wage payments of $5.0 billion; and policy C, a decrease in the average aggregate personal tax rate of 2 percentage points (about $4.5 billion in revenue). The economic conditions that were present in 1964 are taken into the model with the data together with the initial policy shock so that the model incorporates the underlying economic characteristics that prevailed.

The dynamic paths of the three policies simulated indicate that the effects of increased federal wage payments on GNP and unemployment peak much more rapidly than an increase between policies: Monetary policy depresses interest rates, while fiscal policies tend to nudge rates higher. Table 22.1 is included here to suggest the magnitude of dollar change associated with policy change in one of these models.[32]

One problem observers have had in comparing the performance of different models is that conditions and assumptions vary dramatically. A group of econometricians have been simulating different models under more uniform conditions and then comparing results. Table 22.2 presents the dynamic multipliers for a number of the models that are being compared. The dynamic multipliers suggest the amount of stimulus a given policy would have over time. In Table 22.2, multipliers are reported by comparing the changes in nominal GNP over time that result from a given increase in nondefense federal government expenditure (fiscal policy).

With the exception of the Federal Reserve Bank of St. Louis' model, most of the current GNP-nondefense government expenditure multipliers are at or near 2 after 4 quarters. Thereafter, they exhibit a rising pattern with fluctuations due in part to price increases and pressures. The St. Louis model stands in sharp contrast. It reveals multipliers that are much smaller, reflecting an entirely different theoretical basis.

It is important to emphasize that the results from econometric models are still quite imprecise. Over time, the accuracy of predictions seems to deteriorate. The models are continuing to be revised and refined; new models are being developed; better results are being obtained. It seems that model builders "are beginning to converge on a common and acceptable range of

Table 22.1. Effects of Three Expansionary Policies, Initial Conditions of First Quarter, 1964

Quarter	Real GNP (Billions of 1958 Dollars)			GNP Deflator			Money GNP (Billions of Current Dollars)			Corporate Aaa Bond Rate (Percent)			Unemployment Rate (Percent)		
	A	B	C	A	B	C	A	B	C	A	B	C	A	B	C
1	$0.7	$6.6	$1.4	—	—	—	$0.8	$7.3	$1.6	-.27	.06	.03	—	-.2	—
2	2.0	8.3	2.9	—	—	—	2.3	9.4	3.4	-.14	.05	.02	-.1	-.5	-.2
3	3.6	8.7	3.6	.1	.2	.1	4.3	10.3	4.4	-.12	.05	.02	-.2	-.6	-.2
4	5.4	8.9	4.0	.1	.2	.1	6.6	11.2	5.2	-.16	.06	.03	-.3	-.6	-.3
5	7.0	9.0	4.5	.2	.4	.2	8.9	12.0	6.1	-.19	.08	.04	-.4	-.6	-.3
6	8.3	8.7	4.8	.3	.4	.2	11.1	12.4	6.8	-.22	.09	.05	-.5	-.6	-.3
7	9.3	8.0	5.0	.4	.6	.3	13.2	12.6	7.6	-.23	.10	.06	-.6	-.6	-.3
8	10.0	7.9	5.2	.6	.7	.4	15.1	13.5	8.5	-.24	.12	.07	-.6	-.6	-.3
9	10.4	7.6	5.3	.8	.9	.5	16.9	14.1	9.3	-.25	.14	.09	-.7	-.5	-.4
10	10.7	6.8	5.4	.9	1.0	.6	18.6	14.3	10.1	-.26	.16	.10	-.7	-.5	-.4
11	10.3	6.1	5.4	1.2	1.1	.7	19.9	14.5	10.9	-.24	.17	.12	-.7	-.4	-.4
12	9.4	5.6	5.2	1.4	1.3	.8	20.6	15.2	11.6	-.25	.19	.14	-.6	-.4	-.3
13	7.9	5.8	4.7	1.7	1.4	.9	20.6	16.5	11.8	-.25	.20	.14	-.6	-.4	-.3
14	6.1	6.2	3.9	1.9	1.6	1.1	20.1	18.2	11.7	-.23	.22	.15	-.5	-.4	-.3
15	3.9	5.7	2.8	2.1	1.8	1.2	19.0	18.8	11.3	-.23	.24	.16	-.3	-.4	-.2
16	1.4	5.0	1.6	2.2	1.9	1.2	17.2	19.2	10.6	-.23	.25	.18	-.2	-.3	-.2

A indicates step increase in unborrowed reserves of $1.0 billion.
B indicates step increase in real federal wage payments of $5.0 billion.
C indicates step decrease in personal taxe rate of .02 (about $4.5 billion in revenue).
SOURCE: F. deLeeuw and E. Gramlich, "Channels of Monetary Policy," Federal Reserve Bulletin, June 1969, p. 479.

Table 22.2. **Dynamic Multipliers**

Quarters of Change	GNP/G (Current Dollars)					
	BEA	Brookings	Resources Data	FRB St. Louis	MPS (U. of Pa.)	Wharton Mark III
1	$1.1	$1.8	$1.4	$0.6	$1.2	$1.2
4	1.9	2.8	2.0	0.7	2.5	1.8
8	1.9	2.9	1.9	0.1	3.0	2.2
12	1.9	3.0	2.3	0.1	2.2	2.4
16	2.1	3.1	2.9	0.1	1.8	2.6
20	2.5	3.0	3.1	0.1	—	2.5
24	2.9	3.1	1.8	—	—	2.3
28	3.1	3.3	2.7	—	—	2.3
32	3.1	3.4	4.6	—	—	2.3
36	3.2	3.7	4.4	—	—	2.8
40	3.3	3.8	3.8	—	—	3.9

SOURCE: G. Fromm and L. R. Klein, "A Comparison of Eleven Econometric Models of the United States," *American Economic Review* 63, no. 2 (May 1973), 391.

errors for respectable models."[33] It appears likely that forecasts will soon have confidence intervals attached to them. Results now being obtained show that econometric model building is a productive approach to the evaluation and understanding of the impact of monetary policy on the economy.[34]

Conclusions. It is difficult, however, to draw any firm, quantitative conclusions from the evidence on the sensitivity of aggregate demand to monetary policy. The trend in the evidence is in the direction of a rejection of the extreme pessimistic position of the early postwar years. The results of recent attempts at large-scale model building suggest stronger effects than anticipated by most economists who earlier rejected research done in the quantity theory tradition. The challenge of the monetarists and their models is formidable. However, given the imperfect nature of these models, it seems likely that the issue will not be settled definitively in the immediate future.

HOW LONG ARE THE LAGS IN THE OPERATION OF MONETARY POLICY?

An important subsidiary question in the analysis of the impact of monetary policy relates to the timing of its effects. Granted that monetary policy may have a significant impact on the level of economic activity, it is vitally important to know whether those effects can be achieved within a short period or only after a prolonged time lag. If the time lags are short, monetary policy can be a flexible instrument for short-term economic stabilization. If time lags are long, the effective use of monetary policy for such purposes depends on reliable economic forecasting. If monetary policy is powerful but the time lags are long and forecasting is unreliable—and particularly if the time lags are unstable—we may have to abandon the discretionary use of monetary policy for short-term economic stabilization and relate monetary policies to the longer-term growth potentials of the economy. Such an approach to monetary policy has been argued vehemently by some economists, and we will examine it in the next chapter. However, before we turn to it, what is the empirical evidence on time lags in monetary policy?

THE NATURE OF TIME LAGS

It has become customary in discussions of time lags in monetary policy to distinguish between *inside lags* and *outside lags*. Inside lags reflect time taken in decision making and implementation by the authorities, that is, the lapse of time between the emergence of a need for a change in policy (which may become apparent long after the event) and the taking of action. The authorities make their decisions to alter policy on the basis of their readings of various economic indicators. While some indicators are available with only short delays (e.g., banking statistics), others, such as unemployment figures or statistics on industrial production, are available only after considerable delay. Moreover, all these statistics do not move in unison, and as a consequence the authorities initially may be presented with data that paint a conflicting picture of the state of the economy's health. Even once all of the indicators, or a majority, seem to be pointing in a particular direction, the authorities must decide how critical the situation is and what possible moves are required. They may hesitate out of concern to avoid excessive overreaction, which could by itself generate disequilibrium in the economy. In an open economy with a fixed exchange rate, flexible adjustment of monetary policy may also be inhibited by balance-of-payments considerations.

The outside lag relates to the response of economic activity to the measures taken by the monetary authorities. Part of this lag may occur within the financial system (e.g., in the reaction of the money supply or interest rates to changes in the monetary base), but most attention has been focused on lags in the adjustment of expenditures in response to changes in financial variables. As in the case of the inside lag, the time involved in the recognition of the new situation and in formulating new expenditure plans in light of it accounts for part of the outside lag. In addition, however, the outside lag has a major technical component. A new construction project, by its very nature, will be spread out over several months (or perhaps years). Time will be required to draft plans, acquire land, call for tenders for equipment and construction, as well as to carry out the actual construction itself. Similarly, a decision to reduce capital expenditures will initially affect only new orders. For some time, the continuing flow of expenditures resulting from past decisions will dominate the statistical record, obscuring the effects of the new decisions.

It is generally accepted that the lags in question will be not *discrete lags* but *distributed lags*. That is, there will not be a discrete lapse of time between the implementation of policy and the appearance of the effects.

Rather, the effects will emerge gradually, building up to a peak and eventually stablizing (or perhaps tapering off).

THE EVIDENCE ON TIME LAGS

Inside Lags. It is generally argued that inside lags are themselves subject to control by the monetary authorities and hence should not be considered as given data in assessing the potential effectiveness of monetary policy. Improved forecasting techniques, coupled with more decisive decision making, are assumed to be effective in reducing inside lags.

Outside Lags. Most of the empirical research on time lags in monetary policy has focused on the outside lags. On these, evidence is gradually accumulating to suggest that the lags are relatively long.

The classic study is that of T. Mayer, published in 1958.[35] From an assortment of microeconomic evidence, Mayer concluded that "A restrictive policy reaches only half its effectiveness five months after the change in credit availability and reaches three-quarters effectiveness only after nine months. An expansionary policy takes even longer—seven months to reach the 50 percent level and ten months to reach the 75 percent level."[36] Thus, "although a monetary policy itself may be quickly reversed, its effects may not."[37] The persistence of the effects of prior policies can therefore have a serious perverse effect on the economic activity.

This theme has been developed vigorously by Friedman and his collaborators in several studies, some of which have already been referred to.[38] From a comparison of changes in the rate of growth of the money supply and cylical changes in economic activity, Friedman has concluded that the average lag in the United States ranges between 12 and 16 months, but that the lag is highly variable.

Recent studies at the St. Louis Federal Reserve Bank suggest that a 1 percent increase in the rate of growth of the money supply (M_1) provides its maximum stimulative effect to aggregate output within 4 quarters. After that period, the effect on output diminishes rapidly. The stimulation is completely gone after 24 quarters. The effect on the price level is different, and after a slight diminution in the rate of increase in the price level for 6 quarters, the price level begins to rise and reaches a new permanent rate of increase in 24 quarters.

Andersen, of the St. Louis Federal Reserve, thus concludes that, while expanding the rate of growth in the money supply kicks the output of the economy temporarily into higher gear, the long-run effect is to return to the starting point. However, a permanent legacy is left behind: a higher rate of increase in the price level.

The Friedman type of analysis of time lags (which involves simply the comparison of turning points in time series) has been severely criticized as involving a grossly simplified and unacceptable methodology. The analysis makes the assumption that the observed fluctuations in economic activity are always caused by prior fluctuations in the rate of growth of the money supply, an assumption that, it is argued, is unwarranted. However, it is interesting that the results of econometric studies tend to confirm Friedman's conclusions.

As noted earlier, partial econometric studies of expenditures have found little evidence of the impact of monetary policy. However, to the extent that such effects have been identified, they normally occur with a time lag of two or three quarters.

Recent results from simulation experiments on econometric models, however, suggest even longer lags. Thus, in both the Brookings and Federal FRB-MIT models of the U.S. economy the effects of monetary policy on gross national product are very small initially and only gradually increase to a peak that may be as much as 6 (Brookings) or 12 (FRB-MIT) quarters after the initiation of the policy. Thus, describing the FRB-MIT model, Rasche and Shapiro observe that "proponents of aggressive monetary policy as an instrument of cyclical stabilization will be disappointed to note that it takes almost two years (7 quarters) for 50 percent of this twelve quarter effect to be realized. Only 17 percent is realized after one year."[39]

Conclusions. For various technical reasons, the measurement of time lags is difficult. Considerable uncertainty must surround the estimates summarized here. However, there is a steadily accumulating body of evidence that suggests that the effects of monetary policy are distributed over an extended period, perhaps more than two or three years. Moreover, the evidence implies that the effects are very slow to build up to their maximum—much slower, for example, than the effects of various fiscal policies. It has also been argued that the lags are highly variable, a matter that is not resolved by available econometric studies.

SUMMARY

Early discussions of the effectiveness of monetary policy tended to focus on the sensitivity of expenditures to such financial variables as interest rates. Evidence of low sensitivity led many economists to reject monetary policy as an effective tool for stabilizing the economy. It was argued by some economists that this pessimism was unwarranted because the degree of sensitivity of expenditures to monetary measures simply indicated how powerful the monetary measures would have to be to achieve any given real effect. Small sensitivity merely implied massive monetary changes would be necessary. However, there remained concern about the implications of such massive monetary measures for the stability of the financial system. Thus, the estimated low sensitivity of expenditures to monetary measures remained the basis of earlier monetary pessimism.

Recent empirical studies suggest much greater sensitivity of aggregate demand to monetary measures. They partly dispel this pessimism. However, the accumulating empirical evidence that there are long and potentially variable time lags in the operation of monetary policy raises another type of issue regarding the use of monetary policy to stabilize the economy. Will the effects of monetary policy inevitably be perverse? These issues are considered further in the next chapter.

NOTES

1. R. Roosa, "Interest Rates and the Central Bank," in *Money, Trade and Economic Growth, Essays in Honor of J. H. Williams* (New York: Macmillan, 1951), pp. 270–295.

2. Board of Governors of the Federal Reserve System, "The Influence of Monetary Policy on Lenders and Borrowers," *Federal Reserve Bulletin*, March 1953, reprinted in L. Ritter, ed., *Money and Economic Activity: Readings in Money and Banking*, 3d ed. (Boston: Houghton Mifflin, 1967), p. 258.

3. Commission on Money and Credit, *Money and Credit* (Englewood Cliffs, N.J.: Prentice-Hall, 1961), p. 52. Unlike the British Radcliffe Committee and the Canadian Porter Commission, both of which were appointed by governments, the American Commission on Money and Credit was a private body, established by the Committee for Economic Development and financed by the Ford Foundation and the Merrill Foundation.

4. United Kingdom, Committee on the Working of the Monetary System, *Report* (London: H.M.S.O., 1959), p. 134. (Hereafter called the Radcliffe *Report*.)

5. Commission on Money and Credit, op. cit., p. 113.

6. Ibid., p. 108.

7. The seminal paper in this line of analysis is that of Professors J. G. Gurley and E. H. Shaw, "Financial Aspects of Economic Development," in *American Economic Review* 45 (September 1955), 515–538. An explicit statement of the above analysis of velocity is presented in J. G. Gurley, "Discussion of 'Agenda for a National Monetary Commission,'" *American Economic Review* 48 (May 1958), 103–105. More difficult is J. Tobin and W. C. Brainard, "Financial Intermediaries and the Effectiveness of Monetary Controls," *American Economic Review* 53 (May 1963), 383–400.

8. The standard discussion of the theory of debt management is J. Tobin, "An Essay on the Principles of Debt Management," in Commission on Money and Credit, *Fiscal and Debt Management Policies* (Englewood Cliffs, N.J.: Prentice-Hall, 1963), pp. 143–218. It is not an easy paper to read, however.

9. M. J. Hamburger, "The Demand for Money by Households, Money Substitutes and Monetary Policy," *Journal of Political Economy* 74 (December 1966), 600–623.

10. T. H. Lee, "Substitutability of Non-Bank Intermediary Liabilities for Money: The Empirical Evidence," *Journal of Finance* 21 (September 1966), 441–457; "Alternative Interest Rates and the Demand for Money; The Empirical Evidence," *American Economic Review* 57 (December 1967), 1168–1181.

11. H. Galper, M. J. Hamburger, and T. H. Lee, "Alternative Interest Rates and the Demand for Money: Comments and Reply," *American Economic Review* 59 (June 1969), 401–407.

12. Lee presents several different estimates of the elasticity of the demand for money with respect to the rate of interest on near money. Most of these estimates fall in the range −0.4 to −0.7.

13. I. Friend, "The Effects of Monetary Policies on Non-Monetary Financial Institutions and Capital Markets," in Commission on Money and Credit, *Private Capital Markets* (Englewood Cliffs, N.J.: Prentice-Hall, 1964), pp. 1–172.

14. A. Benavie, "Intermediaries and Monetary Policy," in *Michigan Business Reports*, no. 48 (Ann Arbor, Mich.: University of Michigan, Bureau of Business Research, 1965).

15. F. Modigliani and T. Sutch, "Innovations in Interest Rate Policy," *American Economic Review* 56 (May 1966), 178–197.

16. T. E. Holland, " 'Operation Twist' and the Movement of Interest Rates and Related Economic Time Series," *International Economic Review* 10 (October 1969), 260–265.

17. See W. H. White, "Interest Inelasticity of Investment Demand—the Case from Business Attitude Surveys Re-examined," *American Economic Review* 46 (September 1956), 565–587.

18. Econometrics is a highly technical field, not readily accessible to the beginning student in economics unless he has had substantial background in mathematics and statistics. A relatively readable introduction, which does not take the subject very far but nonetheless requires attentive study on the part of most students, is provided by A. A. Walters, *An Introduction to Econometrics* (London: Macmillan, 1968).

19. T. Wilson and P. W. S. Andrews, eds., *Oxford Studies in the Price Mechanism* (Oxford: Clarendon Press, 1951), pp. 16–31.

20. Joint Economic Committee, *Staff Report on Employment, Growth and Price Levels* (Washington, D.C., 1959). Two important survey papers were also published by the Commission on Money and Credit: D. B. Suits, "The Determinants of Consumer Expenditure: A Review of Present Knowledge," in Commission on Money and Credit, *Impacts of Monetary Policy* (Englewood Cliffs, N.J.: Prentice-Hall, 1963), pp. 1–57 and R. Eisner and R. H. Strotz, "Determinants of Business Investment," op. cit., pp. 60–337. See also R. H. Strotz, "Empirical Evidence on the Impact of Monetary Variables on Aggregate Expenditures," in F. Horwich, ed., *Monetary Process and Policy: A Symposium* (Homewood, Ill.: Irwin, 1967), pp. 295–315.

21. M. Friedman, "The Supply of Money and Changes in Prices and Output," reprinted in *The Optimum Quantity of Money* (Chicago: Aldine, 1969), p. 173.

22. M. Friedman and A. J. Schwartz, *A Monetary History of the United States, 1867–1960* (Princeton, N.J.: Princeton University Press, 1963). Another important paper also emerged from this collaboration at the same time: "Money and Business Cycles," in *Review of Economics and Statistics* 45 (February 1963), supplement reprinted in *The Optimum Quantity of Money*, op. cit., pp. 189–235.

23. M. Friedman and D. Meiselman, "The Relative Stability of Monetary Velocity and the Investment Multiplier in the United States (1897–1960)," in Commission on Money and Credit, *Stabilization Policies* (Englewood Cliffs, N.J.: Prentice-Hall, 1963), pp. 165–268.

24. J. Tobin and C. Swan, "Money and Permanent Income: Some Empirical Results," *American Economic Review* 59 (May 1969), 285–295.

25. M. Keran, "Economic Theory and Forecasting," *Federal Reserve Bank of St. Louis Review*, March 1967.

26. L. Andersen and J. Jordan, "Monetary and Fiscal Actions: A Test of Their Relative Importance in Economic Stabilization," *Federal Reserve Bank of St. Louis Review*, November 1968.

27. For example, see D. B. Suits, "Forecasting and Analysis with an Econometric Model," *American Economic Review* 52 (March 1962), 104–132.

28. J. S. Duesenberry, G. Fromm, L. R. Klein, and E. Kuh, *The Brookings Quarterly Econometric Model of the United States* (Chicago: Rand McNally, 1965).

29. G. Fromm, "An Evaluation of Monetary Policy Instruments," in J. Duesenberry, G. Fromm, L. R. Klein, and E. Kuh, *The Brookings Model: Some Further Results* (Chicago: Rand McNally, 1969), pp. 475–511. Fromm reports the following "elasticities" of gross national product with respect to the three policy instruments: open-market operations, 0.346; increase in government expenditures, 0.093; reduction in personal income tax rates, 0.143.

30. F. de Leeuw and E. Gramlich, "The Federal Reserve-M.I.T. Econometric Model," *Federal Reserve Bulletin* 540 (January 1968), 11–40; R. H. Rasche and H. T. Shapiro, "The F.R.B.-M.I.T. Econometric Model: Its Special Features," *American Economic Review* 58 (May 1968), 123–149.

31. Andersen and Jordan, op. cit., p. 22.

32. F. deLeeuw and E. Gramlich, "Channels of Monetary Policy," *Federal Reserve Bulletin*, June 1969, pp. 472–491.

33. G. Fromm and L. R. Klein, "A Comparison of Eleven Econometric Models of the United States," *American Economic Review* 63, no. 2 (May 1973), 386.

34. Ibid., pp. 385–393.

35. T. Mayer, "The Inflexibility of Monetary Policy," *Review of Economics and Statistics* 40 (November 1958), 358–374.

36. Ibid., p. 370.

37. Ibid., p. 371.

38. See particularly Friedman, "The Supply of Money and Changes in Prices and Output," op. cit.; and Friedman and Schwartz, "Money and Business Cycles," op. cit. Friedman has also defended his methodology in an essay, "The Lag in Effect of Monetary Policy," *Journal of Political Economy* 69 (October 1961), 447–466.

39. Rasche and Shapiro, op. cit., p. 145.

THE QUEST FOR A
MONETARY CONSTITUTION

Rules vs. Authority
in Monetary Policy

The discussion of monetary policy in this book has begged a fundamental question. We have implicitly assumed that the central bank has the authority to manipulate the money supply at its own discretion and that the best contribution monetary economics can make to the formulation of policy is to provide theoretical and empirical guidance for the more timely and effective intervention on the part of the central bank in its pursuit of "generally agreed" policy objectives. However, this is a position that does not command universal support among monetary economists. It has been vehemently argued that the central bank ought to have no discretion in the management of the money supply but ought to be bound to a simple monetary constitution that involves a fixed rule for changes in the money supply. In this view, the task of monetary economics is to devise, test, and refine money supply rules. The long-standing debate over this issue has come to be known as the "rules vs. authority" controversy.

THE CASE FOR A MONEY SUPPLY RULE

The case for a fixed money supply rule has two roots, one philosophical and one empirical.

THE PHILOSOPHY OF THE FREE-MARKET ECONOMY

The foundation of the "rules" position is a philosophy of the appropriate role of government in the economy. It is argued that in general an economy in which production and distribution are organized and directed by competitive markets will simultaneously maximize individual freedom and economic efficiency.[1] This is not to say that the government does not have a vital role to play in the economy. However, with some exceptions, the appropriate role of the government is simply "to provide a stable framework of rules within which enterprise and competition may effectively control and direct the production and distribution of goods."[2] Free markets cannot function efficiently in the face of extreme uncertainty. It is important, therefore, that the rules be simple, comprehensible, and stable.

Production of Money. Control over the creation of money is one of the important exceptions to the general rule that the government should not intervene directly in economic activities. Economic efficiency argues for the use of fiat money rather than commodity money: Both perform the same functions, but the former absorbs much less of the scarce real resources of society. However, if money is virtually costless to produce, and hence its value in the market vastly exceeds its costs of production, we cannot rely on profit calculations in competitive markets to produce the optimum quantity of money. In all likelihood, the result would be an explosive inflation. That is, failure of the government to control the money supply would lead to an extreme type of uncertainty, in the face of which competitive markets could not function effectively.

In some early expositions of the argument, this conclusion was followed by the advocacy of "100 percent reserves" for the banking system.[3] It was argued that if commercial banks were required to maintain 100 percent cash reserves behind all monetary deposit liabilities the money supply could be completely divorced from private profitability calculations and placed entirely in the hands of the government. Modern advocates of the free-market position recognize that 100 percent reserves are not required for governmental control over the total money supply, even though part of the money supply is produced by private banks. It is sufficient that reserve ratios be relatively stable, or at least predictable, and that the government have direct control over the monetary base.

The Government and Monetary Uncertainty. Lodging control over the money supply in the hands of the government will not necessarily remove monetary uncertainty, unless the actions of the monetary authorities themselves are fully predictable. Thus, in the words of H. C. Simons, an early proponent of the rules philosophy,

An enterprise system cannot function effectively in the face of extreme uncertainty as to the action of monetary authorities . . . where every business venture becomes largely a speculation on the future of monetary policy.

. . . [D]efinite, stable, legislative rules of the game as to money are of paramount importance to the survival of a system based on freedom of enterprise.[4]

Simons considered various possible rules, including the fixing of the quantity of money at some arbitrary level. Although he was not completely happy with it (because it left the central bank with a considerable amount of discretion), he finally settled on one that focused on the results of governmental intervention—stability of the price level. That is, he argued that as a simple and comprehensible rule the central bank ought to be compelled to manage the money supply in such a way as to achieve stability of the general index of prices of goods and services.[5]

It is important to note that this "rule" involves an important empirical judgment. It presumes that the central bank can in fact manage the money supply in such a fashion as to achieve stability of the price level. Doubts on the empirical side in recent years have resulted in the advocacy of a different type of rule—one relating to the form of central bank intervention rather than the results.

THE EMPIRICAL BASIS OF THE MONEY SUPPLY RULE

Recent advocates of a rules approach to monetary policy have not doubted Simons' assumption that the money supply affects economic activity, particularly the price level. Indeed, their position is that of the modern quantity theory, which, as we saw in Chapters 19 and 22, implies that monetary policy has a very powerful impact. It is the very power of money that makes discretionary monetary policy such a threat to freedom, stability, and efficiency, because central banks are inherently incapable of harnessing this power to achieve the desired results.

Time Lags and Discretionary Monetary Policy. The problem is not that central bankers are devious or antisocial in their intentions. They are trapped by the fact that the timing of the impact of their actions is uncertain. Thus, time lags come to the fore of the debate. It is not simply that such lags exist and may be distributed over an extended period of time. If that were the only problem, improved techniques of prediction would presumably contain a solution. It is argued, however, that the lags are both long and irregular, and it is the latter attribute that causes the trouble.[6] If the timing of the impact cannot be predicted with any degree of accuracy, a discretionary monetary policy is likely to be perverse, imparting contractionary forces when expansion is the order of the day and expansionary forces when contraction is appropriate. The central bank is as likely to be a source of economic instability, and the central banker cannot do better because he cannot know when his actions will affect economic activity.

The Money Supply Rule. It therefore follows that if monetary policies affect the economy with long and variable time lags and it is difficult to see these effects on national income, output, employment, and prices in the short run, then intermediate criteria must be set by which day-to-day operations can be guided. Monetarists argue that the money supply is a far more reliable guide than interest rates, for example. The exact linkage between changes in interest rates and income levels, output, and prices is still not clearly substantiated. Thus, given the present state of knowledge, perfection cannot be expected. However, monetarists claim that a simple rule of thumb, such as increasing the money supply at a constant rate, would vastly improve the performance of monetary policy and its effect on the economy. As Friedman says, "thus, a fixed rate of increase in the stock of money would almost certainly rule out . . . rapid and sizeable fluctuations, though it would not rule out mild cyclical or secular fluctuations (in economic activity), and it would give a firm basis for long range planning on the part of the public."[7]

The central issue is the growth rate. It is argued that the money supply should be allowed to increase at approximately the same rate as that at which the demand for money would increase if the general level of prices were constant. In practice this means a rate of growth roughly equal to the long-run rate of growth of productivity in the economy, with perhaps a slight upward adjustment to allow for the empirical finding that money is a "luxury" good for which the demand increases as per capita income rises (Chapter 18). Precision is not essential. The economy is capable of adjusting to moderate upward or downward trends in the general level of prices without any serious loss of efficiency.[8] Thus, Friedman proposes a rate in the range of 3 percent to 5 percent per annum.[9] However, what is essential is that the rate, once chosen, be stable and hence predictable.

Other monetarists modify the Friedman stance somewhat. They suggest controlling the variability in the growth rate of the stock money over specific periods and making this the target for monetary policy. Then a range of fluctuations in interest rates could become a limiting condition. Allan Meltzer writes:

> In this way, we move away from an approach based on money market or credit market conditions toward an approach based on control of money as a means of affecting economic activity and prices. By gradually widening the range of acceptable fluctuations in interest rates, we take additional steps away from the money market conception toward a system that is far more consistent with monetary theory.[10]

This raises several technical questions. How should the money supply be defined? What is the appropriate growth rate? What should be done about seasonal, weekly, and daily fluctuations in the demand for money. The exact definition of the money supply is not important, as long as it contains the major monetary media, currency and demand deposits (although advocates of the rule usually include time deposits at commercial banks). Seasonal and similar adjustments are appropriate, provided that they are made to accommodate regular shifts in the demand for money and hence are fully predictable.

It is not argued that this money supply rule will provide the best of all possible worlds. However, it will protect us from major blunders and will neutralize the central bank as a source of monetary instability. As experience accrues with the operation of such a rule, our knowledge of the functioning of the monetary system will improve, and we should be able to devise still better rules for controlling the money supply.

THE CASE AGAINST A MONEY SUPPLY RULE

Attacks on the proposal for a fixed money supply rule have not been lacking. Thus, the distinguished British scholar of central banking, R. S. Sayers, has asserted that "we are doomed to disappointment if we look for rules that are applicable to all times and places. We have central banks for the very reason that there are no such rules.[11] Elsewhere he states that "the essence of central banking is discretionary control of the monetary system."[12]

In a slightly different vein, P. Samuelson has derided the black-and-white contrast drawn between "discretion" and "rules":

> For when men set up a definitive mechanism which is to run forever afterward by itself, that involves a single act of discretion which transcends, both in its arrogance and its capacity for potential harm, any repeated acts of foolish discretion that can be imagined.[13]

In other words, the quest for immutable rules—attractive as they may be —is at best idle dreaming and at worst highly dangerous.

What analytical content can we put into the objections to a fixed money supply rule?

STABILITY OF THE DEMAND FOR MONEY

As we have noted at various points in our exposition of the theory of monetary policy, the key issue is the nature and stability of the demand for money. The critics are in effect arguing that the money supply rule rests too much on one debatable empirical finding: Friedman's conclusion that the demand for money is a stable function of permanent income and is little affected by availability of or yields on other financial instruments. This gives the demand for money long-run stability and provides the underpinning for a long-run money supply rule. It is accepted that monetary instability may affect the demand for money, either by engendering extreme uncertainty, and hence precautionary demands for money, or by generating expectations of price level changes. But these are not autonomous shifts in the demand for money. They are induced by the behavior of the money supply. They are a by-product of inappropriate central banking policies.

Whereas the advocates of a money supply rule find the source of all monetary instability on the supply side—that is, with the central bank itself— the critics are in effect arguing that central bank discretion is essential to offset independent shifts in the demand for money or to neutralize the effects of substitutions beween money and near money. Whereas proponents of the rule emphasize a stable long-run relationship between income and money demanded, critics assert that the short-run instability of the ratio is the central banking problem. We have here an empirical issue on which, as we have seen, the evidence is inconclusive (but perhaps this in itself tips the balance against a money supply rule).

The Money Supply Rule in an International Setting. As we saw in Chapter 20, given the assumption of fixed exchange rates, the monetary policy required for balance-of-payments equilibrium, except by chance, will be inconsistent with an arbitrarily adopted money supply rule. Assume that the Federal Reserve achieves a given money supply goal consistent with the domestic economic growth. However, this policy leads to outflows in either the current or the capital account. Then either exchange reserves will be rapidly depleted, direct controls on trade and/or capital will have to be instituted, or the dollar will have to be repeatedly devalued against other currencies. Thus, it follows that a fixed money supply rule is inconsistent with a commitment to fixed exchange rates. In the absence of fixed exchange rates, does it follow that a fixed money supply rule should be followed? It is not by accident that the major exponent of the rules approach to monetary policy is also a major exponent of flexible exchange rates.[14]

Tests of the Money Supply Rule. It is difficult to devise discriminating empirical tests for the effectiveness of such a sweeping change in the conduct of monetary policy. Since the experiment has not been conducted, history provides no direct evidence. However, several economists have attempted to evaluate the relative effectiveness of rules and discretion, basically by analyzing the behavior of the money supply in relation to aggregate economic activity (a measure of the degree of monetary ease or tightness) during various periods and comparing this behavior to what would have happened to the relationship under various hypothetical money supply rules.

The results of this research are inconclusive. In an early study, E. S. Shaw concluded emphatically that a simple money supply rule (a stable growth rate) would have been in the "right" direction more often than the Federal Reserve System over the entire history of that system.[15] Bronfenbrenner considered a variety of rules and reached less clear-cut conclusions. He tentatively accepted the superiority of a modified money supply rule but agreed that the evidence was not strong.[16] Modigliani, pursuing the Bronfenbrenner study further, came to the opposite conclusion, arguing that the empirical record favored discretion, provided that the monetary authorities use the discretion in the pursuit of clearly defined goals.[17]

This range of empirical findings (a problem to which we should be well conditioned by now) is disquieting, particularly given the importance of the issues at stake. However, in a sense, all the evidence may be irrelevant. The tests presume that central bankers cannot improve on their past performance. It can be argued, however, that much of the historical record was in fact a learning process. It contains errors in judgment; misconceptions of the nature, purpose, and effects of monetary policy; and conflicts (or confusions) over the objectives to be pursued, rather than (or as well as) inherent defects in discretionary policy emanating from long and variable time lags. Objectives can be clarified and conflicts in priorities resolved, and techniques of central bank decision making and intervention can be refined.[18] The point is not that perfection is just around the corner but rather that the historical record may be a poor guide to what can be achieved in the future.

NOTES

1. For a highly readable but sophisticated exposition of the general thesis, see M. Friedman, *Capitalism and Freedom* (Chicago: University of Chicago Press, 1962). This work is a modern economics classic.

2. H. C. Simons, "Rules Versus Authorities in Monetary Policy," *Journal of Political Economy* 44 (1936), 1–30; p. 1.

3. Simons, op. cit., reprinted in American Economic Association, *Readings in Monetary Theory* (Philadelphia, 1952), pp. 337–368. Subsequent page references are to the latter publication.

4. Ibid., pp. 338–339.

5. Ibid., p. 351.

6. M. Friedman, "The Supply of Money and Changes in Prices and Output," in *The Optimum Quantity of Money* (Chicago: Aldine, 1969), pp. 171–187.

7. M. Friedman, *A Program for Monetary Stability* (New York: Fordham University Press, 1960), p. 92.

8. Friedman, "The Supply of Money and Changes in Prices and Output," op. cit., p. 186.

9. Friedman, *A Program for Monetary Stability*, op. cit., p. 91.

10. A. Meltzer, in Federal Reserve Bank of Boston, *Controlling Monetary Aggregates* (Boston, 1969), p. 99.

11. R. S. Sayers, *Central Banking After Bagehot* (Oxford: Oxford University Press, 1957), p. 7.

12. Ibid., p. 1.

13. P. Samuelson, "Reflections on Central Banking," *National Banking Review* 1 (September 1963), 16.

14. M. Friedman, "The Case for Flexible Exchange Rates," in *Essays in Positive Economics* (Chicago: University of Chicago Press, 1953), pp. 157–201.

15. E. S. Shaw, "Money Supply and Stable Economic Growth," in N. H. Jacoby, ed., *United States Monetary Policy*, rev. ed. (New York: American Assembly, 1964), pp. 73–93.

16. M. Bronfenbrenner, "Statistical Tests of Rival Monetary Rules," *Journal of Political Economy* 69 (February 1961), 1–14; "Statistical Tests of Rival Monetary Rules: Quarterly Data Supplement," *Journal of Political Economy* 68 (December 1961), 621–625.

17. F. Modigliani, "Some Empirical Tests of Monetary Management and Rules Versus Discretion," *Journal of Political Economy* 72 (June 1964), 211–245.

18. See also H. G. Johnson, "Alternative Guiding Principles of the Use of Monetary Policy," in *Essays in International Finance*, no. 44 (Princeton, N.J.: Princeton University Press, 1963).

INDEX

A

Acceptances, commercial banks and, 196

Accounting, wealth and, 60–62

Adjustments. *See* Financial adjustments; Real adjustments

Advances. *See* Reserve bank advances

Aggregate demand. *See also* Demand
exports and, 483
financial adjustment and, 417–418
government expenditures and, 443–444
international trade and, 481–483
Keynesian theory and, 428–429
monetary variables and, 564–568
taxes and, 444
transfer payments and, 444

Aggregate income, Keynesian theory and, 429–430

American banking. *See* United States banking system

American banking system. *See* United States banking system

American financial markets. *See* United States financial markets

American money supply. *See* United States money supply

Andersen, L., 569, 571

Arbitrage
defined, 48–49
foreign exchange ratio and, 149
international, 473

Asset demand
interest rates and, 400–401
transfer costs, 400
interest elasticity of the income velocity of circulation, 401–402

Assets. *See also* Liquid assets
defined, 9, 61

75 76 9 8 7 6 5 4 3 2 1